Georg Lukács and the Possibility of Critical Social Ontology

Studies in Critical Social Sciences

Series Editor

David Fasenfest (SOAS *University of London*)

Editorial Board

Eduardo Bonilla-Silva (*Duke University*)
Chris Chase-Dunn (*University of California-Riverside*)
William Carroll (*University of Victoria*)
Raewyn Connell (*University of Sydney*)
Kimberle W. Crenshaw (*University of California, LA, and Columbia University*)
Raju Das (*York University*)
Heidi Gottfried (*Wayne State University*)
Karin Gottschall (*University of Bremen*)
Alfredo Saad-Filho (*King's College London*)
Chizuko Ueno (*University of Tokyo*)
Sylvia Walby (*Lancaster University*)

VOLUME 148

The titles published in this series are listed at *brill.com/scss*

Georg Lukács and the Possibility of Critical Social Ontology

Edited by

Michael J. Thompson

BRILL

LEIDEN | BOSTON

Cover illustration: Georg Lukács (Budapest, September 5, 1945) by MAFIRT. MTI-FOTO-754398. Permission granted by MTI Zrt. Photo Archive (archivum.mtva.hu).

Library of Congress Cataloging-in-Publication Data

Names: Thompson, Michael, 1973- editor.
Title: Georg Lukács and the possibility of critical social ontology / edited by Michael J. Thompson.
Description: Leiden ; Boston : Brill, [2020] | Series: Studies in critical social sciences, 1573–4234 ; volume 148 | Includes index.
Identifiers: LCCN 2019037960 (print) | LCCN 2019037961 (ebook) | ISBN 9789004357600 (hardback) | ISBN 9789004415522 (e-book)
Subjects: LCSH: Social sciences--Philosophy. | Ontology. | Critical theory. | Communism--Moral and ethical aspects. | Lukács, György, 1885–1971.
Classification: LCC H61.15 .G466 2020 (print) | LCC H61.15 (ebook) | DDC 300.1--dc23
LC record available at http://lccn.loc.gov/2019037960
LC ebook record available at https://lccn.loc.gov/2019037961

Typeface for the Latin, Greek, and Cyrillic scripts: "Brill". See and download: brill.com/brill-typeface.

ISSN 1573-4234
ISBN 978-90-04-35760-0 (hardback)
ISBN 978-90-04-41552-2 (e-book)

Copyright 2020 by Koninklijke Brill NV, Leiden, The Netherlands.
Koninklijke Brill NV incorporates the imprints Brill, Brill Hes & De Graaf, Brill Nijhoff, Brill Rodopi, Brill Sense, Hotei Publishing, mentis Verlag, Verlag Ferdinand Schöningh and Wilhelm Fink Verlag.
All rights reserved. No part of this publication may be reproduced, translated, stored in a retrieval system, or transmitted in any form or by any means, electronic, mechanical, photocopying, recording or otherwise, without prior written permission from the publisher.
Authorization to photocopy items for internal or personal use is granted by Koninklijke Brill NV provided that the appropriate fees are paid directly to The Copyright Clearance Center, 222 Rosewood Drive, Suite 910, Danvers, MA 01923, USA. Fees are subject to change.

This book is printed on acid-free paper and produced in a sustainable manner.

Contents

Contributors VII

Introduction 1

PART 1
Fundamental Aspects of Lukács' Ontology of Social Being

1 Ontology and Labor in Lukács' Late Thought 13
   Antonino Infranca and Miguel Vedda

2 Lukács and the Reshaping of Marxism: From Hartmann's to Lukács' *Ontology* 28
   Endre Kiss

3 Lukács' Ontology of Social Being and the Material Basis of Intentionality 41
   Matthew J. Smetona

PART 2
Hegelian-Marxist Dimensions of Lukács' Social Ontology

4 György Lukács' Ontological Interpretation of Marx's Labor Theory of Value 81
   Murillo van der Laan

5 The Ontology of Alienation: Lukács' Normative Theory of History 116
   Andreas Giesbert

6 Lukács' Late Appropriation of Hegel's Philosophy: The Ontology of Materialist Dialectics and the Complexities of Labor as Teleological Positing 152
   Michalis Skomvoulis

PART 3
Lukács' Social Ontology and Contemporary Philosophy

7   On the "Constitution of Human Society": Lukács' versus
    Searle's Social Ontology   183
       Claudius Vellay

8   Why Still Reification? Toward a Critical Social Ontology   223
       Thomas Telios

9   Unlikely Affinities: J.L. Borges, Kuhn, Lakatos and
    Ontological Critique   267
       Mario Duayer

10 The Politics of Nature, Left and Right: Comparing the Ontologies of
    Georg Lukács and Bruno Latour   289
       Christoph Henning

PART 4
Toward a Critical Social Ontology

11 From Critical Theory to Critical Ontology: Back to Lukács!   321
       Michael Morris

12 Normativity and Totality: Lukács' Contribution to a
    Critical Social Ontology   366
       Titus Stahl

13 Lukács and the Problem of Knowledge: Critical Ontology as
    Social Theory   392
       Reha Kadakal

14 Marx, Lukács and the Groundwork for Critical Social Ontology   419
       Michael J. Thompson

    Index   457

Contributors

Mario Duayer
retired professor from the Fluminense Federal University, Department of Economics (Rio de Janeiro State, Brazil), is currently associated with the University as a Visiting Professor at the Graduate Program of Education. Working within the Marxist tradition, his research interests include Marxian critique of political economy, ontological critique (Lukács, Bhaskar), philosophy of science, methodological issues in economic science. His writings on these subjects have appeared in diverse journals in Brazil, Argentina and the U.K. He was in charge of the first edition in Portuguese of Marx's *Grundrisse*, to the translation of which he also contributed. He has also participated in the translation into Portuguese of Lukács' *Zur Ontologie des gesellschaftlichen Seins*.

Andreas Giesbert
studied Philosophy and History of Art at both Ruhr-University Bochum and the University of Kansas. His primary research lay in topics related to Critical Theory, Western Marxism and Classical German Philosophy. He is currently a Ph.D. student at the Ruhr-University, writing a thesis on the reception and practical application of Hegelian philosophy in the United States during the 19th century.

Christoph Henning
is Philosophy Fellow at the Max Weber Centre for Advanced Cultural and Social Studies, University of Erfurt, Germany. Earlier he had positions in St. Gallen (Switzerland), Zeppelin University (Friedrichshafen) and Dresden (Germany). His latest books include *Marx und die Folgen* (Springer 2017); *The Good life Beyond Growth: New Perspectives* (with Hartmut Rosa, eds., Routledge 2017), *Theories of Alienation* (in German, Junius Hamburg 2015), and *Philosophy after Marx* (Brill 2014). Currently he is working on New Materialism, Aesthetics and philosophies of nature.

Antonino Infranca
graduated in Philosophy from The University of Palermo (1980), and specialized in Philosophy at the University of Pavia (1985). He obtained his Ph.D. at the Hungarian Academy of Science (1989) and the University of Buenos Aires (2017). In 1989 he received the Lukács Medal for Philosophical Research. He is the author of *Giovanni Gentile e la cultura siciliana* (L'Ed 1990); *Tecnecrate:*

Dialogo (Arlem, 1998); *L'Altro Occidente: Sette saggi sulla realtà della Filosofia della Liberazione* (Aracne 2010), and *Lavoro, Individuo, Storia: Il concetto di lavoro in Lukács* (Herramienta 2005, 2 editions). He is also the author of many essays on Lukács, Bloch, Gentile, Gramsci, Croce, Kerényi, Heidegger, as well as on the philosophy of liberation, and the history of Sicily. He has translated and edited Italian editions of books by Ricardo Antunes and Enrique Dussel, and has edited numerous editions in Spanish and Italian of books by Lukács.

Reha Kadakal
is an Assistant Professor of Sociology at California State University, Channel Islands. His recent publications include "History, Critique and Progress: Amy Allen's 'End of Progress' and the Normative Grounding of Critical Theory" (*Current Perspectives in Social Theory*, 2018); "Toward a Critical Ontology of the Social: Hegel, Lukács, and the Challenge of Mediation" (in *Globalization, Critique and Social Theory: Diagnoses and Challenges*, Harry F. Dahms (ed.), Emerald Publishing 2015), and "Truth, Fact, and Value: Recovering Normative Foundations for Sociology" (SOCIETY, volume 50, issue 6, 2013).

Endre Kiss
Doctor of the Hungarian Academy of Sciences (D.Sc.), Ph.D. dr. habil., is Senior Professor at the Department of Modern Philosophy of the Humanities Faculty of the Eötvös Loránd University Budapest and Professor at the OR-ZSE (Budapest). He is also a fellow at the Alexander von Humboldt-Foundation; visiting fellow at Yale University (New Haven), and a member of the Scientific Commission for Statistics and Future Research of the Hungarian Academy of Sciences.

Michael Morris
is Associate Professor of Philosophy at the University of South Florida. His recent book, *Knowledge and Ideology* (Cambridge 2016), develops and defends a theory of social knowledge that draws heavily on Hegel, Marx, Lukács, and Mannheim. His recent articles include "The French Revolution and the New School of Europe: Towards a Political Interpretation of German Idealism" (*European Journal of Philosophy*, volume 19, issue 4, 2011) and "The Superfluous Revolution: Post Kantian Philosophy and the Nature of Religious Excess" (*Intellectual History Review*, volume 26, issue 2, 2016).

Michalis Skomvoulis
received his Ph.D. in Philosophy from the University of Paris 1-Sorbonne with the thesis "Hegel and Political Economy: The Economy of the System and the

System of Political Economy." He conducted postdoctoral research at the Aristotle University of Thessaloniki. He teaches Political and Social Philosophy at the University of Patras. His most recent publications in English include "Hegel Discovers Capitalism: Critique of individualism, Social Labor and Reification during the Jena Period (1801–1807)" (in *Hegel and Capitalism*, Andrew Buchwalter (ed.), SUNY Press 2015), and "The critical function of Hegel's system: Philosophy of Right and the possibility of a systematic critical theory" (*Hegel-Jahrbuch*, forthcoming).

Matthew J. Smetona
is Assistant Professor of Instruction in the Intellectual Heritage Program at Temple University. His research interests center on German Idealism, Marxism, and critical theory. His first book, *Hegel's Logical Comprehension of the Modern State*, was published in 2013 by Lexington Books.

Titus Stahl
is Assistant Professor of Philosophy at the University of Groningen. He works on social and political philosophy, critical theory, privacy theory and social ontology. His book *Immanent Critique* will appear with Rowman and Littlefield in 2019.

Thomas Telios
is Lecturer of Philosophy at the University of St. Gallen, Switzerland. He has studied Law, Music Performance, Political Theory and Philosophy at the National University of Athens, the Anton-Rubinstein-Akademie, Düsseldorf, Germany and the Goethe-University, Frankfurt/M., Germany. His Ph.D. (obtained at the Chair of Social and Political Philosophy, Goethe-University, Frankfurt/M., Germany and the *Centre for Research in Modern European Philosophy*, Kingston University, London, U.K.) on the collective agency of the decentred subjectivity will appear shortly as a monograph under the title *Das Subjekt als Gemeinwesen. Zur sozial-ontologischen Konstitution kollektiver Handlungsfähigkeit* (Nomos 2018). He has also recently published: "Putting Oneself Out There. The 'Selfie' and the Alter-Rithmic Transformations of Subjectivity" with Jörg Metelmann, in *Transparency, Society and Subjectivity*, Emmanuel Alloa and Dieter Thomä eds., (Palgrave 2018), *Kollektivitäten im Zwiestreit: Verheißungen, Ambivalenzen und Fallstricke* (co-edited – Transcript: 2018), "Collectivity as Critical Model: Pace Adorno?" (*Zeitschrift für Kultur- und Kollektivwissenschaft*, volume 4, issue 1, 2018), and *The Russian Revolution as Ideal and Practice: Failures, Legacies and the Future of Revolution* (co-edited, Palgrave 2019, forthcoming).

Michael J. Thompson
is Professor of Political Theory in the Deptartment Political Science at William Paterson University. His recent books include *The Domestication of Critical Theory* (Rowman and Littlefield 2016), *The Palgrave Handbook of Critical Theory* (Palgrave 2017), *Hegel's Metaphysics and the Philosophy of Politics* (Routledge 2018), and the forthcoming *The Specter of Babel: A Reconstruction of Political Judgment* with SUNY Press.

Murillo van der Laan
studied Social Sciences at University of Londrina (UEL – Brazil) and concluded his Master in Sociology at University of Campinas (Unicamp – Brazil). Currently he is a Ph.D. candidate in Sociology at Unicamp, researching the idea of value in Lukács' *Ontology*, with the support from Fundação de Amparo à Pesquisa do Estado de São Paulo (FAPESP). He is also editor of the Cadernos Cemarx journal and was a visiting researcher at the Carl von Ossietzky University of Oldenburg (Germany).

Miguel Vedda
is a full Professor of the chair of German Literature (University of Buenos Aires); Principal Investigator of the National Council of Scientific and Technical Researchs (CONICET) and Director of the Department of Comparative Literature (University of Buenos Aires). He was Director of the Department of Literature of the University of Buenos Aires and President of the Latin American Association of German Studies and a member of the Marxist collective "Herramienta." His recent publications include *La irrealidad de la desesperación. Estudios sobre Siegfried Kracauer y Walter Benjamin* (Gorla, 2011), *Placeres de la melancolía. Reflexiones sobre literatura y tristeza* (Gorla, 2014), *Lukács: Estética e Ontologia* (Alameda, 2014, with Ester Vaisman), *Leer a Goethe* (Quadrata, 2015). He has translated and edited works of Goethe (*Faust*), Marx and Engels (*Paris Manuscripts*), Kafka (*The Trial, The missing Person*), Lukács (*Taktik und Ethik; Lenin; Ontologie des gesellschaftlichen Seins; Von der Armut am Geiste und andere Jugendschriften,* among others) and Siegfried Kracauer (*Die Angestellten, Ginster*), among other authors. He is also the co-editor of *Anuario Argentino de Germanística* and the *Ibero-amerikanisches Jahrbuch für Germanistik*.

Claudius Vellay
is a German economist living near Paris. He is currently working on a Ph.D. dissertation on Lukács' *Ontology of Social Being*.

Introduction

The tradition of critical theory has charted an acute and steady departure from its foundation in Marx over the past several decades. At stake is nothing less than our capacity to comprehend the objective, social forms that are shaped and oriented by capitalist economic imperatives and the ways that capitalism is able to reshape and reform the social organization of society as well as the shapes of consciousness and culture. Central to this aversion to Marxism has been a persistent view of it as reductionist, economistic, insensitive to complex forms of social action, overly dependent on structure and not enough on agency, and as possessing a misguided attachment to a philosophy of "materialism." More and more, this can be seen as crude caricature. A more nuanced and responsible reading of Marx's work displays a complex ethical theory, a deep sensitivity to problems of human agency, and a rich and deeply explanatory power of the ways that human social relations and structures are rooted in forms of power and control conferred by capturing social wealth as private capital.

A deeper, more philosophically rich understanding of Marxian ideas was undertaken by Georg Lukács, particularly throughout the 1950s and 1960s and his turn to the question of social ontology as a means to unify Marxist philosophy. What Lukács sought to achieve was a philosophical exposition of Marxian philosophy with and eye toward developing an ethics that would be able to judge and to guide practical action and social development. From the vantage point of "actually-existing" communist societies, it was becoming clear that the lack of ethical forms of judgment were increasingly leading it astray and away from the humanist goals posited by Marxism. In this sense, the development of a Marxist ontology was to be the foundation for a new mode of normative thinking, a foundation for an ethics for Marxism. This ethic would not be a separate normative doctrine, it was to be understood as dialectically related to the specific, philosophical-anthropological ideas that Marx developed throughout his work. For Lukács this was contained in the idea of labor itself, in the idea of labor as a distinctively human capacity to realize his cognitive concepts in the world via praxis. Lukács argues that this is the nucleus of a new interpretation of Marxism that will not only unite its various philosophical doctrines, but also provide a rational foundation for ethical and normative forms of thought.

Lukács died in 1971 and left his two volume *Zur Ontologie des gesellschaftlichen Seins* (*Toward an Ontology of Social Being*) incomplete only to be published in 1986 in Germany and then only selected chapters translated into English. Even more, he did not elaborate in any systematic way how a Marxian ethics would be articulated from this social-ontological theory. But a resurgence of interest in his ontological project has been gaining traction. One reason is that a new interest in Marxian theory has once again raised issues about the way that capitalist society is itself constituted and how this shapes and affects the construction of social reality itself. But another is that there is keen interest in building a form of critical theory that is able to develop a higher link between a rational understanding of social reality on the one hand and our evaluation of it on the other. The sharp division between "facts" and "values" in modern social science has led to the hegemony of analytic and positivist trends in terms of method, a vacuum of moral-evaluative critique, and a reification of the prevailing social reality.

It should be noted that the very term "ontology" is itself a contested one – or at least a polyvalent one. Marx's ontological ideas are primarily derived from Aristotle who saw a fundamental distinction between the aggregation of matter and higher forms of reality. In Aristotle's metaphysical scheme, objects possess a material substrate as matter (ὕλη) but they also achieve more complex statuses of being based on their relative *form* (μορφή) and *purpose* (τέλος). Being (ὄντος) therefore refers to a richer conception of reality than mere matter itself. Just as the essence of what a house actually is cannot be captured by an understanding of its material components – bricks, wood, etc. – but only in terms of its non-physical properties, such as its purpose, or what its purpose is, so for any object can we inquire into its metaphysical dimensions. This tradition of inquiry was sharply attacked with the rise of the Enlightenment and analytic forms of empiricism and nominalism. Hegel and Marx, however, reworked this ontological form of inquiry in their attempts to provide a conceptual grasp of the totality and to turn it toward against the alienation of human life.

For much of twentieth-century philosophy ontology has been associated with the philosophy of existentialism. In this sense, it was reframed by the work of Martin Heidegger and his project of re-orienting the course of western philosophy and western metaphysics more specifically.[1] For Heidegger, ontology was a term that referred to the phenomenological realm only, to the domain of experience and subjectivity. It was no longer an inquiry into objective reality (the ontical), but an exploration into authentic subjectivity, of Being as such (*Sein*). In this sense, both Heidegger and Lukács can be seen as reviving an interest in ontology, although from deeply differentiated points of view.[2]

---

[1] For a discussion of Heidegger's reworking of Aristotelian ontological categories, see Werner Marx, *Heidegger and the Tradition*. (Evanston, Ill.: Northwestern University Press, 1971).

[2] See the important study by Lucien Goldmann, *Lukács and Heidegger: Towards a New Philosophy*. (London: Routledge and Kegan Paul, 1977).

Even more, the Heideggerian critique of western metaphysics was used in the rise of postmodernism as a further critique of the kinds of basic philosophical categories that postmodern theorists saw as encoding power into knowledge. Categories such as "essence," "substance," "being," "objectivity," and "existence," were now to be called into question for resting on pre-critical notions of reality and an outdated epistemology. The core thesis of the postmodern attack on modernist forms of knowledge and the categories that undergirded them was the thesis that social reality was constructed and contingent. There was no essence of human life let alone any kind of ontology with objective dimensions.

But more recently, the project of articulating a theory of social ontology has once again become vibrant. Against the postmodern turn, the new social ontology has several divergent fields, but two stand out as particularly influential. First, the *critical realist paradigm* offers a theory that is based on the thesis that social reality has a generative structure that produces the phenomena of social reality.[3] We cannot have adequate cognitive access to social reality through empirical investigation of it but, rather, must insist on an underlying social ontology that has causal powers over our agency and social structures themselves.[4] Social structure is therefore causal with respect to our agency as individuals, but it is also open to transformation as the *object* of our agency.[5] The ontology of our sociality can be grasped in the ways that structure and agency interact. The key insight of the critical realists is that our relations with one another and the practices that are enacted by these relational structures gives rise to forms of social reality with their own ontological properties and powers. The concept of "emergence" is introduced to capture this thesis: namely that the structures and relations and practices give rise to forms of social reality with their own ontological properties.

Second, there is the *analytic paradigm* that essentially builds a theory of social ontology from cognitive and linguistic structures of thought and mind. According to this approach, human practices help construct our social reality whether based on speech-act theory or on forms of coordination of collective

---

3 See Roy Bhaskar, *A Realist Theory of Science*. (London: Verso, 1975).
4 See Roy Bhaskar, *The Possibility of Naturalism: A Philosophical Critique of the Contemporary Human Sciences*. (Atlantic Highlands, N.J.: Humanities Press, 1979); Dave Elder-Vass, *The Causal Power of Social Structures: Emergence, Structure and Agency*. (Cambridge: Cambridge University Press, 2011); as well as Tuukka Kaidesoja, "Exploring the Concept of Causal Power in a Critical Realist Tradition." *Journal for the Theory of Social Behaviour*, vol. 37, no. 1 (2007): 63–87.
5 Cf. Bhaskar, *The Possibility of Naturalism*, as well as the important elaboration by Margaret S. Archer, *Realist Social Theory: The Morphogenetic Approach*. (Cambridge: Cambridge University Press, 1995).

action. Our social world can be seen to be a collection of individuals who construct different forms of reality based on some kind of collective acceptance of certain rules. Hence, for John Searle, it is the acceptance of certain rules for assigning meaning or functions to things that grants them a social-ontological status. But these statuses are constructions of our collective intentions, not actually distinct forms of reality. They remain in the mind, albeit collectively in the sense that we all come to follow a set of accepted collective rules for status attribution. Only when we collectively accept and use such rules do we possess collective intentionality, or a shared form of meaning that possesses an ontological status in the sense that we accept, say, books as books and not piles of paper, or paper weights as paper weights and not pieces of stone, and so on.[6] The paper weight or the book achieve their social-ontological status from our mental rule-following; they do not, however, possess emergent properties, as the critical realists maintain. Social reality is the result not only of these forms of collective intentionality, it also leads to theories of "group agency" where we coordinate our activities according to plans and shared ideas and norms.[7] One key difference between this analytical approach and the critical realist approach concerns the issue of "emergence" and the thesis that social reality possesses its own ontological properties and powers. Critical realists insist on this, analytic theorists do not.[8]

Given this current state of the field, how can Lukács' project be situated or even contribute to these debates? One way to view this is to see that for Lukács, the essential category that he puts forth, that of "teleological positing," possesses features of the two dominant perspectives in contemporary social ontology. This means that his ontology is both an account of objective social structures as well as an account of the constructive basis from which those social structures are generated. For Lukács, a distinctive concept of labor is employed to accomplish this task. Social being, for Lukács, is a specific sphere of reality, one that is dependent upon inorganic nature. Since human social

---

6 The literature here is large, but see especially: John Searle, *The Construction of Social Reality*. (New York: The Free Press, 1996) as well as John Searle, *Making the Social World: The Structure of Human Civilization*. (New York: Oxford University Press, 2014).

7 See Raimo Tuomela and Kaarlo Miller, "We-Intentions." *Philosophical Studies*, vol. 53, no. 3 (1988): 367–389; Raimo Tuomela, *Social Ontology: Collective Intentionality and Group Agents*. (Oxford: Oxford University Press, 2013); as well as Michael E. Bratman, *Intention, Plans, and Practical Reason*. (Stanford: CSLI Publications, 1987).

8 See the interesting exchange between John Searle and Tony Lawson on this issue: John Searle, "The Limits of Emergence: Reply to Tony Lawson." *Journal for the Theory of Social Behaviour*, vol. 46, no. 4 (2016): 400–421, and Tony Lawson's reply, "Some Critical Issues in Social Ontology: Reply to John Searle." *Journal for the Theory of Social Behaviour*, vol. 46, no. 4 (2016): 426–437.

reality itself depends on the inorganic material substrates of nature in a dual sense: (i) it is constituted by inorganic material substrates for its physical existence, and (ii) it is the substance that is manipulated by our activities.[9] Social being is therefore nested within a broader ontology of material reality, but it is not determined by material reality in some crude mechanistic sense. Rather, Lukács wants to explore the ways that subjective agency transforms the material world and how this activity of transformation lies at the heart of social reality and the ways that social forms are articulated. Even more, his premise is that this capacity for intentional activity – understood as the positing of purposes and ends realized through the transformation of nature – is an essential power marking humans off as a species.

For Lukács, labor is not simply a practice in the simple sense of the term, it is a complex act of consciousness and material activity that is distinctive to human beings. In this sense, labor is the primary concept that mediates the conscious and intentional acts of the subject and the realm of nature. The nucleus of this thesis is the foundational concept of "teleological positing" (*teleologische Setzung*) which is the projection of a cognitive concept or idea that is realized in the world through the manipulation and reordering of the material world. As Lukács lays out the thesis, it is "a mental plan achieving material realization, in the projection of a desired goal bringing about a change in material reality, introducing a material change in reality that represents something qualitatively and radically new in relation to nature."[10] This is a unification of the Idealist premise of the primacy of the cognitive pattern of thought and the materialist thesis of the primacy of the material world as the necessary field of objective reality.

The ontological is therefore, as Lukács sees it, a synthesis of both ideas brought together to see social reality as a distinct kind of reality. Labor is therefore not epiphenomenal to, but *essentially constitutive of* social reality, it is the distinctive capacity that marks us off as a species.[11] This concept is meant to cover not simply the narrow understanding of labor that orthodox versions of Marxism put forth, but rather of any structural relation between cognitive ideas and the material world. Praxis, in its broadest sense, is captured by this

---

9   See the interesting discussion by Barbara Tuchanska, "Marxism as the Foundation of Philosophies of Science: The Case of G. Lukács' *Ontology of Social Being*." *Studies in Soviet Thought*, vol. 41 (1991): 1–17.

10 Georg Lukács, *Zur Ontologie des gesellschaftlichen Seins*, vol. 2. (Darmstadt: Hermann Luchterland, 1986), 51.

11 Note the interesting discussion by Ernest Joós, "Alienation in Georg Lukács's Ontology." In Ernest Joós (ed.), *George Lukács and His World: A Reassessment.* (New York: Peter Lang, 1987), 99–113.

Hegelian-Marxist thesis, from language to physical labor. All are to be seen as distinctively human and to be at the center of ever more complex structures of relations between human beings, constituting the essence of social reality. But also, the project touches on the capacity for human praxis to constitute higher forms of being and an implicit theory of progress at the heart of a critical social ontology.

Lukács is therefore developing what was already implicit in the philosophical projects of Hegel and Marx. Hegel's own approach to metaphysics was meant to overturn the pre-critical understanding of metaphysics as a transcendental structure within which objective forms of reality participated. It was also meant to advance Kant's critical project insofar as it remained trapped in epistemology and eschewed any attempt to provide a *de re* account of the structure of reality itself. Hegel's *Phenomenology* therefore provides us with an account of consciousness' development toward the cognitive grasp that human reality is the result of the collective forms of practices that constitute it. Later in his *Science of Logic* and in the *Encyclopedia*, there is an attempt to systematically elaborate the categories that bind subjective reason and objective rationality.[12] Metaphysics now was immanent to the structure of reality itself. Rational structures could be grasped cognitively, i.e., conceptually, but these concepts grasped by consciousness were also the undergirding structures of reality itself.[13] Objective reality therefore possesses a rational structure that can be discerned by subjective intelligence, it was not merely a thing in itself that subjective reason constructed as a rational object of cognition. Rather, cognition was the sharing of the subjective mind with the object's rational structure. The implication of this thesis was that for reason to be rational, it needed to be accountable to the objective structures of reality. This entailed a kind of practical reasoning that led to a critical justification of modern forms of "ethical life" (*Sittlichkeit*) and the ways that it was a realization of the rational structures of human forms of interdependent agency and individual development.[14]

---

12 For a defense of the essential relation between the systematic and metaphysical dimensions of Hegel's project, see Kevin Thompson, "Systematicity and Normative Justification: The Method of Hegel's Philosophical Science of Right." In Thom Brooks and Sebastian Stein (eds.), *Hegel's Political Philosophy: On the Normative Significance of Method and System*. (New York: Oxford University Press, 2017), 44–66.

13 See the important discussion by Stephen Houlgate, "Hegel's Logic." In Frederick Beiser (ed.), *The Cambridge Companion to Hegel and the Nineteenth-Century*. (Cambridge: Cambridge University Press, 2008): 111–134 and Robert Stern, *Hegelian Metaphysics*. (New York: Oxford University Press, 2009), 45ff.

14 See Michael J. Thompson, "The Metaphysical Infrastructure of Hegel's Practical Philosophy." In M. Thompson (ed.), *Hegel's Metaphysics and the Philosophy of Politics*. (New York:

But Marx, too, was concerned with the ontological status of social facts. Marx always maintained a distinction between his conception of "materialism" and the "crude materialism" of French thought of the eighteenth century. His theory of materialism emphasizes a conception of social reality as constructed by intentional subjectivity mediated by praxis.[15] The key idea was that the ontology of our social reality could only be properly grasped once we had in view the structure of reality as material objectivity mediated by praxis and conceptual thought. It is ontological because it is richer than the material substrates that underlie it. In other words, social reality is the objectification of intentional practices that manipulate and transform the material world of raw nature into a new, higher form of reality that is distinctly human. When these activities are coordinated among us as social practices, we magnify our powers and social relations become the backdrop to all social reality.

Since our species is inherently social (*essentially* social and practical, Marx would say) the products of our social-relational practices constitute a transformed natural world that has its own form of being and its own ontological status. Tables, books, computers, electrical systems and so on are more than the trees, metals and so on that constitute them materially; they are also and, perhaps more importantly, forms of reality that obtain their being via our practices and enactments. Once we lose sight of this, we reify our social world and sustain an alienation of ourselves *from* ourselves. This critical social ontology is in strong distinction from those theories of social ontology that seek explanation of social facts in other social facts.[16] Although such projects may be coherent as an *explanans* for social facts, they do not grant us any *critical-theoretical insight*. What is lost in this alienation is the underlying reality of our social world and all social facts: that they are produced by our cooperative, interdependent forms of activity.

The ends of such activity can be judged based on how they serve the developmental capacities and needs of the species rather than the expediency of

---

Routledge, 2018): 101–141; as well as Heikki Ikäheimo, "Ethical Perfectionism in Social Ontology – A Hegelian Alternative." In Italo Testa and Luigi Ruggiu (eds.), *"I That is We, We That is I," Perspectives on Contemporary Hegel*. (Leiden: Brill, 2016): 49–67.

15   See the important discussion of the relation of Marx's materialism to ontology by George L. Kline, "The Myth of Marx's Materialism." In H. Dahm, T.J. Blakeley and G.L. Kline (eds.), *Philosophical Sovietology. Sovietica*, vol. 50. (Dordrecht: Springer, 1988): 158–203. Also see the discussion by Norman D. Livergood, *Activity in Marx's Philosophy*. (The Hague: Martinus Nijhoff, 1967), 20ff. For a discussion of Marx's materialism in this context, see Alfred Schmidt, *The Concept of Nature in Marx*. (London: New Left Books, 1971), specifically 19–93.

16   See, for example, Brian Epstein, "A Framework for Social Ontology." *Philosophy of the Social Sciences*, vol. 46, no. 2 (2015): 147–167.

those able to control it. Individuality is therefore a function of the social-relational nexus of our sociality, not something that exists prior to society itself.[17] Capitalism therefore can be critiqued based on the ways that it orients, shapes and organizes these cooperative and interdependent forms of life. Private control of capital is therefore the invasion of private interest over what is genuinely, indeed, *ontologically*, social. Indeed, even more, a richer account of concepts such as "value," "wealth," "labor," and "capital" becomes possible once we grasp the social-ontological underpinnings of these categories: they each are different ways that human activities have been organized and congealed in our normative and objective valences of social reality. A rational form of human organization – both with each other in society and society with nature – would therefore be one where the organization of society was designed for the optimal development of the individuals that constitute it rather than as an adjunct to the interests and projects of a particular subset of the community, something private ownership of capital sustains.

In many ways, Lukács' earlier work had anticipated the need for a more developed understanding of social ontology. As early as *History and Class Consciousness*, there was an implicit ontology of sociality in that the essence of the concept of class consciousness was understood to be the cognitive grasping of the essential structure of labor as the constitutive activity of modern society. Class consciousness was therefore the explicit knowledge of the way that the processes of labor had been co-opted by private control (i.e., by capital). The labor process was therefore to be brought to its fruition as a social process once the chasm between causality and teleology was overcome. Later, in his study of the young Hegel, Lukács seems to move closer to what he would later see as the central category of social reality: the labor process as a structure uniting the subjective-intentional aspects of consciousness and the practical-material realization of our intentions and plans in the objective world. Lukács also saw the implicit ontological thesis in Hegel's writings and their connection with Marx's ideas. As he notes in his study of the young Hegel: "Hegel's concrete analysis of the dialectics of human labor annuls the unyielding antithesis of causality and teleology, i.e., it locates conscious human purposes concretely within the overall causal network, without destroying it, going beyond it or appealing to any transcendental principle."[18]

---

17   For an important recent development of this thesis, see Michael E. Brown, *The Concept of the Social in Uniting the Humanities and Social Sciences*. (Philadelphia, Pa.: Temple University Press, 2014), 183ff.

18   Georg Lukács, *The Young Hegel: Studies in the Relations between Dialectics and Economics*. (Cambridge, Mass.: MIT Press, 1975), 345.

The Marxian aspect of this argument is not difficult to see. The ontology of our social reality should be viewed as shaped and determined by the ways that this subjective-intentional structure is organized. Social relations, institutions, norms and so on are all shaped by the ways that this ontological capacity of human life is oriented and patterned. And here is where the critical dimension of Lukács' project comes into play. Indeed, in opposition to the analytic approaches that dominate much of the field of social ontology today, Lukács insists on a *critical social ontology* in the sense that it is not merely descriptive of the ways social facts are constituted. Rather, labor is not merely an activity that generates social reality, but its organization expresses the extent to which human beings are able to develop and progress as a community.[19] The concretization of freedom in actual human life – in the institutions, practices and so on of our social reality – is advanced to the extent that our creative-productive powers are organized in accordance with the development and enhancement of the human individual and not alienated from us or exploited for private surplus extraction. There is, then, a theory of progress that accompanies the development of the capacities for labor insofar as the social forms that we inhabit can either promote an enriched individuality or a stunted, debased particularity. It is not only material but ethical and cultural progress that has to be in view. As Lukács remarks on the young Hegel: "what is expressed in labor, in tools, etc., is a higher, more universal, more social principle. A new terrain is conquered which leads to a broader and deeper understanding of nature; and this conquest redounds to the advantage of not just one single man, but of mankind as a whole."[20]

In this sense, Lukács' critical social-ontological project is circumscribed by its concern with the ways we can discern a relation between value judgments and ontological reality. The key here is to overcome the separation between facts and values, between our objective conceptions of reality and our evaluation of that reality. It is not enough to embark on a project of explanation – we must be able to chart a path toward a critical insight into the realm of social reality itself. In this sense, a critical theory of social reality can be seen to be the core project Lukács was after – one he was never to bring to fruition. But at its base it means generating a theory of social ontology that will enable us to see how social and individual development are shaped and affected by the shapes that out social-relational practices take. We are not after a mere explanation of social facts, in this sense, but rather a critique of the social-relational forms

---

19 This theme of progress is emphasized in the study of Ernest Joós, *Lukács' Last Autocriticism: The Ontology*. (Atlantic Highlands, N.J.: Humanities Press, 1983).
20 Lukács, *The Young Hegel*, 348.

that are constitutive of our social reality. Indeed, it is with this latter, critical project in mind that these essays seek to elaborate and to map out Lukács' ideas and the possibility of deriving a critical social ontology from them.

To be sure, this idea goes sharply against the grain of modern philosophy, in particular with respect to the post-metaphysical turn toward pragmatism and intersubjective ethics.[21] This, after all, was the aim of Lukács' project. In his scattered notes left after his death is scribbled the line "*keine Ethik ohne Ontologie*," which indicates that he was pursuing his ontology for the purpose of building a system of ethics. In inheriting this project of a critical social ontology, we are therefore engaged in the project of placing ontological concerns back at the center of critical philosophy, of constructing a paradigm of critique that is rooted in the questions of social being and the objective traits of human sociality. This reworking of Marxian materialism as critical social ontology therefore has in its sights many of the exaggerated claims made by the neo-Idealist turn in critical theory.

Despite the differences between his and the analytic approaches to social ontology, Lukács' thesis and the ideas he develops out of it in his *Ontology of Social Being* are remarkable for their prescient anticipation of the ideas put forth by contemporary social ontology theorists. Although his philosophical language is quite different, he puts forth a theory of intentionality, of social relations as well as of planning and ideas about collective intentionality and about human praxis. His ideas explode any traditional or dogmatic form of Marxism and is engaged with rich project of understanding critical forms of thought in relation to a comprehension of relevant features and capacities of the human species. Many of these chapters were initially presented at an international conference, co-organized by János Kelemen and myself, on Georg Lukács' work and legacy that took place over the course of several days at both Eötvös Loránd University and the Central European University in Budapest in May of 2017. As a whole, these studies seek to develop Lukács' ontological ideas and show their relevance for contemporary philosophy and, most importantly, the possibility for a new form of critique. At the center of the concern of these essays is the potential and promise of a critical social ontology and the ways that Lukács' ideas about social ontology can provide us with a new, more compelling and satisfying form of critical reflection and consciousness.

---

21 See in particular the argument put forward by Hilary Putnam in his *Ethics without Ontology*. (Cambridge, Mass.: Harvard University Press, 2004). This is also the perspective adopted by others in the postmetaphysical and pragmatist turn in ethics such as the different views of Jürgen Habermas and Richard Rorty, among others.

PART 1

Fundamental Aspects of Lukács' Ontology of Social Being

∴

CHAPTER 1

Ontology and Labor in Lukács' Late Thought

Antonino Infranca and Miguel Vedda

1[1]

It is a known and well-documented fact that, later in life, Lukács sought with increasing clarity and conviction to construct a genuine philosophical system, an idea that took on an even more defined shape when, looking to give proper form to his aesthetic and critical-literary reflections, he began to draft the *Aesthetics*.[2] This was the beginning of the 1950s, when, in Stalinist Hungary, Lukács was involved in the so-called "Lukács debate." Thanks to a prompt and diplomatic self-criticism, Lukács was able to withdraw from politics and teaching in private life and dedicating himself to writing his *Aesthetics*. Although he interrupted his labors to participate in the Hungarian uprising of 1956, he resumed his work on the *Aesthetics* after his return from exile in Romania in the Spring of 1957 and, at the beginning of 1960, the work was finally completed. On that occasion he wrote to Frank Benseler, his German publisher, a letter in which he states his intention to write a volume with the title *Die Stelle der Ethik im System der menschlichen Aktivitäten* (*The Place of Ethics in the System of Human Activity*), and adds that it was "the project on which I am now working."[3] While preparing to write the ethics, he felt the need to define the framework which would in turn structure ethical concepts, and in this way a determination was made to compose, as a step before the *Ethics*, an *Ontology of Social Being*.

The first mention of his intent to write this work is found in a letter to Benseler written on September 19, 1964: "I find myself in the middle of working on the *Ethics*. But it seems that the first part of the *Ethics* will be much larger than I had imagined. It would most likely be expanded into a book, starting from various perspectives, of no less than 300 pages. When it is finished, we will have to decide whether the book should appear as an independent work,

---

1 This chapter is translated from the Italian by Elena Mancini.
2 Note the dedication of the Aesthetics to his wife Gertrud, in which she refers to the intention of writing a wider aesthetic comprising two other volumes and an ethic.
3 Cited in the "Nachwort" to *Prolegomena. Zur Ontologie des gesellschaftlichen Seins*, edited by F. Benseler, (Darmstadt und Neuwied: Luchterhand, 1986), 731.

perhaps in the edition of the complete works, or, provisionally, as a separate volume. The title of the work is *Toward an Ontology of Social Being*."[4]

In yet another letter to Benseler, this time dated January 22, 1965, Lukács writes that he has changed the original project and is now working on an Ontology and adds: "Not before I complete this can I approach a true Ethics." Lukács worked incessantly on the manuscript between 1964 and 1968. On May 27, 1968, he wrote to Benseler: "I have finished the last chapter of the *Ontology*. Now there remains the dictation and, later, the revision of the entire manuscript. I hope to finish everything in the Summer or Fall. At long last!"[5] However, the revisionary phase was frequently interrupted by other concerns that were difficult for Lukács to avoid.

It should be pointed out that a preoccupation with ethical problems already appears in the *Aesthetics*, where Lukács delineated a clear distinction between the "whole man of everyday life" (*der ganze Mensch*) and the "totally committed man" (*der Mensch "ganz"*). In this sense, the *Aesthetics* can be considered a sort of introduction to the planned philosophical system which would come to include the *Ontology* – the second work of the system that he was able to complete – and then finally the *Ethics*. In this sense, his approach is reversed and becomes more classical in orientation.

The Aristotelian philosophical system is generally taken as a model for any other philosophical system. As we know it today, it is the result of the work done by Andronicus of Rhodes and it is difficult to reconstruct exactly the chronology of the writing of the single works that compose it. However, the organization that Andronicus gave Aristotle's work shows an inherent rationale. The first work is the instrument (ὄργανον) itself of thinking, i.e., Logic, then follow the various theoretical sciences (Physics and Metaphysics) and then the human sciences (Ethics, Politics, Rhetoric and Poetics). Lukács did not write a logic. Undoubtedly he would have used the Marxian dialectic which was itself a reversal of the Hegelian dialectic. One could perhaps argue that this is achieved in his *The Young Hegel*, the work that represents the moment of clarification of the methodological use of the Hegelian and Marxian dialectic.

As is known, ontology is one of the forms of metaphysics and the *Ontology* is a metaphysics. Nicolas Tertulian emphasizes precisely this essential aspect of the work when he writes: "Lukács intended to value both the tradition of Aristotle's *Metaphysics* and that of Hegel's *Logic* to erect his ontology. His work, therefore, wanted to be a 'metaphysics' and a 'critique of historical reason'

---

4 Ibid.
5 Cited in ibid., p. 736.

simultaneously."⁶ The work of building the Lukácsian system would have continued after the *Ontology* with ethics and political philosophy. On this last subject, Lukács offered an early glimpse in his essay "Demokratisierung Heute und Morgen" ("Democratization Today and Tomorrow"), a pamphlet in which he critiqued the Central Committee of the Hungarian Socialist Workers Party, who had decided that Hungarian troops would participate in the occupation of Czechoslovakia in August 1968.

This classical approach may seem out of step with modern philosophical approaches. But in truth, there is nothing deviant in the classical approach of a philosopher who has founded his conception of philosophy on the classics. In his autobiography, Lukács recalls his first meeting with Ernst Bloch, using classical philosophy as the category for judging the thought of a fraternal friend: "I encountered in Bloch the phenomenon of someone who philosophized as though the entirety of contemporary philosophy did not exist, that it was possible to philosophize in the manner of Aristotle or Hegel."⁷ Classical philosophy is above all a systematic philosophy. That Marxism can be seen as the heir of classical philosophy, with Lukács' own attempt at a systematic philosophy, is only a natural consequence of a conception of Marxism that goes back to its founders. Only they who interpret Marxism arbitrarily, that is to say without a rigorous and scientific method and categorical system, can think of it as a radically new system of thought, without any philosophical lineage, and therefore arbitrary. Such thinkers are also particularly prone to theoretical synthesis, that is, sparing categories and concepts, arriving at hasty conclusions, skipping over important and fundamental steps, reading the philosophers halfway, choosing in the philosophers' thinking that which best suits their particular ruminations, and so on.

The metaphysical character of the *Ontology of Social Being* has attracted countless criticisms, all of them united by a substantial lack of knowledge of the work.⁸ Even more drastic have been the criticisms that came from the

---

6   N. Tertulian, "Teleologia e causalità nell'ontologia di Lukács." In *Critica marxista*, n°. 5, September-October 1980, a. XVIII, Rome, p. 90. Also Ferenc Tökei recognizes the classical and at the same time innovative character of the Marxist ontology of the late Lukács. Cf. F.T., "L'ontologie de l'etrè sociale. Notes sul l'œuvre posthume de György Lukács (1885–1971)." In *La Pensée*, n°. 206, July-August 1979. Paris: 29–37.
7   G. Lukács, *Pensiero vissuto. Autobiografia in forma di dialogo*, edited by I. Eörsi, Italian translation edited by A. Scarponi, (Rome, 1983), 27.
8   Let us take a simple consideration, to understand the method of current philosophical research: the first ontological text of Lukács appeared in 1969 in Hungarian ("Az ember gondolkodás és cselekvés ontológiai alapzatai" [Ontological foundations of human thought and activity] in *Magyar Filózofiai Szemle*, no. 13, 1969, pp. 731–742); in 1971 the first chapters of the work appeared in German, exactly the chapters on Hegel, on Marx and on the work. The first

philosophical circles of orthodox and dogmatic Marxism,[9] where the idea that one could write a Marxist ontology was considered unacceptable.[10] To make matters worse, there is also the fact that it is a work of about 1,500 pages, written in a redundant and long-winded style. What is more, Lukács' students fought to boycott the project because they preferred *History and Class Consciousness*, undoubtedly an important work, but even more important because it is an indispensable presupposition of the *Ontology* itself, as we will show below.

complete edition of the Anthology is the Hungarian translation in 1976. In the same year the Italian translation of the first part came out and in 1981 the Italian translation of the second part. The complete edition in the original language, that is in German, of the Anthology appeared in 1984. Yet G. Bedeschi, based on a book-interview (*Conversations with Lukács*, De Donato, Bari, 1968, pp. 207), in to which the space dedicated to the Ontology does not go beyond 40 pages, it is liquid in two pages (see G. Bedeschi, Introduction to Lukács, Laterza, Bari, 1970, II ed.:1976, pp. 78–80) a work over 1500 pages. Even more Colletti, judges it "a late nineteenth-century metaphysics" and nothing else, giving the impression that such a superficial judgment corresponded to an equally superficial knowledge work. Consider then the reception in Germany on the basis of the account of the meeting between Heller and Habermas in Frankfurt (see F. Feher, A. Heller, Gy. Markus, M. Vajda, "Introduction to the 'Notes on the ontology for the Comrade Lukács' (1975)." In *Aut Aut*, no. 157–158, January-April 1977, p. 14). On that occasion Heller exposed to Habermas the main theses of the Anthology and the German philosopher answered with a strong negative judgment. Given the opposition of Heller to the project of the work, the first suspicions emerge as to how the main themes of the Anthology were exposed. Then the same judgment of Habermas leaves puzzled, because a philosopher of his prestige on the simple oral story struck a work of over 1500 pages. Yet on the basis of such judgments the work was subsequently almost ignored. On the genesis and reception of the *Ontology* cf. F. Benseler, "Zur Ontologie von Georg Lukács." In *Georg Lukács. Kultur, Politik, Ontologie*, edited by U. Bermbach and G. Trautmann. (Opladen, Westdeutscher Verlag, 1987), pp. 253–262.

9   See the criticisms of real socialism, in particular of Bayer and Klopkine, who have called "anachronistic" and "idealistic" a work such as Ontology respectively (see W. Beyer, "Marxistische Ontologie -eine idealistische Modenschöpfung." In *Deutsche Zeitschrift für Philosophie*, no. 11, Volume XVII, 1969, Berlin, pp. 1310–1331, the criticisms of Klopkine are reported by F. Tökei, op. cit., p. 35). Even in Hungary, a country from which some defense of the Anthology could be expected, a few weak defenses have come from the Lukács Archive. In general, the blockade imposed by the communist regime on the publication of most of the materials conserved in the Lukács Archives, such as all the correspondence, was substantially lost in its diffusion. The substantial disinterest in the thinking of Lukács, in general, and of the *Ontology*, in particular, by the researchers of the Lukács Archive can be seen from the almost absolute abandonment of Lukácsian studies after the fall of communism in Hungary.

10   Keep in mind the sociology of daily life of Agnes Heller that proposes many themes and contents of the same Ontology of the social being, often tracing it.

On the basis of this negative judgment, the intellectual circles of the left, who had been formed by *History and Class Consciousness*, despised the *Ontology*. These same students of Lukács then ended up pillaging the *Ontology* without restraint. It may seem paradoxical that the dogmatists have agreed with the proponents of *History and Class Consciousness*, but the paradox is only on the surface; both currents of Marxism were used to dogmatism. Add to this the crisis of Marxism and the collapse of real socialism, which, instead of freeing the intellectuals from the hesitations of confronting an anti-democratic and illiberal regime, freed them from hesitations toward democratic thinking and intellectual freedom. Indeed, to date, a complete edition of the work has yet to appear in English, French and Spanish. Following the criticism of the students of the so-called "Budapest School," Lukács responded with another, shorter volume, *Prolegomena to an Ontology of Social Being* but did not have time to revise the text because of his death on June 4, 1971. Of the proposed *Ethics*, only the preparation notes that were published in 1994 with the title *Versuche zu einer Ethik* (*Attempts Toward an Ethics*) remain.

2

If the project of an ontology was initially outlined by Lukács in 1960, the interest in a more fundamental conception of Marxist philosophy – that is, using a deeper reading of social phenomena, more direct to the search for foundational categories and principles – had occupied Lukács since 1930 when in Moscow he had been able to read Marx's 1844 *Economic and Philosophical Manuscripts*, which were only to be published in 1932. This constituted a real "illumination on the road to Damascus" by Lukács. Until then he had not understood the theoretical depth of Marxian philosophy, now he was faced with a real, if not implicit, ontology, with a metaphysics of historical reality coupled with a critique of political economy. Indeed the critique of political economy was itself based precisely on the definition of some fundamental ontological principles that Marx had used methodologically as points of reference for a critique of the existing social reality. As a result, the Lukácsian conception of Marxism was thoroughly transformed. In fact, on the basis of this encounter with the texts of the young Marx, some of the structuring principles of Lukács' aesthetics can be explained. Thus, for example, his arguments concerning the ability of art to rise above the contingent and the transitory are extremely developed in the *Aesthetics* and in the *Prolegomena to a Marxist Aesthetic*. It is certain that these considerations square with the thought developed in his youthful aesthetics. Above all in his *Theory of Literary History* (1910) and in the section "The Subject–Object Relationship in Aesthetics" of his *Heidelberg Aesthetic* (1916–1918). But there exists, in his later work, an important difference to the extent that, thanks to the appropriation of the philosophy of the young Marx, Lukács succeeds in overcoming the vagueness and oscillations of his youthful thinking. On this point, the key concept is that of "species being" (*Gattungswesen*) a concept that we often find in texts such as *On the Jewish Question* (1843) or in the *Economical-Philosophical Manuscripts of 1844*. Marx had pointed out that, among the main prejudices caused by alienated labor, there are those which strip us of our genuinely human life and reduce it to a simple game of egoism. But also on the epistemological level we can say that the cognitive function of praxis determines the scope of the interests of the social being which confirms, in this way, a genuinely human existence.

Marx, on the other hand, opposed any attempt to fix "society" as an abstraction opposed to the individual. The individual itself is the social essence; in the concrete and acting human being, there exists a dialectical interrelation between "the existence of the species" (*Gattungssein*) and "species consciousness" (*Gattungsbewußtsein*), so that, as Marx claims, one confirms one's social life through their consciousness of their species and reproduces its real being in thought and, at the same time, the species being of man is confirmed in general consciousness. Agnés Heller pointed out the extent to which the concept of *Gattungswesen* allowed Lukács to criticize the mythology of proletarian class consciousness developed in *History and Class Consciousness*: "Lukács often told us disciples, how crucial it was for him to read the *Economic-Philosophical Manuscripts* of 1844: the discovery of the concept of mankind and the central role that Marx developed in the 'species being' greatly impacted intellectually. 'Class' could not occupy the place of 'gender' – in this way he had come to accept Marx's position, and this very substitution was his specific mark in *History and Class Consciousness*."[11]

In a letter to Benseler dated 26 February 1962, Lukács himself points out, in relation to the intense debates caused by *History and Class Consciousness* during the 1920s, that the reading of Marx's Manuscripts restrained him, when he proposed to carry out an exhaustive defense of the positions he advocated: "I immediately understood that, like Hegel, I had confused reification and objectivity, so that this complex of problems was not solved in my book, instead it was even more tangled."[12] If it seems accidental that Lukács interpreted the

---

[11] Agnés Heller, "Lukács' Later Philosophy." In A. Heller (ed.), *Lukács Revalued*. (Oxford, Basil Blackwell, 1983), 177.

[12] "Briefwechsel zur Ontologie zwischen Georg Lukács und Frank Benseler." In R. Dannemann und W. Jung (eds.), *Objektive Möglichkeit. Beiträge zu Georg Lukács' "Zur Ontologie des gesellschaftlichen Seins. Frank Benseler zum 65 Geburtstag."* (Opladen: Westdeutscher Verlag, 1995), 93.

difference between the Marxian idea of transformative praxis and the basic claims proposed by social democracy according to the concepts of *species form* (*Gattungmässigkeit*) and *species being*, Tertulian has pointed out that when Lukács maintains that "to see, in the immanence of the practical and short-term claims of the proletariat, objectives that aim at the human condition in its universality; or, when it refuses to dissociate the program of small reforms from the final objective, which is the leap from the realm of necessity to that of freedom, [...] it seeks to make visible the generic consciousness of humanity as constitutive reality of the proletarian movement."[13]

The insistence on the concept of species being allows Lukács to avoid social democratic conformity as the fallacious mythology of the proletariat put forward by Soviet Marxism. With regard to the latter, it must be remembered that Marx conceived the revolution not as a simple process of liberation of the working class subjugated by capitalism, but as a way of concluding the prehistory of humanity and opening a new phase of history so that once classes are abolished, human beings will be able fully to realize their human essence as a species.

The political situation did not allow Lukács to immediately express his changed conception of Marxism. This was at the beginning of the most ferocious period of Stalinism and Lukács had to flee to the Soviet Union since an extradition request was pending in Hungary where a death sentence awaited him because of his participation in the Council Republic of 1919. Only Austria and Germany had offered him political asylum and, after them, there was only the Soviet Union. Hitler's rise to power forced Lukács to take refuge in Moscow where he began an intellectual association with Mikhail Lifschitz and dedicated himself to literary criticism and preliminary writings for the vast research on irrationalism that would later be become *The Destruction of Reason*. At the end of the 1930s, he wrote *The Young Hegel*, but even this book – one of the highest points of Lukács' philosophical production – was not in line with the Stalinist interpretation of Hegel and the book was only published in 1948 in Switzerland.[14] In 1941, Lukács was also arrested and detained for a month by the Stalinist police who seized his book on Goethe and dialectics, which has subsequently been lost. In 1945, Lukács returned to Hungary and was able to start regular philosophical research.

---

13   Nicolas Tertulian, *Georges Lukács. Etapes de sa pensés esthétique*. Translated by F. Bloch. (Paris: Le Sycomore, 1980), 257.
14   Composed during the first half of the 1930s, the book was completed as early as the autumn of 1937. In 1942 he presented it as a doctoral thesis in Moscow, but only succeeded in publishing it in 1948 in Zurich.

Thus the changed perspective of the 1930s marks about forty years of his intellectual production and can be considered an even more profound change than his transition to Marxism at the end of 1918. We reject the idea that in Lukács' intellectual development there are fractures. Rather, we should see them as only changes of perspective, and this shift in the 1930s is undoubtedly the most significant so much to that it would bring Lukács to attempt to re-ground Marxism, an attempt that unfortunately remained unfinished also because of the distractions that the criticism of the students of the "School of Budapest" caused him. If not for all of this, it is very likely that Lukács could have left a more detailed Ethics than the notes we now possess.

3

In the philosophical framework following the "ontological turn," Lukács defines labor as "the original phenomenon [*Urphänomen*], the model [*Modell*] of social being."[15] *Urphänomen* is a term that belongs to Goethe's theory of science. Goethe also spoke of a *pure phenomenon* (*reines Phänomen*) or a *main phenomenon* (*Haupterscheinung*). The term refers to the perceptible essence governing the *same phenomena*. The original plant and animal, metamorphosis, magnetism, polarity and progression, but also creative love and productivity, the ethical will, etc., are presented as physical or ethical *Urphänomene*. But the original phenomenon is not simply an ideal concept; it is not *behind* the phenomena, but is immediately found in *singular things* (*rebus singularibus*). It is not revealed through abstract speculation but by direct observation of the object. This careful consideration of the object, aimed at describing the original phenomenon, is accompanied according to Goethe by "amazement," in accordance with the Platonic and Aristotelian concept of θαυμάζειν. It could be argued that Goethe's thesis about what drives our interest in the objective world, one where we are driven to recognize in it the ways that objective reality can be developed by the subject, is one of the foundations, not only for the theory of realism developed in Lukács' *Aesthetic*, but also for the conception of labor at the center of the *Ontology*. Indeed, this influence of Goethe's seminal idea was already present in Hegel who had already integrated Goethian principles into his philosophical thought.[16]

---

15   Cf. G. Lukács, *Ontologia dell'essere sociale*, tit. or. *Zur Ontologie des gesellschaftlichen Seins*, tr. It. A. Scarponi, vol. II, (Rome: Editori Riuniti, 1981), Chapter 1, p. 13.
16   The relationship between Goethe and Hegel was studied in details by Karl Löwith in his "Goethes Anschauung der Urphänomene und Hegels Begreifen des Absoluten" included in his classic *Da Hegel a Nietzsche*. Translated by G. Colli. (Turin: Einaudi, 1979).

But in the *Ontology*, Lukács also indirectly refers to labor with the term "original form" (*Urform*).[17] In *The Aesthetics* he had called it "fundamental form"[18] and in the *Prolegomena to the Ontology of the Social Being*, labor is called "foundation" (*Fundament*) and "model case" (*Modellfall*).[19] We are faced with what appears to be a terminological confusion because, beyond the different terms employed, Lukács' intention clearly is to interpret labor as an original principle of human development, as indicated by the terms "original phenomenon," "original form," "foundation," or "fundamental form." Lukács means that with labor an organic being has set in motion a process that will lead him to become fully human. Organic being, in turn, arose from inorganic being, but the complexity of organic being is a more developed level of being than the previous one, that is, than inorganic being. The same relationship occurs between social being and organic being: social being is a complex of complexes that manifests a level of complexity greater than mere organic being.

Since labor also becomes the "model case" from which some complexes are formed, such as language or value, then we can also define labor as an "overlapping moment" (*Übergreifendes Moment*). In fact, language emerges from labor as the necessity for communication between human beings participating in the same productive process or, originally, on the same hunting trip. Value also emerges from labor, when individuals perceive alternatives among objects that can be useful to them if those objects are transformed into instruments of labor. The object's property of alternative character – or its ability to be made into different ends or uses – forces one to choose, but the choice can be made only if one is able to be clear about what is useful. The character of choice causes one to confront the freedom of their own choices and the freedom of their own acts. Of course, a free choice can cause tragedies, such as, for example, choosing a food that can be dangerous to one's health. At first humans interact with the surrounding environment on the basis of adapting this environment for the reproduction of life. They recognize the necessity in which they find themselves working and the free character of their choices grows parallel to their ability to recognize the usefulness of their actions and the objects that surround them.

From these brief considerations we can see that ethical values have an almost joint origin with the rise of human beings themselves. Perhaps at an

---

17   Ibid., 73.
18   G. Lukács, *Estetica*. Translated by A. Marietti Solmi. (Turin: Einaudi, 1970), p. 9.
19   G. Lukács, *Prolegomeni all'Ontologia dell'essere sociale. Questioni di principio di un'ontologia oggi divenuta possible*. Original title: *Prolegomena zur Ontologie des gesellschaftlichen Seins. Prinzipienfragen einer heute möglich gwewordenen Ontologie*. Translated by. A. Scarponi. (Milan: Guerrini, 1990), Chapter 3, p. 175.

initial stage these ethical values may be limited by individual selfishness or egoism, but then they tend to turn to the common interest of mankind, because they help to reproduce human life. On the contrary, respect for ethical values, as well as the ability to communicate, that is, the possession of a common language with others, is the foundation for the continuous reproduction of belonging to the human race by an individual human being. Each individual reproducing his or her life at the same time reproduces the human race and labor is the main instrument of this reproduction. Collective labor or the specialization of labor increases even more the possibility of reproducing one's life and raises the reproduction of mankind to ever higher levels. In this way the individual human being feels increasingly a sense of greater belonging to a wider species, and belonging to a complex that is increasingly more differentiated, recognizing himself as a member of the human race to the extent that his own experience becomes part of a common heritage and the experience of others becomes part of his own patrimony. Thus the individual is born, which is an *in-dividuum*, that is, a being whose nature is composed of inseparable elements which are its singularity and its belonging to the human race. In practice every human being is a community, because it is in a relationship of reciprocal relating (*Gemeinschaft*, which in German is also "community") with itself, with others, and with its kind. This is the most innovative conception that Lukács' *Ontology* presents to us and we see the individual born in labor, as a being that belongs to a species; it is a new conception of subjectivity that originates from labor and in labor. All of the ethical values that distinguish singularity, community and universality can be traced back to the moment when labor became the original principle of human beings.

Labor is therefore the original form of practice. Every human activity imitates or reproduces, in different forms, the original act of labor. The model structure is that of teleology which Lukács takes from Hegel and Nicolai Hartmann. In the chapter on Hegel contained in the first part of the *Ontology*, Lukács maintains that there is a false and true ontology in Hegel. The real ontology is Hegel's recognition of concrete categories and structures of man's everyday life and their interpretation in historical terms, while the false ontology consists in the idealist and hierarchical transformation of these categories and structures. The most emblematic case of this idealist transformation is found in the category of teleology contained in Hegel's *Science of Logic*. Naturally Lukács also takes into consideration the concept of teleology that Marx emphasizes in the famous passage from *Capital* on the distinction between the bee and the architect. In this way, Lukács demonstrates that he has learned the Marxist lesson that led Marx to overthrow Hegelian philosophy.

Teleology, for Hegel, is divided into three moments: the position of the subjective purpose, the investigation of the means to accomplish such purpose, and the purpose achieved, with consequent preservation of the means used. According to Hegel, teleology presupposes a concept: "The relation of purpose is therefore more than a judgment; it is the syllogism of the free concept in itself that reconnects with itself through objectivity."[20] The concept is presented as the realization of the goal, as a unit of objective being with an ideal aim. The only way to connect a purpose with objectivity is the means to accomplish this purpose. The means, therefore, performs the same function as a middle term of a formal syllogism, that is, it is both an immediate object and an extrinsic relation to the end of the goal; the latter provides the external means of determining the object and transforms it from a mechanical object into an instrument.[21] The teleological aspect of labor is, therefore, the moment in which subjectivity becomes objectivized or the rational becomes real.

Lukács recognizes the depth of analysis of Hegelian philosophy and recovers the concept of the "cunning of reason" (*List der Vernunft*) in its original meaning expressed in the *Science of Logic*.[22] With an astuteness of reason, Hegel dialectically explains the rise of the new from the relationship of two natural entities: the means and the object to be transformed by labor. Lukács, in resuming the categorical structure of Hegelian teleology,[23] emphasizes Hegel's interest in the instrument of labor, considered as a means of dominating nature and through which the teleological process can be considered as the translation of the concept into reality. Hegel went beyond such an interpretation by grasping the character not only of the medium of the instrument, but also the fact that it represents the continuation of labor over time, thanks also to the preservation of the instrument of labor once labor is complete. Hegel recognizes that the instrument has a validity superior to the purpose, because the instrument can serve different singularities. This interpretation of Hegelian teleology allows Lukács to express the conceptual nodes around which the Marxian conception of the development of history was formed as a consequence of the relationship of labor with the objective ownership of the instruments of production.

---

20 G. Hegel, *Scienza della logica*. Italian translation by A. Moni revised by C. Cesa. (Bari: Laterza, 1974) Book III, Section 2, Chapter 3, p. 840.
21 Cf. ibid., 846.
22 "What then the purpose is put in the relationship mediated with the object and interposes between itself and the object another object, which can be regarded as the astuteness of reason." Ibid., 848.
23 In the *Prolegomena*, Lukács calls the Hegelian teleology of work a "brilliant episode." Cf. Lukács, *Prolegomeni all'ontologia dell'essere sociale*, op. cit., 23.

Marx reported clearly, but with a revolutionary valence and an up to that moment unprecedented practical-theoretical centrality, what Hegel had expressed *in nuce* in his system. Lukács' attempt to point out a continuity between the two German philosophers emerges on this aspect of the dialectic of labor in an even clearer form than on other occasions. Already in *The Young Hegel*, Lukács had grasped the importance of the instrument in the works of the early Hegel: "The concrete analysis of the dialectic of human labor exceeds in Hegel the antinomy of causality and teleology, showing the concrete place that conscious human purpose occupies in the overall causal context without breaking this context, without having to go out and appeal to a transcendent principle, but also ... without losing the specific determinations of the purpose of labor."[24] The fact that Lukács was also attentive to Hegel's early works, particularly the *Phenomenology of Spirit*, and has analyzed this work above all in *The Young Hegel*, can be due to two reasons. The first is historical. In 1938, when he wrote *The Young Hegel*, the old Hegel was considered by the Stalinist critics an apologist of the Prussian reaction, rendering it therefore impossible to reevaluate. The second is more complex: a careful analysis of the Hegelian text shows us that Hegel's approach to teleology is ontological in the *Science of Logic*, while it is phenomenological in the *Phenomenology of the Spirit*. Lukács had addressed the phenomenological aspect of the concept of labor in *History and Class Consciousness*, while in the *Ontology* he analyzes the original principle of labor, which required a careful reading of the logical-scientific structure of the *Science of Logic* rather than the historical-phenomenological thesis of the *Phenomenology of the Spirit*. In fact, in *History and Class Consciousness* labor presented itself under the phenomenal form of the commodity, as wage and alienated labor, in turn a reified and estranged form of praxis. In the *Ontology*, labor is, instead, the fundamental principle of the individual and of his subjectivity, that is, of man who makes history and reproduces his own humanity in consciousness and in the practice of his daily life. This explanation allows us to link the two major Marxist works of Lukács in a relationship of continuity and not of opposition, as the students of the "Budapest School" have sought to do.

The aim set in labor is, for Marx as well as for Lukács, the moment in which the ideal becomes a fundamental element of social-material reality as it determines the causal series of the determinations of being. It is the moment when Marx takes up the ideal moment and recovers it within his materialistic perspective. The role of teleology is increased by the fact that it, through labor and

---

24   G. Lukács, *Il giovane Hegel*. Italian translation by R. Solmi. (Turin: Einaudi, 1975), Chapter 3, §6, p. 481.

its principle function, becomes the founding element of sociality. Therefore, the genesis of society is also in the thought of man. Placing himself on this line of continuity between Hegel and Marx, Lukács traces all of the stages of Marxian thought on the dialectic of labor and locates in Aristotle's concept of potentiality (δύναμις), as Marx himself had done, the instrument for the emergence of a new objectivity. Aristotle plays an important role in the theoretical framework of the *Ontology* and the reading that Lukács gives of the Greek philosopher is particularly "modern."

From Aristotle, Lukács takes up the theory of mimesis or mirroring. The idealist moment also presents itself in the theory of mirroring, which has aroused the strongest criticisms in philosophical circles. Already in the *Aesthetics* Lukács had dealt with the argument by claiming that mirroring is the re-production in the human mind of external objects. Reproduction that is conducted according to the specific capacities of the human mind and, therefore, not according to the objective nature of objects. Lukács emphasized with particular insistence that, in art and literature, mirroring means, first of all, that the facts represented are mimesis, that is, an imitation in which the practical function is suspended as well as is the need to reproduce an external original. In the *Aesthetics* it should be noted that aesthetic activity arises when the interest is placed in the image reflected as such, and not in the fidelity of this image to an external original. To take an example, given by Lukács himself: dance became an authentic art, that is, an autonomous art, when men, distancing themselves from the immediate needs of everyday life, stopped practicing it for magical-religious purposes and began to experience an immediate interest in the *mirroring itself*, that is, in very the act of dancing. Here the immediate-concrete connection between the reflected element and the external reality remained suspended and the artistic product constitutes its own objectivity.

In the praxis of labor and in knowledge – which are tightly linked to each other – man interprets objects according to their own purposes and values, then substantially according to the use value that an object can have or not for the labor activity. So Lukács himself points out the almost inseparable relationship of mirroring and teleological positing (or the projection of the idea in consciousness into the objective world via labor), although they are heterogeneous.[25] The mirroring in the act of reproducing in consciousness of natural objects overcomes the separation between subject and object; it is an

---

25 "The two heterogeneous acts we are talking about are: on the one hand, the most exact reflection possible of the reality taken into consideration, on the other, the correlative act of putting into place those causal chains which, as we know, are indispensable for

overcoming that, at this stage of the process of labor, is present only in consciousness, in the ideal world. The overcoming shows us the exactness of the mirroring of an object in the human mind, the exactness necessary to pass to the positing of the object and to the production of objects, so that they may be spiritual possessions of social being. The mirroring is based on the category of *possibility*[26] as it can create a reality and make it interact with the natural reality, transforming it into a new objectivity. Thus, a third moment is generated with respect to the subject and the object that acts as a mediation, as noted in a paper of Lukács titled, "On the Ontological Basis of Human Thought and Activity."[27] Lukács conceives the mirroring within conscience as the first step to differentiate man from animals, in fact with mirroring consciousness plays a primary role for the fixation of the purpose to be realized, while in animals it is a mere epiphenomenon. In this way a dialectical process is created which is set in motion by the mirroring of the natural object in human consciousness. It creates a causal chain which becomes a new objectification and determines the acquisition of other properties of social being and represents the new which has formed in consciousness as a consequence of the act of mirroring. Here we can grasp the dialectical character of the Lukácsian conception of consciousness.

4

The *Ontology of Social Being* is a work that not only renews the tradition of great classical philosophy, but also allows the extension of philosophical

---

realizing the teleological position" (G. Lukács, *Ontologia dell'essere sociale*, vol. II, Chapter 1, §1, p. 36).

26 Here I limit myself to pointing out how Lukács is linked to the category of possibility starting from History and class consciousness, when it attributes to the proletariat a possible class consciousness, even if it has not yet reached maturity and full expression. On the other hand, the possibility is a category of the intellect starting from Kant and Leibniz's principle of sufficient reason is nothing other than the anticipation of possibility as a logical category. Lukács recognizes an attenuation of the necessity of Kant (Cf. G. Lukács, *Prolegomeni all'ontologia dell'essere sociale*, Chapter 3, p. 154) and, therefore, bearing in mind that the possibility, together with necessity and existence, make up the group of modality, then one can deduce that a diminished character of necessity leaves more room for the category of possibility in defining an object's mode.

27 "Knowledge in general distinguishes very clearly between the objectively existing being-in-itself of objects and their cognitive process" (G. Lukács, "Le basi ontologiche del pensiero e dell'attività dell'uomo." In G.L., *L'uomo e la democrazia*. Italian translation by A. Scarponi. (Rome: Editori Riuniti, 1975), 27.

interests to branches of science that had remained substantially marginal in contemporary philosophical reflection, particularly to that of paleo-anthropology. Here we cannot adequately elaborate on Lukács' reflections on the process of *man's* humanization, but there is no doubt that a distinctly Lukácsian reflection on the transition from organic to social being arises from paleo-anthropological research. It should be borne in mind that the *Ontology* is a work from the early 1960s, when the most advanced theories concerning human development had not yet been elaborated and, therefore, Lukács considered labor, in essence praxis, as the dominant principle explaining the passage from animal to man.

Today the situation has changed considerably and labor, or the capacity to manipulate the environment, as the paleo-anthropologists would say, is no longer considered the dominant element of this passage because the concept of standing erect has been added, the skeletal structure of man, the monthly fertility of women, the size of the skull and the smallness of molar teeth with the consequent greater size of the human brain, the use of hands and anterior vision and, last but not least, the genetic heritage of the human being. In our opinion, however, none of these factors are dominant, but these taken together, along with others that we have omitted here for reasons of space, have determined the slow process of human development. However, labor was a factor of great synthesis among all of these other factors because labor remains a unique feature of the species. No other animal labors, even if it can use tools. An animal can also improve nature according to a purpose that has been set, but they do not preserve them for subsequent acts of labor. Only man retains the tools of labor and uses them. No other philosopher before Lukács had used labor as the principle of human development and more than any other philosopher, including the theologian and philosopher Teilhard de Chardin, Lukács used the research of paleo-anthropology to derive fundamental concepts for his theoretical reflection. This is also why Lukács may in fact be a dwarf, but one who stood on the shoulders of giants.

CHAPTER 2

Lukács and the Reshaping of Marxism: From Hartmann's to Lukács' *Ontology*

Endre Kiss

1

Although it is true that both Hartmann's and Lukács' ontologies have been critiqued, we cannot rule out that both thinkers nevertheless instantiated the most important *ontological turns* in twentieth-century thought and can be compared on this basis. Their historical situations set the context for their discoveries, something that does not occur very frequently in the same way in modern philosophy. In Hartmann's case and time, this ontological turn came to almost prevail as the leading trend of its time, which cannot be said about Lukács' approach (which itself does not mean that the turn in his case would not also have had very sophisticated, albeit at the same time also very complex historical and philosophical background).

That both these ontologies expressed a strong protest against the other philosophical currents of their time might be soon forgotten; moreover, just a uniformly conceived ontology in the 20th century cannot necessarily be interpreted as a protest act. Both comprehensive ontologies bear the character of a turn; both are fundamental protests and strategic rescue operations for the whole project of "philosophy." Both are conscious of the fact that alone they are seeking to answer an enormous challenge simply because of their basic concept, and thereby are choosing for themselves an approach that is perhaps indispensable and that can, however, no longer have behind it the traditional legitimacy of previous philosophy.

The question remains concerning which threads of Hartmann's ontology could concretely be relevant for Lukács (in the position of the real solution of the fateful dilemmas of Marxism). There are some remarks in the literature and there are also a few legends about this. Hartmann's exact relation to Lukács would, however, throw much light on the way we interpret Lukács' thought and the future of Marxism.

This ontological turn not only means a turn at the level of the overall concept, in which Lukács reacts against quite numerous philosophers and philosophies, which have hitherto constituted his main orientations. We first of all put the question of the philosophical contents of this tremendous turn, but it would be equally fruitful to also put the question of the political contents, perhaps also probably (and rather!) of the political motives. Lukács' transformation of Hartmann bears the traits of an unmistakable and even very devoted and convinced loyalty to Marx. *The possible political contents and motives can undoubtedly be based on the historical and also the philosophical perspectives of actually existing socialism.* In contrast to the relative transparency of this attitude, a multitude of further philosophical-political moments appear in an even greater number.

Apart from its purely systematic importance, this *Ontology* is characterized by multiple philosophical-political initiatives. On the one hand, they are directed in a broad sense against Soviet Marxism, but also against the previous development of Marxist philosophy itself. On the other hand, the philosophical-political concept of Lukács' work is directed against a large number of representatives of non-Marxist philosophy, for instance with the intention that the new *Ontology* must be the clearly leading and hegemonic philosophy in comparison with them, the Marxism for the whole Marxian movement, but in a new philosophical form.

It is precisely the totality of the philosophy-political concept, the conquest of a new millenarian hegemony of Marxism within philosophy that represents its singular enterprise. One side of this singularity consists in the fact that such a vast enterprise extends to several periods of political and philosophical history, thereby this concept is developing in a way that is not only independent of the intra-Marxist but also of the non-Marxist processes. *Such a concept lives its own life.* The embedding of this attempt to renew Marxism thereby gained a decisive importance in actual history by the fact that it emerged from the real history of the late 1960s. *But the work was late.* When the new concept was established, the long-lasting low flight of Marxism/neo-Marxism had already begun. Lukács himself, however, took the encounter with real history so seriously that he wrote his *Ontology* first in German and in addition a whole *Prolegomenon* in Kantian style prefaced the work, in which he provided a clear overview and summary of the content.

For Hartmann, the great complex of neo-Kantianism formed his background and played a most active role in the constitution of his *Ontology*. He summed up the boundless relativism of the other side as the insistence on epistemology, which, *in toto*, blocked the path of philosophy to reality, which path must be opened precisely in the midst of the unique historical circumstances of the post-war time in the twenties.

For Lukács, there existed a large complex of non-ontologically established, non-Marxist philosophies (the detailed representation of which we shall return to), the background of which played the most active role in the constitution of his *Ontology*. But for him there exists also another side: the new Marxist *Ontology*, which must become the master of the non-ontologically established non-Marxist philosophies as well, comes first in the circumstances of being able to become master in the midst of the Marxist philosophical world.

A curious asymmetry becomes visible here: the precondition of the domination in the Marxist philosophical world consists in the already conquered rule in the non-Marxist, non-ontological established philosophical world. Hartmann had to cross the Rubicon of epistemology, while in his turn Lukács on the one hand (in the field of the non-ontologically established non-Marxist philosophies) repeated this step, he used it in his other fields (in the non-ontologically established Marxist philosophies) also productively, which practically constituted his turn against Hegel and against all the Hegelian concepts already included in the different Marxisms.

In his work, Lukács clearly identifies without any hesitation those non-ontologically non-Marxist directions which he wants to overcome with the ontological turn. Neopositivism (usually symbolized by Carnap) rises from the circle of the contemporary philosophies of his time. Lukács' peculiar embedding in the just described "two-front war" might be the cause of the fact that his work is also polemical throughout. Both ontologies also differ in the fact that Hartmann's reformulation of the strata of being (*Seinsschichten*) aims to set up a complete new ontology, while for Lukács the newly-created ontology means only a new framework in which he reformulates Marxism and, as we will see, fulfils this mission with a quite loyal attitude towards Marx. For Lukács, the real matter of *Ontology* is therefore Marx; it is not determined freely from tradition and own research.

2

Hartmann, as in all the great ontological concepts of his time, often refers to the extensive crisis of civilization and of society. With the interpretation of his position as a product of crisis, it is largely more difficult for Lukács. On the one hand, Marxism in its transition from the Stalinist to the post-Stalinist phase might by no means be regarded "officially" as a crisis, while the same process (or, perhaps, crisis) in relation to the neo-positivistic turn of Western philosophy – from a Marxist point of view – could (and should) have been obligatorily considered as quite problematic.[1] Both processes would each

---

1 Lukács considered this emergence of neo-positivism above all from the genre of the Vienna Circle more or less as a scandal. This is an attitude that only a very differentiated investigation can thoroughly explore.

receive a separate specific investigation. However, it seems to us that Lukács' consciousness of the crisis has above all grown out of the insight into the fantastic and hardly communicable (real-existing) juxtaposition of late-Stalinism and neo-liberalism/neo-positivism. His consciousness of the crisis, therefore, does not concern *in toto* Marxism, for he would not have written the ontology with this consciousness.

Lukács must, but also cannot, identify this situation as a crisis, although his *feeling of a danger* can be experienced. However, by no means might he have thought that the historical processes are accelerating to the point that *the new form of Marxism he developed will already be without any echo.* The unexpected turn (the adoption of Hartmann's ontology in the reconstitution of Marxism) just has to work, so that the new hegemonic position must always prove its power in both directions. On the one hand, it has to overcome the newly emerging late-Stalinism and, on the other, the complex of the new international currents (with neo-positivism at the top).

This double intention promises to yield *unique fruit*. The simultaneous renewal of Marxism (the loyal reformulation of Marx's content in the new *framework* of Hartmann's ontology) and the victory, considered as definitive, over the non-ontological, non-Marxist currents grants this new Marxism a lasting and undisputed framework. (With regard to this dimension, we cannot go into any further detail ... how this new concept also even promises an advantageous social, ideological and sociological position ... how this new Marxism can be more or less without any problem be propelled even in the direction of the larger masses, and so on.)

However, the aforementioned double intention (we could perhaps even say *double engagement*) also leads to a further and deeper background intention. Clearly or not, consciously or not, that the philosopher who undertakes this double intention, who with the true Marxian material overcomes post-Stalinism just as definitively,[2] like the new philosophy (characterized by neo-positivism as the ideal type) ... *this philosopher can rightly look at himself as the new Marx.*

It goes without saying that this concept is connected with Lukács' deeper *self-image.*[3] Marx, as a leading philosopher in a new way, refers to Lukács, who is also a leading philosopher entering the tradition. The old and the new leading figure of philosophy is mediated by Nicolai Hartmann. The most striking

---

2 Lukács' critical debate includes official and public Marxism, and it was evident at that time! For the numerous currents of post-Marxian Marxism did not belong at that time simply to the tradition! *If Lukács would today work out this concept, he would do it in a completely different way.*
3 It is clear, however, that he wanted to reach the central position ("master thinker") in world philosophy through this transformation – it might be psychologically trend-setting that in this ambition of his juvenile genius consciousness and loyalty to Marx could find an equilibrium.

change between the Lukács of the *Ontology* and that of the *pre-ontological* period is undoubtedly the clear elimination of Hegel from all possible philosophical contexts, which had previoiusly been dominant in his previous work. With Hegel, the period of *History and Class Consciousness*, that of *the Young Hegel*, as well as numerous individual studies disappeared, but also the Hegelianizing elements of Soviet Marxism disappeared from other authors as well.[4] In spite of the complexity of Soviet Marxism itself, Hegel and his influence alone are considered as a mainly determining element of Soviet Marxism because of Lenin; the actual discussions about Hegel also begin just when we want to put Hegel, already independently of Lenin, into the centre. Hegel's slight farewell is considered the psychologically most complex problematic in this transformation. Even a Marxian paraphrase is perceptible – this break with Hegel also meant a break with his philosophical past (also within the Marxist period), the possibility of the Marxian paraphrase arising in connection with the "break with the philosophical conscience."

Paradoxically, in the eyes of his immediate contemporaries, the annihilation of post-Stalinist Marxism, associated with the elimination of Hegel, was still widely taught (which exercised a clear effect on the wide public).[5] We should not underestimate the personal or psychological significance of these attacks, for these openly stated and devastating-ironic attacks are likely to make Lukács himself personally experience a new attitude of the double intention. While with Lukács the break with Hegel leads to Hartmann's *Ontology* (in which he then transforms Marx), in the case of Marx the same break (with Hegel) has led to a modern form of theoretically motivated positivism.

3

In such a unique philosophical project, the terms are always assuming a new meaning. Lukács appears here as a radical innovator, but simultaneously also as an *orthodox*, for the construction of the *Ontology* allows both definitions. The image of a leading philosopher is always relative. Within philosophy it always involves something other than that found in non-philosophical contexts. Moreover, that specific difference is always dominating, according to which

---

4   We do not disregard the contradictory character of the Hegel discussions of the Soviet time (such as the position of a *Deborin*, or the figure of *Iljenkov*, which was important later), but all this did not change the general embedding of the Hegelian tradition in Soviet Marxism, the leading source of which was the citatological power of Lenin himself.

5   *Ad absurdum*, these devastating remarks might show the innovator of Marxism also as a *politically oppositional* thinker.

the real "time window" for the real hegemony of a philosophy always passes faster than what is required for an effectively mature philosophical solution to be worked out for the same situation.

The one way for success (*Anerkennung, Geltung*) would have consisted in the fact that the whole *Ontology* was quickly published in German, since one could have seen whether the proof of the pudding was in the eating or not. We know that way was not really used. With this failure of the normal reception, the systematic insight should be accidentally shaped in the philosophical community. *And this systematic insight produces a possibility other than the original ambition of Georg Lukács' double intention.* While this intention has determined whether it could be possible to transform the essential positive contents of Marxian philosophy within the framework of Hartmann's ontology, the systematic insight, on the basis of its own perspective, immediately reaches the critical point concerning whether Lukács has not thus navigated a real philosophical *no man's land.*

We see that it is a completely different starting point. This thematization of a possible philosophical no man's land is not at all identical with the earlier attempts of typologization (such as the *double intention* or the others). This question arises from the fact that for the main line of the philosophical evolution either the *positivistic* philosophical family understand in the broad sense or the *Hegelian* philosophical family understand in the broad sense created the real integration and organization of philosophy.

It is crucial for our argumentation that this duality was (and is) by no means perfect. It is also not a comprehensive typology; it corresponded, however, practically perfectly to the philosophical general consciousness of those years (which was for the most part filled fully with Marxism). The concept of "no man's land" was therefore – regardless of the possible nuances of the former and the later typologies – actually the most important reason why one has hardly understood Lukács' conception immediately according to the knowledge of the individual parts of the *Ontology*! To this time-bound situation, it must be added that at Lukács' determining time in this discussion (which was dominated by post-Stalinist Marxism, the Frankfurt School, Existentialism – and not yet even by early neo-positivism) Nicolai Hartmann hardly might have been a philosopher to whom the *decisive word* in the reformulation of Marxism is due.

Let us imagine again a *royal way* of the *Ontology* in relation to the dissemination and reception. In this case, the discussion should have taken the path whereby one begins long and thoroughly discussing from both sides ("Hegelian" and "positivistic"), whether the overcoming of one, of the other or of both school(s) is even possible, and only then one would have been able to start with a more thorough study of Nicolai Hartmann, with which one can understand and according to which model Lukács had imagined the reconstitution of the Marxian paradigm.

It also means, that the philosophical reception in a "royal way" case would have been a very broad and differentiated one, which above all would have been dependent on the recipient's own decisive philosophical position. We have to realize fully that at the important time for Lukács' decision, "Marxism" and "positivism" in the typological consciousness of contemporaries were in very strong conflict with each other. This conflict was a commonly shared construction, whereas numerous strong arguments could have been produced (such as the entire positivism of Marx's *Capital* itself). Independently of the relative bases of this typological conflict, this one however was appearing at that time as a strong opposition.

If this was so, we must turn our attention to Lukács' earlier oeuvre. In fact, positivism (in its numerous forms) is considered as the philosopher Lukács' permanent opponent, *an adversary of whom he gets rid, while often referring to his identity in his existing opposition to it*. The fact that Marxism, being understood as philosophy, also regards positivism as a decisive opponent, highlights Lukács' decision from another new angle. In the context of the constitution of the new *Ontology*, we thus discover a comprehensive dilemma of the whole history of Marxism, which dilemma was also quite characteristic for Lukács (both in his youth and in his mature years). The decided, albeit often hidden, anti-positivism connects such different works as *History and Class Consciousness* and the *Ontology*.

History and Class Consciousness was also understood in its time as a radical reform of Marxism which aimed to redirect the whole process of Marxist thought. As a radical new birth, this work even formulates a quite extended critique of positivism, one of modern rationality in a generalized form, the destruction of which was the main mission of messianic Marxism. Here, scientific terms appear as one-sided, abstract and false – in the *Ontology* Lukács chooses for them the comprehensive term "realization." The intention is here clear, because that category is for Lukács more a dynamic concept than a fixed term, which from the beginning is not reminiscent of objectification (*Vergegenstaendlichung*) and alienation (*Entfremdung*).

The reason for the *compromised* and therefore also *falsified* character of the existing categories lies in *History and the Class Consciousness*, in the non-existent adequacy vis-à-vis the principle of philosophical totality, while the same reason in the *Ontology* lies in the non-existing adequacy in relation to the specific constitution rules of the ontological concepts. In *History and Class*

Consciousness no epistemology exists and the fixed philosophical categories are confronted with a permanent methodological suspicion. In the *Ontology* the categories are determined by those motives which are ontologically relevant for Lukács. In *History and Class Consciousness* the higher value of the totality method is declared, just as in the *Ontology* the higher value of the declared ontological position is clearly represented and demonstrated.

The Marx of *History and Class Consciousness* is the whole and true Marx, the Marx of the *Ontology* is also that. *History and Class Consciousness* is a comprehensive reaction to a new crisis caused by world history and the crisis of philosophy itself; the *Ontology* is also a total reaction to an apparently not so spectacularly emerging new crisis of humanity. *History and Class Consciousness* creates a central position for Lukács in the necessary renewal of Marxism. The *Ontology* also raises Lukács to the central position in the necessary renewal of Marxism. Both works are lacking the *in statu nascendi* exercised *effort of analysis*, in addition, a *methodological reflection* is only present here and there. Both works are a declared execution of a methodological framework that has already been thoroughly thought through in a secret way, in which legitimate and well-identifiable contents of Marxian philosophy have been removed. In *History and Class Consciousness* epistemology is replaced by a concrete interpretation of the subject–object relation and thereby also removed. In the *Ontology*, the epistemological question is excluded by the outcome of Hartmann's ontology. Both works (in seemingly astonishingly different historical situations) experience a shocking vacuum, while *History and Class Consciousness* seeks to break up this vacuum with a messianistic concept of *Praxisphilosophie* and the *Ontology* with a decidedly anti-messianistic, historical-genealogical conception.

Another significant component of the new *Ontology* is that Nicolai Hartmann, otherwise not really well known in a wide circle, had to appear as a *crypto-Marxist* from the beginning, reflecting the usual attitude of those years, because his *strata of being (Seinsschichten)* in the judgment of the philosophical community came very close to Marxism (base-superstructure relation). It is certainly possible to discuss this kinship without mentioning that such a perception can very quickly become different in the historical change of the determining philosophical contexts. Lukács was quite conscious of this proximity. In his largely unconventional comparison of Ludwig Feuerbach and Nicolai Hartmann, he demonstrates the relevant existence of a positivity constructed without epistemological reference, while, on the other hand, he sets Hartmann in relation to the analogy regarding Feuerbach, almost in the same similar position of a *backwards-oriented* intellectual antecedent of Marx.

4

If one wishes to formulate the summarizing thesis that Lukács transforms the new Marxism into the framework of Hartmann's ontology through the transformation of the Marxian content, this thesis still says little about the *magnitude* of that systematic work which Lukács finished. The *extent* of this work also lets us indirectly draw some conclusions from the history of the work's evolution. It also makes the assumption imaginable that Lukács began to develop the idea, maybe even the preparations, much earlier than generally assumed. On the possible effect, or recommendation of Harich and/or Szigeti, he might have already designed the basic idea of this concept even in the turbulent time, which was partly still open to dialogue, of the late 1940s. Thus we also address our hypothesis, that ultimately the *Ontology* might not (or not completely) be understood as a clear and problem-free "prolegomenon" for an upcoming Marxist ethic. If this insight were later corroborated, one would still have to find the systematic position of the *Aesthetics* in this evolution. After all, there is a quite visible bridge between the *Aesthetics* and the *Ontology*, namely the introductory chapter on *everyday consciousness* clearly pointing to a social ontology, which thematic approach had never before appeared as an introduction to a classical philosophical aesthetics.

As regards the oeuvre, both these mighty works (*Aesthetics* and *Ontology*) are an admirable overall achievement – one thinks of the political events and constraints determining the biography, or also the numerous other works. This order of magnitude of the systematic work means that in carrying out this transformation, Lukács adopted a position in relation to hundreds of individual systematic problems, and these positions had to come from his own philosophical workshop. This part of the transformation work is considered as *Lukács' own personal systematic achievement*. This work gave him the opportunity to be consistently strategic and strategically consistent, to avoid the epistemological question and to justify every alternative possibility.

In this context, Lukács becomes really a co-author of Marx, because he has to adapt his theses to the often new questions, but so that the respective necessity of an epistemology is eliminated and numerous systematic places are positively carried out.

The teleology is moving in the central position in the so conceived object constitution. Hartmann's relation to Marx appears clear, the teleology of the work is the model of all sociality in Marx. It is not only a model, but also the "original form of it" (11.18). He calls this teleology "an indestructible component of every thought" (which also underlines again the strength of the relationship to the problematic and relevance of everyday consciousness). The generalization of the thus conceived idea of the teleology during the simultaneous reduction of it in the working process is that step which leads without obstacles into the new Marxian ontology. Only such a proficient *connoisseur* of classical idealism such as Lukács could engage with it, such that he himself brings a Kant into play in an anti-epistemological conception! Kant's teleology (with the "*Zweckmaessigkeit ohne Zweck*") is aimed at the recognition of organic nature, while the Kant of the *Critique of the Pure Reason* stands diametrically opposed to this ontology concept.

Lukács also tries to attribute the duality of the epistemological and ontological approach to the difference of the sciences standing behind philosophy. This idea is creative, because the so-called physicalist and so-called biologically-oriented periods always followed each other in the history of philosophy, and this idea also deserves to be treated further. The only problem is that the concrete duality of the background sciences does not fully correspond to the difference between the epistemological and ontological attitude.

Lukács' transformation work can clearly demonstrate his systematic knowledge and ability; moreover, its purpose consists in the extreme consequence of the exclusion of any open or hidden epistemological reference. In the determination of this occurrence, a very complex difference between Marx himself and Lukács already exists. Marx's position rested on a multitude of historical moments, most of which are historical today. Lukács' motivation is however completely up-to-date and present-day, in which Marx's and his own philosophical and personal interests coincide. Lukács imagines that the widespread integration of the results of modern research can be possible without any explicit philosophical epistemology, partly because the close connection between modern research and epistemology has already been clearly resolved, and partly because other philosophical schools neglect this priority.

5

For these reasons relating to the closer contexts, it follows that Lukács' *Ontology* is distinctly more polemical than Hartmann's. A similar difference also exists in the basic intention: despite its polemical accents, for Hartmann the task consists in providing a new interpretation of being through the reformulation of the individual strata of being (*Seinsschichten*), while Lukács' main task is much more complicated. He assumes that he reformulates Marx's work in terms of a new philosophical science of being and existence. The difference consists in the fact that he does not want to build this ontology "without any presuppositions," but already considers this framework as an instrument in advance.

This instrumentalization (now in a non-negative sense) makes its orientation quickly visible. Put in a much more generalized form, Lukács re-establishes a "classical" (not orthodox, non-selective, not "renewed" or somehow updated) Marxism in the framework of Hartmann's *Ontology* against the irresistibly presented neo-positivist challenge – one cannot talk about the lack of presuppositions.

Like every ontological attempt of his time, Hartmann also experiences a profound crisis and defines his work as a reaction to and overcoming of this crisis. The articulation of a crisis is more difficult for Lukács. Actual socialism is not, in his eyes, living in a crisis. If he had seen it in that way, it would have been completely impossible to formulate it publicly. We can be sure that the Marxism in his mind could also not have been in a crisis; not only Lukács' work speaks against that, but also the content and the whole spirit of the *Ontology*, with his deeply loyal and equally deeply learned Marxism. Thus the result slowly appears that this very differentiated picture of the crisis anticipates in Lukács a crisis that will determine the competitive position of late Stalinism in an opening international discussion, which will face a neo-positivism simultaneously plausible and supported by big powers.

Lukács transforms Marxism in this new framework without any further presuppositions (which stands clearly in contradiction with his previous philosophy). He is thus pursuing a very concrete goal and, indeed, creating in this context a quite new philosophy, which did not exist before him, a new philosophy which, in holistic terms, reminds us neither of Hartmann nor of Marx. This new philosophy is also a preparatory work of Marxism.

Lukács' *Ontology* is simultaneously a philosophical revolution and a philosophical reform. As far as the philosophical systematics is concerned, it is certainly a revolution, a clear opposite of all interpretations, that were, not so long ago, simply condemned (amongst others also by Lukács himself!). The *Ontology* is however, for the most part, also a careful and responsible reform of philosophy, for Lukács wants to transpose the *uncompromised* part of Marxism into Hartmann's structure, which is not only a possibility, but also a reality of the reform.

6

The polemical character in general and the individual concrete polemics are so alive in the *Ontology* that sometimes it (they) can distract the attention of the reader from those outcomes which Lukács effectively achieves in incorporating Marx's results into Hartmann's framework of the *Ontology*. The duality between the multiple polemics and the positive construction runs through the whole work. The polemical face of the *Ontology* also successively divides the history of philosophy into two parts. The outlines of a mighty offensive against the original Kant (that is to say, not against Kant's interpretations), against the whole project of epistemology, against the classical and against neo-positivism, are quite consistently marked.

In this context, if we try to think together about the common contents of these criticized schools, we are astonishingly confronted with those disciplines which – in summary – prepared, or even realized the *rationality* or the *disenchantment* (Entzauberung). Against these disciplines, Lukács represents in the *Ontology* no "re-enchanting" philosophical option (for which he felt a great inclination in his pre-Marxist period). Instead he carries out a *double action*. He wants to shake the (finally) complete philosophical modernization in such a way *that he puts forward another, an "alternative," a "secondary" philosophical modernization.* Thus he wants, *inter alia*, to admit Hegel is right (even if the individual concrete results of this secondary modernization again make Hegel obsolete) and to again bring Marx into the most central position with Hartmann's assistance (both in the Marxist and also in the non-Marxist philosophical universe).

The fact that Hegel and Marx fell away from the Kantian tradition can be interpreted many times. In the fifties and sixties of the twentieth century the exclusive confrontation of Hegel *and* positivism, or of Marx *and* positivism should, however, already occur as more than an increasingly *forced* step. Thus if Lukács was not interested in raising Marx again to the position of sole ruling and leading philosopher, he would have plenty of opportunities to deal with the polemically treated line of the "disenchantment" (*Entzauberung*) of the thinking in the common domain of Hegel and Marx.

After all, through this process Lukács also justifies a new tradition in the history of philosophy. *Lukács changes the legitimacy of the whole Marxian thinking already considered as definite.* In the legitimation of this philosophy, the image of the philosophical greatness was living in an inseparable unity with the comprehensive critique that had delegitimized capitalism. Therefore, this philosophical legitimacy really possessed a double justification, the components of which strengthened each other very strongly: *Marx is the greatest philosopher because he had dealt the most effectively with capitalism – Marx could account most effectively for capitalism because he was the greatest philosopher.*

7

Lukács' *Ontology* breaks with the legitimacy having almost become evident. He wants to base the hegemony of Marxism entirely on the *philosophical superiority* of Marx's philosophy. The problematic of the class struggle or of the labour movement is, therefore, not necessarily appearing on the periphery – the goal is the autochtone philosophical explanation. Sociologically, it is also a clear proof that *philosophy belongs to the philosophers*; the effect of the insight in the particular quality of Marxism should first of all convince philosophers themselves.

In any case, the young Lukács absorbed much of Kant, although presumably his neo-Kantian-coloured environment also prevailed upon him to rebel critically against it. The impression is that he has worked more thoroughly and understood the second and the third criticism in relation to the first one. For the period 1918–1919, Lukács may, after all, be considered as a profound Kant *connoisseur*, whose already massive anti-positivism and anti-scientism of the time should have limited this knowledge of Kant. It can be an important motive that Lukács' way to communism meant also a *direct break* with Kant's ethics. One of the greatest personal frustrations of Lukács' life was also related to neo-Kantianism. His habilitation plans in Heidelberg also failed in (and because of) a largely neo-Kantian environment.

As generally formulated, positivism belonged to all of Lukács' periods as a rather despised adversary, a superficial thinking of the bourgeoisie. The later philosophical and historical research must demonstrate in which relationship his attitude stood then vis-à-vis the always relevant other Marxist waves of anti-positivism. Neo-positivism might have appeared as an incarnation of those tendencies which, in Lukács' eyes, were unacceptable in Kant and in positivism, namely *the overemphasis on epistemology to the detriment of a philosophical attitude directed towards reality.*

As I have already argued, in this confrontation between neo-positivism and late-Stalinism, in the opening world and in the context of an ever-freer philosophical communication, Lukács no doubt realized that neo-positivism would (or could) be victorious in this competition. This was not only the reason for his criticism of this philosophy, but also the reason for the elaboration of the whole new *Ontology* itself.

CHAPTER 3

Lukács' Ontology of Social Being and the Material Basis of Intentionality

Matthew J. Smetona

> Wie überhaupt bei jeder historischen, sozialen Wissenschaft, ist bei dem Gange der ökonomischen Kategorien immer festzuhalten, daß, wie in der Wirklichkeit, so im Kopf, das Subjekt, hier die moderne bürgerliche Gesellschaft, gegeben ist, und daß die Kategorien daher Daseinsformen, Existenzbestimmungen [...].
>
> KARL MARX, "Zur Kritik der politischen Ökonomie"[1]

∴

1 Introduction

Lukács' *Zur Ontologie des gesellschaftlichen Seins* (hereafter *Ontologie*), his ontology of social being, on the reading offered in this essay, explains how any understanding of *intentionality*, if that concept referring to any mental state which is *of* or *about* something – in particular the directedness, aboutness, or reference of that state – is to be truly comprehended at its most fundamental level, requires reference to its material basis in the activity of laboring. This necessity of reference back to the original laboring act as an interaction with and transformation of nature, in conjunction with the necessity of a genetic account from that act to the most complex social formations, together form the commitments of the most systematic and sophisticated articulation of the ontology of Hegelian Marxism. In understanding the human labor process as consciously goal-directed, Lukács explains our intentionality, linguistic discursivity, and normativity in terms of the structural process whereby the goals of our laboring activities are formulated, executed, and evaluated. The political implication of this explanatory strategy is that the freedom and personality of

---

[1] Karl Marx and Friedrich Engels, *Karl Marx / Friedrich Engels Werke*. (Cited as MEW by volume and page number). Band 13. Edited by the Rosa-Luxemburg-Stiftung. (Berlin: Karl Dietz Verlag, 2006), 637.

individuals within any given social totality are to be understood in terms of their participation in this process.

This essay contends that Lukács' ontological framework, in according priority to the labor process in this way, critically reveals the limits and distortions at work in the accounts of intentionality in the historical and contemporary discourses of analytic philosophy. Indeed, the prevailing philosophical aversion to and dismissal of ontological arguments as such is itself symptomatic of those limits and distortions. Thus Lukács in this respect occupies a position which parallels the one which Marx occupied. Just as the classical economists of Marx's time presented their economic laws in abstraction from their material presuppositions in the production process, thereby introducing the possibility of a critique of political economy, the analytic philosophers of Lukács' time and ours present their conceptions of intentionality in abstraction from their material presuppositions in the labor process, thereby introducing the possibility of an ontological critique of the philosophy of intentionality.

The essay will begin with an overview of how intentionality has been conceived in the analytic philosophical tradition and the various questions that have been raised within that tradition. It will then outline Lukács' ontology precisely as a critical response to that tradition's treatment of intentionality. His ontological framework is a systematic construction that can be understood on its own terms, but it is at the same time presented by him, in a number of crucial passages, as a *critique* of the philosophical paradigm about the nature of mental states that was dominant at the time of his writing, a positivistic and logicized paradigm from which the contemporary analytic paradigm is derived directly. Indeed, throughout the *Ontologie*, Lukács refers to both Marx's standpoint and his own as that of "ontological criticism," for reasons that will become clear in the following discussion.

2 Philosophical Explanations of Intentionality

The contemporary philosophical discussion of intentionality has its historical basis in Franz Brentano's 1874 *Psychology from an Empirical Standpoint*. This text presents a number of distinct theses about intentionality, which he identifies below with "every mental phenomenon." Consider the following passage from this foundational text:

> Every mental phenomenon is characterized by what the Scholastics of the Middle Ages called the intentional (or mental) inexistence of an object, and what we might call, though not wholly unambiguously, reference to a content, direction toward an object (which is not to be

understood here as meaning a thing), or immanent objectivity. Every mental phenomenon includes something as object within itself, although they do not do so in the same way. In presentation, something is presented, in judgment something is affirmed or denied, in love loved, in hate hated, in desire desired and so on. This intentional inexistence is characteristic exclusively of mental phenomena. No physical phenomenon exhibits anything like it. We can, therefore, define mental phenomena by saying that they are those phenomena which contain an object intentionally within themselves.[2]

This well-known passage (1) understands the intentional in terms of directionality toward or reference to a content or object; (2) understands all intentional objects as *in*existent; and (3) defines the mental as such in terms of the intentional. The first claim raises the questions of whether directionality can be identified with reference and whether contents can be identified with objects. The second claim raises the question of whether inexistence should be understood as existing in the mind or as not existing at all. If the claim implies the latter meaning, then this would require positing the ontological category of intentional objects, or *the existence of nonexistent objects*. This question of *intentional inexistence* has animated discussion in analytic philosophy for over a century, and a brief sketch of this general development will be offered in this section.

But it must first be noted that the reference to the Scholastics in the first sentence of the above passage is instructive. One can already observe how the late nineteenth-century foundation of all subsequent philosophical treatments of intentionality sets an agenda that is, from its very beginning, purely *theoretical* in character. All such treatments contrast strikingly with the framework established by Marx and inherited by Lukács, i.e., the practical standpoint or the standpoint of (revolutionary) practice. Consider Marx's second and eighth theses on Feuerbach:

> The question of whether objective truth can be attributed to human thought is not a question of theory, but rather a *practical* question. One must prove the truth, i.e., the reality and power, the this-sidedness [*Diesseitigkeit*] of his thinking, in practice. The dispute over the reality or nonreality of thinking which is isolated from practice is a purely *scholastic* question.[3]

---

2 Brentano, *Psychology from an Empirical Standpoint*. (London: Routledge, 1995), 68.
3 MEW 3: 533.

> All social life is essentially *practical.* All mysteries which lead theory to mysticism find their rational solution in human practice and in the comprehension of this practice.[4]

From this view, the entire debate over the necessity of positing an ontological category of intentional objects is beside the point. If theoretical problems about minds and mental phenomena can only find their solutions in the practical activities of human beings, then the necessity of an ontology of social being, an ontological and genetic account depicting the development from the most basic of practical activities to the most complex forms of social life, becomes apparent. The theoretical, in short, must be explained, both ontologically and genetically, in terms of the practical in its most basic form, and that form, for both Marx and Lukács, is the activity of laboring. These are the terms according to which Lukács' Hegelian Marxist ontology can be understood as a critique of philosophical explanations of intentionality.

Brentano's framework, however, represents only the starting point of such explanations. His student, Edmund Husserl, extends this framework along the lines of the phenomenological form of analysis which he founded by introducing the concepts of *noema* and *epoche,* both of which contribute to a paradigm in which intentional mental acts are not to be understood as necessarily directed toward a "real," independent object.[5]

At the same time, Gottlob Frege revolutionizes the philosophical treatment of intentional thought by explaining the structure of such thought in terms of the logical structure of the language through which it is expressed. His distinction between *Bedeutung* (reference) and *Sinn* (sense) constitutes the philosophical foundation of his argument that the essential element of any thought or proposition expressed in the form of a sentence containing a singular term is its *Sinn,* not its *Bedeutung.* Thus, from this view, the constituent elements of sentences are not individuals (concrete particulars), but rather senses (by virtue of which singular thoughts are individuated).

Bertrand Russell extends this analysis in epistemological terms by establishing "acquaintance" with something as a condition of using it in a logical sense. If one is not acquainted with a proper name of a language, then it cannot be understood in logical terms. If such names cannot be understood logically, then, Russell claims, they are "definite descriptions." From this view, mental

---

4   MEW 3: 535.
5   See Edmund Husserl, *Logical Investigations.* Trans. J.N. Findlay. (London: Routledge and Kegan Paul, 1970); *Ideen zu einer Phänomenologie und phänomenologischen Philosophie.* (Halle: Niemeyer, 1913).

states that appear to be about concrete individuals are not in fact singular thoughts, but rather general existentially quantified propositions.[6]

In the more contemporary context, some philosophers have reacted against Frege and Russell on the question of the role played by concrete individuals in individuating singular thoughts. This reaction, one which seeks to ascribe a greater role than the earlier philosophies permitted, is represented by Saul Kripke's theory of "direct reference."[7] This theory is based on a distinction between those designators that are "rigid" (i.e., those which refer to one and the same individual) and those that are not, as well as a distinction within the category of rigid designators itself, with some being rigid in a *de jure* sense (e.g., proper names) and others in a merely *de facto* sense (e.g., definite descriptions).

Nevertheless, contemporary philosophers who subscribe to the Fregean view, such as John McDowell[8] and Robert Brandom, have responded to this theory with a notion of the *de re* sense for singular terms (where "of" marks ascription *de re*, whereas "that" without "of" marks ascription *de dicto*; thus "S believes that Φ[t]" is the *de dicto* form, whereas "S believes *of* t that Φ[*it*]" is the *de re* form).[9] From this view, *de re* ascriptions are the fundamental representational locution of natural languages. As Brandom explains, this locution "comprises the idioms we typically use to express the intentional directedness of thought and talk—the fact that we think and talk *about* things and states of affairs. Words such as 'of' and 'about' play their characteristic intentional, semantic, or representational expressive role in virtue of the way they figure in *de re* ascriptions of propositional attitudes. It is these ascriptions that we use to *say* what we are thinking and talking of or about."[10]

This neo-Fregean position represents, in a way that can be outlined here only schematically, a rapprochement between analytic philosophy and the tradition of German Idealism, not only in its Kantian form, but even in its Hegelian one. Kant, in insisting on the primacy of judgment (*Urteilskraft*), is

---

6   See Bertrand Russell, *The Problems of Philosophy*. (Oxford: Oxford University Press, 1997); *The Principles of Mathematics*. (London: George Allen and Unwin, 1964); "On Denoting." In R. Marsh (ed.), *Logic and Knowledge: Essays, 1901–1950*. (New York: MacMillan, 1956).

7   See Saul Kripke, *Naming and Necessity*. (Cambridge: Harvard University Press, 1980).

8   See John McDowell, "De Re Senses." *The Philosophical Quarterly*, vol. 34, no. 136 (July 1984): 283–294.

9   This framework implies that "*de re* ascriptions may be thought as formed from *de dicto* ones by exporting a singular term from within the 'that' clause, prefacing it with 'of,' and putting a pronoun (or other anaphoric dependent) in the original position" (Robert Brandom, *Making it Explicit: Reasoning, Representing, and Discursive Commitment*. [Cambridge: Harvard University Press, 1998], 502).

10 Brandom, *Making it Explicit*, 499–500.

understood as explaining representations (whether they be particular or general), concepts, and intuitions in terms of the functional role they play in judgments, while judgments themselves are understood as having the primacy which he ascribes to them because of the normative role they play. It is on the basis of this framework that Frege developed the position of semantic holism, as indicated by the "context principle" he articulates in his *Foundations of Arithmetic*, in which the meaning or content of a word or name cannot be understood on its own terms, but only "in the context of a proposition"[11] or sentence. This explanation of sense or meaning in terms of propositional context is also adopted by Wittgenstein, as one can observe in statements 3.3 and 3.314 of his *Tractacus*. But this is not yet conceptual holism in the Hegelian sense. Quine, in his "Two Dogmas of Empiricism" essay, extends this semantic holism beyond the propositional form:

> Any word worth explicating has some contexts which, as wholes, are clear and precise enough to be useful; and the purpose of explication is to preserve the usage of these favored contexts while sharpening the usage of other contexts. In order that a given definition be suitable for purposes of explication, therefore, what is required is not that the definiendum in its antecedent usage be synonymous with the definiens, but just that each of these favored contexts of the definiendum taken as a whole in its antecedent usage, be synonymous with the corresponding context of the definiens.[12]

In understanding the minimum unit of conceptual content as the contextual "wholes" within which they are situated, Quine can be read as approximating not only (1) Hegel's holistic understanding of concepts, but also (2) his (Hegel's) understanding of what he terms the Concept (*der Begriff*) – i.e., the entire holistic system of inferentially-interrelated concepts – as the minimal unit of conceptual content. Hegel understands determinateness or conceptual contentfulness as derived from a process of modally robust exclusion induced by relations of material incompatibility. Consider his following description of his holistic understanding of concepts: "If a specific content ... is determinate, [then] it is in a manifold with another content; it is not a matter of indifference to it whether a certain other content with which it is in relation is, or is not, for

---

11   Gottlob Frege, *The Foundations of Arithmetic: A Logico-Mathematical Enquiry into the Concept of Number*. (Evanston: Northwestern University Press, 1980), 73.
12   V.O. Quine, *From a Logical Point of View: Nine Logico-Philosophical Essays*. (Cambridge: Harvard University Press, 1980), 25.

it is only through such relation that it essentially is what it is."[13] To use Brandom's clarifying example, the concept "circular" is only determinate insofar as it is grasped in relation to the concepts "triangular," "square," "polygonal," etc., or, in the final analysis, "not-circular."[14]

Furthermore, for Hegel, it is not just that grasping one concept requires grasping many concepts, it is that grasping any concept at all implies, at bottom, a comprehension of the totality of concepts, which is itself the Concept (the definite article distinguishes this totality of subjective concepts from those individual concepts of which it is constitutive). So while Hegel begins the third book (or second volume) of the *Science of Logic* with a demonstration of how "the act of judgment necessarily implies an underlying concept,"[15] his analysis finds its completion in "the truth ... that the different determinate concepts, far from falling apart into number, are simply only one and the same Concept."[16]

The Hegelianism of McDowell and Brandom is reflected in a number of ways which cannot be rehearsed here. Nevertheless, it is immediately observable in McDowell's argument that experiential content is conceptual and thus, unlike the "Given," it is able to enter into relations of justification with other elements of the conceptual domain, i.e., it is able to enter into "the space of reasons." He explains concisely: "the conceptual is unbounded; there is nothing outside it."[17] Brandom's Hegelianism, meanwhile, is evident throughout the writings which constitute his ambitious philosophical project that has been described as a kind of rationalist-expressivism or normative inferentialism. His project centers on demonstrating that "[l]ogical vocabulary endows practitioners with the expressive power to make explicit as the contents of claims just those implicit features of linguistic practice that confer semantic contents on their utterances in the first place,"[18] such that "[l]ogic is the organ of semantic

---

13   G.W.F. Hegel, *Wissenschaft der Logik. Erster Band. Die objektive Logik. Erstes Buch. Die Lehre vom Sein* (1832). (Cited as WL 21); *Erster Band. Die objektive Logik. Zweites Buch. Die Lehre vom Wesen* (1813). (Cited as WL 11); *Zweiter Band. Die subjektive Logik oder die Lehre vom Begriff* (1816). (Cited as WL 12). Cited by volume and page number in G.W.F. Hegel, *Gesammelte Werke*. Edited by the Rheinisch-Westfälischen Akademie der Wissenschaften. (Hamburg: Felix Meiner Verlag, 1968–); *The Science of Logic*. Trans. A.V. Miller. (New York: Humanities Press, 1999) (cited as SL). WL 21: 73; SL 86 (emphasis added).
14   Robert Brandom, "Some Hegelian Ideas of Note for Contemporary Analytic Philosophy." *Hegel Bulletin*, vol. 35, no. 1 (2014): 11.
15   WL 12: 54; SL 624.
16   WL 12: 43; SL 613.
17   McDowell, *Mind and World*. (Cambridge: Harvard University Press, 1994), 44.
18   Brandom, *Making it Explicit*, xix.

self-consciousness."[19] At the same time, his project is concerned with demonstrating that normative statuses cannot be reduced to nonnormatively specifiable dispositions, or, more concisely, that it is "norms all the way down."[20] The Hegelianism of this project can be grasped by considering Brandom's basic claim that "what a judgment makes explicit, its content, is conceptual all the way down."[21]

Would the later Lukács, the writer of the *Ontologie*, have been sympathetic to this Hegelian turn in the treatment of intentionality in contemporary analytic philosophy, a treatment which, as the above discussion illustrates, is inseparable from treatments of the nature of conceptual content, holism, modality, and normativity? The answer to this question is critically important and deserves to be addressed here because it illumines precisely why he began the project of the *Ontologie* in the first place. The crucial text for answering this question about the later Lukács is his 1967 Preface to his 1923 *Geschichte und Klassenbewußtsein* (hereafter *Geschichte*), wherein he explains that he was led to return to Marx's writings during the first World War by his "general philosophical interests and under the influence of Hegel rather than any contemporary thinkers."[22] Yet the thoroughgoing character of that earlier, path-breaking text's Hegelianism represents the source of its philosophical "misconceptions" (*Schiefheiten*)[23] in the eyes of the 1967 Lukács, whose commitment to Marx's position that objectivity is the primary material attribute of all things and relations meant that the "theoretical foundations" of his 1923 text were "completely shattered," and it is as a consequence of this that he made the decision to "start again from scratch,"[24] i.e., to begin the project of the *Ontologie*.

This development should be described in greater detail. The "problematic premises" on which *Geschichte* itself is based, result from "a failure to subject the Hegelian heritage to a thoroughgoing materialist reinterpretation and hence to transcend and preserve it."[25] The consequence of this failure is that the "decisive questions," e.g., the relation of theory to practice and subject to object, could not be answered in *Geschichte*; they would have to receive their proper treatment in the *Ontologie*. Lukács explains that a return to Hegel for

---

19   Brandom, *Making it Explicit*, xix.
20   Brandom, *Making it Explicit*, 44.
21   Brandom, *Making it Explicit*, 616.
22   Georg (György) Lukács, *Gesammelte Werke*. (Darmstadt: Luchterhand, 1968–1981) (cited as GW by volume and page number), 2: 11; *History and Class Consciousness*. (Cambridge: MIT Press, 1971) (cited as HCC), ix.
23   GW 2: 22; HCC, xx.
24   GW 2: 39; HCC, xxxvi.
25   GW 2: 23; HCC, xx.

anyone wishing to "return to the revolutionary traditions of Marxism" is "obligatory," and he maintains the position that *Geschichte* was an attempt to "restore the revolutionary nature of Marx's theories [in opposition to the revisionism of Kautsky and Bernstein] by renovating and extending Hegel's dialectics and method."[26] But, as the above outline illustrates, "dialectics and method" are precisely those elements of Hegel's thought which have been excluded from incorporation in contemporary analytic philosophy.

Contradiction is the central principle of reality according to Hegel according to Lukács (as made clear in the *Ontologie* and as reduced, instructively, to semantics in analytic philosophy), and the central contradiction of Hegel's philosophy, according to Lukács following Marx and Engels, is that between system and method. The closed system of logic, nature, and mind – or, in social and historical terms (the terms of "objective mind"), the closed system of the family, civil society, and the state – stands in opposition to the dialectical method, which, as a logical movement from universality to particularity to individuality, necessarily extends beyond any of its particular instantiations. The critical point is that Hegel identifies determinate or concrete universality with individuality, or an individual thought-content is understood by Hegel to be a *determinate* conceptual universal. Consider Hegel's definition of "individuality" in the *Science of Logic*: "Individuality ... is already posited by particularity; this is determinate universality and therefore self-related determinateness, the determinate determinate."[27] Individuality is Hegel's term for determinate (or "concrete") universality, or it is the realization or actualization of the universal that was merely formal or indeterminate in its first moment. However, in every sequence of dialectical cognition, the completion of a syllogism in individuality or determinate universality is at the same time the movement to the first moment of another syllogism, and so the thinking through of determinate universality or individuality reveals it to be indeterminate universality – *its completion reveals its incompleteness*, or *its determinateness reveals its indeterminateness*. Thus dialectical logic reveals that the negation of the modern constellation of social institutions is *necessitated*, and, consequently, it is only through a return to Hegel's dialectics that we can return to the correct, revolutionary understanding of Marx's critique of political economy. *This* is what the later Lukács understands as the meaning of the Hegelian Marxism he inaugurated, and the revolutionary, i.e., *dialectical*, character of that Marxism is expressed clearly in the following sentence from Marx and Engels' 1850 Address (*Ansprache*) to the Central Committee of the Communist League: "Our concern

---

26 GW 2: 23; HCC, xxi.
27 WL 12: 49; SL 618.

cannot simply be the modification of private property, but its elimination, not the covering-up of class antagonisms, but the abolition [*Aufhebung*] of classes, not the improvement of the existing society, but the establishment of a new one."[28] Thus the Hegelianism of Lukács' Hegelian Marxism is not only distinct from that of the analytic philosophical tradition, it is antithetical to that tradition.

In his 1923 *Geschichte*, Lukács erroneously, according to his 1967 standpoint, followed Hegel in identifying alienation (*Entfremdung*) with objectification (*Vergänglichung*) as such. This identification occurs only naturally when the former concept is "taken to its logical conclusion,"[29] but Marxist analysis requires a materialist explanation of that concept on its own terms. This understanding was the basis of the 1967 Lukács' "plan to investigate the philosophical connections between economics and politics," such that he could "discover a real solution to this whole problem in the ontology of social existence."[30] This solution, he later specifies, would not be characterized by the philosophical misconceptions he inherited from Hegel in *Geschichte* (not only the identification of alienation and objectification, but also the very idea of the identical subject–object); rather, this plan for an *Ontologie* would be a "scientific, Marxist account."[31] All of this indicates, quite obviously, that the later Lukács, the writer of the *Ontologie*, would not have been sympathetic to this Hegelian turn in contemporary analytic philosophy. For this turn, in its selective incorporation of only those elements of Hegel's philosophical system that are compatible with *bourgeois* thought, simply reproduces its ideological mystifications in the contemporary terms of logic and semantics.

Indeed, in the most general sense, the analytic aversion to any ontological commitments at all, and the consequent attempt to understand ontological questions as merely terminological ones, only further illustrates the distinction between that tradition and Lukács' framework. When one considers how those who have argued in favor of the existence of intentional objects – not only Russell, but also Meinong,[32] his student Ernst Mally,[33] and more recently

---

28 MEW 7: 248.
29 GW 2: 26; HCC, xxiii.
30 GW 2: 38; HCC, xxxv.
31 GW 2: 39; HCC, xxxvii.
32 See Alexius Meinong, "The theory of objects." In R. Chisholm (ed.), *Realism and the Background of Phenomenology*. (Glencoe: The Free Press, 1960).
33 See Ernst Mally, *Gegenstandtheoretische Grundlagen der Logik und Logistik*. (Leipzig: Barth, 1912).

Parsons[34] and Zalta[35] – do not represent the dominant paradigm that was inaugurated by Quine, further developed by Chisholm,[36] and accepted by Dennett,[37] this distinction becomes even more apparent. This paradigm, one which understands intensionality as a criterion of intentionality, is based on the presumption that the movement from understanding intentionality in ontological terms to understanding it in semantic terms represents an "ascent" in the respect that it proceeds from talk about things to talk about talk about things, thus purportedly "solving" the "problem" of ontology.

3   Lukács' Ontological Criticism

3.1   *Hegel*

After discussing a wide range of topics – including neopositivism, existentialism, Wittgenstein's philosophy, the philosophy of presence (*Gegenwart*), and Nicolai Hartmann's ontology – Lukács begins to lay the groundwork for his ontology of social being. He does so with Hegel, for the reason that the latter's philosophical system is understood as representing an original, singular, and path-breaking unification of logic and ontology. Hegel neither projected the conception of ontological form, conditioned teleologically through labor, onto nature, as occurred with Aristotle, nor did he reject the ontological as such on the basis of a subjectivism presupposed to be transcendental in character, as occurred with Kant. Lukács' criticisms of Hegel's philosophy are relatively equal in importance to the insights he gleans from him, and thus the overall image that emerges from his analysis is remarkably balanced. The concern here will be twofold: (1) to explain just how Hegel's ontology, despite its subordination to logic, represents the foundation of Lukács' philosophical project; and (2) to illumine how Lukács' criticisms of Hegel's logicized ontology can be mobilized as a critique of the general drift of contemporary analytic philosophical treatment of intentionality.

As noted above, Lukács follows Marx and Engels in understanding Hegel's philosophy as characterized by an irreducible opposition between system and

---

34   See Terence Parsons, *Nonexistent Objects*. (New Haven: Yale University Press, 1980).
35   See Edward N. Zalta, *Intensional Logic and the Metaphysics of Intentionality*. (Cambridge: MIT Press, 1988).
36   See Roderick M. Chisholm, "Perceiving: A Philosophical Study." In David M. Rosenthal (ed.), *The Nature of Mind*. (Oxford: Oxford University Press, 1990).
37   See Daniel Dennett, *Content and Consciousness*. (London: Routledge and Kegal Paul, 1969).

method. The nature of that contradiction is specified and explained in great detail in this section of the *Ontologie*. It can be understood first in the practical terms of the philosophy of history. The dialectical method, in extending beyond any of its instantiations by necessity, contradicts the closed character of Hegel's system, a character which indicates (at least in a provisional sense) finality or completeness. This problem is described by Lukács in the following manner: "the present can only acquire a genuine ontological foundation as the bridge between past and future; but if the present is the real fulfillment of the inherent potentialities of the dialectic, then this process must come to an end in its fulfillment."[38] At the same time, the vast critical potentialities at work in Hegel's thought are immediately indicated by Lukács and will be fruitfully appropriated by him. One particularly illuminating notation is Lukács' reference to Hegel as both possessing and systematically articulating "knowledge of the contradictory character of the present, not just as a problem of thought, but equally as a problem of reality itself; as a problem, however, which, primarily ontological, points far beyond the present, insofar as it is conceived as the dynamic basis of reality as a whole, hence the foundation not only of reality, but also of any rational ontological thought about this."[39]

Despite such potentialities, the contradiction in Hegel's philosophy is presented by Lukács in this section of the *Ontologie* predominantly as one between logic and ontology. The basic problem can be understood as a subordination of the latter to the former, but Lukács offers a more detailed analysis of Hegel's philosophical system, one which accounts for how the two are presented therein as holistically interrelated. As he explains, for Hegel, "genuine ontological relationships only find their adequate mental expression in the forms of logical categories, while on the other hand these logical categories are not conceived simply as determinations of thought, but must be understood as dynamic components of reality."[40] This represents a "collision of two ontologies."[41] in Hegel's system according to Lukács. In his analysis of this "collision" (*Zusammenstoß*), he understands the latter ontological commitment as representing a genuine insight, one which he will appropriate as foundational to his own

---

38   Georg (György) Lukács, *Gesammelte Werke*. (Darmstadt: Luchterhand, 1968–1981) (cited as GW by volume and page number); *Ontology of Social Being, Vol. 1: Hegel's False and his Genuine Ontology*. (London: Merlin, 1978) (cited as O1); *Ontology of Social Being, Vol. 2: Marx's Basic Ontological Principles*. (London: Merlin, 1978) (cited as O2); *Ontology of Social Being, Vol. 3: Labour*. (London: Merlin, 1980) (cited as O3). GW 13: 470; O1, 20.
39   GW 13: 469; O1, 3.
40   GW 13: 483; O1, 21.
41   GW 13: 483; O1, 21.

project, whereas the former commitment is understood as an impermissible extension of logic that should be dispensed with.

This combination of appropriating Hegel's ontological conception of logic and dispensing with his logical subordination of ontology appears in Lukács' analysis as praise invariably accompanied by criticism. For instance, he praises Hegel for becoming "ever more intensively aware of the contradictory structure and dynamic of all objects, relations, and processes." But, in the same laudatory passage, he proceeds to explain that "the Hegelian logic, besides its genuine wealth of categories, also treats objects of the real world and their relationships as logical objectivities and relationships, even though the logical can be here at most one moment of their many-sided, essential, and material constitution."[42]

This general impermissible extension of logic is important because it parallels the particular one of teleology. While Hegel is credited by Lukács with discovering the teleological character of the labor process, he is criticized for incorrectly extending the category of teleology beyond that process, depicting the concept in universal terms by means of his logical system. Thus Hegel "discovered labor as the principle which expresses the genuine form of teleology, the positing and actual realization of the end by a conscious subject; on the other hand, this genuine ontological category is structured into the homogenous medium of a system dominated by logical principles."[43]

Continuing with this mode of analysis, Lukács will explain that he was compelled to detail the "distortions" (*Entstellungen*) caused in Hegel's ontology by "the methodological predominance of principles of logic." But, even if the "distorting effect of the methodological priority of logic in his system" must be indicated, "this in no way alters the predominantly positive character of the analyses that have become so necessary."[44] Only in this way can we observe Hegel's "path-breaking originality, his acute relevance for those questions that ontology has to solve today, particularly an ontology of social being."[45]

The "collision" between two ontologies is referred to later in the *Ontologie* as Hegel's "dual ontology" (*doppelte Ontologie*). Again, Lukács expresses his standpoint vis-à-vis Hegel in terms of what might be referred to as a dialectic of praise and criticism: "He is on the one hand one of the precursors of those who sought to conceive reality in its entire contradictory complexity – as the complex and dynamic mutual relation of dynamic complexes – while on the other

---

42 GW 13: 496; O1, 38.
43 GW 13: 508; O1, 53.
44 GW 13: 515; O1, 62.
45 GW 13: 515; O1, 62.

hand the over-extension of reason, which in various forms dominated many earlier philosophies, is still strongly at work in his own."[46]

If Hegel's system, in way that parallels a number of his predecessors, incorrectly "over-extends" reason (*Vernunft*), the very fact that *this* is the standpoint represented by his system – in contrast to the Kantian standpoint of understanding (*Verstanden* or *Verständigkeit*) – is praised by Lukács in unconditional terms. He explains that the "epochal significance" of Hegel's epistemological path from understanding to reason consists in the fact that he "managed to lay the foundations for knowledge of a complex, dynamically contradictory reality, consisting of totalities, something that had defeated the epistemology of his predecessors."[47] Here Lukács is referring to how Hegel shifted rational knowledge neither to the realm of the thing-in-itself, as occurred with Kant, nor to the realm of irrationalism, as occurred with Schelling.

Furthermore, Hegel's "great advance" consisted in his "conception of form as a reflection determination,"[48] a conception which was based on a rejection of the Kantian conception of the categories of modality as "categories of mere knowledge."[49] Hegel is thus to be commended because he "decisively directly himself to their ontological interpretation."[50] The consequence of this directing is the revelation that, in both logical and epistemological terms, "necessity must form the focal point of a consideration of modality, while for any genuine ontology, reality is the totality to which all modal determinations, including necessity, must be subordinated."[51]

Lukács' understanding of Hegel's philosophy, and in particular of what constitutes its virtues and faults, sharply distinguishes his standpoint from those represented by the "analytic" understandings of that philosophy outlined above. This distinction is illumined by a consideration of the fact that his understanding is based on the adoption and development of Marx's original analysis of Hegel's philosophy, as the following passage indicates:

> The entire Hegelian philosophy is essentially oriented to the knowledge of society and history. Hence its categories are by their very nature adapted to this sphere of being. The fact that they are almost invariably generalized far beyond this sphere, as a consequence of their subordination to

---

46 GW 13: 545; O1, 97.
47 GW 13: 530; O1, 78.
48 GW 13: 542; O1, 93.
49 GW 13: 544; O1, 95.
50 GW 13: 544; O1, 95.
51 GW 13: 544; O1, 95.

logic, and that they are thus distorted as far as the ontology of being-in-itself is concerned, is more than a mere form of appearance of the system. But no matter how severely a critical ontology exposes what is theoretically awry, it should never lose sight of the important underlying intention. The Marxist classics were therefore right to speak, not of rejecting the Hegelian dialectic, but of 'inverting' it, and 'placing it on its feet.'[52]

Lukács' Marxism thus determines the character of his appropriations from Hegel's philosophy, in that he understands his project of a "critical ontology" in terms of an extension of the classical Marxist "inversion" of the Hegelian dialectic. The virtue of that dialectic is the ontological character of its logic, whereas its fault consists in the "subordination" of its ontological categories to logic. One might note here how even Hegel's logical ontology or ontological logic distinguishes him from the analytic reduction of ontology to semantics and logic. Such a reduction is observable, to take just a few examples, in Russell's theory that mental states appearing to be about concrete individuals are in fact general existentially quantified propositions, represented by the logical formula $\exists x[Px \ \& \ \forall y(Py \to y = x) \ \& \ Qx]$, in Parsons' assertion that there are nonexistent objects that can be represented without contradiction by the logical formula $\exists x(\sim E!x)$, and in Brandom's attempt to understand Hegel's holistic idealism or idealistic holism as limited to a claim about sense dependence, rather than one about reference dependence, where "Concept **P** is *sense dependent* on concept **Q** just in case one cannot count as having grasped **P** unless one counts as grasping **Q**" and "Concept **P** is *reference dependent* on concept **Q** just in case **P** cannot apply to something unless **Q** applies to something."[53] Hegel, it should be noted, understood the idealism of his philosophical system as implying that any sense dependence claim about meaning (conceptual contentfulness) *entails* a reference dependence claim about (ontological) existence.

Lukács' Marxist appropriation of Hegel's philosophy thus illumines how the contemporary philosophy of intentionality can only be understood as "Hegelian" if the ontological character of Hegel's logic is dispensed with entirely. From this view, the problem with Brandom's following self-characterization becomes immediately apparent:

---

52   GW 13: 503; O1, 47.
53   Robert Brandom, *Tales of the Mighty Dead: Historical Essays in the Metaphysics of Intentionality*. (Cambridge: Harvard University Press, 2002), 194–195.

> Wilfrid Sellars once said that he hoped that an effect of his work would be to begin to move analytic philosophy from its Humean to its Kantian phase. And Rorty has characterized my work, and that of John McDowell, as aimed at helping to begin to move it from its incipient Kantian to its inevitable Hegelian phase.[54]

The nature of Lukács' return to Hegel vis-à-vis Marx makes apparent the fact that the aim of such contemporary works remains unfulfilled, that analytic philosophy has not yet moved to its Hegelian "phase," that the "inevitability" of such a movement is questionable, and that such works arguably represent the assumptions and commitments of Kantianism, if not those of scholasticism.

At any rate, returning to Lukács' project of a critical ontology and its foundation in an analysis of Hegel's philosophy mediated by Marxist commitments, we can observe how the core of that project in the labor process and, more precisely, the intentionality at work in that process, have their basis in Hegel's dialectical unity of spontaneous causality and posited teleology:

> [I]f Hegel's example of teleology is treated as a relationship exclusively within the context of social being, which is where it alone belongs, then we have a genuine relationship of reflection determinations, which forms the ontological basis for what Marx calls the metabolism between society and nature. However independent, different, and even opposed causality and teleology may be for the understanding, their reflection relationship in labor creates what are for the time being inseparable processes, in which spontaneous causality and posited teleology are dialectically united. Since labor provides the original pattern for social practice, a fundamental determination for the ontology of social being is to be found in Hegel's conception of labor teleology, when this is interpreted in this way.[55]

As we have already observed, however, Hegel's social philosophy contains "the distorting rule of his purposive ontology" and "distortions of the real facts in the light of the historical prejudices of his time." Thus Lukács concludes his discussion of Hegel by noting that his analysis has been limited to the task of indicating "the general validity and methodological fertility of the reflection determinations for a dialectical ontology, and especially for one of social

---

54 Brandom, "Some Hegelian Ideas of Note for Contemporary Analytic Philosophy," 4.
55 GW 13: 555; O1, 110.

being."[56] It is with this indication that he transitions to his treatment of Marx in the *Ontologie*.

3.2 Marx

Lukács begins with Hegel rather than Marx not only because he deploys Hegel's ontological framework as foundational his own project, but also because Marx himself similarly takes the basic infrastructure of that framework for granted in his critique of political economy. Lukács begins his discussion of Marx by noting that he never articulated his own ontological framework, he never explicitly addressed ontological questions on their own terms. The fundamental reason for this omission is Marx's acceptance of Hegel's framework and, as is familiar, his "inversion" of the dialectical method through which Hegel articulated that framework, thereby dispensing with the subordination of ontology to logic and the extension of teleology beyond labor. This fact is expressed publicly of course in the 1873 afterword to the second German edition of the first volume of *Capital*. It is also demonstrated comprehensively and systematically in Marx's 1857–1858 *Grundrisse*. Furthermore, while they appealed to the necessity of this inversion to distinguish their own new materialism from Hegel's idealism, the later Marx and Engels (and Lenin) nevertheless came "to stress energetically the effectively materialist tendencies that were already latent in objective idealism."[57] Such stressing is apparent in Marx 1873 afterward (and as early as the first of his 1845 theses on Feuerbach), as well as in Engels' 1888 *Ludwig Feuerbach* essay.[58]

With Marx's rejection of Hegel's subordination of ontology to logic, however, what becomes "paramount"[59] for understanding his new materialism is that social reality becomes the "ultimate criterion"[60] for the existence or non-existence of a phenomenon. This framework allows for the "increasing concretization"[61] of forms and relationships, a decisive development that was precluded by the logical character of Hegel's system. So, despite the Hegelian inheritance on the part of Marx and Lukács, we can observe through the following passage how Marx's own ontological foundation in the production and reproduction in human life – and, thus, in labor – represents the decisive foundation of Lukács' ontology, for the latter, as will be explained below, is ultimately one based fundamentally on the according of priority to labor:

---

56   GW 13: 555–556; O1, 110.
57   GW 13: 559; O2, 2.
58   See MEW 21: 259–307.
59   GW 13: 561; O2, 3.
60   GW 13: 561; O2, 4.
61   GW 13: 562; O2, 4.

> Labor, then, as the creator of use-values, as useful labor, is a condition of human existence which is independent of all forms of society; it is an eternal natural necessity which mediates the metabolism between man and nature, and therefore human life itself.[62]

Thus labor (*Arbeit*) is the category that, for both Marx and Lukács, contains all other determinations within itself *in nuce*. This "metabolism between man and nature" is singularly original, nothing precedes or accompanies it, and even the most complex of social mediations are to be explained in terms of it. Now this interaction, this metabolism between persons and nature that precedes any such metabolism that is mediated by an interaction between persons, must be understood in teleological terms, as what Lukács terms a teleological "positing" (*Setzung*). This understanding is also derived directly from Marx. The key passage indicating this derivation is the following, justly well-known, one:

> Labor is, first of all, a process between man and nature, a process by which man, through his own actions, mediates, regulates, and controls the metabolism between himself and nature. He confronts the materials of nature as a force of nature. He sets in motion the natural forces which belong to his body, his arms, legs, head, and hands, in order to appropriate the materials of nature in a form adapted to his own needs. Through this movement he acts upon external nature and changes it, and in this way he simultaneously changes his own nature. He develops the potentialities slumbering within nature, and subjects the play of its forces to his own sovereign nature. We are not dealing here with those first instinctive forms of labor which remain on the animal level...We presuppose labor in a form in which it is an exclusively human characteristic. A spider conducts operations which resemble those of the weaver, and a bee would put many a human architect to shame by the construction of its honeycomb cells. But what distinguishes the worst architect from the best of bees is that the architect builds the cell in his mind before he constructs it in wax. At the end of every labor process, a result emerges which had already been conceived by the worker at the beginning, hence already existed ideally. Man not only effects a change of form in the materials of nature; he also realizes [*verwirklicht*] his own purpose in those materials. And this is a purpose he is conscious of, it determines the

---

62 MEW 23: 57; *Capital: A Critical of Political Economy, Volume I: The Process of Production of Capital.* (New York: Penguin, 1990) (cited as K1), 133.

mode of his activity with the rigidity of a law, and he must subordinate his will to it.[63]

The teleological character of the original labor process is indicated by Marx's reference in this passage to the worker's own "purpose" (*Zweck*) being realized in the materials of nature. Indeed, and the significance of this cannot be overstated, Marx defines labor or work (*Arbeit*) itself as "purposive activity" (*zweckmäßige Tätigkeit*) in the same section of *Capital*.[64]

This is the material basis of intentionality. Any talk about the directedness or reference of mental states, if it does not refer back to this original purposive activity, is an abstraction. It is an abstraction because, as Marx explains,

> A being which has no object outside itself is not an objective being. A being which is not itself an object for some third being has no being for its *object;* i.e., it is not objectively related. Its being is not objective. A nonobjective being is a *non-being*.[65]

This *materialist* formulation sharply distinguishes Marxist ontology from that of Hegel. It also, for our purposes, concisely articulates the central problem with the analytic debate over the existence of intentional objects. If the obvious problems associated with positing the existence of absurdities such as round squares or golden mountains are revealed by analytic philosophy, the very fact that such absurdities represent the terms of the debate over the existence of inexistent objects underscores the fact that this discourse operates in total abstraction from its *material base*, a form of operation that will arguably never be overcome. Just as there are reasons to question the notion that analytic philosophy has in fact moved from its incipient Kantian phase to its "inevitable" Hegelian phase, there is every reason to question that it will ever reach – for reasons which are ultimately ideological in character – a Marxian phase.

Of course, Marx's critique of political economy combines historical and conceptual analysis, but he knew well according to Lukács that the interaction between these modes of analysis is only possible "on the basis of a permanent ontological criticism at every step, since these two methods deal with the same real complexes and grasp them from different aspects."[66] An analysis of social

---

63   MEW 23: 192–193; K1, 283–284.
64   MEW 23: 193; K1, 284.
65   MEW 40: 578.
66   GW 13: 581; O2, 29.

reality that is purely conceptual in character, concerned exclusively with the abstract and systematizing laws and tendencies at work in society, will invariably abstract from its ontological basis and therewith abandon any critical potential it might have possessed. So while the first volume of *Capital* is a conceptual analysis of the value-form (*Wertform*), it is necessarily accompanied by a historical (genetic) account of the origin of this form in "primitive accumulation," i.e., the expropriation of the objective conditions of production from laborers.

For Lukács, the "central thesis" of all materialism is that "being has ontological priority over consciousness."[67] There can be being without consciousness, but there cannot be consciousness without being. He is referring in particular to Marx's concise statement indicating the determination of consciousness by social being in the *Vorwort* to his 1859 text, *On the Critique of Political Economy*.[68] Importantly, and this is ultimately what distinguishes Marx's new materialism from the old materialisms to which he refers in his first thesis on Feuerbach, this ontological priority of being over consciousness "does not involve any kind of value hierarchy between being and consciousness."[69] He analogizes this relation to the ontological priority of the production and reproduction of human life over all other social activities. Whether one appeals to Engels' speech at Marx's graveside noting the "simple fact…that mankind must first of all eat, drink, have shelter and clothing, before it can pursue politics, science, art, religion, etc.,"[70] or Walter Benjamin's notation that "[t]he class struggle, which is always present to a historian influenced by Marx, is a fight for the crude and material things without which no refined and spiritual things could exist,"[71] the crucial point is that this ontological priority in no way implies that consciousness is to be understood as an epiphenomenon. It is true of course that the "sum total of the relations of production" constitutes the "real foundation… to which correspond definite forms of social consciousness," and it is also true that "[t]he mode of production of material life conditions the social, political, and intellectual life process in general."[72] But neither this correspondence nor this conditioning implies such a reduction of consciousness to the totality of social existence; it implies, rather, that the two are *inextricably related*, and that the former must be understood in terms of the latter, in the final analysis, in

---

67 GW 13: 582; O2, 31.
68 MEW 13: 9.
69 GW 13: 582; O2, 31.
70 MEW 19: 335.
71 Walter Benjamin, *Gesammelte Schriften*. Band 1.2 (Frankfurt am Main: Suhrkamp Verlag, 1972–1989), 694.
72 MEW 13: 8–9.

order to be comprehended properly. This ontological framework is to be contrasted with the philosophical explanations of Lukács' time and our own. As he explains,

> The theoretical cul-de-sacs of bourgeois idealist social philosophy, which are continually re-emerging, very often originate in an abstract and antinomic contrast between the material and the mental, the natural and the social, which inevitably leads to the destruction of all genuine dialectical connections and thus makes the specific character of social being incomprehensible.[73]

This incisive critique might be applied not only to analytic philosophy and bourgeois social philosophy, but also to critical theory itself, in particular to that tradition's shift away from the Marxist dialectical and materialist analysis of capitalist society, and therewith the abandonment of its critical character, whether it be Adorno and Horkheimer's abstract criticisms of "instrumental reason,"[74] Jürgen Habermas' "communicative turn,"[75] or Axel Honneth's "recognition-theoretical" model of reification.[76]

Later in this part of the *Ontologie*, Lukács indicates his adoption of what he terms "the Marxian conception of reality."[77] This conception consists in a commitment to the position that "the starting-point of all ideas is the actual expressions of social being."[78] He is careful to indicate that this conception does not involve any kind of empiricism. Rather, it entails conceiving "every single fact as part of a dynamic complex standing in reciprocal relation to other complexes, and determined internally as well as externally by a variety of laws."[79] This materialist and dialectical conception needs to be further specified. While this mode of analyzing reality must always proceed from the "primary heterogeneity of the individual elements, processes, and complexes," it must also

---

73   GW 13: 589; O2, 39.
74   See e.g., Theodor Adorno and Max Horkheimer, *Dialectic of Enlightenment: Philosophical Fragments*. (Stanford: Stanford University Press, 2002); Max Horkheimer, *Critique of Instrumental Reason*. (London and New York: Verso, 2013).
75   See Jürgen Habermas, *The Theory of Communicative Action. Vol. I: Reason and the Rationalization of Society.* (Boston: Beacon Press, 1984); *The Theory of Communicative Action. Vol. II: Lifeworld and System.* (Boston: Beacon Press, 1990); and *Moral Consciousness and Communicative Action.* (Cambridge: MIT Press, 1990).
76   See Axel Honneth, *Reification: A New Look at an Old Idea*. (Oxford: Oxford University Press, 2012).
77   GW 13: 611; O2, 68.
78   GW 13: 611; O2, 68.
79   GW 13: 611; O2, 68.

grasp "the compulsory character of their intimate and penetrating correlation in every concrete social and historical totality." Concreteness in thought requires avoiding abstractions in terms of both "lawfulness" (*Gesetzlichkeit*) and "uniqueness" (*Einmaligkeit*).[80]

These considerations are only a part of Marx's "ontology of social being"[81] according to Lukács. The final decisive part is a comprehension of the "historicity" (*Geschichtlichkeit*)[82] of such totalities. While Lukács claims that "the historical does not just contain a motion in general, but also and always a direction of change,"[83] he later explains that this ontology is based on a rejection of "any generalized form of teleology"[84] in society. Such a generalization of teleology beyond labor is integrally related to the subordination of history to logic, as occurs in Hegel's system. History for Lukács is a process that involves "the unfolding of human abilities and needs,"[85] and this unfolding is the "objective foundation" of value, and thus the source of its objectivity. History is thus a directional process in that human capacities increase over time. This process is integrally related to the concept of value, a concept which exists only within social being. Value is based either "directly or indirectly"[86] on labor, and the latter is what "precisely constitutes the realm of the human."[87] Understanding history from the ontological point of view (the only correct one, according to Lukács) requires that one recognize

> the way that forms of relationships such as development, progress, etc. are linked up with the ontological priority of complexes over their elements. History can only have the character of a complex, since the concrete components out of which it is composed, such as structure, structural change, direction, etc. are only possible within such complexes.[88]

If history is to be understood as a complex, it is itself constituted by social complexes which have their origin in the teleological positings that constitute labor. Such projects "flow into a contradictory but unitary causal process of

---

80 GW 13: 612; O2, 69.
81 GW 13: 612; O2, 69.
82 GW 13: 612; O2, 69.
83 GW 13: 614; O2, 72.
84 GW 13: 615; O2, 74.
85 GW 13: 620; O2, 79.
86 GW 13: 621; O2, 80.
87 GW 13: 621; O2, 80.
88 GW 13: 624–625; O2, 85.

social complexes and their totality, and in general give rise to law-like relationships."[89] Thus it becomes possible, to use Marx's description of his project in *Capital*, "to reveal the economic law of motion"[90] of a particular social formation, i.e., mode of production. This ontological framework implies that abstractions and generalizations are just as indispensable to ontological criticism as the specification of concrete complexes and relationships. Equally important to note is that the grasping of the most general laws in a logical sense does not entail the ascription or reduction of them to logic. The key issue, for Marx and Lukács, is that analysis must always begin with a commitment to the position that the individual categories which form general laws "can only be understood in their historical concreteness, in the historical specificity that the existing social formation ascribes to them, and never simply in terms of their logical characteristics."[91]

One can observe here just how derivative Moishe Postone's "reinterpretation" of Marx's critical theory is of Lukács' ontology, as well as how misleading it is to categorize Lukács as representative of what he terms "traditional Marxism" for failing to grasp the historical-specificity of Marx's categories. According to Postone, Marx understood capitalism to be an abstract form of social domination based on an alienated structure of social mediation. The abstract categories of time, labor, and value which form the object and content of Marx's critique of political economy are the historical categories of capitalist society, and they are the source of its particular form of social domination. Thus Postone interprets Marx as conceiving capitalism not as the domination of one class of persons by another per se, but rather as the domination of persons by categories which appear to be objective and transhistorical but in fact are particular to the capitalist organization of society.[92] Postone believes that all those whom he claims to be representatives of "traditional Marxism" wrongly understand labor to be a transhistorical category and they wrongly identify

---

89   GW 13: 627; O2, 89.
90   MEW 23: 15–16; K1, 92.
91   GW 13: 644; O2, 110–111.
92   Postone interprets Marx as conceptualizing capitalism in terms of a "historically specific form of social interdependence with an impersonal and seemingly objective character. This form of interdependence is effected by historically unique forms of social relations that are constituted by determinate forms of social practice and, yet, become quasi-independent of the people engaged in those practices. The result is a new, increasingly abstract form of social domination – one that subjects people to impersonal structural imperatives and constraints that cannot be adequately grasped in terms of concrete domination (e.g., personal or group domination), and that generates an ongoing historical dynamic" (*Time, Labor, and Social Domination: A Reinterpretation of Marx's Critical Theory*. [Cambridge: Cambridge University Press, 1993], 3–4).

the subject of capitalist society as the proletariat rather than the capital relation itself. In so doing, Postone claims, they do not accurately grasp Marx's project in the *Grundrisse* and *Capital*. This categorization of Lukács does not comport with his understanding of Marx's project as early as 1923 as a "historical critique of economics which resolves the totality of the reified objectivities of social and economic life into *relations between men*,"[93] nor does Postone's critique of those "traditional Marxists" who understand labor as a transhistorical category as failing to grasp Marx's project comport with Marx's own statement in *Capital* itself that "[l]abor, then, as the creator of use-values, as useful labor, is a condition of human existence which is independent of all forms of society; it is an eternal natural necessity which mediates the metabolism between man and nature, and therefore human life itself." These passages indicate that Lukács is in fact following Marx in these crucial respects.

We have already seen how it is a concern of Lukács' in the final part of this section to depict history as constituted by "the increase in human capacities."[94] His final concern in this section is to depict "the integration of the species."[95] Individual persons in any society are always already integrated in the respect that the production and reproduction of human life is a social process, and the completion of the process whereby production is socialized under capitalism is one of its distinguishing features. It is only a function of bourgeois ideology that individual persons take themselves to be isolated from and independent of one another, consequently taking society to be an "external" entity that is merely "constructed" of individuals and thus reducible to them *as* abstractly understood individuals. The reality, by contrast, is that "[s]ociety does not consist of individuals, but expresses the sum of interrelations, the relations within which these individuals stand."[96] This crucial sentence from the *Grundrisse* is situated within a critique of Proudhon, where Marx explains that persons are only abstract "human beings" outside society, whereas in society they are masters and slaves, feudal lords and peasants, capitalists and workers, etc. Another key passage from the *Grundrisse* elaborates on this contradiction between the unprecedented integration associated with the capitalist form of production and the concomitant emergence of an ideological presupposition of individual independence:

---

93   GW 2:221; *Geschichte*, 49.
94   GW 13: 678; O2, 153.
95   GW 13: 678; O2, 153.
96   MEW 42: 264–265; *Grundrisse: Foundations of the Critique of Political Economy*. (New York: Penguin, 1993) (cited as G), 189.

> The more deeply we go back into history, the more does the individual, and hence also the producing individual, appear as dependent, as belonging to a greater whole…Only in the eighteenth century, in 'civil society,' do the various forms of social connectedness confront the individual as a mere means towards his private purposes, as external necessity. But the epoch which produces this standpoint, that of the isolated individual, is also precisely that of the hitherto most developed social (from this standpoint, general) relations. The human being is…an animal which can individuate itself only in the midst of society.[97]

Capitalism is the most socially integrated form of society, and yet it does not necessarily follow from this that the members of capitalist societies are conscious of that fact. It is on this basis that Lukács develops a thesis about the "realization of the species-character in the individual."[98] The process by which this realization occurs, he explains, is inseparable from, and can only arise through, the social activity of persons, their cooperation, mediated by production relations, in the process by which "the individual produces and reproduces his own existence."[99] Thus the realization of this consciousness, and with it the development of the individual's "individuality" (*Individualität*)[100] itself, ultimately leads the analysis to labor. It is with this that Lukács transitions to his analysis of that category on its own terms, in the first section of the second and final part of his *Ontologie*.

3.3 Labor

Now that the foundational character of Hegel and Marx for Lukács' ontology has been articulated, the distance between that foundation and the philosophical explanations of intentionality outlined above should be apparent. The highly selective character of the appropriations from Hegel by those within the analytic philosophical tradition, on the one hand, and the extreme implausibility of an eventual Marxian "phase" of that tradition, on the other, illumines not only the incompatibility between that tradition and the Lukácsian ontology at its very basis, but also the *critical* character of that ontology. This critical

---

97 MEW 42: 20; G, 84. See also Marx's sixth thesis on Feuerbach: "The essence of man is not an abstraction inherent in each separate individual. In its reality it is the aggregate of social relationships" (MEW 3: 5).
98 GW 13: 668; O2, 140.
99 GW 13: 668; O2, 140.
100 GW 13: 668; O2, 140.

character is articulated by Lukács in remarkably concise way. Every "problem of knowledge," he explains, "conceals an ontological problem."[101] Thus the very fact that his analysis of social being is presented in the form of an *ontology* and, furthermore, the very fact that this ontology is presented in *materialist* terms, as an ontology of social *being*, illustrates just how the analytic attempt to reduce ontological questions to terminological ones represents an ideological abstraction, as well as how, no matter how much contemporary discourse might be dominated by talk of "pragmatics," analytic philosophy retains its *scholastic* character. This scholasticism is made apparent by the fact that Lukács' ontology of social being explains social being, in all its determinations, in terms of the ineliminable aspect of human life that is *labor*.

There is nothing more basic than labor – all other things are reducible to it, and it is not reducible to any other things – and this basic character derives from the fact that the production and reproduction of human life is logically prior to any other activity. Furthermore, the original act of labor, the most practical of activities, is purposive in character, and this purposiveness is integrally related to the fact that it is a human interaction *with* nature, as the external object to which this purposiveness is *directed*. This *directedness* or *reference* at work in the purposive activity that *is* labor brings us to the central contention of this essay, that the critical character of Lukács' ontology consists in the fact that it articulates the material basis of our intentionality, linguistic discursivity, and normativity. All of this is made explicit in the first section of the second part of the *Ontologie*, as will be outlined below.

The following sentence discloses how labor is the basis of the project of the *Ontologie*: "In seeking to present the specific categories of social being ontologically, how they arise out of earlier forms of being, how they are linked with these, based on them and yet distinct from them, we must begin with an analysis of labor."[102] Labor and language (*Sprache*) are listed as "decisive" categories of social being, and, crucially for our purposes, these categories are "indissolubly intertwined;" none of them can be "adequately grasped when considered in isolation."[103] Already, one can observe how any one-sided "linguistic turn" or "semantic ascent" precludes the possibility of adequately comprehending this element of social being (or any other) in Lukács' analysis.

His project, by contrast, centers on depicting the transition "from the predominantly organic to the predominantly social," or the general development

---

101   GW 14: 23; O3, 17.
102   GW 14: 7; O3, i.
103   GW 14: 7; O3, i.

that Marx referred to as the "retreat of the natural boundary."[104] The natural boundary never recedes completely according to Lukács following Marx, and labor consequently remains an ineliminable aspect human life. This is not to say that the role of labor in social being can be understood in naturalistic terms. Even if the original laboring act has its origin in the Darwinian struggle for existence, all "steps of its development" are to be understood as "products of man's own self-activity."[105] This increasingly socially-determined character of being motivates Lukács' interest in depicting the "genetic leap" that gives rise to "the concrete complex of the social as a form of being."[106] This leap constitutes the transition to humanity as a distinct category, and the nature of this transition to "the social as a form of being" can only be grasped by means of an analysis of labor for the reason that

> [A]ll other categories of this form of being are already by nature purely social in character; their properties and modes of efficacy develop only in a social being that is already constituted, and however primitive may be the manner of their appearance, they thus presuppose the leap to have already been achieved. Only with labor does its ontological nature give it a pronounced transition character.[107]

Understood in this way, labor, as the original, purposive interaction with nature that is unmediated by the social interactions which give that interaction a qualitatively different character, is the decisive factor for comprehending social reality. This original form of labor cannot be understood without reference to the intentionality at work in it, and intentionality *as such* consequently requires reference to this form. Labor in this sense is directed toward the end producing use-values, objects of utility which serve the needs and wants of human beings. Use-value (*Gebrauchswert*) is thus for Lukács an original, *objective* concept. It "means nothing more than a product of labor which man is able to make use of in the reproduction of his existence."[108] This form of value will of course become holistically and dialectically interrelated with the irreducibly social concept of exchange-value (*Tauschwert*), but this interrelation occurs only at a much later stage of development, one which is based on an entire complex of social mediations of the labor interaction. Despite the

---

104   GW 14: 8; O3, ii.
105   GW 14: 9; O3, iii.
106   GW 14: 9; O3, iv.
107   GW 14: 9; O3, iv.
108   GW 14: 10; O3, v.

complexity associated with all such mediations, and, as Marx explains, "[b]ourgeois society is the most developed and the most complex historic organization of production,"[109] Lukács seeks to demonstrate that "[a]ll those determinations which we shall see to make up the essence of what is new in social being, are contained *in nuce* in labor. Thus labor can be viewed as the original phenomenon, as the model for social being."[110]

Lukács understands labor as teleological positing, and thus as an irreducible *intentional* activity. He begins his articulation of this understanding by first noting the correctness of Engels in "deriving social life and language directly from labor."[111] Labor as teleological positing is always "realized within material being," and the key consequence of this materiality is that labor can alone serve as "the model for any social practice,"[112] no matter how complex the social mediations of the practice, for the reason that any such practice invariably retains its material dimension. Thus Lukács is clear in his disclosure of the *materialist* character of his explanatory strategy. Though the two concepts at work in the labor process are dialectically interrelated, teleology is distinct from causality because, whereas the latter is an objective concept with a reality outside the human mind, teleology, by contrast, is "a [purely] posited category"[113] (though it must be noted that through the process of labor causality also becomes a [partially] posited category). All labor is preceded by such positing, as explained by Marx in his notation above that "[a]t the end of every labor process, a result emerges which had already been conceived by the worker at the beginning, hence already existed ideally. Man not only effects a change of form in the materials of nature; he also realizes [*verwirklicht*] his own purpose in those materials."

The inference Lukács draws from this framework he appropriates from Marx is far-reaching in its implications. Properly social being, and thus the human character of humanity, can only be adequately grasped through an understanding of the fact that "its genesis, its elevation from its basis and its acquisition of autonomy, is based on labor, i.e., on the ongoing realization of teleological positings."[114] Such positings must be understood in ontological, rather than epistemological terms for the reason that while the latter form of positing contains within it, and thus allows for, the possibility of being incorrect, the ontological form does not. In the ontological form, the goal is

---

109   MEW 42: 39; G, x.
110   GW 14: 10; O3, v.
111   GW 14: 11; O3, 2.
112   GW 14: 12; O3, 3.
113   GW 14: 13; O3, 5.
114   GW 14: 17; O3, 9.

either achieved or it is not, and, if it is not, then it is not in fact a positing in this sense.

Lukács acknowledges that consciousness precedes labor as teleological positing, but this prior existence can only be understood in epiphenomenal terms. He explains that, "[w]ith labor, human consciousness ceases to be an epiphenomenon, in the ontological sense."[115] Thus the consciousness of non-human animals is epiphenomenal because it is natural, biological, instinctual, etc., whereas the distinctly human form of consciousness achieved in virtue of labor cannot be understood in these terms. Lukács' justification for this claim is that

> [o]nly in labor, in the positing of a goal and its means, consciousness rises with a self-governed act, the teleological positing, above mere adaptation to the environment...and begins to effect changes in nature itself that are impossible coming from nature alone, indeed inconceivable. Since realization thus becomes a transforming and new-forming principle of nature, consciousness, which has provided the impulse and direction for this, can no longer simply be an ontological epiphenomenon.[116]

The meaning of this passage, and thus the validity of Lukács' justification, depends on this concept of "realization" (*Verwirklichung*). He defines realizations simply as "the results of human practice in labor."[117] This concept is thus key for Lukács' entire project, for it "produces both the genetic linkage and the basic ontological distinction and antithesis."[118] He explains further that it is "a category of the new form of being [social being],"[119] and thus any realizations that appear "as new forms of objectivity [are] not derivable from nature."[120] Lukács further specifies the structure of the labor process, on the basis of this concept of realization, as involving "the inseparable correlation of two acts that are in themselves mutually heterogenous, but which in their new ontological linkage compose the specific existing complex of labor, and...form the ontological foundation of social practice, even of social being in general."[121] These two acts are (1) "the most precise possible reflection of the reality in question" and

---

115   GW 14: 26; O3, 21.
116   GW 14: 27; O3, 22–23.
117   GW 14: 28; O3, 23.
118   GW 14: 26; O3, 21.
119   GW 14: 26; O3, 21.
120   GW 14: 28; O3, 23.
121   GW 14: 28–29; O3, 24.

(2) "the subjoined positing of those causal chains which are indispensable...for the realization of the teleological positing."[122]

With this specification of the structure of the labor process, and therewith the materiality of human purposive activity, Lukács deduces a number of critical conclusions of philosophical importance from this analysis. His first key claim is that reflection, and the distinction between subjectivity and objectivity through which any reflection occurs, is "a necessary product of the labor process" and "the basis of the specifically human mode of existence."[123] Reflection gives rise to conceptual thinking and the construction of a conceptual world, which in turn gives rise to "perception" (*Anschauung*) and "representation" (*Vorstellung*).[124] One can observe here just how much is presupposed in philosophical treatments of these latter concepts. The manifold theories of perceptual experience and the various representational theories of consciousness in contemporary analytic philosophy all presuppose the ontological basis of these concepts, and it is this basis that Lukács articulates in this section.

What must be specified further, however, is the conceptual content of this reflection. What intentional object confronts the reflective, conscious human mind in the original act of laboring, thereby giving form to the process by which this purposive activity is formulated and executed? Here Lukács introduces the concept of the alternative, and he refers to the "ontological structure of the labor process" as "a chain of alternatives."[125] Similar to the concept of teleology, the alternative is a posited category. It is "an act of consciousness," "a category of mediation," and, with the reflection of reality, it "becomes the vehicle for the positing of an existence."[126] Nevertheless, this category cannot be understood in general, on its own terms as an epistemological concept, as would be presupposed in conventional philosophical explanations. Rather, Lukács explains that the alternative (or any chain of alternatives) must be understood as

> a concrete selection between ways to realize a goal that has not been produced by a subject deciding for himself, but rather by the social being in which he lives and acts... [and thus] any concrete decision about a teleological positing can never be completely derived, with rigorous necessity, from its antecedent conditions.[127]

---

122   GW 14: 29; O3, 24.
123   GW 14: 29; O3, 24.
124   GW 14: 29; O3, 25.
125   GW 14: 36; O3, 33.
126   GW 14: 36; O3, 34.
127   GW 14: 39–40; O3, 38.

Lukács concludes this section with a derivation of human self-control from labor and its specific requirements. Labor requires that the laborer "attempt to exclude everything merely instinctive, emotional, etc. that might obscure objective insight. This is the very way in which consciousness comes to be dominant over instinct, knowledge over mere emotion."[128] As will be explained below, the philosophical significance of this derivation is that human self-control is the basis of our normativity, for the presence of such control represents the condition of possibility for the bindingness of any norms at all.

The second chapter of the section on labor begins to make explicit the implicitly critical character of its derivations from the structure of the labor process as articulated in the first chapter. Lukács begins with a passage that is worth including here, as it directly addresses just how his project can be understood as a *critique* of the philosophical presentation of the problems discussed in this essay:

> [P]roblems which at an advanced level of human development assume a very generalized, dematerialized, subtle and abstract form, and for this reason later come to constitute the major themes of philosophy, are already contained *in nuce*, in their most general but most decisive determinations, in the positings of the labor process. We believe therefore that it is right to see labor as the model for all social practice, all active social behavior.[129]

This framework illumines how conventional philosophical treatments of topics such as intentionality and consciousness; the nature of conceptual mental content; meaning holism; modal logic and the varieties of modality; and the normativity of meaning and content should be understood in radically different terms, precisely, as *derivative* of a process whereby the positing of the teleological goal and the causally functioning means of its realization in thought are brought together dialectically.

In this second chapter of the *Ontologie*, the teleological positing identified by Marx and developed by Lukács in the first chapter as unmediated purposive activity is presented in its "second form" (*zweite Form*),[130] that is, as mediated by relations between persons. This mediation takes the consequently abstract form of the laboring person positing a goal *for* other persons, in contrast to the "first form" (*erste Form*) of labor, the process that "defines the character, role,

---

128 GW 14: 42; O3, 41–42.
129 GW 14: 46; O3, 46.
130 GW 14: 46; O3, 47.

function, etc. of the individual concrete and real positings that are oriented toward a natural object."[131] Thus we can already observe how the concept of exchange-value only arises from the production of use-values, as well as the contradiction at work in capitalist society, in which use-values are produced only insofar as they can be realized as exchange-values, and exchange-values are only produced insofar as surplus-value can be derived from their sale. The reality, Lukács explains, is that the first form of labor (the production of use-values) constitutes the "insurpassable real foundation" of the second form, for "out of the original labor more complicated forms of this kind must necessarily develop, from the dialectic of its own properties."[132] Thus we can observe how Lukács provides an ontological justification for the order in which Marx presents the forms of value in the first chapter of *Capital*.

Now that the basic form of social being has been reached, Lukács' discussion shifts to the articulation of a number of ontological commitments, deductions from the framework he established in the first chapter of this section. These deductions are crucial for our purposes because they illumine the critical potentialities of his framework.

He first explains that "word and concept, language and conceptual thought belong together as elements of a complex, the complex of social being, and they can only be grasped in their true nature in the context of an ontological analysis of social being, by knowledge of the real functions that they fulfill within this complex."[133] Thus the analytic attempt to understand "word and concept, language and conceptual thought" on their own terms, independent of the "real [social, ideological] functions" they perform, precludes the possibility of a true understanding. One cannot explain these phenomena, however, in terms of a single historical "moment" of a social complex. Thus Lukács argues for the necessity of a "genetic derivation of language or conceptual thought from labor."[134] This "from" is critical, as he goes on to explain that while "the execution of the labor process poses demands on the subject…that were already present into language and conceptual thought, […] this cannot be understood ontologically without the antecedent requirements of labor, or even the conditions that gave rise to the genesis of the labor process."[135]

Thus a dialectical interrelation exists between thought and labor, with ontological priority being accorded to the latter. Lukács then traces the ontological

---

131   GW 14: 47; O3, 47.
132   GW 14: 47; O3, 48.
133   GW 14: 48; O3, 49.
134   GW 14: 48; O3, 49.
135   GW 14: 48; O3, 49.

genesis of conceptual thinking. The transferability of the experience in one concrete labor situation to others gives rise to observations that "acquire a certain universal character" and become "relatively autonomous" determinations about "natural processes in general."[136] The iteration of confrontations with those elements of nature which relate directly to the posited goal of the labor process introduces the possibility of raising knowledge of those elements "to a higher level of generalization [*Verallgemeinerung*]." But Lukács explains that "this is not possible without ontological categories of intention increasingly intervening in the reflection of nature, linked as these are with human social life."[137]

Thus we can observe how intentionality increasingly intervenes in human thought, so much so that it will later come to be understood as *the mark of the mental* in contemporary analytic philosophy. But it is only through Lukács' analysis that we can trace this mark back genetically to the reflection of nature in labor and it is only through that analysis that we can be reminded of how this mark can only be understood properly if it is linked ontologically with concrete human social life.

The integral relation between logical positivism and analytic philosophy is well-documented, and Lukács' explicit critique of the former deserves attention. He is clearly aware of how Carnap was strongly influenced by Frege, Russell, Wittgenstein, and neo-Kantianism in attempting to separate logical and linguistic forms of analysis from any metaphysical commitments, as illustrated by his reference to "neopositivism, with any reference to being in the ontological sense being rejected as 'metaphysics,' and hence unscientific, and increased practical applicability being taken as the sole criterion for scientific truth."[138] The last part of this critique, the criticism of attempting to explain scientific truth in terms of "practical applicability" is part of a more general critical theory of how science is subordinated to the production process of capitalist society. In indicating earlier in the *Ontologie* how science is derivative of labor,[139] he mentioned that the contemporary sciences perform "the preparatory work for industry."[140] Later, he noted in passing that "[e]conomy and technique" are characterized by a "contradictory dialectic of end and means."[141] Now, more precisely, he speaks of this "false ontological consciousness in the realm of science" being "clearly rooted in the prevailing social needs," providing the most

---

136 GW 14: 49; O3, 51.
137 GW 14: 54; O3, 57.
138 GW 14: 58–59; O3, 63.
139 GW 14: 25; O3, 19.
140 GW 14: 25; O3, 20.
141 GW 14: 38; O3, 36.

important example of how "manipulation in the economy has become a decisive factor for the reproduction of present-day capitalism."[142] Later, he will explain how science directly contradicts its social application in the form of technology.[143] Lukács will also express this contradiction as an "antithesis between knowledge of being and its mere manipulation."[144] Thus the framework developed by Habermas in *Knowledge and Human Interests*[145] is clearly derivative of Lukács' critical insights here, even if Marx had already indicated in various ways that capital only increases productivity through "incorporating... natural science."[146] The contradictions at work in this social reality of "practice as the criterion for theory" cannot be grasped if one attempts to understand the relation in "epistemological, formal-logical, or methodological" terms.[147]

The solution to this problem – i.e., the problem that theory is subordinated to the practice of capitalist exploitation, rather than the practice of satisfying human needs – is "conscious ontological criticism." Such criticism "must intervene if the fundamentally correct property of this criterion function of practice is not to be endangered."[148] Furthermore, "[o]ntological criticism...must be oriented to the differentiated totality of society – differentiated concretely by class – and to the mutual relationships in the types of behavior that thus arise. Only in this way can the function of practice, which is of decisive importance to intellectual development, and for all social practice, be correctly applied as a criterion of theory."[149] This orientation toward the "differentiated" totality of society is essentially antithetical to those of the analytic and logical positivist traditions for ideological reasons which should already be apparent.

Lukács concludes this second chapter with a derivation of normativity from labor. This derivation is accompanied by a critique of how the category of the "ought" (*Sollen*) is conceived in Kant's philosophy. Despite this historical framing, Lukács' criticism applies directly to understandings in contemporary analytic philosophy of meaning and content as essentially normative in character. First, Lukács explains that "the categorically decisive moment" in the teleological positing and realization of goals in the labor process "involves the emergence of a practice determined by the 'ought'."[150] Thus "the indubitable genesis

---

142   GW 14: 59; O3, 63.
143   See GW 14: 108–109; O3, 126.
144   GW 14: 109; O3, 127.
145   See Habermas, *Knowledge and Human Interests*. (Boston: Beacon Press, 1972).
146   MEW 23: 408; K1, 509.
147   GW 14: 59; O3, 63.
148   GW 14: 60; O3, 64.
149   GW 14: 60; O3, 65.
150   GW 14: 61; O3, 65.

of the 'ought'" is located "in the teleological nature of labor," and the labor process is consequently to be understood as the "ontological foundation" for any normatively-determined practices.[151]

In conventional philosophical explanations of normativity, "[t]he 'ought' is thus torn away from the concrete alternatives" confronted by persons; rather, social practices are understood "as adequate or inadequate embodiments of a kind of absolute commandment, a commandment which therefore remains transcendent towards man himself."[152] This criticism can be applied to a number of contemporary accounts of normativity. Take, for instance, Brandom's explanation of the expressive role words indicating intentional directedness (such as "of," "about," and "represents") in terms of a discursive (deontic, in fact) scorekeeping account with a substitution-inferential structure. This account

> takes the form of a specification of the particular sort of inferential structure social scorekeeping practices must have in order to institute objective norms, according to which the correctness of an application of a concept answers to the facts about the object to which it is applied, in such a way that anyone (indeed *everyone*) in the linguistic community may be wrong about it.[153]

Thus one can observe the contemporary relevance of Lukács' criticism of how social practices are understood in conventional philosophies of normativity "as adequate or inadequate embodiments of a kind of absolute commandment, a commandment which therefore remains transcendent towards man himself."

The conclusion to this chapter offers some crucial insights about the necessity of analysis from the standpoint of concrete, historically-specific sociality. Lukács first presents us with the following succinct formulation of this commitment: "There is no human problem that is not ultimately raised and determined by the real practice of social life."[154] One might argue that Lukács' own analysis, itself a form of theoretical generalization, contradicts this principle. But he himself acknowledges that the "alternatives" which he introduced above as confronting the laborer and as representing the "indelible foundations for specifically human social practice" can be divorced from individual

---

151   GW 14: 66; O3, 72.
152   GW 14: 63; O3, 69.
153   Brandom, *Making it Explicit*, xvii.
154   GW 14: 80; O3, 90.

decisions "only by abstraction."[155] In elaborating on this notion of "social practice," he talks of the "true social context," the one on which analysis must be based, as "always anchored in the social needs of the time."[156]

The third and final chapter of the labor section of the *Ontologie* is concerned with articulating how "the subject–object relation" is "a direct consequence of labor." What is critically important for our purposes, however, is his explanation of how the distancing implied by this relation originating in labor "creates both an indispensable basis for human social existence, and one that is endowed with a life of its own: language."[157] The relative autonomy of language must be explained in ontological and genetic terms, and the following passage provides that explanation:

> Man always speaks 'about' something definite, thereby contrasting it in a double sense with his immediate existence. Firstly, by positing it as an independently existing object, and secondly – and here the distancing process comes even more sharply to the fore – by striving to indicate the object in question as something concrete; his means of expression and his descriptions are constructed in such a way that each sign can equally well figure in completely different contexts. In this way what is depicted by the verbal sign is separated from the objects it describes, and hence also from the subject uttering it, becoming the mental expression for an entire group of particular phenomena, so that it can be applied in a similar way in completely different contexts and by completely different subjects.[158]

The key revelation in this passage is Lukács' understanding of linguistic discursivity, and therewith the mental states which such discursivity makes explicit, in terms of *intentional directedness*: words are always "about" (*über*) something definite in his analysis. Language, from this view, in performing its expressive role, expresses what is thought *about*, what a belief *represents*, or what a claim is true *of*. This can be read as a commitment to the position that the intentional is the mark of the mental.

Lukács cites Engels' notation that "[n]ecessity created the organ," but he explains that this biological explanation does not answer the question on which his analysis in this final chapter is centered: "[W]hat exactly does it mean to

---

155   GW 14: 84; O3, 95.
156   GW 14: 85; O3, 96.
157   GW 14: 88; O3, 100.
158   GW 14: 88; O3, 100.

have something to say?"[159] This question can only be answered through reference to the socially and historically-specific complexes within which persons speak to one another, and, by appealing to human sociality and historicity rather biology, Lukács is laying the groundwork for the achievement of his final task in this section: the derivation of freedom from labor. Thus we can observe, by understanding the project of Lukács' *Ontologie* as articulating the material basis of intentionality, the critical possibilities of that project.

---

159   GW 14: 88; O3, 100.

PART 2

*Hegelian-Marxist Dimensions of
Lukács' Social Ontology*

∴

CHAPTER 4

György Lukács' Ontological Interpretation of Marx's Labor Theory of Value

Murillo van der Laan

This chapter aims to critically assess the category of economic value in György Lukács' *The Ontology of the Social Being* and the interpretation of Marx's labor theory of value underlying it. To do this, after closely reading the *Ontology* – especially the chapters about Marx and about labor – I will address some of Lukács' comments on this topic in his essay *The process of democratization*, written in 1968, in the same period and spirit of the *Ontology*.

I will also follow the analysis made by Antonino Infranca, Sérgio Lessa, Ronaldo Vielmi Fortes, Ana Selva Albinati and Mariana Alves de Andrade, which I consider important contributions to the comprehension of the *Ontology*. Nevertheless, my reading here contrasts with theirs, as I will try to locate some problematic points in Lukács' arguments about economic value.

For a critical reading of this category I will draw on Peter Hudis' brief comments and István Mészáros' sharp critique of Lukács' interpretation of the Marxian labor theory of value. However, here I will also present some minor differences. Furthermore, I will recur to Marx's and Engels' works and briefly refer to classical and contemporaneous commentators and contrast their reading with Lukács' own.

The argument developed here is that the category of economic value in the *Ontology* is fruitful, since it draws an articulation between objectivity and subjectivity in economic valuations. Through a philosophical development of Marx's take on labor and practice, Lukács presents an immanent reading of values that helps to complement Marx's own position by stressing, on one hand, the causality which individuals must face in order to realize successful objectifications; and, on the other hand, the evaluation between the alternatives opened to them and the processes through which they internalize these demands – expressed by the category of ought.

However, Lukács' peculiar reading of Marx's labor theory of value generalizes it to every social formation. In doing this, Lukács also presents a generalization of several aspects that, in our view, are specific of capitalism: (1) the compulsion to reduce labor time; (2) the opacity of economic valuations; (3) the socially necessary labor time. Moreover, the interpretation of economic values in the *Ontology* neglects Marx's distinction between social formations based directly on an organization of social labor and capitalism, in which the social aspect of labor asserts itself indirectly, through exchanges in the market. In our view, this can jeopardize not only the comprehension of pre-capitalist social formations, but also the perspective of human emancipation.

To develop our arguments, we will start with some brief general comments about Lukács' *Ontology*; we will then move to his philosophical reading of use value and to the category of ought; subsequently, we will present his idea of economic value, and will address each of the aspects we consider problematic in his interpretation; finally, we will present an alternative approach to understand economic value as a trans-historical category.

1   The Lukácsian Ontology

Since at least the end of the 1940s, Lukács had been collecting material to write a Marxist Ethics. Nevertheless, it was only about 10 years later, in the last decade of his life, that he could finally start this project, after working on his *Aesthetics*.[1] The new project, however, took him to a detour through an ontological approach that was meant to serve as a solid ground for his investigations, which represented also his different view of the word "ontology" itself. Before the 1960s, Lukács referred to the latter in a negative sense, especially opposing the heideggerian use of it. However, influenced by the works of the German philosopher Nicolai Hartmann, he approached the word differently. In the middle of the 1960s, already engaged in this ontological project – that instead of a prelude, as was previously imagined, became an autonomous work – Lukács refers to "ontology" as a "beautiful word."[2]

Despite all his efforts, the ontological project was not finished. The immense manuscript of about 1,500 pages that he left, *The Ontology of Social Being*, according to some witnesses did not satisfy him due to the way he presented the matter – especially the separation between a "historical part" (that is not

---

1   Besides offering an important account about the philosophical roots of Lukács' ontological thinking – that could be traced to his first contact with Marx's *Economic-philosophical Manuscripts* – Guido Oldrini also summarizes chronologically Lukács' explicit references to the *Ontology*, in the 1960s. See Guido Oldrini, "Em busca das raízes da ontologia (marxista) de Lukács." In György Lukács, *Para uma ontologia do ser social*. (São Paulo: Boitempo, 2013), 9–37.

2   György Lukács, *Werke*, vol. 18. (Darmstad und Neuwied: Luchterhand, 2005), 240. See also Guido Oldrini, "Em busca das raízes da ontologia (marxista) de Lukács." In György Lukács, *Para uma ontologia do ser social* (São Paulo: Boitempo, 2013), 9–37.

organized exactly in a chronological form since, for instance, the chapter on Nicolai Hartmann precedes the one about Hegel) and a theoretical or systemic part. The *Prolegomena to the ontology of the social being*, that he wrote later, despite suppressing that dichotomy, was also left without revision.[3]

Nevertheless, the ontological project advanced by Lukács at the end of his life was proposed to critically mediate the different sciences, taking as its object "what really exists" and to assume the task of "investigat[ing] existence with the concern of understanding its being and finding the different levels and connections inside it."[4]

"What really exists" means here an open defense of the objectivity of the world outside the mind and also the capacity of human cognition, already in its first manifestations in labor, of reflecting – at least minimally and always in an approximate way – the determinations of the real. This is how Lukács, defending that Marx inaugurated a new ontology, interprets his assertion that "the categories express forms of being, determinations of existence."[5] They exist objectively outside of consciousness and it is possible – even inevitable – to reproduce them in different ways in the human mind. Against the exaggerations of formalism and logicism – especially the ones that come from neopositivism[6] – it is to this primacy of objectivity that human cognition must attend in its development. Lukács posits himself, thus, against any absolute separation between reality and knowledge and against any closure of logic and

---

3 Nicolas Tertulian, "Introduzione." In *Prolegomini all'ontologia dell'essere sociale*. (Napoli: Guerini e Associati, 1990), X–XI.
4 György Lukács, *Werke*, vol. 18 (Darmstad und Neuwied: Luchterhand, 2004), 237. The word "ontology" appears with different meanings in Lukács' last work. As João Leonardo Medeiros Gomes argues, it resembles the use of "economy" and "history," which could refer both to the economic *science* or the *discipline* of history, but also to the economic relations and history themselves. Thus, the ontology refers to categories of reality and also to the various world images that reflect this reality. The idea that Lukács equates ontology with *Weltbild* is stressed by Matteo Gargani. See João Leonardo Medeiros Gomes, "As implicações da teoria do valor de Marx para a ética: uma interpretação a partir da obra ontológica de Lukács." In *Política e Sociedade*, vol. 10, no. 19 (2011): 278; Matteo Gargani, *Produzione e filosofia: sul concetto di ontologia in Lukács*. (Hildesheim: Georg Olms Verlag, 2017), XXI.
5 Karl Marx and Friedrich Engels, *Collected Works*, vol. 28. (London: Lawrence & Wishart, 1986), 43. See also György Lukács, *Werke*, vol. 13. (Darmstad und Neuwied: Luchterhand, 1984), 311–312.
6 Lukács considers neopositivism as the purest form of a theory of knowledge based on itself, since it rejects any ontological perspective and evaluates statements by their form, using only criteria immanent in consciousness. This reduces the theory of knowledge, and philosophy itself, to a mere technique to regulate language. See György Lukács, *Werke*, vol. 13. (Darmstad und Neuwied: Luchterhand, 1984), 343–370.

gnoseology in themselves. While they are instruments to human knowledge and practice, they need to be subsumed to ontology.

We cannot address here the complex lukácsian analysis of philosophy and science. But this ontological approach already gives us insight of the road taken by Lukács to address human valuations. He rejects any kind of aprioristic or logicist perspective and stresses the need to comprehend immanently the problem of values inside human activities and relations with the environment itself.

This environment is delineated in the *Ontology* in its "different levels" and searching for the various "connections inside it," highlighting, at the same time, the historical character of the ontological development. Valuations appear in the *Ontology* mediated by this development and by the connections between the different levels of being. To comprehend this process, Lukács – basing his reflection on Marx's method used in the *Introduction of 1857*[7] – employs genetic and abstractive procedures to delineate the various levels, categories, and connections of the being.

Thus, the primacy of objectivity has to be understood inside a processual development of the being that, despite forming a totality, is divided into three great spheres: the inorganic being, the organic being, and the social being. These spheres have, of course, discontinuities between them, but also necessary continuities. From the interactions inside the inorganic being emerges the organic being and, from these two, the social being. The ontological leap from one sphere to the other implies to "carry" the categories of the previous sphere and, at the same time, qualitatively surpass it. In other words, in the ontological development, if the biological reproduction figures as a novelty when compared to the inorganic being, its processuality can only take place interacting internally and externally with this previous sphere. Similarly, with the social being emerges the new capacity of reproducing itself through teleological acts, but this reproduction is necessary and can only take place because of the continuities that the social being has with the previous two ontological spheres.[8]

Throughout the *Ontology*, Lukács tries to indicate the genesis, complexification and, in some cases, the possible disappearance of different categories, according to the particularities of each of the ontological spheres. Despite his focus being on the social being, and that he stresses that he is a mere dilettante on the issues concerning the natural sciences, Lukács presents some philosophical accounts about the inorganic and organic being. These are thought

---

7   Karl Marx and Friedrich Engels, *Collected Works*, vol. 28. (London: Lawrence & Wishart, 1986).
8   See, for instance, György Lukács, *Werke*, vol. 13. (Darmstad und Neuwied: Luchterhand, 1984), 326–327. Sérgio Lessa, *Sociabilidade e individuação*. (Maceió: Edufal, 1995), 22–23.

inside the processual movement of the totality – that Lukács describes as a complex of complexes – and according to what he calls "ontological priorities." By this Lukács means that the ontological determinations are not organized in any arbitrary way (based on logical or gnoseological perspectives, nor according to any set of values), but they have an existence supported by ontological precedents that necessarily serves as a base and acts on the posterior categories.[9] Concerning specifically the social being, this means that its development depends on the possibility of reproducing, primarily, his biological needs, in interaction with the two previous ontological spheres. The biological needs, though, are met in a different way in the social being as compared to the organic being.

This ontological approach takes Lukács, in his first steps analyzing the social being, to abstract the complex of labor and characterize it as the original phenomenon [*Urphänomen*] or the model of the social being[10] [*Modell des gesellschaftlichen Seins*]. Even though labor could be understood properly only in relation to the totality of the social being, it is the complex that is responsible for the urgent task of the biological reproduction of the individuals. As a category of "transition" between the organic and the social being, labor would also have a "methodological advantage" to investigate praxis.[11] According to Lukács, here it is already possible to approach the new articulation that characterizes the social being: the one between teleological acts and causality. On the one hand, the human ability to posit goals that were previously idealized, and on the other, causality understood as a "principle of motion on its own basis."[12]

The articulation between these two moments, through objectification of goals that were previously idealized, does not lead to any kind of identity between teleology and causality. Subject and object remain different entities. Nevertheless, through the relation between them, new nexus are inserted in reality.

In the chapter on labor in the *Ontology*, Lukács develops a complex analysis of praxis. Although we cannot retrace his arguments here, in order to move to his analysis of values we would like to briefly highlight that in the labor process, in order to satisfy a determinate necessity, humans are capable through reflection [*Widerspiegelung*] to reproduce, minimally at least, the determinations

---

9   See, for instance, György Lukács, *Werke*, vol. 13. (Darmstad und Neuwied: Luchterhand, 1984), 582.
10 About the designations of labor in the *Ontology*, see Antonino Infranca, *Trabalho, indivíduo, história*. (São Paulo, Boitempo, 2014), 26.
11 György Lukács, *Werke*, vol. 14. (Darmstad und Neuwied: Luchterhand, 1986), 10.
12 György Lukács, *Werke*, vol. 14. (Darmstad und Neuwied: Luchterhand, 1986), 13. See also Sérgio Lessa, *Mundo dos Homens*. (São Paulo: Instituto Lukács, 2012), 61.

of objects and to foresee the possibilities present in causality. This capacity demands decisions between alternatives to be made during the entire process of objectification. Making choices between these, in turn, requires, on the one hand, valuation processes and, on the other, that the laborer must behave such that his goals can be successfully achieved. This implies, therefore, *value* and *ought*.

2   Ought and Value

Ought [*Sollen*] and *value* are presented in the *Ontology* as two categories that are intimately connected. They are also related to what Lukács considers the first manifestation of *freedom* in the social being. The possibilities inscribed in reality demand from the worker a choice between concrete alternatives. Once chosen, the realization of the alternative necessarily implies a determinate behavior of the one who objectifies what was previously idealized. Therefore, freedom is connected to *ought* since the achievement of a goal requires that every step realized by the subject has to be verified in order to decide how (and if) it can help satisfy a particular need.[13]

When compared to the previous spheres of being, there is now a change in the temporality of the ontological interactions. In the organic being, for instance, past determines the present: "adaptation of the living being to a changed environment," says Lukács, "takes place with equal causal necessity, since the properties produced in the organism by its past react on such a change to maintain or destroy it."[14] There is, of course, a continuity in this relation in the social being. Nevertheless, a qualitative change takes place with the emergence of teleology. The behavior of the subject is now determined by the future, by the realization of a previously idealized goal. Ought, to Lukács, refers to the acting that is directed by what was previously idealized.[15]

In the case of labor, ought is related to the metabolism between humans and nature and is articulated to the decisive demands put forward by causality. This happens in connection to other moments of the teleological positing, like reflection, the investigation of the means of labor, the constitution of goals, etc. Nevertheless, in this complex relationship, Lukács highlights the role

---

13   György Lukács, *The ontology of social being: labour*. (London: Merlin Press, 1980), 65–66. György Lukács, *Werke*, vol. 14 (Darmstad und Neuwied: Luchterhand, 1986), 61.

14   György Lukács, *The ontology of social being: labour* (London: Merlin Press, 1980), 66. György Lukács, *Werke*, vol. 14 (Darmstad und Neuwied: Luchterhand, 1986), 60–61.

15   György Lukács, *The ontology of social being: labour* (London: Merlin Press, 1980), 66. György Lukács, *Werke*, vol. 14 (Darmstad und Neuwied: Luchterhand, 1986), 60–61.

played by the objectivity facing the worker and his ability to develop himself during the process of objectification:

> In so far as the 'ought' also applies to certain aspects of the subject's internal life, and this is unavoidable, its claims are posed in such a way that the internal transformations provide a vehicle for the better control of the metabolism with nature. Man's self-control, which necessarily emerges first of all as the effect of the 'ought' in labor, the growing command of his insight over his own spontaneous biological inclinations, habits, etc., is governed and guided by the objectivity of this process; but this is founded essentially on the natural existence of the object and means, etc., of labor. If we want to understand correctly the aspect of the 'ought' that affects and modifies the subject in labor, then we must proceed from this objectivity as the regulative principle.[16]

Ought determined by this causality facing the subject that realizes the teleological positing influences the worker's behavior in labor, but also his behavior with himself. In this sense, it also "arouses" and "promotes" in human beings predicates that could be important to the more developed praxis. Lukács, nevertheless, stresses only the possibility, though it is a great one, that this takes place, and not any certainty that the changes in the subject put forward by *ought* during the labor process will immediately and necessarily affect the totality of the individual.[17]

The genetic investigation of this category contrasts both with the idealist and the "old materialist" approaches to the matter. The way Lukács analyzes ought as present already in the original moment of labor attempts, on the one hand, to not lose sight of its simplest manifestations that are articulated to the totality of the social being and, on the other, to highlight the qualitative novelty of this category that belongs exclusively to the social being.[18]

According to Lukács, the way idealism addresses this question, in a logical or epistemological manner, takes into account only its "most highly developed,

---

16 György Lukács, *The ontology of social being: labour*. (London: Merlin Press, 1980), 72–73. György Lukács, *Werke*, vol. 14 (Darmstad und Neuwied: Luchterhand, 1986), 66.

17 György Lukács, *The ontology of social being: labour*. (London: Merlin Press, 1980), 73. György Lukács, *Werke*, vol. 14 (Darmstad und Neuwied: Luchterhand, 1986), 66–67.

18 See also Ana Selva Albinati, "Ontologia do ser social: considerações sobre o valor e o dever-ser em Lukács." In Ester Vaisman and Miguel Vedda (ed.), *Lukács: estética e ontologia*. (São Paulo: Alameda, 2014), 126–137.

most spiritualized and subtle forms of appearance."[19] In this way, the ought already present in the most elementary practice of the social being is not only obliterated in idealist philosophies – together with the complex mediations towards the more spiritualized activities – but is also conceived in a way antithetical to its more developed manifestations. The result is that it is delineated "an artificial and rootless sphere of the 'ought' (of value)" that is then "contrasted with man's allegedly purely natural being, even though both are in fact equally social from the ontological point of view."[20]

The "vulgar materialism," on the other hand, interprets these problems based on the model of "pure natural necessity," ignoring the role of *ought* in the social being.[21]

In summary, to Lukács, therefore, *ought* emerges already in the practice that he considers to be the original phenomenon in the social being: labor. It refers to a future direction that is put forward by the goal previously idealized in the labor process, and it is necessarily determined by the objective the worker has in front of herself, such that her behavior is conditioned in the attempt to reach her goal. This can also change her relation to herself. Ought, nevertheless, as with other categories in the *Ontology*, must be regarded in relation to the specific complex where it manifests itself: labor, politics, law, etc. Here, as far as we are aware, Lukács only indicates the development and transformation of this category in the other activities of the social being, not addressing the particular way in which this occurs.

As we said, intimately connected with *ought* is *value*. In the practice of the social being, what determines its future behavior can only do so, since what it aims to objectify is, in a certain way, valuable. Furthermore, value can only realize itself if it can activate in the worker ought as the "guiding thread of his practice."[22] Despite the close connection of these two categories, the moments which they refer to are different: while value acts on the goal that is idealized and on the evaluation of what was objectified, *ought* is connected to the regulative process of objectification.[23]

---

19 György Lukács, *The ontology of social being: labour.* (London: Merlin Press, 1980), 68. György Lukács, Werke, vol. 14. (Darmstad und Neuwied: Luchterhand, 1986), 63.
20 György Lukács, *The ontology of social being: labour.* (London: Merlin Press, 1980), 68. György Lukács, Werke, vol. 14. (Darmstad und Neuwied: Luchterhand, 1986), 63.
21 György Lukács, *The ontology of social being: labour.* (London: Merlin Press, 1980), 68. György Lukács, Werke, vol. 14. (Darmstad und Neuwied: Luchterhand, 1986), 63.
22 György Lukács, *The ontology of social being: labour.* (London: Merlin Press, 1980), 75. György Lukács, Werke, vol. 14. (Darmstad und Neuwied: Luchterhand, 1986), 68.
23 György Lukács, *The ontology of social being: labour.* (London: Merlin Press, 1980), 75. György Lukács, Werke, vol. 14. (Darmstad und Neuwied: Luchterhand, 1986), 68. See also:

Dealing with value, the question Lukács poses regards the definition of what is valuable; as realized by the worker, is this evaluation objective or only subjective? "Is value," asks Lukács, the "objective property of a thing, which is simply recognized by the subject – correctly or otherwise – in the valuing act, or does value arise precisely as the result of valuing acts of this kind?"[24]

To answer this question, Lukács turns his attention to what he considers to be the most elemental form of valuations: use value. Even in this case, where there is a closer and "indelible" relation with natural existence, he considers that "it is certainly true that value cannot be obtained directly from the naturally given properties of an object,"[25] but he also stresses that values are not the "mere result of subjective acts of judgement."[26] It is from the articulation between teleology and natural causality that emerge the valuations expressed in use values. Despite the existence of exceptions where these valuations are not related to labor – like the "air, virgin soil, natural meadows, etc.,"[27] mentioned by Marx in *Capital* –, valuations emerge inside concrete relations of labor.

Value is not present in nature – since there is no teleology there – but the latter necessarily determines the valuation processes that are manifested in use values. This creates a "social form of objectivity," a concrete relation of utility or inutility in the attempt to satisfy a necessity through teleological positing. In the case of use values, this process necessarily has to refer to the natural causality. Thus, through an analysis of use values, Lukács responds to the question about the objectivity of values, saying that it is not "a mere result of subjective acts of judgement, but these simply make conscious the use value's objective utility; their rightness or wrongness is established by the objective properties of the use values, and not vice versa."[28]

Ana Selva Albinati, "Ontologia do ser social: considerações sobre o valor e o dever-ser em Lukács." In Ester Vaisman and Miguel Vedda (ed.), *Lukács: estética e ontologia*. (São Paulo: Alameda, 2014), 126; Ronaldo Vielmi Fortes, *Trabalho e gênese do ser social na "ontologia" de Georg Lukács*. (Belo Horizonte: UFMG, 2001), 101; Sérgio Lessa, *Mundo dos Homens*. (São Paulo: Instituto Lukács, 2012), 114; Mariana Alves de Andrade, *Lukács: reprodução social e valor*. (Rio de Janeiro: UFRJ, 2016), 180–181.

24 György Lukács, *The ontology of social being: labour*. (London: Merlin Press, 1980), 75. György Lukács, *Werke*, vol. 14. (Darmstad und Neuwied: Luchterhand, 1986), 68.
25 György Lukács, *The ontology of social being: labour*. (London: Merlin Press, 1980), 75. György Lukács, *Werke*, vol. 14. (Darmstad und Neuwied: Luchterhand, 1986), 68.
26 György Lukács, *The ontology of social being: labour*. (London: Merlin Press, 1980), 77. György Lukács, *Werke*, vol. 14. (Darmstad und Neuwied: Luchterhand, 1986), 70.
27 Karl Marx and Friedrich Engels, *Collected Works*, vol. 35. (London: Lawrence & Wishart, 1986), 50.
28 György Lukács, *The ontology of social being: labour*. (London: Merlin Press, 1980), 77. György Lukács, *Werke*, vol. 14. (Darmstad und Neuwied: Luchterhand, 1986), 70.

The interpretation of values, according to Lukács, depends on an adequate analysis of labor and its role in the emergence of the social being. The articulation of causality with teleological acts is important in order to address values philosophically. Ontological perspectives based, for instance, on a teleological definition of reality conceive values in relation to a transcendental creator.[29] Furthermore, the opposition that emerged during the Renaissance to this teleological conception of valuations gave emphasis to the subjective dimension of values. Lukács considers this development to have reached its "philosophical summit" with the Enlightenment and with the attempts of the Physiocrats and the English economists of the 18th century to give value an economic foundation.[30]

In this sense, the approach to values in the *Ontology* tries to defend a third possibility to interpret them, which differs from the conceptions that support either values that are "refinedly spiritual" or "immediately material." Despite their opposition, these two approaches, according to Lukács, have in common the rejection of "socially real systems of values" in the social being and an ultimately unitary perspective of valuations. To Lukács,

> only the dialectical method can provide the tertium datur to these two extremes. For this alone makes it possible to explain how the decisive categories of a new mode of being are already contained in its ontological genesis which is why its rise means a leap in development; but also why these are initially present only implicitly (an sich), and the development from the implicit to the explicit (fur sich) must always be prolonged, uneven and contradictory historical process. This superseding of the implicit by its transformation into an explicit involves the most complex determinations of negation, preservation and raising to a higher level, which seem incompatible with one another from the standpoint of formal logic. It is necessary therefore, even in comparing the primitive and the developed forms of value, to bear in mind this complex character of the supersession.[31]

In sum, when interpreting what he considers to be the genesis of values, Lukács focuses first on use values and analyzes them by stressing the social objectivity

---

29 György Lukács, *The ontology of social being: labour*. (London: Merlin Press, 1980), 77–78. György Lukács, *Werke*, vol. 14. (Darmstad und Neuwied: Luchterhand, 1986), 70.

30 György Lukács, *The ontology of social being: labour*. (London: Merlin Press, 1980), 78–79. György Lukács, *Werke*, vol. 14. (Darmstad und Neuwied: Luchterhand, 1986), 71.

31 György Lukács, *The ontology of social being: labour*. (London: Merlin Press, 1980), 79–80. György Lukács, *Werke*, vol. 14. (Darmstad und Neuwied: Luchterhand, 1986), 72.

that characterizes valuations in the social being. This social objectivity is located in the articulation between teleology and causality in labor, which realizes the urgent task of the metabolism between humans and nature. Centered in the positing of goals and in the evaluation of what was objectified, values demand a certain behavior of the worker – they demand ought – so that the positing of goals can be realized successfully. But this is only a first manifestation of both categories. Rejecting the philosophical systems that give importance only to the either "refinedly spiritual" or "immediately material" values, Lukács proposes a dialectical approach to them that stress their development and unity. As far as we understand, this is not completely developed in the *Ontology*. Nevertheless, let us follow Lukács as he unfolds his approach to values.

3 Economic Value

The next step in Lukács' argument is the introduction of the category of *economic value* [*ökonomischen Wert*]. In the *Ontology*, this is related to the control of labor time in the social being. Here, therefore, we are dealing with a more complex moment than the previous one. Nevertheless, Lukács tries to argue that, in relation to the analysis of use values, there is a certain continuity, in the sense that economic values are characterized also by a particular kind of objectivity. Use values emerge in the articulation between teleology and natural causality, and in this articulation the objectivity of this relation can be shown. Economic values, in turn, present an objective dimension supported not only by this relation with use values, but also by another based on the social relations between individuals and time in the different labor tasks demanded by the social being.

The manner in which Lukács delineates this characterization and the results he achieves are simultaneously fruitful and problematic. However, before stressing our reservations about Lukács' take on economic values, let us follow his argumentation in the *Ontology*.

In his attempt to show the objectivity of economic values, Lukács resorts to the example, "in its most general form," of the simple purchase and sale of commodities, presented by Marx in Chapter 3 of *Capital*, in the section *The metamorphosis of commodities*. Lukács' goal here is to "indicate methodologically the manner and direction of the newly arising mediations and realizations."

The economic acts of this example take place according to a division of labor in which the activities of the individual owners of commodities have become unilateral, in contrast to the diversity of their needs. To satisfy the latter, therefore, these individuals need to resort to the market. Here, despite the purchases and sales being acts that represent a unity – since for each purchase a sale is realized at the same time – they can be separated and generate crisis. As Marx stressed, contrary to the idea of an equilibrium between purchases and sales, "no one is forthwith bound to purchase, because he has just sold" and this configuration implies "the possibility, and no more than the possibility, of crises."[32]

From this example, Lukács abstracts the complex objective synthesis that configures a totality of social relations, but also that this totality is the result of singular teleological positing and of alternatives chosen and realized. The multiple valuations that determine the decisions of purchase and sale, in the simple exchange of commodities, can result in crisis that acts objectively against buyers and sellers.

Compared to use values, this is a much more complex moment. The objectivity here is stressed in the synthesis of these diverse acts, which underlies the valuation and the decisions made.[33] This is to say, it is from this synthesis that economic valuations emerge and to it that must report to verify the potential success of a particular act. Furthermore, Lukács says that the individuals involved in this process are not able to adequately evaluate their own practice:

> [totality in process] can no longer be so directly grasped, by the positing individual economic subjects who decide between alternatives, that they could orient their decisions to the world around them with the same complete certainty as was the case with the simple labor that created use values. In most cases, indeed, man can scarcely follow correctly the consequences of their own decisions. How therefore could their positings of value constitute economic value? But value itself is still objectively present, and its very objectivity also determines – even if without complete certainty on the objective side, or adequate awareness on the subjective – the individual teleological positings that are oriented by value.[34]

---

32   Karl Marx and Friedrich Engels, *Collected Works*, vol. 35. (London: Lawrence & Wishart, 1986), 123–124.
33   Ronaldo Vielmi Fortes, *Trabalho e gênese do ser social na "ontologia" de Georg Lukács*. (Belo Horizonte: UFMG, 2001), 118; Mariana Alves de Andrade, *Lukács: reprodução social e valor*. (Rio de Janeiro: UFRJ, 2016), 186–187.
34   György Lukács, *The ontology of social being: labour*. (London: Merlin Press, 1980), 83. György Lukács, *Werke*, vol. 14. (Darmstad und Neuwied: Luchterhand, 1986), 74–75.

Connected to this objectivity of economic values is a compulsion of decreasing labor time. "The division of labor" – says Lukács – "mediated and brought about by exchange-value produces the principle of control of time [*Beherrschung der Zeit*] by a better subjective use of it" and to support his claim, Lukács refers to the following passage of Marx's *Grundrisse*:

> ultimately, all economy is a matter of economy of time. Society must also allocate its time appropriately to achieve a production corresponding to its total needs, just as the individual must allocate his time correctly to acquire knowledge in suitable proportions or to satisfy the various demands on his activity. Economy of time, as well as the planned distribution of labour time over the various branches of production, therefore, remains the first economic law if communal production is taken as the basis.[35]

The interpretation of this passage in the *Ontology* is that Marx refers here to a "law of social production" [*Gesetz der gesellschaftlichen Produktion*], which is the result of various teleological acts. The synthesis of these acts produces a causal effect that retroacts in the same individuals who produced them and they need to adapt to this law or "*perish*"[36] [*bei Strafe des Untergangs*].[37] This constitutes the objective relation that underlies the valuations in the economic complex, but must be comprehended as the attempt of Lukács to grasp the processual development of the social being:

> economy of time, however, immediately involves a relation of value. Even simple labor, oriented just to use value, was a subjugation of nature by and for man, both in its transformation to suit his needs and in his attaining control over his own merely natural instincts and emotions, and is thus a mediating factor in the initial elaboration of his specifically human abilities. The objective orientation of economic law to the saving of

---

35 Karl Marx and Friedrich Engels, *Collected Works*, vol. 28 (London: Lawrence & Wishart, 1986), 109.
36 György Lukács, *The ontology of social being: labour* (London: Merlin Press, 1980), 84. György Lukács, *Werke*, vol. 14 (Darmstad und Neuwied: Luchterhand, 1986), 75.
37 As Tertulian notes, "*bei Strafe des Untergang*s," or "under penalty of ruin," is a Marxian expression used repeatedly by Lukács. Marx referred to it, for instance, when commenting about the need capitalists have "to improve production and expand its scale merely as a means of self-preservation." See Karl Marx and Friedrich Engels, *Collected Works*, vol. 37 (London: Lawrence & Wishart, 1998), 243; Nicolas Tertulian, "Introduzione." In *Prolegomini all'ontologia dell'essere sociale*. (Napoli: Guerini e Associati, 1990), xx.

time immediately gives rise to whatever is the optimal social division of labor at the time, thus bringing about the rise of a social being at a higher level of a sociality that becomes ever more pure. This movement is thus an objective one, independent of how those involved might conceive it, a step towards the realization of social categories from their initial implicit being into an explicit being that is ever more richly determined and effective.[38]

A first difficulty in interpreting Lukács' arguments comes in understanding how he delimitates the category of economic values. As mentioned before, we understand it as related to labor time in social being. Therefore, it should be a trans-historical[39] category. That is to say, it should present a certain continuity, but express itself historically in qualitatively different ways. Nevertheless, in his attempt to demonstrate the complexification of valuations in the social being – which started with use values and now moves to address economic values –, despite referring to a trans-historical movement, he resorts "methodologically" to the simple exchange of commodities and says that individuals "can no longer" understand adequately their decisions in the economic complex. To exactly when this moment refers is not clear in the *Ontology*.

After that, Lukács conflates exchange values with Marx's comments on communal production in the passage of the *Grundrisse* reproduced above. This should not be a problem, since he is interested in Marx's indication of a trans-historical law that points to a decrease in production time. However, his conflation of exchange values with communal production, without further remarks, contrasts with Marx's explicit differentiation between these two moments, made immediately after the passage quoted by Lukács:

> economy of time, as well as the planned distribution of labor time over the various branches of production, therefore, remains the first economic law if communal production is taken as the basis. It becomes a law even to a much higher degree. However, this is essentially different from

---

38 György Lukács, *The ontology of social being: labour*. (London: Merlin Press, 1980), 84. György Lukács, *Werke*, vol. 14 (Darmstad und Neuwied: Luchterhand, 1986), 75.

39 Despite not using the term "trans-historical," we consider that Fortes' and Andrade's reading of economic value point in that direction. Furthermore, we also think is possible to interpret Infrancas' comments in the same way, as we will see below. See: Ronaldo Vielmi Fortes, *Trabalho e gênese do ser social na "ontologia" de Georg Lukács*. (Belo Horizonte: UFMG, 2001), 116; Mariana Alves de Andrade, *Lukács: reprodução social e valor*. (Rio de Janeiro: UFRJ, 2016), 185–189.

the measurement of exchange values (of labors or products of labor) by labor time.[40]

Furthermore, and this is what is most problematic, Lukács understands the law indicated by Marx in a compulsory way, a law to which individuals "must adapt themselves" or "perish."

In the two passages by Lukács mentioned above, at the same time that we see an attempt to grasp a category in its trans-historical movement, we also see a generalization of three characteristics that belong to capitalist relations of production: the opacity of economic values, the indirect social character of labor, and the compulsion to a reduction of labor time. It is interesting that when Lukács starts to argue about economic values, instead of referring in broad general terms to examples of how other social formations related to the question and evaluation of their labor time, he turns his attention "methodologically" to the simple exchange of commodities. As we contend, the result is to transform a category that was supposed to be trans-historical in an ahistorical one. Despite Marx's intellectual development not being progressively linear, we understand that Lukács' approach contrasts with Marx's own when dealing with the question of value and labor time.

This attempt to grasp a trans-historical movement of economic values and at the same time generalize to it characteristics that are specific of capitalist relations of production is also found in Lukács' interpretation of Marx's idea of socially necessary labor time. In the chapter about Marx in the *Ontology*, when commenting about the relation between economic and non-economic values, Lukács says that the latter:

> always presuppose sociality, as an existential characteristic that is already present and in the process of development, whereas economic value has not only originally created this sociality, but permanently produces and reproduces it anew, always on an extended scale. In this process of reproduction, economic value time and again receives new patterns, and even quite new forms of categories can emerge [...]. Yet in this continuous process of change, their basic forms remain essentially unaltered.[41]

---

40   Karl Marx and Friedrich Engels, *Collected Works*, vol. 28. (London: Lawrence & Wishart, 1986), 109.

41   György Lukács, *The ontology of the social being: Marx's basic ontological principles* (London: Merlin Press, 1978), 154. György Lukács, *Werke*, vol. 13 (Darmstad und Neuwied: Luchterhand, 1984), 679.

In a note in this passage, he comments on what would be the basic forms that remain essentially unaltered: "Marx shows in Capital how socially necessary labor time remains essentially unchanged in the most varied formations."[42]

Lukács here first stresses his attempt to understand economic value in a processual trans-historical way, referring to the different forms in which the category manifested itself in different social formations. Nevertheless, when defining the essence of these forms, he generalizes another particular feature of capitalist relations of production, namely, socially necessary labor time. In our view, underlying these incorrect generalizations is another still: the one concerning the understanding of Marx's labor theory of value as valid to all social formations. We will try now to address each of these generalizations.

4   The Compulsion to Reduce Labor Time

It is certain that the passage of the *Grundrisse* mobilized by Lukács should be interpreted as Marx indicating a trans-historical tendency of labor time to decrease. At the same time, this same passage stresses the need every social formation has to *organize* labor time. While this second meaning is self-evident – despite all the various complex forms different societies had distributed its labor time – the first should be taken carefully.

Analyzing the so-called *Forms which precede capitalist production* in the *Grundrisse*, Ellen Wood indicates that, at the time it was written, Marx still has remnants of the concept of progress, coming from the Enlightenment and the Political Economy, that distinguishes modes of subsistence based on a trans-historical tendency towards a more complex division of labor and technological development. This progress could also be characterized by the "commercialization model," which sees capitalist exchange as already present in earlier commodity exchange. This would only need to be liberated of the external constraints so that capitalism can emerge. In the *Grundrisse*, however, there is also a focus on property relations and on the separation between labor and the conditions of its realization, which leads Marx to later rely less on these anachronic trans-historical claims and to reflect more on the specificities of each

---

42   György Lukács, *The ontology of social being: Marx's basic ontological principles*. (London: Merlin Press, 1978), 172. György Lukács, *Werke*, vol. 13 (Darmstad und Neuwied: Luchterhand, 1984), 679.

social formation. Among these, only the capitalist relations of production have a specific drive to improve labor productivity.[43]

Thus, while it is more acceptable to understand economy of time as the organization of time, to claim that a trans-historical law pushes to reduce labor time is problematic because, taken by itself, it lacks the explanation of the social relations that could point in that direction. Despite the fact that Lukács indicates a set of categories that are present in labor – reflection, valuations, ought, etc., – related to the cognition of objects, to decisions during the execution of labor and to the human control of its own instincts, behavior, etc., what is decisive to mobilize these categories in the sense of reducing labor time are the relations of production that are specific in a social formation. In a well-known letter to Ludwig Kugelmann, from July 11, 1868, Marx refers to the question of the organization of social labor without mentioning, however, any tendency towards a reduction of labor time:

> every child knows that any nation that stopped working, not for a year, but let us say, just for a few weeks, would perish. And every child knows, too, that the amounts of products corresponding to the differing amounts of needs demand differing and quantitatively determined amounts of society's aggregate labor. It is self-evident that this necessity of the distribution of social labour in specific proportions is certainly not abolished by the specific form of social production [*gesellschaftlichen Produktion*]; it can only change its form of manifestation. Natural laws [*Naturgesetze*] cannot be abolished at all. The only thing that can change, under historically differing conditions, is the form in which those laws assert themselves. And the form in which this proportional distribution of labor asserts itself in a state of society in which the interconnection of social labor expresses itself as the private exchange of the individual products of labor, is precisely the exchange value of these products.[44]

In our view, however, Lukács not only quotes a problematic claim of Marx about the trans-historical tendency of labor time to decrease, but he goes on to transform this claim into a compulsory relation to which individuals must adapt themselves or "perish." This coercion to reduce labor time is a

---

43   See Ellen Meiksins Wood, "Historical Materialism in 'Forms which precede capitalist production.'" In Marcello Musto *Karl Marx's Grundrisse: foundations of the critique of political economy 150 years later*. (London: Routledge, 2008).

44   Karl Marx and Friedrich Engels, *Collected Works*, vol. 43 (London: Lawrence & Wishart, 1988), 68.

characteristic of capitalist relations production, but cannot be stretched to pre-capitalist formation – despite the *possibility* here of improvements in productivity. More importantly, this compulsory relation cannot be pushed, as far as we understand, to the idea of an emancipated society. Here, despite the importance of the development of the productive forces, to claim the decrease of labor time as a coercive relation contrasts with the idea of a "community of free individuals" guided by the principle of "each according to his ability, to each according to his needs."

5   The Opacity of Economic Values

The question about the opacity underlying Lukács' characterization of economic values also contrasts with Marx's position. We mentioned above how the synthesis between the various teleological positing is the basis of the objectivity of economic values. According to Lukács, however, this happens in a "totality in process" that "can no longer be so directly grasped, by the positing individual economic subjects who decide between alternatives"; they are then guided by economic value without a "complete certainty" of their choices and, "in most cases," "can scarcely follow correctly the consequences of their own decisions." Under these conditions, the relations of economic values that guide ought produce the "optimal social division of labor," despite this not being clear to the subjects involved in the process.

Again, to when exactly Lukács refers here, in this very abstract representation of the movement of economic value, is not entirely clear in the *Ontology*. Nevertheless, the reduction of labor time imposes itself, despite the evaluation individuals can make of it. In the chapter about Marx in the *Ontology*, commenting about this tendency, Lukács states: "it is an important ontological characteristic of economic value and the tendencies of its development that it is possible to establish the objectivity of a development of this kind [i.e., the reduction of labor time], its complete independence of the value judgements made by men."[45]

Here, we also see the generalization of specific capitalist relations and its attribution to the trans-historical category of economic values. It is under the production realized by private producers, characteristic of capitalism, that valuations in the economy acquire the opacity Lukács sees in different social

---

45   György Lukács, *The ontology of social being: Marx's basic ontological principles.* (London: Merlin Press, 1978), 75–76. György Lukács, *Werke*, vol. 13 (Darmstad und Neuwied: Luchterhand, 1984), 617.

formations. The realization of labor-value, the confirmation of the social validity of the labor time spent privately, occurs only *post festum*, and the division of labor that develops based on this relation – and the compulsory reduction of time –, takes place "behind the back" of the producers. So, as a specific trait of capitalism, the opacity of economic values cannot be generalized to the different social formations.

In the section of *Capital* about commodity fetishism, Marx takes a different position on this issue. In the examples of Robinson on his island, of feudalism, of the patriarchal peasant family and of the "community of free individuals," the immediate social character of relations of production is different from the fetishistic one that is realized through the mediation of abstract labor. In the former cases, the allocation of labor and the distribution of its products are clearer to individuals – "perfectly simple and intelligible"[46] in the "community of free individuals" –, while in the latter, the indirectly social character of the capitalist relations of production supports the commodity fetishism. The possibility of overcoming this social configuration in an emancipated society is stressed by Marx when he highlights how economic relations can be not only clear to the individuals involved, but also under their control:

> the religious reflex of the real world can, in any case, only then finally vanish, when the practical relations of every-day life offer to man none but perfectly intelligible and reasonable relations with regard to his fellowmen and to Nature. The life-process of society, which is based on the process of material production, does not strip off its mystical veil until it is treated as production by freely associated men, and is consciously regulated by them in accordance with a settled plan.[47]

What is decisive, then, in determining the opacity of economic values is the *post festum* character of the capitalist market – something that is not present in other social formations. Furthermore, there is not a tendency here that imposes itself and is completely independent of the evaluations made by individuals.

It is possible, however, to take another path concerning the economic values, following Lukács' own arguments in the *Ontology*. As we saw, his intention is to demonstrate the continuity of the objectivity also in the economic values.

---

46   Karl Marx and Friedrich Engels, *Collected Works*, vol. 35 (London: Lawrence & Wishart, 1986), 90.
47   Karl Marx and Friedrich Engels, *Collected Works*, vol. 35 (London: Lawrence & Wishart, 1986), 90.

As a category related to the organization of labor time, economic value depends on the development of the productive forces. As we argued before, it also depends – and this is more crucial – on the forms in which labor time and its products are organized and distributed. These forms, indeed, stabilize and constitute a "second nature," a social objectivity that surpasses any individual valuation. As Lukács explains elsewhere, this depends especially on the teleological position that is directed not to the organic or inorganic being, but to the conscience of other individuals in order to influence a particular teleological positing.[48]

In this sense, it is difficult to see how economic values and the tendency to reduce labor time are completely independent of "value judgements." On the one hand, the continuity of the forms that support the objectivity of economic values in a particular social formation depends on their constant actualization by individuals; on the other hand, these forms themselves can be consciously evaluated and changed collectively. It is this possibility that underlies the "community of free individuals" envisaged by Marx.

6   Socially Necessary Labor Time and Indirect Social Labor

The compulsion to reduce labor time and the opacity of economic values are related to a third generalization made by Lukács in his ontological reading of Marx: that which concerns socially necessary labor time. This is connected, in turn, with Lukács losing sight, or at least not highlighting, the distinction made by Marx between direct and indirect social labor.

We previously mentioned Lukács' interpretation of the first chapter of *Capital*, where, according to him, Marx indicates that "socially necessary labor time [*gesellschaftlich notwendige Arbeitszeit*] remains essentially unchanged in the most varied formations." However, when Marx refers to pre and post-capitalist formations in the section mentioned by Lukács, he mentions labor time [*Arbeitszeit*] and not "socially necessary labor time." This is a significant difference.

In a society where the private production of commodities is generalized, the *post festum* validation – in the process of exchange – of the labour time spent, is not determined by the actual number of hours engaged in the creation of a use value but, in general terms, by the social average of intensity in the execution of that particular kind of labor. This average is established by the market

---

48   György Lukács, *The ontology of social being: labour*. (London: Merlin Press, 1980), 129–132. György Lukács, *Werke*, vol. 14 (Darmstad und Neuwied: Luchterhand, 1986), 110–112.

and "forcibly asserts itself like an overriding law of Nature."[49] This pushes the private producers to search for the reduction of the labor time effectively spent to create a commodity – which can give them advantages in the exchange – and results in a further decrease of the average, put forward "behind the backs of the producers."

Despite reaching its developed form in *Capital*, the distinction between labor time and socially necessary labor time is already present, in a non-developed form, in *The poverty of philosophy*. In this work, Marx criticized Proudhon's position, which, taking into account labor as the source of value, claimed that the "constituted value" of a commodity was determined by the labor time spent in its production. Proudhon stated that the capitalist exchange process distorted this determination of value. The result was that workers received only a part of the price of the commodity and not the value of its labor. Proudhon's solution to this distortion was to alter the capitalist exchange relations so the workers could receive a "fair" equivalent of their labor, through labor-tokens that contain the amount of hours spent in production. This would be, then, a substitute for money, since the latter could not represent the number of hours one had worked. The labor-tokens, then, would be exchanged by goods that contained the same quantity of labor realized by the worker.[50]

Marx criticizes Proudhon for his attempt to use a central aspect of capitalism, the determination of value by labor, as the foundation of a "fair" post-capitalist society. Furthermore, despite accepting labor as the source of value, he does not consider that it is the labor time effectively spent in production that determines value, but instead "the *minimum* time it could possibly be produced in, and this minimum is ascertained by competition."[51] As we said, this will be developed later with the idea of socially necessary labor time. However, already in *The poverty of philosophy*, Marx considers that with the establishment, through competition, of this minimum amount of time to produce a use-value, the workers are forced to submit to it independently of their needs or capacities:

> If the mere quantity of labor functions as a measure of value regardless of quality, it presupposes that simple labor has become the pivot of industry. It presupposes that labor has been equalized by the subordination of

---

49   Karl Marx and Friedrich Engels, *Collected Works*, vol. 35. (London: Lawrence & Wishart, 1986), 86.
50   Peter Hudis, *Marx's concept of the alternative to capitalism*. (Leiden: Brill Books, 2012), 95.
51   Karl Marx and Friedrich Engels, *Collected Works*, vol. 6. (London: Lawrence & Wishart, 1976), 136.

man to the machine or by the extreme division of labor; that men are effaced by their labor; that the pendulum of the clock has become as accurate a measure of the relative activity of two workers as it is of the speed of two locomotives. Therefore, we should not say that one man's hour is worth another man's hour, but rather that one man during an hour is worth just as much as another man during an hour. Time is everything, man is nothing; he is, at the most, time's carcass.[52]

The passage of the *Grundrisse* quoted by Lukács which we mentioned above, is in the context of Marx's discussion with other perspectives of the labor movement of his time, addressing especially the bank reform proposed by the proudhonian Alfred Darimon. Just before the excerpt used by Lukács, it appears for the first time in Marx's writing, according to Peter Hudis,[53] the distinction between indirect and direct social labor – a distinction that underlies the discussion about the communal production. The proudhonian perspectives of emancipation, since they maintain the capitalist relations of production and try to alter only some aspects of the exchange of commodities, cannot offer a real solution to the contradictions of capitalism. In this sense, labor continues to reveal its social character only by mediation of market exchange and socially necessary labor time still subsumes the individuals to its imperative.

In contrast, communal production is based on a directly social labor that is distributed taking into account the qualitative capacities and necessities of the freely associated individuals, and not on the coercive relations of socially necessary labor time. Even though Marx delineated only in very broad terms the aspects of this social formation, it is not based on a reduction of labor time to which the individuals have to adapt or perish, as Lukács claims. Even if this decrease in labor time is important to the social development of the individuals, it must be subsumed to their conscious control.

In sum, the indirect social character of labor, the opacity of economic values and the compulsion to reduce labor time through the imposition of a socially necessary labor time are certainly determinations of capitalism, but they cannot be generalized to other social formations. Above all, they cannot be considered present in an emancipated society. In this sense, we agree with the strong critique made by István Mészáros to his friend and former professor. According to him,

---

52 Karl Marx and Friedrich Engels, *Collected Works*, vol. 6. (London: Lawrence & Wishart, 1976), 127.
53 Peter Hudis, *Marx's concept of the alternative to capitalism.* (Leiden: Brill Books, 2012), 109.

in Lukács's reading of the passage quoted from the *Grundrisse* the Marxian idea of *communal* production and consumption – and the corresponding use of time in a *qualitative/liberating* sense, in contrast to its tyrannical *quantitative imposition* on the producers, which happens to be inseparable from the value-relation – radically changes the meaning of the original. For in Marx's vision the qualitative use of time under the communal form of reproductive interchange represents the historically attainable level and mode of quite *unique mediation* of the associated producers, at the highest stages of socialism.[54]

Nevertheless, we would like to point out some minor differences we have with Mészáros' interpretation of value in the *Ontology*. According to him, the passage of the *Grundrisse*

> directly contradicts [Lukács'] claim that the principle of 'economy of time' is the product of *exchange-value*. For in Marx's view the principle in question both precedes and survives the dominance of exchange-value, asserting its own validity, even if in *qualitatively* different ways, under *all* forms of production, including the *communal* system.[55]

The way we understand it, Lukács also interprets "economy of time" as a transhistorical tendency that is present in every social formation. In the *Ontology*, he repeatedly refers to the "pressing back of the natural boundary" and this is based, above all, on the development of the productive forces that entail this economy of time. In the passages we mentioned above, for instance, he refers to it as an objective tendency of economy and articulates it with economic values, claiming that its essence is socially necessary labor time, which is present in different social formations. Thus, when Lukács refers to exchange-values, he wants to indicate that with its emergence and the division of labor that follows it, there is a better "subjective use" of time – though this use is also subsumed to the opacity of valuations – and not that the "economy of time" takes place only with the emergence of exchange-values.

Futhermore, Mészáros also claims:

> the tendency in Lukács's line of argument is to eliminate the qualitative distinction made by Marx between *social* and *communal* (the latter being 'gemeinschaftliche' or 'not *post festum* social') production and to

---

54 István Mészáros, *Beyond Capital.* (New York: Monthly Review Press), 749.
55 István Mészáros, *Beyond Capital.* (New York: Monthly Review Press), 748.

subsume the latter under the former. In other words, Lukács's approach is characterized by a tendency to subsume the communal system under a form of social production which remains always subjected to and dominated by the constraints of the value-relation.[56]

As we understand it, the problem here is not exactly a qualitative distinction between social production [*gesellschaftlichen Produktion*] and communal production [*gemeinschaftlichen Produktion*]. The difference between these two terms in Marx's use concerns only the different abstract levels of his analysis. While social production is a generic term used to every social formation, indicating any society's production, communal production is one of its specific forms. Therefore, Lukács does not distance himself from Marx when he says that economy of time is a "law of social production."

As we mentioned before, our objection to Lukács' interpretation is that the trans-historical tendency to the decrease of labor time – shared by him, Marx in the *Grundrisse* and Mészáros himself –, must be considered carefully because it states something that must be explained by the specific relations of production in each social formation and, what is more problematic, because Lukács transforms this tendency into a coercive relation. In the letter to Kugelmann, however, we see Marx using the abstract term social production [*gesellschaftlichen Produktion*] and referring to it as a "natural law" [*Naturgesetz*], but pointing only to the need every social formation has to distribute social labor in a determinate proportion, not to any trans-historical law to reduce labor time.

In this last sense, we will argue later that it is possible to understand economic values as a trans-historical category, as long as they are not related to a tendency to decrease labor time that is not explained by relations of production nor to an interpretation of this tendency as a coercive one. However, before this argument, we still have to address another generalization made by Lukács, the one concerning his interpretation of Marx's labor theory of value.

7   Lukács' Interpretation of Marx's Theory of Labor Value

Underlying the generalization in the *Ontology* of aspects of the capitalist social relations we mentioned above is also a comprehension of Marx's labor theory of value as valid to all social formations. As we will argue below, for us this is

---

56   István Mészáros, *Beyond Capital*. (New York: Monthly Review Press), 747.

valid only in capitalist production. Nevertheless, Lukács says the following in the chapter on Marx in the *Ontology*:

> Marx demonstrated the genesis of the most general of these, the law of value, in the introductory chapter of his master-work. This is indeed immanent to labor itself, in so far as it is linked by labor-time with labor itself as the development of human abilities and is already implicitly present when man has only reached the stage of useful labor, when his products have not yet become values; it remains just as implicitly valid after the sale and purchase of commodities have come to an end.[57]

A bit further, Lukács insists on the permanence of the law of value beyond capitalism, linking it with the continuity of socially necessary labor time:

> It is only at a higher phase, the economic preconditions of which Marx indicates, as well as the human preconditions made socially possible by the economy, that the situation "From each according to his ability, to each according to his needs" becomes objectively possible. The structure of commodity exchange, the effectiveness of the law of value for individual men as consumers, now ceases. It is evident of course that in production itself, socially necessary labor-time and hence the law of value as regulator of production must remain unchanged in their validity even with the growth of the productive forces.[58]

In *The Process of Democratization*, essay written at the end of 1968, in the same period, therefore, of the *Ontology*, Lukács also refers to the trans-historical character of the law of value, interpreting it as valid to different modes of production:

> Marx isolates at least three distinct forms of the law of value; for example, with Robinson Crusoe, or with a self-supporting peasant family in the Middle Ages, or, finally, in socialism itself. Labor time, i.e., the present socially necessary labor time, the immediate economic materialization of value, has a double function.

---

57 György Lukács, *The ontology of social being: Marx's basic ontological principles* (London: Merlin Press, 1978), 93. György Lukács, *Werke*, vol. 13 (Darmstad und Neuwied: Luchterhand, 1984), 631.

58 György Lukács, *The ontology of social being: Marx's basic ontological principles*. (London: Merlin Press, 1978), 166. György Lukács, *Werke*, vol. 13. (Darmstad und Neuwied: Luchterhand, 1984), 689.

And immediately, to describe this double function, he refers to the following considerations of Marx in the section on fetishism in *Capital*:

> its apportionment in accordance with a definite social plan maintains the proper proportion between the different kinds of work to be done and the various wants of the community. On the other hand, it also serves as a measure of the portion of the common labor borne by each individual, and of his share in the part of the total product destined for individual consumption.[59]

We consider this a peculiar interpretation of Marx take on the labor theory of value. As we see it, after his initial rejection of this approach, as put forward by the classical political economists, Marx accepts it critically but opposes its use as a fundament of an emancipated society. As we mentioned, already in *The Poverty of Philosophy*, considered by Marx himself as containing "the seeds of the theory developed after twenty years' work in *Capital*,"[60] there is opposition to Proudhon's attempt to use the labor theory of value as the basis of an emancipated society. Marx emphatically states that "relative value, measured by labour time, is inevitably the formula of the present enslavement of the worker, instead of being, as M. Proudhon would have it, the 'revolutionary theory' of the emancipation of the proletariat."[61]

Moreover, in the *Grundrisse*, in the famous *Fragment on Machines*,[62] Marx also stresses the historical validity of the labor theory of value. Although here he did not yet fully develop the categories that appear in *Capital*, this indication of the historicity of labor value continues in his later remarks. In the letter to Kugelmann mentioned above, for instance, he refers to the law of value as the one that governs the distribution of social labor, which takes place indirectly through the "private exchange of the individual products of labour." Implicit in this is that the law of value would not operate in societies that

---

59   Karl Marx and Friedrich Engels, *Collected Works*, vol. 35. (London: Lawrence & Wishart, 1986), 89–90.
60   Karl Marx and Friedrich Engels, *Collected Works*, vol. 24. (London: Lawrence & Wishart, 1989), 326.
61   Karl Marx and Friedrich Engels, *Collected Works*, vol. 6. (London: Lawrence & Wishart, 1976), 125.
62   Karl Marx and Friedrich Engels, *Collected Works*, vol. 29. (London: Lawrence & Wishart, 1987), 90. About the *Fragment on Machines*, in the context of Marx's research developments, see Michael Heinrich, "The Fragment on Machines: a marxian misconception in the *Grundrisse* and its overcoming in *Capital*." In Riccardo Bellofiore, Guido Starosta and Peter Thomas (ed.), *In Marx's Laboratory*. (Leiden: Brill, 2013).

organize labor directly, but are instead mediated by the exchange of commodities. In the *Critique of the Gotha Program*, Marx refers once again to how the law of value is characteristic of the indirect social labor of capitalism, which changes in a society based on the common ownership of the means of production.[63] Finally, in the *Notes on Wagner's Lehrbuch der politischen Oekonomie*, Marx denies the claim of Adolf Wagner that the labor theory of value is the "cornerstone of his socialist system."[64]

Engels has a similar position in this sense, to which we will return below. In any case, the divergence of the most important interpretations of Marx's labor theory of value is based on whether they consider its validity to commodity production, or to capitalism only. In contrast to these two kinds of interpretations, Lukács considers the labor theory of value to be present in every social formation, as we find in the *Ontology* and in *The Process of democratization*.[65]

Against Lukács' reading of the section on fetishism in *Capital*, both Mészáros[66] and Hudis[67] stressed that he obliterates Marx's intention of only drawing a "parallel with the production of commodities" and, to this end, suppose that "the share of each individual producer in the means of subsistence is determined by his labour time."[68] Moreover, Hudis comments:

> Marx mentions this parallel only to emphasize the role that labor-time would play in the future. But what does he mean by labor-time? The actual labor-time that operates *after* capitalism is far from identical with the socially-average necessary labor-time that operates *in* capitalism.

---

63 Karl Marx and Friedrich Engels, *Collected Works*, vol. 24. (London: Lawrence & Wishart, 1989), 85.
64 Karl Marx and Friedrich Engels, *Collected Works*, vol. 24. (London: Lawrence & Wishart, 1989), 533.
65 To name only a few of those interpretations, Isaak Rubin made some comments about the possibility of labor-value existing, in an embryonic form, in pre-capitalist societies; Octavio Colombo offers an excellent analysis of this possibility. On the other hand, Roman Rosdolsky, Ronald Meek and Ernst Mandel stressed how the labor-value would not exist in an emancipated society. See Isaak Rubin, *Essays on Marx's theory of value*. (Montreal: Black Rose Books, 1990), 256; Octavio Colombo, "Simple commodity production and value theory in late feudalism." In Laura da Graca and Andrea Zingarelli, *Studies in pre-capitalist modes of production*. (Leiden: Brill, 2015); Roman Rosdolsky, *The Making of Marx's Capital*. (London: Pluto Press, 1977), 428–436; Ronald Meek, *Studies in the labour theory of value*. (New York: Monthly Review Press, 1973), 257–284; Ernest Mandel, *The formation of the economic thought of Karl Marx*. (New York: Monthly Review Press, 1971), 49–51.
66 István Mészáros, *Beyond Capital*. (New York: Monthly Review Press), 744.
67 Peter Hudis, *Marx's concept of the alternative to capitalism*. (Leiden: Brill Books, 2012), 109.
68 Karl Marx and Friedrich Engels, *Collected Works*, vol. 35. (London: Lawrence & Wishart, 1986), 89.

In Lukács's reading the two become conflated, even though the latter implies value-production whereas the former implies its transcendence. Marx never mentions value or exchange-value in discussing the new society in Chapter One, and for a good reason: he holds that the new society's social relations are 'transparent in their simplicity.' Lukács does not mention Marx's discussion of the 'transparent' nature of social relations in the future, even though Marx repeats it on several occasions. If Lukács had paid greater attention to this issue, he would have recognised that Marx is not referring to socially necessary labor time in discussing the operative principles of a postcapitalist society.[69]

We agree with Hudis' critique, but would like to add, following our previous considerations, that Lukács' generalization of the labor theory of value imputes the socially necessary labor time to all social formations. Moreover, Lukács' not only *does not mention* the "transparent" social relations in an emancipated society, but he *claims* the opposite when he generalizes the opacity of economic values.

Contrary to Hudis' interpretation, Antonino Infranca argued in favor of Lukács' reading of the labor theory of value criticizing Mészáros' position:

> about Mészáros's critique of Lukács's theory of the permanence of value in a socialist society, I recall that exactly there [in *The Process of Democratization*], Lukács addressed this problem. In this essay, he claims that Stalin did not considered, even minimally, Marx's clear orientations, in the first volume of *Capital*, which stressed that the labor time indicates the value of a commodity and, since it is labor that creates wealth, is impossible to eliminate value. Therefore, in a socialist system of wealth production value is indispensable to production. In this way it depends not on the market, but on labor time. Lukács explains also why Stalin related the disappearance of value to its elimination of the market: 'For Marx, the law of value is not dependent upon commodity production. Yet Stalin insisted on this interconnection, and it was by no means a mere slip of the tongue. Stalin's distortion of the methodology of Marx had practical consequences, for it led him to distort the definition of socialism. A fallacious definition of the construction of socialism was presented in a propagandistic fashion, as if Stalin consciously wanted to substitute a false interpretation of Marx for the true one. For this purpose, Stalin used the trick of depicting classical economic categories as if they were merely

---

69 Peter Hudis, *Marx's concept of the alternative to capitalism*. (Leiden: Brill Books, 2012), 158.

historical manifestations of capitalism and thus no longer operative in socialism.'[70]

Infranca does not refer here to the problems with the lukácsian interpretation we mentioned above. He misses Marx's intention of only drawing a parallel with commodity production in the section on fetishism in *Capital*; he takes Lukács' word about the permanence of the law of value without contrasting it to Marx's own claims; and he does not mention how Lukács conflates labor time with socially necessary labor time – the latter being a specific capitalist relation. Furthermore, there is no indication about the generalization of the opacity of economic values and the compulsion to reduce labor time. Although these appear in a more explicit form in the *Ontology* – which is not the focus of Infranca above – they are implicit in the *Process of Democratization* and, as we understand, cannot serve as the basis for an emancipated society. Nevertheless, we think a trans-historical category of economic value related to labor time is indeed possible, as Infranca seems to indicate. This cannot be conflated, however, with the labor theory of value and cannot generalize the aspects of capitalism that we have mentioned so far.

8   Economic Value as a Trans-historical Category

To offer an alternative possibility, based in the *Ontology*, to consider economic values as a trans-historical category, without generalizing the particular relations of capitalist production, we would like to refer here to some of Engels' passages about the labor theory of value. First, about how he delimitates the validity of this theory in the *Anti-Dühring*:

> the concept of value is the most general and therefore the most comprehensive expression of the economic conditions of commodity production. Consequently, this concept contains the germ, not only of money, but also of all the more developed forms of the production and exchange of commodities.[71]

We do not want to address here the problem of whether the labor theory of value should be considered as valid to commodity production in different

---

70   Antonino Infranca, *Trabalho, indivíduo, história*. (São Paulo, Boitempo, 2014), 94–95.
71   Karl Marx and Friedrich Engels, *Collected Works*, vol. 25. (London: Lawrence & Wishart, 1987), 295.

social formations or only to capitalism. What is important for us to highlight, however, is that while Lukács resorts "methodologically" to the simple commodity exchange to abstract from there the "mediations" and "realizations" that are, then, used to approach economic value, Engels finds in the relationship among private producers that labor value is a fundamental category which can have a historical development, but remains circumscribed to commodity production. Moreover, Engels states that:

> Commodity production, however, is by no means the only form of social production. In the ancient Indian communities and in the family communities of the southern Slavs, products are not transformed into commodities. The members of the community are directly associated for production; the work is distributed according to tradition and requirements, and likewise the products to the extent that they are destined for consumption. Direct social production and direct distribution preclude all exchange of commodities, therefore also the transformation of the products into commodities (at any rate within the community) and consequently also their transformation into *values*.[72]

Engels echoes then the section on fetishism in *Capital*, and refers to the possibility of the law of labor value being extinguished in an emancipated society – and, with this, advances the possibility of establishing direct and transparent relations of production:

> From the moment when society enters into possession of the means of production and uses them in direct association for production, the labor of each individual, however varied its specifically useful character may be, becomes at the start and directly social labor. The quantity of social labor contained in a product need not then be established in a roundabout way; daily experience shows in a direct way how much of it is required on the average. [...] It is true that even then it will still be necessary for society to know how much labor each article of consumption requires for its production. It will have to arrange its plan of production in accordance with its means of production, which include, in particular, its labor-powers. The useful effects of the various articles of consumption, compared with one another and with the quantities of labor required for their production, will in the end determine the plan. People will be able

---

72   Karl Marx and Friedrich Engels, *Collected Works*, vol. 25. (London: Lawrence & Wishart, 1987), 294.

to manage everything very simply, without the intervention of much-vaunted 'value.'[73]

In these last two passages from Engels, we would like to highlight that when commenting about pre-capitalist societies, he stresses that the distribution of labor and its products is determined "according to tradition and requirements." On the other hand, when dealing with an emancipated society, he claims that "even then," in this post-capitalist society, a plan will be necessary to determine "the useful effects of the various articles of consumption, compared with one another and with the quantities of labour required for their production." Although these relations are not at all determined by the law of value and are not opaque or realized "behind the backs" of the producers, they nevertheless demand evaluations in order to choose between concrete alternatives that will, then, push individuals to the indelible realization of the metabolism between nature and society.

In a letter to Karl Kautsky, from 20 September 1884, in which Engels points to the passages of *Anti-Dühring* mentioned above, he opposes Kautsky's attempt to search for a trans-historical "economic value" [*ökonomische Wert*]:

> you do the same kind of thing in the case of *value*. Present value is that of the production of commodities, but with the suppression of the production of commodities, value 'changes' or rather, *value as such* remains and merely changes its form. But in fact economic value is a category that appertains to the production of commodities, *disappearing* with it, just as it did not exist before it. The relation of labor to product prior to and after production of commodities no longer expresses itself in the form of *value*.[74]

We do not want to suggest here a substantial proximity between Lukács and Kautsky, but only indicate that the *search* for a broad category of value related to the metabolism between society and nature is also, as we saw it, attempted by Lukács in the *Ontology*. On the other hand, the procedure denied by Engels is similar to the way Marx refers to the economic or "natural" law in the *Grundrisse* and in the letter to Kugelmann. That is to say, an indication of a trans-historical determination that manifests itself in different forms based on

---

73 Karl Marx and Friedrich Engels, *Collected Works*, vol. 25. (London: Lawrence & Wishart, 1987), 294–295.

74 Karl Marx and Friedrich Engels, *Collected Works*, vol. 47. (London: Lawrence & Wishart, 1995), 194.

particular historical relations. These forms, immersed in the social relations of their own time, are what is decisive to determine the kind of valuations that occur in the economic complex. Nevertheless, however they change, the demand to choose between the alternatives to distribute labor and its products remains. Engels himself appears to address this question when, immediately after referring to the overcoming of the "much-vaunted 'value'" in a post-capitalist society, he writes in a footnote in *Anti-Dühring*:

> as long ago as 1844 I stated that the above-mentioned balancing of useful effects and expenditure of labor on making decisions concerning production was all that would be left, in a communist society, of the politico-economic concept of value. The scientific justification for this statement, however, as can be seen, was made possible only by Marx's *Capital*.[75]

Therefore, although Engels delimits the law of value to commodity production and denies the idea of a trans-historical economic value, he recognizes the necessity of a "balancing of useful effects and expenditure of labor" in the process of production, which will occur according to a conscious plan in an emancipated society or, for instance, "according to tradition and requirements" in some pre-capitalist societies. In other words, even if production and distribution are not determined by the exchange between private commodity producers, nor by socially necessary labor time, nor by any compulsion to reduce labor time, nor by the expression of this in the exchange values and in money, they still need, nonetheless, valuation processes – socially and historically determined – to the economic decisions that will guide the ought of individuals.

That is why we claimed above that the category of economic value put forward by Lukács is fruitful. Besides drawing a whole set of mediations in the *Ontology* – which are decisive to valuations – when Lukács indicates that the "economy of time," to which Marx refers, is a "value relation," he points to an interesting articulation between objectivity and subjectivity. When Marx in the *Grundrisse* and, especially, in the letter to Kugelmann mentioned above, points to the necessity of organizing labor and the distribution of its products, he does so from a macro and objective perspective. Lukács, on the other hand, through an analysis of praxis, shows how those relations pass through – and, in our view, also depend on – the actualization of these values realized by the alternatives put forward by individuals. Furthermore, once again, economic value is articulated with ought, that is, with the demand of self-control that has to

---

75   Karl Marx and Friedrich Engels, *Collected Works*, vol. 25. (London: Lawrence & Wishart, 1987), 295.

be internalized, in one way or other, by individuals. Despite its abstraction, this approach of the *Ontology* could constitute an interesting way to address both the objective and subjective sides of concrete historical relations.

Nevertheless, as we argued, Lukács jeopardizes the category of economic value when he characterizes socially necessary labor time as its essence and generalizes the opacity of economic valuations – positing a coercive transhistorical tendency to the reduction of labor time, imposed upon individuals. Underlying this is his interpretation of the labor theory of value as valid to all social formations. This is important, above all, because it compromises any perspective of human emancipation. So, a category that could be set as a transhistorical one, and its movement grasped by referring, however generally, to different social formations, ends up as an ahistorical one. In this sense, we agree with Mészáros when he analyzes Lukács' reading of the *Grundrisse*, which obliterates:

> the diametrical opposition between the *directly general* organization of the communal labor process and those in which the social character of labor can only be posited *post festum*, through the intermediary of exchange value. Indeed, it is almost incomprehensible that Lukács, who is as a rule highly appreciative of the encountered historical specificities, should pursue his ahistorical line of reasoning on this set of issues, despite the fact that the *qualitative* differences separating the societal reproductive systems are made quite explicit in the quoted passage of the *Grundrisse*.[76]

The division of social labor among the different activities mentioned by Marx as a "natural law" requires then the "balancing of useful effects and expenditure of labor." These take place in different historical forms and a category as abstract as the economic value proposed by Lukács has to be able to refer to these different moments – be it determined by the direct social labor, as in the pre and post-capitalist society, or by the indirect one, as in capitalism. In this sense, to be a "reasonable abstraction," which "actually emphasizes and defines the common aspects and thus spares us the need of repetition," as Marx put it in the *Introduction of 1857*,[77] the economic value must only refer to the time related to the division of social labor and the distribution of its products. The specific forms can only be indicated concretely by a historical analysis.

---

76 István Mészáros, *Beyond Capital*. (New York: Monthly Review Press), 751.
77 Karl Marx and Friedrich Engels, *Collected Works*, vol. 28. (London: Lawrence & Wishart, 1986), 23.

Furthermore, to refer to its processual movement demands, at least, a general indication of its heterogeneity and, more important, cannot generalize to other social formations the features of capitalist production.

There is, nevertheless, another moment in the *Ontology* that seems more interesting to reflect on regarding these valuations. To address this, let us refer, once again, to the distinction between direct and indirect social labor. In the pre and post-capitalist societies, the metabolism with nature is determined by the direct relation with social labor – either tradition, physical coercion or the free communal acknowledgement of social needs and the necessary activities to satisfy them. If there is, here, a set of relations that stabilize at some point and can be referred to as "economics," they seem to be more imbricated with other social relations – politics, religion, ethics, etc. – that also exercise an important role in the ought of individuals.

With the emergence of capitalism, the distribution of social labor and its products takes place, above all, indirectly, by the market, and this assumes a more independent dynamic in relation to the other dimensions of social life. More independence, however, does not mean, obviously, a complete separation. The social dimensions which are not directly economic are not only influenced by the economy, but also determines it. Here we can mention, for instance, the economic importance of the multiple oppressions under capitalism. Although most of them cannot be reduced to an economic effect, they are determined by the economy and also play an important role in the accumulation of capital.

In the chapter of the *Ontology* about Marx, despite considering the economy a fundamental complex of the social being, Lukács argues that the "economic and extra-economic phenomena in social life continuously transform themselves into one another, and stand in an insuperable relationship of interaction," in a way that does not lead "neither to a lawless once-and-for-all historical development, nor to a mechanically 'law-like' rule of the abstract and purely economic."[78] Since this development is comprehended based on Lukács' characterization of the economic value, we regard it as a having its historicity compromised.

Nevertheless, abstracting the problematic generalizations of economic value, and approaching it based on this dynamic relation between the economic and the non-economic, can offer an alternative path to understand the different social formations; this approach not only effectively takes into account the

---

78   György Lukács, *The ontology of social being: Marx's basic ontological principles*. (London: Merlin Press, 1978), 34. György Lukács, *Werke*, vol. 13 (Darmstad und Neuwied: Luchterhand, 1984), 585.

directly social organization of labor of pre and post-capitalist societies, but also is open to reflect on the importance of the extra-economic valuations to the reproduction of capitalism.

Acknowledgements

I would like to thank Sylvana Insúa-Rieger for proofreading this text. This research received the support from Fundação de Amparo à Pesquisa do Estado de São Paulo (FAPESP).

CHAPTER 5

The Ontology of Alienation: Lukács' Normative Theory of History

Andreas Giesbert

1   Introduction

Lukács can be regarded as the thinker of alienation par excellence. His voluminous oeuvre can obviously not be confined to such a relatively narrow question; still, his theory of alienation stands out as a dominant theme of his work. Already his early pre-Marxist works deal with "the petrifaction of the dynamic potentiality of man,"[1] the problem is even more prominent in his Marxist works. Alienation is the core problem of his influential chapter on Reification in *History and Class Consciousness* from 1923 and remains central in the final chapters of his posthumous *Ontology of Social Being*. During all phases of his theoretical work, Lukács "never abandoned the central theme of achieving wholeness and overcoming alienation."[2]

However, Lukács significantly developed and changed the conception of his core theme over time. He openly criticizes his influential concept of "reification" in his critical foreword to *History and Class Consciousness* from 1967, where he regrets a broad and Hegelian usage of this concept, what he describes as an error that "has certainly contributed greatly to the success"[3] of his work. Thus, at least he shifts his terminology, restricting the broad usage of the term reification of 1923 to a specific problem that only partly coincides with the phenomenon of alienation in his later work. Nothing else can be expected of a man who deeply connects intellectual integrity to the ability to change one's mind, when "confronted by weighty arguments."[4]

This paper will shed light on Lukács' later theory of alienation. This focus has two main reasons. First, Lukács' later concept of alienation is simply not

---

[1]   Michael J. Thompson, "Introduction: Recovering Lukács' Relevance for the Present." In Michael J. Thompson (ed.), *Georg Lukács Reconsidered*. (London / New York, N.Y.: Continuum, 2011), 3.
[2]   Ibid., 6.
[3]   Georg Lukács, *History and Class Consciousness*. Translated by Rodney Livingstone. (Cambridge, Mass.: The MIT Press, 1971), xxiv.
[4]   Georg Lukács, *Record of a Life*. Translated by Rodney Livingstone. (London: Verso, 1983), 122.

the subject of a lot of scholarly work. There are relatively few papers concerning his *Ontology* in general and even fewer dealing with the last – and currently untranslated – chapters of this work.

The second argument is Lukács own theoretical assessment. As mentioned above, Lukács found his early conception of alienation not compelling, despite its popularity. This self-criticism is often ignored or even dismissed as a sign of a new dogmatism by Lukács. Such a dismissal is problematic, ignoring the fact that Lukács constantly reworked his conceptualization of alienation. The few pages of self-criticism that he gives in his foreword to *History and Class Consciousness* are backed up by constant theoretical work, culminating in his concept of alienation in the posthumous *Ontology*. This does not entail that Lukács' later concept of alienation is necessarily better and ought to replace his earlier theory of reification, but it clearly gives ample reason to take a closer look at it and to take Lukács' reservations about his earlier concept seriously.[5]

To present his later theory on alienation I will proceed as follows. In a first step I will outline the importance of the concept of alienation in general (1) and give a brief overview of the shift of Lukács' early concept of reification to his later concept of alienation (2). I will then locate the place of alienation in Lukács later work and asses its importance and restriction (3). Following this, I will give a first sketch and definition of his later concept of alienation (4) that is tightly connected to Lukács anthropologic foundation (5). It will be shown that his definition of man refers to the human species as a historical species being with labor as its key feature. Thus the description of the labor-process (6) allows for a presentation of Lukács theory of history that has labor as its vehicle of progress (7). This progress is reached through the sacrifice of individuals in history (8) and an uneven development of human personalities (9) what is the root for alienation. This reconstruction of Lukács theory of man and history allows for a final conclusion and assessment of Lukács later concept of alienation (10).

2   The Importance of Alienation

Lukács work is constantly concerned with the problem of alienation. More than that, he was in a way even the inventor of the concept of alienation and beyond any doubt highly responsible for its importance. Even if only one essay in his collection *History and Class Consciousness* is concerned with the prob-

---

5   Cf. Nicolas Tertulian, "Lukács' *Ontology*." In Tom Rockmore (ed.), *Lukács Today. Essays in Marxist Philosophy*. (Dordrecht: Reidel Publishing Company, 1988), 249.

lem of alienation, this three part essay on reification makes for more than a third of the total pages and can be regarded as the most influential essay in the book. Lukács himself guesses that the reason for this is that it deals with the "question of alienation [...] for the first time since Marx"[6] from a revolutionary perspective.

This assessment by Lukács holds true. It can even be regarded as cautious as he could not rely on an elaborated theory of alienation by Marx himself or a developed concept of alienation by other Marxists. Rather he had to root his theory of reification in Marx' theoretical framework by using scattered passages in Marx' earlier works and the short but dense chapter on "The Fetish of Commodities" in the first volume of the *Capital*. Thus, it is correct of him to state that Marx was in some way the inventor of this analysis, but it is important to notice that the core of Marx' theory of alienation – the Economic-Philosophic Manuscripts – was not yet published[7] and that there was by no means any serious debate about this concept before Lukács. Therefore Lukács' concept of alienation is an original one. Lukács did not merely rephrase Marx' theory of alienation but invented this concept by combining scattered passages of Marx with an analysis of rationalization by Max Weber and the vitalism of Georg Simmel.[8]

From this fact, two important conclusions follow. First, Lukács can implicitly prove continuity between the early and the late Marx. Thus he rejects a hard split between an early philosophical Marx and a late scientific, economic one, an interpretation most prominently applied by Althusser and sometimes used to incorporate the young Marx into a harmless philosophical canon. Second, it shows the originality of Lukács' concept.

We may still wonder why alienation became such an important topic. As Lukács states in retrospect, the concept has hit a nerve: "[T]he problem was in the air at the time."[9] Many socio-historical factors can be named as reasons for this interest. The time between the two world wars saw rapid changes in industrial work, rising unemployment, different economics crises and substantial shifts in academia.[10] From a theoretical standpoint it can also be added, that the broadness of the term of alienation had an affinity to a manifold application.

---

6   Georg Lukács, *History and Class Consciousness*, xxii.
7   The *Manuscripts* were published in 1932. In his critical foreword Lukács notes, that he had access to the manuscript from 1930 on. Cf. Georg Lukács, *History and Class Consciousness*, xxxvi.
8   Cf. Georg Lukács, *History and Class Consciousness*, ix.
9   Georg Lukács, *History and Class Consciousness*, xxii.
10   Cf. Axel Honneth, *Reification: A New Look at an Old Idea*. Translated by Joseph Ganahl. (Oxford / New York, N.Y.: Oxford University Press, 2008), 17.

It can already be seen in Marx how the term of alienation was used to connect a strict economic analysis with problems of everyday life. This function was especially important in contrast to vulgarized forms of Marxism that either excluded aspects of culture and everyday life or derived them from the economic foundation as part of a superstructure; a problem that Lukács still addresses in his later works.[11]

The concept of alienation – especially Lukács' theory of reification – allowed expanding Marx's radical critique to aspects of everyday and cultural life. This transfer was partly responsible for a lasting influence of the concept. Joós, one of the first academics concerned with the later Lukács, comes to the explanation that "[t]he proliferation of the use of the term alienation is due to the confusion sociologists and psychologists inherited from the Marxist tradition, namely to label alienation such phenomena which are observable in the social or cultural fabric of life and which are always termed as having a negative effect on its victims."[12]

Sometimes lacking a theoretical foundation, the term alienation allowed for a broad critique of modernity, garmented with Marxist terminology. By opening Marx' theory to such applications, Lukács became one of the founding fathers of a "Western Marxism."[13] It is even possible to characterize this tradition – or at least the sub-current of "Critical Theory" – by applying the concept of alienation: "No concept has been more powerful in defining the character of early Critical Theory than that of alienation."[14]

It cannot be overemphasized how groundbreaking Lukács' early Marxist work and especially his introduction of reification was. In a word: Lukács'

---

11   Cf. Georg Lukács, *Zur Ontologie des gesellschaftlichen Seins*, vol. 1. (Darmstadt: Hermann Luchterhand Verlag, 1984), 74.

12   Ernest Joós, "Alienation in Georg Lukács' *Ontology*." In Ernest Joós (ed.), *Georg Lukács and His World: A Reassessment*. (New York, N.Y.: Peter Lang, 1987), 104.

13   This thesis would need a more detailed analysis as a multitude of intellectual figures were relevant for this development. I feel legitimated to overstress Lukács significance by a statement of Martin Jay, who describes the "larger tradition of Western Marxism [as] inaugurated by Lukács." Martin Jay, "Introduction." In Axel Honneth, *Reification*, 13 fn. 7. The term Western Marxism can be problematized. I use it as it is the most popular term and as it is also wide enough to include different, sometimes conflicting thinkers and theories.

14   Axel Honneth, "Foreword." In Rahel Jaeggi, *Alienation*. Translated by Frederick Neuhouser and Alan E. Smith. (New York, N.Y. / Chichester: Columbia University Press, 2014), vii. Honneth adds at another occasion, that this influence was not confined to Western Marxism: "In the German-speaking world of the 1920s and 1930s, the concept of reification constituted a leitmotif of social and cultural critique." Axel Honneth, *Reification*, 17.

chapter on reification introduced the phenomenon of alienation to the academic world and even formed a core concept of Western Marxism.

Thus it is not surprising that *History and Class Consciousness* is still the most prominent text by Lukács in Marxist debates. Even if it was rejected by Lukács in his later years, the influence of this book alone legitimizes continuing studies of this work. Nonetheless, there is no excuse for the fact that this historical significance completely overshadows his later work. This is especially problematic when it comes to systematic approaches. More recent endeavors to revive the concept of reification from a systematic sociological standpoint refer only to his earlier works and usually ignore his later position completely, barely taking notice of his overt self-criticism.[15] This is problematic, not because they would be obliged to Lukács' authority, but because it ignores theoretical reasons that lead Lukács to reject his earlier point of view. A current revitalization of the theory of alienation should at least be able to learn something from the later work of Lukács, even if his own reservations would be eventually rejected.

What holds true for systematic approaches to the concept of alienation holds true for the broader debate as well. The *Ontology* is subject of few studies and the exposed chapters on alienation share the same fate. Lukács' last autocriticism,[16] as Joós calls it, is not taken seriously.

This cannot only be attributed to a lack of interest. Lukács' work is not easy on its potential readers. Some aspects can be highlighted here. First, Lukács chooses the relatively dry topic of ontology. Instead of the revolutionary vigor of his earlier work, he elaborates a necessary "theoretical operation" that aims to establish "the basis for an ontology of social being."[17] This is especially problematic as the term ontology is burdened with a rich history of dogmatism that is even more suspicious to Marxist readers, who are often informed by the radically anti-essential philosophies of Critical Theory and a general shift in social studies.[18]

---

15 Cf. Axel Honneth, *Reification*, 53f.
16 Ernest Joós, *Lukács's Last Autocriticism: The Ontology*. (Atlantic Highlands, N.J.: Humanities Press, 1983).
17 Cf. Nicolas Tertulian, "Lukács' *Ontology*," 244.
18 Benseler quotes a fitting statement by Ernst Bloch: "One cannot express the word ontology in front of normal Marxists; it reminds them of Heidegger, of fundamental ontology, and when ontology is used in another context, it only leads to head-shaking and quarrel." ("Man kann vor normalen Marxisten das Wort Ontologie nicht aussprechen; es erinnert sie an Heidegger, an Fundamentalontologie, und wenn nun Ontologie sonst noch gebraucht wird, gibt es immer Kopfschütteln und Krach.") Frank Benseler, "Nachwort." In Georg Lukács, *Zur Ontologie des gesellschaftlichen Seins*, vol. 2. (Darmstadt: Hermann Luchterhand Verlag, 1986), 744. As large parts of the Ontology are not translated into

A second problem is the voluminous extent of Lukács' magnum opus. The two volumes consist of roughly 1400 pages that bear some redundancies and lengthy digressions concerned with examples in philosophy, history and art. It is also demanded that the reader has the whole project in mind as Lukács is constantly referring to the general framework and other chapters of his work.

Finally, he often refers to his unfinished ethics that should answer problems that cannot be solved in the *Ontology*. After all, the *Ontology* can be seen as "a vast introduction to a future Ethics."[19]

Part of those problems may be attributed to a premature end of Lukács' studies due to his illness and eventual death. Authorized by Lukács, the *Ontology of Social Being* was published in German as part of Lukács' collected works but was compiled out of his manuscripts.[20] This might explain some of the stylistic problems, but the book can still be regarded as more or less complete and finished. The *Ontology* as presented in the edition of "Luchterhand" is a text that can be regarded as Lukács own product that only needed some reediting. It is not suggested that Lukács planned to fundamentally change the theoretical framework of his last work. Still, the two volumes of the collected works edition of Luchterhand were only published in 1984 and 1986, roughly 15 years after the authors dead. Before that, only three parts were published separately, due to the pressing of the author who saw the need to present his final theoretical revision to the public sphere.[21] Lukács did everything in his power to reach an audience for his later theory. He published three separate chapters in advance and explicitly chose a paperback edition for this purpose.[22] Besides that, he gave numerous interviews, some of them published separately, like his biographical *Record of a Life* and the theoretically more fruitful *Conversations with Lukács*.

The scarce publicity is even more severe in the international debate. Even today, the *Ontology* is not completely translated in English. Only translations of the three separately published chapters mentioned before are available. The meritorious translations date back to 1978 and are mostly concerned with the first – historical – part of Lukács' magnum opus. Only the important first chapter of the second, systematic part is translated. This chapter, which gives a treatment of labor, is crucial to the understanding of Lukács' later theory in

---

English, some translations are mine. Whenever I translate myself, I give the original quote in footnote or parentheses.

19   Nicolas Tertulian, "Lukács' *Ontology*," 269.
20   Cf. Frank Benseler, "Nachwort," 731–743.
21   Lukács explicitly decided for a paperback edition to reach a broader audience. Cf. ibid., 742f.
22   Cf. Frank Benseler, "Nachwort," 741.

general and the concept of alienation in particular. As the chapter on alienation itself remains untranslated, it is not surprising that there are even fewer articles on Lukács' later concept of alienation in the English language than in German.[23]

Such problems of publication and style can help to understand why Lukács' newer approach to alienation was not received with the same enthusiasm as his earlier work; however it does not say anything about the theoretical value of the two approaches. It might explain, but not excuse that Lukács' autocriticism is often simply put aside in favor of his earlier concept.[24]

There are few exceptions. Joós is one of the few proponents who did substantial work on Lukács project of ontology in English. His insightful works date back to the late 1980's, but like Tertulian[25] he does not focus on the theory of alienation.[26] For the problem of alienation Joós' shortened translation of the Vienna paper is his most useful contribution.[27] This paper – originally intended as a lecture – is probably the most concise presentation of Lukács' concept of an ontology and especially the ontological foundation of his theory of history. As it is crucial for Lukács concept of alienation that it is rooted in general tendencies of history the Vienna paper might be the best text by Lukács himself that is translated to get a grasp on his later concept of alienation. Also worth mentioning is a more recent article by Dannemann that is concerned

---

23 Three articles are specifically concerned with Lukács' later concept of alienation in German: Claudius Vellay, "Die Entfremdung aus Sicht der Lukácsschen Ontologie – Materialistische Ethik diesseits von Religion und Glauben." In Christoph J. Bauer et al. (ed.), *"Bei mir ist jede Sache Fortsetzung von etwas." Georg Lukács. Werk und Wirkung.* (Duisburg: Universitätsverlag Rhein-Ruhr, 2008), 153–185; Maik Puzić, "Lukács' späte Entfremdungskonzeption. Natur- und gesellschaftsontologische Grundlagen." In Rüdiger Dannemann (ed.), *Lukács 2016: Jahrbuch der Internationalen Georg-Lukács-Gesellschaft.* (Bielefeld: Aisthesis Verlag, 2016), 125–142; Andreas Giesbert, "Menschwerdung. Der Begriff der Entfremdung beim späten Lukács." In Christoph J. Bauer et al. (ed.), *Georg Lukács. Totalität, Utopie und Ontologie.* (Duisburg: Universitätsverlag Rhein-Ruhr, 2012), 93–121.

24 Tertulian is outspoken on this topic: "[T]he apologists of the young Lukács have still not furnished the least plausible argument for the willful decision to ignore these two works [Aesthetics and Ontology – A.G.]." Nicolas Tertulian, "Lukács' *Ontology*," 268.

25 Tertulian gives a rough and insightful interpretation of the phenomenon of alienation that he regards as "the most original part" of Lukács' theory of subjectivity but does not discuss alienation in detail. Cf. Nicolas Tertulian, "Lukács' *Ontology*," 263ff.

26 Admittedly Joós is the author of the only article in English that is especially devoted to Lukács theory of alienation in the Ontology. Unfortunately this short article does not give a detailed analysis of this concept. Ernest Joós, "Alienation in Georg Lukács' Ontology."

27 Georg Lukács, "The Ontological Foundations of Human Thinking and Action." Translated by Ernest Joós. In Ernest Joós, *Lukács Last Autocriticism*, 135–149. The translation has to be used with care. Beside some omissions, Joós gives at least one severe mistranslation. See my footnote 175.

with the concept and current adaptions of reification. As an expert on the early as well as the later Lukács, he takes the later concept of alienation into consideration, but treats the chapter more or less as an addition to his earlier theory of reification.[28]

3 From Reification to Alienation

Before we proceed with a discussion of the later theory, it is important to give a rough picture of the differences between his early and later concept of alienation. The first thing to mention is a shift in terminology. Where the young Lukács makes the term "reification" the center of his argument, the later one tends to use "alienation." This all too simple difference in terminology is seriously confused as soon as we have a closer look at the texts themselves. The essay on reification sparsely uses the term "alienation," mostly in quotations from Marx that are used to corroborate a theory of reification. It is actually a good indicator for the originality of Lukács' work that he tries to reformulate a concept of Marx by applying a term that is rarely used by him.[29] The fact that Marx used the term alienation rather than reification is not a sufficient reason for a shift in terminology, though. There has to be profound reasons that Lukács constantly applies the terminology of alienation when he speaks about his earlier concept in retrospect. As quoted earlier, in review, Lukács saw the importance of his earlier work in the fact that it deals with "the question of alienation,"[30] not that it introduced the concept of reification. In his autobiographic interviews he affirms this view, using the same terminology, in reference to *History and Class Consciousness*, stating that "[i]t is generally acknowledged that the problem of alienation was raised for the first time there."[31]

Although both terms are relatively interchangeable, this terminological shift nevertheless points to a shift of theory. The later Lukács precisely differentiates between the phenomena of reification and alienation. Both terms are

---

28   Cf. Rüdiger Dannemann, "Georg Lukács' Theory of Reification and the Idea of Socialism." *Contours Journal*, vol. 8 (Spring 2017). The journal is an online publication: http://www.sfu.ca/humanities-institute/contours/issue8/theory/3.html (30.04.2018).
29   There is no quote given by Lukács where reification is used by Marx. Instead the concept of reification is backed by a quote from the chapter on fetishism, introduced by the words: "Marx describes the basic phenomenon of reification as follows." Cf. Georg Lukács, *History and Class Consciousness*, 86.
30   Ibid., xxii.
31   Georg Lukács, *Record of a Life*, 77.

interconnected but do not coincide. According to his own statement,[32] Lukács was motivated to this clarification by Marx' *Economic Philosophical Manuscripts* that famously deal with the terms "alienation" or "estrangement"[33] and also introduce the term "objectification" (*Vergegenständlichung*). It is in fact the confusion between objectification and alienation that he deems his "fundamental and crude"[34] but influential error of his earlier work. Lukács argues that his earlier theory of reification gives a negative description of the fact that humans objectify themselves through labor, what is highly problematic: "For objectification is indeed a phenomenon that cannot be eliminated from human life in society."[35]

For the later Lukács, objectification is a conditione humaine, an anthropological fact. As Lukács proceeds, if the simple fact that humans objectify themselves is identified with the fundamentally critical concept of alienation, the solution to overcome alienation can only be an idealistic one. Lukács consequently had to import the idea of an identical subject–object that does not objectify itself anymore. According to the later Lukács, the materialistic identification of this subject–object with the proletariat was able to cover up this basically idealistic approach, but was reason for further messianic implications and was eventually "an attempt to out-Hegel Hegel."[36] His later criticism, that his earlier concept was mostly Hegelian and thus not a materialistic one, hits a nerve, but seems to be an oversimplification. It was always specific – alienated – forms of objectification that Lukács described with his concept of reification and not a general identification of objectification and alienation. The intriguing power of his earlier concept is grounded in the ability to identify alienated forms of objectification, even if the theoretical base might not sufficiently allow for a distinction between "good" and "bad" forms of objectification or in Hegelian terms: forms of realization and alienation. Especially his implicit attack, that this fundamental confusion was uncritically applied by the cultural debate can be doubted. Nevertheless it should alert us, that the founding father of the concept of reification warns us of such a severe theoretical problem. At least there is a theoretical vagueness at the root of one of the most famous concepts of 20th century Marxism. A fact that can explain applications of alienation that use forceful terminology, but that tend to fall apart when the question is addressed, what alienation exactly consists of. As Lukács

---

32   Cf. Georg Lukács, *History and Class Consciousness*, xxxvi.
33   See my footnote 132.
34   Georg Lukács, *History and Class Consciousness*, xxiv.
35   Ibid., xxiv.
36   Ibid., xxiii.

has the problem clearly in mind, it can be expected that his later theory of alienation will give a sufficient answer to this problem. It is to be hoped, that his later conceptualization avoids idealistic arguments as well as mysterious formulations.

4 The Location of Alienation

The complex of alienation always enjoyed an exposed place in Lukács works. The problem of alienation makes for the last three chapters of his *Ontology of Social Being* and is referred to as a central problem of this work.[37] Even the last notes in his autobiographical sketch *Gelebtes Leben* – only followed by general notes concerning the epochs of his life in Hungary – concern problems deeply connected with the problem of alienation. As the core thoughts of his *Ontology* – and "the deepest truth of Marxism"[38] – he presents us the idea of "humanization of man as the content of the process of history which realizes itself – in a myriad of varieties – in each individual human life."[39] According to Lukács, this makes for a historical tendency that appears subjectively as a "progress toward the practical realization of one's own being (= the real unfolding of individuality)."[40] This real unfolding of individuality will be the central problem for his concept of alienation. History is conceived as a fragile progress that is only realized in a myriad of individual struggles. In the very last words of his notes he describes the individual "conduct of life as a struggle between (genuine!) curiosity and vanity – vanity as a principal vice: it nails people firmly to their particularity. (Frustration as fixation at the level of particularity.)"[41] Even if Lukács does not use the term alienation in this context, this problem is the general framework of Lukács later concept of alienation in nuce. Alienation is the unreal unfolding of individuality; it is the chief obstacle in a principally progressive history of mankind.

As claimed before, the concept of alienation is an often overstretched theory. It seems that the term either remains vague or loses its theoretical background and its revolutionary implications. Proponents of Western Marxism tend to use the concept in the broadest possible sense, making it hard to pinpoint the phenomenon, whereas approaches in the social sciences miss what

---

37 Cf. Georg Lukács, *Zur Ontologie des gesellschaftlichen Seins*, vol. 1, 193.
38 Georg Lukács, "Gelebtes Denken: Notes toward an Autobiography." In Georg Lukács, *Record of a Life*, 169.
39 Ibid.
40 Ibid.
41 Ibid.

Lukács was intending, sometimes indeed focusing on objectifications in general.[42]

The concept of alienation in the *Ontology* tries to avoid both pitfalls. Lukács does not give us a checklist of phenomena of alienation as specific pathologies of modern capitalist society while directly addressing the theoretical foundation of alienation. He wants to understand "the phenomenon of alienation in reality, without mythological ingredients and distortions."[43] Lukács does indeed present us with a clear concept of alienation that can at least function as a corrective. His later theory of alienation lacks the suggestive force of his earlier concept, but is able to exemplify the normative assumptions implied in most concepts of alienation.

In accordance with his aversion against a broad and merely suggestive usage of alienation, the first thing to notion is Lukács tendency to disempower the term in various ways.[44] Similar to his critique of his earlier work he first delimits the concept of alienation to a strictly socio-historical manifestation. To make this point, he criticizes Hegel's identification of alienation with objectification, what would only allow for the abolition of objectification in general as the only opportunity to overcome alienation.[45] Lukács refuses this concept with Marx, quoting the *Economic Philosophic Manuscripts*: "A non-objective being is a non-being."[46] Connecting the Hegelian approach to concepts that regard alienation as a condition humaine,[47] he then locates the problem exclusively in the realm of social being. In opposition to objectification, alienation is a strictly socio-historical phenomenon that arises at a specific state of human history and can therefore be abolished.

This confinement is mostly negative and does not say much about the concept of alienation in particular. Only later in the text does Lukács present us with additional specifications of the ontological place of alienation. Here, Lukács adds that alienation is "one of the social phenomena that are most

---

42 Dannemann sees this exemplarily in Martha Nussbaums theory of reification. Cf. Rüdiger Dannemann, "Georg Lukács' Theory of Reification and the Idea of Socialism."
43 "Will man also das Phänomen der Entfremdung wirklich, ohne mythologische Zutaten und Verzerrungen begreifen." Georg Lukács, *Zur Ontologie des gesellschaftlichen Seins*, vol. 2, 513.
44 Cf. Maik Puzić, "Lukács' späte Entfremdungskonzeption. Natur- und gesellschaftsontologische Grundlagen," 131.
45 Cf. Georg Lukács, *Zur Ontologie des gesellschaftlichen Seins*, vol. 2, 501ff.
46 Karl Marx, *Economic and Philosophie Manuscripts of 1844*. Translated by Martin Milligan and Dirk J. Struik. In Karl Marx and Friedrich Engels, *Collected Works. Volume 3*. (Electric Book: Lawrence and Wishart, 2010), 337.
47 Cf. Georg Lukács, *Zur Ontologie des gesellschaftlichen Seins*, vol. 2, 501.

decisively centered on the individual."[48] He does not specify what the other social phenomena are; instead he reaffirms that the problem of alienation is concerned with the single individual (*Einzelmensch*) and its personality in an emphatic sense. He closely links the problem of alienation with the "subjective factor of a revolution,"[49] a phrase adopted from Lenin.

This should not lead to the idea that Lukács shifts from an all-encompassing objectivistic concept of alienation to a mere subjective one. He immediately repels such a notion by mentioning that the concept of personality is strictly a social category. An isolated human being outside of society is a purely abstract concept for him. As Marx and Engels had put it in their theses on Feuerbach: "[T]he essence of man is no abstraction inherent in each single individual. In its reality it is the ensemble of the social relations."[50] Or in the words of Lukács: "[T]here is no form of subjectivity that is not social in its deepest roots and definitions of its being."[51] This focus on the concrete person is accompanied by a further specification of alienation. Not only is the single individual a mere abstraction, so is the phenomenon of alienation. According to Lukács, alienation in general is a useful concept, but in reality we have to deal with alienations in plurality that affect each individual in strictly individual and therefore different ways. "Alienation is a scientific abstraction, certainly an indispensable one for theory, therefore a rational abstraction."

A last restriction and clarification regards the importance of alienation. As mentioned, Lukács disempowers the term in comparison to his earlier theory of reification. Already in his critical foreword, it becomes clear that he refuses a broad application of his concept to all areas of social life. Thus he feels the urge to clarify that alienation is only one of many problems, but adds that it is still a very important one.[52] For him this applies in particular to his own time,

---

48 "Entfremdung [ist] eine der der entschiedensten auf das Individuum zentrierten gesellschaftlichen Erscheinungen." Georg Lukács, *Zur Ontologie des gesellschaftlichen Seins*, vol. 2, 507.
49 Georg Lukács, *Zur Ontologie des gesellschaftlichen Seins*, vol. 2, 523.
50 Karl Marx, "Theses on Feuerbach." Translated by W. Lough. In Karl Marx and Friedrich Engels, *Collected Works. Volume 5*. (Electric Book: Lawrence and Wishart, 2010), 4. Lukács does not refer to this thesis in the context of alienation, but quotes the phrase in his Prolegomena. Cf. Georg Lukács, *Zur Ontologie des gesellschaftlichen Seins*, vol. 1, 38.
51 "Es gibt keine Art von Subjektivität, die in den tiefsten Wurzeln und Bestimmungen ihres Seins nicht gesellschaftlich wäre." Georg Lukács, *Zur Ontologie des gesellschaftlichen Seins*, vol. 2, 510.
52 "Alienation is only one of many social conflicts, sure enough a highly significant one. (Die Entfremdung ist nur einer der gesellschaftlichen Konflikte, freilich ein höchst bedeutsamer.") Ibid., 513.

in which he recognizes a "generalization of the alienation of mankind" that will "revolutionize our relationship of labor."[53]

Despite its importance, "alienation never encompasses the complete totality of the social being of man."[54] This approach to narrow the concept of alienation in its significance is contrasted by an adherence to its theoretical importance. He still holds that the concept of alienation is crucial for the understanding of the theory of Marx in all its stages. It is by no means "a special problem of the young (still philosophical) Marx."[55] Explicitly refusing a cut between the early and late Marx, Lukács refers to notions of alienation in Marx' *Theories of Surplus Value* and defends a usefulness that is not restricted to the bourgeois intelligence (*bürgerliche Intelligenz*).[56]

Another problem becomes virulent in regard of the historical place of alienation. Lukács does mention that alienation is a socio-historical phenomenon that could only come into being at the stage of a specific development of the division of labor. Throughout the text, he deeply connects the problem of alienation with economic developments, without deriving alienation solely from economic factors.[57] He especially refuses to limit the problem of alienation to capitalist societies. This does not only allow him to refer to examples of alienation and de-alienation from ancient Greek, but even more important as an attack on nominal socialistic societies, including Soviet Russia in the late 60s. More or less unnoticed he confronts the reality of soviet Marxism with the (Marxist) demand of a non-alienated form of socialism.[58] He explicitly criticizes that Stalinism "took the view, that the mere induction of socialism automatically brings an end to alienation."[59]

---

53   Georg Lukács, "The Ontological Foundations of Human Thinking and Action," 145.
54   "[Entfremdung] umfaßt bei all ihrer Wichtigkeit nie die volle Totalität des gesellschaftlichen Seins des Menschen." Georg Lukács, *Zur Ontologie des gesellschaftlichen Seins*, vol. 2, 510.
55   "[E]ine Spezialfrage des jungen (noch philosophischen) Marx." Ibid., 503.
56   Cf. ibid.
57   This is resembled by the statement: "I am not convinced that economic progress is all-determining-that the abundance of material goods and the steady improvement of living standards will solve all problems and will automatically produce communism." Georg Lukács, "An Interview with George Lukács." Translated by Ernest Joós. In Ernest Joós, *Lukács Last Autocriticism*, 128.
58   The Ontology was scarcely studied in the GDR and Hungary. Cf. Frank Benseler, "Nachwort," 746.
59   "[D]en Standpunkt vertreten, daß die bloße Einführung des Sozialismus ein Ende der Entfremdung mit sich führt." Georg Lukács, *Zur Ontologie des gesellschaftlichen Seins*, vol. 2, 551.

5 What Is Alienation?

The placement of alienation helps to avoid too narrow or broad applications but does not answer the question what alienation exactly is. In his later theory, Lukács still gives no clear definition, but rather uses implicit ways to define alienation. After a few pages of his chapter on "The General Features of Alienation," he states: "The development of productive forces is necessarily at the same time the development of human capacities. Albeit – and here the problem of alienation comes into the open – the development of human capacities does not necessarily leads to a development of the human personality."[60] The dialectic tension between the development of capacities or skills on the one hand and man's development as a person on the other will be seen as the center of his theory of alienation. It is the discord between both sides that form the core of alienation. This is further confirmed by an indirect statement in context of his discussion of the importance of alienation. There he notes in passing: "The dialectic contradiction of the development of capacities and of personality, thus alienation."[61] This is the shortest definition of alienation given by Lukács and is restated in different variations. In another passage he refers to the "central phenomenon that concerns us here" – alienation – "the societal originated conflict between the development [*Entwicklung*] and unfolding [*Entfaltung*] of the capacities of humans and the formation [*Ausbildung*] of his personality as man."[62] The shift from the societal development of capacities of humans in plural to the formation of personality of a single individual is especially important, as it can once more affirm the deep connection between the subjective phenomenon of alienation and its objective

---

60 "[D]ie Entwicklung der Produktivkräfte ist notwendigerweise zugleich die der menschlichen Fähigkeiten.
    Jedoch – und hier tritt das Problem der Entfremdung plastisch ans Tageslicht – die Entwicklung der menschlichen Fähigkeiten muß nicht notwendig eine Entwicklung der menschlichen Persönlichkeit herbeiführen." Ibid., 504.
61 "Der dialektische Widerspruch von Fähigkeits- und Persönlichkeitsentwicklung, also die Entfremdung." Ibid., 510.
62 "[D]as Grundphänomen, das uns jetzt beschäftigt, um den gesellschaftlich entstandenen Konflikt zwischen der Entwicklung und Entfaltung der Fähigkeiten der Menschen und der Ausbildung seiner Persönlichkeit als Mensch." Ibid., 514f. Lukács' terminology is deeply rooted in the humanist tradition. He often uses the term *Entwicklung* that can only roughly be translated as development. The German *Entwicklung* implies progress and development as well as unfolding. Lukács appeals to the latter, when he adds the specific term of *Entfaltung*, that can be translated as "unfolding." By that the (technical) development of skills is already connected to the humanist unfolding of capacities in an emphatic sense.

preconditions. The socio-historical grounding of human development and personality will be central for the description of Lukács theory of history.

The given definition(s) of alienation are still relatively vague and it is once again only possible to clarify its meaning in negation. We learn that a difference between the capacities of human beings and the development or formation of personality is the core of the problem of alienation. Lukács implies that the difference between a possible realization of personality – thanks to historically developed skills and capacities – to a currently realized level of personality (*Persönlichkeit*) is the benchmark for alienation. After explaining that both developments do not necessarily go hand in hand, he adds: "In opposite: It [the development of productive forces – A.G.] can distort, debase etc. the human personality, precisely through the higher development [*Höherentfaltung*] of single capacities."[63] That Lukács only gives an enumeration followed by etc. shows, that he only wants to paint a rough picture. Indeed the terminology that he uses – distortion (*verzerren*) and debasing (erniedrigen)[64] – is full of moral implications and implicitly refers to an undistorted or undebased norm without exemplifying it. Alienation is a strictly negative term – morally as well as logically.

Before we proceed to explain this normative benchmark it can be helpful to present at least some of the examples that Lukács gives as forms of alienation. Lukács himself sees the need for such examples throughout the text. To explain what he means by debased or distorted formations of personality, he refers to the "many team-specialists of today [...], in which the wily [*raffiniert*] bred special skills [*Spezialgeschicklichkeiten*] work as personality-destructing in the highest degree."[65] Once again does he use morally loaded terminology and his implication that there are (wily) agents who are responsible for such

---

[63] "Im Gegenteil: Sie kann gerade durch die Höherentfaltung von einzelnen Fähigkeiten die menschliche Persönlichkeit verzerren, erniedrigen etc." Ibid., 504.

[64] *Erniedrigen* can hardly be translated without losing meaning. It literally means lowering but is mostly used in the sense of debasing or even humiliation. Both meanings work well in Lukács' framework. I am convinced that Lukács is aware of both meanings, but does use the term in this case in a more morally loaded sense. *Erniedrigung* (debasing) can be read as a reference to Marx' *"categorical imperative to overthrow all relations* in which man is a debased, enslaved, forsaken, despicable being." Karl Marx, "Contribution to Critique of Hegel's Philosophy of Law. Introduction." Translated by Martin Milligan and Barbara Ruhemann. In Karl Marx and Friedrich Engels, *Collected Works. Volume 3.* (Electric Book: Lawrence and Wishart, 2010), 182.

[65] "[V]iele Teamspezialisten der Gegenwart [...], bei denen die raffiniert gezüchteten Spezialgeschicklichkeiten in höchste m Grad als persönlichkeitszerstörend wirken." Georg Lukács, *Zur Ontologie des gesellschaftlichen Seins*, vol. 2, 504.

forms of alienation is more than problematic. The example can nevertheless help to understand the central form of alienation: An uneven and erratic development of personality contrasted to a wholesome, genuine human personality.[66] Lukács backs up this observation by referring to the historian Ferguson who described manufactural work with the famous saying that "ignorance is the mother to industry as well as of superstition."[67]

Lukács gives many different examples for types of alienation. We learn that specific character types like bureaucratic-petrified routiniers, strivers, or household tyrants can be described as alienated formations of personality.[68] We are also informed that conspicuous consumption or a life that tries to establish an "image," foster forms of alienation.[69] The main issue is here, that Lukács gives examples rather than criteria. We can say in advance, that all these forms are in some way characterized by particularity, like Lukács notes most figurative in his cryptic autobiographic sketches: "Vanity as a principal vice: it nails people firmly to their particularity. (Frustration as fixation at the level of particularity.)"[70]

The criterion of particularity alone is not sufficient though. Even when he discusses needs and vices, he tends to add the criterion of (in)humanity: "the satisfaction of unreal needs – private property, graft – renders one inhuman."[71]

6   What Is Human?

The reference to an undistorted and uneven developed human being, narrow perfections (*bornierte Vollendungen*)[72] of individuality or even to a particular man (*partikularer Mensch*),[73] show that Lukács' concept needs a benchmark of

---

66   Lukács adds that directedness to wholesomeness or totality is no guaranteed cure for alienation. Referring to the USSR of Stalin and old Prussia, he adds that "unconditional commitment to a matter of objective societal meaningfulness can lead to alienation sui generis." ("[Das] bedingungslose Hingabe an eine Sache von objektiv gesellschaftlicher Bedeutung, zu Entfremdungen sui generis führen kann.") Ibid., 527.
67   "Unwissenheit ist die Mutter der Betriebsamkeit sowohl wie des Aberglaubens." Ibid., 505.
68   Cf. ibid., 529.
69   Cf. ibid., 627.
70   Georg Lukács, "Gelebtes Denken," 169.
71   Georg Lukács, "An Interview with George Lukács," 128.
72   Cf. Georg Lukács, *Zur Ontologie des gesellschaftlichen Seins*, vol. 1, 91; 158; 206; 231, and Georg Lukács, *Zur Ontologie des gesellschaftlichen Seins*, vol. 2, 274; 295f.; 508; 542; 546; 623; 642; 648; 661; 703.
73   Lukács uses the term in different forms, sometimes highlighting the aspect of isolation. He does not emphasize the term as a *terminus technicus* but uses it frequently, most explicit in the passages concerning alienation. Cf. ibid., 363.

a successful, undistorted form of personality: The real unfolding of human individuality. This implication is a core problem for the theory of alienation in general and an obvious and convincing point of critique. Especially the anti-essentialist strains of Marxism – that Lukács significantly helped to form – are firmly opposed to essentialist anthropological arguments as to non-dialectic references to (human) nature.

Although Lukács presents us a concept of anthropology, he does not give a simple normative foundation that relies on a non-historical human nature or static ontological dogmas. In fact, he is skeptical of any such approach. When asked "What is human?," he leaves no doubt of his skepticism: "I shrink away from this term, because each and everyone understands something different by it."[74] The subsequent argument begins with the notion that "the term 'human' has become fashionable phraseology."[75] Instead he refers to the short theses on Feuerbach where "the essence of this term"[76] is given. This essence is again a historical one. It is not a fixated essence but one that is constantly in becoming. Consequently, Lukács describes the essence of man as an aim to reach: "every man should live a life befitting the species, a life that allows the full development of individuality."[77] We will have to specify this goal furthermore to understand what alienation – as the distance to this aim – precisely is. Before we proceed to do so, it is important to understand the essential anthropological assumptions that Lukács applies with the help of Marx and Engels.

While refusing to give a fixated idea of a human nature, humans are still basically natural beings. They have to survive in biological – and social – circumstances that they have not chosen themselves.[78] The specific human device of this struggle is labor or vice versa: "The essence of labor consists precisely in the biological struggle of living beings against the limitations of their environment."[79] In other words, human existence is dependent on lower ontological levels: "Social being is dependent on organic being and the latter owes its existence to its inorganic foundation."[80] Man is dependent on levels of organic and inorganic being, but is discerned from the other levels by the way in

---

74 Georg Lukács, "An Interview with George Lukács," 128.
75 Ibid.
76 Ibid.
77 Ernest Joós, *Lukács's Last Autocriticism: The Ontology*, 129.
78 E.g., "'Men shape their history themselves,' says Marx, 'but not under circumstances they have chosen themselves.'" Georg Lukács, "The Ontological Foundations of Human Thinking and Action," 146.
79 Ibid., 138.
80 Ernest Joós, *Lukács's Last Autocriticism: The Ontology*, 52.

which he organizes his "metabolism with nature."[81] This is due to labor, what "can be viewed as the original phenomenon, as the model for social being."[82] This does not mean, that all expressions of human beings has to be understand as acts of labor, but rather that labor has to be understand as the "model for any social practice."[83] It "is the new master concept, because it includes everything within itself."[84] This leads to the question what characterizes labor exactly and what allows for it to be the "the generative cell of social life" or even the "key to anthropogenesis."[85]

7 What Is Labor?

Lukács famously refers to Marx's definition of labor given in *Capital*. In contrast to animals (e.g., spiders and bees) which work in the general way, that they transform inorganic being into organic being, human labor in a specific sense is distinguished by the fact "that the architect builds the cell in his mind before he constructs it in wax."[86] Obviously this figurative example is not restricted to the construction of honeycombs. The important aspect is that the labor process produces a result "which had already been conceived by the worker at the beginning, hence already existed ideally."[87] In Lukács words: "labour is the realization of a teleological positing."[88]

By that a new and crucial element comes into reality: Teleology. Teleology makes for the crucial difference between nature in a narrow sense (inorganic and organic being) and social being. Society does build on the ontology of nature, but with the category of teleology it adds a fundamentally new principle to it that has its exclusive place in man and society. There is no teleology in

---

81   Georg Lukács, *The Ontology of Social Being: Labour*. Translated by David Fernbach. (London: Merlin Press, 1980), 20. Alfred Schmidt highlights and discusses the terminology of a "metabolism of man and nature" in his classic study on the concept of nature in Marx. Cf. Alfred Schmidt, *The Concept of Nature in Marx*. Translated by Ben Fawkes. (London, New York: Verso, 2014), 76–93.
82   Ibid., v.
83   Ibid., 3.
84   Georg Lukács, *Record of a Life*, 141.
85   Nicolas Tertulian, "Lukács' *Ontology*," 256.
86   Karl Marx, *Capital Volume 1*. Translated by Samuel Moore and Edward Aveling. In Karl Marx and Friedrich Engels, *Collected Works. Volume 35*. (Electric Book: Lawrence and Wishart, 2010), 188.
87   Ibid.
88   Georg Lukács, *The Ontology of Social Being: Labour*, 3.

nature. By that the act of labor even introduces a new form of necessity. Through labor, natural causality is transformed into a posited causality.[89]

With Hegelian terminology, Lukács further describes this transformation. Man is able to do so by making nature's own blind activity purposive by the cunning of reason.[90] As a limited, natural being, man cannot transform nature by the power of his mind alone, but only by utilizing the forces of nature against each other. In the Prolegomena to the *Ontology*, Lukács quotes Engels: "[F]reedom does not consist in any dreamt-of independence from natural laws, but in the knowledge of these laws, and in the possibility this gives of systematically making them work towards definite ends."[91] This is similar to a note that Lukács gives in his book *The Young Hegel* from 1938: "Every working man knows instinctively that he can only perform those operations with the means or objects if labour that the laws or combination of laws governing those objects will permit. That is to say, the labour-process can never go beyond the limits of causality."[92]

Nevertheless, this cunning utilization of nature against itself introduces the teleological element of purpose. Thus a strictly new – human – element arises in reality. Man does not only realize its purposes in nature like every natural being, but does so with consciousness. This role of consciousness is an aspect of labor that Lukács constantly underlines: "With labour, human consciousness ceases to be an epiphenomenon, in the ontological sense."[93] This is in accordance to Marx, especially his more emphatic description of the category of labor in the *Economic Philosophic Manuscripts*. Where an animal is considered "immediately one with its life activity," man "makes his life activity itself the object of his will and of his consciousness. He has conscious life activity. It is just because of this, that he is a species-being."[94] For Marx – who is confident that "the whole character of a species [...] is contained in the character of its life activity"[95] – this goes hand in hand with other implications that Lukács happily accepts. Human labor is (potentially) universal instead of one-sided

---

89 Cf. ibid., 15.
90 Cf. ibid., 12.
91 Friedrich Engels, *Anti-Dühring*. Translated by Emile Burns. In Karl Marx and Friedrich Engels, *Collected Works. Volume 25*. (Electric Book: Lawrence and Wishart, 2010), 105; Georg Lukács, *Zur Ontologie des gesellschaftlichen Seins*, vol. 1, 21.
92 Georg Lukács, *The Young Hegel. Studies in the Relations between Dialectics an Economics*. Translated by Rodney Livingstone. (Sussex: Merlin Press, 1975), 345. Puzić emphasizes this argument. Cf. Maik Puzić, "Lukács' späte Entfremdungskonzeption," 129.
93 Georg Lukács, *The Ontology of Social Being: Labour*, 21. This is even the exact point where "dialectical materialism cuts itself off from mechanical materialism." Ibid., 23.
94 Karl Marx, *Economic and Philosophie Manuscripts of 1844*, 276.
95 Ibid.

and can be regarded a "free activity." Man is not confined to the immediate need of the species, but "man knows how to produce in accordance with the standard of every species."[96] He even "forms objects in accordance with the laws of beauty."[97]

Lukács stresses this aspect as well. Labor as a conscious way of transforming nature – the humanization of nature[98] – is also "a freeing of man from his environment, a distancing, which is clearly revealed in the confrontation of subject and object."[99] We might suspect a trace of Lukács' earlier concept of reification when he describes this process as a distancing. Indeed, the process of labor includes the danger of reification, but the later Lukács rather emphasizes the element of freedom. As the central model for social practice, labor contains even "the ontological kernel of freedom"[100] in so far as it is constantly concerned with choices and alternatives. Even the – at first sight – simple act of selecting a fitting stone as an instrument is a conscious act that has to make a deliberate choice between alternatives: "By observation and experience, i.e., by reflection and the operations of consciousness, certain properties of the stone have to be recognized which make it suitable or unsuitable for the planned activity."[101] Obviously this example is only the most basic one. The role of consciousness and the importance and pure sum of choices increase on a more developed level of laboring. Thus the importance of alternative choices and freedom rises with the complexity of processes of labor and its division. Lukács is not concerned with the abstract concept of the freedom of the will here, which he simply asserts. Instead he underscores that this process is inherently directed as it includes valorization.

As labor is always connected to a goal – usually the fulfilling of a need according to a preconditioned plan – it also introduces an "elementary form of appearance of value."[102] Reduced to this aspect, Lukács' idea is simple: As the labor-process is connected to a teleological posit, there is an aim to which the process can be compared and therefore be measured. Labor can succeed or

---

96   Ibid., 277.
97   Ibid.
98   "Only here [with the appearance of social man – A.G.] has what is to him his natural existence become his human existence, and nature become man for him. Thus society is the complete unity of man with nature – the true resurrection of nature – the accomplished naturalism of man and the accomplished humanism of nature." Ibid., 298.
99   Georg Lukács, *The Ontology of Social Being: Labour*, 26.
100 Ibid., 39; cf. Georg Lukács, "The Ontological Foundations of Human Thinking and Action," 146.
101 Georg Lukács, *The Ontology of Social Being: Labour*, 32.
102 Ibid., 76.

fail. On the subjective side this means that the individual has to act and think in a "correct" way. With labor appears "the concept of 'Ought,' which in Hungarian we call 'Legyen.'"[103] Lukács describes this "should-be"[104] with the help of a concrete example: "Each individual movement in the process of sharpening, grinding, etc., must be considered correctly (i.e., must be based on a correct reflection of reality), be correctly oriented to the posited goal, correctly carried out by hand, etc. If this is not the case, then the posited causality can cease at any moment to be effective."[105]

Due to the constant feedback of the labor process, man sharpens his senses and abilities in a progressive way, the development – or unfolding – of human capacities. This development is not an individual one, but a historical development of the human species in general.

8 Lukács' Theory of History

Lukács' Anthropology is a non-essentialist one that is based on labor as its key feature. The teleological directedness of labor is the materialistic basis for the conscious life activity of human beings. Man is – in the strict sense presented before – an animal that organizes its metabolism with nature in the way of labor. In opposition to animals, mankind is a social and historical being in an emphatic sense: It is a "species being" (*Gattungswesen*). As mentioned before, the human being is conceived by Lukács as the ensemble of the social relations. Thus the historical development has two sides to it. It is at the same time the ontogenetic development of the species in general, but also the phylogenetic development of the individual.

We can once again refer to the brief notes in Lukács' autobiographical sketch, where he presents "the humanization of man as the content of the process of history."[106] This already implies a progressive directedness of history that connects general historical tendencies of the human species with individual development. To understand the latter, we have to take a closer look at these general historical tendencies first. The best overview of this is probably given in Lukács' Vienna paper of 1968.[107] Here Lukács presents "three [...]

---

103   Georg Lukács, *Record of a Life*, 77; cf. Georg Lukács, *The Ontology of Social Being: Labour*, 65–75.
104   Cf. Nicolas Tertulian, "Lukács' *Ontology*," 258.
105   Georg Lukács, *The Ontology of Social Being: Labour*, 33.
106   Georg Lukács, "Gelebtes Denken," 169.
107   A shorter and more or less similar description is given in a *Provisional Summary* given by Lukács as part of an interview with Hans Heinz Holz and Wolfgang Abendroth. Cf. Hans

directions in the evolution of economics"[108] that are rooted in the structure of labor itself.

The first one is, that "the duration of labor socially necessary for reproduction is steadily decreasing."[109] This core Marxist insight is easy to accept and Lukács adds nonchalant, that "this general tendency would be recognized by all as a fact."[110] It will reappear in the discussion of the realm of freedom and is noted in Lukács discussion of alienation as well, where he deems the appropriate organization of free time as a central problem for the development of unalienated forms of being.[111]

The second tendency is, that human reproduction has "become more and more socialized."[112] This analysis is given in Lukács' treatment of labor on several occasions. For Lukács it even defines Marx's genuine historicism: "'Pushing back the limits of nature' as the principle of progress."[113] Even if the "retreat of the natural boundary"[114] can never be complete, it is a core feature of human labor.

The third tendency – one that Joós does not bother to translate in detail – is the increase of globalization, a growing integration of smaller social entities into a world society, a unified humanity that is currently only economically realized in the form of the world market.[115]

Lukács uses these three tendencies of history to paint the historical process as progressing in a directional way. All these developments are presented in a positive way. The growth in free time is a progressive fact as well as the retreat of natural boundaries and globalization. Thus his theory is not compatible to essentialist or conservative approaches that try to identify alienation with technology or modernity. Lukács criticizes capitalist modernity and does so "without devolving into Romantic fantasy."[116] He does not ask for a more rudimentary – a more "natural" – way of labor or a regionalization of production. Instead he clearly takes position for the progressive tendencies in history

---

Heinz Holz et al. (ed.), *Conversations with Lukács*. Translated by David Fernbach. (London: Merlin Press, 1974), 119–123.
108   Georg Lukács, "The Ontological Foundations of Human Thinking and Action," 144.
109   Ibid.
110   Ibid.
111   Cf. Georg Lukács, *Zur Ontologie des gesellschaftlichen Seins*, vol. 2, 702.
112   Georg Lukács, "The Ontological Foundations of Human Thinking and Action," 144.
113   Georg Lukács, "Gelebtes Denken," 151.
114   Georg Lukács, *The Ontology of Social Being: Labour*, 34. Lukács lends this phrase by Marx and uses it steadily throughout his later works. Cf. Karl Marx, *Capital Volume 1*, 516.
115   Cf. Georg Lukács, "The Ontological Foundations of Human Thinking and Action," 144.
116   Michael J. Thompson, "Ontology and Totality: Reconstructing Lukács' Concept of Critical Theory." In Michael J. Thompson (ed.), *Georg Lukács Reconsidered*, 245.

as a "process of becoming more and more human,"[117] without ignoring that these tendencies currently only appear in distorted ways. He clearly states: "I believe in progress, even if it does not mean an overall improvement. The uneven nature of progress does not exclude, in spite of its negative aspects, positive sides."[118]

The unevenness of this progress can only become clear on the individual level. As mentioned before, the three general tendencies of history – rooted in labor – are only one side of a twofold historical progress. The development of productive forces can only be conducted by humans and thus is always accompanied by the development of concrete human beings as well.

Lukács once again refers to Marx as his crown witness: "[T]he forming of the five senses is a labour of the entire history of the world down to the present."[119] Lukács frames this "transformation of the working subject"[120] in terms of the unfolding of inherent possibilities. He considers the labor process as "essentially a systematic awakening of possibilities that were previously dormant in man as mere possibilities."[121] This systematic awakening is grounded in the master concept of labor: "There are very probably few movements used in labour, e.g., ways of handling an object, etc., that were known or used at all before the labour process began. Only through labour were these raised from mere possibilities into capacities that enabled ever new possibilities in man to become realities, in a permanent process of development."[122]

This dynamic is not only a mere possibility, but follows with necessity out of the value structure inherent in labor mentioned above. In the context of his chapter on "The Ontological Features of Alienation," he states, that the aim of the labor-process – the objectification – "is imperative unambiguous prescribed by the respective division of labour and the necessary capacities for this purpose, are evolved with necessity."[123] Thus he can conclude that "development and improvement belong to the essential and ontological characteristics of labor; that is, how labor perfects itself or calls into being a higher order of social structure."[124] As humans formulate (possible) aims to fulfill their

---

117   Georg Lukács, "The Ontological Foundations of Human Thinking and Action," 148.
118   Georg Lukács, "An Interview with George Lukács," 129.
119   Karl Marx, *Economic and Philosophic Manuscripts of 1844*, 302.
120   Georg Lukács, *The Ontology of Social Being: Labour*, 42.
121   Ibid., 123f.
122   Ibid., 124.
123   „[D]ie Vergegenständlichung [ist] von der jeweiligen Arbeitsteilung imperativ eindeutig vorgeschrieben [und entwickelt] daher die dazu notwendigen Fähigkeiten in den Menschen notwendig." Georg Lukács, *Zur Ontologie des gesellschaftlichen Seins*, vol. 2, 506.
124   Georg Lukács, "The Ontological Foundations of Human Thinking and Action," 141.

needs, they necessarily produce capacities to reach them, develop new and more complicated laboring processes and a more specialized division of labor.[125] This can be understood best, if we think again about Marx' definition of labor. His definition is accompanied by the forceful remark that labor is a demanding process that reacts upon the worker:

> He not only effects a change of form in the material on which he works, but he also realises a purpose of his own that gives the law to his modus operandi, and to which he must subordinate his will. And this subordination is no mere momentary act. Besides the exertion of the bodily organs, the process demands that, during the whole operation, the workman's will be steadily in consonance with his purpose. This means close attention. The less he is attracted by the nature of the work, and the mode in which it is carried on, and the less, therefore, he enjoys it as something which gives play to his bodily and mental powers, the more close his attention is forced to be.[126]

This description is presented in a negative way by Marx, but ought not to be confused with alienation. The permanent subordination of momentarily needs and desires is a painful act for sure, but also crucial for cultivation. Indeed, Lukács highlights the positive aspects of this subordination, the forming of the five senses and the accumulation of skills, the "growth of capacities"[127] that form the "indispensable ground"[128] for the development of higher forms of human personality. The process of labor is a permanent dialectical process between the laboring subject and nature. By that it is a steady learning-process in which the worker actively uses his skills and cunning to form a new – humanized – product out of mere nature. By that he gets a permanent feedback that culminates in a sharpening of skills that is necessary by the "penalty of ruin."[129] This initiates a progress that takes place on the individual level as

---

125 This holds even as Lukács notes that the tendencies can only be attested in retrospect and are not teleological in a strict sense. Cf. Georg Lukács, "The Ontological Foundations of Human Thinking and Action," 144. At another occasion, he states that "these three great processes can be established as objective economic tendencies, and that they should be considered as necessary ones." Hans Heinz Holz et al. (ed.), *Conversations with Lukács*, 123. Also cf. Nicolas Tertulian, "Lukács' *Ontology*," 260.
126 Karl Marx, *Capital Volume I*, 188.
127 Georg Lukács, "The Ontological Foundations of Human Thinking and Action," 146.
128 Ibid.
129 Karl Marx, *Capital Volume III*. Translated by Ernest Untermann et al. In Karl Marx and Friedrich Engels, *Collected Works. Volume 37*. (Electric Book: Lawrence and Wishart, 2010), 243.

well as at the socio-historical level. Practical knowledge of nature in the way of science and technology is passed on to further generations. This altogether allows for Lukács to analyze with Marx a "historical trend of development, an upward movement that for example develops the merely physiologically effective hunger to an already societal appetite."[130] Thus the development of capacities and skills – triggered necessarily by the development of productive forces – is the base of the development of human nature in an emphatic sense.

This idea is so crucial for Lukács, that he sees need for a differentiation of the labor-process into the objective process of objectification (*Vergegenständlichung*) and a simultaneous process of the externalization (*Entäußerung*) of a subject.[131] The idea of objectification has already been outlined. It is the realization of a teleological positing in reality. The means and objects of this objectification develop steadily as clearly indicated by the technological progress. The realm of objectification is therefore associated with a clear and measurable progress that proceeds with necessity based on an "ought" and valorization. It cannot be the realm of objectification, where alienation takes place; instead the developing possibilities of objectification are a space of possibilities (*Möglichkeitsraum*) for a higher developed human personality.

The process of externalization is the more crucial part for the phenomenon of alienation and not as easy to grasp as objectification. Lukács states that "alienation can only originate out of externalization."[132] Thus it is not surprising that the term externalization is introduced relatively late by Lukács. While he suggests that the laboring process is always an act of objectification and externalization at the same time, he does not refer to externalization in his description of the labor-process at all. The term occurs for the first time in the

---

130 "[E]ine Aufwärtsbewegung [...], die z. B. den bloß physiologisch wirkenden Hunger zu dem bereits gesellschaftlich gewordenen Appetit erhebt." Cf. Georg Lukács, *Zur Ontologie des gesellschaftlichen Seins*, vol. 2, 517. Another example is the development of sexuality from a means of reproduction to erotic. Ibid., 532.

131 Lukács remarks that this differentiation can be already seen in Marx description of the labour process, but that the terminological differentiation is applied by him. I am not convinced that externalization is the best possible term, as Marx uses externalization and alienation in similar ways. The English translators of the *Economic Philosophic Manuscripts* note precisely: "In this manuscript as in the other works published in this volume Marx frequently uses two similar German terms, 'Entäusserung' and 'Entfremdung,' to express the notion of 'alienation.' In the present edition the former is generally translated as 'alienation,' the latter as 'estrangement,' because in the later economic works (*Theories of Surplus-Value*) Marx himself used the word 'alienation' as the English equivalent of the term 'Entäusserung.'" Karl Marx, *Economic and Philosophic Manuscripts of 1844*, 588.

132 "[D]ie Entfremdung kann nur aus der Entäußerung entspringen." Georg Lukács, *Zur Ontologie des gesellschaftlichen Seins*, vol. 2, 354.

chapter on "The Realm of Ideas and Ideology" where he discerns between "the objectification of the object and the externalization of the subject, which constitute the foundation of human theory and praxis as a homogeneous process."[133] He immediately adds at this first occurrence of the term, that the importance of externalization is deeply connected to the problem of alienation.

This does not mean for him that both phenomena are identical.[134] Instead he underlines, "that ontological, the origin of alienation out of externalization does not remotely mean an unambiguous and unconditional cohesiveness of both ontological complexes: specific forms of alienation can only originate out of externalization, those can very well be and act without originating alienations."[135] In fact, externalization can be the origin of un-alienated forms of human personality as well. It is the development of externalization that allows for the raising of the problem of the humanization of man and the ideal of a species being that is not speechless anymore.[136] Externalization is therefore potentially also the "vehicle for the development of the subject."[137] This argument becomes clearer if we keep in mind, that externalization encompasses the whole subjective side of the labor-process, thus also the development of the five senses and needs.[138] At the same time, this idea of externalization allows for a more qualified definition of alienation that is extracted by Tertulian:

> The non-coincidence between objectification and exteriorization is pursued this time in the interior of the act of exteriorization itself, postulated as the possibility of a contradiction between the development of qualities (of capacities of the individual which can accumulate themselves in

---

133 "[D]ie Vergegenständlichung des Objekts und die Entäußerung des Subjekts, die als einheitlicher Prozeß die Grundlage von menschlicher Praxis und Theorie bilden." Ibid., 353.
134 This usage is in conflict to Marx' terminology, see my footnote 132.
135 "[D]aß seinsmäßig der Ursprung der Entfremdung aus der Entäußerung keineswegs eine eindeutige und un bedingte Zusammengehörigkeit beider Seinskomplexe bedeutet: bestimmte Formen der Entfremdung können zwar nur aus der Entäußerung entstehen, diese kann aber sehr wohl sein und wirken, ohne Entfremdungen hervorzubringen." Ibid., 355.
136 Cf. ibid., 362.
137 "[D]ie Entäußerung [ist]das Vehikel der Entwicklung des Subjekts." Ibid., 361.
138 Lukács' terminological usage of externalization is not as clear as desirable. He seems to discern between externalization and the retroaction of externalization mediated through its objectification. Cf. ibid., 364; 507; 583. This usage is so nuanced, that Benseler comes to a definition of externalization as the retroaction of the act of labor onto the subject. Cf. Frank Benseler, "Nachwort," 748. The definition helps to understand the complex of externalization but is unprecise as Lukács usually refers to the repercussion of externalization. Thus externalization can not be understood as the repercussion itself.

heterogeneous fashion) and their synthesis in the homogeneous unity of the personality.[139]

Without this possibility, the described process could easily be understood as a success story. The development of productive forces proceeds necessarily on a socio-historical level. With the concurrent accumulation of skills and work experience of the whole human species, new skills, qualities and even qualities of senses arise and allow for a potentially more and more perfect form of society and humanity. The concept of labor allows identifying a general historical progress that is mirrored on the subjective level.

As shown before, Lukács would indeed agree to an optimistic interpretation of history. He believes in the idea of progress but confines this progress to an economic or technical level. He still does not treat this progress lightly. It is in fact the most important development and the indispensable ground for the development of the "real unfolding of individuality."[140] The core problem for Lukács is that this potentiality remains in latency. It is exactly the task of his concept of alienation to explain why this realization does not take place.

9   The Sacrifice of History

Lukács has a conception of history as progressing, but sees an "uneven nature of progress."[141] To understand this "brutal unevenness"[142] (*brutale Ungleichheit*) it is important to see how Lukács conceives the connection of the general historical progress and its connection to the individual. Lukács notes that the general "development of the process of labour and the broadening of the fields of activity [has] still other indirect consequences: the emergence and unfolding of human personality."[143]

The core argument here is that the historical development of mankind is the base for higher forms of human personality and the emergence of personality altogether. Where the evolving of human skills and capacities is a necessary trend, it is important to note that the unfolding of human personality is presented as an indirect consequence. Thus the unfolding of human personality does not necessary follow out of the historical progress like the human

---

139   Nicolas Tertulian, "Lukács' *Ontology*," 264. I follow more recent translations by translating *Entäußerung* as externalization instead of exteriorization.
140   Georg Lukács, "Gelebtes Denken," 169.
141   Cf. Georg Lukács, "An Interview with George Lukács," 129.
142   Cf. Georg Lukács, *Zur Ontologie des gesellschaftlichen Seins*, vol. 1, 190.
143   Georg Lukács, "The Ontological Foundations of Human Thinking and Action," 146.

capacities. The historical progress on the ontogenetic and phylogenetic level is only the "indispensable ground"[144] for the development of higher forms of human personality, not its guarantee.

This idea is best presented in a passage by Marx that Lukács uses extensively.[145] In a passage of *Capital III*, Marx introduces the terminology of a realm of freedom and a realm of necessity. The realm of (physical) necessity encompasses the human needs as well in its rudimentary as in its historically developed forms. It is therefore the ineluctable ground for the realm of freedom. In the realm of necessity, freedom

> can only consist in socialised man, the associated producers, rationally regulating their interchange with Nature, bringing it under their common control, instead of being ruled by it as by the blind forces of Nature; and achieving this with the least expenditure of energy and under conditions most favourable to, and worthy of, their human nature.[146]

Even if Marx argues in anthropological and moral terms, when he defines this kind of freedom with conditions that are the most worthy of (*am würdigsten*) and most favorable to (*am adäquatesten*) the human nature, this realm of necessity is even in its best form not the human realm in its emphatic sense. It is only beyond that realm – be it as effective and favorable to mankind as possible – that the true species being of humanity – the realm of freedom – begins: "Beyond it [the realm of necessity – A.G.] begins that development of human energy which is an end in itself, the true realm of freedom, which, however, can blossom forth only with this realm of necessity as its basis."[147]

This idea is clearly compatible to Lukács concept of human development. It argues in a strict sense that the realm of necessity is the eternal basis for the human race, but that it has not to be confused with the human nature. Labor to fulfill ones needs is not the fulfillment of man's capacities; it is only a necessary means for the actual realm of humanity. In a short sentence Marx even describes the reduction of the realm of necessity as a condition for the blossoming of the realm of freedom: "The shortening of the working day is its basic prerequisite."[148] Lukács highlights exactly this by adding, that the shortening

---

144 Ibid.
145 Cf. Georg Lukács, *Zur Ontologie des gesellschaftlichen Seins*, vol. 1, 683f.; also cf. Georg Lukács, *Zur Ontologie des gesellschaftlichen Seins*, vol. 2, 118; 152f.; 365; 457ff.; 476; 479; 486; 646.
146 Karl Marx, *Capital Volume III*, 807.
147 Ibid.
148 Ibid.

of socially necessary labor time, thanks to the development of the productive forces is the fundamental condition for the realm of freedom. Thus the historical development of productive forces and the concurrent development of human capacities presented before, make for the necessary ground for real human individuality. Lukács – and Marx – emphasize, that this is only a possibility and that this progress is paid for by harsh labor-conditions under capitalism. Capitalism and the whole prehistory of mankind only allow for the development of technology and capacities but usually not for the higher development of human personalities. Instead "the higher development of individuality is [...] only achieved by a historical process during which individuals are sacrificed."[149] This price is not only paid in the past, but is still a core aspect of present times. In his Vienna paper, he reaffirms this estimate in a general statement: "Nowadays, it seems as if the constantly increasing differentiation and development of capacities were the direct obstacle of becoming a person and the vehicle of the alienation of human beings."[150] Under capitalism, the "tendency to freedom of man is actually unfreedom."[151]

Here, Lukács does not give a clear analysis how capitalism actually turns the necessary development towards freedom into real unfreedom, but only refers to Marx in general. Thus we can assume that Lukács does not see the reason for this turn in a "wily" plan by "evil" corporations. The unfreedom of capitalism has its basis in the form of capitalist production itself, which is profit-making. Here we can apply Marx' analysis of the form of capitalist production: "The production of surplus value is the chief end and aim of capitalist production."[152] This leads to a "restless never-ending process of profit-making."[153] The capitalistic mode of production follows a strictly inhuman end-in-itself in so far as it coincides only randomly with the needs of human beings. By that, capitalism degrades the "spontaneous, free activity to a means" and "makes man's species-life a means to his physical existence."[154] This early definition of alienation

---

149   Karl Marx, *Economic Manuscript of 1861–63*. Translated by Emile Burns, Renate Simpson and Jack Cohen. In Karl Marx and Friedrich Engels, *Collected Works. Volume 31*. (Electric Book: Lawrence and Wishart, 2010), 348. Lukács quotes this passage on several occasions. Cf. Georg Lukács, *Zur Ontologie des gesellschaftlichen Seins*, vol. 1, 595; Georg Lukács, *Zur Ontologie des gesellschaftlichen Seins*, vol. 2, 459; 503.
150   It is important to note that Lukács does not argue here, that the evolvement of skills and capacities is itself the reason for an alienated human personality, it only *seems* to be the reason for this aberration.
151   "[...] daß die so entstehende Tendenz zur Freiheit des Menschen im Kapitalismus faktisch eine Unfreiheit ist." Georg Lukács, *Zur Ontologie des gesellschaftlichen Seins*, vol. 1, 157.
152   Karl Marx, *Capital Volume 1*, 238.
153   Ibid., 164.
154   Karl Marx, *Economic and Philosophic Manuscripts of 1844*, 277.

given by Marx implies a form of free activity that is not a mere means but an end-in-itself. It was already quoted, that Marx' definition of the true realm of freedom is that of the "development of human energy which is an end in itself."[155]

The philosophic idea of an end-in-itself is crucial for Lukács' argument as well as for Marx.' It is powerful as it applies the idea of an end-in-itself to the law of production under capitalism as well as to the realm of freedom. The two opposites – the alienated pre-history of capitalism and the realized true history and humanity under communism[156] – are both characterized as societies that follow an end-in-itself. The latter develops human capacities as the ultimate goal, whereas the first produces for the sake of production. Once again we encounter the idea that capitalism lays the groundwork for true humanity. In some way, capitalism even develops the ideal of human activity as an end-in-itself in its twisted, narrow form:

> In fact, however, if the narrow bourgeois form is peeled off, what is wealth if not the universality of the individual's needs, capacities, enjoyments, productive forces, etc., produced in universal exchange; what is it if not the full development of human control over the forces of nature – over the forces of so-called Nature, as well as those of his own nature? What is wealth if not the absolute unfolding of man's creative abilities, without any precondition other than the preceding historical development, which makes the totality of this development – i.e. the development of all human powers as such, not measured by any previously given yardstick – an end-in-itself, through which he does not reproduce himself in any specific character, but produces his totality, and does not seek to remain something he has already become, but is in the absolute movement of becoming?[157]

This is powerful as it shows that capitalism already begets the idea of true human development. Neither Marx nor Lukács refer to a utopic dream or an obscure nature of human; instead it is history itself that produces this ideal and even the requirements for the objectification of this goal in latency. The

---

155   Karl Marx, *Capital Volume III*, 807.
156   Cf. Georg Lukács, *Zur Ontologie des gesellschaftlichen Seins*, vol. 1, 210.
157   Karl Marx, *Outlines of the Critique of Political Economy*. Translated by Ernst Wangermann. In Karl Marx and Friedrich Engels, *Collected Works. Volume 28*. (Electric Book: Lawrence and Wishart, 2010), 411f. Lukács quotes the complete passage. Cf. Georg Lukács, *Zur Ontologie des gesellschaftlichen Seins*, vol. 1, 620.

development of the productive forces as an end-in-itself is the progressive function of capitalism that Lukács and Marx defend against regressive criticism:

> Ricardo, rightly for his time, regards the capitalist mode of production as the most advantageous for production in general, as the most advantageous for the creation of wealth. He wants production for the sake of production and this with good reason. To assert, as sentimental opponents of Ricardo's did, that production as such is not the object, is to forget that production for its own sake means nothing but the development of human productive forces, in other words the development of the richness of human nature as an end in itself.[158]

Passages like these bear two further implications. First, they imply a specific historical development as the necessary condition for free humanity. It is exactly this passage where Marx adds that "at first the development of the capacities of the human species takes place at the cost of the majority of human individuals and whole human classes."[159] This is put in terms of historical necessity and followed by the assertion that "in the end it breaks through this contradiction and coincides with the development of the individual; the higher development of individuality is thus only achieved by a historical process during which individuals are sacrificed, for the interests of the species in the human kingdom."[160]

As shown before, Lukács follows this line of argumentation but leaves a shallow messianic trace. As alienation is a phenomenon strictly concerned with individuals, they themselves can overcome it. In great art and philosophy as well as in acts directed at higher forms of species being are permanent possibilities to overcome alienation or at least foreshadow forms of un-alienated being: "[G]reat philosophy and great art (as well as the attitudes and behaviors of exemplary individuals) work in the direction of a species in itself."[161] Second, the problem of real individuality reoccurs. Marx only hints at the question how the "development of all human powers as such"[162] looks like. There is good reason that Marx – and with him Lukács – refuse to give a clear definition of such forms of real individuality. Still, they are the implicit yardstick to determine what forms of human being can be considered alienated.

---

158   Karl Marx, *Economic Manuscript of 1861–63*, 347.
159   Ibid.
160   Ibid.
161   Georg Lukács, "The Ontological Foundations of Human Thinking and Action," 148.
162   Karl Marx, *Outlines of the Critique of Political Economy*, 411f.

10 The Universal Species Being

As pointed out, Lukács later idea of alienation depends on an idea of undistorted humanity that is historically produced in latency. The goal of such progress remains relatively unclear. It is mostly formulated in negativity. Alienation is a form of particularity, a one-sided, uneven formation of individual personality. The freedom to be realized cannot be determined in the state of unfreedom, therefore Lukács shies back from a restricting, positive definition of the goal. Nevertheless he occasionally hints at such forms of real individuality. This is not only important as it helps to clarify what alienation is, but because a vague knowledge of these forms is important to overcome alienation and thus to reach a higher developed form of society.

Lukács' core idea of a real species being is tightly connected to an idea of universality. He refers to universality in to ways. True individuality is first a well-rounded development of human individuality. The real individual is not particular anymore; true individuals are not divided in an intellectual and physical part[163] or defined by a particular capability. Instead a real individual should be – in the words of Marx – a "fully developed individual"[164] (*total entwickeltes Individuum*). This is a reverberation of the humanistic ideal of a renaissance man that seems like an extrinsic argument but can again be backed up by the development of the productive forces. The fully developed individual is not presented by Marx as a mere ideal, but as a requirement of modern production:

> Modern industry, indeed, compels society, under penalty of death, to replace the detail-worker of to-day, crippled by life-long repetition of one and the same trivial operation, and thus reduced to the mere fragment of a man, by the fully developed individual, fit for a variety of labours, ready to face any change of production.[165]

Another argument by Marx goes in the same direction. Like Lukács he attests alienated forms of labor. In 1847 he writes: "What characterises the division of labour inside modern society is that it engenders specialities, specialists, and with them craft-idiocy [*Fachidiotismus*]."[166] Lukács uses the terminology of

---

163 Cf. Georg Lukács, *Zur Ontologie des gesellschaftlichen Seins*, vol. 2, 622.
164 Cf. Karl Marx, *Capital Volume 1*, 490.
165 Ibid.
166 Karl Marx, "The Poverty of Philosophy. Answer to the Philosophy of Poverty by M. Proudhon." Translated by Frida Knight. In Karl Marx and Friedrich Engels, *Collected Works. Volume 6*. (Electric Book: Lawrence and Wishart, 2010), 190.

craft-idiocy[167] in his *Ontology*, but makes no use of the optimistic tendencies that Marx adds:

> What characterises the division of labour in the automatic workshop is that labour has there completely lost its specialized character. But the moment every special development stops, the need for universality, the tendency towards an integral development of the individual begins to be felt. The automatic workshop wipes out specialists and craft-idiocy.[168]

The second usage of universality concerns the relation of the human individual to its species being. True individuality is characterized by directedness towards species being. As Lukács notes in his last notes: "Progress towards species being in individual life represents the true convergence of two real but inseparable paths of development,"[169] referring to the ontogenetic and phylogenetic development. True history is only possible "if both poles of social being, man and society, cease to act in a spontaneous antagonistic way onto each other: When the reproduction of society nurtures the humanity [*Menschsein*] of man, when the individual realizes itself consciously as species being."[170] This idea is very prominent in Lukács' thinking and is not restricted to his theory of alienation. Labor itself is "the objective elevation of particular man to its species being [*Gattungsmäßige*]."[171] History once more implies the ideal of a perfection of the species being that is realized in each individual. History is concerned with the "development of man to a real species being."[172] Such development is an objective one that has to be realized actively and consciously.

Lukács phrases large parts of his chapter on alienation in such terms of species being. Here he differentiates in Hegelian terminology between the species

---

167   Cf. Georg Lukács, *Zur Ontologie des gesellschaftlichen Seins*, vol. 2, 718.
168   Karl Marx, "The Poverty of Philosophy. Answer to the Philosophy of Poverty by M. Proudhon," 190.
169   Georg Lukács, "Gelebtes Denken," 169.
170   "Diese Vorgeschichte, die Geschichte des Menschwerdens des Menschen, des zum adäquaten Gattungsausdruck Werdens der Gesellschaft, kann nur zu Ende gehen, wenn die beiden Pole des gesellschaftlichen Seins, menschliches Individuum und Gesellschaft, aufhören, aufeinander spontan antagonistisch zu wirken: Wenn die Reproduktion der Gesellschaft das Menschsein des Menschen fördert, wenn das Individuum in seinem individuellen Leben sich bewußt als Glied der Gattung verwirklicht." Georg Lukács, *Zur Ontologie des gesellschaftlichen Seins*, vol. 2, 362.
171   "[D]ie objektive Erhöhung des partikularen Menschen ins Gattungsmäßige." Ibid., 161.
172   "Entwicklung des Menschen zu einer echten Gattungsmäßigkeit." Ibid., 514.

being in latency as the "species in-itself" (*Gattungswesen an sich*) and the possible, currently unrealized[173] "species for-itself" (*Gattungswesen für sich*).[174] According to Tertulian, this "tension between what he [Lukács – A.G.] regards as the two fundamental levels of the human species: the human species-in-itself and the human species-for-itself" is even "the center of gravity of Lukács' reflections."[175]

Alienation can then be reformulated as the difference between the possible species being for-itself and the realized level of species being in-itself on a subjective level. The different forms of alienation then present obstacles for the realization of a higher developed form of species being. It is the task for every single individual to resist against such forms: "Species being for-itself utters itself first and foremost in everyday life as individual discontent with the respective prevailing species being in itself, occasionally as a direct uprising against it."[176]

Such an uprising and directedness towards species being for-itself is the best remedy that Lukács prescribes: "Above all, what matters here is that both society and individual men reject those tendencies that threaten this process of becoming more and more human."[177] Even if Lukács is mostly concerned with general historical tendencies and the revolutionary struggle for a better, more human society, the problem of alienation is deeply connected to highly developed forms of ideology. In the end, it is extraordinary philosophy, art and moral behavior of exemplary individuals, that most clearly anticipates a higher developed form of species being.[178] It can even be supposed that this

---

173 Cf. ibid., 524.
174 English articles sometimes confuse both forms of species being and occasionally identify the species being in-itself (*an sich*) with the higher developed form that Lukács describes as for-itself (*für sich*). This error is likely initiated by Joós. In his translation of the *Vienna* paper he translates that "great philosophy and great art (as well as the attitudes and behaviors of exemplary individuals) work in the direction of a species in itself." Georg Lukács, "The Ontological Foundations of Human Thinking and Action," 148. Joós even gives the German term *Gattungsmäßigkeit an sich* in parentheses where Lukács does not use this term in this sentence at all. By that Joós deforms the argument and errantly introduces the species-being in itself as the higher developed species being.
175 Nicolas Tertulian, "Lukács' *Ontology*," 264.
176 "Die Gattungsmäßigkeit für sich äußert sich vorerst und zumeist im Alltagsleben als individuelle Unzufriedenheit mit der jeweils herrschenden Gattungsmäßigkeit an sich, zuweilen auch als direkte Auflehnung dagegen." Georg Lukács, *Zur Ontologie des gesellschaftlichen Seins*, vol. 2, 524.
177 Georg Lukács, "The Ontological Foundations of Human Thinking and Action," 148.
178 Cf. ibid.

directedness towards species being for-itself is the core for Lukács' unfinished ethics.[179]

11 Conclusion

Lukács' later theory is not a vein of gold for the research of alienation. It does not give a detailed and applicable analysis of modern forms of alienation despite its exposed position in Lukács final work and its voluminous extent. Lukács does not conduct a systematic social study, nor do his few examples suffice to understand what alienation exactly composes of. Still, Lukács later work is worth noticing, as its strength lies in a relatively clear and plain foundation for the concept of alienation. Without mystifications, alienation is now simply defined as the difference between the historical possible development of a real individuality and current – alienated, thus deformed and debased – realizations of human personalities. Like in Marx it is an outcry against forms of social being that do not treat human activity as an end-in-itself. This legitimate and necessary outcry is brought forward by Lukács with cautiousness. He does not present us with the messianistic solution of an identical subject–object. Instead he relies on his large ontological framework, especially his concept of history. Lukács theory of alienation still has to deal with the problem, that it is dependent of a concept of an un-alienated, wholesome real form of being. It fulfills this demand by referring to a goal that is given and realized by history itself, although in mere latency. His twofold theory of history that encompasses general and individual development is convincing and allows for the identification of an immanent goal. Here, the concept of alienation is crucial to avoid simple teleology. Even if Lukács occasionally runs into the danger of legitimizing sacrifices in the name of progress, he emphasizes the daily need to overcome a form of production that forces such sacrifices.

Lukács general framework of history does not rely on many assumptions. If one agrees on the Marxist backdrop and the focus on material praxis, Lukács conclusions are easy to accept. Problems occur, when this theory is bodied out and applied to concrete societal or political phenomena. This is particularly true for Lukács concept of alienation. Even his concise later definition of alienation leaves ample room for interpretation and needs to complement the general theory of history with humanist assumptions.

---

179 Cf. Michael J. Thompson, "Ontology and Totality: Reconstructing Lukács' Concept of Critical Theory," 244; cf. Claudius Vellay, "Die Entfremdung aus Sicht der Lukácsschen Ontologie," 178f.

Lukács' humanist understanding of Marx demands a realization of communism that allows for the growth of each individual. By that, it is a forceful corrective against alienated forms of socialism and is still helpful to discern Marx' idea of socialism and communism from its historically "realized" forms. It keeps the idea of a radical new form of social being alive and delegates this task to each and every one without forgetting about the overwhelming power of cultural habits and economic reality.

Acknowledgements

I would like to thank Leo Niehorster-Cook for proofreading and extensive advice and Yoonoh Kye for helpful remarks.

CHAPTER 6

Lukács' Late Appropriation of Hegel's Philosophy: The Ontology of Materialist Dialectics and the Complexities of Labor as Teleological Positing

Michalis Skomvoulis

1 Late Lukács and Hegel's Philosophy: What Is at Stake

The discussion of Hegel's presence in Marxist philosophy and the project of historical materialism in general has been one of the most heated, antinomical and ultimately – in terms of philosophy – decisive discussions in the history of this theoretical and political tradition. From a certain point of view, the attitude of the Marxist theoreticians before the Hegelian dialectic defined their positioning in the different tendencies of Marxism, thus having explicitly political consequences. After the disdain that the first generation of Marxist theorists manifested against Hegel's philosophy (encouraging scientism and evolutionism), it was Lukács himself with his emblematic *History and Class Consciousness* (from now on HCC) which posited the "Hegel question" as an unavoidable question of any theoretical Marxist discussion.[1] According to a well-established distinction it was precisely the attitude adopted for or against Hegelian dialectics that categorized the different trends of materialist-critical thought as either "critical theory" or "scientific (and later structural) Marxism."[2] It goes without saying that Lukács was always the central figure amidst these discussions, with his personal theoretical shifts functioning as general indicators of the antinomies and frequently of the impasses of this historical movement during the 20th century.

In any case, Lukács never abandoned his interest on Hegel during the evolution of his thought (leaving aside his "young" phase before HCC). During this evolution we can discern three phases each of them marked by an important

---

[1] On the relative lack of interest of the first generation of these theorists for the Hegelian philosophy and on the importance of Lukács' intervention on this subject as a gesture of renewal for Marxist philosophy, see Perry Anderson, *Considerations on Western Marxism*. (London: NLB, 1976), Chapter 3.

[2] On the importance of Hegelian dialectic for this division, see Alvin Gouldner, *The Two Marxisms: Contradictions and Anomalies in the Development of Theory*. (London: Macmillan, 1980), p. 71–77.

intervention concerning Hegel's philosophy: In his first "revolutionary" period of the HCC, it is precisely the introduction of Hegelian dialectics that will distance his view from naturalist-evolutionist certainties of official Marxist doctrine, introducing the exigencies of a "critical theory" based on the immanent contradictions of socio-historical world. The second phase is undoubtedly marked by his (forced!) engagement with Stalinism and the soviet type of philosophy. Nevertheless, it is during this very phase that Lukács will write his voluminous study on *The Young Hegel*, a book which, first of all, can legitimately be (and has been) considered as high-quality Hegel scholarship. Engaging into a detailed polemic against the metaphysical-theological interpretations of Hegel (popular during the first three decades of twentieth century), Lukács introduces pioneering insights about the development of Hegel's thought, favoring the importance of his socio-economic studies and the discovery of the historical structures of modern society as decisive for the emergence of dialectical method as a new form of philosophy. Finally, the final phase of his thought (developed in the slightly safer and free environment of the post-stalinist era) dominates his great project on the *Ontology of Social Being* (from now on, *Ontology*). For the constitution of this project the appeal to Hegel's philosophy plays again a fundamental role, not only for the construction of his general theoretical context – as the initial book-length chapter on "Hegel's false and his genuine ontology" testifies – but also for the more concrete parts of his social ontology, with recurrent references to Hegel's work being placed at crucial points of his argument. It is interesting that although this last account of Hegelian philosophy can be considered as Lukács' most mature – and rich in determinations – appropriation of dialectics (given that it integrates, as we will see, important reflections on the *Science of Logic*), it remains almost unstudied, following more or less the general faith of Lukács' last great systematic work.

This continuous interest for the study of Hegel's philosophy indicates consequently that Lukács never doubted the importance of Hegelian dialectics as the philosophical presupposition of historical materialism (resisting thus the existential, Nietzschean, analytical or other temptations, very common to postwar critical theory). In contrast, he worked through the difficulties and the contradictions of a method that corresponded to the exigencies of historical materialism as a critical theory of the socio-historical world, namely a method which bases itself on the *real* historical dynamics. Already in his essay on the "reification and the consciousness of the proletariat," he praised Hegel for laying the foundation of this method which can thematize praxis as the "genesis" of the historical new.[3] And if these references, within the framework of HCC,

---

3 HCC. Translated by Rodney Livingston. (London: Merlin Press, 1971), 143–146.

remain undeveloped and hidden behind an appeal to a partially metaphysical consciousness of a revolutionary class subject, it is to the aforementioned late appropriation of Hegel that we should turn our attention in order to find a much more developed and conceptually demanding version of what Lukács wanted to realize throughout his work: a project where the methodological foundation of historical materialism can be articulated *as a critical social ontology*.

An initial interest of this paper is to examine to which extend the engagement with Hegel in *Ontology* presents elements of continuity with the problematics of Lukács' previous treatments, but also to which extend there is such a differentiation that permits us to speak of a new philosophical view on Hegel. First of all, *Ontology* marks a clear differentiation with the elements of a certain naturalist (and mechanistic) materialism, present in the *Young Hegel*. The insistence of *Ontology* on the exclusively social character of its ontological assertions and the praise of Hegel in that direction, states a reevaluation of Hegelian thought as a warranty for the autonomy of the socio-historical, without reducing it to its "idealist limits."[4] Furthermore, labor (the fundamental concept of social ontology, whose philosophical origins are to be found for Lukács in Aristotle and principally in Hegel) is not presented as the major gateway for the constitution of a quasi-transcendent subject[5] (as in HCC, according to its critics) but rather as this dynamic socio-historical specificity which drives towards a teleological social positing more and more mediated and complex in terms of its structures; consequently, more and more differentiated and contradictory in terms of the *social alternatives* that society has to posit as its explicit goals. In contrast to the revolutionary impulse of the HCC (inspired explicitly by the "bacchantic orgy" of the equally driven by revolutionary inspiration *Phenomenology of Spirit*),[6] the project of *Ontology*, through its materialist insistence on the non-reducibility of social complexity and especially of social alternatives, leaves open an important space for the political choices that society as a whole has to make. If for Lukács of the HCC the dialectical

---

4   There are plenty of passages in the *Young Hegel*, where Lukács denounces the "idealist limits" of Hegel's philosophy, externally opposing him to the classics of Marxism. Nevertheless, already in this works, he makes the important observation that Hegel's idealist "self-deception" was a necessary condition for the emergence of dialectical method, see Georg Lukács, *The Young Hegel*. Trans. Rodney Livingston. (London: Merlin Press, 1975), 283. In the *Ontology* the critique of Hegel's idealism continues, but on a significantly different basis, much more internal to Hegel's philosophy itself as we will see.
5   A subject more of a Fichtean than of a Hegelian kind, Tom Rockmore, *Irrationalism. Lukács and the Marxist view of reason.* (Philadelphia: Temple University Press, 1992), 114.
6   For that reference HCC, 145.

transformation of the objectively projected labor to the unified proletarian subject contained thus a certainty of being the "truth" of the dynamics of Hegelian dialectic[7] (as against its systemic reification) for Lukács of the *Ontology*, the differentiated social objectivity based on the positing activity of labor, designs a subject that can never be complete: it constantly presupposes a preserved divide between a subject and an object,[8] whilst simultaneously the permanent presence of a certain natural materiality as the necessary condition of social ontology does not eliminate the fact that this material presence is always noematically conceived within the context of the social world; immersing in the final instance this materiality to the dynamic of social contradictions. It is this centrality of the social that will define *Ontology* as the distinctive phase of Lukács' thought that we can call *critical materialism*, equally differentiating it from the historicism present in the HCC and the mechanistic tendencies of his intermediate "orthodox" period. Additionally, it is this centrality that distances his project from any kind of criticism claiming that his appeal to ontology signifies a heyday of his metaphysical (or even religious!) tendency.[9] As we argue, for the constitution of this materialist and simultaneously dialectical-critical social ontology, a crucial role should be attributed to the mode of his appropriation of Hegelian philosophy.

At this point, and before proceeding to a more detailed account of late Lukács' Hegelianism, we can summarize the two main subjects that come up with this reconstruction:

a) Firstly we should consider the status of Lukács' interpretation of Hegel's philosophy, especially within the framework of Marxist tradition. Lukács was not the first critical theorist who tried to link the ontological element in Hegel's thought with a certain conception of historicity.[10] However, we

---

7   For moments of this transformation in HCC, see HCC, 170–172, 177, 188–190.
8   The negation of an identity between subject and object in the *Ontology* constitutes a crucial point of the critique against Hegel's tendency towards the autonomization of Logic, see Georg Lukács, *The Ontology of Social Being: Hegel*. Trans. David Fernbach. (London: Merlin Press, 1980), 28–29. At the same time, the preservation of the subject–object divide will be proved to be product and at the same time indispensable condition for the constitution of the teleological force of labor, Georg Lukács, *The Ontology of Social Being: Labour*. Trans. David Fernbach. (London: Merlin Press, 1980), 24.
9   For these objections against *Ontology* which frequently came from Lukács' disciples or other authors close to "critical theory," see Sergio Lessa, "Lukács' Ontology: a return to medieval ontology?" *Jaargang* 45, nummer 4 I, Winter 2011. We are generally in agreement with Lessa's effort to respond to these criticisms highlighting the active side of essence-formation through the determinations of reflection (*Reflexionsbestimmungen*) and underlining the *radical historicity* of essence in Lukács' ontological conception.
10 We have particularly in mind Marcuse's initial effort to relate a dynamic conception of the ontological element in Hegel with historicity, where at the same time nonetheless he always conditioned this relation with a highly metaphysical general understanding of being

can admit that the particularity of his intervention is to be found on his insistence about the non-metaphysical, socially confined and historically determined employment of Hegelian dialectical motives. Additionally, we should underline that this interpretation does not limit itself to the hermeneutically "convenient" texts of the Jena period, resulting in the historical contents of the *Phenomenology of Spirit* (a period in generally considered by critical theorists as being more close to real contradictions and respecting "living history," against the later fixation of dialectic in the system).[11] Without abandoning the priority of *Realphilosophie* over the Logic, Lukács claims a highly original appropriation of Hegel's *logical* motives: his interpretation integrates a reconstruction of crucial parts of Hegelian *Logic*, where the *logic of essence* (and especially the *determinations of reflection*) takes the privileged role of contextualizing conceptually the dynamics of labor's positing activity, offering simultaneously the materialist basis for an interpretation and critique of Hegel's Logic, orientating the latter toward the exigencies of social reality.

b) Secondly, it is equally important to address the question of whether Lukács' conception of dialectics in the *Ontology* produces consequences as a kind of intervention within the fundamental problems of historical materialism and its conception of capitalist society. As we will see, Lukács' late Hegelianism offers a highly encompassing response to one of the most important dualistic problems of historical materialism: how to conceive the autonomy of social structures in a developed capitalist society without abandoning the *unifying dynamic* of economic factor. As implied Lukács' Hegelian inspiration to conceive labor as the specifically social teleological positing of social structures proposes an integral answer to this fundamental question.

Before considering the integration of Hegel's philosophy to the argument of the *Ontology*, we shall first reflect on how Lukács recognized in the development

---

in Hegel as "living mobility," see Herbert Marcuse, *Hegel's Ontology and the Theory of Historicity*, trans. Seyla Benhabib. Studies in Contemporary German Social Thought (Cambridge, Mass.: MIT Press, 1987), 228–249.

11 "As we know, spirit, the substratum of his philosophy, is not intended to be a separate, subjective idea; it is intended to be real, and its movement to be real history. Nevertheless, with incomparable tact, even the later chapters of the *Phenomenology* refrain from brutally compacting the science of the experience of consciousness and that of human history into one another. The two spheres hover, touching, alongside one another. In the *Logic*, in accordance with its thematics and no doubt also under the pressure of the later Hegel's increasing rigidity, external history is swallowed up in the inner historicity of the exposition of the categories." Theodor Adorno, *Hegel: Three Studies*. Trans. Shierry Weber Nicholsen. (Cambridge: MIT Press, 1993), 142.

of Hegel's philosophy, the privileged framework in order to thematize the dynamic social structures of capitalism and the particularity of *modern labor processes* within them. For this purpose we will initially turn our attention to the *Young Hegel*.

2 Labor and History in the *Young Hegel*: The Hegelian Ontological Transformation of Traditional Philosophical Categories

The *Young Hegel*, the longest text of Lukács on Hegel, was written (in Moscow) under peculiar theoretical and political circumstances: first of all, we should take into account the concrete limitations posited by the Stalinist dogmatism. Thus, Lukács' perspective in this book unavoidably reflects the rigid general intellectual environment of the Soviet Union at the epoch.[12] On the other hand, we have to consider the influence of young Marx's humanism on Lukács through the recently discovered Paris *Manuscripts*. The result of these two heterogeneous influences is indeed pretty peculiar: Lukács interprets Hegel's philosophical development following a materialistic philosophical anthropology, taken from the Manuscripts, while at the same time this anthropology is distilled through the filter of the naturalist and mechanistic evolutionism, dominant in his intellectual surrounding. Lukács' perspective, presents this twofold pressure, especially in his interpretation of the totality of *Phenomenology of Spirit*, where the movement of the figures of consciousness translated as the "externalization" of forces of humanity in history, coexists with the call to take into account the objectivity of the development of productive forces, which Hegel only partially and inadequately (due to his "idealism") can thematize.

Lukács' book remains, after all, extremely rich in content and well researched, yielding important results, given its lucid polemic against irrationalism and what he aptly calls "reactionary" appropriations of Hegelian philosophy. Our reconstruction, however, will be limited in finding these elements that already prefigure the later aspects of the appropriation of Hegelian philosophy in the *Ontology*, which are already to be found in the *Young Hegel*. The conception that especially has to be stressed is undoubtedly the way Lukács attempts, through Hegel's texts of the Jena period, to integrate the labor

---

12   In many places of the book Stalin is proclaimed a great dialectician (among Marx, Engels and necessary Lenin), even to the point of being considered as the one who with Lenin "liberated historical materialism from this mechanical vulgarization [of the Second International] and restored and extended the teachings of Marx and Engels on this respect too," Georg Lukács, *The Young Hegel*, op. cit., 357.

processes and its outcomes as a transformative moment for the philosophical tradition.

Although the ideological rigidities under which Lukács writes this book have a clear impact in affiliating his interpretation to the dogmatics of dialectical materialism, we should not underestimate that his main interest in studying Hegel's development, remains a critical approach that appeals to a socio-historical inspiration. It is precisely in the idea of historical rupture that gives birth to the modern capitalist society where Lukács found the main modality in order to criticize the irrational-theological interpretations of Hegel, interpretations which completely omit the social-economic supports of his thought, but also these interpretations which inversely recognize the importance of history for Hegel, just to theologize it.[13] According to Lukács, the social and historical studies that Hegel wrote during the Frankfurt and the Jena period remain the *most valuable source* to prove that the essential shift in Hegel's thought toward dialectical philosophy went hand in hand with his acknowledgement of the irreversible transition to modern world and with his understanding of the dynamic specificity of this world as a historical era.[14] Lukács shows in great detail that these studies distanced Hegel from the romantic sanctification of the ancient Greek political organization and its "beautiful ideal" as inappropriate for the modern capitalist societies. At the same time, these studies also distanced his thought from the kind of irrationalism found in Schelling's influence, thus turning the historical element into the new unavoidable presupposition that philosophy has to take into account. In this way, both the philosophically innovative and the *politically progressive* characters of Hegel's philosophy are corroborated, making it the heyday of "bourgeois horizon,"[15] upon which the Marxist critique should turn itself.

At this point we address a movement which is equally important for the understanding of the "Hegel chapter" in the *Ontology*: before considering any kind of ontological assumptions about the objective results of labor activity,

---

13   This is what K. Löwith expresses when he writes "[Hegel] is the last philosopher of history because he is the last philosopher whose immense historical sense was still restrained and disciplined by the Christian tradition." Karl Löwith, *Meaning in History: The Theological Implications of the Philosophy of History*. (Chicago: University of Chicago Press, 1957), 56. This identification of Hegel's historical sense with a theological philosophy of history epitomizes the theological neutralization of the Hegelian introduction of the historical element in philosophy.

14   On this point see particularly, *The Young Hegel*, op. cit., 171, 309–313, 401–403.

15   The defense of the politically progressive character of Hegel's philosophy is nonetheless considered excessively in some cases as the main contribution of the book, see T.I. Ojzerman, "Lukács' Hegel interpretation." In Tom Rockmore (ed.), *Lukács Today* (Dordrecht and Boston: Reidel, 1988).

we have to acknowledge the presupposition of the historical rupture marked by the passage to capitalist modernity. Even though Lukács' language is stigmatized by the aforementioned Soviet orthodox, we can assume that at the same time many of the elements that will be later evaluated as the genuine dialectical core of his argument in the *Ontology* are already present in the *Young Hegel*. In this context we will proceed to a necessary sketchy summary of these elements:

a) The supersession of the divide between causality and teleology as an important Hegelian innovation during the Jena period will become a powerful dialectical scheme. Their mediation relativizes traditional metaphysically orientated philosophical schemes, introducing a new form of philosophical rationality.[16] Hegel found the material for such a conceptual discovery in his studies of *Realphilosophie*. Lukács stresses the pivotal role of Hegel's studies of the real (socio-economic) objects in producing conceptual results, as a testimony for the superiority of its constant dynamic – being found in these real procedures of modern capitalist societies – over any abstract philosophical-logical system. It is the realities of modern labor procedures and their *durable* technical outcomes (the tools, the machines or even the dynamic real-abstract mediums like money) that should be considered as the incentives for the concepts-formation of a dynamic dialectical ontology of the real social relations.

b) Indeed, the influence of political economy – that Lukács brings forward in his detailed study of Hegel's Jena texts – and especially the thematization of the modern capitalist concept of labor, as represented in Adam Smith's views, highlights for Hegel a new conception of the *human praxis* that goes beyond the abstract and dualistic practical subject of Kant and Fichte:

> As is well known the 'pure will' is the central category of the ethics of Kant and Fichte. If Hegel now sees tools as the first expression of the human will it is evident that he is employing the term in a way directly opposed to theirs; for him, it implies a conception of the concrete totality of man's activity in the actual world. And if he describes will as abstract this just means that he intends to proceed from there to the more complex and comprehensive problems of society, to the division of labor, etc., i.e.

---

16   For a more detailed account of this subject see our text, Michalis Skomvoulis, "Hegel discovers capitalism. Critique of Individualism, Social Labor and Reification during the Jena Period (1801–1807)." In A. Buchwalter (ed.), *Hegel and Capitalism*, (Albany, N.Y.: State University of New York Press, 2015).

that one can only talk concretely of these human activities by talking of them as a whole.¹⁷

It is evident that we have here the germ of a genuine materialistic dialectic which finds its basic patterns in Hegel's insightful transformation of traditional philosophical categories through the structural reconstruction of socio-historical realities. Lukács exemplifies the prominent attribute that this transformation offers to the ontological conception of the world: the "lower strata" (the lower "forces") of the world are restituted and re-introduced to the higher levels as necessary moments within a dynamic relation.¹⁸ In this context it does not come as a surprise that Lukács already in the *Young Hegel* already articulates the difference between the "genuine and the false" features of Hegel's ontological views: on the one hand stands the tendency which produces dialectical forms through the contradictions of the concretely particular, and on the other hand the tendency which subsumes all particulars under the idealistically hypostasized pseudo-universals.¹⁹

c) Lukács' discussion of the difference between alienation (*Entfremdung*) and externalization (*Entäußerung*), although today it appears to be dated, indicates an important shift in his thought, which is absent in HCC. The part of the book where he systematizes this discussion is his threefold distinction in the use of the Hegelian concept of externalization.²⁰ We consider as the most important issue of this distinction precisely the recognition of an externalization which is *not immediately* identified with capitalist alienation (fetishism) is: the non-identification between externalization and alienation attributes also to Lukács' ontological thought a more positive and optimistic tonality, as far as the progress of technology is concerned.²¹ Simultaneously, Lukács differentiates himself from what he considers Hegel's "expansionist" conception of externalization as an externalization of spirit which completely identifies with objectivity in general,²² eliminating subject's action and absorbing nature

---

17   Georg Lukács, *The Young Hegel*, op. cit., 322–323.
18   Ibid., 412–413.
19   Ibid., 393.
20   Georg Lukács, *The Young Hegel*, op. cit., p. 539–541.
21   On this issue see Vittoria, Franco, "Lukács: L'ontologie, l'éthique et le renouveau du marxisme." In *Réification et utopie. Ernst Bloch & György Lukács un siècle après. Actes du colloque*, Goethe Institut de Paris, 1985, Paris: Actes Sud, 132–133, reference in Paul Browne, "Lukács' Later Ontology." *Science and Society*, vol. 54, no. 2 (summer 1990): 199.
22   In the *Phenomenology of spirit*, Hegel indeed tends, in the section of "Absolute Knowing," to adopt an overextended use of externalization as completely identified with objectivity. The opening paragraph of the section acquires thus a programmatic character "The overcoming of the object of consciousness is not to be taken one-sidedly, as showing that the

and finally history as "externalization of spirit in time."[23] For Lukács, the most appropriate conception of externalization – as non-identified with alienation – is what he refers to as:

> the complex subject–object relation inseparably bound up with all work and all human activity of an economic or social kind. What is involved here is the problem of the objectivity of society, of its development, of the laws governing that development, all this in the general context of the idea that men make their own history themselves.[24]

As it can be easily understood this conception prefigures the later social-ontological conception. He opens up a space of wider importance for differentiated structures as possible of being conceptually thematized in a critical ontology, not necessarily referring to a total "reificatory faith" which condemns any kind of externalization in capitalist societies (a conception with which Lukács flirts especially in the first part of his "reification" essay in HCC). Alienation in capitalism can then assume a twofold meaning: apart from the element of domination, it can also integrate an element of *augmented rationality*, based on the enhancement of creative-practical possibilities contained in the social character of modern labor. The claim for a *determinate negation* of alienating aspects of capitalist procedures can be attained in a more concrete way than the one prefigured in the abstract revolutionary potentialities of a unified proletarian subjectivity. The preservation of the possibility of determinate negation presupposes the respective protection of this possibility of externalization as not fully alienated. Thus the maintenance of the difference between a

---

object is returning into the self, but rather, it is to be taken more determinately, both that the object as such exhibited itself to the self as vanishing, as well as being instead the self-relinquishing of self-consciousness that posits thinghood, and that this self-relinquishing does not only have a negative meaning but rather a positive one as well, and not only for us, or in itself, but also for self-consciousness itself. For self-consciousness, the negative of the object, or its self-sublating, has as a result a positive meaning. Self-consciousness knows this nullity of the object as a result, on the one hand, of self-consciousness relinquishing itself of itself – for in this self-relinquishing, it posits itself as object, or, on account of the inseparable unity of being-for-itself, it posits the object as itself." G.W.F. Hegel, *The Phenomenology of Spirit*. Trans. Terry Pinkard. (Cambridge: Cambridge University Press, 2018), 454. It is interesting to note that also later there are moments where Hegel himself explicitly adopts such an overly idealistic conception, when for example in the *Introduction to the Philosophy of History*, he defines history as "expression of spirit in time." See G.W.F. Hegel, *Lectures on the Philosophy of World History, Introduction: Reason in History*. Trans. H.B. Nisbet (Cambridge: Cambridge University Press, 1975), 128.

23 *The Young Hegel*, op. cit., 542.
24 Georg Lukács, *The Young Hegel*, op. cit., p. 539.

subject and an object, where this externalization can take place without completely annihilating finite subject and without absorbing objectivity, becomes the priority for dialectical-materialist ontology. Lukács' criticism for the point of view of the absolute knowledge at the end of the *Phenomenology of Spirit* implicates already in the *Young Hegel*, his resistance to accept a final "negation of negation."[25] In other words, he refuses to accept the elimination of the material objective presuppositions of externalization. His insistence that the objective presuppositions are always mediated by social activity does not invalidate his claim for the *permanent resistance* of the subject–object divide.

Lukács' interpretation, of course, is characterized by *certain limits* determined by the framework within which he is obliged to express himself. The treatment of the relation between teleology and labor indicates the dependence of his thought on certain motives of dogmatic Marxism, where the "objective" priority of productive forces is presented as an automatic justification for the rationality or the non-rationality of a theoretical position, pushing Lukács on several occasions to reduce Hegelian dialectics to a mechanics of "objective conditions." Although Hegel is praised for raising contradiction as the fundamental principle ruling the conditions of capitalist modernity, his idealism nonetheless leads him to "spiritualize" its reconciliation and translate the contradictions of capitalist development within the framework of the progress of human culture.[26] In contrast, Lukács states, it was Ricardo who fully depicted in his thought the importance of the steady development of the forces of production abolishing all contradictions. Ricardo was not simply at the historical and "class objective" position to understand that "only under socialism" this non-contradictory steady and linear development of productive forces can be attained.[27] As we will see, the view, proposed in the *Ontology* leaves a much wider space to the self-reflective and relational character of the social element, also including the possibility of the *non-linear teleological development*.

Additionally, for all the importance that Lukács attributes to the historical factors, his interpretation of the *Phenomenology of Spirit* as the "externalization

---

25   Ibid., 559. Lukács clearly finds the initial motive on this subject in the Feuerbach-based criticism of young Marx against the Hegelian "absolute knowledge" in the *Manuscripts* [see Karl Marx, trans. Martin Milligan, *Economic and Philosophic Manuscripts of 1844*. (Amherst, N.Y.: *Prometheus* Books, 1988), 162–163], but according to our view he draws the criticism of the finality of "negation of negation" much further than the motive of the "alienation of human forces" and especially later in the *Ontology* he subsumes it in a whole new framework.
26   Ibid., 401.
27   Ibid., 402.

of the forces of humanity" succumbs to a certain anthropological evolutionism. Lukács reconstructs *Phenomenology* as the externalization of the forces of humanity projecting to it the concept of species (*Gattung*) that the young Marx makes fundamental,[28] while this concept is received through the lenses of latent soviet Marxist motives. The deployment of the figures of self-consciousness – which for Hegel was not a linear evolution but rather representational structure (a recollection) referring indirectly to the representational structure that marks the transition to a "new world" (namely the modern world) – tends to become an evolutionary (even idealist) testimony of human progresses in the final part of the *Young Hegel*. According to Lukács' presentation the only deficit of this progression is that it places spirit as its ultimate leading subject, disregarding *productive forces* as the carriers of the quasi-natural forces of human species. In this way, Lukács actually hides a metaphysical crypto-teleology,[29] common in the Soviet dogmatic thought, which to a great degree will be absent from the text of the *Ontology*, giving its place to a real and we may say scientific (in the sense of social sciences) social teleology based on the complexities of social labor as positing activity.

3   Lukács' Hegel in the *Ontology*: Toward a Genuine Materialist Interpretation

The Hegel chapter is placed at a crucial point of the *Ontology of Social Being*. Lukács concluded his assessment on the "actual state" of philosophy (his critical chapter on Neopositivism and Existentialism and his much more positive chapter on Hartmann's effort for the foundation of a new ontology). The chapter on Hegel seems to be placed to the point where Lukács starts to unfold his argument about the modalities of a contemporary ontological thought and uses his reconstruction of Hegelian dialectics as the initial motive of this unfolding. In our view, the decisive points of this reconstruction can be divided in three levels: the first point concerns the connection that Lukács draws between

---

28   For this projection of young Marx's motives to the interpretation of the Phenomenology of spirit, as seen from the historical perspective of the reception of Hegel's social philosophy, see Henning Ottman, *Individuum und Gesellschaft bei Hegel, vol. 1: Hegel im Spiegel der Interpretationen.* (Berlin: De Gruyter, 1977), 91.

29   Even in the strict sense of the aim of his book, the interpretation of Hegel's development, a crypto-teleology is implied given that it seems like "Lukács' Hegel is forever trying to become Marx but failing." James Schmidt, "*Recent Hegel Literature*: General Surveys and the Young Hegel." *Telos* 46 (Winter, 1980–1981), 141.

historical actuality and the ontological potential of Hegel's thought (a), subsequently we will focus on these very ontological possibilities, how they transform traditional philosophical categories and in which respect they correspond to the exigencies of historical materialism (b), finally we will present what we consider to be the essential points of Lukács' critical appropriation of Hegel's *Logic*. As we will see, the "logic of essence" and especially the concept of reflection as well as its determinations lie behind his project for a dialectical ontology (c).

(a) Against the possible assumption that Lukács adopts a general ontological point of view expressing another "ontology of human being"[30] (so common in the philosophy of mid-twentieth century) he begins his important chapter on Hegel by reconstructing the historical framework within which Hegel's efforts for the new philosophical practice take place. The post-revolutionary present (after the French Revolution) and the dynamics of capitalism give Hegel the historical resources to raise the claim for a new philosophical practice. The introduction of the *historical present* (as a structural historical horizon) in the ontological claims of philosophy, not only has the value of taking into account historical presuppositions, but also it has direct philosophical consequences, announcing the possibility of a *new* (dialectical) ontology.[31] Taking into account historical specificity to properly evaluate the social dynamics relative to modern capitalism, it also means accepting the presuppositions that this historical horizon posits for the very logical core of philosophy:[32] above all, the need to respond to the new real and social historical dynamics with a philosophy which goes beyond traditional dualism and fixed given identities and corresponds to the standards raised by the non-linear and

---

30 For a presentation of Lukács' critique to this general ontological ("existential") argument, see Nicolas Tertulian, "Aliénation et désaliénation: une confrontation Lukács-Heidegger." In *Les Nouvelles Alienations, Actuel Marx*, no. 39, mai 2006. We have to admit, nevertheless, that Tertulian in his account of the whole of Lukács' ontological project overstresses the importance of the "individual practice." Nicolas Tertulian, "Lukács' Ontology." In Thom Rockmore (ed.), *Lukács Today*, op. cit.

31 Georg Lukács, *The Ontology of Social Being: Hegel*, op. cit., 13–14, 27.

32 That is why we consider that recent attempts to revitalize the ontological aspect of Hegel's thought [Stephen *Houlgate, The Opening of Hegel's Logic: From Being to Infinity* (West Lafayette, Ind.: Purdue University Press, 2006), particularly Chapter 6], conceiving it as the linear unfolding of determinations which constantly has as its reference the abstracted "sheer" Being (ibid., 42–53), are clearly at odds with Lukács' historical and content-informed project. We believe that the perspective of unfolding the determinations of "sheer" Being succumbs finally to a form of empiricism.

non-empiricist conceptualizations of contemporary sciences.[33] Thus, neither prevalent positivist empiricism that uncritically accepts the *sosein* nor the transcendental dualism that separates the *sosein*, perceived equally positively, from abstract and empty *solen*, can attain this goal. Hegel's efforts to turn philosophy toward reality in general and especially toward historical reality as the horizon of philosophical thought has as its main consequence a new philosophical conception of the historical present as a dynamic process, where every static identity is subjected to transformation or, repeating *Communist Manifesto*'s apt expression, "everything solid melts into air."

Nevertheless, Hegel's reconstruction of traditional philosophical identities through the introduction of the historical temporality of the present and its real contradictions hides a new danger for the transformation of dialectical ontology into a metaphysical positivity. Hegel's claim to *harmonize* idea and socio-historical element leads him to the sanctification of his historical present,[34] to the transformation of his dialectical presentism – where the emergence of the new is the subversive motor of dialectics – to a new form of conservatism. Capitalist modernity is logically produced as the much desired eternal harmonic form of adjustment for the relationship between history and concept.

Lukács then connotes, for the first time, the existence of Hegel's *two ontologies*: that of the logically-centered conservative ontology which reduces content complexity and functions as rational *reconciliatory justification* of the historical present and the other which functions as the philosophical incitation of a materialist dialectical ontology,[35] given its effort to understand reality within its constant movement as a contradictory and differentiated totality. In this way, dialectical thought comprehends itself as a complex *processual* production which should accomplish the exigencies posited by the equally complex multi-level, real processes: "The processual (*Prozeßartigkeit*) character of thought is only the consequence of the processual character of all reality."[36]

---

33   "The great discoveries of the natural sciences, the historical experience of centuries teeming with revolutions, had shaken, even in the concrete, everyday image of the world, the age-old supremacy of a eternal, stationary, unmoved substantiality, the absolute predominance of a primary, thing-like objectivity, as against a motion conceived as secondary [...] but the basic philosophical categories still remained for all that on the level of a world of things that was in and for itself unchangeable." Georg Lukács, *The Ontology of Social Being: Hegel*, op. cit., 64.

34   Ibid., 15–16.

35   Ibid., 37–39.

36   Ibid., 22 (trans. modified). The term processual already appears in HCC (Lukács speaks of "Prozessartige eines jeden Phänomens." See *Geschichte und Klassenbewusstsein, Studien*

(b) Before passing to a more detailed account of the principles that Lukács accepts as the essence of the Hegelian dialectics pointing toward a new materialist ontology of the social, it is crucial to ponder on the elements that Lukács considers of the false side of this dialectics. It is interesting to acknowledge that, according to Lukács, the "false ontology" of Hegel is to be found especially in the autonomization of logical categories against their link to the real procedures. In this way, the real ontological phenomena that should have been respected in their differentiated autonomy are violated and subsumed under these logical categories. Although, the Hegelian dialectic introduced the construction of logical categories through their continuous contact with real-content dynamics as its pioneering achievement, it is a structural problem of Hegelian philosophy that logical element autonomizes itself "dictating" to reality its direction. One of its characteristics that Lukács criticizes is the overextension of the use of the concept of *negation*:[37] when negation remains a methodological function in order to perform the transitions into a system of dynamic movement, it is a legitimate and powerful methodological instrument. The use of the term instrument here is deliberate, helping us to understand the broader ontological horizon into which the concepts of the Hegelian dialectic are evaluated. At this point, we once again note that the instrument is the outcome of technically-produced mediation where the mechanical and the teleological are simultaneously posited as socially enduring dimensions of the real.[38]

When, adversely, negation is autonomized as a pure logical modality, it isolates only the negative side of every concept, trying to proceed in their dynamic logical unification. This way, it omits the autonomy that ontologically is implicated in every real complex, especially when it is transformed into an implicit (or explicit in some cases) logical normativity, which directs and submits the real. The pseudo-dynamics of logical transitions in its idealist constant movement finally preserve the ontologically real as eternal, thus giving a conservative tonality to Hegel's system.

> The Hegelian logic, with its abstractly universal logical generalization of negation into a fundamental moment of any dialectical process, thereby

---

    über marxistische Dialektik. (Neuwied: Luchterhand, 1970), 319), representing more a methodological promise that it is never sufficiently developed in the text.

37 Ibid., 40–42.

38 For the technical (originating from cunning) means as what endures ("preserves itself") through the mediating processes, see G.W.F. Hegel, *Encyclopedia of the Philosophical Sciences in Basic Outline, Part 1: Science of Logic*. Trans. Klaus Brinkmann and Daniel O. Dahlstrom. (Cambridge, U.K.: Cambridge University Press, 2010), § 209, p. 281.

obliterates the specificity of social being, even though Hegel generally intended to make, and actually did make, his biggest effort precisely in elucidating this.[39]

Against this possible domination of a systemic logicist dimension over the ontology, Lukács underlines that for the materialist dialectics revolutionary movement should be found into the *movement of the real object* of research within its practical interaction with the subject; in the case of the ontology of the social into the *historical reality* which earns the primacy, before any logical reconstruction.[40] We should thus note that Lukács' insistence on a non-linear materialist dialectic, where the *absolute primacy is accorded to the real object*, parallels the chronologically respective efforts for a "finite" dialectic by other important representatives of western Marxism (presented as critiques of Lukács' initial "teleological historicism") like Adorno and Althusser.

The difference of Lukács' perspective is to be found in the systematic character he accords to his materialist dialectics.[41] The systematic character acknowledged as essential for this reassessment of dialectics means that for the late Lukács the criticism of Hegel does not lie anymore on the traditional Marxist distinction between the revolutionary character of his *method* and the conservative character of his *system*. Although Lukács refers to the conservative direction which the prevalence of the logical element imposes to dialectics transforming it into a mode of speculative justification of the present historical horizon, he does not oppose the dialectical systematicity *per se*. It is precisely the relativization of the distinction between a dynamical method and the system that gives him the capacity to reassess Hegel's *Logic* and reintroduce in critical theory the ambition for a new dialectical systematicity, advancing further from the Hegelian one.[42] In other words, Lukács' relativization

---

39 Georg Lukács, *The Ontology of Social Being: Hegel*, op. cit., 44.
40 We have to note that through this criticism Lukács does not hesitate to criticize even Engels for a certain logicistic metaphysics, when he applies directly Hegelian categories and logical schemes (ibid., 45). Rockmore remarks correctly that this critique against even the classics of historical materialism, emphasizes the degree of freedom that Lukács claims in this book in order to express his own genuine materialist dialectics (Tom Rockmore, *Irrational. Lukács and the Marxist view of reason*, op. cit., 219–221).
41 Anderson remarks the similarities that could be identified between Adorno and Althusser, but he fails to accord the deserved importance to Lukács' *Ontology* on these issues, see Perry Anderson, *Considerations on Western Marxism*, op. cit., 72–73.
42 As a counterexample we can think of Ernst Bloch's very creative appropriation of Hegel, which nevertheless fully retains its faith to the relevance of the Hegelian method as the framework for Marxist thought. For his clear formulation of the "subversive" character of dialectical method, see Ernst Bloch, "Subjekt-Objekt." In Ernst Bloch, *Subjekt-Objekt*.

of the system/method divide in the Marxist interpretation of Hegel[43] does not only mean that he retains the possibility of systematicity as a plausible mode of thinking for Marxism and critical theory in general. It means also that his criticism touches the *very core of the sacralized Hegelian method*, highlighting thus the importance of his critical engagement with the Hegelian logic in the *Ontology*, as a path to revitalize historical materialism.

Toward that direction, Lukács argues that a new Marxist critical ontology must be produced theoretically, only by finding its conceptual basis on the *real procedures of the social being* respecting thus the *distinct ontological framework* that social being should acquire in relation to first-order natural stratum.[44] Any possible reduction to a logical priority as well as any naturalist reductionism should be avoided. We see thus that Lukács' battle against the idealist insights of Hegelian philosophy is accompanied, in this mature phase of his work, with the respective battle against mechanistic naturalism (including the one that was taken for granted in the framework of official Soviet Marxism).

At this point, it is worth mentioning the difference of Lukács' critique of Hegel in this text in comparison to his previous critiques, and especially with his important theoretical approach in HCC. While there is indeed a common base for the two critiques in asserting a conservative speculatively driven political position that can result from Hegelian idealism, the conclusions that Lukács draws in these two phases are different. For the revolutionary dialectics of the HCC, finding the limits of Hegelian idealism led to the radicalization of the claim for negative dynamics, through its realization to a historically abstract unified subject, while for the systematic (and we could say more materialist) approach of the *Ontology*, the confirmation of these limits constitutes more of a call for the formation of a dialectic that could thematize the dynamic aspects of differentiated social complexes. The primacy of movement is thus clearly attributed to the immanent differentiation of the very specific objective reality of social being. The fact that we are dealing here with social objects attaches additional importance to the claim of respecting multi-level complexity, given that the subject in Lukács' dialectical ontology can emerge

---

Erläuterungen zu Hegel. (Frankfurt a. M., Suhrkamp, 1962. Gesamtausgabe. Bd. 8), 123–126 – although we have to admit that simultaneously he presents materialism as the discontinuity (unterbrechung – ibid., 135) of the idealist dialectical movement. For his account of Hegel's systematicity as all-encompassing ontology which suppresses history, see ibid., 466–467.

43   See Paul Browne, "Lukács' *Later Ontology*." *Science and Society*, op. cit., 202.
44   Georg Lukács, *The Ontology of Social Being: Hegel,* op. cit., 61–62.

only by establishing and maintaining a differentiated relation to social objectivity.[45]

Lukács definitively abandons the Hegelian assumption for a possible unification between subject and object, contrary to the first phase of his thought. The development of Lukács' argument about the actual realization of the subject through its labor-based teleological positing will demonstrate that the (social) object includes an indispensable structuration of free choices (or better yet of *social alternatives*) and raises concrete exigencies to the self-comprehension of social subjects. This question will preoccupy a significant part of Lukács' conceptual exposition in the more "real" parts of his ontology, especially the parts which treat the concrete articulation of differentiated social structures and their complex mediated relation with the teleological results of labor. We will return to this question in the final part of our reconstruction. At this point we can already acknowledge that the dialectical core of the relation between labor positing and material limits that the already accumulated, already posited complex social structures raise against this positing, consists in conceptualizing the normative meanings (values) that come up during this teleological positing not as abstract normative claims but as concrete social alternatives, making them possible to be defined as stakes of socially structured *political struggles*.

The question then for the philosophical framework of Lukács' materialist ontology is which moment of Hegelian dialectics presents a privileged pertinence in order to impel the comprehension of the concrete relation between the dynamic of subject's teleological positing and the complex autonomy of the real structures. Lukács claims that he found such a moment in the Hegelian dialectic, concentrating on the *logic of essence* and particularly on Hegel's development the concepts of *reflection* and the *determinations* of reflection.

(c) Determinations of reflection are, according to Lukács, the most important methodological discovery[46] of Hegel from the point of view of materialist dialectics. As an introductive point it is worth noting that Lukács finds particularly appealing the fact that Hegel attributes an objective character (consciousness-independent) to the determinations of

---

45 The assumption thus that Lukács proposes a genuine dialectical social theory inspired by Hegel should not be taken as a given, but should always presuppose the thoroughly critical transformation of Hegel's ontology that Lukács undertakes, see Reha Kadakal, "Toward a Critical Ontology of the Social: Hegel, Lukács, and the Challenge of Mediation." In Harry F. Dahms (ed.), *Globalization, Critique and Social Theory: Diagnoses and Challenges*. (Emerald Group, 2015).

46 Georg Lukács, *The Ontology of Social Being: Hegel*, op. cit., 74.

reflection,[47] correlating them additionally with the objectively orientated immanent dynamic that acquires the Hegelian exposition of the forms of reflection[48] (from *positing reflection* to the *external reflection* and then to *determining reflection*). This correlation should be crucial for Lukács' argument because it would allow us to conceive reality as an objective dialectic of a real totality, which at the same time is *susceptible to the dynamics of the endogenous genesis of the new, in other words, to the logic of the self-posited and self-transformed subject.*
The determinations of reflection are henceforth the basis of a real dialectic because they, first and foremost, destroy any theologically orientated conception which reproduces unaltered a transcendent dualism as an immediate given.[49] The immediacy, Lukács declares, is a phenomenon of consciousness, where mediation is an *objective ontological category*.[50] Simultaneously, the merit of the particular nature of the determinations of reflection within Hegel's logical exposition is that they *moderate the harmonizing image of dialectics that Hegel wants to present as far as the unity of dialectical logic is concerned*.[51]

---

47 It is not perhaps without importance to note how enthusiastic Lenin was in emphasizing this objectivist tendency. V.I. Lenin, "Notebooks on Hegel." In *Collected Works*. (London: International Publishers, 1976), 38, 134. What is also interesting is that he underlines the reproduction of this objective tendency in the "noble parts" of the *Logic of Concept* as highly important from a materialist point of view. See especially his notes on the importance of the concept of "tool" in the treatment of teleology, where dialectical conceptual treatment is referred to human practice as a *real process*, (ibid., 189–191, 198–200). The reproduction of reflective determinations in the most conceptually "advanced" parts of Hegel's *Logic* will be, as we will see, a basic motive of Lukács' argument.

48 See Hegel's statement: "But at issue here is neither the reflection of consciousness, nor the more specific reflection of the understanding that has the particular and the universal for its determinations, but reflection in general. It is clear that the reflection to which Kant assigns the search of the universal for a given particular is likewise only an external reflection which applies itself to the immediate as to something given. – But the concept of absolute reflection, too, is implicit in it. For the universal, the principle or the rule and law, to which reflection rises in its process of determination is taken to be the essence of the immediate from which the reflection began; the immediate, therefore, to be a nothingness which is posited in its true being only by the turning back of the reflection from it, by the determining of reflection. Therefore, what reflection does to the immediate, and the determinations that derive from it, is not anything external to it but is rather its true being." G.W.F. Hegel, *The Science of Logic*. Trans. George di Giovanni. (Cambridge: Cambridge University Press, 2010), 350.

49 Georg Lukács, *The Ontology of Social Being: Hegel*, op. cit., 83.

50 Ibid., 90.

51 Hegel in the §81 of the Encyclopedia criticizes the "exteriority" in its relation to the object that necessarily carries any reflective activity, opposing it to the fluid "immanent transition" of dialectical movement, see G.W.F. Hegel, *Encyclopedia of the Philosophical Sciences in Basic Outline, Part 1: Science of Logic*, op. cit., 129. It is clear that Lukács retains this

The determinations of reflection are categories that constantly engage *real contents* with different (material-objective) determinacies: these contents being mediated through the presupposition of the positing activity of a self-reflexive subject, they are not possible to be reduced into a unified identity, but can be conceived only by studying *concrete complexes* of real determinations.

The real dialectic of determinations of reflection is inserted in all logical levels, destroying its harmonic self-sufficiency. On the one hand, Lukács shows in detailed example how Hegel is obliged to implicitly introduce the reflexive activity in the parallel static existence of the conceptual entities in the logic of being, attempting to mobilize the transitions between them. On the other hand, the Hegelian presentation (*Darstellung*) cannot avoid retaining the reference to reflexive determinations even in the most advanced and conceptually integrated parts of his logic of the concept.[52] This last observation is of particular importance for the materialist dialectics because it shows the presence of the non-linear objective reflexivity even in the most "noble" parts of the Hegelian logic:

> In the doctrine of the notion itself, universality, particularity and individuality emerge a specifically new categories. The philosophical content of these categories is extraordinarily important and consequential for Hegel's entire view of the world, but this also seems frequently to be obscured by logicism, in so far as the decisive applications of these categories are built into the doctrine of notion, judgment and syllogism. It is easy to see, none the less, that Hegel essentially employs these categories as reflection determinations. This is already clear from the fact that,

---

residual exteriority of the logic of reflection as a materialistic moderation of Hegel's ambitious teleological assumptions. We could say that at this point materialist dialectics indeed inverses Hegel's dictum "every finitude consists in its self-refutation," responding that "every infinity has its finite conditions of existence."

52 For instances in the development of logical exposition where the reflective modality appears implicitly in the transitions within the sphere of Being, see for example Hegel's reference in the implicit presence of positing activity of reflection during the transition to Determinate Being, an activity that at this stage of development cannot be thematised as a concept and remains external, G.W.F. Hegel, *The Science of Logic*, op. cit., 84. On the other hand, for the reproduction of the reflection theme within the more advanced spheres of the Concept, see Hegel's implications in the analysis of the concept of the syllogisms of reflection, "where the externality of reflection is still here." Later, Hegel clarifies, that "reviewing the course of the syllogism of reflection, we find that mediation is in general the *posited* or *concrete* unity of the form determinations of the extremes; reflection consists in this positing of the one determination in the other." Ibid., 616.

although he presents them as domiciled in the logic of the notion, he already deals with their first dialectical relationships at the conclusion of the doctrine of essence, and the sense of his presentation is certainly to present them as reflection determinations [...] The further the Hegelian system progresses, from the notion to the Idea, the more clear it becomes that the structural basis of the complexes appearing here, and their contradictions lies always in the determinations of reflection.[53]

Determinations of reflection involve then an active element of moderation against the ambitious claims of the Hegelian dialectic for the self-sufficiency of the concept. They reintroduce the non-linearity of the objective constitution of the concepts as a contradictory multi-level procedure, which finally refers itself in the *concrete articulation of its structure*. The case of the analysis of the determination of form, which Lukács explicitly refers to,[54] is from this point of view characteristic: the form is obliged to re-introduce the multiplicity and the non-teleological nature of matter. Only in this way it can be established as a *reflected form relation*, only being mediated by the matter, but not unified with it.[55] So, a causal relation between form and matter can be constituted only through the mode of their *concrete articulation*.

As a conclusive remark and before referring ourselves to the more concrete consequences of the Lukács ontological evaluation of Hegel's logic and especially of the logic of essence *for his ontology of the social*, we have to note the two fundamental points that Lukács tries to co-articulate in his treatment: the objective appeal of the determinations of reflection to the real that opposes any logically linear harmonious teleology and simultaneously the emergence of subjectivity as a self-reflective positive activity. It is a crucial point of Lukács' argument that he will resolve these antinomical claims with the introduction of the *specificity of the social element*.

In the materialist view of Lukács' dialectical ontology society is the particular objective reality with internal contradictions, impossible to be reduced to a logicist teleological scheme. At the same time, the objective reality is a *second order* reality. It is produced as social objectivity (in the sense of the Hegelian *Gegenständlichkeit* as opposed to sheer *Objektivität*) through the teleological

---

53   Georg Lukács, *The Ontology of Social Being: Hegel*, op. cit., 108–109.
54   Ibid., 93–95.
55   This positing of unity by the active form which simultaneous presupposes the non-teleological disunity represented by matter refers clear to the conceptual structure of reflection. It is besides Hegel himself which notes that form-determinations resume previous determinations of reflection, naming form "the completed whole of reflection." G.W.F. Hegel, *The Science of Logic*, op. cit., 391.

positing activity of labor, which for its part has these objective social structures as the presupposition of its positing activity. Lukács' conception of objective social reality takes thus its conceptual incitation from Hegel's *logic of reflection*, where especially the *determining reflection* presents a version of the dialectical scheme of the *positing of the presuppositions* as also integrating the *presupposing of positing reflection*. In other words, determining reflection contains simultaneously[56] the subjective dynamic of positing reflection and the external objectivity of external reflection by assimilating (as *reflected in itself*) its own negatively related external objectivities as specific conditions of its posited being (*Gesetztsein*) and of its self-reflected capacity of positing.[57] There is here a model of thought which parallels to thinking synthetically the non-reducible teleological aspect of labor positing as *self-reflected* relation with its objectified products which also function as its *external structural presuppositions*. Subject's teleological activity emerges only as being negatively related/limited by these objective conditions, while at the same time its activity constitutes the specificity of these objective conditions as being *social* structures.

The labor-emerging subject includes potentially a relative control on objective social contradictions by giving rise to social consciousness not as a metaphysical entity, but as active social mediation that can *organize social contradictions* and reified differentiations as meaningful *social alternatives*. Lukács' complex dialectics subsequently open up a space that has to do with a form of consciousness which can attain an *objective understanding* of social structures, introducing to its ontological positioning as producer of social normativity a *political interest* similar to his strong interest in political subjectivity in HCC, but less subjected to revolutionary certainties. The examination of the Hegelian

---

56 On the importance of including the presupposed immediacy as part of the positing activity and on the importance of *determining reflection* as the point of synthesis of the argument of reflection, see the classical analysis of this subject in Dieter Henrich, "Hegels Logik der Reflexion." In *Hegel im Kontext* (Frankfurt a. M.: Suhrkamp Verlag, 1971), particularly 151–153.

57 As Hegel puts it: "[P]ositedness (*Gesetztsein*) is at the same time immanent reflection, the determinateness of the reflection is the reference in it to its otherness [...]. Rather, the determination of reflection is within it the determinate side and the reference of this determinate side as determinate, that is, the reference to its negation [...]. The determination of reflection [...] has taken its otherness back into itself. It is positedness – negation which has however deflected the reference to another into itself, and negation which, equal to itself, is the unity of itself and its other, and only through this is an essentiality. It is, therefore, positedness, negation, but as reflection into itself it is at the same time the sublatedness of this positedness, infinite reference to itself." G.W.F. Hegel, *The Science of Logic*, op. cit., 353.

influence to Lukács' complex dialectical adjustment of the relation between the differentiated social structure and the unificatory force of labor will thus concern the last part of our reconstruction.

4 Hegelian Dialectics in the Ontology of the Social: Structural Complexities of Labor and Social Emancipation

The importance of Lukács' engagement with Hegelian dialectics in his social ontology appears in the three elaborated forms of dialectical relations, upon which we can organize the general relation that is developed between the social dynamics of labor's teleological positing and its structural presuppositions. The mode of adjustment between the structural presuppositions and labor concerns precisely Lukács' effort for a (re)foundation of historical materialism on a new dialectical ontology. We discern thus three forms of these dialectics: (a) the relation that consciousness builds with its biological-ontological fundament, the degree of its autonomization and the raising of its self-propelled limits within the social structure, (b) the relation that labor establishes, as a socio-economic procedure (including a strong material-technical element), with the genesis of values into its teleological activity, (c) the totalizing relation that is developed between the unificatory function of the economy (as the field where labor unfolds its dynamic *par excellence*) and the autonomized social spheres in the advanced highly differentiated modern societies.

a) Lukács never ceases to acknowledge that the biological element constitutes the undeniable fundamental stratum which conditions any consciousness activity, even if this concerns the construction of mediated social structures.[58] As a consequence Lukács frequently oscillates during the exposition of his argument between understanding labor as the driving force social specificity and subjecting it to an anthropological quasi-biological general ontology.[59] According to our view, and taking our previous analysis on the character of Hegel's reception by Lukács in the *Ontology* as a point of departure, the main burden of Lukács' argument equally evades the possibility of an unhistorical biologism and the possibility of transhistorical ontology of the human being, based on an

---

58 Georg Lukács, *Zur Ontologie der Gesellschaftlichen Seins*, vol. 2, 208.
59 This oscillation of considering labor sometimes as the holistic social framework of a historical ontology, sometimes as quasi-anthropological transhistorical founding is clearly discernable in Lukács treatment of labour, see for example Georg Lukács, *The Ontology of Social Being: Labour,* op. cit., 83, 111, 129. For a thematization of this oscillation see Bruno Gulli, *Labor of Fire. The Ontology of Labor between Economy and Culture.* (Philadelphia: Temple University Press), 43–49.

abstract and perpetual "metabolism" between man and nature. As we have already established, Lukács highlighted the historical presuppositions as a necessary condition for understanding his reception of Hegel's philosophy. We can now clearly ascertain that he respectively contextualizes labor's formative power (which from the Marxian point of view, also means value-forming power) as a historical outcome, where the socially defined (labor-produced) value posits itself as the matrix where a subjective ought emerges as "valuable" social alternative. In order to formulate the complex relation between the social objectivity of value and the subjectivity of the "ought" Lukács makes use of the Hegelian conceptualization of positing the presuppositions:

The problem of value is inseparably linked with the problem of the 'ought' a category of social being. For just as the 'ought' can only play this specifically determining role in the labour process as a determining factor of subjective practice because the goal aimed at is valuable for man, so value cannot be realized in a process of this kind if it is not in a position to posit the 'ought' of its realization to the worker as the guiding thread of his practice.[60]

The crucial element is not thus that a natural-biological element is unavoidably reproduced in social forms (as their unsurpassable limit) but rather how labor *internalizes reflexively* this limit, creating the capacity of its continuous transposition, expanding thus the field of social understanding and knowledge. The social dynamics of labor is not manifested only in the production of complex social structures (highly independent of its natural references), but also through the expansion of *social consciousness* by internalizing new ontological social forms as new forms of meaningful understanding.[61]

Inspired by Hegel's treatment of the genesis of self-consciousness in *Phenomenology of Spirit*, and especially of the transition of this genesis to the master–slave dialectic, Lukács shows how labor activity finally exercises a *control* over the physical biological instincts.[62] In this way, the

---

60 Georg Lukács, The Ontology of Social Being: Labour, op. cit., 75. Lukács goes on bringing out the socio-historical character of use value and utility as integrating normative claims, ibid., 77–78.
61 On the internalization and the transposition of the natural limit: ibid., 76. On the dynamic enrichment and autonomization of social consciousness, see ibid., and Georg Lukács, Zur Ontologie der Gesellschaftlichen Seins, vol. 2, 162–163.
62 See especially on labor as a capacity of control over biological instincts, G.W.F. Hegel, *Phenomenology of Spirit*, op. cit., 115.

refutation of the biological desire constitutes a fundamental element for the genesis of the *autonomy of consciousness* and henceforth for the genesis of the autonomy of social element.[63] What is interesting is that Lukács does not limit the mediating character of the socialization of consciousness only to this dialectic between dependence and independence on a biological element, but complexifies the range of this mediation. He introduces forms of quasi-natural restrictions that come up this time in the *proper social field*, namely he thematizes the problem of the *second nature* within societies,[64] focusing on the fact that consciousness, albeit autonomous, is always subject to the limitations of social structures functioning as second nature. The historical process of what Lukács calls "socialization of society," namely the development of a differentiated society presents henceforth itself as *second nature*, which is reproduced through its own elements, through its own *second-order metabolism*, becoming a complex of complexes (*Komplex aus Komplexen*).

b) The detailed analysis that Lukács undertakes in order to show the relative autonomy of language as a distinct structure of social consciousness which at the same time finds its resources and its limitations on *material* social structures is a characteristic example of how Lukács evaluates this dialectic in the general plan of the *Ontology*.[65] At this point, it is worth returning to the fundamental condition for the emergence of this dialectic: the realization and the perpetuation of the divide between *subject and object* should be considered again as the fundamental relation where the social specificity that labor manifests is consolidated. Although, the object always maintains some kind of a materialist primacy in this phase of Lukács' work, we should not underestimate that the object, in an already mediated social environment, refers to *other social individuals* and to *other social relations*.[66] From this point of view we understand that the teleological element in labor does not, from now on, principally refer to a certain "first order" biological reproductive metabolism between humans and nature. Its teleological positing is already mediated by its reference

---

63 Georg Lukács, *The Ontology of Social Being: Labour*, op. cit., 45.
64 Ibid., 129. The *enlightening* aspect of *Ontology* emerges thus as claiming the dereification of this second nature, providing the possibility of better understanding the transformation of society as self-transformation and thus of *conscious social choices*. That is besides the possible political implication of his critique of "irrationalism," see Michael J. Thompson, "*Ontology and Totality: Reconstructing* Lukács' Concept of Critical Theory." In Michael J. Thompson (ed.), *Lukács reconsidered. Critical essays in politics, philosophy and aesthetics*. (New York/London: Continuum, 2011), 242.
65 Georg Lukács, *Zur Ontologie der Gesellschaftlichen Seins*, vol. 2, 173–179.
66 Georg Lukács, *The Ontology of Social Being: Labour*, op. cit., 47.

to *other social subjects* and its production of teleological forms, in differentiated social activities, subsequently takes the character of (non-reducible and frequently contradictory) *values* that are generated via different social perspectives, representing thus different social alternatives, finding their *common ground* in the socially constitutive social practice of labor. The specificity of the social world is thus constituted, in late Lukács' perspective, as a *subjectively practical mediated objectivity* (i.e., as *Gegenständlichkeit*) and not as an intersubjective sphere. The constitutive sphere of labor, becoming the substance of a highly mediated social conception of the economy, takes the role of bringing the different social values, produced by the autonomized social spheres, back to the their real essence of genuine creative (*eidetical*[67]) social activity. The integration of the different social values finally becomes connected to the *real bases* of social alternatives which have to do (Lukács does not hesitate to make this connection) with different *class positions* generated as social alternatives in the fundamental sphere of labor.[68]

c) This is probably the most important reason why Lukács insisted on the conservation of the Marxist primacy of the economy. Lukács unfolds a very meticulous argument on the autonomy of the highly differentiated social spheres in complex capitalist societies and simultaneously utilizes the traditional dialectics of "final instance" in order to reintroduce the *primacy of the economy in a totally different way* than the technicist perspective which favors the quasi-automatic development of the means of production. Without negating a certain technical element and a general privileged connection between technique and economy, Lukács differentiates the core of the social character of the economy as *ontologically different* from its technical presuppositions. The economy can attain a certain primacy in the reproduction of social structures as the sphere which acquires a particular *dynamic* in organizing the different value perspectives of the general social activity and concentrating their knowledge, becoming a uniquely reflexive sphere not in spite of the presence of the social character of labor in its interior *but because of it*.

Lukács explicitly criticizes those who identify economy with technicity excluding thus its particular dynamic place in social ontology.[69]

---

67 "*Gattungsmäßigkeit*," writes Lukács, *Zur Ontologie der Gesellschaftlichen Seins*, vol. 2, 205.
68 Georg Lukács, *The Ontology of Social Being: Labour,* op. cit, 131–132.
69 "The so frequent, in historical and social sciences, idealist and fetishist representation of an absolute autonomy of social complexes takes as its point of departure an impoverished and reified representation of the economic sphere." Georg Lukács, *Zur Ontologie der Gesellschaftlichen Seins*, vol. 2, 219. It is worth noting that this point of Lukács retains its

Lukács asserts that social ontology should adopt a more refined view on the economy, making its social character its distinctive element,[70] and this can happen because labor retains the capacity to concentrate different social values in a social structure of *conscious co-operation*. This *synthetic* quality of the labor-based economy then moves between the epistemological aspect of knowing the complex social causal chain of a differentiated social reproduction and the practical aspect of opening up the possibility of conscious co-operation. This movement transforms the socialized-developed forms of labor into the sphere where genuine social alternatives and fundamental social stakes are posited, equally in the epistemological and socio-ontological level.[71] So, the possibility of a de-alienated co-ordination between individual practices and social structures can be considered never as a final "accomplished" condition, but as an open project (traversed by social contradictions and strong elements of contingency[72]) for new social experimentation and formation of new institutions and thus as a call for a creative political emancipation.[73]

From this point of view, Lukács' insistence on the objective character of social dialectics and of the genesis of subjective transformative action, only through the

---

full validity as a relevant framework of criticism against the (highly complex and refined) contemporary systemic social theory of N. Luhmann from a critical materialist point of view.

70   This argument, thus, already constitutes a strong objection against the criticism of Lukács' students (Feher, Heller, Markus, Vajda) who in their critical "Notes on the Ontology" take a position against Lukács' choice to maintain the dynamic primacy of the economy (Ferenc Feher, Agnes Heller, Gyorgy Markus, MihalyVajda, "Notes on Lukács' Ontology." *Telos*, issue 29, 1976, p. 176). Lukács' argument clarifies that the rejection of economy's primacy is frequently accompanied with a simplistic and technicist view on the economy, which underestimates its social dynamics.

71   Lukács, implying the epistemological consequences of the emergence of self-consciousness in the *Phenomenology of spirit*, explicitly negates to completely separate the epistemological and the ontological level of knowledge, see Georg Lukács, *The Ontology of Social Being: Labor,* op. cit., 41–42.

72   Ibid., 124. The acceptance of the fact that the complex procedures of developed socialized labor include inevitably a strong determination of social contingency, against any kind of historicist teleology, is equally a distinctive feature of Lukács' materialism in the *Ontology*. A feature where, once again, the importance of his antimetaphysical appropriation of Hegel's philosophy plays a crucial role. Lukács reiterates the importance of Hegel's philosophy (manifested in his criticism of Fichte's authoritarian subjectivism) for the integration of the element of contingency in social reproduction even in the most advanced moments of his *Ontology* (see his reference to Hegel on this subject in the chapter on "The problem of Ideology," Lukács, *Zur Ontologie der Gesellschaftlichen Seins*, vol. 2, 430).

73   On the importance of proposing and integrating new institutions in order for Lukács' ontological project to take an *ethical* (in Hegelian sense) political-normative translation, see Michael J. Thompson, "Ontology and Totality," op. cit., 245.

dialectic of these objective conditions, presents a clearly heterogeneous character in relation to the actually dominant theoretical trends. That is why the neglect of his late great work is totally *comprehensible* and *predictable*. Especially, when this ontological materialist perspective is juxtaposed against a dominant neoliberal theory which considers the market as the only institution being able to accumulate and distill social knowledge: Lukács counterposes labor procedures as an alternative for the social concentration of knowledge and conscious co-operation, capable to provide *individuals with reflexive self-understanding* of social structures. Simultaneously, the Lukácsian "persistence of dialectics" could be juxtaposed to the dominant critical theory, which in its formulation constitutively presupposed the rejection of any kind of objective dialectics[74] and insisted on the obsolescence of the "paradigm of production." As we already implied, against the dualistic turn of critical theory Lukács' paradigm resists any idealistic detachment of a communicative normative sphere from a systemic economic sphere. Taking into account these last observations on the actuality of Lukács' *Ontology* and above all on his insistence on social alternatives (as indicators of the possibility of social *freedom*), we can conclude this paper acknowledging that Lukács' ontological dialectics (despite being written in a much more sober environment and formulated in a much more conceptually systematic mode than his previous original philosophical work of *History and Class Consciousness*) fully retain their political radical consequences.

---

74 For Habermas' rejection of any kind of objective dialectics as being identified with metaphysical "objective spirit," see Jürgen Habermas, *The Theory of Communicative Action: Volume One: Reason and the Rationalization of Society*. Trans. Thomas McCarthy. (Boston: Beacon Press), 363–365, 368.

PART 3

Lukács' Social Ontology and Contemporary Philosophy

∴

CHAPTER 7

On the "Constitution of Human Society": Lukács' versus Searle's Social Ontology

Claudius Vellay

1   Introduction

John R. Searle, one of the leading philosophers of Anglo-Saxon style analytic philosophy, is probably more correct than even he suspects with the diagnosis that ontological questions, especially concerning social ontology, will replace epistemological considerations at the heart of 21st century philosophy. The overall task of rational philosophy at the present time is to contribute to the very existence of mankind, now threatened by global problems such as war, destruction of the environment and social inequality. It is real existential problems which force humanity not only to be one integrated biological species but to become a unified "subject" of our own destiny – as well as that of other species. Therefore ontology is still, *mutatis mutandis*, the grounding branch of philosophy, as it had been in the ancient Greek tradition, and could be expected to have a comeback as the principal preoccupation of philosophers against the still-strong neo-Kantian tradition.

It is his "great sense of reality,"[1] which enables Searle to avoid and criticize quite convincingly many of the prevailing dead-ended philosophies, from overall skepticism to postmodern relativism. This sense of realism makes Searle, objectively, one of the most precious allies within dominant contemporary philosophy in the combat against obscurantism and mounting irrationalism in society.[2] His general ontology defends the independent existence of nature as

---

1   Lukács praised in this manner the German philosopher Nicolai Hartmann, who developed his ontology in the first half of the 20th century without being heavily compromised by the Nazis in the way his irrationalist counterpart Heidegger was, and who despite serious differences inspired much of the late ontological theory of the Marxist thinker, Georg Lukács, *Zur Ontologie des gesellschaftlichen Seins*, vol. 1. (Darmstadt, Neuwied: Luchterhand Verlag, 1984), 464. Concerning their relationship see also Claudius Vellay, "Von Hartmann über Harich zu Lukács. Einige Besonderheiten der ontologischen Wende im Marxismus." In Andreas Heyer (ed.), *Wolfgang Harich in den Kämpfen seiner Zeit.* (Hamburg: LAIKA Verlag, 2016), 53–84.
2   Concerning mounting irrationalism and the Marxist concept of rationality see Claudius Vellay, "Vernunft, Vernunftlosigkeit und Unvernunft, Rationalismus und Irrationalismus. Zur

the foundation of scientific knowledge. And even if I consider his view on social ontology to be fundamentally erroneous, he still treats social issues with a sense of reality well above that of his colleagues. Not only by expressing his point of view clearly – which is unusual in philosophy nowadays – but also by avoiding obscuring real debates by over-technical hairsplitting, as is very common especially in analytic philosophy. Even where he fails, it is worth reading Searle.

But by reading Searle we should not expect a critical theory of contemporary society, which he acknowledges after all as a capitalist society, but holds a rather conservative[3] apologetic view of it. We find in society, as well as among philosophers, all kinds of political and ethical stands combined with different, sometimes strange,[4] explicit or implicit ontologies. Unfortunately, it is quite common that critical positions combine with so-called "anti-realist" views.[5] Without a realist ontological foundation, social critique risks missing applicable solutions especially of global problems.

The core of Searle's social ontology is the idea that social reality "exists only because we think it exists."[6] Human civilization is what it is because of our way of "seeing" things, in the metaphorical sense of how we think of them. That is not because Searle pretends that we are doing nothing, other than thinking. Rather he holds that our intentional action could be analyzed in terms of the

---

Klärung einiger Kategorien vor dem Hintergrund des Lukácsschen Werks von der *Zerstörung der Vernunft* bis zur *Ontologie*." *Marxistische Blätter*, vol. 56, no. 1 (2018): 35–46. For Searle's quite different concept of rationality see John Rogers Searle, *Rationality in action*. (Cambridge: MIT Press, 2001).

3   This is not meant to be a statement of endorsement regarding the recent allegations of questionable conduct by Searle whose philosophical merit should be treated separately.
4   Consider for example Lukács' severe judgment about his longstanding friend, Ernst Bloch, whom he certified a "fascinating Italian salad of subjectivist thoughts" while welcoming his leftist ethics, see Frank Benseler, "Nachwort des Herausgebers." In Georg Lukács, *Zur Ontologie des gesellschaftlichen Seins*, vol. 2. (Darmstadt, Neuwied: Luchterhand Verlag, 1986), 731–753, 733. Concerning the relation Bloch-Lukács and especially Lukács' critique of utopianism, see Claudius Vellay, "Der Marxismus proklamiert keine Utopien. Plädoyer für eine marxistische Ontologie mit der Wirklichkeit als Zentralkategorie." In Hermann Kopp (ed.), *Wovon wir träumen müssen. Marxismus und Utopie*. (Hamburg: LAIKA Verlag, 2013), 219–236; and Claudius Vellay, "Nochmals dazu, warum der Marxismus keine Utopien verkündet. Für eine realistische Ontologie des Marxismus: Lukács statt Bloch." Marxistische Blätter, vol. 53, no. 6 (2015): 66–75.
5   Later (2.7) I explain why in Marxist tradition "anti-realism" is appropriately called "subjective idealism" and "materialist" replace "realist."
6   John Rogers Searle, *Philosophy in a new century. Selected essays*. (New York: Cambridge University Press, 2008), 27.

logical structure of speech-acts, which gives us the key to understand how we *constitute* social reality.

In opposition to this view, I will argue on the basis of Lukács' *Ontology of Social Being* that logical analysis is not the right approach to understand what human society is. Ontology has to tell us what there really is. It has to show the real being in its most fundamental structures and categories by studying its genealogy, the way it has evolved. Social ontology then tells us that social reality exists because we made it. It is the way we make things intentionally, i.e., teleologically-guided, that produces human society and enables the development of our thinking and communication, including acts of speaking.

To show this I will confront the general philosophical views of Lukács and Searle. In the second section I will expose the fundamental differences between the Marxist and the analytic concepts of ontology along major categories (2.1–2.7). After calling attention in a brief "interlude" to the puzzle of social being, I confront in the third section Searle's and Lukács' social ontologies (3.1–3.7). The discussion is centered by their fundamental paradigms, language and labour. I conclude with a brief outline regarding critical theory and the crucial notion of human liberty.

2 Marxist versus Analytic Concept of Ontology

2.1 *Searle and "Constitution" of Reality*

Searle's worldview is grounded in the acknowledgement of independent reality. He consequently rejects the concept of an ideal "constitution" of reality concerning brute facts and the related skepticism concerning the existence of the external world independent of humanity. He has a too-large sense of reality, at least concerning the physical facts, to be tented by the solipsist implications this philosophical stance of traditional constitution theory bears. Searle accepts on the contrary this notion for social entities, for instance in formulations like "human society is largely constituted by distinctive institutional structures";[7] even so the titles of his major books on social ontology avoid this kind of idealistic connotation. However, "construction of the social world"[8] or "making the social world"[9] are in a way ambiguous, because they suggest a voluntarily-produced genealogy of what Searle calls the "social world."

---

7   John Rogers Searle, *Making the social world. The structure of human civilization.* (Oxford, New York: Oxford University Press, 2010), 200.
8   John Rogers Searle, *The construction of social reality.* (New York: Free Press, 1995).
9   Searle 2010, op. cit.

There are two problems with those titles:

On the one hand, even in a Lukácsian perspective with labour as the fundamental category of social being, there never is a "making" or "constructing," understood as "acting on purpose," concerning society as a whole, i.e., "social being" according to Lukács or "social world" according to Searle. First there is no such thing as an overall subject capable to conceive and produce on purpose society altogether, or society as a totality. Surely it makes sense to say that society and especially its constraints are due to human action as opposed to the natural and in that way unchangeable eternal conditions of human life (think of Thatcher's purely ideological TINA-formula: "there is no alternative"). We might even say with Engels and Lukács, that by labour man has not only produced society but himself (see 3.4). But interpreting the whole of society as a single project, consciously conceived and realized by a single subject, humanity, does not have even a metaphorical sense.

Secondly, as Lukács further explains in his *Ontology*, even by the most basic and limited acts of labour, the real outcomes never coincide exactly with the prior ideally, i.e., mentally, conceived purpose. Generally speaking: foreseeing "absolute" or "total" completeness of conditions is limited to cases of idealizations, which we make use of in mathematics or logic. But we should not forget that reality itself proceeds with an infinity of conditions both in every aspect and as "totality," whereas our ideal reflection of reality is never more than – at best – a finite approximation of it. So even if we would, for strictly pedagogical purposes, imagine society reduced to a single social act, the actual outcome would not even then be identical with the ideal plan, because real causal acting consists always of interfering in (a very tiny part of) the infinite causal interdependent relations of natural reality. But social being is of course not only the very large number of all kinds of individual actions at a given moment of historical social development, on purpose or not, coordinated or not, with all its interferences among people and with ever more transformed objects of organic and inorganic nature. It is actually the totality of the historical development of humanity. Clearly, there is no such thing as "constructing" or "making" the "social world" as a whole.

It is also clear that Searle does not have labour in mind when he talks of "constructing" or "making" the social world. Labour for him is at best a certain subclass of "social action." His "making" is more an attributing, seeing as, interpreting and so forth, which he analyzes in the logical form of speech acts (see 3.1). Thus, for him the social "world" is constituted by the according of meaning to things or states of affairs in the (physical) world, including whatever we are doing. Though there are some interesting insights to gain, Searle's view is not that of an actual "making" or "constructing" the social being, but rather that of ideally "constituting" the social "world."[10]

2.2 Skepticism and Epistemic Bias

The most precious feature of Searle's philosophy is his clear acknowledgement of the independent existence of reality, of "brute facts," as he calls it. This has to be, according to Searle, the starting point of contemporary philosophy, by endorsing scientific knowledge, especially (atomistic) physics and (evolutionary) biology. That is why he is confident that ontology will again occupy the center of philosophy in the 21st century.[11] It is precisely this turn to ontology based on the independent existence of reality which is the main common point between Searle's, Lukács' and incidentally Nicolai Hartmann's philosophies. It should be emphasized that accordance on this point is rather exceptional even among the followers of the recently-renewed interest in ontology, especially within analytic philosophy.[12] Searle and Lukács both argue against the hegemony of epistemology in philosophy, even if Lukács analyzes this tendency and its historical background much more profoundly and comprehensively in his critique of the principal currents of contemporary philosophy, which occupies a large part of the first volume of his *Ontology*.[13]

For Searle the dominance of epistemology is driven by skepticism starting with Descartes' systematic doubt. Occidental philosophy struggles with the question of how to ensure certainty of knowledge, leading to fundamental false dualist worldviews and its equally erroneous materialist alternatives (I will discuss materialism vs. idealism in 2.7). Searle's rather weak rejection of skepticism is based on the diagnosis of "sheer growth of certain, objective, and

---

10   Compare his following formulation: "I am not asking what *caused* [...], but rather what facts about them *constitute* their being money," Searle 2008, op. cit., 115 (emphasis in original).
11   Ibid., 4ff.
12   Critical theory generally endorses what used to be called an "anti-realistic" stance concerning independent nature, in for instance the Frankfurt School, largely inspired by Lukács' famous youth opus *History and Class Consciousness* (1923), which among other major errors in his Marxist apprenticeship rejected dialectics of (independent) nature. Lukács himself criticized – not only – this point from an ontological perspective in his introduction to the re-publication in 1967, see Georg Lukács, "Vorwort." In Frank Benseler (ed.), *Frühschriften II, Geschichte und Klassenbewußtsein*. (Berlin, Neuwied: Luchterhand, 1977), 47–78.
13   Lukács 1984, op. cit., 325ff.

universal knowledge" distinguishing our times, so that it is no longer possible to "take seriously arguments that attempt to prove that it [the world, CV] doesn't exist at all."[14] We could not "send men to the moon and back and then seriously doubt whether the external world exists."[15] Being thus of no epistemic interest, Searle believes it possible to reject skepticism.[16] But this argument misses the point of skepticism, which has never been pretending to doubt knowledge of this or that concrete aspect of reality; as Searle knows, even accumulating scientific knowledge should always allow for the possibility of failure in any particular question. The skeptical interrogation is not epistemic; by showing the impossibility of absolute knowledge it gains a semblance of respectability to subjective idealism, leading consequently to solipsism.

The still appealing stance of skepticism – which in a sense seems even more captivating than in Descartes time, if we consider the much greater number of people who are paying attention to philosophical questions – does not concern knowledge at all. No more than the ancient paradoxes of motion are designed to prevent Zenon or whoever to put one foot before the other. Skepticism concerns the possibility of knowledge altogether, in pretending that we cannot exclude – logically! – that everything could be completely different than we actually think it is, e.g., that everything is just an idea in the mind and there is no such thing as reality. The science fiction film *The Matrix* is a popular adaption of a skeptical idea in philosophy, namely the "brain in a vat"-argument. Searle is badly advised when trying to find a logical solution,[17] because we cannot actually exclude the skeptical hypothesis logically. And indicating the growing knowledge of scientific facts will not change it any more than appealing to the well-established knowledge of any particular fact. Otherwise, first Descartes or the ancient skeptics and then everyone would have much more convincing arguments literally at hand than the existence of the moon. Evoking the moon landing is an unfortunate example, since skepticism of the first moon-landing is a popular internet conspiracy theory, asserting that the landing is somehow made up. I do not want to suggest that philosophers arguing about skepticism is exactly like conspiracy gossip, a phenomenon, which is to be explained – like growing irrationalism on the top political level – with regard to the crisis-prone capitalist system. Nevertheless there is a rather obvious

---

14 Searle 2008, op. cit., 5f.
15 Ibid., 110.
16 Searle 2015, op. cit., 157.
17 Ibid., 156ff. He is right to not be "sure" himself about his logical "solution," ibid., 160, because none of his theory, including intentional content being "satisfied" or not, could escape from the "brain in a vat" fantasy.

link between disseminating the skeptical idea and a spreading fragility within society in the face of irrationalism.

Historically it would be a crude anachronism to associate Cartesian rationalism with irrationalism. Descartes' doubt marked a milestone in liberating thinking from theological dominance at a crucial moment of early capitalism with its thirst for uninhibited development of productive forces and thus for scientific knowledge liberated from the dogmatism of the ruling Christian church. The resulting dualism, even as the Kantian inaccessible thing-in-itself, first and foremost strongly promoted the liberation of material affairs and of the natural sciences from religious interference. In this sense the young Marx hailed Descartes in *The Holy Family* as an early representative of French materialism, precursor of the Enlightenment. Searle from his logisticist throne cannot judge dualism and other philosophical views but as continuous mistakes with disastrous consequences,[18] whereas Lukács, due to his historical approach, could adequately appreciate the initial progressive role of dualism and German idealism. But, as Lukács further explains, the dualistic mode of thought opens the door to religious dominance concerning the core being of man, his thinking and soul, leading to a lasting acceptance of double truths:[19] on one hand scientific truth for practical affairs, while on the other the truth of one's essence – and initially the world – left to religious faith and the church.[20] This "historical compromise" continues to be influential. It has inspired a double mode of thinking that combines the need for perfect technical knowledge and mastery but with a certain vagueness and uncertainty concerning humanity and social being. This double truth, to which I will return in the discussion of free will (3.7), fits with the overall irrational organizing of a capitalist society based on competition, where gigantic inequality is supposed to serve the general public. For instance, does this ideology permit that hyper rationalist economists, (whose standard model of rational utility maximization ignores against all evidence the economic crisis in capitalism) are Nobel-prized while no one

---

18 Ibid., 10ff. He is even tempted to imagine how the philosophy of the last 300 years would have been, if this kind of "error" had been avoided, for example ibid., 31.

19 Lukács reminds us of the double truths claimed by the Cardinal Bellarmin in confronting Galileo, see Lukács 1984, op. cit., 337ff. As a modern adaptation of the medieval doctrine of the two truths, the theory of double truth will continue in different forms till the present day, as Lukács discusses on various occasions, see for example Lukács 1984, op. cit., 31, 34, 344ff., 418f., 533; see also Georg Lukács, *Zur Ontologie des gesellschaftlichen Seins*, vol. 2. (Darmstadt, Neuwied: Luchterhand Verlag, 1986), 58f., 108, 386, 631.

20 Lukács 1984, op. cit., 533. See also ibid., 249 where Lukács qualifies the liberation process opening with Descartes and the Renaissance as still remaining inside a renewed but continuing form of alienation.

really believes that people act like their theories pretend. They are widely accepted as perfectly calculable models, whose political outcome – while seldom mentioned aloud – happens to serve the particular interest of the dominant class. We have to distinguish between the motives which lead someone to invent a certain theory and the reasons why a particular theory becomes influential and carries on to spread in society; a difference what sometimes even Lukács seemed to have neglected in his eagerness to find the social-historical roots of philosophies and ideologies. The need being served, for instance a religious need for the immortality of the soul which was pleased by the dualist worldview, did not necessarily coincide with the motivation Descartes and other philosophers had in mind.

Searle's argument is nevertheless right that the skeptical fantasy is leading nowhere and that it cannot serve a philosophy attuned to real problems people encounter in dealing with nature and society. Nevertheless there is one objective skepticism could serve, which the analytic philosopher leaves aside, possibly not by pure chance. As any reasoning pushed to its limit, such as the traditional thought-paradoxes of the ancient philosophers, skepticism also reminds us that logical reasoning is not omnipotent and especially cannot alone provide the solution to questions of real existence. Logic is a very powerful tool of our reasoning especially serving heuristic purposes, but if we want to know what there really is "out there," we have to look at reality. Just reasoning logically will not do the job. Pure thought-experiences could show us reasonable avenues for further research, but to know if something really exists we cannot leave out the empirical part. It cannot be otherwise, because logic belongs to our thinking, to our rationality, to the ideal reflection, but not to reality itself. Reality is not functioning logically, but causally. This is what the skeptical "puzzle" really reminds us, instead of solely illustrating the ontological distinction between subjective consciousness and objective reality, as Searle pretends.[21]

For Searle, similar to the philosophical current of critical realism associated with Roy Bhaskar,[22] it is the skeptical stance toward knowledge about reality which leads to the epistemic bias of modern philosophy since Descartes. For

---

21 Searle 2015, op. cit., 78 and 156ff.
22 Roy Bhaskar, *A realist theory of science*. (London: Verso, 1997). There have been also some attempts to associate critical realism with Marxist thinking, see e.g., Alex Callinicos, "Critical Realism and Beyond, Roy Bhaskar's Dialectic." In Jacques Bidet and Eustache Kouvélakis (eds.), *Critical companion to contemporary Marxism*. (Leiden, Boston: Brill, 2008), or even, especially in Brazil, to Lukács' *Ontology*, see e.g., Mário Duayer, João Leonardo Medeiros, "Lukács' critical ontology and critical realism." *Journal of Critical Realism*, vol. 4, no. 2 (2005): 395–425.

them, the epistemic fallacy consists of basing philosophy on skepticism and thus discrediting ontology, instead of starting from our scientific knowledge of the world. It is worth noting that the ontologies of Lukács and Hartmann, in sharp opposition to the contemptuous ignorance of Heidegger, endorses science as an important means to get true knowledge about reality, even if they maintain, in deference to Searle, the necessity of an ontological critique of certain scientific theses, especially as they result from extrapolation and analogies across different domains.[23] But Lukács analyzes the epistemological hegemony in contemporary philosophy principally as a result of Kantian subjective idealism. The assertion of the inaccessibility of the thing-in-itself and its post-Kantian radicalization to the inexistence of the thing-in-itself, i.e., the independent reality, has long discredited all ontology as "naïve" and simply impossible after Kant's *Critique*. This epistemic bias aims to limit all philosophy to worry about the knowledge of appearances, but it is perfectly compatible with scientific progress. Both neo-positivists as well as pragmatists, to take only two philosophies in the Kantian tradition, have an encouraging attitude toward science as long as it abstains from any "metaphysical" claims of actually explaining the world as it is, i.e., reality-in-itself.[24] We encounter here an adaptation of double truths already mentioned above: an openness to mathematical-technical manipulation in science and its application at will, provided it works, combined with noble abstinence concerning world views.

To review and summarize: it is not so much the Cartesian skepticism about knowledge altogether which nourishes the epistemological dominance in modern philosophy and to which the sheer amount of accumulated scientific knowledge could be opposed, but the establishment of neo-Kantian double truths, which leaves science methodically unscathed but declares as impossible access to reality as such, which condemns philosophy to the methods of logical analyses concerning knowledge, i.e., epistemological enquiry.

Lukács' analysis of what is really at stake in the epistemological hegemony lets us clearly see that analytic philosophy altogether is concerned by the epistemological bias, including its recent rather strange turn to "ontology" and even Searle's philosophy.

---

23 See e.g., Lukács 1984, op. cit., 19.
24 It is quite interesting to see that Searle also establishes the rejection of the independent and objective world as the converging point of such different and ideologically opposed philosophical traditions like phenomenology and logical positivism, Searle 2015, op. cit., 224 and 227.

2.3 The Notion of Ontology: Analytic Logic vs. Marxist Genealogy of Categories

They inherit the Kantian transcendental methods which try to logically figure out what are the conditions of possibility of an encountered entity. The emblematic question of Kantian transcendentalism is: how is it possible that X? This question does not enquire about the real historical way an entity, X, came into being. Rather they analyze the *a priori* conditions, which logically are supposed to exist in order to make it possible to encounter X. The answer to the analytic question consists in deductively filtering out some principles, which are presumed to constitute the logical structure of the phenomenon in question, but not to discover the real historical genealogy of it.

That is why neo-Kantian philosophies tend to replace the correspondence notion of truth, which supposes an access to independent reality in order to compare it with our theories about this reality, by that of logical coherence. Therefore they emphasize the logical enquiry and formal analysis of language which characterizes the linguistic turn in analytic philosophy.

Finally, analytic social ontology tries to establish the constitutive principles of social facts. We see the same scheme in the lead question of Searle's social ontology, which he believes to be "the single overriding question in contemporary philosophy":[25] "How is it possible in a universe consisting entirely of physical particles in fields of force that there can be such things as consciousness, intentionality, free will, language, society, ethics, aesthetics, and political obligations?"[26] He tries to answer the question in his "social ontology," as we will see in the second section, by analyzing the logical structure of social facts, which is supposed to tell us how they are possible.

But despite Searle's attachment to the philosophical tradition of analytic philosophy, we have to acknowledge the difference to most of his colleagues. For them, in contrast to Searle, it is commonly admitted that perception and action depend on language which structures mental entities, and therefore the linguistic access to the world is not a detour but the central way to reveal reality.[27] According to Jansen, understanding ontology with Quine as "what there is" or social ontology with Pettit as "an account of what there is in the social world" would be a naïve and boring undertaking.[28] Instead, analytic social ontology must ask of which kind of entities cooperation is constitutive. Therefore

---

25   Searle 2010, op. cit., 3.
26   Ibid. See also e.g., Searle 2008, op. cit., 26ff. and 108.
27   See for example Ludger Jansen, *Gruppen und Institutionen. Eine Ontologie des* Sozialen. (Wiesbaden: Springer, 2017), 17.
28   Ibid., 12.

he includes in his definition of social entities Martians, angels or hyper-intelligent androids, provided that they rely on cooperation for "metaphysical" reasons. He excludes individual activities, for which he makes an example of a four-handed cook able to prepare alone a very complicated cake.[29] Obviously Jansen's logisticist "ontology" is an awful lot concerned with exhaustive definitions, not with reality. Even if Searle shares the logical approach to social "ontology," he is distancing himself from this kind of dominant analytical philosophy due to his sense of reality.

Lukács also tries sometimes to discover the requirements for a certain phenomenon, such as the existence of language as a condition of the maintenance and continuity of the social being.[30] But for him, logic is "just" of heuristic utility to find candidates for empirical research to get access to reality, and not the only way to acquire *a priori* and thus absolute certain knowledge about otherwise inaccessible things in themselves, as for analytic philosophy. Lukács' genealogical method might as well encounter the problem of missing empirical evidence, especially concerning the first stages of humankind, but he takes it not as a proof of metaphysical inaccessibility of reality, but as a task for further research. For Lukács, ontology is a theory of categories on its most fundamental level. Marxist ontology understands categories primarily as forms of being (*Daseinsformen*) or characteristics of existence (*Existenzbestimmungen*), as inherent determinations of objects and their relations which constitute the material, or the same, real being.[31] Only secondarily, if they become part of our comprehension of reality, are they forms of our ideal reflection. Conceiving the categories as inherent to and developing within real being distinguishes sharply the Marxist ontology from other philosophies;[32] I will come back to this difference concerning the traditional problem of universals (2.7).

Most of the recent return to "ontology" in contemporary philosophy, and even to a certain extent Searle's social ontology, continues in fact as a variation within the neo-Kantian logisticist approach, whereas Lukács develops the Marxist ontology of materialist and developing being.

---

29   Ibid., 9ff.
30   Lukács 1986, op. cit., 166.
31   Lukács 1984, op. cit., 36, 127, 144, and passim. See for example 310f. where he indicates explicitly the primary use by Marx of the notion "category" as form of being despite the etymological meaning of prediction.
32   See István Eörsi, "Gelebtes Denken. G. Lukács im Gespräch über sein Leben." In Frank Benseler and Werner Jung (eds.), *Georg Lukács. Autobiographische Texte und Gespräche.* (Bielefeld: Aisthesis, 2005), 49–223, 196f. See also the English translation Georg Lukács, *Record of a life. An autobiographical sketch.* (London: Verso, 1983), 142.

2.4 Three Spheres of Being: Inorganic, Organic and Social

Searle takes it as a condition of the adequacy of social ontology to avoid postulating multiple realms or worlds, as in dualist or "trialist" world-conceptions.[33] He aims at the representatives of philosophy of language like Frege or Habermas, but mentions also the three-world concept of Popper and Eccles composed of the physical, the mental and the ideal reality of objective knowledge. For Searle, on the contrary, there exists only one world and the overall task in philosophy is to give a unified concept of ourselves being part of the natural world so that human reality is not only consistent with but a natural consequence of the behavior of physical particles and evolutionary biology. From a Marxist point of view Searle is right to say that there is only one natural world, if by that is understood the inexistence of any supra-natural beyond or transcendence. Likewise Lukács shows that it is erroneous to suppose, as in objective idealist philosophies, an independent existence of an ideal or spiritual sphere, which precedes the natural world (Hegel) or has an objective existence as ideal being apart from it (Nicolai Hartmann). That we live in one unique world does not mean that there are not substantial variations in it. Searle also admits this when, in addition to physical particles, he counts evolutionary biology as "basic facts." For Lukács, this distinction reveals not only an epistemic difference to structure our scientific knowledge but reveals a fundamental differentiation operated within natural being itself. Even if we still do not know exactly how life on earth began – the unique life form we know – it is more than reasonable to accept life, or in Lukács' jargon the organic sphere, as having emerged with its proper functioning laws out of the fundamental inorganic sphere, whose basic functioning and laws are integrated into the higher sphere. This ontological view of the real genesis is in complete accordance with scientific knowledge and is precisely the rational alternative to a supernatural "explanation."

But nature is not all that there is. There is also human culture or in Lukács' words the "social being," as emerged over time out of the organic sphere with its proper operating mechanisms and laws by integrating those of the lower level. Lukács' main objective of his ontological turn in Marxism is to show the operating of the basic categories of social being by emphasizing the importance of the emerging subjective side and hence of humane individuals, too often neglected in traditional Marxism. Especially the extensive *Prolegomena*[34]

---

33   See for instance Searle 2010, op. cit., 3f.
34   Lukács 1984, op. cit., 7–324. Lukács wrote the voluminous *Prolegomena* as an explanation after controversial discussions with his Budapest scholars which simply failed to grasp till the present day the ontological approach to Marxism altogether, see Claudius Vellay, "Die

of the first volume of his *Ontology of Social Being* is dedicated to the articulation between natural and social ontology, joining their respective central categories of causality and teleology. The main part of the first volume treats the philosophical-historical roots of Lukács materialist ontology, from Hartmann and Hegel to Marx.[35] Articulated around the central category of being, it is opposed to epistemic-logisticist philosophy, whose central category is necessity. The second volume then addresses the main complexes of social ontology, namely labour as its founding category, reproduction, ideal and alienation.[36]

What is important to see at this point is that there are higher forms of being, first the organic and then, with humans, the social sphere, emerging from the everlasting inorganic nature and constituting an ever more complex structure of real being. So e.g., consciousness is well an emerging feature within the higher forms of organic being, but becomes its fully developed form only in social being with human thinking and teleologically-guided action. Even if it starts with animal life, consciousness is not essential to the organic sphere but becomes a central feature, no longer just an epiphenomenal one, in the development of human being and society. To see this development, we have to understand the central category of labour in which an *ideal* teleological element is joined to *real* transforming action and permits auto-development from the real social sphere and its ideal component (see 3.4). Reality means foremost that it functions causally, which implies among other features being directed in time and spatially located. In that sense, all three spheres of being are, despite their differences, overall functioning causally, i.e., they form three spheres of real being. But inside the social being is developing an ideal feature, located in human brains, which is no longer functioning causally but able to guide teleologically our action.

Entfremdung aus Sicht der Lukácsschen Ontologie. Materialistische Ethik diesseits von Religion und Glauben." In Christoph J. Bauer et al. (eds.), „*Bei mir ist jede Sache Fortsetzung von etwas*". *Georg Lukács – Werk und Wirkung.* (Duisburg: Univ.-Verl. Rhein-Ruhr, 2008), 153–185, 155. As important as the *Prolegomena* are to better understand the whole project of Lukács' ontology, it is a pity that Lukács left the ontology unfinished and without final editing.

35   Lukács 1984, op. cit. Only two chapters from the first volume are translated to English: Georg Lukács, *The ontology of social being. Vol. 1 – Hegel's false and his genuine ontology.* (London: Merlin Press, 1978), (cited furthermore as O1, following in parenthesis the German reference) and Georg Lukács, *The ontology of social being. Vol. 2 – Marx's basic ontological principles.* (London: Merlin Press, 1978), (cited as O2).

36   Lukács 1986, op. cit. From this second volume only the first chapter is translated into English: Georg Lukács, *The ontology of social being. Vol. 3 – Labour.* (London: Merlin Press, 1980), (cited as O3).

But before addressing the specific features of the social sphere, other basic categories of general ontology, such as causality, determinism and infinity, are discussed, as well as the notion of *being-in-itself*.

2.5 *Being-in-Itself: Causality, Determinism and Infinity*

Another problem with Searle's view of the social being as the natural consequence of the behavior of the physical is that it suggests an overall inherent determinism, in the sense of Laplace, which implies a closed and finite universe with a common origin of everything. This classic version of a deterministic universe has roots in a teleological concept of nature, in which causality is a means to a goal, i.e., the world as it actually is at every moment since its creation. On the contrary stands a concept of an infinite universe which comprises the totality of reality. The infinity is not only understood temporally in both directions, but the causal influences are also extensively and intensively infinite.[37] It excludes the existence of any "outside" or transcendence of reality as well as an absolute beginning or ending of something, a fortiori of everything, out of or into nothing. Reality, or in Marxist jargon *matter*,[38] thus understood as all-encompassing and continuously transforming its internal structures, infers that causality goes along with probabilism. In this concept, causality means just that there is no *real* phenomenon – leaving aside the mental or *ideal* phenomenon of representational content – out of nothing, i.e., without antecedent (or successor), thus in this sense the – infinite – universe is causally "closed," by concomitantly excluding an all reality encompassing determinism. Any real phenomenon, whose continuously transforming existence as a unit is always relative concerning its limits, has an infinite number of determining factors which all have an infinite number of antecedents. This real infinity of causal heterogenic influences means that there is always an

---

37 This type of consideration about the totality of all that exists encompasses necessarily a speculative element, which – at best – extrapolates adequately on the basis of our knowledge to a coherent worldview.

38 A classical dialectical-materialist account of causality of *matter* is emphasizing the natural existence excluding miracles, see Vladimir Ilyich Lenin, *Materialism and Empiriocriticism. Collected Works*, vol. 14. (Moscow: Progress Publishers, 1977), 26off. That causality is additionally directed in time and located somewhere, as well as in all dimensions infinitely, is more bound to the notion of *real* being or *being-in-itself* developed by Lukács. Searle rejects the notion of "being" as confused in his critics of phenomenology, see Searle 2008, op. cit., 110. In a way this is correct because phenomenologists confuse precisely *ideal* representations and *real* being into conscious phenomena. But Searle as well confuses both, although into real (biological) being. But it is fundamental to distinguish (real) *being* and (ideal) *representations* in its heterogeneity.

inevitable element of real contingency, which enables the existence of real possibilities, especially the emerging of something fundamentally new.[39]

Any phenomenon is, strictly speaking, unique; it always belongs to one (or generally several) essential type(s), expressing one (or several) law(s), whose existence is strictly inherent to the real phenomena and their relationships to each other. Real causality does not include the rationalistic fallacy of an all-encompassing determinism.[40] Lukács therefore rejects the logisticist conception of absolute necessity, which projects a constituent of our logical reasoning onto the functioning of the world. In reality we only encounter strictly conditioned necessity, or as he says "if-then-necessity,"[41] i.e., the causal factors producing the natural processes in their *being-so* (*Sosein*) as they actually are. All in all reality or *being-in-itself* is throughout a historical process,[42] i.e., in continuous causal transformation, which, due to its infinite character, is not subjected to global determinism and thus open to emergent phenomena.

Searle is right to think of consciousness as a biological feature[43] as opposed to an independent "free-floating" ideal entity. He also is correct when he considers as a "useful heuristic device"[44] that from the seventeenth century on consciousness was excluded from being part of the natural world; it helped to liberate the understanding of nature from the teleological explanation, a crucial turn which was achieved by Darwin's theory of evolution. But by treating consciousness just "as much a part of the natural biological order as any other

---

39   An incorrect ontological understanding of modal-categories such as necessity, probability, possibility and, embracing all others, reality, is often a major source of misleading philosophical conceptions, not only in Marxism, see Claudius Vellay, "Les catégories modales dans l'Ontologie de Georg Lukács – une confrontation avec Nicolai Hartmann et Ernst Bloch." In Pierre Rusch and Ádám Takács (eds.), *L'actualité de Georges Lukács. Actes du colloque organisé les 28 et 29 octobre 2010 á Budapest* (Paris: Archives Karéline, 2013), 227–241.

40   To see this there is no need of probabilism or indeterminism in the sense of quantum mechanics. Incidentally Searle regards it as a scandal that philosophy of science has "not so far given us a coherent account of how quantum mechanics fits into our overall conception of the universe," Searle 2008, op. cit., 24.

41   See Lukács 1984, op. cit., 103f. and 151ff. See also Wolfgang Abendroth, Hans Heinz Holz and Leo Kofler, "Gespräche mit Georg Lukács (1966)." In Frank Benseler and Werner Jung (eds.), *Georg Lukács. Autobiographische Texte und Gespräche*. (Bielefeld: Aisthesis, 2005), 233–351, 241f.

42   We should not be troubled that the timescale of change could vary to the point that things appear unchanging and practically stable. Lukács holds as "the most important part of Marxian theory" that historicity is a fundamental characteristic not only of social reality but of being altogether, Eörsi 2005, op. cit., 196 or in English Lukács 1983, op. cit., 142.

43   John R. Searle, *The Rediscovery of the Mind*. (Cambridge: MIT Press, 1992), 90.

44   Ibid., 93.

biological features such as photosynthesis, digestion, or mitosis,"[45] Searle assumes that consciousness remains subordinate to the causal processes of biological reproduction. He fails to see that in the social sphere, which developed solely with humans, the initial biological feature of consciousness could overcome its epiphenomenal limitation and play a central role in social being by gaining a certain degree of autonomy relative to its natural basis. Without suggesting any necessity of development to the higher form, it is important to see that among all biological features, consciousness is the only one to have the inherent possibility to play this role, even if it could only develop within the human social sphere (See 3.4–5). That is not just to state a logical truism that what has come to being, had to be possible in the first place, but also to see that "other biological features such as photosynthesis, digestion, or mitosis" never could have played this role of possible distancing from solely causal processes.

What developed as the central part of social being is not the biological feature of consciousness as such and its causally functioning organ, the brain, but rather the ideal content the conscious human is able to produce by thinking. In a way, Searle grasps this difference superficially by distinguishing the ontological objective from the subjective as two modes of existence. The latter he defines as existing "only insofar as experienced by a human or animal subject," whereas the former "have an existence independent of any experience."[46] Leaving to the forthcoming discussion (see 3.4–5) the undifferentiated attribution of the subject character to humans *and* animals, the point here is that on first sight his objective domain could be confused with what Lukács called *being-in-itself* (*Ansichsein*), because both philosophers make reference to its independent existence. Searle also names it observer-independence or in his first book on social ontology "intrinsic features of reality."[47] Independence, though adequate in opposition to subject-dependent features, remains a kind of indirect and negative qualification. To see the weak point, just suppose that life exists only on earth, so that before our planet came into existence some 4.5

---

45   Ibid., 90. But Searle does not feel really comfortable in treating the brain as any other organ "as a completely deterministic system," at least when he comes to reasoning about "free will," see Searle 2001, op. cit., 296.

46   Searle 2015, op. cit., 16. He correctly differentiates from these ontological modes of existence the epistemic claims, which for their part are either objective, i.e., truth or falsehood could be settled, or subjective, i.e., an opinion based on individual evaluation.

47   Searle 1995, op. cit., 12. Concerning the observer-independence, see for example Searle 2008, op. cit., 78ff.; in which he explains he has dropped the term "intrinsic" because it caused frequent confusion, which is not surprising when analytic philosophers are asked to treat reality as it is.

billion years ago, there was definitely no conscious subject from which the already existent stars of the galaxy could have been independent. To call them "intrinsic" sounds like a positive qualification of reality, but it leaves open the question of what kind of "extrinsic" entities it might be opposed, since Searle wants consciousness, and especially his master concept of intentionality, to be treated ontologically as natural phenomena.[48]

In a way it is the same negative concept as defining the Marxist philosophical notion of matter, which is identical to the notion of reality or being, as independent and outside of (human) consciousness.[49] All these qualifications express the idea of objective existence, as does Lukács' positive notion of *being-in-itself*. But for the latter this is just one fundamental characteristic among others. Notably does *being-in-itself* convey determinations like proceeding causally, including being as transforming processes directed in time and located spatially; being in reciprocal interrelation (*Wechselwirkung*) and reflexive determination (*Reflexionsbestimmung*) as the fundamental dialectical concept, which are both concretizations of being objectivity (*Gegenständlichkeit*, literally what stands in front of) and implies universal generality as well as unique concretion, being essence and phenomenon, form and material, quantity and quality, etc. The full panoply of fundamental categories of being as its positive determinations are included in the notion of *being-in-itself*, leaving aside just the categories which belong merely to human thinking or to the purely social domain of *being-for-itself* (*Fürsichsein*). The notion of independence of consciousness is just one aspect of *being-in-itself*, concerning our relation to it. But being "real" (*wirklich*), or in Marxist terms "material," as the most fundamental characterization of *being-in-itself* implies all other categories and concrete determinations.[50] N.B.: It is a *real* biologically-evolved phenomenon that people (and to some extent animals) have consciousness and a mind, that people have the capacity to think and thus *ideally* reflect objects of the world.[51] But herein lies the veritable difference to Searle,[52] the content of

---

48 See for example Searle 2015, op. cit., 42. See also John Rogers Searle, *Intentionality, an essay in the philosophy of mind.* (Cambridge, New York: Cambridge University Press, 1983), 14f., 230 and 264, in which he labels his view "biological naturalism."
49 See Lenin 1977, op. cit., 260f.
50 This means Leibniz by his notion of total determinacy of reality which Searle refers to, see 2015, op. cit., 68.
51 In this sense Lenin critiques the otherwise appreciated "worker-philosopher" Joseph Dietzgen that "thought and matter are 'real,' i.e., exists" but it is false "to say that thought is material," Lenin 1977, op. cit., 244.
52 Searle uses the notion of (intentional) content inside the "head," see for example ibid., 56, which he opposed to the (intentional) object outside, which is (re-)presented, see ibid., 37, and writes that conscious states have "subjective mode of existence," Searle 1992, op.

the thinking is ideal and its development from just being an epiphenomenon of real biological processes to making a substantial difference in guiding the real action of humans, is shown by Lukács as a social (*gesellschaftlicher*) process.

2.6 *Ideal Reflection*

It lies beyond this essay to discuss extensively the role of the *ideal* in social being, to which Lukács dedicates a whole chapter in his *Ontology*, or his concept of reflection or mimesis theory, discussed in his so called Great Aesthetics.[53] Reflection theory does not mean that the *ideal* is just a mechanical duplication in the mind of objects in the real world, as a naïve or corrupted version of photographical copy-theory of knowledge might suggest and which Lukács explicitly rejects as his complex mimesis theory.[54] The *ideal* reflection has a finite character and therefore could grasp at best only an approximation of the infinite complexity of interrelated objects of reality; it is also inevitably a homogenization of heterogenic reality.[55] For example, Lukács confronts the types of homogenized mimesis of art and math, where the former is anthropomorphic, qualitatively referring to the totality, atomistically closed for itself, etc.; the latter by contrast is desanthropomorphic, quantitative and possibly referring to parts, and forming an expanding continuum, etc. The homogenizing medium, for example visibility in case of a picture, is an important reason why a mimetic reflection can never coincide with its object, beside the fact that the one is *ideal* and the other is *real,* which puts a qualitative abyss between them. Leaving for later (see 3.1–2) Searle's major error of treating intentionality as a logical problem, we note that Searle makes an interesting differentiation between representation and presentation. Desires, thoughts or words for example represent the object indirectly, or Lukács would say mediated, whereas perception presents the object directly. Especially vision and touch "give us direct access to the determinate character of reality,"[56] in Leibniz's sense of its total determinacy, as Searle clarified. Whereas the descriptive word "brown" suggest vaguely a range, a representational visual image leaves less, and the

---

cit., 94. The contrast to Lukács is that he treats mental states as "real biological phenomena" and supposes an "identity relation between mental phenomena and the brain," Searle 1983, op. cit., 264f.

53 Georg Lukács, *Die Eigenart des Ästhetischen.* 2 Volumes. (Berlin, Neuwied: Luchterhand, 1963).
54 Lukács 1984, op. cit., 454f. See also Lukács 1963, op. cit., vol. 1, 332ff. and vol. 2, 273f.
55 To the necessarily homogenizing character of thinking see Lukács 1984, op. cit., 454f., 505 and 540.
56 Searle 2015, op. cit., 69.

direct seeing presents all shades of brown hair. Even if I doubt that all variations of shading will be present in the seeing, the difference to the representational word is as obvious, as the fact that a perception is not up to us, at least not in the same way "we can shuffle representations around at will."[57] Nevertheless, is it not the object in all of its determinations which is perceived, even in seeing or touching and not only, as Searle concedes, because the limits of our perception apparatus excludes for example seeing infrared and ultraviolet. What we see at a given moment, and even this only accurate to a certain degree, is just one of the infinite number of appearances belonging objectively to the real object: by touching we perceive yet another appearance the object presents. But not only has any real object infinitely more appearances than we could possibly grasp by our senses, but it has an infinite number of further intensive as extensive determinations other than its appearance, which in reality all proceed in their determinate totality. This totality of determinations from every relatively singular existing aspect of reality could never be extensively grasped, neither in perceptional "presentations" nor in thought or spoken "representations." Even perceptions are always subject to specific homogenizations, for example sounds to comprehend pressure waves or colors to comprehend light rays, which reinforces the fundamental difference between *ideal* reflection and *real* being. The *ideal* is not only limited in its capacity to reflect reality, it also could reach beyond reality. Examples are the invention of very powerful *ideal* tools man has developed to get to know reality, like the category of negation,[58] the logic of our thinking or mathematics as a homogenized way to apprehend structural components of reality.

Whereas general ontology enquires about all ramifications of the fundamental categories of reality, the category of the *ideal* belongs to the regional ontology of social being. It is absolutely crucial to understand that the *ideal* "exists" only as a function of the brain and principally as the content of conscious thought,[59] leaving as secondary the unconscious brain processes such

---

57 Ibid., 63f.
58 Lukács, in contrast to Searle but similarly to Searle's predecessor Wittgenstein, rejects an objective existence of negative "facts." In reality we find only affirmative processes which transform one positively existing entity into another one, never bare absence or sheer negation. Reserving negativity solely to logical thinking, Lukács critiques Engels' concept of "negation of the negation" as an inappropriate Hegelian heritage to a Marxist dialectic of nature, Lukács 1984, op. cit., 114ff., see also Eörsi 2005, op. cit., 144ff. or in English Lukács 1983, op. cit., 102f.
59 By the *ideal* is here only meant the content of human conscious thinking, in contrast to the approach of evolutionary or cognitive biology which treats also unconscious "cognitive processing" by animals as "thinking," see for example William Tecumseh Fitch, *The evolution of language*. (Cambridge: Cambridge University Press, 2010), 151f.

as sentiments, which are primordial in the biological genesis of intentionality, but continue to influence our conscious processes, as wholly integrated living organisms. The crucial point to emphasize here is that as fundamental as the all-encompassing category of reality (*Wirklichkeit*) is, the totality of *being-in-itself* as causally functioning reality, regardless of whether it is of purely natural or of social origin, is not all that "exists." Emerging out of reality and opposed to it as "non-being" is the *ideal* as the content of thinking. To say that something does not exist means that it is not *real*, not part of reality, which in fact means that it has an *ideal* "existence." The unique place of something non-real or non-being is as part of our thinking, and its mode of "existence" is solely *ideal*.[60] Thus that we could *ideally* "transcend" the causally functioning reality, that e.g., in our thinking we are no longer bound to the here and now, that we could reverse the temporal flow, comprehend real possibilities, etc., is an essential aspect of teleology, without which there would be no social being including one's self and one's thinking (see 3.4–5).

2.7 *Materialism versus Idealism*

If we now come to name the overall worldview, we first have to agree with Searle that the usual oppositions between monism and dualism or materialism and idealism are not satisfactory to either side, because they cannot deliver an accurate account of the ontological objective and subjective domain. But acknowledging the subjective just as the conscious experiences of humans and certain animals by treating it concomitantly as a strictly natural biological phenomenon, we will still not be able to grasp the real complexity of being.[61] Being firmly tied to the Anglo-Saxon tradition of analytic philosophy of mind, he takes not even into consideration the Marxist dialectical materialism.[62] Marx and Engels affirmed primarily their materialist answer to the fundamental philosophical question disputed since ancient philosophy concerning the two conflicting world views: materialism and idealism. Together with Feuerbach

---

60 That we could *ideally* invent objects which have no corresponding reality is the valid aspect of Searle's statement that e.g., in the belief in Santa Claus "there is no intentional object," Searle 2015, op. cit., 38.

61 Of course, by opposing supra-natural existence it is trivially true when Searle proclaims that "humans are continuous with the rest of nature," Searle 1992, op. cit., 90; but it is an ontological fact that living organism are not in the same way "continuous with nature" as stones are and humans not in the same way as animals. It is this fact, which in Searle's jargon we could state epistemically objective, which he cannot grasp with his logical approach.

62 For an introduction to Marxist philosophy see Claudius Vellay, "Dialektik und historischer Materialismus." In Ingrid Artus et al. (eds.), *Marx für SozialwissenschaftlerInnen, Eine Einführung*. (Wiesbaden: VS Verlag für Sozialwissenschaften, 2014), 29–50.

they opposed German Idealism to affirm the material priority of the world. But reaching behind Feuerbach and his atheist combat, Marx and Engels conceived their materialism incorporating a dialectical component of Hegelian origin. On the one hand, in this way they captured the dynamism of dialectically-conceived historical development of all being, including the emerging of something new as a dialectical leap. On the other hand they rejected the teleological orientation of Hegel's objective idealism, who thought of the becoming of the world as originated out of the negation of nothingness.[63] It is the overcoming of the teleological concept of reality which led them to enthusiastically welcome Darwin's theory of evolution as complementing their theory of historical materialism.[64] But they opposed as well the subjective idealism of their Young Hegelian colleagues, who basically thought that just imagining the world as changed would effectively change it.[65] The authors of the *Communist Manifesto* took from the idealist tradition the active element, the human subject, to orient it toward really changing the world by revolutionizing social relations. Lukács, in the footsteps of Lenin, reinforced the Marxist worldview by showing the adaptive continuity of the traditional conflict between objective idealism and mechanical, or more precisely reductionist, materialism. Where

[63] See Georg Wilhelm Friedrich Hegel, *The science of logic*. (Cambridge, New York: Cambridge University Press, 2010), 59f. For Lukács' critique of the transposition of the logical category to ontological formation, see Lukács 1984, op. cit., 115ff., in which he explains that Spinoza's formula *Omnis determinatio est negatio* has a certain justification in his logic which it fails in Hegel's "false ontology," see also ibid., 121f. and 498ff. (for the latter see O1, 40ff.).

[64] Marx and Engels expressed their delight about Darwin's "mortal blow" to teleology in the conception of nature in various letters, see e.g., Karl Marx, "Letter to Ferdinand Lassalle in Berlin (16 January 1861)." In Karl Marx and Frederick Engels, *Collected Works (MECW)*, vol. 41. (New York: International Publishers, 1985), 245; see also Frederic Engels, "Letter to Marx in London" (11 or 12 December 1859). In Karl Marx and Frederick Engels, *Collected Works (MECW)*, vol. 41. (New York: International Publishers, 1983), 550. For a critique of a serious but nevertheless erroneous Marxist attempt at a teleological comprehension of nature and society in the wake of Hegel and Leibniz from the Bloch scholar Hans Heinz Holz, see Claudius Vellay, "Hans Heinz Holz' metaphysische Idee des Gesamtzusammenhangs. Eine kritische 'Dekonstruktion' vor dem Hintergrund der Ontologie von Georg Lukács." *Aufhebung – Zeitschrift für dialektische Philosophie (Salzburg)*, vol. 2, no. 3 (2013): 10–48.

[65] From the neo-Kantian tradition, passing irrationalistic thinkers such as Schopenhauer and Nietzsche to post-modernism today are examples belonging to the subjective idealistic tradition, whose concepts in one or another way amount to the idea that reality depends on our interpretation. Searle is correctly admonished for naming just "idealism" positions, who postulate that "human reality is more basic than the basic reality" of nature, Searle 2008, op. cit., 124, because those positions e.g., in phenomenology are "subjective idealism."

the former declares the ideal as ontologically primary (the religious transcendental, Plato's static reality of substantial ideas, Hegel's dynamic world spirit etc.),[66] the latter comprehends the world as entirely material (Democritus and Epicurus,[67] the materialists of the Enlightenment, and largely Anglo-Saxon philosophy of mind).

The dominant philosophical discourse tends to replace the traditional appellation materialism vs. idealism by realism vs. antirealism, which is not satisfactory for at least two reasons. First, would antirealism only cover the subjective branch of idealism which is dominant today, especially in its openly irrational versions.[68] Secondly would realism, since it is a necessary but insufficient condition, not coincide with materialism, as for example the objective idealism of Hartmann or Hegel shows.[69] A good illustration is found in the medieval dispute concerning the problem of universals. The "realists" in this theological discussion have been objective idealists, who attributed to the universals an independent and prior existence to the world, whereas the "nominalists" saw only names given by people, but after all obtained as *universalia post rem* by thought which abstract them from the individual things. The Marxist materialist-dialectical concept of categories as inherent ontological forms of being, as Lukács defends it, renews the Aristotelian realist view of *universalia*

---

66 See Lukács 1984, op. cit., 427. There are also contemporary forms of objective idealism, e.g., conceiving the profound character of reality as mathematical (Badiou) respectively of informational character (transhumanists) or speculating about the reality of counterfactual or possible worlds. For an update of an objective-idealist teleological vision of modern physics from a theological standpoint, see the book by Werner Heisenberg's daughter and Thomas Mann's grandchild, Frido Mann and Christine Mann, *Es werde Licht. Die Einheit von Geist und Materie in der Quantenphysik*. (Frankfurt a. M.: Fischer, 2017).

67 The young Marx wrote his dissertation about the differences between the materialism of Democritus and Epicurus, favoring the latter particularly for his rejection of determinism and thus opening the worldview to enable conceiving of human liberty, see Karl Marx, "Difference between the Democritean and Epicurean philosophy of nature." in Karl Marx and Frederick Engels, *Collected Works (MECW)*, vol. 1. (New York: International Publishers, 1975), 25–108; see also Georg Lukács, *Der junge Marx. Seine philosophische Entwicklung von 1840 bis 1844*. (Pfullingen: Neske, 1965).

68 The so-called "new realism" confuses even more. His "realism" concerns equally physical entities as unicorns because for partisans of this "new" theory, "existing" means "appearing in a field of sense." So there "exist" an infinity of worlds imagined by humans except the one all-reality comprehending world (since it cannot appear altogether as suggested even in the following title), see Markus Gabriel, *Why the world does not exist*. (Cambridge, U.K.: Polity Press, 2015), 50ff.

69 That is the reason Lenin prefers "materialism" to "realism" to characterize the Marxist world view, see Lenin 1977, op. cit., 60. For a more precise discussion especially concerning Hartmann's alleged "realism" beyond materialism and idealism, see Vellay 2016, op. cit., 61ff.

in rebus by avoiding his teleological concept of being. Lukács' analyzes additionally the historical stages of the philosophical development of the conflict between materialism and idealism and how it is articulated with the development of society and its social, particularly class conflicts. This permits him to see the idealist philosophy not simply as a false or socially reactionary theory, but also to appreciate its contributions to the increasing mastery of reality by human knowledge. He sees the preponderance of the teleological mode of explication in religion and secularizing philosophy as a heritage of earlier mythological explication of nature and society, raised to a higher stage of de-anthropomorphizing and universalization, which contributed to the gradual and contradictory formation of scientific thinking. A clear affirmation of a materialist stand in principle thus does not preclude a nuanced appreciation of the idealist bequest.

It is in this sense that Lukács cites Lenin in an opening epigraph to the chapter of his *Ontology* concerning Hartmann: "Intelligent idealism is closer to intelligent materialism than stupid materialism."[70] It is tempting to think as well of Searle's social ontology in these terms, but that would incline towards subjectivism.[71] He rejects, in a sense correctly, materialism as well as idealist monism and dualism. For him the materialist negates the existence of the subjective, the idealist on the contrary negates the objective – which reduces idealism inadequately to solipsist subjectivism and permits Searle to quickly desert the terrain as irrelevant –, and the dualist supposes erroneously a multiplicity of worlds.[72] We should be reminded that Descartes' dualism, though it permits progress towards autonomous materiality for scientific research, saw the world constituted of two substances, the extended object (*res extensa*) and thinking thing (*res cogitans*). But there is no substance, or worse principle, that the world is "made" of; and even less several of them, each "floating" autonomously and independently, immutable and eternal. The overall Cartesian picture remains inside a teleological framework where the world is made by God out of certain elements which could be figured out by logical reasoning, rather than

---

70 Lukács 1984, op. cit., 421; Lenin makes this remark to qualify the dialectical idealism of Hegel, Vladimir Ilyich Lenin, *Philosophical Notebooks*, Collected Works, vol. 38. (Moscow: Progress Publishers, 1976), 274.

71 Maybe in traditional Marxist classification the unusual rubric of "subjectivist materialism" would fit to Searle, as for example to thinkers of critical realism as Toni Lawson, in spite of its apparent contradiction in terms because they try to reconcile a materialist view of a subject-independent world (natural *being in itself*) with a subjectivist view of in fact subjective-idealist origin concerning the "social world."

72 See e.g., Searle 1992, op. cit., 6ff. and John Rogers Searle, *Mind, A brief introduction*. (Oxford, New York: Oxford University Press, 2004), 2ff., 41ff. and 83ff.

trying to comprehend the real history of a transformed and multiple-structured reality. Up to this point Searle is right that the mind-body problem is, and continues to be, based on the ontological false presupposition of logically incompatible principles. The dominant "materialist" monism of the philosophy of mind which denies the existence of the *ideal* altogether by pretending to reduce it to the causal functioning of its organ, the brain, is no more a solution to be taken seriously[73] than idealist monism. Neither is the *ideal* content an epiphenomena of biological or even physical processes,[74] nor does reality entirely consist of our *ideal* appearances. In fact, no part of reality itself exists in an *ideal* mode: ideas could refer to reality (in Searle's jargon, they have intentionality), but their mode of existence is not *real* and the mode of existence of reality is never *ideal*. To accept the *ideal* as a central feature of human reality, as any other person does, and trying to understand its genesis inside of social being, does not lead to Cartesian dualism but requires dialectical materialism. This is demonstrated by Lukács all over in his *Ontology of Social Being*, especially concerning its foundational category labour, as shall be discussed in Section 3.

2.8 *Interlude: What Should Be Explained?*

Searle begins his book about perception by asking his readers to close their eyes to realize what seeing means.[75] Right now I also want you to stop reading for a moment. But leave your eyes open and look closely at your surroundings. If you are indoors you can see the book you're reading or a computer screen, a table, a chair and other furniture, walls, a door and window. If you are outdoors you might see a human-shaped landscape, trees and other plants, perhaps streets, cars and houses. None of these objects you see (or hear, feel or otherwise

---

73 The relevance of this kind of "materialism" is solely ideological, since it is neither meant to inhibit the authors to produce theoretical outpourings highly charged with the denied *ideal* content of their thinking, nor to incite any practical change whatsoever. Virtually the whole discussion of philosophy of mind falls under the admonishment of the 27-year old Marx addressing his Young Hegelians friends in the second Thesis on Feuerbach: "The dispute over the reality or non-reality of thinking which is isolated from practice is a purely scholastic question." Karl Marx, "Theses on Feuerbach." In Karl Marx and Frederick Engels *Collected Works* (MECW), vol. 5. (New York: International Publishers, 1976), 3–5, 3.

74 That Searle takes Marx as a reductionist thinker for whom only "material" interest counts and the subjective is an ideological epiphenomena is less surprising than the prevailing objectivist interpretation in traditional Marxism itself; for a critic of the dominant dualism of economic determinism and political voluntarism in traditional Marxism see Lukács 1986, op. cit., 298f.

75 John Rogers Searle, *Seeing things as they are. A theory of perception.* (Oxford, New York, Oxford University Press, 2015), 3 and 11.

perceive) would be there, without humans having made them. Consider even the things you are doing, from putting your shoes on, chatting on the internet, to the relations you have with other people. None of that would have been possible or even conceivable some 7 million years ago which is about the time our common animal ancestor of the great apes, like chimpanzees or bonobos, lived. In fact most of your surroundings are relatively recent inventions. Despite the enormous variety of experience in the ordinary lives of the 7.5 billion humans on earth today, they are all quite different from the life conditions we imagine at the time of the beginning of the adventure of human kind. Compare these differences to the changes in living conditions of our closest animal relatives, the evoked chimpanzees or bonobos. Surely there would be changes, but they are not obvious to a lay person, leaving aside the mortal danger caused by human interference. And how few of these changes might be produced by the animals themselves?

Searle has said that being a philosopher starts in being astonished about things many others take for granted. So let us at least be curious about how much of our lives is shaped by us, humans, especially if we compare the distance covered to our animal "cousins." Despite the common thoughtless saying that humankind is just a special animal among other special animals, this striking difference between human development and animal evolution should be taken into account in any further consideration about the character of social beings.

3 Social Ontology

Searle is right to say that social ontology has to clearly distinguish the human from the animal way of living[76] and that the evolutionary explanation prevailing in biology since Darwin fails to explain the development of human society, since fossils tell us that the gene-pool of humans has not changed for at least 30,000 years. The same biological basis cannot explain the enormous variety of mankind's social organization, even if we consider just the last 3,000 years. This becomes even more surprising if we compare the essentially unchanged living conditions of great apes, due to the much slower mode of biological

---

76 See his critique of Tony Lawson's social ontology, which does not explain what distinguishes the social ontology, John Rogers Searle, "The Limits of Emergence. Reply to Tony Lawson." *Journal for the Theory of Social Behaviour*, vol. 46, no. 4 (2016): 400–412, 400f. See also Tony Lawson, "Comparing Conceptions of Social Ontology. Emergent Social Entities and/or Institutional Facts?" *Journal for the Theory of Social Behaviour*, vol. 46, no. 4 (2016): 359–399 and 426–437: "Some Critical Issues in Social Ontology. Reply to John Searle."

evolution, with the dramatic pace of change in human cultural development. Social ontology should allow one to understand this difference.

3.1 Searle's Concept of Social Ontology

Searle considers social reality to include all mental facts involving collective intentionality, which subsumes animals with the capacity to engage in cooperative behavior and to share intentional states such as beliefs, desires and intentions.[77] Humans as well as certain animals can assign functions to natural phenomena, e.g., when primates use a stick as a tool to get food.[78] Hyenas' skillful coordination of hunting a lion and Congress passing legislation are social facts for Searle, but only the latter is an institutional fact.[79] Institutional facts as a subclass of social facts are appropriate only to humans because they rely on language. Their assigned status functions can be performed only by collective agreement or acceptance.[80] People are not necessarily aware of implicitly assigning a status function. They may create institutional facts by, for example, buying, selling, or exchanging; they may even accept a function on false assumptions (alleged gold-backed money; divinely-authorized kings, etc.).[81] As long as recognition continues, the institutional fact is created and maintained. Institutional facts carry deontic powers like rights, obligations, or duties, which give "desire-independent reasons for action."[82]

Searle's main question is: "How is it possible that human beings can, by their subjective thought processes, create an objective social reality?"[83] His answer is that except for language itself, "all of institutional reality, and therefore, in a sense, all of human civilization, is created by speech acts that have the same logical form as Declarations," even without being an explicit declaration.[84]

---

77 Searle 1995, op. cit., 23. By intentionality Searle understands the biological capacity of representations to be about something or directed at something, and he insists that for him intentionality "has no special connection with intending" conceived as "just one kind of intentionality," ibid., 7.
78 Ibid., 40.
79 Ibid., 38.
80 Ibid., 39 and 46. Only in virtue of collective acceptance and not of the physical structure attributed status functions are "the basic social mechanism, the glue that holds human society together," Searle 2008, op. cit., 1.
81 Searle 1995, op. cit., 47.
82 Searle 2010, op. cit., 123ff. For Searle the creation of desire-independent reasons for action and deontic powers depend on language as a conventional symbolic device, see Searle 2001, op. cit., 203f.
83 Searle 2008, op. cit., 109.
84 Pushing a beer in someone's direction could also signify "it's yours" without being an explicit speech act, which Searle conceives as changing reality by just representing it as being so changed.

Sometimes we just "think about an object in a way that creates a reality by representing that reality as created." Therefore "all of human social-institutional reality has a common underlying structure": it "is created in its initial existence and maintained in its continued existence by a single, logico-linguistic operation," the "status function declaration." Its unrestricted recursive application creates "all of the complex structures of actual human societies" and thus explains "the enormous diversity and complexity of human civilization."[85]

Let us leave aside for now that Searle includes animals in the field of the social. If we assume that Searle's unique logical scheme is applicable to the huge variation in human civilization, so what? Would we by that understand the ability to perform a single social act? Not at all! Even in performing a simple speech act like "The meeting is adjourned," a wealth of social development is needed. One needs to share a language, the concept of "meeting" has to exist, speaker and audience have to know what the speech means, and how to then act (and actually act so it becomes social reality, but this is beyond the scope of Searle's argument). Searle assumes this knowledge by the notion of "background,"[86] meaning to live under determinate social conditions, at a certain place and time. Meetings have not always existed; you cannot speak of a future social activity not yet even known. All social being is, even more emphatically than the natural being, historical!

If Searle was right with his "single, logico-linguistic operation" applicable to all human reality, we would still not understand why early humans lived in small hordes in very different ways than in ancient slave-owning society, or in feudalism of the middle ages or in a modern capitalist society. His logical principle cannot even explain why it was not an early human, just after "language" supposedly fell into the lap of mankind, who conceived Searle's theory. In the light of his logical and thus ahistorical principle, all variations of social development are transformed into miracles, owing their existence to the will of anyone possessing the necessary "linguistic apparatus."[87] Animals, lacking the appropriate "apparatus," cannot see a "person scoring a touchdown" in an American football game, whereas humans have the necessary "cognitive apparatus" to

---

85 Searle 2010, op. cit., 12f.
86 Searle differentiates two presuppositions of intentions: a network of mostly unconscious intentional states (desires, beliefs, etc.) and a background of capacities, ways of doing things and general know-how, see ibid., 31f. From an ontological point of view it is the "presupposing" of both that not only leaves out what actually has to be explained, the social history enabling a human subject to think and act in a certain way, but further more reduces the real social history to its – conscious and unconscious – traces in the individual mind, i.e., treats it exclusively as a subjective phenomenon.
87 Searle 1995, op. cit., 66.

(learn to) see such social facts.[88] But here the pointing finger seems to hide the moon: it is not just the "linguistic apparatus" which animals lack to represent such social facts. They lack social being altogether, i.e., the whole human history of social praxis which enables us to conceive of such social facts and represent them linguistically in a certain way. As essential as thinking is to social praxis, it is not enough to say that social facts like a "football game or a promise or a president can only exist as such [...] if they are thought of as such."[89] Social praxis has to be developed to the point that permits this kind of thought. When Searle defines rationality as "a biological phenomenon [...] which enables (certain) organisms [...] to have conscious selves, to coordinate their intentional contents, so as to produce better actions,"[90] he treats rationality as an unchanging feature from the beginning ("biological phenomenon") to an already well-developed stage of social being ("conscious selves"). By ahistorically reducing consciousness and rationality to the biological starting point, he leaves out the whole development of social being, a gap which cannot be filled just by introducing language.

3.2   What Searle Is Really Doing

Similarly, Searle reproaches phenomenalists for confining their enquiry to phenomenology, whereas for him the subjective experience is just a "good beginning"[91] of his analytic method. But even if Searle is reaching a higher level by analysis of the logical structure, his "social ontology" remains on the subjective side of ideal reflection. Husserl seeks the essence of "things" by introspective intuition (*Wesensschau*) of a subjective experience (whose relation to reality he leaves out by his famous "bracketing" or "transcendental reduction"). But essence and categories belong ontologically first to reality, as inherent determinations (see 2.3), and only secondarily we might consciously reflect them. To determine if an essence is represented correctly, one has to look into reality instead of just scanning the phenomenological experience. That is not what Searle does either. He indeed differentiates human concepts from categories, but the latter he sees belonging to the biological consciousness of animals instead of conscious independent being. The "prelinguistic conscious experiences of animals [...] are already *structured* by metaphysical categories such as space, time, individuation, object, causation, agency, and so on."[92] Searle is not

---

88   See Searle 2008, op. cit., 36.
89   John Rogers Searle, "Durkheim and the waves of thought. Reply to Gross." *Anthropological Theory*, vol. 6, no. 1 (2006): 57–69, 63.
90   Searle 2001, op. cit., 141f.
91   Searle 2008, op. cit., 116.
92   Searle 2010, op. cit., 68 (emphasis in original).

limiting himself to the phenomenological experience, but his "social ontology" reduces to the logical structure of intentional states, presentations and representations. The social he is concerned with is located in individual minds, similar to the Austro-Marxist theory of Max Adler, which Lukács critiques for making any material element of the social being (*gesellschaftliches Sein*) disappear so that the socialisation exists in a Kantian individual consciousness as condition of its historical development, instead of the other way around.[93]

The apparent strength of Searle's theory results from the simplicity of a unique principal of explication. But how does it keep a certain plausibility, if it fails entirely as ontology of the social? The answer is found in the object of his logical analyses. He is not analyzing social being altogether, but just the ideal part where the meaning is located, which indeed plays a crucial role especially in teleologically-guided action and linguistic communication. The persuasiveness of pretending that a certain logical form explains social entities has its roots in the fact that the ideal content of thinking effectively is a matter of logic. Not the real social history, but the stages of the development of human logical thinking are revealed by his analyses. Starting from its biological roots in animal forms of intentionality (hunger, thirst, perception) and collective coordination of behavior, over the relative autonomy gaining *ideal* in developing teleological action, which shaped the meaning of human perceptions, representations and linguistic communications, to its full development in attributing functions, building institutions and deontology. Searle is analyzing the rationality and the logic of thinking itself as it is developing inside ever-more-complex human society. Not social ontology, as he pretends, but the development of the ideal is the real subject of his theory.

3.3 Lukács' Social Ontology

By contrast, Lukács shows in his ontology how social being has been raised out of two basic spheres, the inorganic and the organic being; he analyzes in the second volume the development and inner articulation of categories in four principal complexes: labour, reproduction, ideal and alienation. I cannot convey here the complexity of Lukács' ontology, which he considered as his main contribution to Marxism,[94] but will express the main argumentation. The distinctive character of social being is the teleological moment, which has no equivalent in inorganic being and just some precursor biological forms among

---

93 See Lukács 1986, op. cit., 298f.
94 Frank Benseler, Werner Jung, "Nachwort, Von der Utopie zur Ontologie – Kontinuität im Wandel: Georg Lukács." In Frank Benseler and Werner Jung (eds.), *Georg Lukács. Autobiographische Texte und Gespräche*. (Bielefeld: Aisthesis, 2005), 471–487, 483.

animals. The teleological moment is developing in labour, which therefore is the original form of human practice[95] and remains the foundational category of social being from which all the complexity of human society took off.

3.4 *Labour as Foundational Category of Social Being*

Among the reasons why Lukács finds labour to be the foundational category of social being are the classical Marxist arguments that labour is, as a creator of use-value in all societies, "an eternal natural necessity which mediates the metabolism between man and nature, and therefore human life itself,"[96] as Lukács cites Marx. Labour and nature are the source of all wealth and thus the "prime basic condition for all human existence," and also, as Engels put it, creating "man himself."[97] In following Marx and Engels, Lukács takes labour as the "decisive motor of man's humanization" and as an "exclusively human characteristic,"[98] due to the teleological moment to choose between different means for a certain end. In *Capital*, Marx formulated that in contrast to animals, a human builds the labour-product first in his mind before he constructs it in reality.[99] The point is actions of animals are guided by instinct and that attempts to reach beyond the animal realm, like tool use, remain confined to biological determination.[100] Only the human species has been able to develop the first half-conscious attempts of teleological guided action in conscious labour, which resulted in the development of a separate sphere of being, social being. Even where the use of tools by animals and the "cultural" transmission of learned techniques is established, like with great apes, it has not changed

---

95   Lukács 1986, op. cit., 28 (O3, 23).
96   Ibid., 10 (O3, IV).
97   Frederic Engels, "The Part Played by Labour in the Transition from Ape to Man." In Karl Marx and Frederick Engels, *Collected Works* (*MECW*), vol. 25. (New York: International Publishers, 1987), 452–464, 452.
98   Lukács 1986, op. cit., 12 (OS, 3).
99   See Karl Marx, "Capital. A Critic of Political Economy. Vol. 1." In Karl Marx and Frederick Engels, *Collected Works* (*MECW*), vol. 35. (New York: International Publishers, 1996), 188. Lukács cites extensively this famous passage from *Capital*, in which Marx distinguishes the labour of "the worst architect" from the honey-comb cells building of "the best of bees."
100 It shows again Searle's high sense of reality when he takes the speech about queens and slaves from so called "social insects" as harmless metaphors, because their "behavior is construed solely in terms of bodily movements." That he attributes the difference only to the lack of "a system of representation such as language," shows the limits of his approach, see Searle 1995, op. cit., 37. Lukács on the contrary points out that concerning social development the biologically-fixed differentiations in so-called animal societies are "blind alleys" and "the more perfectly this 'division of labour' […] is biologically rooted, the less its future potential," Lukács 1986, op. cit., 11f. (O3, 2).

radically their biologically-determined animal way of life.[101] The question is not to try to establish, as in analytic philosophy, a logical sharp distinction between animal and human being but to see which features, by changing radically its character, historically permitted the radically different mode of development between the biologically-determinate lives of great apes and human civilization.

Earlier I noted that all the objects, doings and relations of daily living needed a very long social development. That is also true of our "interior life." Early humans could not have conceived of our complex thoughts, and even less, as Searle put it,[102] could they freely "shuffle" them around like we do. The ability to think as we do is itself a product of social development. It is a long way from the first uncertain, apprehensive attempts to a tiny aspect of reality as useful to one's need, to choose a certain stick or stone; to extract this premise of "knowledge" from its particular situation and generalize it as a causal characteristic useful to construct new and previously nonexistent entities, which serve to satisfy all kinds of already-developed social needs; to finally arrive at the full human being which is able to comprehend reality and its own social being, including scientific inquiry, philosophy and even the ethical task of one's fulfillment. This has been the mode of the development of social being, wherein "social" means much more than collectively-coordinated behavior as in analytic philosophy, and whose development is lined up with horrendous social contradictions of new possibilities and destructive elements, which humanity must learn to master at the risk of perishing.

This development should be understood as a long and difficult, tentative process of change for the emerging social being, with increasing teleological mastering of the natural environment by means of labour and the resulting complexity of social relations which constitutes society. This long process is ontologically nevertheless a dialectical leap from naturally determined consciousness to consciously determining nature by intent. The emerging process is full of contradictions concerning both the mastering of the external object and the development of the subjective self, in which the new social being is "struggling" against the "old" biologically-determined living processes.[103] As a result, we can see a clear distinction between consciousness as a biological phenomenon with the "simple" possibility to *ideally* reflect objects and states

---

101 According to Fitch "we can safely assume that tool use and toolmaking [...] were present in our common ancestor with chimpanzees" some 7 million years ago, Fitch 2010, op. cit., 154.
102 Searle 2015, op. cit., 63.
103 See Lukács 1986, op. cit., 114f. (O3, 134f.).

of affairs in the world and consciousness as a central feature of social being with the emerging of labour, language and thinking. *Until then,* all phenomena are dominated by natural determination; even animal consciousness is subordinate to the objective imperative of biological reproduction, which Lukács calls the essential muteness of biological species.[104] The animal consciousness is apprehensive and can act only within the limits of its immediate biological interests, and thus this basic possibility to *ideally* reflect remains confined to the biological *being-in-itself* (*Ansichsein*) in its causal functioning. *From there on* the reality of a dialectical subject–object-relation is emerging, which progressively lessens its biological barrier (*Naturschranke*),[105] without ever completely disrupting the bond to nature, and by that opening the perspective of actively and consciously transforming into a social *being-for-itself* (*Fürsichsein*).

I refer to labour mainly in the form of transformation of nature and its crucial role in the emerging of social being. But labour is also the "model for social being," which contains "in nuce" all essential determinations of the new form of being.[106] There are also "secondary teleological positings" (*sekundäre teleologische Setzungen*), which aim not to transform nature directly but to influence others in their teleologically-guided action.[107] These forms of social being are increasingly orientated toward the transforming of social relations itself, conveying increasingly important weight to ideology. As teleologically-guided activity is labour not only central at the beginning of the hominization-process of man, but its importance is constantly expanding, even if necessary work will be drastically reduced and exploited work abolished. It is this larger sense in which Marx projects that in a communist society, when the class-divided "pre-history" will be concluded and the genuine history of humanity begins, labour becomes "not only a means of life but life's prime want" (*erstes Lebensbedürfnis*).[108]

3.5 *Labour versus Language?*

Why could not the social being not just be created linguistically with the advent of language, as Searle imagines? There is no way to know whether the content of our thoughts corresponds to something in reality, regardless how logically correct our thinking might be. Even if we communicate with others, we reach at best collective or intersubjective agreements, not yet objective

---

104 See ibid., 161 and also 115 (O3, 135).
105 See ibid., 8 (O3: ii; where it is translated as "retreat of the natural boundary").
106 See ibid., 10 (O3: v).
107 See ibid., 47 (O3, 47).
108 Karl Marx, "Critique of the Gotha Programme." In Karl Marx and Frederick Engels, *Collected Works* (MECW), vol. 35 (New York: International Publishers, 1996), 75–99, 87.

knowledge about reality. To acquire knowledge, we have to confront our ideas with reality, referred to as practice-criterion of truth in Marxist' epistemology. This is still valid for modern knowledge, where we need the confrontation of our theory with reality in scientific experimentation. This is more obviously so if we consider the early beginnings of social being, where thinking and communicating and the ideal content is just elementary. Only in the practical confrontation with the "hardness of the real," as Nicolai Hartmann puts it, is there an external corrective to the thinking, which permits humans to progress. If biological reflection in animal consciousness fails, either the failure is fatal for the individual, or the possible adjustments reinforce the biologically-determined reactions, reinforcing its acquaintance[109] with a specific aspect of reality, namely how it is *for* the animal and its biological needs. By contrast, teleological thinking of humans fails always at least a little bit (this is the grain of truth in Poppers theory of falsificationism), since ideal reflection can never grasp exhaustively the infinite causal connections of reality (see Section 2.6). But the failure is the starting point of a dynamic towards real knowledge of *reality-in-itself*, in exploring and generalizing new causal properties of reality with new opportunities for reiterated teleologically-guided transformation of reality.[110] Thus labour reinforces the constant distancing of thought from the actual existent here and now, because in teleologically-guided action one has to learn not only to foresee the result of the transforming action and to choose the appropriate means between real alternatives, but also that there is a past, that actions could be different, apprehend real possibilities and impossibilities, and so on. Furthermore, as our practice is based on knowledge of *reality-in-itself*, it tends to be universal by overriding the limitation of our initial biological niche, especially by technical mediation. Searle recognizes the human capacity to "order time" as an essential difference from animals, but "forgets" that we have

---

109   Lukács uses the Hegelian term acquaintance (*Bekanntsein*) to characterize the animal being familiar with its environment which for that very reason lacks the distanciation from here and now necessary to human knowledge (*Erkanntsein*). He follows Hegel's concept that the words of a language aim per se to express the essence of objects and state of affairs, transcending the immediately given reality, see for example Lukács 1986, op. cit., 168. Searle also notes that "verbal descriptions [...] assimilate the determinate to the general category," see 2015, op. cit., 68. This generalizing by the words on one side comes for Lukács on the other side together with growing particularizing of language, with the invention of new words, see Lukács 1986, op. cit., 175.

110   See Lukács 1986, op. cit., 35ff. (O3, 32ff.). The teleological positing has always to grasp *ideally* some relevant causal aspects of reality, if its realization is not to fail altogether. But Lukács mentions several times the wheel as a remarkable early invention in the Stone Age, based on a certain apprehension of real possibilities long before any scientific comprehension of its actual causal functioning is evidenced.

this capacity only *ideally* and ties it instead to the existence of language.[111] His ahistorical method does not acknowledge that language arose where, as Lukács cites Engels, humans had "something to say to each other,"[112] especially as an indispensable medium of communication inside of the social division of labour.[113] It is the cooperative, intentional changing of living conditions which provides the need to communicate, and thus boosts the development of language. Searle names this openness to development the "principle of expressibility," meaning "that whatever can be meant can be said."[114] But his logical method remains powerless about how there is meaning in the first place and that it is developing. Although he criticizes that others (Bourdieu, Foucault and Habermas) take language for granted, he confines himself strictly to logical analysis for which it would be "only marginal relevant" whether human language "was the result of a single evolutionary Big Bang."[115] Of course, Searle does not believe in miracles. But a logical analysis which is indifferent to whether language and human reality have somehow developed or is it just fully-developed thrown into the world out of nowhere, cannot pretend to be an ontology, regardless of its merits in other respects.

Searle ironically takes it as "not essential to language that it be spoken," but "whether spoken or not" it "must be thinkable."[116] He would be right in the sense that teleological thinking is the first and necessary ingredient in labour and thus in social being. We do not know whether the "naked ape," beginning the hominization process, could have survived and developed the social being and thus his capacity to think, without articulated speech, especially to coordinate human action. But we do know, as an ontological rather than logical question, that labour, language and thinking did actually develop together as essential components of social being.

---

111 "For nonhuman animals, there really are only immediate reasons, because without language you cannot order time," Searle 2001, op. cit., 202. For some interesting discussions concerning transcending the bond to here and now, but equally limited to the use of language see also ibid., 2; Searle 2008, op. cit., 191 and Searle 2015, op. cit., 65.
112 Lukács 1986, op. cit., 88 (O3, 100). For the original see Engels 1987, op. cit., 455.
113 See Lukács 1986, op. cit., 118ff. It is principally in his chapter on reproduction that Lukács describes the place of language in social being, among others as organ and medium of its continuity, see ibid., 166ff., as central for the formation of the human species character (*Gattungsmäßigkeit*), 169ff., and as organ of different cultures with a distinct development, 176ff.
114 John Rogers Searle, *Speech acts. An essay in the philosophy of language*. (Cambridge: Cambridge Univ. Press, 1969), 19.
115 John Rogers Searle, "What is language. Some preliminary remarks." *Etica & Politica / Ethics & Politics*, vol. XI, no. 1 (2009): 173–202, 178.
116 Ibid., 176.

3.6 Social Objects

Searle reduces the social to the ideal part by conceiving of the social only as existent insofar as we think of it as existent. Thus he reject the notion of "social objects" for two logisticist reasons.[117] First because an object could be both, social and natural (e.g., a dollar bill and a piece of paper) and second because an institutional deontology, like an obligation following a promise, carries on even after the "demise of it physical creation" by the utterance. On one hand, is it specious to count paper as a "non-social object," albeit it is being produced by humans for a certain usage, and on the other hand, the obligation as much as the promise is not a *real* object but, as any *ideal* meaning, a matter of conscious interpretation. If it continues after the *real* utterance, it is only as *ideal* content of thinking. Searle is at least ambiguous to say that "something is a sentence of English or a piece of American money only because people have certain attitudes toward it. Those attitudes are ontologically subjective."[118] It is ambiguous because sometimes Searle seems to believe that it is a certain real use of an object that makes it being, e.g., money,[119] which is close to a Marxist understanding of how humans created money. But predominantly he insists over and over again that it is the people's thinking which creates and maintains social facts. So when he says that the social fact "screwdriver" depends on our attitude and thus "is ontologically subjective," but the "sheer existence of the physical object [...] does not depend on any attitudes we may take toward it."[120] Here it is clear that Searle does not mean *real* "acting" by the "attitudes of people" but only *ideal* "thinking." Otherwise, interfering with the "sheer existence of the physical object" would be as much a "social fact" as bringing it into "sheer existence" in the first place by producing it. But producing something on purpose, in other words labour, is not what "social ontology" of analytic philosophers is about.

It is because Searle fails to distinguish *real* and *ideal* that he cannot see that speech acts change reality only marginally, namely as "trivial acoustic blasts"[121] coming out of the mouth. It is not that "we all think of them as sentences and speech acts" which makes them "remarkable features";[122] rather it is the fact that they have a meaning which people generally understand and may act in consequence. But meaning is *ideal*, it is only realized as thinking in someone's

---

117 See Barry Smith and John Searle, "An Illuminating Exchange. The Construction of Social Reality." *American Journal of Economics and Sociology*, vol. 62, no. 1 (2003): 285–309, 302f.
118 Searle 2015, op. cit., 42.
119 See for example Searle 1995, op. cit., 22.
120 Ibid., 10.
121 Searle 2001, op. cit., 207.
122 Ibid.

brain, whereas acoustic blasts, marks on paper, and so on are *real*, causally functioning objects. Their particular causal functioning includes the objective possibility of conveying the structural elements to which we attribute a certain meaning (under determined cultural circumstances, especially by using the same language). The important point is that meaning is always *ideal* and it needs the interpretative realization by a subject (in the "heads" of individuals), whereas communicating meaning needs changing something in the *real* world, especially in labour to transform nature, even if in the case of communicating the changing of reality (air-waves in the case of speaking, putting ink on a sheet of paper in the case of writing) is purely instrumental to convey a certain message.

It is one of the convergent points of Lukács and Searle that human thinking is not epiphenomenal but essential to social being, and further that consciousness is a purely individual phenomenon.[123] Their approaches differ sharply when Searle pretends that "all social and institutional reality exists in individual minds" and "all of the material objects and other features" belong to the "context in which those minds operate."[124] For Lukács the whole context – how people relate to each other, their social relations, and also the artificial material objects – not only belongs to the social sphere of human beings, but that is what *real* social being actually is. Its very existence is due to teleologically-guided action, where the *ideal* interpretative thinking holds the central place. It is not only obvious that produced artefacts form more and more the human-shaped environment – which sometimes is poorly referred to as the "second nature" of humans precisely because in nature nothing exists on purpose or "teleologically" – but that everything humans make use of belongs, exactly to that extent, to the sphere of social being, regardless how little they transform it. In that respect Tony Lawson's account of "social ontology" seems initially more reasonable since he insists on a "practical dimension" of social reality[125] and critiques Searle for his linguistic reductionism which excludes social objects. But ontologically it does not make much sense when Lawson counts the emerging "organizing structure" of gardens or zoos as social entities but not

---

123 Lukács in his ontology left behind the Hegelian heritage of collective consciousness, central to his youth opus *History and Class Consciousness* (1923).
124 Searle 2006, op. cit., 59.
125 Lawson 2016, op. cit., 367. When he defines this "practical dimension" as "mind-dependent but not mind determined" it is to say that he also remains inside of logical preoccupations of analytic philosophy rather than in social ontology, otherwise he would see that human action is (teleologically) determined but its *real* outcome, once produced, is mind-independent.

their "wild" elements i.e., the supposed "natural" plants or animals.[126] Assumed there are no "super-natural" entities, then all *real* entities are "natural," regardless if organic, inorganic or social. Or "natural" is contrasted to "social" and then zoo-animals or garden-plants certainly do not remain "virgin" natural organisms. Going for a walk in "nature" rarely means a primeval forest but rather an artefact of obviously transformed countryside. And global climate change is an objective social fact, whose destructive power will only worsen if high profile politicians take the "attitude" of denying it. It is our *real* doing, speaking included, which, depending on our *ideal* "attitude," brings the social into being. The genealogy differentiates natural objects from social objects in the sense that only the latter are produced by the teleologically-guided action of humans. But once produced, social objects are as much *real* and purely causally functioning, as natural objects.[127]

3.7 *Human Freedom*

Searle's negation of the objective side of real social objects leads to incoherencies also on the subjective side. As outlined above, Searle reduces the social to consciousness and treats intentional action as a minor subset of animal intentionality. Moreover, his sense of reality is betrayed by his logisticist method when it comes to the existence of freedom and a subjective self.

Searle knows that his whole theory depends on humans "endowed with a capacity for free action"[128] and that *"rationality applies only where there is free choice, because rationality must be able to make a difference."*[129] Nevertheless, he pretends not to "know whether free will exists."[130] Searle's concept of "free will" looks much like Hume's skepticism, for whom even if there is no such thing, nevertheless we have to suppose causality. It shows the logical method inadequate to explain ontological problems.[131] Searle's "argument" starts on a

---

126   Ibid., 379.
127   Here we find one of the very few disagreements between Lukács and the world-wide leading specialist of his late work, the French scholar Nicolas Tertulian, who maintains contrary to Lukács that artefacts or products of labour are "sedimentations" of teleology, which he locates somehow inside the labour outcome, see Nicolas Tertulian, *Pourquoi Lukács?* (Paris: Maison des sciences de l'homme, 2016), 371f.
128   Searle 2009, op. cit., 199. See also John Rogers Searle, *Freedom and neurobiology. Reflections on free will, language, and political power.* (New York: Columbia University Press, 2007).
129   Searle 2001, op. cit., 142 (emphasis in original), see also ibid., 202 and 208ff. and on many other occasions.
130   Searle 2015, op. cit., 214.
131   Searle's approach is still ahead compared to positions like "compatibilism" or "soft determinism," which he refutes convincingly, see for example Searle 2004, op. cit., 219ff. See also

questionable metaphysical concept of the world (all-encompassing determinism, see Section 2.5) which leads to the alleged impossibility of "free will." But since our lives require decision-making incompatible with the assumption of determinism, Searle finally seeks refuge in supposing "free will" anyhow.[132] That is the most an analytic philosopher can concede, forced by the logisticist argument that even the refusal of "free will" is intelligible only in terms of "free will."[133] But just to suppose something, in this case "free will" and possible choices in decision-making, against what one takes for established knowledge is nothing more than pure Hume-Kantian subjectivism.

Searle appeals to common sense to "refute" Hume by raising his arm to demonstrate causality in action. But the same common sense refutes his own remaining skepticism about "free will," based solely on logical sophistries not worthier than Hume's. It is absurd to see as the "only argument" against determinism that it would be an "absurd result" of natural evolution to give us the (biologically) expensive illusion of "free will" and rational decision making, if it makes no difference?[134] The reason that Searle maintains the myth of the alleged impossibility of "free will" is found in his reductionist view that humans, including their thinking, are ultimately just a biological phenomenon, which in turn is ultimately just a physical one: if everything in the end amounts just to "physical particles in fields and forces,"[135] it looks like there is no place for "free will." But that is insufficient to account for life, consciousness and the whole social domain, which we know really exist.

Frankly, it is irrational to take "free will" or human freedom as an illusion. It is correct, as Searle holds, that we cannot live under the assumption that "free will" is an illusion. In particular, no science is possible if one is not able to choose a hypothesis, as determinism suggests. But more important than these logical considerations is the ontological reason that we, as fully developed social humans, would not even be what we are without "free will." No one could have come up with curious philosophical theories like the all-encompassing determinism for the simple reason that no complex thinking and thus theory could exist. No thought and actually no humans could have developed if the ability to choose between alternatives and orient our action did not exist, since it is a central element both to build our social reality and to acquire all of our

---

his refutation of the famous Libet-experiences supposed to show the inexistence of "free will," Searle 2015, op. cit., 213ff. or 2001, op. cit., 290ff.
132 Searle links the alternative choices of "free will" to the experience of a "gap" of insufficient causal conditions, see for example Searle 2004, op. cit., 217ff.
133 See for example ibid., and Searle 2007, op. cit., 11 and 43.
134 Searle 2004, op. cit., 233f., see similar Searle 2007, op. cit., 69f.
135 Searle 1995, op. cit., 7.

knowledge. To validate this ontological fact, it does not matter that we do not know how the connection between thinking and the brain exactly works.[136] What matters is the fact that only teleologically-guided acting – as we all experience every day – could be a valid candidate to explain the rapid development of social being, and therefore thinking, making choices and rational decision making cannot be epiphenomenal.

For Searle, "epiphenomenalism is a possible thesis, but it is absolutely incredible,"[137] because he understands by epiphenomenalism that the higher level (consciousness) would not matter at all since it is completely determined by the lower level (neuron-firing). But again this takes an ontological question logically. If we want to see epiphenomenalism, we just have to look at tool use by animals or pre-forms of "labour" of great apes.[138] These phenomena "matter" in the sense that they really change something in the animals' lives, but they remain epiphenomenal to their biologically-determined way of living in contrast to humans, where labour became the dominant way of producing one's own means of subsistence.[139]

It is only "with the greatest reluctance" that Searle feels forced to retreat from his skepticism and accept the existence of a human self,[140] as if the simple fact that one is able to consider such a question does not already answer it. To suggest that the existence of human freedom and self is an open question is just restating a version of double truth, which affirms the technical mastering on the basis of natural science, meanwhile it undermines the very basis of any possible comprehension and thus rational mastering of social reality.[141] Searle's theory not only establishes but legitimizes that "the individual tends to feel

---

136   See Searle 1983, op. cit., 272.
137   Searle 2001, op. cit., 286.
138   Choices between alternatives already existent for animals lacks particularly the dynamic of developing values, which characterizes the choice as the original phenomenon of human liberty, see Lukács 1986, op. cit., 314f.
139   Marx and Engels insist that however one characterizes humans, "they themselves begin to distinguish themselves from animals as soon as they begin to *produce* their means of subsistence," Karl Marx and Frederick Engels "The German Ideology." In Karl Marx and Frederick Engels, *Collected Works* (*MECW*), vol. 5. (New York: International Publishers, 1975), 15–539, 31 (emphasis in original).
140   Searle 2001, op. cit., 75.
141   I discussed elsewhere that Habermas' "language game of responsible authorship" concerning freedom is just another recall of a Kantian concept of double truth, see Claudius Vellay, "Sozialontologie oder Kommunikationstheorie? Die Konzepte von Jürgen Habermas und Georg Lukács zur Grundlegung des Historischen Materialismus." *Junge Welt*, 11.04.2012, 9.

helpless in the face of the institution."[142] If it is questionable whether or not we have "free will," how could we ever imagine to be able to change society by overcoming the social mechanisms of exploitation, alienation and oppression. Just to say that "it is up to us what we say" because speaking is "perhaps the most paradigmatic form of the human freedom of the will"[143] does not even allow understanding of the growing influence of ideology in society nor how it develops including its inner contradictions. Lukács' ontology on the contrary shows the dialectics of freedom in human action as a condition of human-built social constraints up to and including class division and its possible overcoming. Not only is the "rise of freedom" intimately linked to the hominization process,[144] but *humanity-in-itself* so acquired could overcome its self-produced class-contradictions and rationally organize society as a whole to become *humanity-for-itself.* In his ontology Lukács develops a veritable Marxist theory of subjectivity as the central part of contradictory society based on the articulation of social being with nature.

Acknowledgements

I would like to thank Chris Rhinehart and Claudine Falk, without whose help this essay would not have been possible.

---

142 Searle 2010, op. cit., 108, where Searle cites as such an institution "private property" (of means of production, as he should specify). The apologetic character of Searle's thinking is obvious when he "explains" that the capitalist "system will work just fine" as long as everyone shares the constitutive "fantasy" and it is only when these "fantasies cease to be believable" that "economic crises" like those in 2008 occur, see ibid., 201.
143 Searle 2009, op. cit., 201.
144 Lukács 1986, op. cit., 115 (O3, 135).

CHAPTER 8

Why Still Reification? Toward a Critical Social Ontology

Thomas Telios

1   Introduction[1]

In his essay "Why Still philosophy?" (1962) Theodor W. Adorno takes up arms against positivist scientism, as well as against Heideggerian fundamental ontology. What both scientism and fundamental ontology have in common is the wish to counter idealism; a wish justified and shared also by Adorno. Where they both fail is, however, the fact that while trying to do so both scientific positivism and fundamental ontology could not avoid succumbing to essentialism in the form of anthropomorphism, i.e., the assertion that there is a last, infallible and Archimedean point of truth and that this can still be none other than the subject. Against this metaphysical presupposition interwoven and prevalent in western metaphysics since Protagoras' "man is the measure of all things," Adorno brings forward a minimal demand that reorients philosophy by reinvesting it with a concrete utopian character: "If philosophy is still necessary, it is so only in the way it has been from time immemorial: as critique, as resistance to the expanding heteronomy, even if only as thought's powerless attempt to remain its own master and to convict of untruth, by their own

---

1   The first part of this book chapter is based on a lecture given in November 2016 at the University of Vienna during the workshop "Heteronomie – Entfremdung – Verdinglichung. Grundbegriffe philosophischer Sozialkritik" organized by Andreas Gelhard in cooperation with Gerald Posselt and Sergej Seitz. The second part reflects on what was already argued in Thomas Telios, "Vom Ding zur Ware: Lektüren der Verdinglichung und die Fundamente kollektiver Handlungsfähigkeit dezentrierter Subjekte." *EPEKEINA. International Journal of Ontology, History and Critics*, vol. 6, no. 2 (2015): 1–23, and was recently translated in Spanish as "De la cosa a la mercancía: lecturas sobre la cosificación y el fundamento de la capacidad de acción colectiva de los sujetos descentrados." In Gianfranco Casuso and Justo Serrano (eds.), *Las Armas de la Crítica*. (Barcelona: Anthropos, 2018), 320–341. The third part in its main features goes back to a paper delivered on April 2017 at a conference on the legacy of Georg Lukács that took place at the Eötvös Loránd University and the Central European University (CEU) in Budapest. I am thankful to Michael J. Thompson for including this book chapter in this volume and for inspiring me to work further on this very complicated relationship between Lukács, New Materialisms and Bruno Latour.

criteria, both a fabricated mythology and a conniving, resigned acquiescence. [...] It is incumbent upon philosophy [...] to provide a refuge for freedom. Not that there is any hope that it could break the political tendencies that are throttling freedom throughout the world both from within and without and whose violence permeates the very fabric of philosophical argumentation."[2]

Should the apologetic of philosophy rely, according to this account, on providing freedom by means of critique while avoiding essentialism, the argument intended to be disclosed in the first part of this paper is an analogous one. Should the question be "why still reification?," i.e., why should we keep clinging to this concept instead of discarding it alongside the useless rest of parochial terms from the Marxist literature, the answer is a relative unostentatious one: Should we regard reification henceforth as a *process of subjectification* (a), i.e., as a process of subjectivity production and leave behind the more common understanding of reification as a mere social pathology, or distortion of an original human nature, reification is capable of providing an *immanent* critique of subjectivating processes (b) because it does not fall prey to such *anthropomorphic* or *essentialist* pitfalls (c) allowing thus for the individual to convert its determination to *self-determination* (d) by setting in motion dereification processes that – taking into account the collective processes of subjectification (e) – are necessarily equally collective (f) even though contingent in their outbreak (g). The reason is that such an indubitably post-structuralistically inspired understanding of reification is able to obviate the subject-centered essentialisms by extrapolating a notion of the subject that is *collective in its way of becoming* because it emerges as and through a *collective process*. As Lukács points out directly in the preamble of his Reification Essay from his *History and Class Consciousness*, reification is related to the commodity *structure* to which an objective form and a subjective stance correspond. The form out of which subjectivity emerges is the commodity form. Concerning the notion of form, Katie Terezakis brought forward recently a highly insightful and radical proposition according to which "[f]orm is a demonstration of *being-in-relation*."[3] By the latter she did not only radicalize the way that Lukács' commodity form could be understood by aligning the commodity form to a relational understanding of form. She also questioned the metaphysical character of the commodity form, thus immanentizing and rendering it a socio-philosophical

---

2 Theodor W. Adorno, *Critical Models. Interventions and Catchwords*. (Columbia University Press: New York, 2005), 10.
3 Katie Terezakis, "Living Form and Living Criticism." In Michael J. Thompson (ed.), *Georg Lukacs Reconsidered. Critical Essays in Politics, Philosophy and Aesthetics*. (London/New York: Continuum, 2011), 220.

category. With this relational understanding of commodity form as a framework and with Lukács' core notion that the structuration of the subjectivity corresponds to the commodity structure as a starting point, the reified subject can overcome its heteronomous becoming not because it is being driven by historical teleology or out of a dialectical leap of faith. On the contrary, the subject is capable of overcoming reifying processes due to – in a nutshell – the process of its socio-ontological structuration. Should the reified subject be the effect of such forms like exchange that are collective in their development since they unravel out of the interactions of more than one subjects, then the subject cannot be an integral individual but the collective product of such collective processes. Subsequently, the dereifying processes should be equally necessarily collective. The notion of labor as rearticulated by Lukács in the *Ontology of the Social Being* allows us to interpret labor as a productive, immanent process and it is this reinterpretation that will provide the theoretical instruments in order to justify whether reification can be understood as process of subjectification and how necessarily collective in their structuration albeit contingent in their appearance dereifying practices are. Despite the recent renaissance of ontological thinking, especially among the broadly understood Critical Studies, Lukács' late opus magnum, *The Ontology of the Social Being*, has received less than the deserved attention. The scope of this chapter is, seen this way, not only to provide a systematic argument, but also to invite us to re-examine Lukács' last work, that unlike the other works from his later period deserves more the received oblivion.

In what follows, I will offer a brief cartography of the different interpretations that the concept of reification underwent in its tumultuous intellectual history. Founded by Georg Lukács in his groundbreaking, homonymous, essay published the same year in his *History and Class Consciousness* (1923) alongside a series of equally seminal essays, the concept of reification rose to prominence – both amidst the Western Marxist discourse and beyond – as being indispensable for the purposes of a critical social philosophy. Even though it must have sounded completely different to the ears of its original readers, this text still sounds remarkably current; maybe even against the will of its author or to the historical-political context it unavoidably echoes. If we take into account the essay's main enquiry, namely "how far is commodity exchange together with its structural consequences able to influence the *total* outer and inner life of society?"[4] or when we, a couple of pages further, come across such statements according to which in order for the capitalization of society to be

---

4 Georg Lukács, *History and Class Consciousness. Studies in Marxist Dialectics.* (Cambridge, Mass.: The MIT Press, 1971), 84. Hereafter cited as *HCC*.

completed the commodity structure has "to penetrate society in all its aspects and to remould it in its own image,"[5] we cannot avoid but hearing passages precipitating Michel Foucault's *Madness and Civilization* or *Subject and Power*, Judith Butler's *The Psychic Life of Power*, or Michael Hardt's and Toni Negri's *Empire*. Through this cartography, I do not intend to trace such a highly differentiated, constructivist understanding of the subject back to a script that could only prefigure and not explicitly substantiate such claims, demands or frameworks. What I rather intend to make plausible, is that for us, Post-Hegelians and post-metaphysical readers schooled after the end of the grand narratives, such an anti-prescriptive understanding of the subject is worthy of being revisited because it is everything else than rusted, musty, outdated, reductionist, orthodox or reactionary. Having shown that reification in light of Lukács' later work can also be regarded as a process of subjectification and having elucidated the practical-political effects that such a new understanding entails for emancipatory action, is yet not enough without giving a meta-theoretical account of how the epistemological foundations that are engaged in order to meet such a claim emerged also immanently and inherently to those reification processes. Therefore, a method must be devised that explicates immanently how dereifying processes can indeed be instantiated. In order to underpin the latter, a second account must be given as to on what grounds immanent judgements are possible that are still capable of staging dereifying processes. Georg Lukács' ground axioms as laid down in the "Prolegomena" of his *Ontology* seem to point to this direction and it is here that the fundaments for a *critical social ontology* can be found. While subject-centered "philosophies of consciousness" and object-oriented ontologies account for the main adversaries concerning an understanding of reification as a subjectification process, New Materialist tendencies (mainly Karen Barad's epistemological model of diffraction and intra-agency and Bruno Latour's notion of agential symmetricity) will emerge as the main opponents concerning critical social ontology as methodological vector of recasting the subject in the socio-natural nexus. A differentiation and scrutinization of similar projects (like Social Ontology) will be added to the latter in order to clarify the point of convergence and divergence respectively. Should Lukács' philosophy be worthy of rehabilitation and should he be worthy of being vindicated, then – so the quintessence of the chapter – it is precisely by showing that his theory cannot only provide an embankment to the current and reformulated "antinomies of the bourgeois thought," but moreover that his theory can provide reasons, actions and actors that are capable of reversing the tide.

---

5   HCC, 85.

2   Reification: A Cartography

2.1   *French Post-war Philosophy*

It was none other than Gilles Deleuze who declared that Lukács should be regarded as belonging to the chorus of those thinkers who through their writings promoted a new understanding of (socially constructed) subjectivity. As he writes in a footnote in his book on Foucault,

> [o]n the level of currents of thought we must no doubt go back to Lukács, whose *History and Class Consciousness* was already raising questions to do with a new subjectivity; then the Frankfurt school, Italian Marxism and the first signs of "autonomy" (Tronti); the reflection that revolved around Sartre on the question of the new working class (Görz); the groups such as "Socialism or Barbarism," "Situationism," "the Communist Way" (especially Felix Guattari and the "micropolitics of desire").[6]

Such an utterance was certainly not an easy one, especially if we take into consideration how vehemently Foucault himself had criticized Lukács. As Foucault unambiguously unearths in an interview on his just published *Archeology of Knowledge*, what he aimed through that book was to part once and for all with understandings emanating from notions such as "conscience" or envisaging "totalizing revolutions."[7] Under the latter he listed categorically Sartre, Goldman, Dilthey, the Hegelians of the 19th century and above all: Lukács. The very same line of thinkers whom Deleuze assembled as predecessors of this new understanding of subjectivity is reinterpreted by Foucault in order to explicate the limits of the thinking of consciousness and what it entailed, namely totalitarianism and authority. Similar is the case concerning the Marxist father of critique of subjectivity and copyright owner of the notion of subjectification, Louis Althusser. In his writings of the same period, i.e., the glorious 60s, Althusser directly attacked Lukács for his religious conception of the proletariat, his outrageous Hegelianism and his dual understanding of theory and practice. Nothing could be more alien to Althusser's epistemology than Lukács' messianic expectancy of the insurrection of the proletariat, the anthropological assumption of an original, unreified and unreifiable individual who could

---

6   Gilles Deleuze, *Foucault*. (Minneapolis: University of Minnesota Press, 1988), 150 (fn. 45).
7   Cf. Michel Foucault, "Michel Foucault explique son dernier livre (entretien avec J.-J. Brochier)." In François Ewald and Daniel Defert (eds.), *Michel Foucault: Dits et Écrits 1954–1988. I (1954–1969)*. (Paris : Gallimard, 1994), 775. More on this topic cf. Diogo Sardinha, "Réinvention et mort de la subjectivité." *Labyrinthe*, vol. 29, no. 1 (2008): 91–102.

be reinstated should reification processes be aborted, his ethical reading of capitalism running counter to the scientific one that Althusser tried to establish, or the alignment of the revolutionary Marxism back to a dialectical model (Hegel) which Marx himself had tried so fervently to overcome in order to liberate history from its suffocating claws. Given that the differences at least from Althusser's perspective were so ostensible, there is in the whole corpus of his opus not a single passage where Althusser deals thoroughly with Lukács philosophy. When referring to Lukács he normally suffices in referring always in passing primarily to the "young Lukács," in bringing him in relation to the also "young Korsch" and to a lesser extent to Antonio Gramsci in order to finally reject them both (Lukács and Korsch) quickly and summarily.[8] From this perspective, it is not surprising that the biggest follower of both Althusser and Foucault, Judith Butler, chose also not to deal in a more detailed manner with reification as a process of subjectivation. In her contribution to the book edition of Axel Honneth's Tanner Lectures bearing the promising title *Reification: A New Look to an Old Idea* Butler avails herself of this opportunity in order to comment on Axel Honneth's recognitional re-conceptualization of the concept of reification. Yet she misses the chance to reexamine the concept of reification on the grounds of her own theory of subjectification.[9] The second time she was given a similar opportunity, i.e., when asked to write the preface to the new centennial edition of Lukács' *Soul and Form*,[10] she also did not take up the challenge to scrutinize reification as a subjectification process. Irrespective of magnificent and thorough her literary critique may be and how ingeniously she brought elements of her own poststructuralist theory in Lukács' early and still existentialist framework, she did not occupy herself with a more profound reading of Lukács' early structural elements that would later culminate in his reification theory.

2.2 *Feminist Philosophy*

Besides Poststructuralism there is another thread of theory that finds in Butler its crowing point: feminism. For the denominations among the Feminist

---

8   Following quotations should suffice to sustain Althusser's irreconcilable attitude to Lukács: Louis Althuser, *For Marx*. (London: The Penguin Press, 1969), 114 (fn. 29), 221 (fn. 1); *Essays in Self-Criticism*. (London: Verso, 1978), 115 (fn. 11); *Lenin and Philosophy and Other Essays*. (New York/London: Monthly Review Press, 1971), 44, 122; *Reading Capital. Vol. 1*. (London: NLB, 1970), 120, 140, 143, 249.

9   Judith Butler, "Taking Another's View: Ambivalent Implications." In Axel Honneth, *Reification: A new look at an old idea*. (Oxord: Oxford University Press, 2008), 97–119.

10 Judith Butler, "Introduction." In Georg Lukács, *Soul and Form*. (New York: Columbia University Press, 2010), 1–15.

scholars and activists inspired by the Marxist or Marxian literature,[11] not only the essay on reification from *History and Class Consciousness* was of major importance. The essay on class consciousness proved to be equally influential and inspiring. The "Standpoint Theory," lending even its name from Lukács' conceptual arsenal, extrapolated a category of the woman, the female and sexuality analogously to the figure and the aims of the worker and the proletariat.[12] Now, to be sure, the aforementioned chasm between Lukács and the Althusserians could not leave the Feminist discourse intangible. As Catherine MacKinnon, one of the leading figures of this Marxian or Marxist inspired Feminism, put it, Marxist methodology was

> divided between an epistemology that embraces its own historicity and one that claims to portray a reality outside itself. In the first tendency, all thought, including social analysis, is ideological in the sense of being shaped by social being, the conditions of which are external to no theory. [...] In the second tendency, theory is acontextual to the extent that it is correct. Real processes and thought processes are distinct; being has primacy over knowledge. [...] Situated thought is as likely to produce "false consciousness" as access to truth. Theory, by definition, is, on the contrary, nonideological.[13]

The former tendency is attributed to Lukács; the second to Louis Althusser. Embracing Lukács' project of theory which lies in creating "a theory of theory and a consciousness of consciousness"[14] MacKinnon's verdict concerning the practicability of the tension between Lukács and Althusser for the Feminist subject, thought and tactics is undisputable.

---

11   The demarcation lines between Marxist Feminism, Materialist Feminism, Radical Feminism and Standpoint Theory are for the purposes of the current article far too blurry in order to be able to be addressed suitably and with respect to their tremendous differences. The generic term "inspired by Marxist or Marxian literature" introduced so as to speak of all of them together hopefully does not harm the irreducibility and incommensurability of those tendencies more than necessarily.

12   Sandra Harding provides in her *The Feminist Standpoint Theory Reader*. (New York/London: Routledge, 2004) with articles from Patricia Hill Collins, Dorothy Smith, Donna Haraway, Nancy Hartsock, Uma Narayan, Hilary Rose, Alison Wylie, etc., a very condense overview of the debates covering the standpoint theory.

13   Catherine MacKinnon, "Feminism, Marxism, Method, and the State: An Agenda for Theory." *Signs*, vol. 7, no. 3 (1982): 515–544, here 527–528 (fn. 23).

14   HCC, 47.

The problem with using scientific method to understand women's situation is that it is precisely unclear and crucial what is thought and what is thing, so that the separation itself becomes problematic. The second tendency grounds the Marxist claim to be scientific; the first, its claim to capture as thought the flux of history. The first is more hospitable to feminism; the second has become the dominant tradition.[15]

Echoing Lukács, the feminist standpoint, as Nancy Hartsock put it,

> is not an empiricist appeal to or by the oppressed but a cognitive, psychological and political tool for more adequate knowledge judged by the nonessentialist, historically contingent, situated standards of strong objectivity. Such a standpoint is the always fraught but necessary fruit of the practice of oppositional and differential consciousness. A feminist standpoint is a practical technology rooted in yearning, not an abstract philosophical foundation.[16]

As the citation unbosoms and given that Marxist methodological aspirations reached the feminist discourse at a time when feminists where already informed by Foucault concerning technologies of subjectivity, Lukács' theory, as reappropriated by feminism, was always one step ahead of most of Lukács' interpreters who even till nowadays are afraid of betraying the founder of Western Marxism thus ossifying what once dynamically rendered Marxism capable of disambiguating the higher elaborated capitalism of the 20th century. This having been said, Lukács just as Marxian or Marxist inspired feminism and maybe the latter because it was grounded so strongly on the former, received a well-deserved critique from more elaborate and diversified feminist theories and above all from intersectionalist feminism. As long as the more essentialist feminist positions continue to unreflectingly presuppose an ahistorical female subject or set off from a dual gender construction and thus ignore further ways of production of subjectivity like race, origin, religion, nationality, etc. or misinterpret them as deriving solely from capitalist ways of production, there can be no proof of the timeliness of Lukács' philosophy. Despite Fredric Jameson's wishful thinking,[17] as long as it cannot be plausibly shown that Lukács'

---

15   Catherine MacKinnon, "Feminism, Marxism, Method, and the State: An Agenda for Theory." *Signs*, vol. 7, no. 3 (1982): 528 (fn. 23).

16   Nancy Hartsock, *Money, sex, and power: toward a feminist historical materialism*. (New York: Longman, 1983), 236.

17   Fredric Jameson, "*History and Class Consciousness* as an 'Unfinished Project.'" *Rethinking Marxism*, vol. 1, no. 1 (1988): 49–72.

philosophy can indeed provide us with the analytical toolkit to launch not only a capitalist, but also a holistic critique of society encompassing all possible aspects of domination, Lukács will always and on good grounds remain a reductionist, masculinist, white, Eurocentric thinker. As demonstrated shortly, the latter is definitely not the case. The fact that the German section of intersectional Feminists accrued under the hospice of the Frankfurt School with its undisputable bonds to Lukács or projects like the ones pursued by Frederike Habermann or Kevin Floyd should be considered as first indications of Lukács' still unexhausted potential.[18]

2.3 *The Critical Theory of the Frankfurt School*

Parallel to these tendencies that acknowledge in a more or less affirmative manner Lukács' influence and accordingly attempt in a more or less direct way to reconfigure reification in accordance with their own dispositions, there is another strand of thought that made reification its point of reference: the Critical Theory of the Frankfurt School. No matter whether Deleuze declared Lukács to the pioneer of the socially structured subject, or whether Marxist Feminism reappropriated Lukács' conceptual arsenal to substantiate its claims, and finally no matter whether Althuserian Marxism or poststructuralist thinkers like Foucault and Butler more or less tacitly avoided a direct confrontation with Lukács' theory of reification, there is probably no other concept that has haunted the conglomerate of theories we usually tend to identify as the Frankfurt School than that of reification. Hauke Brunkhorst could not be more right when claiming that the different conceptualizations the notion of reification underwent could be regarded as being indicative of the cross paths, bifurcations and modifications that the Frankfurt School's thought itself underwent throughout its entire history.[19] Nevertheless, there is no doubt that in order for the philosophers of the Frankfurt School to abide by the imperative of (a) Critical Theory that is able to inveigh the capitalistic processes of socialization, the concept of reification was a concept they could not avoid to revisit. At the very same time though, in order for reification to be embedded in the theoretical framework of every rearticulation of Critical Theory's fundaments, reification

---

18 Kevin Floyd, *Reifying Desire: Capital, Sexuality, Dialectic.* (Minneapolis: Minnesota University Press, 2015).

19 In accordance with Maurice Merleau-Ponty, who declared George Lukács the grounder of Western Marxism (cf. Merleau-Ponty 1973), Hauke Brunkhorst will also identify Lukács' HCC as the "silent foundational paradigmatic undertaking" of Western Marxism and consequently of the Critical Theory of the Frankfurt School; cf. Hauke Brunkhorst, "Paradigm-core and theory-dynamics in critical social theory: people and programs." *Philosophy & Social Criticism*, vol. 24, no. 6 (1998): 67–110, here 68.

had to be translated in order to meet the new proposed aims, methods and grounds upon which critique ought to be exerted anew. Nonetheless, this "epistemological" reification resulted to a lot but not to a forfeiture of its critical character. The gradual disjunction of capitalism from the notion of totality is indicative of Lukács' approach of reification; the gradual withdrawal from an understanding of capitalism as the only materialized totality to the dispersion of the notion of totality in order to characterize – under the guise of domination, authority, instrumentality, irrationality, pathology, etc. – henceforth societal subsystems even on the microscopic level of intersubjective relationships; the subsequent application of reification also on those subsystems so as to refer, *in addition to* processes of capitalistic socialization, to the absence of reason, identity-thinking, abuse of communicative action, colonization of the life-world and forgetfulness of recognition; last but not least the very transition from a dialectic-epistemological to a social-ontological via a linguistic paradigm, expanded and diversified the spatio-temporal range of reification's application. This longitudinal-latitudinal expansion of the notion of reification, as Martin Jay called those diversified rapprochements,[20] did not result in altering what has always been reification's main specific: the *exchange principle*. Nonetheless, these trajectories relate asymptotically to the question whether reification could be understood as a subjectivation process. They are not incompatible, since due to this continuous shifting of the content and areas of application of the notion of reification they did smooth the way to such an understanding of reification as a subjectivation process. Nevertheless, none of the understandings of reification brought forward by the Frankfurt School went as far as to question the sovereign constitution of the subject.

Even though, e.g., in the case of Theodor W. Adorno, reification was promoted to a transhistorical, structural feature of social coexistence *par excellence*, it did not lose its capitalism-critical punchline, but its specificity as a phenomenon apparent only under capitalist processes of socialization. Reification was henceforth not only a matter of life circumstances, but also a certain way of superimposed, mediated, disciplinary thinking that pertains to the creation of subjectivity by fragmenting it and distracting it from wholeness of its existence (cf. 91). This argument was questioned by Habermas, according to whom Adorno and Horkheimer "see themselves forced […] to sink the foundations of the reification critique still deeper and to expand instrumental reason into a category of the world-historical process of civilization as a whole, that is, to project the process of reification back behind the capitalist beginnings of

---

20   Martin Jay, *Marxism and Totality. The Adventures of a Concept from Lukacs to Habermas*. (Berkeley: University of California Press, 1982), 26, 59.

the modern age into the very beginnings of hominization."[21] In order to reinstate the process of reification at the capitalist beginnings of modernity Habermas extrapolated out of reification his colonization thesis and incorporated it in his theory of communicative action. According to Habermas, reification becomes henceforth apparent not only as a specific worker's problem, but as a problem pertaining not only to workers, but to all subjects who "coordinate their interactions by way of the de-linguistified medium of exchange value rather than through norms and values, as the other side of a rationalization of their action orientations."[22] The third generation, with Axel Honneth as its figurehead, shifted the content of reification once more and expanded its normative orientation with a clear practice-oriented orientation. By going back and reinterpreting Horkheimer's and Adorno's dictum "[a]ll reification is forgetting"[23] as "a 'forgetting' of the elementary recognition originally granted to every human being,"[24] Honneth's success concerning the reactualization of reification lies in broadening up once more the range of reification processes and subsequently the fields where struggles for dereification could accrue. As Martin Jay rightly notes, "[s]tressing the ongoing struggle for recognition – involving the inviolability of the body, legal equality, and respect for discrete ways of life – he [Axel Honneth] believes he can locate the normative kernel of critique in a level of human interaction even more fundamental than the quest for perfect understanding posited by Habermas as a premise of all human communication. Because that struggle is universal, it can motivate social action whenever the desire for recognition is thwarted."[25] In this context, reification divests the power problematic bequeathed to it from Habermas and at the same time is purified from the strong linguistic characteristics attributed to it also by Habermas in favor of an understanding of reification as a normative socio-ontological category. Should the latter be the first set of differentiations with which Honneth furnishes his reactualization of reification, the second one pertains to the fact that he cannot avoid pointing out the productivity of reification. Reification seen this way does not belong constitutively to a certain

---

21   Jürgen Habermas, *Theory of Communicative Action. Vol. 1, Reason and the Rationalization of Society*. (Boston: Beacon Press, 1984), 366.
22   Jürgen Habermas, *Theory of Communicative Action. Vol. 1, Reason and the Rationalization of Society*. (Boston: Beacon Press, 1984), 359.
23   Max Horkheimer/Theodor W. Adorno, *Dialectic of Enlightenment. Philosophical Fragments*. (Stanford: Stanford University Press, 2002), 191.
24   Axel Honneth, *Reification. A New Look at an Old Idea*. (Oxford: Oxford University Press, 2008), 156.
25   Martin Jay, "Introduction." In Axel Honneth, *Reification. A New Look at an Old Idea*. (Oxford: Oxford University Press, 2008), 9.

socio-cultural stage of development like capitalism (as would be in the case of Habermas), nor does it pertain intrinsically to social life as such (as would be in the case of Adorno and Horkheimer). On the contrary, reification is induced structurally by social institutions and is incorporated as a way of thinking. As he states: "if the tendency toward reifying behavior is not to be traced back to processes of mental or cultural development, it will be necessary to identify those social structures or practices that *promote* or *cause* such a tendency [my emphasis]."[26] In spite of this realization though, Honneth directly softens and relativizes this diagnosis by introducing epistemological criteria that my not regress to the consciousness paradigm of the earlier Frankfurt School, but nevertheless pertain to universal pragmatics for which the references to the philosophy of John Dewey furnish proof. In this framework, Honneth may successfully avoid subjectivism, but only at the price of an essentialism that manifests itself in possessing epistemological perceptual criteria and being able to use them arbitrarily in order to overcome the forgetting of recognition that the reification structures have brought about; the latter referring not only in respect of the relation of the subject to nature, the other or itself, but also in respect to its self-relation. A fourth shift could be identified in the theoretical framework of the Frankfurt School, namely Herbert Marcuse's reading of reification in his *One-Dimensional Man*.[27] Nevertheless, even in the work of the most ardent social constructivist among the theorists of the Frankfurt School, Marcuse falls pray to another essentialism since desire and imagination, or even better, the individual upon which Marcuse bestows imaginary potential and socially unrestrainable desire, will at the end find its way out of the one-dimensionality in which automation and reification keep it chained.

Summing up this undoubtedly very sketchy cartography, the following can be stated: With the exception of Deleuze, who alone saw in Lukács' notion of reification the potential for a critique of subjectivity beyond the pitfalls of anthropomorphism, whenever – as in the aftermath of the Marxist-feminist discourse – essentialism was combatted it was done by concurrently departing from the notion of reification and whenever the notion of reification was revisited in order to broaden its content as in the case of the Frankfurt School it seemed that anthropomorphism could not be circumvented. Unsatisfactory as this may be, there is nonetheless another, minoritarian, path of reintroducing reification, that was suggested by Lucien Goldmann and his pupil Nicolas

---

26 Axel Honneth, *Reification. A New Look at an Old Idea.* (Oxford: Oxford University Press, 2008), 75.

27 Herbert Marcuse, *One-Dimensional Man. Studies in the ideology of advanced industrial society.* (London/New York: Routledge, 2002).

Tertulian and rearticulates reification as a productive process based on a firstly phenomenological and then socio-ontological framework. That reification leads to subjectivation is being tackled by questioning self-consciousness as the sole reason of subject formation and by outsourcing the process of the subject formation in order to transfer it firstly to the things and then the labor process as modes of subjectivity production respectively.

3 Reification as Subjectivation

According to Goldmann, Lukács succeeds in overcoming the dualistic view of the world that separates subject and object and thus all problematics related to reification as soon as he establishes that "[t]he real subject of all historical action for Lukács (inspired by Marx), the subject of all human. action, is a plural subject; the subject which at the same time is an object, since it is itself that it understands, and since it acts upon a society of which it forms a part."[28] In this way, the epistemological complications of this problematic retreat in favor of a phenomenological view which holds to no longer seeking the distortions which can be self-reflexively perceived by the subject. On the contrary, we must seek the interactions that emerge between "the world, the significant universe in which men live, and the men who create it [...]. The subject is part of the world and in fact introduces meaning there practically, but this world is part of the subject and constitutes it."[29] Things represent a part of this empirical, material, worldly world, and Goldmann in his *Dialectical Investigations* Goldmann continually returns to the concept of the thing in order to define capitalism from the perspective of things.[30]

---

28   Lucien Goldmann, *Lukacs and Heidegger. Towards a new philosophy*. (London: Routledge, 1977), 32.

29   Lucien Goldmann, *Lukacs and Heidegger. Towards a new philosophy*. (London: Routledge, 1977), 35.

30   The *Dialectical Investigations* (1959) were published fourteen years before his later reflections on Lukács and Heidegger (1973), which remain unfinished due to Goldmann's premature death. Although Goldmann does not address Heidegger directly in the *Dialectical Investigations*, his approach to the phenomenon of reification in this work is more broadly Heideggerian than his later comparative writing. It nevertheless seems sensible to begin the treatment of Goldman's interpretation of Lukács' reification with these highly significant passages from the later work on Lukács and Heidegger, for only in the light of this more mature work can we better understand Goldmann's earlier remarks and in particular those concerning the shift from the epistemological to the phenomenological view of reification.

Furthering Marx's and Lukács' thought, he conceives of capitalism as an economic structure that "strengthens the autonomy of dead things over human activity"[31] and "disguises the social relations between human beings, the mental and psychic realities, by giving them the appearance of natural properties of things or of natural laws."[32] The abovementioned coupling of epistemological object and phenomenological thing – even the very fact that there is a material entity, a thing, under which both the epistemological dimension of the object and the phenomenological dimension of the thing are subsumed – comes to light when Goldmann refers to this entity as the "most important concept for everyday life."[33] In this longer passage, which is worth citing in full, Goldmann alternates between epistemological apperception and the phenomenological physicality of the (thing-) world, interpreting the emergence of theoretical apperception as an attempt to grasp the external, objective natural world of things. This is not derived or inspired from the Heideggerian *world-angst* but is perceived as compensation for meeting and resisting the constantly changing world and the things' effects on the judging subject, through which the latter becomes a subject in the first place. The relevant passage reads as follows:

> In every society, social practice is closely linked to physical objects. People work together on the nonhuman reality that is constantly changing under their influence. It is probable that in every society, in order to effectively act on reality, people have been forced to separate the cognitive aspect of physical reality from their active or affective relationship with it. Thus they create a world of which man can speak *theoretically*, i.e. in the mode of determination [*Feststellung*]. It is also likely that, in order to achieve this, they were always forced to associate the ever-changing images of the immediately empirically given with conceptual invariants, of which the most important for everyday life is the concept of the *object*, the *thing*.[34]

The volatile vicissitude of the argumentative grounds from phenomenology to epistemology obvious in this passage is not attributable to Goldmann's argumentative inconsistency. It is more likely a testament to the inherent

---

31   Lucien Goldmann, *Dialektische Untersuchungen*. (Darmstadt: Luchterhand, 1966), 89. Given that there is still no English translation available of this work all citations – unless otherwise indicated – are mine.
32   Lucien Goldmann, *Dialektische Untersuchungen*. (Darmstadt: Luchterhand, 1966), 87.
33   Lucien Goldmann, *Dialektische Untersuchungen*. (Darmstadt: Luchterhand, 1966), 89.
34   Ibid.

impossibility of distinguishing between epistemological determination and phenomenological observation. This, as the passage reveals, is due to the effects produced by things, which determine not only the cognitive but also the psychic sphere of the subject and lead the subject to reconfigure itself as a defense against these effects. Coming now to Goldmann's treatment of the phenomenon of reification from the perspective of the thing as a commodity, given that he emphasizes the constitutive meaning of things for the total personal structuring of the subject, a process which takes place in the sphere of everyday life, it is all the more surprising that he ascribes to commodities such a limited subjectivating power. He situates commodities as factors that influence economic life alone, which is part of the public life of the subjects. Faithful to his genetic structuralism, which was itself influenced by Piaget's developmental psychology, Goldman argues that things only as commodities develop a subjectivizing character. As soon as the thing that has become a commodity leaves the marketplace, thereby leaving behind its exchange value, entering the private sphere of the subject and recognizable only for its utility value, it loses its reifying character, and thus its subjectivizing function is negated. In addition, the commodities that revert to being things within the private sphere, which, according to Goldmann, include e.g., the family and friendships, are accorded neutral qualities and effects, which not only have no reifying effects but also allow for relationships that are considered as being "withdrawn from the *immediate* influence of the market" and that, "to a certain extent, remain accessible to altruism and solidarity."[35] Thus Goldmann's argument leads to a division of the world, driven by things that have become commodities, into a reified public sphere and an unrelated, indestructible, even de-reified, private sphere. The notion that this leads to a *"psychic dualism that becomes one of the basic structures of man in capitalist society"*[36] should be viewed as a shorthand interpretation of society's subsumption under capitalist ways of production and above all under the commodities rather than a presupposed distinction between an unreifiable, private and a reified, public sphere of life.[37]

---

35 Lucien Goldmann, *Dialektische Untersuchungen*. (Darmstadt: Luchterhand, 1966), 85.
36 Lucien Goldmann, *Dialektische Untersuchungen*. (Darmstadt: Luchterhand, 1966), 94.
37 That there can be a de-commodified private sphere, or that the restoration of the original unity of nature and man requires a form of naïve, unreified access to things, is a notion that is not restricted to Goldmann's dialectic of reconciliation. Representatives of a more open, negative dialectic such as Adorno and W. Benjamin are equally guilty of naïve optimism, which is likely to prove useless against capitalist reification; on this see, among others, Francesca Caligiuri, "Das unwurdige der Welteinrichtung erfahren." In Tobias Goll, Daniel Keil and Thomas Telios (eds.), *Critical Matter. Diskussionen eines neuen Materialismus*. (Münster: Edition Assemblage, 2013).

With regards to the former, i.e., spelling out the effectiveness of the capitalist economic structure inherent in the commodity form, the fruitfulness of Goldmann's thought with regard to the reification problematic stems from his abandonment of the epistemological approach to the issue and his turn towards a phenomenological conception of the thing. The latter manifests itself – as seen – in the fact that there is a world of things that is independent of the cognition of the subject and that these things are the factors that structure subjects. The short-sightedness noted above, as far as the constitutivity of things/commodities in the development of the subject is concerned, is thus located not in the content but in the formal-logical structure of the argument, i.e., in the fact that, despite the phenomenological nature of his approach, Goldmann's reflections are still based on a dialectical strategy. The mental development from the neutrality of the "in itself" mode of being of things as material entities that belong to the natural world (T), to the negativity of things that have become commodities (T-C), to a commodity that has now become a thing again (T-C-T') – one which withdraws its negative effects within the private sphere, preserves its exchange character and has affirmative effects – points to a logic of dialectical reconciliation which Goldmann seems yet to have abandoned. The problem here, as will become apparent, is neither the dialectical, operative train of thought nor the synthetic consideration of the thing as both a thing and a commodity. What is limiting is the above-suggested original unity of the fabricated, reconciling world of the private sphere to be achieved through the teleological self-movement of the thing from a neutral disposition to the social self-determination of the commodity that has again become a thing. Nicolas Tertulian rightly viewed this explanatory model as being too brief. Following Goldmann's thought, he turns to the late Lukács and takes the *Ontology of Social Being* as a starting point for his reflections on the phenomenon of reification.

While Lukács remains within an epistemological framework in his earlier to middle writings, including *The Young Hegel* and *The Young Marx*,[38] Tertulian notes that a break takes place at least by the time of *The Ontology of Social Being*, which Lukács himself applies to his earlier exposition of the concept of reification. Reification is now understood not as a "category of historical philosophy" but as a "category of personality theory." Subtle distinctions between objectification and alienation, between generated abilities and their synergy in the synthesis of personality, last but not least between phylogenetic

---

38   Cf. Georg Lukács, *Der junge Hegel. Uber die Beziehungen von Dialektik und Okonomie.* (Frankfurt a. M.: Suhrkamp, 1949); *Der junge Marx. Seine philosophische Entwicklung von 1840 bis 1844.* (Stuttgart: Neske, 1965).

humanity (*Gattungsmäßigkeit* species character in itself) and the ontogenetic individual (*Gattungsmäßigkeit* for itself) testify to this "mutism,"[39] this transformation of personality, that Tertulian detects as being set in motion by the process of reification. This mutism is to be attributed to the neither epistemological, nor phenomenological but, henceforth, social-ontological approximation of the phenomenon of reification, which Lukács presents in the *Ontology of Social Being*. As will be shown more thoroughly in the next section of this chapter, Lukács asserts inorganic nature, organic nature (life) and society as modes of being. However, Lukács observes these three modes of being as mere analytical categories aiming only to describe the complexity of the genesis of the social being (i.e., the subject). The three modes of being are only seemingly opposing facts,[40] since in reality they condition each other regardless how irreducible they may remain to each other. Fictitious is therefore not the ontological irreducibility of those modes of being, but the fact that they should be conceived of as being not related to one another. As a matter of fact, inorganic nature, organic nature (life) and society are interrelated and emerge as equally original. Lukács according to Tertulian succeeds in this by proclaiming that their relationship is a reciprocal constitution which depends on the ontological, i.e., *productive*, character of the labor process, during which the subject produces itself. The fact that Lukács identifies every change brought about both by and during the labor process as a new positioning [*Setzung*][41] makes possible to rethink this subjectivation process as having a never-ending, reiterating character. The fact that subjectivation is a process that must be every time reiterated makes evident not only the productive but also the *performative* character of this relationship. This reasoning leads to the notion that we can distinguish neither between the natural and the social world on the one hand nor between the public and the private on the other – as was the case with Goldmann.[42] Because of this, not the exchange of commodities on the market is to be held responsible for the effects of reification. On the contrary, it

---

39 Nicolas Tertulian, "Alienation et Desalienation: Une confrontation Lukacs-Heidegger." *Actuel Marx*, vol. 39 (2006): 36.
40 Georg Lukács, *Zur Ontologie des gesellschaftlichen Seins. Die Arbeit*. (Darmstadt: Luchterhand, 1973), 125; henceforth *Ontology/Labor*. The quotations from the labor chapter are taken from the German separate edition of this chapter and not from the posthumously appeared second book of the *Ontology* of which it is a part. Again, unless otherwise indicated, I decided to provide my own translations instead of referring to the existing English translation.
41 Cf. *Ontology/Labor*, 24.
42 From this point of view, it is easy to see why the notion of everyday life was so fundamental to deciphering the problems of capitalist socialization in the writings of the Budapest School; see Heller 1980 and 1981.

is labor as a socio-ontological and teleological, i.e., self-defining, category, that is to be held accountable for the subjectivating effects reification deploys. The reason is that through labor inorganic nature, organic nature (life) and society come to contact with one another and that through these interactions the social being is being brought about.

To be sure, and against Tertulian, it could be argued that also Lukács' earlier essay on reification from his *History and Class Consciousness* contains elements of a constructivist concept of subjectivity. Primary evidence for this can be found in passages in which Lukács categorically opposes essentialist conceptions of the subject. Lukács subsumes them under the general category "humanism" or an "anthropological point of view," which he views, for example, as underlying modern pragmatism, the revolutionary utopianism developed by Ernst Bloch, and Kant's subjective idealism.[43] In the case of all three, Lukács debunks that, as man becomes absolutized, he is simultaneously mythologized, thereby manifesting the inadequacy of this way of thinking to "understand reality concretely as a historical process."[44] Further evidence for Lukács' anti-humanistic conception of the subject can be found in his rejection of human's natural species character (*Gattungsmässigkeit*). Unlike Marx, who in his declination of the modes of alienation reveals man as a natural being,[45] Lukács states clearly at the very beginning of his essay that "[b]y selling this, his only commodity, he [man] integrates it (and himself: for his commodity is inseparable from his physical existence) into a specialised process that has been rationalised and mechanised, a process that he discovers already existing, complete and able to function without him and in which he is no more than a cipher reduced to an abstract quantity, a mechanised and rationalised tool."[46] Even clearer are the *Ontology*-anticipating ideas on the formal logical level of argumentation. Not only is the later Lukács of the *Ontology* anticipated[47] when the early Lukács claims in the Reification-Essay that Marx

---

43   Cf. *HCC*, 220 (fn. 51; on pragmatism); 222 (fn. 68; on Ernst Bloch); 192 (on revolutionary utopianism). Lukács returns to the "intellectus archetypus" of German idealism in the chapter on labor of the *Ontology*; see *Ontology/Labor*, 18. This also supports the thesis, presented here, that (against Tertulian) we should speak not of a break between the earlier and the later Lukács but rather of a further development of the former in the latter.

44   *HCC*, 187.

45   Karl Marx, *Economic and Philosophic Manuscripts of 1844*. (Amherst/New York: Prometheus, 1988), 69–84.

46   *HCC*, 166.

47   The thesis that Lukács' early thinking already had ontological features – where ontology is used as a metonymy for productive processes – was also advanced by Andrew Feenberg. As he writes: "Lukács' theory can best be understood as a generalization of Marxian fetishism in two dimensions, in sociological breadth through Weber, and in ontological

historicized Hegel by historicizing man, i.e., by making man the "initial abstract category[y] of dialectics,"[48] according to which *"he* [man] *both is and at the same time is not."*[49] It can even be said that Lukács' equation of life with social life,[50] which is to be found in the conclusion of the *Ontology* and according to which "the existence and effectiveness of consciousness are inextricably linked to the biological process of the living organism, such that every individual consciousness [...] emerges together with its body and perishes,"[51] should indeed be understood not as a departure from but as a continuation of his earlier attempt.[52] As a matter of fact and in order to better illustrate this continuation, by staying loyal to the terminology of Hegelian anthropology, e.g., when Lukács ascribes phenomena such as affects, instincts, and needs to the sphere of consciousness,[53] he does not privilege the subsumption of every day, wordly practices and bodily experiences under mental categories but rather grasps the opportunity to address those bodily issues by means of the Hegelian anthropology since the latter was the only back then available conceptual set of tools to theorize such issues. Last but not least, Lukács is in his early writing not content merely to deny in purely formal terms that a certain essence resides in the core of the subject.[54] He more significantly endeavors to

---

depth through Hegel. So generalized, the concept of reification becomes the basis for a critique of capitalist rationality as a system of social thought and organization threatened by its inability to grasp the material substratum of its own formalistic categories and institutional structures"; Andrew Feenberg, *Lukacs, Marx and the Sources of Critical Theory*. (Oxford: Rowman and Littlefield, 1981), 61.

48 *HCC*, 189–190.
49 Ibid.
50 *Ontology/Labor*, 18.
51 *Ontology/Labor*, 125.
52 W.T. Newell already points in this direction when he writes: "Lukács' relation to the Marxist tradition is a complex one. He hegelianises the Marxist maxim that social being determines consciousness by expanding its meaning beyond the idea that the economic base determines the superstructure. [...] This opens up the Marxist critique of capitalism to embrace far subtler kinds of alienation – psychological and aesthetic – than the economic"; Walter R. Newell, "Philosophy and the perils of commitment: A comparison of Lukacs and Heidegger." *History of European Ideas*, vol. 9, no. 3 (1988): 311. On this cf. also Susan Buck-Morss, *The Origin of Negative Dialectics*. (New York: The Free Press, 1977), 26.
53 On this cf. Lukács' thesis that "the rule of human consciousness over its own suffering, [...] extends to one part of the sphere of consciousness, to habits, instincts, affects"; *Ontology/Labor*, 123.
54 As Lukács retrospectively states in his unpublished response to his critics: "The direct forms of appearance of social being are not, however, subjective fantasies of the brain, but moments of the real forms of existence, the conditions of existence of capitalist society"; Georg Lukács, *A Defence of History and Class Consciousness: Tailism and the Dialectic*. (London/New York: Verso, 2000), 79.

draw attention to those specific mechanisms that are immediately elevated to social-ontological modes of subjectivity production. The administration of the capitalist market (whose laws are shaped by the commodity form) and technology (as a centralized and alienated way of organizing labor) are presented by Lukács as two paradigmatic modes of subjectivity production, that like Foucault's *dispositifs* are accorded a productive function within the capitalist discourse. Thus, Lukács radicalizes and concretizes the vague Marxist phrase that barter must strike back into the interior of the community and decompose it[55] by elevating the commodity form to a structural feature and the constitutive form of capitalist socialization. As he claims, in order to complete the capitalization of society, "it would be necessary [...] for the commodity structure to penetrate society in all its aspects and to remould it in its own image. It is not enough merely to establish an external link with independent processes concerned with the production of exchange values."[56] Thus Lukács not only diagnoses the transformation of all human and social relationships into commodities but also notes that man does not remain untouched in this regard: "Just as the capitalist system continuously produces and reproduces itself economically on higher and higher levels, the structure of reification progressively sinks more deeply, more fatefully and more definitively into the consciousness of man."[57] Viewed in this way, the concept of the "contemplative stance"[58] of which Lukács speaks is to be understood not as a passive consciousness, whose possibility to self-reflection has gone astray, but as a consciousness that is generated by the reification process from the very beginning as a reified one. Not a pre-existing consciousness is replaced or distorted by new modes of perception. Rather, a reified consciousness is produced by reification that in its turn is driven by the commodity form. It is due to this diagnosis that Lukács can declare that to the extent that capitalist socialization owes its founding to the exchange of commodities, the consciousness not only of the worker, but of everyone in this thus-constructed sphere of life comes down to equate from the very beginning "the *self-consciousness of the commodity;* or in other words it is the self-knowledge, the self-revelation of the capitalist society founded upon the production and exchange of commodities."[59]

At this point, what becomes clear is that, on the one hand, by virtue of the socialization of the capitalist economic structure, a product owes its

---

55   Cf. Karl Marx, *A Contribution to the Critique of Political Economy*. (Moscow: Progress Publishers, 1977), 53.
56   HCC, 85.
57   HCC, 93.
58   HCC, 200.
59   HCC, 168.

commodity form to the exchange that has taken place between subjects in the marketplace. At the same time though, the reifying commodity form also conveys through its surplus-value the producer whose work has been invested and incorporated in the product. As Lukács, herein again following Marx notes, the labor, that one performs, merges with the product, whereby the producer "by selling this, his only commodity, he integrates it (and himself: for his commodity is inseparable from his physical existence) into a specialised process that has been rationalised and mechanised, a process that he discovers already existing, complete and able to function without him and in which he is no more than a cipher reduced to an abstract quantity."[60] Therefore, the subjectivation effects that – according to Goldmann – the commodities deploy as soon as they start getting consumed by the subject in its everyday life are to be traced back to the labor that the producer has invested in order to produce the commodity that will subjectivate the inner world of the consumer. This second relation that the commodity form brings about occurs through labor whereby labor merges with the product and through this merger the consuming subject comes into contact with the producing subject. Nonetheless, there is a third relation being instantiated through commodification processes. Beside exchange in the marketplace that creates a commodity out of a thing/product, or how labor effects the subject's private world as soon as it becomes a part of its everyday life by getting consumed, there is a third set of relations unravelling from consumption. Through the consumption of a commodity, the consumer determines via the laws of supply and demand the socio-economic sphere of the lifeworld of the subject. The surplus value that is being incorporated though the producer's labor in the commodity-to-be depends on the demand that the consumer determines. Therefore, parallelly to the exchange that lends the produced product its commodity form two further intersubjective relations are being conveyed through exchange: one which traces the transformation of the inner world of the consumer back to the labor of the producer invested in the product and one which traces the determination of the surplus value of the labor incorporated in the product back to the consumer who determines – amidst the capitalist regime of production in which we are still moving – through his/her demand the compensation of the producer's invested labor. In this regard, Katie Terezakis rightly claims that "[f]orm is a demonstration of *being-in-relation* [...]. Being-in-relation is a cognitive condition of experience, insofar as experience is understood via ordering forms, and being-in-relation is the content of experience, insofar as subjectivity is only encountered in

---

60   HCC, 166.

intersubjective involvement and in its productive (and thereby self-productive) objectivations."[61]

The above-described reading of reification as an *intersubjectively driven* and *subjectivating* phenomenon which takes place through the exchange of commodities provides a picture of the commodity as a product of labor and as an economic form between the world of things and the economic sphere of the lifeworld, which is dominated by capitalist exchange relations. This makes it possible to view the productive effects of each object, which is at the same time a thing and a commodity, synthetically, without having to attribute these effects reductively to one or the other sphere. The latter allows to conclude by assuming that there can be also other ways to found collective action. Conventionally, Lukács bases the emancipatory agency of the proletariat on the objectification that the proletariat experiences through reified labor. As soon as the proletariat becomes conscious of this heteronomous determination it is being transformed dialectically to the self-autonomous motor of history. Though this assumption does not have to be discarded, the hitherto analysis provides further foundations concerning collective agency and the possible, subsequent forms of collective practice. The latter pertains to acknowledging the consumer/producer as reciprocally subjectivating factors of the producer/consumer respectively and to integrating consumers and producers respectively in the emancipatory practices that can be derived from such a subjectivation framework. If the producer subjectivates the consumer though the labor invested in the commodity that will form the producer's inner world, then the consumer's emancipation runs through integrating the producer in his/her emancipatory practices. Similarly, if the consumer through his/her needs or demands determines the exploitation of the producer's labor, then also the consumer has to be integrated in the emancipatory practices of the producer in the producers' attempt to liberate themselves from the exploiting mechanism of the surplus value. Seen this way, Not only due to the identification of each proletarian as a member of the proletariat is what makes each proletarian agentially capable of emancipatory practices. Those identity politics can be complemented by acknowledging according to the subjectivation practices illustrated so far the structurally determining role of further subjects and include them in emancipatory practices. The latter obviously broadens up the possible practices suggested by the early Lukács in his Reification-Essay by taking off from the

---

61   Katie Terezakis, "Living Form and Living Criticism." In Michael J. Thompson (ed.), *Georg Lukacs Reconsidered. Critical Essays in Politics, Philosophy and Aesthetics.* (London/New York: Continuum, 2011), 220.

subjectivating effects that commodities social-ontologically deploy as suggested by the later Lukács in his *Ontology of the Social Being*.

4   Towards a Socio-ontological Critique

4.1   *From Ontology to Critical Social Ontology*

What we have seen so far is firstly how – on the grounds of Lukács' later, social-ontological understanding of labor – reification can be read as a subjectivation process. Secondly, we came to realize how this alternative and minoritarian understanding of reification has direct consequences concerning its addressees, i.e., the subjects whose conditions of life it pertains to. As a subjectivation process, social bonds are constituted between the subjectivating other and the subjectivated self and in order for dereification to kick in both relata of the relationship must be transformed. It would seem that such a transformation would be implied already in the early, epistemological understanding of reification as analyzed as early as in the Reification-Essay. Yet, Lukács is *eo loco* categorical concerning the incapability of the bourgeoisie to transform itself due to the fact that bourgeoisie is not reified through the reification process, does not become a part of it and therefore cannot be transformed with it. In contrast, the transition from a phenomenological to a social-ontological understanding of reification examined here seems to be more inclusive and thus provide for a broader range of actors capable of introducing and deploying dereification processes. If subjectivation, as indicated, takes place not only through labor, but also through consumption, then the subjects that could appear as capable of disentangling dereification processes are all participants of both the production and the consumption process. Seen this way, the problem of identity politics, namely the fact that only the proletariat is to be presumed as the only motor of history that arose within Lukács' epistemological understanding of reification, is being rendered obsolete. By observing reification as a social-ontological process of production of subjectivity, what we now, gain is a concept of agency that does not rely anymore on a presupposed epistemological capacity but comes around as an immanent agency arising through social practices. Nevertheless, and though this might already seem like a big step forward concerning Lukács' Up-to-date-ness and a first answer concerning the critical character of his *Ontology* on a praxeological level, we still have not answered the question concerning the critical character of Lukács *Ontology* on a theoretical level. In order to do this we have to take a narrower look at the *Prolegomena* of Lukács' book on the *Ontology of the Social Being*.

To be sure, even in the Left-Hegelian philosophical tradition, ontology and subsequently social ontology could only mean what it has always meant in every school or tendency of philosophy. As Robert Pippin argues, in the case of recognitional relationships, social ontology brings to light "the *ultimacy* of such dependence [...] and so the *necessity* of acknowledging its indispensability in our political theory."[62] The fact that when speaking of social ontology it comes down to interrogating the relationships that unfold between social entities and how they influence social theory and consequently political praxis is a main argument shared almost unanimously by all theories moving in this paradigm independently of their origin (analytical or continental). Concerning the former, the analytical philosophical tradition, according to Raimo Tuomela, "can be broadly understood to cover all kinds of entities and properties that rational study of the social world is taken to need. Understood in this wide sense, social ontology is not only a study of the basic nature of social reality but at least in part a study of what the best-explaining social scientific theories need to appeal to in their postulated ontologies."[63] Along the same lines and emphasizing the praxeological in contrast to the metaphysical character of social ontology, Brian Epstein argues that "[s]ocial ontology should not be thought of as the study of 'ontological claims' such as 'social groups exist' or 'there are no social spirits.' But instead it is the study of *ontological building relations* between different kinds of entities."[64] Should that be the case in the analytical philosophical framework, the continental camp slightly complexifies the field by trying to identify what – in addition to social ontology – a "critical" social ontology could be. Putting aside the impossible and more general question "what critique is?," concerning social critical ontology, two lines of thinking seem to become prevalent in the continental discourse: one concentrating on elements of Marx's critique of capitalism and one taking up some main arguments of the Frankfurt School as enriched by a renewed interest in pragmatist discourse. In regard to the former, the Marxist one, the critical character of social ontology seems to evolve around the notions of historicity and totality. Social ontology is only then critical if it extrapolates out of allegedly ahistoric (ontological) entities historical procedures of (social) becoming and if it accommodates epistemological knowledge that grasps the society in its

---

62 Robert Pippin, "Recognition and Reconciliation." In Bert van den Brink and David Owen (eds.), *Recognition and Power. Axel Honneth and the Tradition of Critical Social Theory*. (Cambridge: Cambridge University Press, 2007), 64.

63 Raimo Tuomela, *Social Ontology. Collective Intentionality and Group Agents*. (Oxford: Oxford University Press, 2013), ix.

64 Brian Epstein, "Framework for Social Ontology." *Philosophy of the Social Sciences*, vol. 46, no. 2 (2016): 147–167, 149.

entirety. As Reha Kadakal states, "[s]ocial theory as critical ontology grasps social reality not simply in terms of a positivist notion of 'facts,' but rather in terms of its very processes of becoming, and it attempts to comprehend these processes through questions that are simultaneously theoretical and normative."[65] To the latter he adds that "[t]he purpose of critical ontology is not only to make intelligible the processes of concrete social reality and social relations, which is a necessary part of any critical social theory, but also to bring to light the categories of thought that such a reality brings into being – categories, that is to say, with their own historicity."[66] In a similar gesture and echoing Marx's understanding of the man as the "totality of human life-activity,"[67] Michael J. Thompson argues that "the critical conception of social ontology has in view the thesis that it is only by understanding the totality of human social life and its potential aims and goals that [such social-ontological processes as] reification can be overcome."[68] Now, to be clear, it is not as if the analytical philosophical approach of social ontology is bereft of any critical inquiry into the existence of the social entities, the relationships among them and/or the ways to overcome them. By asking "[w]hat sets up the grounding conditions for social facts, to be what they are?,"[69] a project that Brian Epstein calls "anchoring," we are given the possibility "if the grounding conditions for a particular social fact are partly anchored by a widely held false belief" to "'debunk' the concept may be by criticizing the anchors."[70] Nevertheless, while merely the possibility of critique or critique as a mere possibility is brought forward here, in the continental tradition social ontology is considered – if not elevated to – a critical project *per se*. The latter is surely the case regarding the second line of thought within the continental understanding of social ontology that can be traced back to emancipatory objectives of the Frankfurt School

---

65 Reha Kadakal, "Toward a Critical Ontology of the Social: Hegel, Lukács, and the Challenge of Mediation." *Globalization, Critique and Social Theory: Diagnoses and Challenges*, vol. 33 (2015): 167.

66 Reha Kadakal, "Toward a Critical Ontology of the Social: Hegel, Lukács, and the Challenge of Mediation." *Globalization, Critique and Social Theory: Diagnoses and Challenges*, vol. 33 (2015): 177.

67 Karl Marx, *Economic and Philosophic Manuscripts of 1844 and The Communist Manifesto*. (Amherst: Prometheus Books, 1988), 105.

68 Michael J. Thompson, "Collective Intentionality, Social Domination, and Reification." *Journal of Social Ontology*, vol. 3, no. 2 (2017): 207–229, 224.

69 Brian Epstein, "Framework for Social Ontology." *Philosophy of the Social Sciences*, vol. 46, no. 2 (2016): 147–167, 158; cf. also Brian Epstein, "History and the Critique of Social Concepts." *Philosophy of the Social Sciences*, vol. 40, no. 1 (2010): 3–29.

70 Brian Epstein, "Framework for Social Ontology." *Philosophy of the Social Sciences*, vol. 46, no. 2 (2016): 147–167, 161.

no matter how irretrievably influenced by pragmatist critical ideals the rearticulation of those ideals appear to be. As Emmanuel Renault e.g., argues,

> for a social theory that thinks of politics in terms of practices rooted in tendencies and contractions, and that thinks of radical transformations in terms of dynamics of social transformation, only the processual ontology is a consistent option. For sure, even a fully articulated processual social ontology could not all by itself provide a direct contribution to the study of the dynamics of social transformation and to practical efforts of transforming the world. What it could do, is to help critical theories in clarifying their principles and to offer conceptual tools for critical reflection on the social sciences as well as for bridging the gap between social theory and practical efforts toward social transformation. In other words, such a social ontology could be useful for the particular kind of self-reflection associated with the very idea of critical theory.[71]

Along the same lines and after acknowledging that it would be highly unlikely that Adorno would succumb to any reading of ontology as a critical project, Italo Testa argues that

> in order to be critical, social ontology should not confine itself to mere description of the constitution of social objects, but should take up from critical social philosophy the task of providing a critical diagnosis of social reification. This means introducing a distinction between necessary mechanisms of objectification constitutive of social objects, and additional mechanisms of reification providing some forms of objectivation and the resulting social objectivity with an appearance of necessity and immutability and thus constraining free, rational agency.[72]

4.2   *The Social-Ontological Foundations of the* Prolegomena

Though Lukács' *Ontology* was intended by its author as a propaedeutic to a bigger and more elaborate Marxist ethic and for which, as a propaedeutic to the "first Marxist ethic"[73] the *Ontology* has received – and still does – enough

---

71   Emmanuel Renault, "Critical Theory and Processual Social Ontology." *Journal of Social Ontology*, vol. 2, no. 1 (2016): 31.
72   Italo Testa, "Ontology of the False State. On the Relation Between Critical Theory, Social Philosophy, and Social Ontology." *Journal of Social Ontology*, vol. 1, no. 2 (2015): 290–291.
73   Rüdiger Dannemann and Werner Jung (eds.), *Beiträge zu Georg Lukacs' "Zur Ontologie des gesellschaftlichen Seins." Frank Benseler zum 65. Geburtstag.* (Opladen: Westdeutscher Verlag, 1995), 49.

acknowledgement,[74] its merit does not lie less in the reorientation of Hegelian-Marxism from an epistemological to a social-ontological project. The latter was precipitated by Lukács' evaluation of the philosophical landscape of his time according to which scientific positivism and analytical epistemology could not be fought differently but through a robust concept of social-ontology capable of taking into account the subject's be(com)ing as processualization of nature and society. Instead of leaving it to falsifiable and more prone to ideology mental categories, "the role of ontology in History and in the Present of the human thinking is concretely determined through the creation of the human being according to its being [seinshaftig] and it is therefore – de facto, not merely abstract-verbally – not able to stamp it out any system of thought, our of any domain of thinking and surely above all out of any type of philosophy."[75] For this reason, Lukács begins by introducing directly the three modes of being that must be taken into account, if we want to elaborate on the general problems of the social being, its essence and it special way of existing: inorganic nature, organic nature (life), and society. Though seemingly still moving in the Kantian dichotomization between a realm of necessity and a realm of freedom, Lukács intends to show that through the reciprocal interplay between all three of them neither necessity is to be applied solely to nature and freedom to society, nor to claim – in a relativist manner – that none of the two exist. Concerning the former, i.e., the question whether necessity resides in nature and freedom in society, Lukács' point of departure matches the state of his critique against Kant and the bourgeois philosophy expressed in his HCC and according to which condoning the epistemological existence of such a thing like the thing in itself makes impossible to be able to criticize societal structures since they quickly acquire such a status like the thing in itself rendering them automatically impossible to grasp and consequently criticize. The *a priori* characterization of nature as the realm of necessity and of society as the realm of freedom entails the same danger. It tends to depict society as an already realized freedom mitigating thus the criticality of social institutions. Concerning the latter, i.e., if there is at all freedom to be realized and/or necessity already at work and/or how they condition each other, Lukács' answer resides in the way we see the interplay between inorganic nature, organic nature (life) and society. If we keep privileging the one mode of being over the other, we will

---

74   Cf. Mário Duayer and João Medeiros, "Lukács' Critical Ontology and Critical Realism." *Journal of Critical Realism*, vol. 4, no. 2 (2005): 395–425.
75   Georg Lukács, *Ontologie des gesellschaftlichen Seins. Erster Halbband.* (Darmstadt: Luchterhand, 1984), 9; henceforth *Ontology I*. Given that there is still no proper English translation of the text, unless differently indicated, the translations are mine.

always be deficient concerning the holistic all-encompassing processes that becoming is. The same happens if we seek to observe the exact transition from nature to life to society, i.e., when (temporally) or to what extent the human is being rather determined by its inorganic elements, its natural traits or its social identity. As he states:

> The three modes of being exist simultaneously, intertwined and exert, accordingly, often simultaneous effects on the human being, on his/her practices. [...] The human being belongs simultaneously (and in a way in which it is difficult to separate theoretically) to both nature and society. Marx most clearly recognized this simultaneity as a process by repeatedly saying that the process of becoming human being carries with it a retreat of nature's barriers. It is important to emphasize that [according to Marx] there is no talk of a disappearance of those barriers nor their complete dissolution, but of their retreat. However, this process never results in a dualistic constitution of the human being.[76]

Interestingly enough, the same arguments brought forward by Lukács to corroborate the relevance and value of reontologization of critical theory were almost literally repeated in the recent years from a thread of thought that was not – necessarily – Marxist: New Materialisms. Certainly, there is no common basis or a manifest to which all New Materialist tendencies found themselves obliged to abide to. Nevertheless, the complications between ethics and ontology, the need to correct epistemology through the return to a non-linguistic materiality, the aspiration to rethink materiality anew in order to spark new forms of (human/non-human, individual/collective) agency – to mention only but the most important of them – are topics that gained the greatest interest amidst the disparate field of what is being called New Materialisms. Just as Lukács apprehended the revitalization of the ontological as a political project capable of counteracting the prevailing academic thinking of his time, New Materialisms, as Coole/Frost argue, are also opposed to the currently prevailing "cultural turn that privileges language, discourse, culture, and values."[77] Further, just as Lukács found himself – due to the aforementioned political motivation – obliged to incorporate developments in the natural sciences in his ontological framework in order to prove the ongoing validity of the Marxist

---

76   *Ontology I*, 13.
77   Diana Coole and Samantha Frost, "Introducing the New Materialisms." In Diana Coole and Samantha Frost (eds.), *New Materialisms. Ontology, Agency, and Politics*. (Durham & London: Duke University Press, 2010), 3.

critique and at the same time show the inadequacy of current critical or from Marx' philosophy inspired theories, New Materialisms – at least in Cool's and Frost's account – take into consideration the "emergence of pressing ethical and political concerns that accompany the scientific and technological advances predicated on new scientific models of matter and, in particular, of living matter"[78] and take off from the diagnosis that "the dominant constructivist orientation to social analysis is inadequate for thinking about matter, materiality, and politics in ways that do justice to the contemporary context of biopolitics and global political economy."[79] Last but not least, just as Lukács points out the necessity to think the complexity of the interactions between inorganic matter, organic life and social being and how each of these instances mitigates the existence of one another, the New Materialists "can hardly ignore the role of *social* construction"[80] and at the same time they cannot but acknowledge that "society is simultaneously materially real and socially constructed: our material lives are always culturally mediated, but they are not only cultural. As in new materialist ontologies, the challenge here is to give materiality its due while recognizing its plural dimensions and its complex, contingent modes of appearing."[81] Apart from this general framework provided by Coole and Frost, some of the most distinctive voices among the new materialist theorists, like Jane Bennett, also seem to echo some of Lukács' positions. Concerning Bennett, it becomes apparent in her pursuit to reinvigorate agential thinking and extrapolate new political subjects. Abandoning the idea of "matter as passive stuff, as raw, brute, or inert"[82] is inherently political, since it questions the epistemological, socially dependent, presumptions concerning matter. The trajectory that has to be followed in order to overcome those presumptions and help develop new political subjectivities is according to Bennet as follows:

> (1) to paint a positive ontology of vibrant matter, which stretches received concepts of agency, action, and freedom sometimes to the breaking point; (2) to dissipate the onto-theological binaries of life/matter, human/animal, will/determination, and organic/inorganic using arguments and other rhetorical means to induce in human bodies an aesthetic-affective

---

78 Diana Coole and Samantha Frost, "Introducing the New Materialisms," 5.
79 Diana Coole and Samantha Frost, "Introducing the New Materialisms," 6.
80 Diana Coole and Samantha Frost, "Introducing the New Materialisms," 26.
81 Diana Coole and Samantha Frost, "Introducing the New Materialisms," 27.
82 Jane Bennett, *Vibrant Matter. A Political Ecology of Things.* (Durham & London: Duke University, 2010), vii.

openness to material vitality; and (3) to sketch a style of political analysis that can better account for the contributions of nonhuman actants.[83]

Transgressing or, rather, demolishing dualities, going back to forms of non- or inorganic life, arguing in favor of overcoming the limits of identity, corroborating nonidentity politics are only some of the methods that could be implemented in order to leave behind individualist politics and give in to what according to Lukács, as sketched in the last chapter, could provide for collective politics and according to Bennett could lead to "politics of assemblages": politics that acknowledge and take into account the socio-political role of things/products, etc., abort the individual as the sole basis and source of transformative action and, last but not least, question the intersubjective communicative intentionality of having to share interests or normative, identity grounds in order to underpin collective action or agency.

So far similarities between Lukács and the New Materialisms have been extrapolated that pertain to (a) the political mission of the ontology, (b) the interdisciplinary methodological rapprochement (comprising of having to take into account the latest achievements in the field of natural sciences and prevailing theoretical discourses in order to do philosophy), and (c) the content of their investigations (revisiting the notion of the subject, what matter consists in, and collective forms of action). Nevertheless, things look different concerning the notion of critique. Both Bennett and Coole/Frost agree with one another that critique ought not to constrain or limit itself to merely revealing, uncloaking or disclosing – a radical turn concerning the notion of critique in the framework of the Critical Theory of the Frankfurt School. Critique should also be able to provide viable alternatives. For Bennet, although "demystification is an indispensable tool in democratic, pluralist politics that seeks to hold officials accountable to (less unjust versions of) the rule of law and to check attempts to impose a system of (racial, civilizational, religious, sexual, class) domination,"[84] demystification is not enough since what we really need is "both critique and positive formulations of alternatives, alternatives that will themselves become the objects of later critique and reform."[85] Similarly, Coole/Frost argue that "the prevailing ethos of new materialist ontology is consequently more positive and constructive than critical or negative: it sees its task

---

83 Jane Bennett, *Vibrant Matter. A Political Ecology of Things*. (Durham & London: Duke University, 2010), x.

84 Jane Bennett, *Vibrant Matter. A Political Ecology of Things*. (Durham & London: Duke University, 2010), xiv.

85 Jane Bennett, *Vibrant Matter. A Political Ecology of Things*. (Durham & London: Duke University, 2010), xv.

as creating new concepts and images of nature that affirm matter's immanent vitality."[86] Though it would seem, at least according to the account that Coole/Frost provide, that the New Materialisms could suffice in assuming that the new concepts they introduce are per se political, the latter is definitely not the case. As they illustrate in their critique of Foucault, though Foucault "contra Foucault's insistence on his own nonnormative positivism, what makes such analyses grist for the critical materialist is the recognition that such dense networks of relationships support socioeconomic structures that sustain the privileges and interests of some rather than others, that these advantages are not randomly, much less fairly, distributed, and that understanding how they operate and are maintained is a crucial task for the engaged social theorist, especially one who eschews any lingering faith in the inevitability of either the present or the future."[87] The fact that critique has to go side by side with "visionary alternatives"[88] is particularly underlined in the account of New Materialisms that Rick Dolphijn and Iris van der Tuin present. In the latter's volume, Rosi Braidotti, yet another leading figure in this thread of thought, asserts unmistakeably that the new materialist turn is characterized by "an oppositional consciousness [that] combines critique with creativity."[89] What is at stake, again according to Braidotti, is "to overcome the boundaries that separate mere critique from active empowerment"[90] and in a combinatory manner take off from the former (critique) and lead to the latter (active empowerment).

The case is different when taking a further prominent figure among the new materialists, Karen Barad. Responding to Dolphijn's and van der Tuin's question whether the notion of agential realism she introduced ought to be understood as a critique of conventional entanglements of matter and meaning both in the natural sciences and the humanities, Barad provides following glaring answer:

> I am not interested in critique. In my opinion, critique is over-rated, over-emphasized, and over-utilized, to the detriment of feminism. [...] [C]ritique is a tool that keeps getting used out of habit perhaps, but it is no longer the tool needed for the kinds of situations we now face. Critique

---

86   Diana Coole and Samantha Frost, "Introducing the New Materialisms," 8.
87   Diana Coole and Samantha Frost, "Introducing the New Materialisms," 36.
88   Rick Dolphijn and Iris van der Tuin, *New Materialism: Interviews & Cartographies.* (Ann Arbor: Open Humanities Press, 2012), 14.
89   Rick Dolphijn and Iris van der Tuin, *New Materialism: Interviews & Cartographies.* (Ann Arbor: Open Humanities Press, 2012), 22.
90   Rick Dolphijn and Iris van der Tuin, *New Materialism: Interviews & Cartographies.* (Ann Arbor: Open Humanities Press, 2012), 23.

has been the tool of choice for so long, and our students find themselves so well-trained in critique that they can spit out a critique with the push of a button. Critique is too easy, especially when a commitment to reading with care no longer seems to be a fundamental element of critique. Thus, as I explain to my students, reading and writing are ethical practices, and critique misses the mark. Now, I understand that there is a different valence to the notion of critique in Europe than there is in the United States; nonetheless, I think this point is important. Critique is all too often not a deconstructive practice, that is, a practice of reading for the constitutive exclusions of those ideas we cannot do without, but a destructive practice meant to dismiss, to turn aside, to put someone or something down – another scholar, another feminist, a discipline, an approach, et cetera. So this is a practice of negativity that I think is about subtraction, distancing and othering.[91]

In this devastating critique of the notion of critique Barad cannot avoid giving away Bruno Latour as the figure she leans against to launch her attack and particularly Latour's "Why Has Critique Run out of Steam? From Matters of Fact to Matters of Concern"[92] where Latour debunks critique as a critical barbarity stemming from the fact that the critic is concerned solely with being right. Addressing his audience Latour ridicules critical projects by following simple – and not that easy to foil – assertion: "Do you see now why it feels so good to be a critical mind? Why critique, this most ambiguous *pharmakon*, has become such a potent euphoric drug? You are always right!"[93] Going back to Alfred North Whitehead and Gabriel Tarde and quoting Andrew Pickering and Isabelle Stenghers, Latour formulates what according to him could consolidate a new critical attitude:

> The solution lies, it seems to me, in this promising word *gathering* that Heidegger had introduced to account for the "thingness of the thing." Now, I know very well that Heidegger and Whitehead would have nothing

---

91   Rick Dolphijn and Iris van der Tuin, *New Materialism: Interviews & Cartographies*. (Ann Arbor: Open Humanities Press, 2012), 49.
92   Bruno Latour, "Why Has Critique Run out of Steam? From Matters of Fact to Matters of Concern." *Critical Inquiry – Special issue on the Future of Critique*, vol. 30, no. 2 (2004): 225–248.
93   Bruno Latour, "Why Has Critique Run out of Steam? From Matters of Fact to Matters of Concern." *Critical Inquiry – Special issue on the Future of Critique*, vol. 30, no. 2 (2004): 239.

to say to one another, and, yet, the word the latter used in *Process and Reality* to describe "actual occasions," his word for my matters of concern, is the word *societies*. It is also, by the way, the word used by Gabriel Tarde, the real founder of French sociology, to describe all sorts of entities. It is close enough to the word *association* that I have used all along to describe the objects of science and technology. Andrew Pickering would use the words "mangle of practice."

Whatever the words, what is presented here is an entirely different attitude than the critical one, not a flight into the conditions of possibility of a given matter of fact, not the addition of something more human that the inhumane matters of fact would have missed, but, rather, a multifarious inquiry launched with the tools of anthropology, philosophy, metaphysics, history, sociology to detect *how many participants* are gathered in a *thing* to make it exist and to maintain its existence.[94]

In the previous section we saw already how Lukács' return to social-ontology parts from the philosophies of solipsistic subjectivity and what kind of collective practices it enables exactly because it takes off from an understanding of the commodity as not a subject, but exactly as a vector, a gathering, of its producers' labour and its consumers' socio-political norms/values/imaginaries. In this section we have seen – so far – what the epistemic object of social ontology is, what the political task of a critical social ontology consists in and after sketching the similarities between Lukács and New Materialisms we came to see what kind of challenges await any updating of Lukács' social ontology should the latter still demand to be critical. The answer lies – so much can already be foreclosed – in the fact that Latour's gathering, or collectivity as will be called here, forms the conceptual and methodological basis of Lukács' taking up social ontology. As will be argued, collectivity as Lukács places it as the fundament of his *Ontology* is (as shown in the last section) in the position to promote collective action beyond the currently prevailing identity or normative politics not only because it provides for a collective epistemology but also because it is because of the latter able to exert social critique by promoting a positive alternative that moves beyond the individualist, solipsistic understanding of subjectivity in favor of collectivist mode of being.

---

94   Bruno Latour, "Why Has Critique Run out of Steam? From Matters of Fact to Matters of Concern." *Critical Inquiry – Special issue on the Future of Critique*, vol. 30, no. 2 (2004): 245–246.

4.3 Collectivization as Form of Social-Ontological Critique

Picking up the thread where we left it concerning the critical character of social ontology, Emmanuel Renault does not randomly attribute the critical quality to any ontology or social ontology. In order for an ontology or social ontology to be critical, it has to be processual. Should social-ontological thinking be able to facilitate (conceiving) transformation in favour of (in order to realize) social change, ontology has to be processual.

> What specifies a processual ontology is not the claim that substances or sets of relations have a genesis [which is the case in mere ontologies, independent whether social or critical], but that this genesis does not have less reality than its results, be they substances or sets of relations, and that these results are only moments of a becoming. To sum up, what is characteristic of processual ontologies is that they give full reality to relations and becoming. This does not mean that they give only a secondary reality to substantial and relational properties. On the contrary, substantial and relational properties are moments (in Hegelian terms) or phases (in Deweyan terms) of processes. [...] [P]rocessual ontologies give full reality to relations and becoming whereas substantial ontologies refuse to give full reality to relations and becoming, and relational ontologies refuse to give full reality to becoming.[95]

That Lukács' social ontology is a processual one should have already become clear given the differentiation he grants to the different modes of being and how they determine reciprocally the be(com)ing of the social being. Through his description of how being emanates at/as the cross-point of organic, inorganic and society, Lukács provides us with a description of socio-ontological structures generating the social being and its *ex post*, epistemological faculties, which depend on those structures. While Lukács reveals himself herein as a thinker moving still in the framework of the (Left-)Post-Hegelian tradition, the pivotal point is that he conceives of them not as expressions of an always already existing spirit awaiting to emanate (entäußern), but as constructions, as products of those modes of being that provide the context in which the social being will accrue; a context, of whom there is no outside. Between Kantian transcendentalism and Hegelian logicism Lukács opts for the latter. However, between Hegelian logicism and Marxian social ontology Lukács favors again

---

95   Emmanuel Renault, "Critical Theory and Processual Social Ontology." *Journal of Social Ontology*, vol. 2, no. 1 (2016): 22–23.

the latter since only this scheme can dictate/describe/articulate immanently its own process. This positioning has an immediate impact both on the understanding of subjectivity with which Lukács will find himself obliged to operate and the epistemological faculties that can be attributed to such a notion of subjectivity. Lukács emphatically affirms what we have already seen in the previous section and what Adorno, in the very beginning of this book-chapter, claimed as the basis of critical philosophy, namely the necessity to break away from anthropomorphic, essentialist understandings of subjectivity. In Lukács' terminology, disanthropomorphization is one of the most important and essential tasks of the analytics of social being since only through disanthropomorphization are we able to grasp the formation of social being as process where the modes of being co-determine the social being's becoming, the momentousness of the social being's current form of being and the prospective actions the social being can engage in. As he states: "Disanthropomorphization is the most important and indispensable means for the understanding of how the being really, in itself is, was and will be."[96] Furthermore, the social-ontological analytics of the social being do not allow subject–object dialectics to perforate the contingency and multiplicity of struggles that arise from this multileveled and plural process of becoming. As products of social processes, the revolutionary/emancipatory, etc. subject cannot be predetermined or bestowed upon a certain emancipatory activity, nor are the demarcation lines or fronts predetermined and ex ante set. Therefore and concerning this subjectivity's epistemological guarantees, not only contingency is at play, but also constructivism (i.e., that the concretization of the social being's epistemological faculties depends on the modes of being), historicism (i.e., that this concretization renders the epistemological faculties reliant to the respective reconfiguration of the modes of being in/through time), fallibilism (i.e., the fact that given the historical dependency of epistemological categories from their time of concretization and the fact that those epistemological faculties are never able to grasp their way of production through time, the epistemological faculties are prone to mistakes and constrained to an unavoidably deficient understanding of the reality's totality), and last but not least partiality (i.e., the fact that it is impossible to grasp epistemologically and implement into praxis the wholeness of ontological processes entangled in the process of the social being's becoming).[97]

---

96   *Ontology I*, 28.
97   For this chain of rather fragmented and not that linear arguments see *Ontology I*, 16, 30, 35: "It is clear that this is ultimately the already treated ontological fact that human practice, even if scientifically sound, can never be realized in the knowledge of all individual

Should just that be the case, namely if Lukács would just decree/suggest/propone contingency, constructivism, historicism, fallibilism and partiality as characteristics of any epistemological undertaking he would just be moving amidst the framework of post-metaphysical relativism, processual metaphysics, etc. Therefore, he could never be rehabilitated as being able to indicate a new direction of thinking and provide the fundaments for an alternative social critique that could in return result in a new emancipatory project. The move that changes the tables comes as soon as Lukács – quoting Marx as a cloak instead of directly expressing himself – argues that the just diagnosed characteristics of epistemological practice are the results of an ontological articulation of reality that is collective in its calibration. Contingency, constructivism, historicism, fallibilism and partiality as qualities are therefore not opposed only to Hegelian or idealistic teleology and metaphysics. Given their collectiveness, i.e., the fact that those qualities arise out of the collective structuration of reality and should not therefore be presupposed, those qualities are opposed also to notions like discontinuity, fragility, epochal closure, irreducibility, etc., that were made prominent from the hermeneutical or genealogical discourse in connection with e.g., Hans-Georg Gadamer, Paul Ricoeur or Michel Foucault respectively. Lukács' notion of the "Geradesosein" is indicative for his grasping the parts of reality as collective reciprocal reconfigurations of the modes of being and therefore neither as moments awaiting to be sublated nor as fragments irrelevant to one another. As he states:

> Centuries later he [Marx] gives precise details about the method of its [historicity's] exploration: the investigation of the processes themselves in their respective dynamic *Geradesosein**. Such a development is not – as the bourgeois way of thinking often asserts – merely a certain change of objects, of their relationships, etc. where the determining categories that express their essence persist essentially unaltered. [...] For the

---

circumstances, assumptions, and consequences. On the other hand, this leads to the conclusion that a practically used scientific thesis can in many respects, indeed in essence, be wrong from the point of view of the total knowledge and its developmental tendency and yet be able to properly solve the given task and on the other hand be correct in certain cases, yes, epochal cognitive tendencies can bring to light." (30) "For now, let us content ourselves with the statement that Marx, even in his youth, has placed this universal validity of historicity for every being at the center of his method." (16) "The totality of the respective ways of the being's determinations, which is impossible to recognize in its completeness, renders both the long, undisturbed functioning of incomplete theories, which contain only partial truths, as well as their overcoming socially possible and necessary." (35).

process of history is causal, not teleological, multi-layered, never one-sided, simply straightforward, always a trend set by real interactions and interrelations of the respective active complexes of developmental tendencies set in motion. [...] This consistently thought-through priority of historicity in its concrete *Geradososein** as a real, i.e. really processing [als reale, weil real prozessierende] way of being is already an explosive criticism of any absolutization of everyday life.[98]

This passus suggests thinking the various modes of being as momentary points of encounter where, as Lukács points out a couple of pages later, the genesis of the mode of social being should never be understood as a unique moment of becoming something different, something permanent, something completely and permanently new in a reality where unity takes hand over multiplicity.[99] It is exactly for this reason why Lukács speaks of the social being as the "ensemble of social relations,"[100] as a "complex"[101] of internal forces being permanently in motion, as the "co-existence"[102] of the different modes of being. Even when upholding the notion of the individual, he differentiates the individual, i.e., the concrete reality of the interplay of the different modes of being, from the particular, i.e., the one-sided realization of the generality, and the general, i.e., the category invented to describe the reality.[103] In a quote illustrating the latter while underlining the overdetermined and at the same time non-sublatable process of the social being, Lukács argues that

> [t]he merely natural biological detail of the individual corresponded to the stage of spontaneous biological reproduction, which in principle was overcome by work. Since their repression [Zurückgedrängtwerden] (never their total disappearance [Verschwindenlassen]) is a protracted, uneven, contradictory process, the increasing domination of the social over the merely natural, the emergence and the augmenting, both subjective and objective ponderousness of individuality in social life must also be a process of similar determinations.[104]

---

98   *Ontology I*, 36.
99   Cf. *Ontology I*, 37–38.
100 *Ontology I*, 38.
101 *Ontology I*, 42.
102 *Ontology I*, 43.
103 Cf. *Ontology I*, 44.
104 *Ontology I*, 56.

As he categorically asserts: "It is therefore ontologically impossible to conceive of an individuality without this origin and without such an outcome, let alone to see the unifying principle that really governs individuality through the lenses of an individuality as isolated being, characterized – seen this way only allegedly – by its own self-movement."[105] Further, it is important to realize that what Lukács diagnoses – as the last quote underpins – is a non-hierarchical structuration of the social being where neither the inorganic, nor the natural or society take a leading role in the social being's collective articulation. Though the subject might seem to privilege and confirm by bringing to light through its actions the one or the other mode of being, this ought to be conceived a coincidental and not a normative matter.[106] Although there is – on the analytical level – a procession from seemingly less complex to supposedly higher and more complex life-forms, nothing changes in the original source of social being as an already-always composition comprising continuously the different modes of being independently of the different reconfigurations that the social being's form and content can acquire.[107] The social being's outline absorbs, integrates, sediments, consolidates, incorporates – to mention only some of the notions Lukács scatters in his *Prolegomena* in order to describe the process of the social being's becoming – but collectivity never goes astray or becomes unified to a sole, synthetic mode of existence.

Through the latter, Lukács ontologizes and by that ventures to also rehabilitate the Marxian notion of class struggle. At the end, there is not much left of class. What Lukács recodifies though is the motive of the struggle as a method. Struggle pertains no more to the relationship of societal structures, like the proletariat or the bourgeoisie, to one another, but henceforth to the disposition of the different modes of being to one another. "Indeed, it must even be said that the immediately most powerful achievement of Marx's method of the class struggle as a real motor of social development, and thus as a decisive motor in the history of the human species, cannot be fully understood as a determining factor, without the complex of decisions from which human individuality emerges fully understood as the overcoming in general of the mere particularity, as judging [wertende] and judged [gewertete] real moments of the overall process."[108] The latter can be applied not only to the relation dictating the intertwinement of the different modes of being with one another, but also concerning the different modes of societal discourses of which society as

---

105   *Ontology I*, 62.
106   *Ontology I*, 56.
107   Cf. *Ontology I*, 129–130.
108   *Ontology I*, 60.

a mode of being consists. Further, it can be applied to the different struggles alongside which the palimpsestic fabric of – this time – societal reality is interwoven. Seen this way, not only the social being is a collectivity of inorganic nature, life and society. Collectivity also forms the basis of the subject's identity which therefore should be considered as comprised of different societal discourses. Last but not least, collectivity indicates how society's (re-)structuration can be accomplished through the collective renegotiation of its current articulation. Therefore, Lukács' social ontology accounts for much more than just a critical stance, i.e., it does not just provide for a ground to assert and evaluate current situation. It also provides for a new project according to which reality could be rearticulated. By asserting the ontological collectivity of the social being's be(com)ing, Lukács did not just contribute yet another understanding of natural and societal reality and of their interrelatedness. At the same time, he extrapolated out of this collective composition of reality second-order epistemological tools that enable us to grasp it.[109] Further, he radicalized the vector of these epistemological faculties, the subject, by disanthropomorphizing and deessentializing and furnishing proof of its heteronomous structuration as a product of inorganic, natural and societal structures and how even on the level of its societal structuration the subject could also be conceived of as the amalgam of different social identities. Last but not least, Lukács suggested how collective struggles running along different lines and fronts are (still) the only viable and immanent way to change social and natural reality since this mode of praxis, i.e., collective practices, corresponds immanently to reality's collective mode of be(com)ing. Seen this way, Lukács not only seems to outdo Latour's critique of the blind and futile barbarity of critique. It also seems to be more practical even in comparison to Karen Barad's notion of diffraction. As Barad summarizes both the methodological and practical-political consequences of diffraction, the epistemological advantages of diffraction as a methodology rest primarily in: "marking differences from within and as part of an entangled state"; in acknowledging the "performativity [of] subject and object [according to which subject and object] do not preexist as such, but emerge through intra-actions"; in proposing an "entangled ontology" or "onto-epistem-ology" according to which by taking off from "material-discursive phenomena" we extrapolate a notion of knowing as "a material practice of engagement as part of the world in its differential becoming"; last but not least in realizing that there is no interacting of separate entities but "intra-acting within and as part of" those entities' way of becoming for which

---

109 For a detailed and thorough analysis of the latter cf. Titus Stahl, *Immanente Kritik. Elemente einer Theorie sozialer Praktiken.* (Frankfurt am Main/New York: Campus, 2013).

reason differences may be "real material differences" but "without absolute separation." Concerning the political impact of diffraction, Barad allocates the latter in "making a difference in the world" which is "about taking responsibility for the fact that our practices matter" given that "the world is materialized differently through different practices (contingent ontology)."[110] While the epistemological advantages of Barad's new materialist methodology of diffraction bear so many similarities that it could even be argued that they were anticipated by Lukács, this does not seem to be the case concerning diffraction's potentiality as a political strategy. Diffraction does not seem possible to support radical politics, but merely exhausts itself in the traditional and conventional Weberian politics of responsibility. Radical politics should not necessarily follow the collective paradigm of practice which we saw that can be mounted according to Lukács' social-ontology, but it should be in a position to account for something significantly more than the poor realization that "our practices matter." They are entitled to take off and underpin, as they do, that "ethics, ontology and epistemology are not separable" in order to craft a viable, effective and powerful political scheme, but this cannot be the place where they end.[111] The latter applies also to Latour's debunking of critique as critical barbarity. Albeit right as he may be therein, namely in the fact that critique ought to never become domesticated as a self-assuring endeavor, and regardless how drastic his critique of conventional onto-epistemological certainties may be, it does not look like that an equally robust articulated and equally drastic political project can be expected anymore. As shown, this is not the case with Lukács. The social being, as an effect and product not only of the modes of being that constituted it but also as a product and effect of the different forms the mode of being society consists of, bears with it the modes of its production. As such, i.e., by emerging as a cross-path, the social being has to be understood as the participation of every mode of being involved in its production. Read this way, Lukács' ontology deploys a political functionality that allows for collective struggles to occur out of the commonality of the subjects' – in plural – production. This is not identity politics since there is no concrete identity that was brought forth, but the subject as a totality of societal relations. Furthermore, read this way Lukács' social ontology though not explicitly addressing sex or gender or race, ecological movements or the undocumented migrants,

---

110   Karen Barad, *Meeting the Universe Half-Way: Quantum Physics and the Entanglement of Matter and Meaning*. (Durham, N.C. & London: Duke University Press, 2007), 89–90.

111   For a more favorable reading of Barad's method of diffraction in contrast exclusively to Lukács' social ontology, cf. the working paper by Waltraud Ernst and Ágnes Kovács: "New Materialisms, Older Ones, and New Genderings."

provides us with a framework to conceive of them as parts and even modes of being of that mode of being that Lukács calls society. Collective agency is thus being grafted to the subject through its social-ontological emergence *as* a collective social being and entering collective struggles is being liberated from having to be a matter of political engagement or normative ethics, just as it does not require legitimization. And the actors in question are as innumerable as the concrete forms that these subjects' social-ontological formation can acquire. Latour may have been the one to have recently propagated in the strongest fashion gathering, association and society, but at the end it seems that Lukács is the one able to sufficiently substantiate the latter both theoretically and politically.

5 Conclusion

The chapter started by scrutinizing wherein the contemporary applicability of the notion of reification could still lie. Drawing on another similar yet broader undertaking, namely Adorno's attempt to ascertain the reasonability of not only reification but philosophy itself, a working hypothesis was established: The ongoing applicability of reification depends on where it could still be able to function as a critical category which can be asserted as such only if it can enable a radical political project. Instead of tarrying in what critique is – an undoubtedly enticing question – Adorno's answer to the question was chosen as point of departure. Just as Adorno qualifies freedom as philosophy's goal and puts an end to essentialist, anthropomorphic approaches as philosophy's method, reification should also be able to account for freedom by putting an end to essentialist understandings of subjectivity. Combining those two criteria, the working hypothesis concerning reification's ongoing topicality was translated as depending on reification being able to function as a subjectivation process that can account firstly for a socially constructed (as opposed to essentialist) understanding of subjectivity and secondly for the theoretical means to graft collective practices as a form of self-determination.

The first part of the chapter was dedicated to mapping the different substantializations of the notion of reification underwent in the course of its existence as soon as it was introduced and firstly corroborated by Lukács in his *History and Class Consciousness*. Three tendencies were detected in the chapter: (1) With the exception of Deleuze, for the French postwar philosophy Lukács' concept of reification remained due to the world-historical role it attributed to the proletariat still rooted in an idealist philosophy of subject; (2) For the feminist discourses, above all for standpoint theory, no matter how consequently they furthered the decentering of the subject and how inspired by Lukács they admittedly were, their notion of choice to operate with was not that of reification, but rather that of false consciousness; (3) For the Frankfurt School reification may have been one of the very few terms that have incessantly accompanied its different generations and paradigmatic turns. However, given the fact that the Frankfurt School, regardless how critical and radical it was in radicalizing the subject–object dialectics and never giving up conceiving subjectivity in its robust Hegelian-Marxian understanding, reification never became a subjectivating phenomenon, but remained a subject-critical one.

In light of this cartography it would seem that the venture to address reification as a subjectivating process should be suspended before it even begins. This would have definitely been the case if a minoritarian, phenomenological line of interpretation of the phenomenon of reification led by Lucien Goldmann and Nicolas Tertulian had not managed to demonstrate how reification had still not exhausted its full potential. As seen, Goldmann's and Tertulian's merit lays in shifting reification from a phenomenon that determines market practices to henceforth apply also to the construction of subjectivity as a historical entity. In order to demonstrate the latter, Lukács' social-ontological understanding of labor in his *Ontology of the Social Being* was accroached. In this context, labor manifests itself not as a self-expressive activity that can be alienated, but as a process of subjectivity production. Further, the subjectivating process of labor was identified as affecting not only the subject in its producer identity, but also in its consumer identity. Through the consumption of commodities, the consumer encounters the economical and socio-cultural laws that determine the transformation of the product to commodity. As argued, the consumer becomes, as a consuming buyer, a co-determining factor of the producer's labor regimes. A new kind of social bond is therefore created between the producer and consumer that results in a shift of the reasons upon which collective practices can be founded. Collective practices do not have to rest necessarily only on production – which was the argumentative strategy of the early Lukács in his HCC concerning the forging of proletariat – which broadens the hitherto rather narrow foundation of collective practices.

Although this broadening and alternativity in founding collective practices could provide an answer to the second leg of the equation concerning reification's contemporary applicability (critique plus self-determining practice), the first leg, that of critique was yet to be answered. For the latter, Lukács' social ontology was revisited as laid down in the Prolegomena of his *Ontology of the Social Being*. At the same time, just as Adorno had to counterattack contemporaneous prevailing notions of what philosophy is, in order to strengthen the validity of his understanding of philosophy. Lukács' fundaments of critique had to be examined through the lenses of currently prevailing notions of critique. New Materialisms and Bruno Latour were accroached as representing the latter. After some introductory remarks concerning where the critical character of processual social-ontologies could lie, various understandings of the notion of critique as well as critical voices against the notion of critique per se stemming from the field of New Materialisms were mentioned. As argued, collectivity as the mode of social-ontological organization of reality was Lukács' solid answer concerning the demand for an alternative understanding of reality that could also account for a different analysis of society and, last but not least provide for practical considerations concerning radical politics. As demonstrated, by starting from reality as the composition of inorganic nature, organic nature (life) and society, Lukács did not just collectivize reality. The social being, i.e., the subject, and society were shown as also having to correspond to this socio-ontological collectivity that lies at the basis of existence. For this reason, self-determining practices must – as corresponding to the collective social being that instantiates them and the society they aim to change – also be collective.

Undoubtedly, there is still a lot to be clarified concerning e.g., the underlying fractions or similarities between Adorno's notion of Constellation and Lukács' understanding of collectivity, the role of networks in Latour's Science-and-Technology-Studies (STS) or Michel Callon's Actor-Network-Theory (ANT) and how they relate to Lukács' understanding of collective action; the conceptualization of the thing according to the early or the late Lukács and the early or late Latour, etc. Furthermore, the chapter decidedly avoided discussing and counter-examining Lukács' social ontology with the ontological, epistemological and political assumptions of the critical realism of Roy Bhaskar which became prolific and increasingly importance.[112] Last but not least, a more elaborate look at the relationship between Lukács' processual social ontology and Whitehead's processual metaphysics or the notion of association in Pragmatism would surely have been insightful in light of recent publications.[113]

---

112   For some first inputs in what should have been a more thorough discussion cf. the public and later printed discussion between Alex Callinicos and Roy Bhaskar in: Roy Bhaskar and Alex Callinicos, "Marxism and Critical Realism." *Journal of Critical Realism*, vol. 1, no. 2 (2003): 89–114.

113   Cf. Anne Fairchild Pomeroy, *Marx and Whitehead. Process, Dialectics, and the Critique of Capitalism.* (Albany: State University of New York Press, 2004); Italo Testa, "The Authority of Life: The Critical Task of Dewey's Social Ontology." *Journal of Speculative Philosophy – Special Issue on John Dewey and Social Criticism* (edited by Federica Gregoratto, Arvi Särkelä, and Justo Serrano Zamora), vol. 31, no. 2 (2017): 231–244.

Nevertheless, such shortcomings can only be promising for prospective projects and do not necessarily change the structure of the argument: that it is still worthy to operate with the notion of reification because as old and parochial as this concept may be considered to be, it can still provide radical critique and facilitate radical political practice.

CHAPTER 9

Unlikely Affinities: J.L. Borges, Kuhn, Lakatos and Ontological Critique

Mario Duayer

> I thought that Argos and I participated in different universes; I thought that our perceptions were the same, but that he combined them in another way and made other objects of them; I thought that perhaps there were no objects for him, only a vertiginous and continuous play of extremely brief impressions.
>
> J.L. BORGES, *The Immortal*

∴

1   Introduction

This article seeks to support the idea that one of the main factors of the lack of alternatives for the various crises that many countries have been facing in recent times is the absence of an ontological critique in which another social world could be envisioned, a social world worthier of humanity and able to captivate people. To uphold the ineluctable nature of the ontological critique for transformative praxis, the chapter firstly explores some of Jorge Luis Borges' essays, in which the writer shows in his own way how ontological notions underlie every social human activity and – differently from what Foucault seems to infer from those essays – emphasizes the objectivity of such notions, which of course are always subject to refutation. From literature to philosophy of science, the chapter also argues that science cannot operate in an ontological vacuum. A brief examination of the conceptions on science and scientific explanation held by logical positivism, Kuhn and Lakatos makes it possible to demonstrate this argument, despite the contempt of those conceptions for ontological issues.

Finally, the chapter argues that Lukács' *Ontology* convincingly demonstrates that genuine science orientates itself by necessity towards the being of things, that is to say, towards truth. Taking into account that a social science cannot operate in an ontological vacuum either, to orientate itself towards the being of things means that social science has to understand what society is, and therefore it means that it is founded, explicitly or implicitly, on an ontology of the social being. Moreover, if social theory is part of society, if it creates an intelligibility based on which people act preserving or transforming society, it is possible to affirm that the dispute between theories and the corresponding practices they foster and support is an ontological dispute. Hence, the ontological critique is an imperative to any emancipation from social structures that oppress, coerce and degrade human beings.

2 Borges and the Ontology

Before justifying the statement that ontological issues represent a central theme for Borges, it is relevant to say that neither a specialist in Borges nor a literary critic developed the interpretation sustained henceforth. It is rather the result of the impressions caused by the writer's texts, especially because his writings deal, in fiction, with the complex relations between word and concept, conceptual thought and language. It would be nonsense to expect that Borges treated ontological issues in an explicit and systematic fashion since these questions are not an explicit theme not even in philosophy. It seems, though, that such matters featured in his major concerns. To show this I believe few of his texts are enough, two of which will be examined more closely: *John Wilkins' Analytical Language* and *Funes, the Memorious*. Nonetheless, a short mention to two other Borges' pieces, *The Aleph* and *On Exactitude in Science*, can function as an introduction to the subject.

In the short story *The Aleph*, the narrator reports the case of a character who is a writer of an endless poem and lives in a house in whose basement there is a point, the Aleph, precisely located on the nineteenth step of the stairs. The Aleph, when seen from a certain angle, is "the place where, without admixture or confusion, all the places of the world, seen from every angle, coexist." Skeptical, the narrator manages to get into the basement and, astonished, sees the Aleph, the infinity, that object of no more than three centimeters in diameter, in which, however, there was the "cosmic space, with no diminution in size… [e]ach thing… was infinite things," because, asserts the narrator, he could see it/them from all sides of the universe. After watching the vertiginous extensive and intensive flow of all things in a "gigantic instant,"

> [...] the teeming sea…daybreak and nightfall…the multitudes of America…a silvery cobweb in the center of a black pyramid, [...] bunches of

grapes, snow, tobacco, lodes of metal, steam...convex equatorial deserts and each one of their grains of sand, [...] at the same time saw each letter on each page [...] the night and the contemporary day [...] tigers, pistons, bison, tides and armies...all the ants on the planet [...] the coupling of love and the modification of death...[1]

Having being the spectator of all this, the narrator expresses his despair as a writer: how would it be possible to tell others about infinity if language is a "set of symbols" that presupposes a shared past among its speakers?[2] If language is successive, how to transcribe all the simultaneity caught from experience? How to deal with the insoluble problem of enumerating an infinite set? Besides being incommunicable, or exactly because it is incommunicable, infinity seems to immobilize the mind with the stunning density of its events flow. Maybe this is the reason why the narrator confesses that he only regained control of himself after spending sleepless nights by reliving what had been seen in the Aleph, when he was "visited once more by oblivion."[3]

It can be said that the crucial point of the story is the world's infinitude and our access to it. The world is obviously inapprehensible in its intensive and extensive totality of things, processes and events. The immediate and magic access to such infinity, supposedly enabled by the Aleph, is more likely to represent nescience than knowledge, for the infinity's limitless details are what they are, namely, an instantaneous and paradoxically simultaneous succession of singular events, objects, etc., that by themselves, as singulars, do not convey the knowledge of totality. To draw a parallel, its infinite profusion is like a sudden and endless collapse of the shelves of a huge and assorted warehouse: a tangle of things.

Knowing the world, just on the contrary, does not come down to identifying singulars. It consists in recognizing the universal and particular determinations of the singulars, the categories that specify the effects that the singulars produce on the world and that the world produces on them. In other words, Borges, in *The Aleph*, performs a remarkable critique to one of the moments of the process of knowledge, the analysis, by absolutizing it, precisely by firstly implying that to know is to access the infinite details of everything that exists and happens, and subsequently by suggesting that to know is to forget the details, that is, to synthesize – the other moment of the process of knowledge.

---

1 J.L. Borges, "The Aleph." In Jorge Luis Borges, *Collected Fictions*. Trans. H. Hurley. (London: Penguin Books, 1998), 93.
2 Ibid.
3 Ibid.

It is not difficult to notice that in *On Exactitude in Science* Borges deals with the same problem. It is a widespread text, largely used as a sort of "methodological" epigraph, so to speak, in many scientific articles in different areas of knowledge, and as object in literary analyses themselves. The short narrative tells about an alleged empire in which cartography had achieved such high level of perfection that its maps were produced in a gigantic scale: the map of a province could cover a whole city; the map of the empire could reach the total extension of a province. Disappointed with the inaccuracy presented by such exorbitant maps, the faculty of cartographers decided to carry out a 1:1 scale map so that the map of the empire had exactly the same extension of the empire. Useless for the following generations, this map was left to degenerative action of time.

As we can see, Borges again addresses the problem of abstraction, of subject–object separation, of distancing of the subject from the object that constitutes the presupposition of practice. Even dealing with a specific mental appropriation of reality – a map, a graphic representation of any extension –, the text has a meaning that holds to any type of representation and to any sector of reality, be it natural or social. In a word, as Borges sums up in another tale, thinking is abstracting. And, in abstraction, as observes Lukács, reality is "reality" as spiritual possession. For this reason, reality constitutes a

> new form of objectivity..., but not a reality, and – precisely from the ontological standpoint –, it is not possible to equate the reproduction with what it reproduces, let alone identify the two. Just on the contrary.[4]

In the short story *Funes, the Memorious*, the narrator talks about a peculiar character, Irineu Funes, who used to entertain and delight whoever he met with his curious ability to precisely guess the hour of the day.[5] One day, however, a horse knocked him down and he became paraplegic. What was quaint in Funes turned into amazing capacity. As a sequel his senses became hypertrophied, and his memory answered to this by swelling up in order to be able to register the immeasurable volume of information offered by the senses. As an effect of the accident, he was now capable of perceiving

> [...] all the leaves and tendrils and fruit that make up a grape vine. He knew by heart the forms of the southern clouds at dawn on the 30th of

---

4 G. Lukács, *The Ontology of Social Being*, 3. *Labour*. (London: Merlin Press, 1978), 26.
5 Borges, "J.L. Funes, the Memorious." In *Labyrinths: Selected Stories & Other Writings*. (New York: New Directions, 1964), 93.

April, 1882, and could compare them in his memory with the mottled streaks on a book in Spanish binding he had only seen once [...]. These memories were not simple ones; each visual image was linked to muscular sensations, thermal sensations, etc. He could reconstruct all his dreams, all his half-dreams. Two or three times he had reconstructed a whole day; [...], but each reconstruction had required a whole day.[6]

Funes' senses were so prodigious that the decimal numbering system seemed excessively prolix to him. Hence, one can understand that he started thinking to develop a more synthetic system, in which each number would correspond to a word. Another project that his phenomenal memory demanded was to build a language in which each singular ("each stone, each bird and each branch") would receive a specific name. The narrator of the tale was right to ponder that such projects, though senseless,

> [...] permit us to glimpse or infer the nature of Funes' vertiginous world. [...] [he] could continuously discern the tranquil advances of corruption, of decay, of fatigue. He could note the progress of death, of dampness. He was the solitary and lucid spectator of a multiform, instantaneous and almost intolerably precise world. [...] no one ...has felt the heat and pressure of a reality as indefatigable as that which day and night converged upon the hapless Ireneo, in his poor South American suburb. It was very difficult for him to sleep.[7]

With an extremely tumultuous mind, it is easy to perceive that Funes was not able to conceive general ideas. That is why it was unthinkable for him that "the generic symbol *dog*" could designate not only all dogs but also all sorts of dogs and each dog in their endless circumstances of life. Funes was a tireless and obsessed spectator of the singular, and kept in his mind all the details of everything that his senses could offer him and of everything that he imagined. In spite of Funes' overburdened mind, Borges suspects he was incapable of thinking, since thinking is "to forget differences, generalize, make abstractions. In the teeming world of Funes, there were only details, almost immediate in their presence."[8]

It is needless to emphasize that the problems dealt with in *Funes, the Memorious* are essentially the same ones treated in *The Aleph*. Later it will be seen

---

6 Ibid.
7 Ibid.
8 Ibid., 97.

that in both stories the observation and/or the identification of the infinite singulars presupposes an ontology, which is implied in the taxonomy from where each of the singulars is identified. If so, the delusion that only singulars are seen in the Aleph or that only singulars matter to Funes is more than evident. Actually, the taxonomy by means of which each singular is captured, seen or identified involves, with its singular, particular and universal categories, relations of identity and difference among the singulars, their specific features and reciprocal connections. In other words, that taxonomy presupposes a notion of the world as totality – namely, an ontology –, even when totality absurdly appears as a mess of atomic singulars, as Borges seems to insinuate. An emphatic evidence of this Borgean conception can be observed in *John Wilkins' Analytical Language*, to be seen next.

In *John Wilkins' Analytical Language*, Borges' advocacy of the objectivity of our knowledge of the world is so clear, so inspired, that it could be placed in the same level of a philosophical treaty. The project of creating a philosophical language, developed by John Wilkins – a character who "abounded in happy curiosities" –, serves as material to discuss the question of objectivity. Wilkins' project aimed at solving the undecipherable and inexpressive nature of the words of any language – despite claims to the contrary. The *Real Academia*, for example, derides Borges, but at the same time mentions the alleged expressive character of the words "in the riches of the Spanish language" and, paradoxically, publishes a dictionary in which the "expressive" words are given a definition.[9] According to Borges, by observing that with the use of "the decimal system of numeration, we could learn in a single day to name all quantities to infinity, and to write them in a new language,"[10] Descartes, in the beginning of the 17th century, thought about something similar: "a language that would organize and contain all human thought. Around 1664, John Wilkins embarked on that enterprise."[11]

Wilkins started from the assumption that people generally share the same principle of reason and the same apprehension of things. That is why it seemed to him that humanity could get rid of such language confusion and its unhappy consequences if the notions in common could be linked to shared written or spoken symbols. Having this purpose in mind, and not without an admitted arbitrariness, Wilkins imagined that forty basic categories or classes subdivided in differences, which in turn were dismembered into species, could

---

9   Borges, "John Wilkins' Analytical Language." In Jorge Luis Borges, *Selected Non Fictions*. (London: Penguin Books, 1999).
10 Ibid., p. 230.
11 Ibid.

compose the symbols of a kind of inventory of the world. To turn his artificial language expressive, Wilkins put forward the following scheme: to each of the forty classes there is a corresponding monosyllable; to each difference, there is a corresponding letter; and to each type, there is also a corresponding letter. This way, each sequence of pronounceable symbols would immediately express a specific item of the world. Borges exemplifies this device as follows: *de* corresponds to the genre "element"; *deb* is the element increased with the letter that expresses the difference (b) – in this case, fire, the first element; by adding the letter that indicates the type (a), it results *deba*, a portion of the element fire – a flame. Another example would be the class "world," represented by the monosyllable *da*. When *da* is followed by the letter that indicates the second difference (d), which denotes "celestial," it results in the notion of sky (*dad*). The symbol for "Earth" is *dady*, which is composed by the same *dad* plus the symbol of the seventh type (y), resulting in the globe of earth and sea.

That is the scheme conceived by Wilkins. What is essential, though, is Borges' critical interpretation. The fundamental question it raises, Borges says, is "the merit of the forty-part table on which the language is based."[12] To offer an answer, the writer points out the ambiguity of some categories:

> the eighth category: stones. Wilkins divides them into common (flint, gravel, slate); moderate (marble, amber, coral); precious (pearl, opal); transparent (amethyst, sapphire); and insoluble (coal, fuller's earth, and arsenic). The ninth category is almost as alarming as the eighth. It reveals that metals can be imperfect (vermilion, quicksilver); artificial (bronze, brass); recremental (filings, rust); and natural (gold, tin, copper). The whale appears in the sixteenth category: it is a viviparous, oblong fish.[13]

The "ambiguities, redundancies, and deficiencies"[14] of this classification remind the classification of animals of an alleged Chinese encyclopedia – *Heavenly Emporium of Benevolent Knowledge* – mentioned by Franz Kuhn, Borges invents. As we will see, such classification of animals exhibited by the presumed "emporium of knowledge" and Wilkins' classification offer the central elements of Borges' arguments. For this reason, despite the fact that such classification is well known, it is reproduced below. The animals are specified as follows:

---

12 Ibid.
13 Ibid., 230–231.
14 Ibid., 231.

a) those that belong to the emperor	h) those that are included in this classification
b) embalmed ones	i) those that tremble as if they were mad
c) those that are trained	j) innumerable ones
d) suckling pigs	k) those drawn with a very fine camel's-hair brush
e) mermaids	l) *et cetera*
f) fabulous ones	m) those that have just broken the flower vase
g) stray dogs	n) those that at a distance resemble flies[15]

Leaving aside Borges' most direct statement, to be seen below, the above passages already unequivocally indicate his conviction in the objectivity of our knowledge and, by extension, in the objectivity of the ontology that it always presupposes.

In fact, the ambiguity, the deficiency and, above all, the anthropomorphism of the classifications express the social, historical and, therefore, fallible character of the ontological notions on which our practice is always based.[16] However, its fallibility does not contradict its objectivity, being, instead, its condition. The mention to the whale, defined as oblong, viviparous fish in Wilkins taxonomy, is not pointless. With such expedient, Borges forces the reader to an involuntary reflection. It leads the reader to immediately realize that the classification does not correctly capture the anatomical-physiological structure of the whale – a mammal, and that, therefore, it is false. At the same time and in the same act, though, he compels the reader to claim the objectivity of his/her own knowledge, or his/her own taxonomy, for he/she can only catch a mistake from a point of view held to be true. From this, it can be said that our

---

15   Ibid., 231.
16   As a moment of practice conditioned by its aims, anthropomorphism must have some objectivity despite its falsity in ontological terms. This objectivity, emphasized by Borges, is also corroborated by Keith Thomas, who points out that "[at] the start of the early modern period, even the naturalists themselves regarded the world from an essentially human viewpoint and tended to classify it less according to its intrinsic qualities than according to its relationship to man. Plants, for example, were studied primarily for the sake of their human uses and perceived accordingly. There were seven kinds of herbs, thought William Coles in 1656: pot herbs; medical herbs; corn; pulse; flowers; grass and weeds." Keith Thomas, *Man and the Natural World*. (London: Penguin, 1988), 52.

classifications based on superficial observations from everyday practice – for example: an animal that swims and lives underwater is a fish – may be superficial, false and can (and should) be corrected. However, they are objective in some degree, for it is on them that daily practice is based. Borges uses the same resource when he resorts to the classification of the Chinese encyclopedia, which provokes laughter exactly because the reader perceives its absurdity. Evidently, the reader can only do so from the point of view of his/her own classification, assumed to be true and objective.

Borges ends the essay in a less allusive way when he declares, with regard to the ambiguities of the classifications quoted, that all classifications of the universe are arbitrary. Nonetheless, he warns that "[the] impossibility of penetrating the divine scheme of the universe cannot, however, dissuade us from planning human schemes, even though it is clear that they are provisional."[17] Being human, knowledge cannot have access to the "divine," to the absolute. However, since human practice is teleological, finalistic, the knowledge of the world is its necessary presupposition. Consequently, nothing can "dissuade us from planning human schemes" indeed. And if human schemes are an inextinguishable condition of practice, it follows that they are objective, despite their fallibility and transience.

This interpretation of Borges, it must be said, totally differs from that held by Foucault regarding the last essay discussed. Even though it is impossible to assert it categorically, the "Analytical Language" seems to owe much of its diffusion to the fact that Foucault, in the preface to *The Order of Things*, reveals that his book was born from the reading of Borges' essay.[18] According to Foucault, the classification of animals shown in the supposed Chinese encyclopedia kept him "laughing a long time, though not without a certain uneasiness that I found hard to shake off."[19] Notwithstanding, the taxonomy provokes very distinct laughters. The first laughter, suggested here, is one that finds humor in the nonsense of the scheme, which it judges, not without mercy, from the objectivity experienced from its own ontology. The second is a laughter of perplexity, of astonishment at a taxonomy that presumably demonstrates the irremediable contradiction of our mental schemes in the face of the impossibility of reaching an objective knowledge of the world. In Foucault's words, such laughter

---

17   Borges, "John Wilkens."
18   Michel Foucault, *The Order of Things: An Archaeology of the Human Sciences*. (New York: Vintage Books Edition, 1994), iv.
19   Ibid., xvi.

shattered, as I read the passage, all the familiar landmarks of my thought – our thought, the thought that bears the stamp of our age and our geography – breaking up all the ordered surfaces and all the planes with which we are accustomed to tame the wild profusion of existing things, and continuing long afterwards to disturb and threaten... In the wonderment of this taxonomy, the thing we apprehend in one great leap, the thing that, by means of the fable, is demonstrated as the exotic charm of another system of thought, is the limitation of our own, the stark impossibility of thinking that.[20]

Foucault's reading seems to be a manifestation of what, in connection with the ideas of the neopragmatic philosopher R. Rorty, I called, in another work, as "longing for God."[21] Departing from the somehow trivial assumption that all knowledge, being human and social, is relative, this position mingles objectivity and the absolute. Being the latter unachievable, it advocates the wholesale relativism. Hence, frustrated the megalomaniac aspiration to know everything, all worldly knowledge is deprived of objectivity.

It is important to explore the deepest meanings of the difference between Foucault's reading and the reading argued for here. This discussion will not be carried out in the specific field of literary criticism, but rather taking into consideration the serious repercussions of the skepticism that underlies Foucault's interpretation. In practice, regardless the intention of who advocates it, skepticism means tacit acquiescence with the *status quo*. Such skepticism does not go unnoticed by Norris, for whom the use of Borges' passage by Foucault unmistakably demonstrates Foucault's anti-realist, conventionalist, and nominalist view. Norris asserts that, in fact, for Foucault, the classification of the animals in the "Chinese encyclopedia" is an indication of the parochial and cultural-determinate character of our concepts and categories. In his critique of Foucault's reading, Norris agrees with the interpretation advocated here, noting that "the possibility of thinking such exotic thoughts is demonstrated clearly enough by [...] our (i.e. the reader's) capacity to perceive it is as just such an instance of wild and zany categorization."[22] Moreover, Norris agrees that such classifications might constitute a fictional allusion to "our naturalized habits of thought and perception."[23] He argues that it is precisely because of this that it is a total mistake to mean, as Foucault does, that the simple possibility of thinking, and in Borges' case of inventing, such "starkly impossible

20   Ibid., xiv.
21   See Duayer 2010: 72.
22   Norris, 169.
23   Ibid.

thoughts" serves as a sufficient basis to suggest that "*all* our concepts, categories, ontological commitments and so forth are likewise fictive constructions out of one of such 'arbitrary' discourse or another."[24]

In Norris' view, these ideas make up the implicit premise of the whole Foucaultian project, already present in its starting point in the "archeology" of knowledge, of structuralist orientation, up to the genealogical approach (post-1970) of the Nietzschean matrix, which certainly nourish the agendas of the postmodernism, neopragmatism and their theoretical adjacencies.

According to Norris, such a premise can be thought of as *reductio ad absurdum* of the anti-realist proposal that

> begins by locating truth in propositions about things, rather than in the things themselves, and ends up – as with Quine, Kuhn, Rorty, Lyotard *et al* – by holistically relativising 'truth' to whatever sorts of language-games happen to enjoy that title.[25]

As can be seen, the use of the Borgean texts analyzed here serves to very different theoretical – and political – purposes.

The interpretations of those texts can illustrate the conception advocated here, according to which we can never think and act "from nowhere." Our practice and the thinking that guides this practice are based on general characterizations of the world, on ontologies that, as seen in Borges, are provisional and fallible, but have their objectivity corroborated by the practices acted upon them. However, such interpretations can also be taken as an example of the notion that all our beliefs, whether theoretical or not, are equivalent, since truth – objectivity – is held to be unreachable. In this way, the readings and interpretations of these and other texts create, reinforce or refute, stimulate or inhibit the current ideas. There is no way to be indifferent to divergent, conflicting readings, since they express ontological disputes whose impact in practice is impossible to neglect, for it is in the general characterizations of the world that we seek our ideas about the desirable, the possible, the feasible.

3 Philosophy of Science and Ontology

As we announced in the Introduction, we will now move from literature to the philosophy of science and will try to show that science, in spite of so many protests to the contrary, cannot function in an ontological vacuum. A brief

---

24   Ibid.
25   Ibid.

examination on the conceptions of science and scientific explanation proposed by Kuhn, Lakatos, and logical positivism allows us to demonstrate that claim, despite the contempt and indifference of those conceptions for ontological issues. For this demonstration, it is worth noting, we will use some schemes that try to show graphically the embargo to ontological questions in philosophy. In this sense, instead of intending to elaborate an exhaustive analysis of currents and authors, the following considerations take the formulations of the main currents and/or authors in the orthodox philosophy of science to illustrate how their interdiction on ontology is purely nominal.[26]

To begin, in the figure below there is a schematic representation of how the roughest empiricism conceives the process of knowledge.[27] Between the horizontal parallel lines it is represented the flow of events, that is, everything that is happening in the world. If knowledge, for empiricism, is a generalization of what the sensorial apparatus allows us to grasp from the world, in the scheme this process is illustrated by the movement that begins at the top of the diagonal line and "crosses" the flow of events. Each of the recurring courses along the line permits us to capture new empirical facts and to generalize them, thus forming the knowledge that practice presupposes and produces. Except for misconceptions in the process of generalization of the empiric experienced by the senses, free from metaphysical speculations – ideas without strictly empirical origin – errors that science should avoid – this cumulative process would imply an increasingly comprehensive knowledge of the world. That is to say, this process would imply a continuous empirical improvement of the "belief systems," "ideological coordinates" or "ontological schemas" which, by principle, could be traced to the original sensations and, therefore, are irrefutable.

It is immediately clear that this conception implies a subject of knowledge that can only be an isolated, atomic, pre-Adamic individual, devoid of relations not only with other individuals, but also with nature. This individual, in consequence of all this, would have neither language nor consciousness. It is this individual that suddenly begins to interact with nature and, from these experiences without ideas, embarks on forming them by noticing the similarities and differences between things caught here and there by his/her senses.

---

26   See Mario Duayer, "Relativismo, Certeza e Conformismo: para uma Crítica das Filosofias da Perenidade do Capital." *Revista da Sociedade Brasileira de Economia Política*, n°. 27, p. 58–83, October 2010, for a more detailed explanation of the arguments elaborated in this section. For a synthetic exposition of Kuhn's and Lakatos' conceptions, see F. Suppe (ed.), *The Structure of Scientific Theories*. (Chicago: University of Chicago Press, 1977).

27   My special thanks to Rômulo A. Lima for the elaboration of the schemes below. I am very grateful for his contribution.

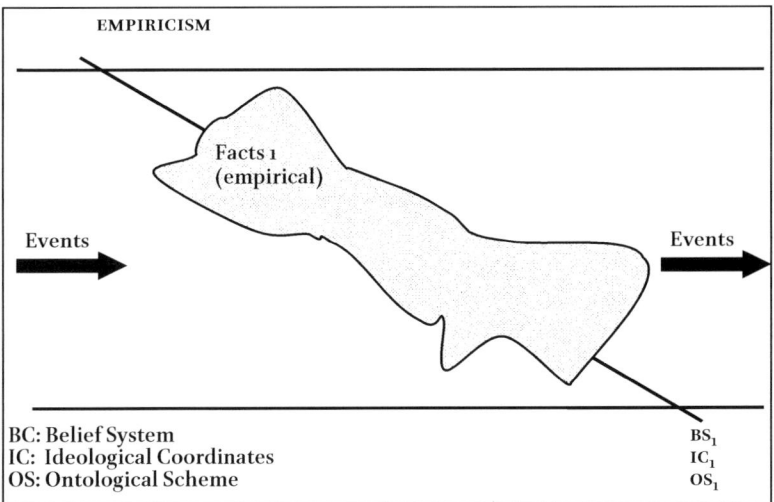

FIGURE 9.1 Empiricism

On that account, this absurd individual gradually constructs particulars and universals, and builds for himself/herself an intelligibility of the world, through which he/she had passed "empirically" and blindly in the beginning, without any intelligibility, as nonsensical as it may seem. Finally, since, according to the empiricist conception, knowledge is a mere mechanical effect of the world captured by our sensorial apparatus – a kind of "drive-thru" effect of the world crossing our senses –, then the belief systems so formed exclusively from the empiric would be free from all "metaphysics." Notwithstanding such a claim, it is not difficult to see, as Bhaskar has shown, that this conception of knowledge implies an empiricist ontology in which the flattened and one-dimensional world, collapsed in the impressions of subjects, is composed of atomic things and events, since their probable characteristics and relations are nothing more than mere concomitances (similarities, empirical regularities, patterns of association) perceived by the subjects. The atomic subject of cognition, therefore, conforms to this implicit ontology.

In logical positivism, the positivist tradition itself sought to overcome the absurd inconsistencies of this conception that, in order to purify the scientific discourse of all metaphysics–its central programmatic point – had to ensure that all items of knowledge could be traced back to the gross empirical datum. This idea implies a sort of creation myth: the isolated individual of cognition, who is none other than the superlative isolated individual of liberal thought, *éminence grise* of so many theories. To reformulate such a position, logical positivism at least admits, albeit in a very curious way, that the subject who perceives things, forms ideas, gives meaning to the data originated from his/her impressions never exists without ideas.

The result of this reformulation of the conception of science and of scientific explanation of the positivist tradition is illustrated in the next scheme. In accordance with the empiricist gnosiology of the positivist tradition, to which all knowledge is derived from sensory experience and justified on the basis of it, logical positivism inherited the function always claimed by that tradition: to operate as a supervisor of the mind in its scientific generalization processes, curbing metaphysical speculations and thereby holding firm the bonds of the mind with the world, here understood as the reality captured by the sensorial apparatus. Logical positivism imagined playing such normative function by postulating a general structure of scientific discourse, supposedly characteristic of the paradigmatic sciences, physics in particular. According to such prescription, every scientific discourse has to present a hypothetical-deductive structure, also known as the H-D model of scientific discourse. Put simply, H-D postulates that every theory consists of an axiomatic hypothetic-deductive structure. This is to say that, from this point of view, a theory is nothing more than a set of axioms, including at least one general law, axiomatic as well, from which a series of propositions about observable phenomena is deduced.

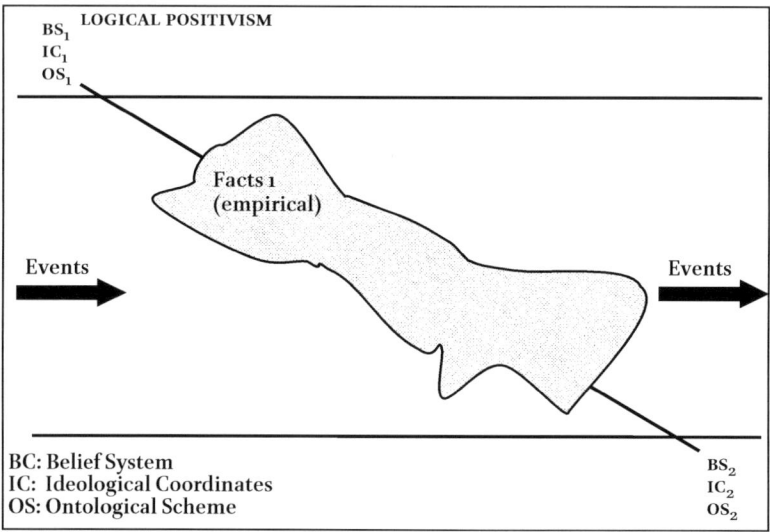

FIGURE 9.2 Logical positivism

It can be seen in the above illustration that, unlike empiricism, in logical positivism the subject of cognition no longer goes to practice devoid of ideas. In a similar way to the previous scheme, the process of knowledge here also begins at the top of the diagonal line and, throughout it, "crosses" the flow of events, capturing new empirical facts in each of the cycles. However, in this case the empirical facts do not give rise to the generalizations. On the contrary, the theories deductively constructed from axioms are postulated generalizations, imagined descriptions of a sector of reality that, according to the positivist injunction, can only consist of empirical regularities among phenomena, or stable functional relations between variables observable from the perspective offered by the theories. The validity condition of the theories, therefore, is its corroboration by means of the observational evidence. In summary, theories postulate empirical regularities or constant conjunctions of events and are validated when the postulated regularities are confirmed by empirical evidence.

Starting from BS_1, OS_1 or IC_1, at the top of the diagonal – that is, from an ontology, a particular figure of the world – the theory "goes across" the flow of events with the purpose to identify the postulated empirical regularities. In each cycle along the diagonal, the theory, based on the same structural axioms, seeks to encompass new empirical phenomena – that is to say, to submit the phenomena to its interpretation. The success of this expansion of the empirical domain of theory is at the same time the empirical validation of the "belief system"– ontology – on which it is founded.

It is not relevant, at this point, to talk about the total absence, in the H-D model, of any mention to the origin of ideas – the set of axioms –, out of which this, so to speak, archetype "belief system," is assembled. For the argument sustained in this article, rather than highlighting all the inconsistencies of this conception of science and scientific explanation, it is mostly important to emphasize that such conception implies a clear refutation of the anti-ontological position of the positivist tradition. Indeed, to uphold that the scientific discourse is axiomatic-deductive is equivalent to saying that every theory is based on a "belief system," on an "ontological schema" or on "ideological coordinates," that is, on an ontology. Consequently, theories can no longer be considered, as the positivist tradition has always intended, the expression of the raw data from experience, for theories are, in fact, interpretation of the world. Thus, it is the theory that conveys meaning to the phenomena captured by the sensorial apparatus and not the phenomena grasped by the senses that naturalistically turn into theory by means of a kind of mechanical process, as empiricism implies. As Bhaskar warns, "[...] facts ... are not what we apprehend in sense-perception, but results of the theories in terms of which our apprehension of things is organized."[28] Hence, for the purpose of this article, it is extremely crucial to bear in mind that logical positivism, while vaguely and ambiguously suggested that the rooting of theories was in the empirical, actually implied the reverse. The apparent anti-ontological attitude conceals an implicit ontology: the empirical ontology uncritically inherited from empiricism, in which the world consists of atomic phenomena.

The next two schemes illustrate the conception of science and of scientific explanation of the post-positivist currents that are now prevalent in the philosophy of science. Post-positivist currents are so called because they stem from the critique of the positivist conceptions. However, it is possible to show that despite the relevance of some of their criticisms these currents do not constitute an effective critique of the positivist tradition. Indeed, taking into account the way post-positivist currents conceive science and scientific explanation, it is possible to say that they hardly differ from the conception of which they imagine to be a radical critique. To support this argument, this paper focuses on the most emblematic authors of post-positivism in the philosophy of science – Kuhn and Lakatos. Their work mainly pays particular attention to natural sciences, but its influence can be seen in the theoretical currents that predominate in social theory today, such as culturalism, postmodernism, pragmatism, constructivism, among others. Currents that directly or indirectly find inspiration in Kuhn's and Lakatos' ideas, especially in the wholesale relativism associated with their theories. The examination of the conceptions of the two authors seeks to highlight the role of ontology in their theories of science. It should not be overlooked, however, that in their theories, just as in logical positivism, the function of science is reduced to the search for empirical regularities among phenomena (variables) and their empirical corroboration. Consequently, from this perspective, the relevant feature of scientific theories is their predictive capacity, not that of offering a true and objective explanation of reality.

The figure below represents the ideas of the "post-positivist" Thomas Kuhn. As widely known, the author affirms that in the dynamics of all science one can observe the pattern shown in the figure. According to him, any science is founded on a paradigm (on an ontology) – BS_1, IC_1 or OE_1 – and is refined in the repeated cycles along the diagonal. Normal science, as Kuhn calls it, distends its empirical domain in this process, as advocated by logical positivism. As pointed out before, science here has the exclusive function of capturing

---

28   R. Bhaskar, *Reclaiming Reality: a Critical Introduction to Contemporary Philosophy*. (London: Verso, 1989), 60–61.

empirical regularities among relevant phenomena that were caught by its interpretive net. Yet, the very logic of normal science of continually expanding its empirical territory eventually causes it to find a limit. After some time, normal science proves to be inadequate, insufficient, because it cannot "explain" new phenomena or incorporate new phenomena into its domain. Such stagnation, according to Kuhn, inaugurates a revolutionary period in which new theories compete for the interpretive hegemony of the existing normal science, which, in the end, is replaced by another theory – in the case of the scheme, represented by the dark area. For the author, we have here what he called paradigmatic shift: the new normal science is based on another paradigm – BS_2, IC_2 or OS_2 –, on another ontology, on another figure of the world, and presents exactly the same dynamics of the theory that it has replaced.

According to this perspective, in which the empirical is internal to each paradigm, it is impossible to justify empirically the supremacy of the theoretical current that at each time holds the hegemony. In fact, as can be seen in the diagram, the checkered area, which indicates the intersection of the currents' respective "empirical" domains, reveals that the currents are equivalent from the empirical point of view, since the "empirical excess" of each one is irrelevant to the other. In this sense, the supremacy at issue can only be ontological, that is to say, it is the supremacy of the ontology on which the new current is founded. That being the case, the post-positivist author explicitly admits what logical positivism implied, namely, that all science posits and presupposes an ontology. More than this, he shows that what is fundamental in the dynamics

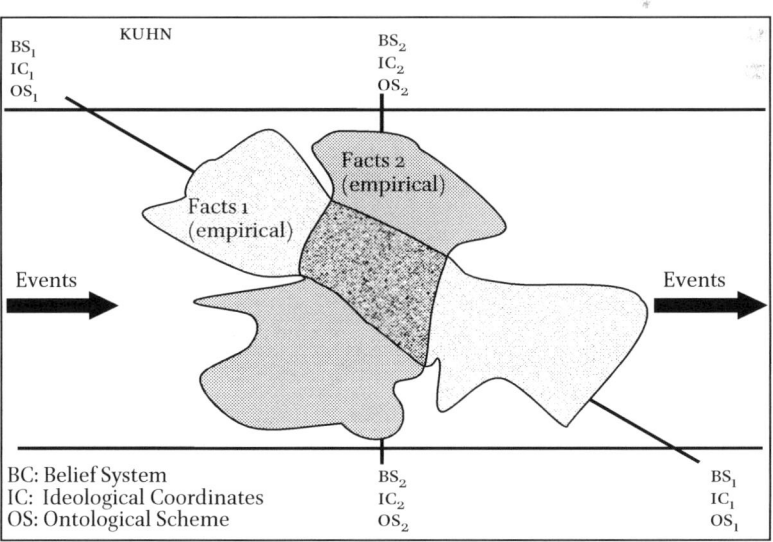

FIGURE 9.3 Kuhn

of sciences is the radical change in the figure of the world, in the ontology that sciences posit and presuppose. Still, this explicit recognition of the absolute relevance of ontology, of its decisive character in substantive scientific disputes, has no theoretical effect in Kuhn's conception of science and scientific explanation, simply because ontology is never thematized in his studies. As can be verified, paradigms, a tag for ontology, are structural elements of any science, but their origin and nature are never analyzed. For this reason, it can be concluded, as did Kuhn's critics, that paradigms are incommensurable, and, therefore, that critique is impossible. This represents a theoretical position whose corollary is the equation of all belief systems and, consequently, the refutation of the objectivity of all knowledge. It is a wholesale relativism of unequivocal sense: truth does not matter, for it is unreachable. Therefore, science can only be legitimized by its effectiveness as an instrument of immediate praxis.

The next figure illustrates the ideas of Imre Lakatos. He substitutes the idea of scientific research programs (SRP) for the polarity "normal science/revolutionary science" of the Kuhnian scheme – not sufficiently nuanced, and, for this reason, incapable of assimilating the coexistence of several theoretical currents competing for the explanatory hegemony in a specific science. In Lakatos' version, science must be understood as consisting of systems or families of theories rather than isolated theories. Science, from this perspective,

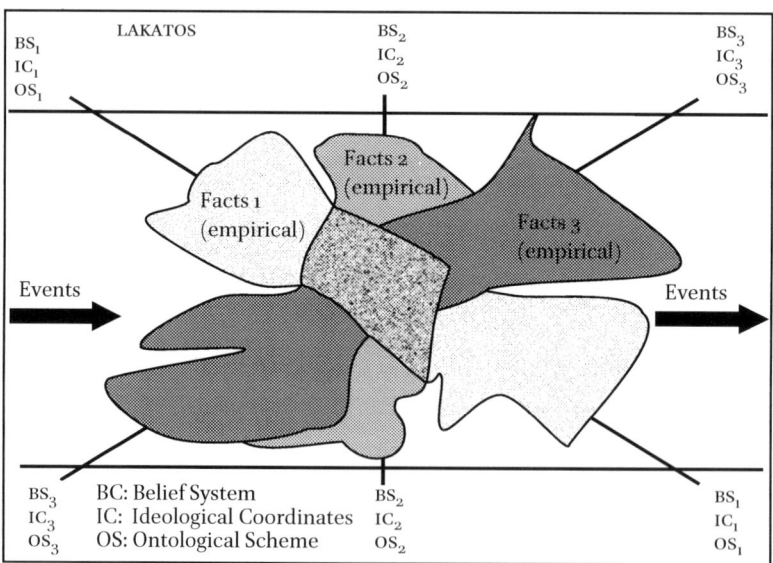

FIGURE 9.4 Lakatos

functions as a system of theories in permanent process of improvement and transformation. Such systems or theoretical traditions, in each particular science, constitute a SRP, so that it is possible to exist in a given science a variety of theoretical traditions in dispute, each evolving according to the protocols of its SRP, illustrated here by BS_1, IC_1 or OS_1; BS_2, IC_2 or OS_2: BS_3, IC_3 or OS_3.

In general terms, in the Lakatosian explanation the SRPs are constituted by two types of methodological rules: a negative heuristic and a positive one. The negative heuristic of a SRP establishes improper investigations within it. Such rules proscribe the examination of the SRP's *hard core* – that is, the set of structural axioms that make up its *irrefutable* part: BS_1, BS_2 and BS_3. The positive heuristic defines the legitimate research lines, endorsed by the SRP, which will constitute the list of guidelines for perfecting and modifying the theories that orbit the hard core. These theories make up the SRP's "protective belt," or its refutable part.

Except for the possibility of coexistence of different theoretical currents, Lakatos' proposal is almost identical to that of Kuhn in its essence. With regard to the dynamics and function of science, one can infer from Lakatos' propositions that theories are constructed to capture empirical regularities among phenomena and that, therefore, each system of theories evolves or not according to its capacity to apprehend new empirical facts under its interpretation. This implies that the function of science is to operate as an instrument of immediate practice. On the other hand, just as Kuhn, Lakatos, while arguing that the difference between the theoretical currents is ontological, *a priori* cancels the possibility of analyzing or discussing the ontological foundations of the different theoretical systems, since the so-called hard cores are irrefutable by definition. Again, if the theories are validated empirically and their hard cores are irrefutable, the result of this conception is the denial of the objectivity of scientific knowledge. In other words, the result is the interdiction of criticism and the consequent equalization of all belief systems – the parity of all ontologies –, whether based on reason and science or on superficial notions of everyday life, on superstition, on magic and mystic.

If not even the scientific knowledge is objective, the conclusion can only being one: the disqualification of truth and the veiled defense of instrumentalism and the conception of science as mere instrument of immediate practice. Lukács had already warned that this was the substantive effect of logical positivism, since in this theory

> it is no longer a question of whether each particular moment of linguistic-scientific regulation ... leads to immediate practical results but,

rather, that the entire system of knowledge is elevated to the condition of instrument of a general manipulation of all relevant facts.[29]

In this context, Lukács could have emphasized the absurd fallacy of the position which claims that science, built in accordance with its prescriptions, does not contribute to form a conception of world, but only offers instruments to manipulate it. As if all the images of the world, hold in modern society, could be composed without the aid of science!

By omitting any mention to ontology in its formulations, logical positivism could evoke the axiological neutrality of science and, consequently, justify its merely instrumental character. Free from any ontology, science could not be at the service of any values or interests. Although such expedient is naturally disallowed to the post-positivist authors examined, it is implicit in their conceptions. Actually it is an irreconcilable inconsistency to sustain that every science is founded on an ontology and, at the same time, to restrict the role of science to an instrument of immediate practice, as Kuhn and Lakatos do. For science, in accordance to their formulations, instead of being axiologically neutral, would always function as an instrument for the realization of the values and interests related to the ontology on which it is founded.

4   Lukács: Labor, Science and Truth

From the foregoing considerations, it is possible to conclude that ontology is inescapable. As Borges wrote, "[the] impossibility of penetrating the divine scheme of the universe cannot, however, dissuade us from planning human schemes, even though it is clear that they are provisional."[30] If we compulsively totalize, if the figure of the world, the general characterization of the world is a fundamental moment of praxis in general, and hence also of scientific practice, it is quite understandable why Marx, already in the *Grundrisse*, goes into the elaboration of a systematic and articulated figure of the capitalist society, critical of the current figurations – scientific or not – that this social form generates and requires. In other words, Marx formulates an ontology of modern society in everything distinct from that which circumscribes praxis to the continuous reproduction of what exists. As Lukács states rightly in the first paragraph of the chapter dedicated to Marx in his *Ontology*,

---

29   G. Lukács, *Para uma Ontologia do Ser Social*, I. (São Paulo: Boitempo, 2012), 58.
30   Borges, *Selected Non Fictions*. (London: Penguin Books, 1999), 231.

the attempt to summarize Marx's ontology, in a theoretical sense, leads one into a somewhat paradoxical situation. On the one hand, it must be clear to any unbiased reader of Marx that all of his concrete statements, [...] are ... intended as direct statements about an existent, i.e., they are specifically ontological.[31]

The reason for this necessary ontological approach Lukács himself helps to understand. Among the numerous notable developments in his examination of the labor complex, there are key indications for understanding the importance of the explicit consideration of ontology. To summarize the point, it should be noted that in the analysis of this complex, Lukács emphasizes the specifically human determination of labor and, following Marx, highlights its teleological character. To deal with the principles related to the "positing of the goal" in labor, Lukács, based on Aristotle and on Hartmann's proposed addition to the ideas of the latter, stresses the two central moments of labor: the "positing of the goal" and the analysis of the necessary means to achieve it. Two moments that in the most primitive work can hardly be distinguished, but that in the development of the social being end up being differentiated – aspect that interests us to highlight here. Lukács asserts that the "positing of the goal" presupposes a spiritual appropriation of reality, oriented by the aim set, because only in this way the result of labor can be something new, something that would not spontaneously emerge from the typical processes of nature. However, Lukács points out that the rearrangement of the materials and natural processes required to give rise to the goal posited demands a better knowledge of these objects and processes, exactly to convert them from natural causalities (processes) into posited causalities. Unlike the typical anthropomorphism of the spiritual possession of reality conditioned by the planned end, here the maximum of desantropomorphism must prevail, since the attainment of the end would not be possible without the knowledge of the properties of the objects and processes involved in the transformation of natural causalities into posited causalities.

Thus, if the examination of the labor complex allows to demonstrate the genesis of knowledge at labor, it is not difficult to understand that these two moments of labor – the positing of a goal and the investigation of the means – become relatively autonomous with the improvement and the development of the complexity of labor processes, or of the production and reproduction of the material conditions of life with the evolution of the social being. In the Lukácsian elaboration, science, whose genesis can be referred to the most

---

31   G. Lukács, *The Ontology of Social Being*, 2. *Marx*. (London: Merlin Press, 1978), 1.

rudimentary labor processes, is the moment of the investigation of the means progressively autonomized in relation to the aims of the particular labor processes. Consequently, even without fully detaching itself from the social determination of ends, by asserting itself as a relatively autonomous sphere, science convert truth into its specific purpose, that is, the most adequate knowledge of reality itself. In an apparent paradox, therefore, even having its origin connected to the socially posited ends (hence, values), by searching truth science contributes to the realization of values, which is not its immediate goal.

This explains the obligatory ontological orientation of genuine science, which could sound like a motto such as: knowing the world as it is in order to change it for our (human) benefit. If it is possible to admit such an interpretation, one can understand why, for Lukács, Marx's statements are "specifically ontological statements" and, to that extent, consist of an ontological critique. In Marx's formulation, the critique of political economy exhibits the mark of the ontological orientation of genuine science: the point is to achieve the most correct knowledge of the social formation governed by capital. Being historical, this social world necessarily changes. For this reason, the adequate social theory for this world must consist in a critique of the theories which, based on an ontology that cuts off historicity, cannot but be confined to the investigation of the structure of modern society and its functioning. By doing so they not only corroborate and convey the impression of a perpetual nature of modern society, but also condition and coach subjects to passively respond to its structural imperatives.

The critique of such theories consists mainly in restoring the effective historicity to the object, to society, in capturing the truth of the historical dynamics of the social form governed by the capital, in elucidating its tendencies, and its possible futures, thereby disclosing new possibilities of practice to the subjects. The relation of humanity with the historicity of the social world produced by its practice is itself historical. It does not have to be an ahistorical relation as it is implicit in postmodernism, post-structuralism and neopragmatism, theoretical currents in which history is conceived at best as pancontingency, as absolute contingency to whose occurrences mankind can only watch and conform to. The ontological critique not only (re)signifies society with its intrinsic historicity, but also opens to the subjects the historicity of the relation between human beings and their own history, in which they are not at all destined to be eternally mere spectators. This truth of Marx's ontological critique is the condition of the transformative praxis: to leave prehistory and reactive praxis behind and actively participate in history, in the construction of a world worth of humanity.

CHAPTER 10

The Politics of Nature, Left and Right: Comparing the Ontologies of Georg Lukács and Bruno Latour

Christoph Henning

When philosophers grow older, some of them seem to develop a tendency to condense their accumulated wisdom in a book on ontology. The philosophical sub-discipline of ontology aims to capture all there is, and the ways in which we can distinguish different spheres of being, including our different modes of knowing them or interacting with them. Obviously, in order to write about such a broad topic as ontology, which somehow includes everything there is, can be or will be, a writer not only needs a lot of self-esteem and a sense of mission; one also has to have a lot of experience as a writer, but also as a person.[1] For this reason Aristotle warned his readers that you should not start dealing with metaphysics until you are at least forty or fifty. Nicolas Hartmann started publishing his *Ontology* at age 53; Hegel, who does not have an ontology (for systematic reasons) was 47 when he published his *Encyclopedia*.[2] But unfortunately, as we will see, old age is not a guarantee to write a good book.

In this paper, I want to compare two such late works on ontology – from different decades, and politically at very different camps: Georg Lukács, aged 80-plus, writing his 1500 page *Ontology of Social Being* in the mid to late Sixties in socialist Budapest, and Bruno Latour at age 65 in the postmodernist Paris of the new millennium. Lukács wrote as a disappointed Communist and silently re-casted the understanding of socialism in his draft. The book was published in German after the author died (1971 in parts, 1984 as a whole), and it met with immediate resistance from his friends, and mainly disinterest by the profession – until recently. Latour, in contrast, is a celebrated writer of the pop-theory-industry who by now can publish almost everything, and the public will

---

1 Kant distinguished school wisdom and world wisdom; here I refer to the latter.
2 Hegel did not see a need for an ontology, because he merged ontology and epistemology in the philosophy of "spirit" (a kind of early speculative network). Hence, most of Hegel's text deal with "everything"; yet compared to the *Phenomenology of Spirit* or the *Logic* the *Encyclopedia* is the most wordly book of his. Lukács sees *two* ontologies in Hegel, one historical, one logical, and complains that Hegel blurs ontology and epistemology. For me this amounts to saying that there is no Hegelian ontology; in fact the resurgence of ontologies in the 19th century (by Friedrich A. Trendelenburg, for instance) was clearly directed *against* Hegel.

appreciate it. But he expresses disappointment as well: he is full of misgivings about the political effects of his earlier work in science studies ("Was I foolishly mistaken?").[3] In a nutshell, his open relativism and constructivism may have inspired others from the political right ("fake news," etc.), including climate skeptics. Yet he is not retreating, instead he is now backing his earlier claims by laying out the *ontological underpinnings* his earlier works often vaguely evoked, but never fully elaborated.[4] (Unadmittedly, though, he *does* change some of his earlier claims.) These elaborations fill more then 650 pages (in German), but they still remain vague and playful.

In spite of these differences, there are interesting similarities between these two ontological works of two famous writers at the twilight of their careers: Both authors gravitate around a philosophical "classic," the subject–object-distinction, which both of them presuppose, problematize, and transform. In this process, both writers follow neo-Hegelian alleys in some way or another. (Some of Latour's more euphoric readers have drawn comparisons to Hegel, and this is no coincidence.) Also, both of them are interested in ontological questions particularly in relation to society. We should not call this "social ontology," because this only captures part of their enterprises – to say the least, the spheres of *nature* and of human *individuality* are also of key importance for them (and they are "social" only in a bended reading). Astonishingly, in their respective enterprises both writers also investigate the practices of the natural sciences – with great respect, but also questioning current interpretations of those sciences. It is here that we can start distinguishing the different political tendencies of these two ontologies.

1   The Politics of Science

The development of the modern sciences had some liberating effects – the rise of the "enlightenment" and of individual autonomy would have been impossible without them: they could explain things that seemed threatening before, they could help curing diseases, and they also helped deconstructing the political theology which often legitimized oppressive feudal power-relations.[5] However, they could also be used by modern political and economic elites in order to sustain or accumulate their power, inducing also a backlash in gender

---

3   Bruno Latour, "Why has Critique run out of steam? From matters of fact to matters of concern." *Critical Inquiry*, vol. 30 (2004): 225–248, 227.
4   Bruno Latour, *Existenzweisen: Eine Anthropologie der Modernen*. (Berlin: 2013).
5   Hans Blumenberg, *The Genesis of the Copernican World*, (Cambridge, Mass.: MIT Press, 1987).

relations.⁶ When the sciences are used for ideological and political purposes, Lukács follows Husserl and Nicolai Hartmann in using "everyday life" as an antidote, as a source of another kind of certainty in order to question scientism.⁷ Latour rejects this phenomenological heritage, not least because he rejects *all* philosophy. For him philosophers in general, the "modern" ones in particular, were not able to bridge the gap between "subject" and "object" that they themselves had erected. We may call this his *standard argument*, which he uses in many different books,⁸ even though it is only loosely connected to the question of political instrumentalizations of the sciences. But just as the philosophers he despises, Latour, too, is after an alternative perspective that can question an overconfidence in the sciences without turning to agnosticism or mere subjectivism.

That Latour and Lukács shared this meta-critical focus on the sciences is quite surprising. That said, this similarity of interest can also show us their political differences very clearly: Latour and Lukács are criticizing the sciences from different political angles. It is interesting, e.g., how Lukács comes back to Robert Bellarmin once and again – the 16th cardinal who negotiated with Galilei in the name of the church, and who was (much to Lukács' discomfort) reinvoked by French philosophers of science Pierre Duhem or Henri Poincaré. For Lukács,⁹ Bellarmin was the founder of modern epistemology in a Kantian understanding – not because he invented something like a subject–object-opposition, but much more concretely, because he managed to *partly* accept the new groundbreaking research of Copernicus and Galilei *without* allowing it to question anything "religious" or political. He established an epistemic double standard. Here we see at once how ontological pluralism may look progressive to postmodern readers, but in practice often had quite conservative political effects, e.g., when it helped to immunize political or religious power structures from a social criticism that employed the sciences for emancipatory purposes.¹⁰

---

6   Carolyn Merchant, *The Death of Nature: Women, Ecology, and the Scientific Revolution*, (San Francisco: 1980).

7   Lukács did not recognize that Henri Lefebvre and the later Wittgenstein were on a similar track, he only sees Wittgenstein's positivist surface. Georg Lukács, *Zur Ontologie des gesellschaftlichen Seins*, vol. 1. (Darmstadt/Neuwied: 1984), 371ff. (1984I, 371f.). Agnes Heller and Habermas later both followed this phenomenological focus of everyday life.

8   Bruno Latour *We have never been modern*, (Cambridge, Mass.: Harvard, 1993), 55ff.; Bruno Latour, *Politics of Nature: How to bring the sciences into democracy.* (Cambridge, Mass.: Harvard, 2004), 73ff.; Latour, *Existenzweisen*, 134ff.

9   Lukács, *Zur Ontologie des gesellschaftlichen Seins*, vol. 1, 7.

10   The separation of different spheres with different grammars had liberating effects as well, for example when Spinoza started to disentangle religion and politics. But Spinoza rather

And it is here where our two writers part ways: Lukács despises Bellarmin's compromise as a cynic catholic power play, a double standard. In discussing the affair of Bellarmin and Galilei politically, Lukács brings epistemology and power closely together (in an almost Foucaultian way), maintaining that this was only a temporary compromise, with the church being forced to further retreats in the future. Latour, however, argues along Bellarminian lines himself: what is true here, must not have an impact on other (say religious) truths there (even though "modern" writers had begun to interpret political relations *more geometrico*, and *etsi deus no daretur*, and notwithstanding that Latour himself argues against "purity" at other places.[11] Bellarmin was a "diplomat" exactly in the way Latour is calling for:[12] he *assessed* the importance of scientific insights and weighed them against other "matters of concern,"[13] issues that concern us;[14] with "us" standing for quite a small group of powerful members of the clergy here. What concerned them in this case was religious power, or the epistemic dignity of catholic practice. Concern for the latter is still in the forefront in Latour's ontology,[15] whereas matters of power are mostly absent from Latour's writing.[16]

So Bellarmin's ambivalent role in Lukács' ontology parallels Latour's efforts to demystify the sciences and bring them into "democracy,"[17] to make them one voice among many others. This is the political ambivalence of Latour's position: Why should such a demystification *not* be read as an invitation to climate skeptics? In his later works, Latour aims to convince his readers that this accusation misfires. But he is not really changing his position: In the 1980s Latour had claimed that Galilei was an unsuccessful scientist because he did not sufficiently manage to enroll networks ("an isolated person builds only dreams, claims and feelings, not facts."[18] Today Latour still wishes to replace the worldview of Galilei (which was already the offending object for Husserl)

---

is an example for the emancipatory use of the natural sciences that Bellarmin stood against.

11 See Latour, *We have never been modern*, 66.
12 Latour, *Politics of Nature,* 225ff.
13 Latour,, "Why has Critique run out of steam?" 231.
14 Bruno Latour *Das terrestrische Manifest*. (Berlin: 2018), 90.
15 Latour, *Existenzweisen*. (2013), Chapter 7; cf. Gunnar Skirbeck, "Bruno Latour's anthropology of the moderns: A reply to Maniglier." *Radical Philosophy*, 189 (Jan. 2015), 45–47.
16 Daniel McCarthy, "Objects in Motion: Marx, Latour, and the Historical Processes of Powerful Things." Draft (2015), online at https://ecpr.eu/Filestore/PaperProposal/13aad5c9-04f8-4906-be81-b1bbb3cdf0ad.pdf.
17 Latour, *Politics of Nature*.
18 Bruno Latour, *Science in Action: How to follow Scientists and Engineers through Society*. (Cambridge, Mass.: Harvard, 1987), 41.

with that of Gaia-adherent James Lovelock.[19] The respectable "green" motive behind this move notwithstanding, this can still be interpreted as an invitation to theoretical esotericism – the Gaia-hypothesis belongs to a spiritual hippie-culture, not so much into the ecological discourse within the natural sciences or the global political green movement. It is particularly hard to digest this postmodernist esoteric move because at the same time Latour is attacking the *existing* ecological moment with heavy ordnance – it is said to be deeply mistaken, in terms of both their sciences and their philosophy (it is in a "state of impotence," suffering from "childhood illnesses";[20] and consequently, their practice. Their mistake: they still believe in an entity called "nature," a realm or force that exists in and by itself. Is it any wonder that Latour meets with resistance from ecological thinkers?[21]

The point of my comparison is to show that Latour's recent turn to a pluralist metaphysical ontology indeed leaves many ontological questions open, and is even deeply problematic in some instances – particularly in his take on nature and on values. So we have good reason to turn to the late Lukács' ideas on nature and the values in our search for better answers.

2 A Mode of Self-Defence: "Modes of Existence" as a Reaction to Criticism

The *science studies*, an academic movement to which Latour contributed for a while, look into the social context of the natural sciences. To the amount that the investigation of the genealogy of scientific practices was used to question the validity of their results,[22] this movement was considered to lead to relativism. Because Latour's tone was even more daring and vague than those of his colleagues, notably his earlier works were often accused of being overly constructivist, relativistic, and too vague or ill-conceived.[23] Indeed the science

---

19 Latour, *Das terrestrische Manifest*, 89.
20 Latour, *Politics of Nature*, 5; Latour, *Das terrestrische Manifest*, 87ff.
21 Cf. John Bellamy Foster, "Marxism in the Anthropocene: Dialectical Rifts on the Left." *International Critical Thought*, vol. 6, no. 3 (2016): 393–421.
22 This was not the general claim – the aim was to explain the phenomenon of "differential credibility," see David Bloor, "Anti-Latour." *Studies in History and Philosophy of Science* vol. 30, no. 1 (1999): 81–112, 102. But of course the findings can be used that way.
23 Bloor cites eight reviews of Latour (from 1990–1995) and judges: "the criticisms in this literature are devastating," as is his own enlightening review of Latour's metaphysics, "Anti-Latour," 95. Other reviews, including more recent ones, could be added to the list, see e.g., Simon Schaffer, "The Eighteenth Brumaire of Bruno Latour (review of Latour 1988)." *Studies in History and Philosophy of Science*, vol. 22, no. 1 (1991), 174–192; Sokal, Alan/

studies (not only Latour's writings), when claiming that our notions of truth (or, by implication, beliefs we hold to be true) are socially constructed and hence need to be dethroned, may have fueled at least some of the anti-scientific sentiments of the climate skeptics, in the Trump-camp and elsewhere. If the theory of man-made climate change is itself man-made, then why do we not simply construct an "alternative truth"? But indignant to recant any of his earlier work, Latour now seems to work out an apologetic web which defends his earlier positions by offering a third way between scientism and skepticism. That alone is interesting enough. He now claims his earlier position was *not* constructivist, relativist, or void of criteria, and in order to show this, he develops his new ontology.

To come straight to the point: this reaction is detouring and gets lost on the way. Latour is not addressing his critics directly, instead he keeps on making fun of them (to the entertainment of his readers), assuming that the criticism was unfounded all along and thus leaving the impression that his critics are too silly to get it.[24] Yet he is not caring too much to explain *why* the recurrent criticism should be unfounded. This is a peculiar way to deal with criticism; and this hints us to a general characteristic of Latour's thinking.[25] It is not only this or that criticism of his works that he ridicules, it is the critical activity *as such*.

It is no secret that Latour, who is currently very popular in the media as well as in the art-schools, politically stands for an anti-critical stance:[26] he not only mocks the ecological movement, for decades he also attacked the current critical thinking in sociology and philosophy (which is in a weak position anyway), trying to defend social spheres like religion or art against a social criticism he

---

Jean Bricmont: *Fashionable Nonsense: Postmodern Intellectual's Abuse of Science*. (New York: 1998); Andrew Brennan, "Review of Latour." *Environmental ethics*, vol. 28, no. 2 (2006): 1–4; Jon Elster, "Holberg-prisen bør nedlegges: Tildelingen av Holberg-prisen til Bruno Latour er et lavmål i prisens sørgelige historie." In *Aftenposten*, 31 March 2013; and "Den uforståelige Latour: Hva betyr det at bjørketrær og slimålen, for eksempel, «lager sin egen mening». Kanskje Bruno Latours norske tilhengere kan svare?" In *Aftenposten*, 24 April 2013; Hylton White, "Materiality, Form, and Context: Marx contra Latour." *Victorian Studies*, vol. 55, no. 4 (2013): 667–682; Daniel Chernilo, "Review of Latour 2013." *European Journal of Social Theory*, vol. 18, no. 3 (2015): 343–348.

24 "Much of Latour's account of anti-fetishism is thus focused on a portrait of the critic as a character governed by fatal flaws and vices. [...] Critics of the fetish are described as puritanically austere, suspicious to the point of paranoia, and barbarically aggressive in their handling of the things they make into targets for their critical attentions." White, "Materiality, Form, and Context," 670.

25 Skirbekk calls it "[s]uggestively repetitive, conceptually vague, and characterized by a blend of inclusive reasonableness and aggressive confrontations." "Bruno Latour's anthropology of the moderns," 46.

26 White, "Materiality, Form, and Context."; Foster, "Marxism in the Anthropocene."

views as mainly destructive.[27] This anti-critical stance can be read in different ways: one could read this sympathetically, claiming that this critique of critical critique in fact is an effort to *strengthen* a critical stance by overcoming some of its weaknesses. (This was how Marx once minted the term in 1845.) So maybe Latour is only aiming at the superficial, socially disconnected and sometimes arrogant academic "criticism" of upper-class liberals who over-moralize the curriculum in literature, cultural and gender studies, who – incomprehensible to Joe Doe – demand political correctness and justice for animals and the third Gender, e.g.; and by prolongation of this empty gesture open a door to the climate skeptics? The fun Latour makes of the critic seems to suggest such an interpretation: "Isn't this fabulous? Isn't it really worth going to graduate school to study critique? 'Enter here, you poor folks. After arduous years of reading turgid prose, you will be always right.'"[28]

At closer inspection, however, we quickly learn that this normalized industry of a sometimes sterile academic criticism is not the main enemy of his. In fact, this industry is the main recipient of his theories and thus contributing to his huge success.[29] When Latour neglectfully talks about the "critical sociology," he aims at another target – at Marx's theory of the fetishism of commodities and money, and Pierre Bourdieu's empirical cultural sociology (notwithstanding the large differences between the two). Against Bourdieu, Latour asks us to take the experiences and narratives of interviewees more seriously, and not to "reduce" them into an objectivist expert-language devoid of meaning, a claim I support.[30] Against Marx, Latour holds something more devastating: Marx seems to be the protestant among the philosophical saints, being responsible for the ongoing "purification" in the social sciences. He seems to be the one who feeds the assumed scientific affect against things, against appearances

---

27 Latour, *We have never been modern*, 5ff., 35ff.; *Politics of Nature*; "Why has Critique run out of steam?," 225. "A 'flat' interaction, focusing on immediate experiences, is a way of avoiding sociological (or psychological) explanations of religious phenomena, and thereby avoiding that kind of criticism of religion which stems from Marx and Freud, as well as from the radicalism of the youth movement in the 1970s." Skirbekk, "Bruno Latour's anthropology of the moderns," 46.

28 Latour, "Why has Critique run out of steam?" 239.

29 Latour admits that the *Science studies* were part of this academic normalization of critique: "entire Ph.D. programs are still running to make sure that good American kids are learning the hard way that facts are made up, that there is no such thing as natural, unmediated, unbiased access to truth, that we are always prisoners of language, that we always speak from a particular standpoint, and so on." Latour, "Why has Critique run out of steam?" 227.

30 Cf. Christoph Henning, "Ontologie bei Marx." In Jan Urbich/Jörg Zimmer (eds.), *Handbuch Ontologie*. (Stuttgart: 2019 (in press)).

and pictures, against fetishes, against everything that goes beyond the meager and meaningless world of social structures.[31] The world is rich, it seems, but after it has gone through an interpretation by the social sciences inspired by Marx and Bourdieu, alas, it is catholicism is "reduced" to only a few entities – social structures in this case. And thus, when Latour alleges a modern "cult of anti-fetishism,"[32] Marx becomes its apostle. For this, however, the Marxian theories are misread in a simplistic and cognitivist way.[33]

Latour is charging critical theory with yet another accusation. Unlike Latour, they are said to be unaware that society is not a pre-given substance, but something that is reproduced by its elements constantly. Critical theorists seem to believe in a given and unmediated substance.[34] This, again, is a peculiar claim. Is not the great bulk of critical theories (including Lukács' ontology) trying to elaborate exactly how the structures of contemporary society emerge from social and economic processes, including asymmetries of property, gender relations of domination, hegemonic ideologies, etc.? Latour's misconception results from the fact that the only operation he *registers* as criticism is the effort to show that something is "made."[35] But that is not all.

So Latour's believes that the moderns have not yet discovered (1) that society is fabricated by other entities and processes, and (2) that construction and truth (or reality) can go together. He ascribes the belief to critical theorists that making and truth are incompatible.[36] This not only explains why Latour esteems the church so much (for this premodern institution knew very well that

---

31   Latour, *We have never been modern*, 36f.; Bruno Latour, *Reassembling the Social: An Introduction to Actor-Network Theory*. (Oxford: 2005), 84.

32   Latour, *Existenzweisen*, 247.

33   "According to Latour, anti-fetishists such as Karl Marx believe themselves to be exposing the illusory projection of human agency onto things. This leads them, says Latour, to overlook the actual roles and powers of nonhuman actors in constructing actor-networks." White, "Materiality, Form, and Context," 667. But, White claims: "There is little correspondence to be found between Marx's critique of the fetishism of commodities and the anti-fetishism that Latourians see in Marxist theory," 668. There is a long prehistory of misreading Marx as a religious writer (see Henning Christoph Henning, *Philosophy after Marx. 100 Years of Misreadings and the Normative Turn in Political Philosophy*. (Boston/Leiden: 2014, 353ff.).

34   Latour (2013) calls this approach "doubleclick," which stands for immediate access; Latour, *Existenzweisen*.

35   Latour, *Existenzweisen*, 230.

36   This is another strange claim: For one, this suggests that "truths" are *only* made, which has to be contested. A "truth" that was fully fabricated, say an election result, would no longer hold true. And secondly, this neglects many other elements of critical theories: e.g., the importance of relations of domination and exploitation *within* these practices, efforts to come up with better theories, which of course are made as well, etc.

their "truths," or dogmas, had to be carefully constructed over and over again). It is also Latour's standard argument against the social constructivism of which he is constantly accused: according to Latour, social constructivism ignores that the "society," which is said to "construct" various things (gender roles, economic trends, or scientific truths), is not simply given. It is itself constantly in the making, assembled and re-assembled by networks of persons, things, institutions, and ideas. So, it seems that Latour wants to beat the accusation of social constructivism by being even *more* constructivist than the social constructivists: he also constructs the social (without claiming that by this it becomes less real; however, it becomes ontologically dependent on something else).

Of course, this leads to the question *from what* we can possibly start such a process. What is the starting point, the foundation to begin with? A simple answer to this would be that before there was a society, there obviously was nature, and some kind of natural beings, the hominids, which at some point started to build large groups. But this is much *too* simple for a new millennium thinker: Latour would call this *another* reductionism. This *other* reduction also drives the purifiers in the social sciences (including Marx), and in the natural sciences as well: you can wrongly reduce things not only to their origin in an assumed "society," but also back to their supposed nature. For these other reductionists, things are not what they seem. In reality they consist of some *natural* phenomena only the experts know about, be they biological (instinct), physical (atoms) or genetic (codes).

Against this side Latour launches a similar objection: for him, there is no such thing as *nature* ("We have succeeded in freeing ourselves from the first nature"[37]). The reason is that nature itself is constructed, so it cannot be said to construct something else. And if it is constructed, neither can it exist *before* the construction.[38] This peculiar claim is a constant one in Latour's books, and here he is very much in line with the postmodernist anti-essentialism of Derrida, Judith Butler and others (see below). However, the claim that nature is constructed because our *knowledge* about it can be traced to laboratories, where a lot of construction is at work, misses a central point – the difference between ontology and epistemology. There is a huge difference between nature and "nature," between the real world that predates us, and our apprehensions of it which may capture some characteristics more or less correctly (this is where science is hoping to progress over time), but which will always be incomplete. Latour is making fun of Tarski's dequotation axiom, but it is exactly

---

37 Latour, *Politics of Nature*, 132.
38 "Before Koch, the bacillus has no real existence." Latour quoted in Sokal and Bricmont, *Fashionable Nonsense*, 97.

Tarski's distinction between nature and "nature" which goes amiss in Latour's overcast claim that nature is constructed. Making fun of a critic is a diversionary tactic which may entertain readers, but does not solve conceptual problems. This is why his critic's keep on deploring this shortcoming over and over again;[39] Latour has not changed this idealistic claim over the decades, not even in *Modes of Existence*, where he rather multiplies the ways in which entities are produced together with their images. That does answer the missing distinction between ontology and epistemology.

Now, a solution to the one-sided and indeed problematic explanatory efforts Latour describes (reducing perceived entities either to society or to nature) might be a *combination* of these two explanatory strategies. Imagine a discussion about some person's violent disposition: some opponents will attribute it to their nature ("it is running in the family"), others to their nurture ("his father was like that," or "society made her what she is"). But most likely *both* factors, together with some of their own decisions, have made them what they are. So, in a Latourian idiom, you can "reduce" in both directions at the same time. Yet for Latour this third way, which he ascribes to Marx,[40] is not a solution either, because now you simply mix the reductions of the phenomena like a cocktail; you move on an axis between two mistakes. Latour seems to assume that two bads do not give us one good.[41] Supposedly this is a wrong path because distinguishing nature and society leads to ontological *depletion*. I cannot articulate the "non sequitur" clearly enough.

The description Latour gives of his enemy, the "moderns," is surprisingly impoverished. For Latour, the "modernists" wish to divide the world ontologically in two, and only two entities: objects and subjects. This is their original sin, and many shortcomings result from this. From this primordial failure, according to Latour – and as we know it from Heidegger – we see the world falling apart into two pieces: one half, so called objectivity, is devoid of meaning and "reduced"

---

39   "The most fundamental assumption underlying Latour's first principle is that we are unable to make any distinctions between things and their representations: Things are what we collectively represent them to be, nothing more and nothing less." Olga Amsterdamska, "Surely you are joking, Monsieur Latour! Review of Latour." *Science, Technology, & Human Values*, vol. 15, no. 4 (1990): 495–504, 497. "Latour slips, without comment or argument, from 'Nature's representation' in the first half of this sentence to 'Nature' tout court in the second half" (Sokal and Brikmont, *Fashionable Nonsense*, 93). "Latour makes no systematic distinction between nature and beliefs about, or accounts of, nature. ... It is as if he has difficulty telling these two things apart. ... He rejects the subject–object distinction, and drawing a boundary between nature, and beliefs about nature, is just a form of this distinction." Bloor, "Anti-Latour," 87.

40   Latour, *We have never been modern*, 36.

41   See the diagram in *We have never been modern*, 58.

to physical basics; the other half, subjectivity, is said to be non-real, "reduced" to a dream, because it is only subjective. What Latour is after while attacking these straw men is another *interpretation* of the world; one that does not impoverish our rich experiences by a minimalist ontology.[42] So far, so good, one might say – this is the familiar philosophical program other writers started out with seven or eight decades earlier: William James' and John Dewey's Pragmatism or Edmund Husserl's and Martin Heidegger's phenomenology had similar goals, and even analytical philosophy has ended up with a re-appraisal of Hegel and his much richer approach.[43] So without need, Latour hastily rejects a respected ontological tradition – philosophical anthropology, natural philosophy and ecological thinking had all tried to bring the effects of nature and society together and balance them against one another.[44]

Various authors demonstrated how Latour often misrepresents the scholars he is depicting: apart from a stereotypical schoolbook interpretation of Descartes, there is no "modernism" in the way Latour assumes, neither among the natural scientists,[45] nor the Marxists[46] or the earlier science studies.[47] The picture-book story of the modern philosopher who foolishly divides the world into purely "objective" and "subjective" sectors, where objective stands for physicalism and subjective for mere phantasy, is an over-simplification, a straw men for rhetorical purposes. Even the young Carnap or the Vienna circle, who really experimented with such assumptions, withdrew them quickly.[48] The thing *most* reductionist in all this is this narrative itself: Latour deduces all kinds of things from this abstract philosophical distinction between subject

---

42   Latour, *Existenzweisen*, 236.
43   The "subject–object dichotomy has been thoroughly criticized from dialectical and phenomenological perspectives through to the pragmatic–linguistic turn and the critique of instrumental rationality, as well as via a focus on different forms of situated rationality (or *Wissenschaft*). If someone claims to have new and interesting contributions to make to such debates, is it too much to expect some clarification as to how these differ from what has already been said and done before?" (Skirbekk, "Bruno Latour's anthropology of the moderns," 47.)
44   Joachim Radkau, *Nature and Power: A Global History of the Environment.* (Cambridge: 2008); Donald Worster, *Nature's Economy: A History of Ecological Ideas.* (Cambridge: 1994); Jost Hermand, *Grüne Utopien in Deutschland. Zur Geschichte des ökologischen Bewusstseins.* (Frankfurt a. M.: 1991).
45   Brennan, "Review of Latour."
46   White, "Materiality, Form, and Context."
47   Bloor, "Anti-Latour."
48   Carnap's reductionist "physicalism" is criticized by Lukács as well (*Zur Ontologie des gesellschaftlichen Seins* I, 367ff.). But Lukács would not have claimed (as Latour) that Carnap is representative for "modernity" as such; one reason for this is that most earlier philosophers knew to distinguish epistemology and ontology.

and object: it seems to determine our views on various fields such as nature and culture, facts and norms, or science and morality. This amounts to a Heideggerian idealism, where an overly abstract ontology seems to magically produce the rest; mind prefigures matter.[49] His claim is that most problems in the contemporary world result from an insufficient understanding, an incomplete *philosophical* picture of the world which he calls "modern." This category is meant to catch almost everybody in philosophy, from Hobbes to Hegel and Husserl, from Locke to Rousseau or Marx.

But if, for argument's sake, we follow Latour so far, what exactly is the alternative? Is there a *tertium datur* between nature and nurture, subjects and objects, facts and fantasies, science and morality? It is here that ontological questions become most pressing. Latour claims that distinguishing nature and society makes no sense since we always already experience them together, not as a mix, but in a synthesis or "hybrid."[50] It is only the mistaken "modern" philosophy of subject and object, mind and matter, or nature and culture that artificially disentangles what in our technological age increasingly grows together. The term "ecology" is henceforth used for *these* networks, for assemblages of technologies, persons, things, and ideas acting together. It no longer means protecting wildlife, the atmosphere and or ourselves from an industry that carelessly exploits and pollutes everything in its reach (or in short: "nature" from "society"), since for Latour these separate entities do not exist. It now refers to the *network* of forests (or what is left of them), coal mines, toxics, and stories about all of them. The political price paid for this "third way" is quite high.

This focus on networks, on combinations of things in practice may have some merit on the descriptive level, when networks of scientific practices and the "construction" of scientific facts are described in great detail. From a sociological perspective, maybe this is all you can ask for. Whether or not such a story is convincing is an empirical question. But note that an early commentator demurred that Latour could only *jump* to his hypothesis of "things" as actants

---

49   "Latour's conception of the political and legal institutionalising of nature looks more like magic than argument" (Brennan, "Review of Latour," 3). See White, "Materiality, Form, and Context," 679ff.: "[S]omehow Latour's examples of these convergences or translations never move beyond a repetitive back-and-forth narrative in which mind is joined to matter and matter subsequently relays, exceeds, or displaces mind. At the post office counter, the agent and the customer interact in accordance with a plan designed in the architect's office [...] much more than critical theory, it is ANT that traps the object in a relationship with mind, instead of placing it carefully in the world of all its historically particular connections."

50   Most prominently in Latour, *We have never been modern.*

within these networks because he failed to analyze the social context fully. To illustrate this point with an example: 'Why did the strongest brother end up with the biggest piece of cake? Because the cake *wanted* to be eaten by the brother.' You can only claim such an agency of the cake if you abstract from the unequal power relation between the brothers.⁵¹ This narrative produces a useful ideology: it is the bigger brother who says the cake was acting.

However sociology evaluates Latour's claims in the long run, philosophically speaking they leave many questions in the dark, particularly questions of normativity and politics, but also regarding ontology. This is the Hegelian element mention earlier: Latourian networks are like a revenant of Hegel's "spirit": a mystical entity that encompasses everything and hence cannot be analyzed by the given theoretical tools: all previous distinctions fail, because we are now in the realm of the indistinguishable ("back to the moment where the distinction has not yet been made.")⁵² Here we can hardly explain, rather we should turn to telling stories or invent a new language, like Heidegger did when describing "Seinsgeschehen."⁵³ This is all the more disturbing because on the way there, Latour asks us to drop most of our philosophical convictions.

3   Problems with Hybridity

Let us list the problems that come with this. First of all, ontologically we do *not* get plurality. Rather, instead of two impoverished realms that were there before for Latour (but only because he fuses epistemology and ontology – in fact the world looked much richer in most earlier ontologies), we now have but one. We have networks – and nothing else. This is an ontological grey in grey

---

51   In his book on Pasteur, Latour neglects the competition between Pasteur and Koch, and locates the events in a process in the laboraty alone – but only in *one* of the two camps. See Bruno Latour, *The Pasteurisation of France*. (Cambridge, Mass.: Harvard, 1988).

"The microbes by no means 'enthusiastically' obeyed the Pastorians in preference to Koch. Indeed, we have no basis for speaking of their wishes if we are to obey the dictates of symmetry: their reported behaviours varied between the two places, in a manner quite familiar to sociologists of scientific controversy." Simon Schaffer, "The Eighteenth Brumaire of Bruno Latour." *Studies in History and Philosophy of Science*, vol. 22, no. 1 (1991): 174–192, 188. So the new discovery (things are actants) is the result of a sociological truncation: "Hylozoism directs our attention towards the items whose action is in dispute. It directs our attention away from the forces which help close that dispute. It therefore disables understanding" (189).

52   Latour, *The Pasteurisation of France*, 252.

53   "The invisible presence at the banquet here is the ghost of Heidegger." Brennan, "Review of Latour," 3.

that hardly accomplishes what Latour meant to achieve in the first place. The second problem is that if there *only* are networks, we have no criteria in order to judge their efficiency: "with the network model and the concept of enrollment we can easily account for anything, no matter what happens."[54] Success in terms of science becomes a matter of social power; only that it now is no longer decipherable as such.[55] That leads to a third problem: the political agenda Latour often evokes in his books – a nebulous "parliament of things" or "political ecology" is called for in order to make the world a better place – lacks meaningful normative criteria:

where are the resources by which we can define ourselves, our values? Indeed, why should the diplomat accept that administrators, scientists, politicians, economists and moralists have any special role to play (as opposed, for example, to businessmen, generals, salespeople, dictators and terrorists)? Where, in in the absence of all differences and forsaking any distinction between the 'rational' and the 'irrational,' does Latour find the very standards by which he is able to commend his own set of solutions to our environmental quandaries?[56]

His late ontology aims to answer these problems – he acknowledges the problem of causal inefficiency, ontological monotony and lack of normative criteria, but he passes it on to another school of thought he claims to have left behind (the science studies). However, the solution Latour offers in his new book is not his own – he retreats back to a philosophy of *values* in order to account for differences between the different networks.[57] But he only goes back half way: he uses the old idea, but he does not subscribe to the old way of writing that came with it – aiming for logical transparency, clear cut differentiation, and a systematic argumentation.[58] So what Latour is getting at in this

---

54 Amsterdamski, "Surely you are joking, Monsieur Latour!" 500.
55 Latour could also account for a success of Lysenko: "Using Latour's logic and his vocabulary, it appears not only that Lysenko was a great scientist but also that the methods he used to assure his victory over Soviet genetics and agriculture are a superb example of sound scientific strategy." Amsterdamski "Surely you are joking, Monsieur Latour!" 502.
56 Andrew Brennan, "Review of Bruno Latour." *Environmental Ethics*, vol. 28, no. 2 (2006): 4.
57 Latour 2013, 39.
58 Reviews of Latour complain: "the book offers neither theoretical discussion nor empirical evidence" (Chernilo 2015, 4). It "constantly teaches and tells the reader (via an imagined female investigator) what he or she has understood at the various stages," aiming at "conversion" rather than arguments (Skirbekk 2015, 45). Indeed, Latour had early on expressed his uneasiness with things like explanation or cause: "the ideal of explanation ... is not a desirable goal" (1986, 164); "the belief in causes and effect is always, in some sense, the admiration for a chain of command or the hatred of a mob looking for someone to stone" (1986, 162).

book is rather conventional: a reinstatement of different value spheres (law, the arts, the economy, technology, religion and personality). What this means ontologically, however, is far from clear. A recent review thus rediscovered the old problem of relativism and ontological poverty even in the new book:

> Instead of a cosmos that is populated in a 'richer way,' Latour has effectively flattened even more the modern ontology. The world is now populated by networks and networks alone. [...] The plurality of modes of existence fails to emerge because it gets subordinated to an endless and ontological unspecific flow of networks; all we can learn and experience we learn and experience because it has successfully become real as a network.[59]

Before we finally have a look at Lukács' alternative conception, let me spell out why this approach is so problematic not only philosophically, but also politically. It is a well-disguised attack on environmentalism, which today is more important than ever. Environmentalism started to have some impact on social democratic governments in the 1970s, but after the global turn to neoliberalism since the 1970s, environmental degradation has increased considerably on a global scale. In order to restore profitability, neoliberalism has sacked environmental regulations, and the power of nation states or other authorities to steer pollution and the waste of natural resources is in permanent decline. In the face of these ecological disasters, it must come as a surprise that Latour, who is clad in an "ecological" dress and borrows green concepts, does *not* pick up from a juxtaposition of nature and society, as progressive movements in the 18th and 20th centuries used to put it, but from an "assemblage" of the two that leaves us with the ontological grey in grey described above. It always already combines elements of both. This claim is euphorically picked up by a group of technophilists and transhumanists today.[60]

Examples for this new techno-monism are found in various fields, art-related ones like post-structuralist feminism and literature studies[61] or aesthetics,[62] as well as in anthropology.[63] Latour is a main inspiration for this new monism. Like Latour, these scholars proclaim an era beyond or "after nature," the reason

---

59 Chernilo, "Review of Latour," 4ff.
60 Timothy Morton, *Ecology without Nature: Rethinking Ecological Aesthetics*. (Cambridge, Mass.: 2007); Rosi Braidotti and Rick Dolphijn, *Philosophy after Nature*. (London/New York: 2017).
61 Braidotti and Dolphijn, *Philosophy after Nature*.
62 Morton, *Ecology without Nature*.
63 Philippe Descola, *Beyond Nature and Culture*. (Chicago: 2013).

being that technology often *influences* it. This idea is highly problematic from a philosophical perspective: it is like claiming that there are not atoms because we have molecules; that there is neither flour nor milk because in many cases it already is backed into cake. For hundreds of years cookbooks have ignored the rich practices of cooks and only looked at "objective" ingredients, they have heedlessly transferred notions of taste into the "subject"! This way of putting it seems to deny the very possibility of abstraction, of thinking beyond appearances. If at the same time, and in a similar intellectual trend, Spinoza has become very popular again (for Deleuze, Althusser, Lordon and many others, clearly in the post-modern political spectrum), his focus on *natura naturans* is unthinkable within a Latourian frame. Maybe such a move would already count as anti-fetishistic and hence "modern" in a pejorative sense; but here we see how unmeaning the term "modern" really is.

The political effects of this ontologically indifferent mishmash are fatal: when there is no more nature for somebody, but *only* interactions, only technologically modified entities, we not only loose one important source of political criticism (see below), this may also trick the readers into technophilia or even phantasmagories of a "technofix" (to climate change, e.g.).[64] There is not much left of social criticism here, neither of an ecology proper. As the following contrast to Lukács will show, this technological mindset, a surface-only-thinking in terms of technical disposability, was very much at the center of Lukács' criticism. For Lukács, the dispositive of "manipulation" results from several ontological mistakes, all of which we can by now attribute to Latour.[65]

4 Georg Lukács as an Alternative

Paradoxically, in comparison to this current ontological turn in one of the most popular contemporary thinkers, Lukács' much older and in many ways old-fashioned *Ontology of Social Being* suddenly becomes significant. As we have

---

[64] "'imbroglios' or technological monsters, modern versions of Mary Shelley's Frankenstein, are a normal part of our relation to nature, and we should accept them and their consequences, while rejecting environmentalism in favor of […] 'post-environmentalism,' which does not challenge capital accumulation and unlimited economic growth, or accept the existence of natural limits, but rather places its emphasis on machines/technology, coupled with the market mechanism." (Foster, "Marxism in the Anthropocene," 398). We will see in a minute that Lukács was clearly opposed to such technological thinking, he called it the mindset of "manipulation."

[65] Lukács, *Zur Ontologie des gesellschaftlichen Seins* I, 355, 367.

seen, Latour's ontological turn did not manage to convey an ontological plurality – different spheres are described, but ontologically they are thrown together, everything became a network. Rather than allowing for plurality, different regions are lumped together, simplified and standardized (nature and society, facts and values, subjects and objects). If everything is renamed as network, it is only by borrowing from an elder school – neo-Kantian philosophies of value, which remain an alien element – that Latour could articulate differences between what was formerly called "value spheres" (Max Weber) or "regional ontologies" (Edmund Husserl). Latour also withdrew the distinction between epistemology and ontology, and as an effect, he politically undermined critical theory in general, and ecological thinking in particular.

In order to save ontology from its new friends, it is almost therapeutic to turn back to Lukács' classical approach, which has not been well received until recently. When Lukács wrote his ontology, his last book, he was about eighty years old. By then he had extensively tackled questions of literature, politics, aesthetics and ethics as well as "bourgeois" philosophy broadly speaking, over a course of over 60 years. So, he was a very experienced writer. Unfortunately, his old age may have been a reason for the over-extensive length and the sometimes missing focus in his last book – often the sentences do not find a close, and the text meanders from topic to topic. So, the book is not an easy read and it stands much in contradiction with his earlier commitments towards the *essay as form*.[66] Nevertheless this is an important document, not least because Lukács here answers questions both from philosophy and politics. If readers have the energy and patience to bear with it for the whole 1500 pages, they are about to discover an impressive draft that covers a lot, from the first human activities back in the stone age (remember that Marshall Sahlins published his *Stone Age Economics* only a view years later, in 1972) up to shortcomings in contemporary societies, both capitalist and communist, and contemporary philosophical schools (including Heidegger, who is something like a godfather to Latour). Some critics maintained that the book is outdated, for all kinds of reasons: most prominently, both Habermas and the Budapest school claimed it would not give "normativity" its proper place and hence was monistic and reductionist. This was a little off target because the book *does* deal with normativity (in fact it was meant to be a preface to another book on ethics). Yet it does not do so in an isolated way: It integrates normativity within a broader framework of co-operation and social labor, so it is no longer "pure" (in Latourian

---

66   This essay ("On the Nature and form of the Essay," 1910), however, anticipated a new "system" (probably by the writer himself); and the late *Ontology*, in spite of its monstrous length, still claims to be preliminary.

terms), but can show the functions of normativity as well as the development of thought *about* those values of cooperation. Note that "bringing together" for Lukács does not mean withdrawing differentiations, as it is Latour's tendency. Let me name three main differences and elaborate why these issues are so important.

(1) The first difference is that unlike Latour, Lukács does differentiate *being and thinking*, ontology and epistemology.[67] Why is that so important? Latour assumes that distinguishing the two is dualistic and leads to an artificial separation which brings our theories out of touch with the lived reality, where everything becomes increasingly hybrid. The solution can only be focusing on what "matters" to us, regardless of distinctions between sciences and morals, nature and culture, subject and object. In a romantic manner, the neglect of ecological issues is attributed to the "cold" and "distant" concept of nature within the natural sciences, which does not mobilize politically.[68] Lukács, on the contrary, argues that the destruction of nature has different ontological roots: it is the idealism that in its quest for unity tries to overcome all distinctions, starting with the most fundamental one between being and thinking. In effect, if everything that is "thought" is made "real" by various truth-procedures,[69] we no longer have a "thing in itself" in the Kantian understanding. This may satisfy intellectual cravings for holism, yet it has some side effects: first, we can no longer account for mistakes. How can you think wrongly, if what you think is real, and made real by this thinking?[70] How can you even *realize* that you might be wrong, if you *think* what you think is – by implication – real? Overcoming the distinction between thinking and being is thus a recipe for hubris. This is the second side effect: a philosophy that believes it has captured all

---

67 Lukács, *Zur Ontologie des gesellschaftlichen Seins* I, 402, 565.
68 Latour, *Das terrestrische Manifest*, 87.
69 This idealism has another revenant in todays "speculative materialism" and the approaches of Karen Barad and others; for a criticism see Elmar Flatschart, "Matter that really matters? New Materialism und kritisch-dialektische Theorie." In Tobias Goll/Daniel Keil/Thomas Telios (eds.), *Critical Matter: Diskussionen eines neuen Materialismus*. (Münster 2012), 96–112, or Paul Rekret, "A Critique of New Materialism: Ethics and Ontology." *Subjectivity*, vol. 9, no. 3 (2016): 225–245.
70 Lukács discusses the possibility of a technology that works in it little segment of reality, but misrepresents other, larger parts of reality (a phenomenon that is typical for the contemporary car industries, etc.). In order to account for this, you have to distinguish epistemology and ontology, as well as philosophy and the sciences. "Diese Dialektikzwischen strenger Richtigkeit im engeren Gebiet der konkreten teleologischen Setzung und möglicher, sehr weitgehender Falschheit im Erfassen der Natur in ihrem vollen Ansichsein hat für das Gebiet der Arbeit eine sehr weittragende Bedeutung" (Lukács, *Zur Ontologie des gesellschaftlichen Seins* II, 21).

there is in its thinking, especially when it claims to be "holistic" (in other words: that it is thinking *is* reality, and all of reality, as Lukács ascribes it to Hegel, but also to Carnaps neo-positivist program of "unified sciences"), neglects the depth of reality.[71] The reason for this is that we will never be able to know everything, so equating knowledge with reality *reduces* reality to what we know about it. So, for Lukács, it is not the distinction between subject and object, or epistemology and ontology, that creates a purification,[72] a neglect, an ontological impoverishment, as Latour claims, but exactly the opposite is the case: it is the *missing* distinction of the two (as we find it in Latour) that leads to this result. This is one reason why Lukács has such a high esteem for Nicolai Hartmann – and would not have welcomed today's "speculative realism": Hartmann was clear from the beginning that for him, there is a reality that is prior to and independent of thought, and thus ontology cannot be reduced to epistemology (and the less so to a sociology of scientific practice).

(2) The next large difference is that Lukács talks about the *subject–object-distinction* in much more detail and concreteness, and does not believe that it can or should be overcome once and for all. It is well known that the young Lukács (as well as Wittgenstein) was suffering from the threat of solipsism.[73] This can be described as a gap between one subject and the rest of the world (other people, but also things and values). Here, subject–object-talk was sociophilosophical, later on Lukács dealt with the specificity of the subject–object-relation in aesthetics or politics.[74] When he covers it in the late *Ontology*, there are at least three dimension of the subject–object-distinction that run at different levels. This differentiation avoids Latourian fallacies. Lukács distinguishes (i) the ontological dimension, the social *reality* of subjectivity and the outside world, from (ii) the developing *awareness* of this subject–object-distinction, and particular philosophical *expressions* of this distinction (iii). Here he finds more diversity than Latour does, without overburdening philosophy (iii) with a "construction" of social realities (i) or persistent patterns of thought (ii).

---

71 "Die ontologische Verschiedenheit der Seinsarten lässt sich aus der wissenschaftlichen Begriffsbildung nur durch eine homogenisierende, die wirkliche Eigenart vergewaltigende Gleichschaltung eliminieren" (Lukács, *Zur Ontologie des gesellschaftlichen Seins* I, 366).

72 Lukács literally mentions an unnecessary "purity" of the sciences (*Zur Ontologie des gesellschaftlichen Seins* I, 368).

73 Andreas Hoeschen, *Das 'Dostojewsky-Projekt': Lukács' neukantianisches Frühwerk in seinem ideengeschichtlichen Kontext.* (Berlin: 2015).

74 G. Lukács, "Die Subjekt-Objekt-Beziehung in der Aesthetik." *Logos. Internationale Zeitschrift für Philosophie der Kultur*, vol. VII, no. 1 (1917/18).

(i) First of all, there is a historical ontology of personhood, of the individuality of subjects. This is a key element for Lukács, not least because the ethics already implicit in the *Ontology* focuses on the possibilities of unfolding this individuality. There *are* subjects in the world (so subjectivity is something objective and ontological, not a "dream" or shadow), and they can and should become ever more like themselves.[75] This is a real phenomenon, but not a natural one: the ontology of subjects is *social*.[76] This does not mean that we can reduce subjectivity to sociality, as it was suggested for a while in Habermas' over-inclusive reading of "intersubjectivity"; it means that the materiality of subjectivity can only develop within certain social conditions which are thus worthwhile to be sustained.[77]

(ii) Secondly, we can reconstruct the process of *becoming aware* of the evolving differences of subjectivity and objectivity – this it no "construct" of some philosopher's brain in the 17th century, as Latour sometimes seems to imagine, but a much older result of the evolution of human practices, and of processes of work in particular. When humans are processing materials, as they have to in order to survive, they experience material resistance and learn to see different paths for acting. Thus, they become aware that there are various "objective" possibilities in the material and the tools, and also various "subjective" desires or needs.[78] At some point they need to be discussed with others, so we even get a third, social kind of possibilities, which Lukács discusses under the cooperative

---

75   We can not elaborate this perfectionism here, but in general see Christoph Henning, *Freiheit, Gleichheit, Entfaltung: Die politische Philosophie des Perfektionismus*. (Frankfurt a. M.: 2015).

76   "Die wirkliche Entwicklung der immer gesellschaftlich, nie bloß naturhaft fundierten Individualität aus der bloß naturhaften Einzelheit ist ein höchst komplizierter Prozeß" (Lukács, *Zur Ontologie des gesellschaftlichen Seins* I, 44).

77   A similar ontological interpretation of subjectivity was developed by critical Realism, e.g., in Margaret Archer, *Being Human: The Problem of Agency*. (Cambridge: 2000). For a comparison of critical realism and Lukács, see Mário Duayer and João Medeiros, "Lukács' Critical Ontology and Critical Realism." *Journal of Critical Realism*, vol. 4, no. 2 (2005): 395–425.

78   "Jede teleologische Setzung ist eine vom Subjekt der Praxis bewußt vollzogene Wahl zwischen zwei (oder mehreren) Möglichkeiten und die daraus folgende, dadurch bestimmte praktische Verwirklichung der gewählten Möglichkeit. Die Polarisation des Aktes auf subjektive und objektive Momente ist bereits in dieser fundamentalen Situation einer jeden menschlichen Praxis mitenthalten. Indem das Subjekt sowohl in der Frage der Zielsetzung wie in der der Verwirklichung vor eine Wahl ist und wählt, müssen sich im Akte selbst die Momente der Subjektivität und die der Objektivität – bei aller unauflöslicher Verknüpftheit – seinsmäßig genau scheiden" (Lukács, *Zur Ontologie des gesellschaftlichen Seins* I, 165).

evolution of *language*.⁷⁹ To the extent that human work activities are embedded in a "metabolism with nature" (Marx), we can call this genesis of a sense of subjectivity and objectivity a natural process.⁸⁰ However, Lukács' phenomenology of labor shows that this metabolism with nature, even if never suspended (but blanked out from view by certain philosophies), is over time shifting to another level, the level of social being. Social being is enabled and persistently influenced by nature, but not reducible to natural laws (*Zurückweichen der Naturschranke*).⁸¹ The political consequences of this ontological decision to distinguish nature and society are far-reaching and need to be discussed in a little more detail.

Analyzing the confrontation with matter as an "interaction" not with objects, but with actant-things which have their own "agency" can be inspiring.⁸² But it is problematic when this is used to abandon well-established critical vocabularies and instead asks these things into our parliaments.⁸³ What would nuclear plants, car factories and glyphosate tanks decide when allowed access there?⁸⁴ Rather than jumping to such speculative conclusions, Lukács carefully spells out the pragmatic consequences of this recurring encounters with matter step by step. The outline Lukács gives of these correlations may be sketchy, but it has a captivating systematic. The awareness of subjective and objective possibilities within the labor process does not only set free the sense of subjectivity and objectivity, but also the concepts of *freedom* (based on the choice between different paths),⁸⁵ of *morality* (anchored in what today is called "affordances" and the need to choose sustainably, even when not

---

79 Lukács, *Zur Ontologie des gesellschaftlichen Seins* I, 46ff., 186f.
80 "The word 'nature' refers to the allencompassing, material system in which human animals and the entire pattern of their interactions, and all the products and consequences of these interactions, have their allotted place. To talk about society explaining nature, when it is but one part of nature, is incoherent. Knowledge itself is just one more natural phenomenon" (Bloor, "Anti-Latour," 87).
81 Lukács, *Zur Ontologie des gesellschaftlichen Seins* I, 69.
82 See Jane Bennett, *Vibrant matter: A political Ecology of Things*. (Durham: 2010).
83 Latour, *Politics of Nature*, 164ff.
84 Borrowing Marx's term "character mask," which Latour despises, we could say that these things already sit in parliament: the influence of lobby firms catering the interesting of chemical, nuclear or petro-industries within parliaments is proverbial, as even Latour recently acknowledged – these lobby groups spend millions of dollars in order to deny climate change. So figuratively speaking, oil, cars and glyphosate already are in charge in our western democracies; but that is a nightmare. For the importance of such "things" and pictures in Marx, see Christoph Henning, "Marx und die Monster des Marktes: Kleine philosophische Bilderkunde." *Allgemeine Zeitschrift für Philosophie*, vol. 3 (2018): 353–374.
85 Lukács, *Zur Ontologie des gesellschaftlichen Seins* II, 40, 97f.

immediately controlled by a collective)[86] and the *values* (as criteria within those choices, anchored in the everyday-experiences of use-values).[87] Further on in the book, he also traces the genesis of the realm of ideas, of alienation and reification. For Lukács these phenomena are no mere "illusions," but ontological phenomena. With this he catches Marx's intentions better then Latour does.[88]

Even more striking is the reflection on the genesis of the *sciences*: Lukács locates them in recurring efforts to explore the "means" of the labor process. But the possibilities of the emerging sciences soon transcend this immediate practical purpose; even if some actors in society would like to restrict the uses of science to this instrumentality. (This leads us back to Bellarmin and the question how much scientific knowledge and philosophical reflection is *allowed* to circulate in society).[89] Lukács also traces ideas like the "human soul"[90] or the religious idea of *teloi in nature itself* back to the mental model of the labor process.[91] The main difference to Latour in all this is not only the richer phenomenology concerning the results (the *explanandum*, e.g., the genesis of freedom, individuality, religion, morality, the values and the sciences are situated within this chapter). It is also a much richer description of the underlying *processes* (the *explanans*): at the center we do not only find the comparatively small field of scientific experimentation (which is present),[92] the main topic and the general explanatory model for Latour, but a much broader range of material human activities. Situating the sciences within this broader range makes it much harder to use insights from science studies *alone* as a blueprint for the rest of social theory.[93]

(iii) Finally, the third dimension of the subject–object-distinction is the variety of ways in which different *philosophies* expressed and interpreted this subject–object-distinction in particular contexts (epistemic, aesthetic, work-related, etc.). Due to difference number 1 (the distinction between ontology and epistemology), for Lukács it is impossible to claim, as Latour seems to do,

---

86 See Lukács, *Zur Ontologie des gesellschaftlichen Seins* II, 61.
87 Lukács, *Zur Ontologie des gesellschaftlichen Seins*, 68ff.
88 "When Latour targets anti-fetishism, he describes it as a misguided epistemic crusade, whereas Marx's account of the fetishism of commodities is an immanent critique of a form of life" (White, "Materiality, Form, and Context," *Victorian Studies*, vol. 55, no. 4 (2013): 667–682, 668; cf. Henning "Ontologie bei Marx."
89 Lukács, *Zur Ontologie des gesellschaftlichen Seins* II, 58f.
90 Lukács, *Zur Ontologie des gesellschaftlichen Seins* II, 92.
91 Lukács, *Zur Ontologie des gesellschaftlichen Seins* II, 14, 24f.
92 Lukács, *Zur Ontologie des gesellschaftlichen Seins* I, 57f.
93 "Latour claims that because laboratory studies are central to understand how the modern world works, then science does mirror society at large: this is a sociological return to pre-sociological certainty" (Chernilo, "Review of Latour," 7).

that these philosophies somehow created the reality and the awareness of subjectivity. The owl of Minerva spreads its wings only with the falling of the dusk: For Hegel, Marx and Lukács, philosophy is a reflective enterprise and comes in post factum; hence it is not, as in Heidegger and Latour, to be made responsible for all the sins of "the moderns." Nevertheless, once we acknowledge the broad spectrum of different philosophies within modernity, and their relations to power structures in a given place and time (both aspects are missing in Latour's perspective), it is indeed important to investigate in some detail how *certain* philosophers characterized our relations to the world, including their interpretation of subjectivity and objectivity.

Lukács also finds examples for an idealism were ontology (including the intrinsic value of nature) is swallowed by a subjectivist perspective – Heidegger; and for a "physicalism" were subjective elements are wiped out and the depth of reality is reduced to mere physical things – Carnap. But these are not traits of modern philosophy (or modernity) *as such*, but examples of particular philosophies under their respective circumstances. Lukács reads the peculiarities of these two philosophies as an effect of a certain stage of capitalism, where industries and political parties increasingly use technologies of mass manipulation (the "hidden" and not so hidden persuaders of the mass media, propaganda, commercials, public relations, etc.).[94] So instead of treating all modernity with an ad hoc, catch all hypothesis, he cares for the differences: not all "modernity" was reductionist like Heidegger or Carnap. As one string of theories that was different Lukács mentions the "Philosophy of Nature" from the Renaissance up to the 19th century.[95] We could fill in the names of Bruno, Spinoza, Schelling, Goethe and Marx here. Another way to paint a more accurate picture of modernity would be an interpretation of literature, which was Lukács' main profession.

(3) Finally, a further major ontological difference between Latour and Lukács is the relation between nature and society. This can be connected to the question of subject and object, but it is far from being the same distinction.[96] In a nutshell, here the difference is the following: In questioning the existence of both nature and society as such, Latour melts them together into his new mega-subject, the network, which is said to produce them both (not as independent entities, but as epiphenomena). We have seen already that this leads

---

94   One is reminded of Herbert Marcuses *One-dimensional man*. Note that Lukács had criticized Heidegger and Carnap as "irrational" already in his *Destruction of Reason* from 1954.
95   Lukács, *Zur Ontologie des gesellschaftlichen Seins* I, 355.
96   Lukács for example illustrates Hegel's disdain for nature with his claim that for Hegel, there is not subjectivity in nature (nature is not a subject–object, as it was for Schelling; Lukács, *Zur Ontologie des gesellschaftlichen Seins* I, 493).

to cynicism with regard to ecological questions. Lukács, however, considers it crucial that society and nature are separate ontological spheres. Relying on Nicolai Hartmann, Lukács develops an emergentist conception of stages, were organic nature is based on, but not reducible to inorganic nature, whereas society is based on, but is not reducible to nature. Nature can exist without nature (and has done so for millions of years), but society cannot exist without nature; in fact it is integrated into nature's metabolism.

> Der Mensch, das aktive Mitglied der Gesellschaft, der Motor ihrer Änderungen und Vorwärtsbewegungen, bleibt im biologischen Sinn unaufhebbar ein Naturwesen: Im biologischen Sinn bleibt sein Bewusstsein—trotz aller auch ontologisch entscheidenden Funktionswandlungen—untrennbaran den biologischen Reproduktionsprozess seines Leibes gebunden; in der allgemeinen Tatsache einer solchen Gebundenheit überhaupt bleibt die biologische Basis des Lebens auch in der Gesellschaft unverändert bestehen.[97]

This is the reason why the current ecological crisis is so alarming: humankind is about to destroy its own foundations. This interpretation can only be questioned if we refuse to consider nature as a realm in its own rights and to think in terms of causation altogether, as Latour tends to do. To close this paper, I would like to briefly demonstrate that this last difference between the two thinkers is politically decisive.

5   Politics of Nature, Left and Right

For many progressive writings from the 17th to the late 20th century, an ontological distinction between nature and society was a driving force.[98] Today,

---

97 Lukács, *Zur Ontologie des gesellschaftlichen Seins* II, 91. "Wenn alle jene höchst komplizierten Lebensäusserungen, die in ihrer Gesamtheit das gesellschaftliche Sein ausmachen, zur Wirklichkeit werden sollen, muss das Lebewesen Mensch vorerst sein biologisches Dasein biologisch reproduzieren können [...] die Kultur in der Zubereitung und in der Aufnahme der Nahrung mag noch so tief gesellschaftlich bedingt sein, das Sich-Nähren bleibt ein biologischer Prozess, der nach den Notwendigkeiten des Menschen als biologischen Wesens abläuft. Darum hat Marx, wie wir bereits gezeigt haben, immer wieder diesen Reproduktionsprozess als die unaufhebbare Grundlage des gesellschaftlichen Seins betrachtet" (Lukács, *Zur Ontologie des gesellschaftlichen Seins* II, 208).

98 Worster, *Nature's Economy*; Joachim Radkau, *Die Ära der Ökologie: Eine Weltgeschichte*, (München: 2011).

however, it has become difficult to maintain this distinction: Western Marxism had given up this distinction in its heyday, thus losing the support of the ecological movement that evolved in the 1970s. The distinction was only slowly rediscovered here – with Lukács being one of the first to re-elaborate a Marxist ontology of nature *separate* from society.[99] But this crucial distinction is under attack once again, in the enormously influential writings of Latour and other postmodernist writers. Therefore, this paper aimed to delineate that even though there are some surprising similarities in the approaches of Latour and Lukács, in the end the differences between their takes on ontology and on politics are enormous, and clearly Lukács' is to be preferred. I would like to illustrate this with some historical observations.

Ever since Edmund Burke published his *Reflections on the Revolution in France*, there seemed to be one reliable fact in the map of political thinking in a world that was rapidly changing: political arguments using "nature" as an ally or a rhetorical trope used to be a conservative language game. This move defended the current state of affairs in society, calling any effort to "move one" or progress an "unnatural" inclination that had to be resisted because it was "against nature."[100] The urge to live according to nature (*secundum naturam*) could even mean to step back in time, to defend backwards-looking politics or withdraw from culture altogether (as in *Walden*). The list of these conservative "politics of nature" is impressive.

Burke maintained that efforts to consciously construct new rules for society would create unruliness and enforce violence. Building on this, Thomas Malthus (1798) claimed that new laws aiming to improve the condition of the poor necessarily would have an adverse effect, due to biological processes: it would only increase the number of poor people and hence *worsen* their condition. Likewise, Social-Darwinist Scholars in the 19th and early 20th century claimed that there is a "natural selection" at work even within modern societies, so overcoming the natural laws of an unequal society would only decrease the hereditary "quality" of the population. In the 20th century, neo-conservatives and the Christian right similarly invoked a "natural order" in order to counteract political and cultural changes[101] – women and gay rights, affirmative action,

---

99 As Foster, "Marxism in the Anthropocene," one contemporary defender of this distinction, openly acknowledges.

100 Frank Hartmann, "Wider Natur. Die Biologisierung sozialer Praxis im naturwissenschaftlichen Monismus." In Harald Welzer (Hg.), *Nationalsozialismus und Moderne*. (Tübingen: 1993), 150–165; Lorraine Daston and Fernando Vidal (eds.), *The Moral Authority of Nature*. (Chicago: 2003).

101 Leo Strauss, *Natural Law and History*. (Chicago: 1953); John Finnis, *Natural Law and Natural Rights*. (Oxford: 1980).

etc. Finally, in a kindred mindset, neoliberal scholars argued that only the free play of market forces would create a "natural order" in society. Interfering with this mechanism in a Socialist or Keynesian way would lead towards totalitarian regimes.[102] Regardless of the variety within these approaches, ontologically they all share one assumption: In all of them, nature and society had been mingled into one "assemblage." Seemingly you could not criticize society without also criticizing the natural order of things, and consequently this had to appear as a preposterous undertaking. You cannot protest against gravity.

Given this unpleasant coalition of conservative, reactionary and neoliberal forces under the banner of a politics of nature from above, it is no wonder that the dominant progressive impulse during these days was to resist this trend and to argue *against naturalism*. Emancipation could then mean to free oneself both from the chains of a repressive society, and from the suggested natural limits it represented and controlled. This motive is a building block of science fiction. For example, we find such a super-naturalist belief in the forces of society in Trotsky's appeal to a Soviet super-human. Here, nature and society seemed to be decoupled, based on the progress of the sciences. Likewise, later Western Marxists disassociated themselves from naturalistic readings of Marx and Engels, claiming that Hegel's "second nature" had nothing to do with the first and was purely social. Similarly, during the neoliberal hegemony of the 1980's, postmodernist Gender-theories de-naturalized their thinking, culminating in Judith Butler's claim that not only our (social) "gender," but even our (so called natural) "sex" is socially constructed all the way down. A Gnostic view of an "unjust" nature led techno-optimists to even picture a technological enhancement of human bodies not as a threat, but as a potential liberation from natural limitations.[103] This undialectical decoupling of nature and society on the left is a surprisingly robust narrative. (So, Latour has to be credited with pointing us in a right direction, even if we neither share his diagnosis nor his therapy.)

Today, however, for two reasons reasons, this mapping of the political discourse no longer holds water. Most obviously, it is incorrect historically to assign arguments of nature only to conservative ideologies and to frame progressive agendas as anti-naturalist: As recent research on "radical enlightenment" thinkers from Spinoza to Rousseau, Helvétius and Marx has shown,

---

102   Friedrich August Hayek, *The Road to Serfdom*. (Chicago: 1944); cf. William G. Sumner before him, Christoph Henning, "Naturalistic Values and progressive politics. A missing link between Pragmatism and Social Theory." *European Journal of Pragmatism and American Philosophy*, vol. IV, no. 1 (2012a): 84–106.

103   Christoph Henning, "Review: Allen Buchanan, *Beyond Humanity. The Ethics of Biomedical Enhancement*." *Journal of Critical Realism*, vol. 11, no. 3 (2012): 395–400.

progressive authors in the 18th century used concepts of nature in a quite different way: nature was framed and experienced as a source of resistance and liberation. After 1789 it was even called "the most dangerous word in the French language."[104] In the late 20th century, another ecological or "green" thinking evolved, mainly (but not only) from the political left. Again, arguments from nature were used in order to *transform* societies towards more equality and ecological sustainability.[105] Note that in both types of a "politics of nature" from below, enlightenment liberation *from* (a repressive) society and an ecological transformation *of* (a destructive) society, nature was understood as a source of criticism, and thus it was conceptualized as ontologically separate from the forces of society.

Let us zoom in a little closer. In the first case, the argument ran like this: All human beings are "created equal," as the *Declaration of Independence* claimed and Adam Smith maintained in the same year (1776). Thus, social differences cannot be attributed to "nature," they result from social forces, such as the division of labor and the resulting segregation of social classes.[106] Consequently, arguments from nature will lead to more – not less – political and social equality.[107] This is evident even in thinkers like Hobbes:

> Nature hath made men so equal in the faculties of body and mind, as that [...] the difference between man and man is not so considerable as that one man can thereupon claim to himself any benefit to which another may not pretend as well as he.[108]

The radical consequences were clear: If people are more or less equal by nature, but an oppressive and exploitative society treats them unequally, this aberration must be overcome. The quest for more equality was thus driven by naturalistic reasoning. This 18th century trend survived in the writings of Karl

---

104 Radkau, *Die Ära der Ökologie*, 38.
105 Jost Hermand, *Grüne Utopien in Deutschland. Zur Geschichte des ökologischen Bewusstseins*. (Frankfurt a. M.: 1991); Ramachandra Guha and Madhav Gadgil, *Ecology and Equity: The Use and Abuse of Nature in Contemporary India*. (Abingdon: 1995).
106 "The difference of natural talents in different men is, in reality, much less than we are aware of; and the very different genius which appears to distinguish men of different professions, when grown up to maturity, is not upon many occasions so much the cause, as the effect of the division of labour. The difference between the most dissimilar characters, between a philosopher and a common street porter, for example, seems to arise not so much from nature, as from habit, custom, and education" Adam Smith, *The Wealth of Nations*, Book I, Chapter 2 (1776).
107 Henning, "Naturalistic Values and progressive politics."
108 Hobbes, *Leviathan* (1651), 183; Book I, Chapter XIII.

Marx and progressive authors of the 20th century like Dewey or R.H. Tawney. A related argument was the *alienation* of human beings from their natures by a society that forced people to work long hours of mechanical repetition in dark and dirty places, without proper food, leisure time or even light, without opportunities to socialize or be creative. However, in order for arguments from nature to function as a corrective of social oppression, nature had to be conceptualized as a distinct power, separate from society. Of course, society depends on nature for its reproduction – Enlightenment thinkers from Spinoza to Helvetius saw that clearly, and that is also the crucial difference between a naturalist Marxism and a supernaturalist utopia. But if society manages to denaturalize social relations, it has to be considered as an entity following its own rules. Lukács' solution to this was dialectical – in modern terms, one could say that society depends on nature, evolving as an "emergent" entity which in turn cannot be explained by nature alone. We cannot reverse the relation: society depends on or emerges from nature, but certainly the opposite is not true.

In the second case, the ecological movement included the experience and evaluation of nature not only as a source of resistance against an oppressive and exploitative society, but also as an *object* of politics: after industrial farming, mining, mass production and massive pollution had changed the faith of the earth to a degree that left both people and wildlife unhealthy, that shortened people's lifespan and deforested the faith of the earth, it seemed obvious that nature itself needed protection and preservation.[109] Arguments from nature were important sources for a progressive mobilization against social mechanisms of oppression, exploitation, plunder, pollution and waste. And again, in order to protect wildlife and the atmosphere from the destructive forces of an unchecked industrialization, forces of society and of nature needed to be distinguished conceptually. An ontological distinction aims to distinguish different factors within the "given" (e.g., when climate research identifies the particular impact of human activities to global warming), it does not exclude interaction between the two; in fact, the very problem at the heart of ecological concern is the *kind* of interaction between the two – here a particularly careless one. We can now access the political relevance of the ontological difference between Lukács and Latour: as we learned today, Marx's thought had a deep naturalistic undercurrent, inspired by romantic philosophies of nature and from early ecological scientists,[110] and Lukács honored this heritage, trying to substantiate it by importing elements from Nicolai Hartmann and

---

109 Radkau, *Die Ära der Ökologie*; Hermand, *Grüne Utopien in Deutschland.*
110 Kohei Saito, *Capital, Nature, and the unfinished Critique of Political Economy. Karl Marx's Ecosocialism.* (New York: 2017), 141ff.

historians of nature. Latour, on the other hand, does decidedly not take up older progressive ideas, but rather the undifferentiated "politics of nature" that we know from conservatives and reactionaries where both were already read into one another. So, the important message is that when we are inspired by the recent material or ontological turn, we have to choose very carefully *which* ontology we would like to rely on. Latour's fancy texts are glittering yet fatal, but Lukács' writings deserve a new reading.

PART 4

Toward a Critical Social Ontology

∴

CHAPTER 11

From Critical Theory to Critical Ontology: Back to Lukács!

Michael Morris

1   Where We Stand

For many years, we have been inundated by strident laments of fascism and ubiquitous Nazi comparisons, which, all too often, reflect and remain mired within the emotivist hyperbole, titillated hysteria, and lack of historical perspective that mar contemporary social discourse. Like the boy who cries wolf, those who endlessly and ignorantly yell "fascist" or "Nazi" have blunted our capacity for thoughtful alarm and hindered more serious reflections upon the ultimate significance, social roots, and persistent threats of fascism. Such facile rhetoric appears unfortunate, particularly to those of us who remain convinced that the Twentieth Century emergence of fascism – I here use the term rather indiscriminately, without considering potential differences between fascism, Nazism, authoritarianism, totalitarianism, etc. – signaled a fundamental shift and persistent crisis in the foundations that support our collective existence. This crisis, we maintain, is systemic, transcultural, and deeply rooted in longstanding historical developments. A proper analysis therefore demands that we interpret particular policies, actions, and actors as the symptomatic manifestations, not as the direct causes, of the threat we face. We must ascertain the foundational shifts that span political parties and even the supposedly dramatic differences between the Continental European and the Anglo-American political traditions. Looking beyond the latest outrage, we must therefore encounter and consider the broader contours of a crisis that emerges as the misbegotten but undeniable progeny of enlightenment, as the disturbing fruition of much that seemed best, not as the atavistic return of an insufficiently vanquished evil.

   In proposing this admittedly grand interpretive framework for the maladies of the present, I wish to echo, partially endorse, and partially transform the rich tradition of analysis provided by many German *émigrés* who fled the Nazis and settled on American or British shores, the analysis developed by members of the Frankfurt School, critical theorists such as Max Horkheimer, Theodore

Adorno, Herbert Marcuse, and Erich Fromm, as well as by other unattached thinkers, such as Hannah Arendt and Karl Mannheim. The *émigré* generation of critical theorists all rather infamously insisted upon the merely superficial divergence between Nazi totalitarianism and post-war American liberalism, at least in their basic tendencies, if not in their bloody extremities. While I shall draw upon and defend this basic thesis, I readily acknowledge that the political sympathies and the temperamental dispositions of early critical theorists create serious obstacles to a sympathetic consideration of their analysis. It is initially tempting to dismiss the Frankfurt School's interpretation of Anglo-American society as the result of traumatically induced paranoia and the anxieties of cultural dislocation. The members of the Frankfurt School never show much familiarity with – let alone genuine sympathy for – the indigenous particularities of Anglo-American political and cultural traditions. Moreover, the structure and tenor of their prose displays a remarkable susceptibility to various forms of atompsheric moodiness. The reader finds many extended passages in Adorno, Horkheimer, and Marcuse that veer amidst a range of discontented moods, from the cranky discomfort of the aging traditionalist, to the anti-democratic disdain fostered by elite cultural privilege, to the exhilarating, self-flattering, conspiratorial, and totalizing suspicion of youthful rebellion. Even if we share and appreciate these moods, they hardly provide a basis for serious social analysis. It may thus be helpful, here at the outset, to recall the comments of more placid observers, such as Arendt and Mannheim, both of whom displayed deep sympathy for selected aspects of Anglo-American political and cultural traditions.

Consider Arendt. Despite her epoch-making appreciation of the republican dimensions of the American Revolution,[1] and despite the striking objectivity or emotional distance that her writings display, she shares the general Frankfurt School interpretation of the Nazi regime as the localized manifestation of deeply rooted, persistent, and geographically ubiquitous social developments. In *The Origins of Totalitarianism*, she interprets the emergence of Nazi and Soviet totalitarianism as the warped fruition and self-destruction of the Western tradition. She concludes:

> We can no longer afford to take that which was good in the past and simply call it our heritage, to discard the bad and simply think of it as a dead load which by itself time will bury in oblivion. The subterranean stream

---

1 Hannah Arendt, *On Revolution*. (New York: Penguin Books, 2006).

of Western history has finally come to the surface and usurped the dignity of our tradition.²

In an apt word of warning to the more Whiggish celebrants of contemporary liberal culture, Arendt insists upon what we might call the dialectical entanglement of the good and bad dimensions of our tradition. This concurs with the analysis of Horkheimer and Adorno, who make a similar point in *Dialectic of Enlightenment*, where they analyze "enlightenment thought" as the source of both human liberation *and* the emergent trend towards totalitarian styles of human management. They rightly argue that the dominant traditions of "critical thinking" ultimately breed a distinctly modern amalgam of acquiescent conformity and unbridled irrationality.³

Without minimizing many nuanced and important differences, we nonetheless see that Arendt, Horkheimer, and Adorno share an interpretation of Nazi Germany as a singular revelation of the inherent tensions in Western social and intellectual life, not as a distinctly German aberration, not as the failure of the German people to appreciate the wisdom of the Anglo-Saxon political tradition.⁴ Elsewhere, Arendt makes the geographical ubiquity and persistence of the problem plain. She first considers and then affirms that "what we usually call the crisis of our century...is no mere threat from the outside, no mere result of some aggressive foreign policy of either Germany or Russia, and...it will no more disappear with the death of Stalin than it disappeared with the fall of Nazi Germany."⁵

We find a similar analysis in Mannheim, a man who expresses his deep sympathy for the liberal political traditions of his adopted home. He is a man, he tells us, for whom "freedom" and "personal responsibility" are "the highest of all values."⁶ Unlike his British and American counterparts, however, he claims to recognize the fragile and deeply imperiled nature of these values. He thus notes the fundamental difference between the Anglo-American and German perspectives on the ultimate scope and nature of the crisis that produced fascism:

---

2 Hannah Arendt, *Origins of Totalitarianism*. (New York: Harcourt, Inc., 1976), ix.
3 Max Horkheimer and Theodore W. Adorno, *Dialektik der Aufklärung*. (Frankfurt am Main: Fischer Verlag), 3.
4 Cf. Isaiah Berlin, *Liberty*. (Oxford: Oxford University Press, 2004), 166–217.
5 Arendt (1976), 460.
6 Karl Mannheim, *Man and Society in an Age of Reconstruction*. (New York: Harcourt, Inc., 1954), 4.

> We should not try to belittle or conceal the difference between these points of view. It is most clearly expressed in the fact that to the Western countries the collapse of liberalism and democracy and the adoption of a totalitarian system seem to be the passing symptoms of a crisis which is confined to a few nations, while those who live within the danger zone experience this transition as a change in the very structure of modern society…those who have first-hand knowledge of the crisis, even if they are keen opponents of dictatorship, are united in the belief that both the social order and the psychology of human beings are changing through and through, and that if this is an evil it is an evil which sooner or later is bound to spread.[7]

The language of "spreading" remains misleading, unduly benign, for Mannheim elsewhere describes the crisis as "the crater which is yawning beneath our Western society."[8] The foundation is gone. We stand upon illusions.

In a time when the reigning orthodoxies of democracy and liberalism once again meet with apathy, disapproval, and skepticism, we face similar questions: do recent events merely reveal the fragility of our cherished ideals in the face of the recalcitrant, backward, and atavistic force gathering *out there*? Or is the problem deeper? Do the things we fear and loathe emerge from the forces and ideals we publically cherish? In response to these questions, I here develop two main lines of argument. First, drawing upon insights from the variations on critical theory developed by Marcuse, Horkheimer, and Adorno, I argue that the persistent threat of fascism emerges directly and inevitably from our complexly intertwined commitments (a) to what I shall here characterize as "doctrinaire liberalism," (b) to positivistic restrictions on science and epistemic authority, (c) and to the forms of commodity production and contractual exchange that constitute free markets. I argue that the noisy and frantic promotion of liberal ideals, scientific forms of expertise, and free markets will only exacerbate the problem of fascism and obscure all possible solutions. While this first argument draws upon and endorses dominant themes from traditional critical theory, my second line of argument suggests the ultimate failure of critical theory to overcome the positivistic conception of reason and the liberal conceptions of freedom, community, and normativity. My second line of argument thus introduces and defends Georg Lukács' *critical ontology* as the successful completion of the basic aims of the project of critical theory. I argue that traditional critical theorists pursue broadly neo-Kantian strategies that

---

7 Mannheim (1954), 3.
8 Mannheim (1954), 5.

already presuppose too many framing assumptions shared by positivism and liberalism. By contrast, Lukács pursues an Hegelian-Marxist strategy that is overtly ontological (rather than epistemological), and that is sociologically and historically concrete (rather than abstract or formal-legalistic) in its approach to questions of individuality, community, and normativity.

2 Positivism: The Epistemic Spirit of the Age

We shall here define and analyze positivism in terms of five central claims. First, positivism follows the modern philosophical insistence upon the prioritization of epistemology over ontology. According to this view, all pre-epistemological ontology is naïve, dogmatic, and dangerous, while the recognition of the priority of epistemology represents the beginning and the essence of critical thought. Second, positivism accepts a rigid distinction between the *a priori* and the *a posteriori*. It thereby posits and endorses the ideal of a clean separation between responsible scientific claims and every tainting admixture of philosophical speculation. Third, positivism rejects the synthetic *a priori*, and it therefore reduces the *a priori* dimension of thought to the tasks of logical and semantic analysis. Fourth, positivism reduces the *a posteriori* task of thought to the formulation of laws that facilitate prediction and the manipulation of material. Fifth, positivism rejects the cognitive status of ethics and the semantic content of metaphysics and religion. It unmasks all three as veiled and manipulative forms of emotive expression. Taken together, claims three through five render reason strictly instrumental. Unable to determine or adjudicate the proper ends of existence and action, reason simply facilitates the manipulation of objects. While early critical theorists repeatedly and rightly elucidate the devastating social implications that follow from the acceptance of the purely instrumental conception of reason [Section Four], they never sufficiently challenge claims one and two. They largely accept both (1) the priority of epistemology over ontology and (2) the basic distinction between the *a priori* and the *a posteriori*. These assumptions render anemic and ultimately unsuccesful their varied attempts to rehabilitate some non-instrumental conception of reason. The following discussion of positivism therefore devotes considerable attention to the Hegelian-Marxist lines of argument that Lukác's employs to dismantle these basic assumptions.

Beginning with Descartes, modern philosophers, including the logical positivists, have generally insisted that the successful completion of epistemology must precede, guide, and limit all ontological claims. Before we can know the nature of being, we must, as responsible thinkers, determine the foundation, method, and limits of knowledge. Over the past 400 years, this epistemology-first strategy has yielded strictly negative forms of criticism, but only minimal positive results. This strategy effectively destroys the epistemic pretenses of the intellectual culprit *de jour*, but it does not positively bolster the reigning consensus, let alone advance our knowledge in new directions. The critical or negative efficacy of this strategy is easy to understand: without being able to presuppose any of the things that we purportedly know, we cannot explain how it is that we might know them. The supposedly responsible bracketing of all first-order knowledge claims inevitably undermines the only plausible basis for articulating and defending second-order claims about the nature of knowledge as such. It seems plain that at least moderately successful cognitive practice must precede and ground the reflexive knowing of epistemology.[9]

The effective critical function of the epistemology-first strategy further derives from the difficulty of self-reflection, from the ways that effective practice frequently – perhaps even permanently and inevitably – outstrips our reflexive attempts at methodological codification. Many fluent speakers of ordinary language cannot reflectively articulate the rules they follow. Many successful scientists profess simplistic caricatures of the history and methodology of science. Excellent judges of human veracity cannot fully articulate the rules that distinguish the lie from the truth. Indeed, our cognitive capacities are remarkably nuanced and complex. They can be relatively trustworthy and objectively sound, even when we are incapable of fully articulating the methods they embody.

While the epistemology-first strategy forms an effective critical front against its hapless interrogees, it tacitly shelters dogmatism and fosters numerous dimensions of the *status quo* epistemic consensus. We must therefore, in the words of Lukács, reveal "the philosophical predominance of epistemology as a necessary ideology."[10] The epistemology-first strategy comes in two forms, both of which ironically tend to bracket and shield their fundamental presuppositions from the realm of rational dispute. In its more rarified or pure form, the epistemology-first project necessarily begins with an illicit and implausible set of ontological assumptions. In various particular ways, the epistemology-first project isolates and identifies some single privileged domain of being which it presumes to be (a) immediately and unproblematically given, (b) fully distinct

---

9 See Michael Morris, *Knowledge and Ideology*. (Cambridge: Cambridge University Press, 2016), 234–239, and Karl Mannheim, *Ideology and Utopia*. (New York: Harcourt, Inc., 1985), 288–289.
10 Georg Lukács, *Zur Ontologie des gesellschaftlichen Seins, 1. Halband* (Darmstadt: Hermann Luchterhand Verlag, 1984), 34.

or separate from all other beings or domains, and yet (c) uniquely able to transcend itself in its drive to comprehend all other beings. In Descartes and the British Empiricists, this privileged being is the mind of the individual knower, a purportedly self-enclosed realm of ideas and images. In this tradition's Twentieth Century positivist redux, language comes to occupy this privileged position.[11] The history of post-Cartesian philosophy offers many other candidates as well, including lived experience, the subject, texts, the self-positing I, etc.

The epistemology-first position simply begins with the *unargued* – often even unrecognized – rejection of ontological holism. It tacitly assumes that some region of being can be completely and adequately given in isolation from all other regions. More specifically, it assumes that the rational activities and normative rules of language or the mind can ultimately be abstracted from and analyzed prior to any application to the domain of empirical fact. In the "Introduction" to the *Phenomenology of Spirit*, Hegel highlights the tacit ontological commitments that structure every form of epistemology. In particular, the epistemology-first project always begins with the (ontological) assumption, "that the Absolute stands on one side and knowing stands on the other side, for itself, divided from the absolute, *but nonetheless something real*" [emphasis added].[12] Mind, language, the subject – these are real. Any claim about the mind or language is already an ontological claim. Such pre-epistemological claims only seem unproblematic if we ignore their ontological status, or, alternatively, if we the accept the further ontological assumption that this special region of being is self-contained and directly given, while all other regions of being are only mediately accessible through it.

More importantly still, there is no generic epistemological project. Terms like "mind" or "subject" only acquire meaning within the context of some particular ontological distinction between mind and world, subject and object.[13] In other words, our conception of and access to the mind or subject always presupposes some prior assumptions that distinguish the subject from the object. Some particular form of this distinction always precedes epistemology proper, shaping the very contours and aims of any supposedly critical inquiry into the possibility, nature, and limits of knowing. For instance, much early analytic philosophy simply begins with the distinction between language and world. This tradition identifies language with thought, and it treats language

---

11   For a forceful critique of these traditions, see Richard Rorty, *Philosophy and the Mirror of Nature*. (Princeton: Princeton University Press, 1980), 131–212.
12   G.W.F. Hegel, *Phänomenologie des Geistes*. (Frankfurt am Main: Suhrkamp Verlag, 1986b), 70.
13   Hegel (1986b), 71.

first and foremost as a series of declarative sentences. The British Empiricists begin with the still more peculiar presumption that private sensations or impressions are more evident, immediate, and susceptible to analytical individuation than are stones, trees, and turtles. Other philosophers provide more thematic guidance in helping us to "discover" the realm of ontologically uncommitted thought. In the "First Meditation," Descartes guides us through a process of doubt that purportedly strips away the world and leaves us with the immediately given realm of the mind. Husserl's *epoché* serve a similar function, as does Fichte's "First Introduction" to the *Wissenschaftslehre*, which teaches the reader to distinguish between the given material of inner sense and the pure spontaneity of the self-positing I.[14]

In *The Ontology of Social Being*, Lukács develops this Hegelian line of criticism: "the methodological starting-point for every 'critical' stance is, in fact," he argues, "the separation of method from reality, thought from being."[15] The supposedly critical stance of the epistemology-first tradition always presupposes the clean distinction between thought and being, where the former is immediate and unencumbered by the entanglements of being. This tradition therefore begins by ignoring or tacitly rejecting the guiding principle of the Hegel-Marxist tradition: "the dialectical [and thus inextricable] relation between subject and object in the historical-process [as a totality]."[16] The social objects in the historical process derive their organizational forms from the initially conscious or semi-conscious aims of the subject, while consciousness itself always emerges as the attempt to guide and uphold these formative processes, particularly in the face of surrounding obstacles that threaten the smooth function of the socialized body and its materially embedded projects. On this view, the subject and the object are not distinct realms that stand in relations of reciprocal cause and effect. Instead, the subject relates to the object as consciousness relates to any embodied action.

Consciousness or attention accompanies and guides activity at many levels, sometimes largely submerged beneath other modes of attention or inattention (I stir the sauce in the pot while thinking of Terrence Malik's latest film.), sometimes focused on the object of the activity (I focus on the sauce congealing on the bottom of the pot.), sometimes focused on the methods or particular decisions that guide the activity (Should I have used a different pot or lower heat?). My consciousness is not a stable or self-enclosed domain that stands in

---

14   J.G. Fichte, *Werke,* vol. 1. (Berlin: Walter de Gruyter & Co, 1971), 412–449.
15   Georg Lukács, *Geschichte und Klassenbewußtsein*. (Berlin: Hermann Luchterhand Verlag, 1968), 174.
16   Lukács (1968), 173.

mechanistic causal relations to the pan via my body. It is the dependent but necessary accompaniment of all voluntary biological action. In many ways, the difference between the ontology and epistemology derives from the difference between direct and reflexive attention. Obviously, reflexive attention must often guide and correct more direct forms of engagement and awareness. Thus every critical approach to natural and social being must consider the modes or rules that inform our attentive directedness towards it. However, this rule-governed attentiveness emerges from, remains entangled within, and is ultimately directed towards material processes in the world.

Moving beyond the basic dialectical structure of the relation between subject and object, we must further remember that the objective or ontological context, ground, and end of thought can only be properly conceived in terms of their further relations to being as *a dynamic or historical totality*. "The objective form of the object of knowledge is determined by its relation to the whole."[17] Neither thought nor the objective processes are ever immediately given. They are always dialectically intertangled and essentially informed or constituted by their relation to the concrete and dynamic totality of being. This commitment to ontological holism leads Marx to develop a novel approach to science, one that rejects the rigid distinctions between philosophy and science, the *a priori* and the *a posteriori*, theory and observation:

> It [Marx's approach] is a construction of an entirely new character: a form of science, which, in the process of generalization, never leaves the realm of science, but which, nonetheless, in every determination of fact, and in every conceptual presentation of concrete relations, always keeps the totality of social being in view. *It is from the standpoint of this totality that it evaluates the reality and the significance of every individual phenomenon.* It never soars above the phenomena under investigation, through the reification of self-evident abstractions, but rather it remains an ontological-philosophical observation of the reality as it itself is, and it [the approach] has therefore obtained the highest level of critical and self-critical consciousness [emphasis added].[18]

There is no subjective, mental, linguistic, formal, logical, or *a priori* realm that precedes, guides, and justifies our access to empirical facts. However, this does not reduce thought to the mere recognition and collection of given empirical facts. Indeed, thought must interrogate and transcend the facts to determine

---

17   Lukács (1968), 185.
18   Lukács (1984), 572.

their true shape and significance, to determine the distinction between appearance and essence. However, this transcendence of appearance seeks neither (a) the noumenal reality *behind* the facts, nor (b) the essence that lies *within* or *under* the facts, nor (c) the universal mental or subjective forms that first *constitute* the facts, nor (d) the Platonic forms that the facts imperfectly imitate. For Marx, thought transcends the initial appearance of the facts through its ability to trace the constitutive relation of the initially apparent facts to the historical totality of being.

If there is no self-evident, isolated, ahistorical, or self-determining starting point within the historical totality of being, then we must reject every temptation to soar "above the phenomena" through "the reification of self-evident abstractions." Abstractions never simply limn the discrete, stable, and directly given joints of reality, as certain forms of naïve or dogmatic ontological realism maintain. Nor do they reflect the self-grounding rules, the given empirical interests, or the self-transparent and autonomous volitions that guide some pristine subjective process of abstraction. The divisions that render reality discrete or given are the product of an empirical subject, which is itself the tangled synthesis of (a) selected objective processes or material practices formed by the historical process and (b) the reflexive and always only partially transparent striving to interpret, harmonize, and transform the same. Critical ontology therefore interrogates the given, the presupposed and often actively maintained divisions that structure our access to empirical facts. However, this interrogation does not turn inward. It does not seek a universal, historical, or pragmatic *a priori* in language, mind, or the subject. This initially plausible move simply reifies and endorse some particular abstract division between the mind and the world, between the *a priori* and the *a posteriori*. Instead, critical ontology pursues a richer but also more tentative strategy: it seeks to integrate some guiding set of articulations within the totality of a broader historical process, the process that itself provides these distinctions with their source or ground, their often distorting context, and their final end.

Having artificially and rigidly separated the mind from the world, the pure forms of the epistemology-first strategy have inevitably failed to unite what they have severed, to show how mind or language comes into contact with something beyond itself. This has led to the development of what we might call *the impure variation of the epistemology-first strategy*. This strategy more or less tacitly (a) selects and analyzes some body of widely accepted knowledge, and then (b) shows how the basic methods and mental operations thus abstracted either may or may not be applied to some further set of objects. Even Descartes already mingles the pure and impure strategies, drawing upon the success of mathematics to provide a basic model for his philosophical quest.

The mingling of the pure and impure strategies finds heightened expression in Kant's critical philosophy. In the *Critique of Pure Reason*, Kant begins by accepting the synthetic *a priori* knowledge of geometry and physics. Through a series of transcendental arguments, he employs the presumed legitimacy of such knowledge claims to determine the forms of intuition and the basic rules of judgment, and he then employs this account of the mind to demonstrate the illegitimacy of transcendent metaphysics and all knowledge of the thing in itself. Of course, Kant also develops alternative strands of argument. In the antinomies, for instance, he argues that metaphysical claims necessarily embroil us in contradiction. In his "purest" moments – the Transcendental Deduction and Chapter Three of the *Groundwork for the Metaphysics of Morals* – he anticipates Fichte's project: the attempt to deduce all knowledge from some very basic and undeniable truth about the self-determination of pure apperception and/or moral agency.

In *Eclipse of Reason*, Horkheimer interprets positivism as strictly impure deployment of the epistemology-first strategy. It begins with "physics" as the paradigm of knowledge, and it rejects all forms of knowing that do not conform with its methods and techniques. "The positivists," according to Horkheimer, "reduce science to the procedures employed in physics and its branches; they deny the name of science to all theoretical efforts not in accord with what they abstract from physics as its legitimate methods."[19] In other words, the positivists accept physics as the model of knowledge. They determine its principles and procedures, identify these with knowledge *tout court*, and then develop a theory of the methods and limits of knowing. Obviously, this procedure threatens to become circular. The positivists claim, "that their own insights are scientific, holding that their cognition of science is based upon the observation of science." But Horkheimer rightly asks: "How is it possible to determine what justly may be called science and truth, if the determination itself presupposes the methods of achieving scientific truth?" The positivists select physics as the model and paradigm of knowledge, and they use this model to abstract and articulate the basic principles that govern knowledge. However, the defense of their initial choice of paradigm must have some ground or basis, and it seems that this could only come from some theory of knowledge. Horkheimer thus accuses the positivists of "begging the question," and he suggests that their position ultimately rests upon the "mere worship of institutionalized science."[20]

---

19   Max Horkheimer, *Eclipse of Reason*. (Oxford: Oxford University Press, 1947), 75.
20   Horkheimer (1947), 76.

In opposition to this circular procedure, Horkheimer defends the primacy of philosophy, arguing that, "science should expect philosophical thought...to account for the nature of truth rather than simply to boost scientific methodology as the ultimate definition of truth."[21] Unfortunately, this suggestion remains ambiguous and underdeveloped. As it stands, this remark recalls and even appears to endorse the pure-epistemology first strategy promulgated by Descartes, Fichte, or Husserl, a strategy that attempts to ground the legitimacy of empirical knowledge in some special form of philosophical or *a priori* inquiry. At times, however, Horkheimer points towards the procedures and questions of critical ontology. In response to the positivists presumptive acceptance of physics, Horkheimer observes that, "the division of all human truth into science and humanities is itself a social product that was hypothesized by the organization of the universities."[22] In "Traditional and Critical Theory," Horkheimer develops this point a bit further. He criticizes traditional theory for accepting "the scientific division of labor," for failing to consider the ways that the divisions (a) between disciplines and (b) between the formal and institutionalized pursuit of knowledge in the university and the varied productive practices that constitute the remainder of society. He then suggests that critical theory must render "the interrelations between the individual activities [of the university and society at large] immediately transparent."[23] Unfortunately, Horkheimer does not sufficiently develop this suggestion. For instance, he never considers how this particular component of critical theory will differ from an institutionally renegade form of empirical sociology. Stated differently, he never develops the kind of holistic and processual social ontology that overcomes the traditional distinction between the *empirical* and the *a priori*.

We might further note that Horkheimer's criticism of positivism is hasty and unfair. Positivism does not merely consist in the "worship of institutionalized science." The positivists can give reasons for privileging physics as the paradigm of knowledge, though these reasons themselves raise further questions. Horkheimer briefly considers such reasons as articulated by Sidney Hook. Hook ascribes the unique essence of science to the fact that its claims are "established by methods of public verification open to all who submit themselves to its disciplines."[24] More importantly, perhaps, these methods of public verification involve the ability to foresee and control the outcome of

---

21   Horkheimer (1947), 73.
22   Horkheimer (1947), 75.
23   Max Horkheimer, *Traditionelle und kritische Theorie*. (Frankfurt am Main: Fischer Taschenbuch Verlag, 2005), 214.
24   Horkheimer (1947), 73.

particular events. Unlike many other types of knowledge claims, the well-established claims of physics can (in principle) be inter-subjectively or publically verified through relatively evident cannons of method, and they can be employed to produce desired outcomes. While *public verifiability* and *utility* play a predominate role in the contemporary evaluation of purported forms of cognitive inquiry, it is not self-evident that they provide the only legitimate criteria. It is not even obvious that public verifiability and utility represent necessary conditions for knowledge. In the allegory of the cave, for instance, Plato presents true knowledge as a kind of useless and discursively incommunicable contemplation of the good that necessarily invites public misunderstanding and mockery. In more mundane terms, Aristotle conceives virtue as an important form of habitualized practical knowledge that can neither be codified nor exhaustively defended in universal and abstract terms.

In actual practice, we employ a very broad range of values in determining our engagement with – and eventual commitment to – particular disciplines or knowledge projects. In complex and tacit ways, we evaluate knowledge projects in terms of the ideal ends of communicability, public justifiability, existential significance, quantifiability, technological applicability, and political implication. We further find ourselves called to inquire by attitudes ranging from anxiety to Aristotelian wonder, from the ephemeral moment of passing curiosity to the life-transforming call of beauty,[25] from the boredom of endless consumption and comfort to the unrelenting anguish of systemic degradation.[26] In every case, the epistemic relevance and ultimate justification of these values derives from the epistemology and ontology we accept (partly under their direction). There is no epistemology- and ontology-neutral way to evaluate these meta-epistemological values. Depending upon our ontological commitments, we might deem communicability, simplicity, and beauty either as signs of truth or as symptoms of bad-faith anthropomorphic projection.

Every particular epistemology thus always comes fraught with tacit commitments to existing forms of inquiry, along with the practical values and the ontological assumptions that frame them. The epistemology-first strategy denies such attachments, thereby uncritically shielding its presuppositions from debate. We should note that our insistence upon the derivative status of epistemology does not foreclose rational deliberation. Instead, the project of

---

25   For a striking discussion of the epistemic role of beauty, see Hans Urs von Balthasar, *Herrlichkeit: Eine Theologische Ästhetik, Band I* (Trier: Johannes Verlag, 1988), particularly 15–42.

26   With regards to this final distinction between boredom and degredation, see the differentiation between the bohemian and proletarian critiques of the bourgeoisie in Morris (2016), 125–178.

critical ontology renders rational deliberation richer, but also more complex, open-ended, and indirect. It forces us into the cycles of dialectic, as we tease out the complex reciprocal relations between epistemology and ontology, between our doxastic and our socio-existential commitments. Every epistemology presupposes an ontology, but every ontology also presupposes an epistemology. Every claim about being emerges from tacit forms of cognitive practice. Likewise, every attempt to articulate and defend a cognitive practice must first identify and characterize that practice, distinguishing it from other practices and domains of being. Moreover, the defense of a particular cognitive practice presupposes a range of social and/or existential commitments, which themselves in turn presuppose a number of claims about being and knowledge. Our social and existential commitments are never brute givens: they only emerge and take articulate form against the background of our beliefs about being and our appraisal of various modalities of human knowing.

Critical ontology comprises the core of this dialectical endeavor. In epistemology, as in politics, theory derives its content from successful practice. There can be no pure political or epistemic theory. The attempt to ground empirical practice in some *a priori* or traditionally philosophical domain yields disconnected abstractions that deny but never fully bracket the commitments to particular epistemic or political practices, which, in fact, guide these *a priori* fantasies and give them their limited content. However, the demise of pure epistemology does not provide invitation or license to reify our *de facto* epistemic and political commitments. As Lukács rightly notes, "the direct, absolute, and uncritical declaration of praxis as the criterion of theory is not unproblematic." The predominance of practice over theory suggests that the strength and content of our epistemological and meta-ethical theories always ultimately derives from our particular cognitive and normative commitments. True criticism therefore cannot precede via some pure strategy of epistemic doubt or moral abstraction. True criticism must be ontological criticism. This "ontological critique must necessarily be concrete:" it must not abstract from the particular practices and commitments under consideration. Instead, it must consider the source, context, and aim of the particular practice within the "social totality."[27]

We must apply critical ontology to positivism, itself conceived as a particular manifestation of the modern prioritization of epistemology over ontology. Here we must consider positivism and the modern prioritization of epistemology within the broader history of philosophy, particularly as that history

---

27   Lukács (1984), 60.

reveals the shifting relationship between philosophy, personal redemption, and political order. In almost all its forms, ancient philosophy is anti-political. It defines itself as a way of life outside and against the political domain. In this sense, ancient philosophy is first and foremost a kind of individual self-formation or self-care. Beginning in the early modern period, philosophy comes to adopt an inherently collective and political aim. It attempts to replace violence with argument, conflictual disagreement with harmonious order. It represents the attempt to construct society in accordance with principles that enjoy universal, rational consent. In pursuit of such consent, it attempts to adjudicate all disagreements and differences upon the basis of previously established, universally accepted, and strictly determinate methods. This explains the social presupposition of the epistemology-first strategy: before we debate particular questions, we must secure the universal principles that shall govern dispute. In this sense, the ideals of the epistemology-first strategy find their overt political analogue in the ideal of the written constitution. In both cases, some idealized universal consent to a set of relatively abstract procedures serves to underwrite and purportedly to ensure the unambiguous rational determination of particular contested cases. In our pursuit of unanimity via rational consent, we thus reify method, treating it as the stable, independent, exhaustive, and self-justifying ground of practice.

In reality, constitutional debate and scientific practice radically outstrip the simple principles and supposedly unambiguous procedures respectively elaborated by the constitution and the methodological cannons of science. While constitutional law thus tends to become a tortured but necessary game forced to obscure its reasoning behind the veneer of an aged document, the scientific practice retains is central epistemic status, largely due to the economic and utilitarian forces that promote the continued spread of its institutional existence. As all areas of business, health, and education become increasingly intertwined with the institutional regimentation of technological development, the sheer omnipresence of scientific practices and results yields an impressive air of sociological reality. It is the social reality and prolific instantiation of cognitive practices that lends them the bulk of their social epistemic force, not some rarified theoretical awareness of the historical arguments that ground them.

3 Liberalism: The Well-Worn Path

Our strong commitment to the priority of method and the possibility of procedurally generated consensus suggests deep affinities between positivism and what we might call doctrinaire liberalism. Here we must carefully distinguish between the modest and the doctrinaire strands of liberalism. In its modest form, liberalism simply recognizes the pluralistic nature of contemporary societies, and it approaches politics as the attempt to cultivate and tend some fragile and ultimately contingent *modus vivendi*. Modest liberalism acknowledges the persistence of disagreement and difference, and it privileges messy compromise, inefficiency, and imperfect political union as the price of non-genocidal coexistence. As a rough working tradition that rests upon a deep preference for non-violent coexistence, modest liberalism has much to recommend it, though I think it now blinds us to the true nature and the deepest problems of contemporary society. In its current form, global capitalism does not ultimately permit the rich co-existence of alternative communities, each with some robust but competing conception of the good. We are not really a pluralistic society, at least insofar as pluralism entails a series of developed but conflicting practices or concrete modes of living together that embody some tacit, cooperative vision of the good. Instead, we are an ever more homogeneous and atomized society, where market exchange increasingly determines all forms of human interaction, where culture increasingly takes the form of the commodified holidays, cuisine, music, or dress; where religion becomes a private form of self-help; and where discussions of the good life founder upon fantastical visions of autonomy and the supposed psychological bedrock of personal preferences and private pleasures.

We should here be very careful to note that a homogenous and atomized global society does not resolve difference and dispute. Such societies will be homogenous, but not harmonious. The dramatic epistemic finitude of the individual, the incoherence of radical self-creation, and the fragility of the self in the face the of interpenetrating totalities of nature and society – these and other persistent dimensions of the human condition compel individuals to seek forms of corporate security, identitarian belonging, and doxastic guidance, though these increasingly come in ideological, politicized, symbolic, and fantastical form. *Much like successful cognitive practice, properly binding communal relations have complex forms that outstrip reflexive formulation.* Highly conscious or reflective forms of communal identity are almost always simplistic, reductive, oppressive, and derivative. Indeed, high levels of communal self-reflection usually derive from acute internal conflict, from external threat, or from the rapid onset of disintegration. Note well: the ideal relative absence of *communal* self-reflection should not be taken to suggest either the possibility or even the desirability of some strictly pre-reflective and "naturally" harmonious form of communal life. There is no natural, pre-reflective, and purely harmonious communal life.[28] All forms of human existence involve conflict and (thus) the need for reflection. However, in a healthy community, the conflict and the resolution focus on *particular* issues or relationships, while the community as such remains a more or less diffuse background. It is like the ecosystem that provides the broader framework and common space for conflict, cooperation, and individual adaptation.

When the ecosystem as a whole is threatened from without; when dominant trends within the ecosystem clash, affecting all individuals and forcing them to take sides; and when the ecosystem disintegrates and leaves individuals without the objective structures that underlie all stable patterns of adaptation – then the identity of the ecosystem as a whole enters into the consciousness of its members, often becoming the object of reductive symbolic construction. In the cases of war and revolution, this simplifying and symbolic instrumentalization of collective identities serves some concrete and potentially necessary purpose. However, in response to atomizing social disintegration, these identities merely exacerbate the underlying problem. They have neither content nor functional end, and they therefore tend to become virulently destructive, demolishing the remaining tissues of localized practices.

In *Origins of Totalitarianism*, Arendt draws a sharp and analytically important distinction between nationalism and biological racism, a distinction that sheds light upon the dynamic formation and varied fruition of alternative forms of collective identity. On the one hand, nationalism is a frequently virulent and inevitably reductive construction. The nation radically transcends the everyday experience of the individual, and it only becomes the object of knowledge, love, and commitment through highly mediated and ubiquitously manipulated forms of symbolic idealization. On the other hand, nationalism often plays a necessary and positive role, particularly in cases of self-defense, internal crisis, and anti-colonial struggle. The term "nation" has some socially, culturally, and politically meaningful referent, even if the process of reference demands reductive and dangerous simplification. By contrast, "race" is a term of dubious biological significance, reducing varied spectrums of genetic diversity to a small and random set of selected markers, such as skin color. Moreover, pure biological racism – i.e., racism stripped of the merely local and contingent cultural associations of race – involves the allegiance to a group without any social or cultural content. In this sense, modern racism is inherently

---

28 See "The Sociological Tradition and the Idea of Community." In Christopher Lasch, *The True and Only Heaven*. (New York: W.W. Norton and Company, 1991).

anti-social. It attempts to construct a group without direct reference to any shared social or cultural identity.

Perhaps stating the point too strongly, Arendt thus rejects the "old misconception of racism as a kind of exaggerated nationalism."[29] Arendt traces the history of racism, showing its frequent opposition to nationalism and its tendency to become an ever more imaginary construct. Comparing the function of race in British overseas imperialism and the aspirations to continental imperialism that animated the Pan-Slavic and Pan-Germanic movements, Arendt observes:

> While overseas imperialism had offered real enough panaceas for the residues of all classes, continental imperialism had nothing to offer except an ideology and a movement. Yet this was quite enough in a time which preferred a key to history to political action, when men in the midst of communal disintegration and social atomization wanted to belong at any prices. Similarly, the visible distinction of a white skin...could be matched successfully by a purely imaginary distinction between an Eastern and a Western, or an Aryan and a non-Aryan soul. The point is that a rather complicated ideology and an organization which furthered no immediate interest proved to be more attractive than tangible advantages and commonplace convictions...This popular appeal, which withstood tangible failures and constant changes of program, foreshadowed later totalitarian groups which were similarly vague as to actual goals and subject to day-to-day changes of political line. What held the pan-movements' membership together was much more a general mood than a clearly defined aim.[30]

The dynamism and instrumental relations of market exchange tend to erode concrete or objective group identities, producing individuals who increasingly seek "belonging at any price." More importantly, as diversified and diffuse social trust – grounded in stable patterns of experiences, longstanding face-to-face interaction, and common ways of life – erodes, individuals become suspicious of everyone. The resulting epistemic vacuum creates a space for conspiracy theory, the psychic need for some hidden "key to history." If I trust no one, there are few remaining constraints upon what I might believe. Individuals in this state cannot readily be united into a political group forged through the fragile compromises that emerge from decades of common interaction

---

29 Hannah Arendt, *The Origins of Totalitarianism*. (New York: Harcourt, Inc., 1994), 160–161.
30 Arendt (1994), 225.

between relatively stable groups. With their need for belonging and their lack of objective social structure, such individuals naturally fall prey to ideologies and movements that express "a general mood," not some "clearly defined aim." As a concept without any fixed social or cultural content, "race" provides the ideal rallying point for an otherwise fluid and featureless mass society.

As concrete phenomena, nationalism and racism fluidly intermingle. Arendt's sharp distinction nonetheless rightly alerts us to the dramatic ruptures in the apparently continuous history of particularistic attachment, one that moves from an attachment to family, town, province, guild, or occupation, to the still content-laden Nineteenth Century identities of nation and class, to the increasingly contentless or strictly symbolic national and racial identities of the Twentieth and Twenty-First Centuries. On the standard capitalist-liberal-cosmopolitan interpretation, totalitarianism emerges from an excess of (a) dogmatic commitment and (b) particularist or "tribal" attachment. In other words, totalitarianism or fascism bespeaks the persistence of the old foes of Enlightenment, which require the renewed commitment to promulgating the highest virtues of Enlightenment: skepticism, detachment, and deliberate calculation. Against this interpretation, Arendt's emphasis upon the novelty of Twentieth Century racism suggests the dialectical relationship between skepticism and fanaticism, between individualistic detachment and the self-effacing drive to absolute belonging, between the instrumental and atomizing tendencies of rational calculation and the appeal of a merely symbolic or atmospheric politics. Arendt rightly argues that our diffuse, particular, and embodied attachments shape the firm but nuanced doxastic commitments that allow for stable compromise and that provide the most effective bulwark against fanatical simplicities.[31] The particularities of local attachment provide the necessary context for rich individuality, and they provide the connective tissues that allow individuals to come together in ever-larger social and political groups. By contrast, the destruction of local and non-instrumental attachments creates unpredictably explosive but contentless individual lives divorced from all possible ties of broader solidarity. *Pace* the Kantian fantasies of doctrinaire liberalism, the rigorous abstraction of the individual self from empirical content and particularistic commitment does not reveal the universal ground of rational agency, the common basis of universal moral duty.

Arendt forcefully articulates an anti-Kantian and anti-liberal vision of sociality and solidarity in *The Human Condition*:

---

31   Arendt (1994), 460–479.

> Under the conditions of a common world, reality is not guaranteed primarily by the "common nature" of all men who constitute it, but rather by the fact that, differences of position and the resulting variety of perspectives notwithstanding, everybody is always concerned with the same object. If the sameness of the object can no longer be discerned, no common nature of men, least of all the unnatural conformism of mass society, can prevent the destruction of the common world...This can happen under conditions of radical isolation, where nobody can any longer agree with anybody else, as is usually the case in tyrannies...To live an entirely private life means above all to be deprived of things essential to a truly human life...to be deprived of an "objective" relationship with them that comes from being related to and separated from them through the intermediary of a common world of things...Under modern circumstances, this deprivation of "objective" relationships to others and of a reality guaranteed through them has become the mass phenomenon of loneliness, where it has assumed its most extreme and most antihuman form.[32]

Following Marx, I would suggest that our *common* human nature comprises a series of highly abstract tendencies that derive from the capacity for labor – i.e., for the collective, non-instinctual, and therefore historical transformation of the material world. Abstracted from all socio-historical particularities, these commonalities provide no basis for solidarity and no guide to action. Taken abstractly or universally, human beings remain aimless, disconnected, and prone to destructive conflict. We first come together through "the intermediary of a common world of things" by which we are both "related to" and "separated from" one another. It is our differential relationship to a shared material environment, our complex social ecosystems, that provides the basis for human individuality and human community. Radical detachment from our concrete and local world produces only the "unnatural conformism of mass society," a state of "radical isolation," where no one "can any longer agree with anybody else, as is usually the case in tyrannies."

Arendt's vision of sociality and solidarity suggests a politics of modest or tentative liberalism, one that vigilantly tends a fragile consensus without guarantees. In doctrinaire liberalism, by contrast, society rests upon some rationally guaranteed form of universal consensus regarding the nature and limits of public reason and thus also of public power. Specifically, all individuals must step back from their particular moral, cultural, metaphysical, and

---

32 Hannah Arendt, *The Human Condition*. (Chicago: University of Chicago Press, 1998), 57–58.

religious commitments; they must recognize that the limits of reason necessarily preclude the possibility of achieving rational consensus on these matters; and they must therefore agree to expunge all questions of the good from politics. The state must remain agnostic about the ultimate ends of human life. Moreover, the state itself, as the rational collective form of society, can have no ultimate aims. Instead, politics and the state must simply provide the necessary means required by individuals in their personal pursuit of happiness. In the libertarian strand of the doctrinaire liberal tradition, the state exhausts its purpose in the protection of individual freedom, particularly as manifest in integrity of body, speech, and property. In the social-welfare strand, the state might further provide a range of goods, including education, health care, pensions, unemployment benefits, etc. However, these further goods fall within the legitimate state power only because they count as universal means – i.e., as allegedly useful or necessary for *any* possible conception of happiness or the good life.

Doctrinaire liberalism binds citizens together in their abstract status as free agents, each of whom pursue some personal or private vision of happiness. It posits the cognitive act of radical detachment or self-distancing as the foundation of political theory and discourse. By contrast, Arendt's vision of sociality and solidarity takes the good, as the shared but also always disputed form of materially embedded human practices, to be the only potential source of human community and solidarity. Like doctrinaire liberalism, this Arendtian position accepts the frequently vehement disputation of the good as rationally ineliminable, but it recognizes that the process of disputation often reveals commonalities and modes of temporary compromise. Unlike doctrinaire liberalism, Arendt's project does not seek to construct some absolute, abstract, and timeless framework for society. Instead, politics always emerges as the procedurally unguided discussion of the ultimate socially embedded or materially embodied aims that always unite and divide us.

We are now finally in a position to see the deep affinities between positivism and doctrinaire liberalism. As we have seen, positivism and other epistemology-first strategies strive to codify the abstract, timeless, and unambiguously applicable rules that govern all rational inquiry and adjudication, and they take the successful deployment of these codified rules to determine the permanent and plainly recognizable demarcation between science and all forms of pseudo-cognitive pretense. These epistemic strategies take universal rational consensus as the supreme condition of knowledge, and they see the universal acceptance of method or procedure as the necessary preliminary step in the acquisition of knowledge with objective content. In its pure form, the epistemology-first strategy seeks to bracket all knowledge-practices and ontological assumptions, claiming that the rules of knowing can be derived from the universal structures of mind, subjectivity, language, etc. These pure forms frequently intermingle with impure content derived from the illicit – or merely tacit, or even explicit – acceptance of particular paradigm forms of knowledge, themselves selected upon the basis of meta-epistemic values (clarity, communicability, beauty, etc.) and ontological assumptions.

Doctrinaire liberalism presents the practical or normative analog of the epistemology-first strategy. It asks individuals to bracket their highest aims and definitive empirical identities in order to achieve an abstract universal standpoint. From this standpoint it then seeks to derive rules and procedures (a) that firmly demarcate the line between the domain of rational public consensus and the domains of private conviction, and (b) that guide the unambiguous adjudication of questions that fall within the former domain. Much like the epistemology first project, doctrinaire liberalism tacitly and illicitly derives much of its actual content from the more or less standard ideals of a particular time and place. It then either formulates abstract rules that generate this presupposed content, or else it simply passes back and forth between the disconnected abstractions of formal principles and the "self-evidence" of broadly accepted content.

The affinities between positivism and doctrinaire liberalism become still more evident when we consider the relationship between means and ends. According to positivism, reason has two functions. In its empirical mode, reason discovers and establishes law-like regularities that hold between variables or sets of events. It is *a priori* capacity, reason analyzes terms by tracing them back to the observation sentences that provide them with content. In this second task, reason is guided merely by the exigencies of clear communication. There is no intrinsically right or wrong meaning for a given term. We must simply connect terms with observation sentences in ways that are readily communicable and universally recognized. Clearly, this form of analytical reason cannot dispute or establish questions of ultimate ends, though it often serves to clarify the implications and extent of specific legal terms. It is equally clear that the empirical determination of law-like regularities cannot tell us what ends we should pursue, though it provides significant guidance in selecting the most efficient means for some predetermined end. In short, positivism reduces reason to a strictly instrumental procedure. It tells us *how*, but it must remain silent before questions of the ultimate *why*.

This purportedly rational abstention from questions of ultimate ends directly mirrors the basic presumption that constitutes doctrinaire liberalism. Isaiah Berlin aptly states the more libertarian variation of this presumption:

Most modern liberals, at their most consistent, want a situation in which as many individuals as possible can realize as many of their ends as possible, without assessment of the value of these ends as such, save in so far as they may frustrate the purposes of others. They wish the frontiers between individuals or groups to be drawn solely with a view to preventing collision between human purposes, all of which must be considered to be equally ultimate, uncritizable ends in themselves.[33]

The disputation of ends or purposes violates the vigorously policed limits of liberal politics, presumably because it raises non-technical or non-instrumental questions that transcend the determinate decision-procedures that facilitate consensus. Liberalism avers an elegant but relatively empty first principle: consenting adults should be allowed to do whatever they want as long as it does not harm anyone else. In the libertarian version, the purpose of the state is simply to police the lines between consent and non-consent, and between the sphere of consenting interaction and the un-consenting spheres effected by this consent. In welfare liberalism, the state seeks to enable consenting adults by providing them the skills and goods presupposed by every consensual project.

In order to provide determinate content for this principle, liberalism violates its own strictures and smuggles in its own presumptions of ultimate ends. There is no purely private space in the social web of human interaction. Every consenting action ripples through society, with diverse and often unforeseeable effects. Gun ownership, smoking, child rearing practices, transportation choices, alcohol consumption, seatbelt wearing, regular attendance of religious services, racist language, pornography, careerism – these activities obviously ramify beyond the private realms of consent, shaping our collective existence, hindering some individual purposes, facilitating others. In evaluating the significance of these activities, we might purportedly rely upon quantitative considerations: how many innocent or non-consenting people are harmed our have their purposes thwarted by gun ownership, by alcohol consumption, by racist language? How great is this harm? Of course, the faux-quantification of utilitarian calculus does little real work in analyzing these collisions between proximate spheres of individual freedom. In reality, our tacit conceptions of the values of different activities or aims must play the dominant role.

In carving out and defending spheres of freedom, the libertarian strand often smuggles in a certain conception of freedom as itself the highest aim or end of human development. Berlin thus accuses Mill of equivocation:

---

33   Isaiah Berlin, *Liberty*. (Oxford: Oxford University Press, 2004), 199.

> Mill confuses two distinct notions. One is that all coercion is, in so far as it frustrates human desires, bad as such...The other is that men should seek to discover the truth, or to develop a certain type of character of which Mill approved – critical, original, imaginative, independent, non-conforming to the point of eccentricity.[34]

Here liberalism illicitly endorses a familiar vision of the good life: it is critical, original, imaginative, independent, and non-conforming. This vision of the good then provides one tacit basis – there are others – for evaluating the omnipresent conflicts between aims or spheres of freedom. In welfare liberalism, the notion of the good life actually moves in the opposite direction. In its pretense to provide citizens with those instrumental goods required by all visions of the good life, it inevitably favors lifestyles and human self-conceptions that emphasize hygienic self-care, social stability, healthful longevity, psychic adjustment, career success, and positive self-esteem.

Significantly, libertarian and welfare liberalism find common ground in the promotion of economic growth, though the former identifies this growth with the creative disruption and destruction of the visionary entrepreneur, while the latter views economic growth as a source of social stability and increased tax revenue. More generally still, doctrinaire liberalism, in all its forms, inevitably foregrounds technical efficiency, particularly in the economic domain. The market is the realm of purely elective or consensual exchange, where objective cultural practices give way to quantified and calculated efficiency, where consensual and reciprocal use of other human beings unabashedly replaces the solidarity of shared goods. The market is in fact the paradigm and source of the liberal political order, which is itself simply the political articulation of more basic economic practices. If the market is the pure model of liberal freedom and "community," it also provides the premier locus of universal consent. The market is the realm of pure instrumental reason, where every factor can be quantified and measured in relation to the ultimate aim of profit, itself mediated by the determinate and objective process of competition. If we reify personal or consumer preference as the only ultimate measure of all economic, political, and ultimately human activity, then market competition adjudicates between alternative means for satisfying these ends, inevitably selecting the most efficient. *The market does what constitutions and epistemic methodologies cannot do: it provides a formal procedure for determining the unambiguous and ultimate solutions to the only legitimate questions that exists, where those*

---

34 Berlin (2004), 175.

questions now concern nothing but the maximally effective satisfaction of individual preferences.

4 Fascism: The End of Enlightenment

Liberalism frequently celebrates itself as the extreme antithesis of fascism or totalitarianism, as the supreme bulwark against the lure of excessive ideological commitment and the temptation to heroic sacrifice and self-effacement. Liberalism contrasts its vision of the free society, characterized by intellectual modesty and the motely diversity of private opinions and ends, with the ideological fanaticism and totalizing corporate ends of Fascist, Nazi, and communist states. Against the lurking temptation to collective irrationality, liberals and their left-wing fellow travelers brandish the traditional weapons of Enlightenment. With its positivistic epistemology and vision of expertise, liberalism relegates comprehensive social theories and ontological inquiries to the discredited realm of metaphysics, myth, or ideology. It likewise rejects all diffuse wisdom rooted in collective local practices, unless that wisdom becomes strictly private, or, alternatively, unless it receives the imprimatur of those who command the paraphernalia and keep the institutional gates of social, psychological, and pedagogical expertise. Against every particularism that transcends the contractual and ephemeral relation between individuals, liberalism enforces an abstract form of individual autonomy as the universal basis of right, duty, and solidarity.

In Hegelian or Marxist terms, we can identify the basic failure of liberalism with its merely formal – not concrete – conception the universal. Lukács aptly characterizes and employs the distinction between the abstract and the concrete universal in his account of the qualitative distinctions between inorganic, organic, and social being:

> With highly sophisticated arguments, the preceding forms of epistemology exhausted themselves seeking to determine (a) how human thought can ascend from the mere sensory acquaintance with particular cases to the abstract universal concept of the species or (b) how it descends from logically established universal concepts to particular cases. In stark contrast to this approach, *Marx views the indivisible unity of species and exemplar as a fundamental feature of being* [emphasis added].[35]

35　Lukács (1984), 40.

Stated more fully, we might say that the individual is always the indivisible unity of the active synthesis of the difference between the exemplar and the species, the particular and the universal. A biological species is a materially embodied, environmentally located, highly complex, largely harmonious, and at least previously successful pattern of living – i.e., pattern of nutritional intake, growth, movement, reproduction, etc. The living individual is a relatively successful attempt to instantiate these common patterns under the highly particular conditions that characterize its body and its immediate local environment. We only comprehend the individual animal when we recognize its activities as more or less successful instantiations of general strategies in a particular context.

When we move from the biological to the social strata of being, the relationship between the universal and the particular remains, but it undergoes certain qualitative changes.[36] In many animal species, there is little differentiation between the tasks of distinct individuals. We might say therefore that the universal, as the total pattern of life, is fully instantiated (though always ultimately imperfectly) in the individual. In some animal species, however, there is significant differentiation in task, and thus the universal only reveals itself in the relation between multiple individuals. The life strategy of an individual ant only makes sense in relation to the different but related activities of other types of ants within the individual colony. Human beings are highly social and cooperative animals, and their existence is early marked by this differentiation of task. However, in contrast to ants or bees, these tasks themselves emerge from a highly conscious and genetically indeterminate form of creativity. The human forms of life do not derive strictly from the genetic material of the individuals, and therefore they must be transmitted through a distinct form of cultural formation.

Positivism and liberalism largely ignore the plain ontological realism of the individual-particular-universal relation in the biological and social spheres of being. Rather than viewing the individual as the dynamic instantiation of an independent and prior pattern that bears some complex and partial relation to the collective totality of human activity, they instead view the universal as a mental abstraction from the independent and prior existence of the individual. This ultimately leads to an existentially, morally, and politically inert universal.

Particulars necessarily have many differences. However, through attentive processes of reduction or abstraction, we can determine the small set of features that some group of particulars share. If we are ontological realists, these

---

36   Lukács (1984), 52.

shared properties may be taken to define the essence of some objective type, those properties that most truly and fully characterize the thing as what it is, which express some ontological bond between the particulars that transcends their differential properties, which are mere "accidents." Of course, we moderns are cradle nominalists. We view concepts as functionally useful but otherwise arbitrary sets, not as attempts to limn the distinctions between natural kinds. Even when we do flirt with ontological realism, our purely descriptive and nomological conception of reason precludes the teleological presuppositions that transform a non-arbitrary set of properties into a true essence – i.e., interrelated behavior patterns that illumines the most important features of a thing. Thus, for instance, even if we assume that some set of properties accurately captures "jade," "ibis," or "human being" as distinct natural kind terms, the abstract conception of the universal provides no reason to think that, when considering this or that particular ibis, jade, or human being, these general properties are inherently more important or central to the individual qua concrete individual.

All of this becomes deeply problematic when we consider the nature and limits of human solidarity. Suppose we begin some massive intellectual and/or socio-economic project of abstraction, whereby we abstract from all human differences. Suppose we then find some limited set of properties that we all share. Here we should first note that genuinely shared properties do not necessarily generate any solidarity or sense of common duty. For instance, the dietetic commonalities of carnivores do not generate any form of solidarity or mutual commitment. Significantly, the commonalities that do generate solidarity or commitment tend to derive from shared contexts or relations, not from the discrete distribution of an abstract property or capacity. If two carnivores share the same habitat or prey, this commonality generates some shared interests (i.e., the preservation of the habitat or the prey-species), but it also simultaneously generates conflict. We should further note that, even if a small set of properties did bind together all human beings in a way that generated common interests, moral duty, or solidarity, there would be no obvious reason to presume the essential or supreme status of these shared properties, to presume that these properties would or should be more important to each individual than the particular characteristics that divide and differentiate them.

Liberalism coincides with a complex amalgam of political institutions, intellectual habits, legal norms, and economic activities that train the individual to abstract herself from the particularities of her context, her past, her body, even her desires. She can and must ask: is this desire really "mine," or is it forced upon me by social expectation or conditioning? If consistent and sufficiently critical, she can and must simultaneously ask: is this desire really "mine," or is it forced upon me by *this* body that *I* so plainly did not choose? On such a view, the individual can only become herself by taking up a critical or discriminating stance towards her social identities and the biological matter so unconsensually affixed to her pure will. Through this process of abstraction, she purportedly discovers the simultaneous source of her individual selfhood *and* the universal human essence. She discovers the universal capacity for self-determination.[37] As Hegel and Kierkegaard document and analyze, the pure possibility or freedom thereby discovered holds a deep fascination and promise of liberation, but it ultimately proves stunting and alienating.[38] The individual can in fact say to any particular feature of her socialized body and her past: *that is not me!* This pure capacity for negation gives a powerful sense of freedom, but it simultaneously reveals the permanent contingency of all particularity. The self therefore remains divided between an explosive capacity for negation and the permanent contingency – thus radical otherness – of every particularity.

When applied to the human person, the pursuit of abstractive universality produces either a limited and morally indifferent set of biological commonalities or the strictly formal capacity for self-definition or self-evaluation, the permanent capacity to always become other by stepping back from or existentially bracketing all that merely *is*. This existential bracketing is the radicalized practical analogue of the total skepticism that grounds the pure epistemology-first strategy. In this epistemological strategy, I bracket all purported knowledge practices in pursuit of some pure and immediately given domain of the mind, from which I can then determine the rules that govern the proper pursuit of knowledge. As we have already suggested, this strategy presupposes that the mind or reason can be immediately given in pristine isolation from the rest of reality. In the practical context, the entangling interpenetration of the mind, subject, or psyche by the rest of reality is still more evident. On the one hand, our internal *cognitive* experience might seem to present us with the immediate and indubitable presence of a special kind of being, about which we cannot be mistaken. Perhaps I cannot be wrong that I currently feel pain, or that the table seems brown to me. Perhaps these internal experiences are genuinely immediate and come with an indubitable seal of the truth. The genuine "mine-ness" or "me-ness" of an internal state is never immediately given in this way. Many psychic experiences often present themselves to me as intrusions, affronts, or

---

37   G.W.F. Hegel, *Grundlinien der Philosophie des Rechts*. (Frankfurt am Main: Suhrkamp, 1986c), §5.
38   Hegel (1986c), §16. Sorin Kierkegaard, *The Sickness Unto Death*. (New York: Penguin, 1989), 65–67.

obstacles to my elusive experience of my personal identity. With even a modicum of reflection, I must further recognize that, even when psychic states *seem* like affirmations or expressions of myself, this seeming always remains highly intricate and mediated. No psychic experience immediately bears the self-evident mark of expressing or revealing *my* identity. Thus while the epistemology-first strategy can at least seemingly fall back upon some realm of mind or immediate experience, the practical retreat from questionable commitments very soon finds itself left with nothing but the formal structure of negating and positing, with the abstract capacity to set ends. With every *particular* act or instantiation, even this abstract capacity falls under suspicion. The individual positing is always particular and thus contingent, not abstract and universal. More to the point, every individual act of positing is always highly mediated. Despite our occasional attempts to be arbitrary or unprecedented, our particular self-interpreting posits always come laden with the tangled threads of historical and social contexts. Blissful ignorance of history and the structures of social totality do not negate their effective persistence in the rarified chamber of abstract self-reflection.

The demise of the epistemology-first strategy does not end the possibility of genuinely critical reflection and rational deliberation. It does however end the dream of securing rational consensus through the prior codification of method. It shows that rational reflection must content itself to articulate the imperfect norms imbedded in particular examples of successful cognitive practice, while simultaneously recognizing and reflecting upon the ontological and meta-epistemological assumptions that guide our designation of *these* particular cases as paradigmatically successful. In a very similar way, the incoherence of the practical strategy of abstraction and existential bracketing does not preclude the genuinely critical examination and rational discussion of our self-defining commitments, but it does redirect these discussions towards the particular institutions, roles, and practices that always already bind us, both *connecting us with* and *dividing us from* our interlocutors. There is no universal, abstract, rational, and self-determining capacity of the self that can itself generate, underwrite, or normatively limit empirical family structures, economic practices, social institutions, legal norms, etc. When we criticize or defend a social order, we must do so based upon what we consider the successful elements of that order, while recognizing that our judgments of success must themselves be elaborated in terms of some ontological framework that ultimately incorporates history, society, and nature.

Liberalism attempts to construct a peaceful, harmonious, and consensual social order by privatizing the particular social and doxastic commitments that divide people. It thereby more or less tacitly presupposes some universal structure of reason and the self that underlies these particularizing commitments, a structure that yields a cognitive and moral consensus sufficient for the political sphere. Against this pursuit of the abstract universal, Hegel, Marx, and Lukács elaborate and advocate the concrete universal. Here the link between the individual and the universal proceeds through the concrete or materially embedded particulars. This strategy relies upon mediation, not abstraction. While abstraction tends to atomize or dissect, mediation traces the interconnections between the apparently discrete entities and their constitutive contexts. Abstraction necessarily presupposes a non-holistic ontology. If abstraction can reveal particular truths, then these truths can be rightly stated in isolation from broader contexts or relations. By contrast, mediation presupposes a holistic ontology. In a discrete or atomistic world, mediation would simply represent an unfortuitous change of subject, not the revelation of false immediacy. As a rational strategy, mediation assumes that the proper or complete recognition of a thing comes through the recognition of its inherent connections with broader contexts and processes.

Abstraction, existential bracketing, and pre-epistemological skepticism presume the mere particularity and immediacy of all individuals. On this approach, the particular is merely particular, simply and immediately given, and as yet unconnected with reason or the universal. It must therefore initially be rejected in pursuit of reason or the universal, though it may turn out that reason or the universal will ultimately legitimate the particular. By contrast, mediation presumes that the individual is always more than a mere particular. Every individual includes a universal-particular relation within itself, where that relation might variously be described as the relationship between general life-pattern and particular instantiation, between form and matter, between norm and fact, between rule and practice. Instead of bracketing the purported universality in the particular, mediation first attempts to understand the particular on its own terms, through the acceptance of its internal standards. It then considers the emergence of these standards and the tensions between standards and practice in terms of the broader ontological context from which the particular emerges and in relation to which it maintains itself.

Through this process of integrative-mediation, the original social individual becomes transformed: she comes to realize, and thus to become more fully and truly, what she is. Hegel remains a wild optimist, suggesting that this mediation proceeds until it incorporates and harmonizes the latent truth in all discourse and the latent rationality or goodness in all particular practices and identities. However, we must emphatically note that the basic coherence and socio-epistemic effectiveness of Hegel's project *does not depend* upon this sanguine conclusion. If we think that only the finality of absolute spirit and the perfect harmony of the state can justify every sub-ultimate claim to truth and goodness, then we force Hegel's philosophy back into a framework that rigidly divides the universal from the particular, the norm from the practice, and that then claims the justification of the latter depends entirely upon some ultimate grounding of the former. Hegel's strategy of mediation derives from a realistic assessment of the concrete nature of knowing and acting, of epistemology and solidarity. The reflective justification of cognition and solidarity can never radically outstrip the current practices of knowing and relating. Our current practices of knowing and relating can be criticized, but this criticism must come from dialectical mediation, not from totalizing skepticism or detached abstraction. We may fall tragically short – or potentially succeed – in our rational pursuit of the final unity of truth and the fullness of human solidarity, but neither the inherent limits nor the ultimate success of these endeavors can be determined from the outset or from any particular point along the way.

Failing to recognize the path of critical mediation and the nature of the concrete universal, liberal and fascist tendencies develop through a dialectical exchange. In defense of political consensus and the abstract universal, liberalism attacks all forms of cognitive and practical particularity. Such particularity must acknowledge its pure particularity, transforming itself into a mere personal opinion or preference. Otherwise, it must be destroyed as a form of illiberal fanaticism. In doing so, liberalism seeks the universal form of human agency and the indisputable bedrock of public consensus. In fact, it creates a rational and existential vacuum. In the absence of justified knowledge, people flee to flattering myths and thrilling conspiracies. In the absence of particular commitments, people seek vacuous symbolic identities, the fabrications of crude demagogues and their sophisticated consultants, the natural fruit of a political discourse untethered from pre-political forms of materially embedded coexistence. Then, in response to the horrors of fascist politics, even the sterilities and repeated failures of the liberal project regain some appeal, for the second, the third, or the fourth time. Indeed, it was only the horrors of Hitler and Stalin that served, in the forties and fifties, to revive the otherwise moribund and discarded rhetoric of liberalism and the old metaphysical visions of natural or universal human rights.[39]

This dialectical interpretation suggests that the strength and appeal of fascism derives from the dramatic successes of liberalism and positivism, themselves construed as the ultimate fruition of Enlightenment. In *Dialectic of*

---

39   For a genealogical history of human rights in the Twentieth Century, see Samuel Moyn, *The Last Utopia: Human Rights in History*. (Cambridge: Harvard University Press: 2012) and *Christian Human Rights*. (Philadelphia: University of Pennsylvania Press).

Enlightenment, Horkheimer and Adorno therefore suggest, "that the cause of the regression from Enlightenment to mythology does not principally lie in the nationalistic, pagan, and other modern mythologies devised to promote this regression, but rather in the fear of truth that rigidifies Enlightenment itself."[40] In its critical pursuit of liberation, Enlightenment embraced a "false clarity."[41] In its attacks on myth, metaphysics, tradition, and ideology, it ironically wielded mythological or illusionary standards of clarity, consensus, abstract universality, and methodological codification. These standards ultimately lead to "the perplexed self-destruction of Enlightenment,"[42] that is, to "the transformation of Enlightenment into positivism."[43] This ultimately leads to the final "metamorphosis of critique into affirmation." In pursuit of clarity, certainty, method, and universal consensus, radical critique becomes problematic; normative discussion becomes anemic; the good becomes a matter of personal taste; and society increasingly turns its attention to concrete problems of a technical or instrumental nature.

Horkheimer provides a succinct expression of the interrelation between the Enlightenment conception of reason, the technical problems of positivistic social management, and the personal preferences that ground liberal policy and discourse. "When the ordinary man is asked to explain what is meant by the term reason," Horkheimer suggests, he "will say that reasonable things are obviously useful, and that every reasonable man is supposed to be able to decide what is useful to him." According to this practically ubiquitous assumption, reason "is essentially concerned with means and ends, with the adequacy of procedures for purposes more or less taken for granted and supposedly self-explanatory. It attaches little importance [or even semantic content or rational coherence!] to the question of whether the purposes as such are reasonable."[44]

This strictly instrumental or technical conception of reason has three implications. First, it labels every radical or wholesale critique of society as a dangerous ideology, a beautiful illusion, and/or an idiosyncratic personal preference. Second, it gradually undermines all rational support for the liberational aims of liberalism and Enlightenment.[45] Third, it leads to a strictly regimented or managed society, where individuals become the objects of scientific observation and technical manipulation. Horkheimer captures the first and second implications as follows:

---

40   Horkheimer and Adorno (2009), 3–4.
41   Horkheimer and Adorno (2009), 4.
42   Horkheimer and Adorno (2009), x.
43   Horkheimer and Adorno (2009), 1.
44   Horkheimer (1947), 3.
45   Morris (2017), 65–94.

> Justice, equality, happiness, tolerance, all the concepts that, as mentioned in passing, were in preceding centuries supposed to be inherent in or sanctioned by reason, have lost their intellectual roots. They are still aims and ends, but there is no rational agency authorized to appraise and link them to an objective reality. Endorsed by venerable historical documents, they may still enjoy a certain prestige, and some are contained in the supreme law of the greatest countries. Nevertheless, they lack any confirmation by reason in its modern [i.e., instrumental] sense. Who can say that any one of these ideals is more closely related to truth than its opposite? According to the philosophy of the average modern intellectual, there is only one authority, namely science, conceived as the classification of facts and the calculation of probabilities. The statement that justice and freedom are better in themselves than injustice and oppression is scientifically unverifiable and useless. It has come to sound as meaningless in itself as would the statement that red is more beautiful than blue, or that an egg is better than milk.[46]

Enlightenment reason and the doctrinaire liberal state proscribe all forms of rational or public deliberation that do not unfold in accordance with determinate and universally accepted procedures or methods. It takes such formal procedures as the necessary condition for all knowledge and for every consensual and therefore just society. With these assumptions in place, it ultimately recognizes (a) "the classification of facts," (b) "the calculation of probabilities," and (c) the facilitation of communication through the stipulative clarification of concepts as the only legitimate tasks of reason, the only proper modes of public discourse. Every question that transcends these methods concerns a matter of opinion, and thus the defense of justice become rationally equivalent to the preference for city-life, the sea shore, or wide open spaces.

The exclusive pursuit of instrumental reason has a third, still more devastating effect: it increases the capacity for regimented control. Just as instrumental reason draws a fundamental distinction between the rationally determinate questions of efficient means and all strictly arational considerations of ultimate ends, it also breeds a similarly rigid distinction between human beings (a) as empirical objects of administrative control and (b) as sources of pure subjectivity or absolute spontaneity. In short, instrumental reason knows only law-like regularity and pure contingency. In its official pronouncements regarding human agency, contemporary society respects the elusive freedom and mysterious self-determination of the individual, a freedom located

---

46   Horkheimer (1947), 23–24.

somewhere safely beyond the reaches of empirical science and scientific management. Beneath the veneer of official pronouncements, however, the social scientists, bureaucrats, administrators, and managers that determine the shape of our society continue to amass probabilistic regularities and to construct environments that facilitate smooth and efficient production. Thus instrumental reason constructs an "administrated world,"[47] where, "technological rationality becomes the rationality of domination itself."[48] Marcuse develops this theme in *One Dimensional Man,* where he observes how, "technological rationality reveals its political character as it becomes the great vehicle of better domination, creating a truly totalitarian universe."[49] With the unchallenged supremacy of instrumental reason, "the world tends to become the stuff of total administration," where "the web of domination has become the web of reason itself," and where "the transcending modes of thought seem to transcend Reason itself."[50] In service of varied and sometimes even conflicting efficiencies, we collectively construct corporate, legal, administrative, educational, and media environments that predictably correlate positive and negative incentives with desired outcomes.

Fascism thus emerges from the metastasis of instrumental reason, a process that maximizes the technical power of society, while simultaneously eroding the rational resources available to direct this power. These effects do not derive from definitive epistemological arguments that limit reason to an instrumental function. Nor do they derive from a well-established and exhaustive ontology that excludes binding ends or aims from the objective structure of reality. Beneath these positivistic assumptions lies the dubious presupposition that a clear methodological consensus must precede and determinately resolve all rational disputes concerning the nature of beings and the appropriate forms of human society. This emphasis upon formal methods and procedures receives further reinforcement from the rejection of ontological holism and the indivisible unity of the universal and the particular as an ontological feature of reality. Tacitly rejecting or simply ignoring these possibilities, liberal society attempts to combat positivism through the determination of highly abstract features that are purportedly shared by all human beings, and that some provide binding claims that are genuinely normative but not objective – i.e., not rooted in the objective structure of reality. In a similar fashion, liberal-enlightenment thought seeks to undermine all particular knowledge claims that cannot

---

47 Horkheimer and Adorno (2009), ix.
48 Horkheimer and Adorno (2009), 129.
49 Herbert Marcuse, *One Dimensional Society*. (New York: Routledge, 2008), 20.
50 Marcuse (2008), 173.

likewise be justified from some universal and thus highly formal standpoint. Ironically, both strategies actually facilitate the emergence of fascism by destroying the concrete – and therefore particular – human connections and doxastic commitments that provide the necessary starting point for larger forms of solidarity and broader forms of rational deliberation.

5   Critical Ontology: The Challenge That Remains

Fascism derives from the confluence of humanity's ever-increasing capacity for rational control and its ever more anemic capacity for rational guidance. The point here is not simply that our increased capacity for control renders our arbitrary or rationally unconstrained aims more destructive, though this is surely true. Barbarians with trains, tanks, and airplanes, not to mention atomic bombs and genetic engineering, are surely more frightful than their sword-wielding and horse-riding counterparts. Beyond this basic point, however, we must recognize that our increased capacity for control both derives from and breeds a host of institutional and attitudinal accompaniments, which themselves then render our individual and political aims increasingly chaotic, arbitrary, violent, and explosive. I at least shall argue that the construction of an instrumentally ordered and hyper-efficient society renders our ultimate selection of aims increasingly disordered, ephemeral, collectively disharmonious, and existentially contingent. The drive for rational control thus ironically breeds explosive moments of individual and collective eruption that thwart all prediction and that radically redirect our apparatus of socio-technical control.

In the face of this persistent threat, the dominant and more developed lines of traditional critical theory remain inadequate. Programmatically stated, critical theory traditionally pursues a range of broadly Kantian strategies in its engagement with the threat posed by positivism. With Kant and the positivists, the critical theorists generally accept the priority of epistemology over ontology. More importantly, they generally assume or explicitly maintain that the critical insights of modern epistemology preclude traditional ontological inquiries concerning the fundamental categories, the ground, and the totality of being, as it is in itself, beyond or behind the formative processes of language or the subject. Thus considering the threats posed by instrumental reason and its fascistic fruition, Horkheimer warns: "Ontological revivals are among the means that aggravate the disease."[51] With an equally blunt confidence,

---

51   Horkheimer (1947), 163–164.

Habermas assures us that, "the good and true life can be preserved today only on the ruins of ontology."[52]

Finally, with Kant and the positivists, the mainlines of traditional critical theory accept the instrumentally or technologically motivated determination of nomological regularities as the legitimate and exhaustive task of the traditional empirical science, and they further advocate for the continued instrumental organization of many social domains, particularly the domain of human labor. For instance, both Horkheimer and Marcuse tend to criticize the non-universal and oppressive ends that instrumental efficiency currently serves, while fully embracing the legitimacy of the nomological social sciences and the institutional structures that facilitate their social application. After excoriating instrumental reason and its seemingly inherent drive towards "total administration" for more than two-hundred pages, the final sections of *One-Dimensional Man* make a surprising turn: Marcuse embraces instrumental reason. "Self-determination in the production and distribution of vital goods and services," he says, "would be wasteful. The job is a technical one, and as a truly technical job, it makes for the reduction of physical and mental toil."[53] Similarly, he says: "The more technological rationality, freed from its exploitative features, determines social production, the more will it become dependent on political direction – on the collective effort to attain a pacified existence, with the goals which the free individuals may set for themselves."[54] These passages plainly suggest that the fundamental problem resides in the oppressive deployment of instrumental reason, not in its essence. Technology, the social sciences, and the methods of institutional organization are neutral: they can serve aims of oppression or liberation.

Horkheimer does at least occasionally flirt with the suggestion that critical theory must revive a concern with totality,[55] and that it must demonstrate the inherently dialectical nature of social being,[56] but he ultimately leaves these suggestions undeveloped and falls back upon a rather lame formulation of the distinction between critical and traditional theory. "Critical theory," he assures us, "has the happiness of individuals as its goal," and thus, unlike activities of "the scientific servants of the authoritarian state," its activities "cannot be reconciled with the persistence of misery."[57] Critical theory reveals the *particular interests* that human knowledge and organization currently serve, and it seeks

---

52 Habermas (2002), 313.
53 Marcuse (2008), 256.
54 Marcuse (2008), 240.
55 Horkheimer (2005), 228.
56 Horkheimer (2005), 225.
57 Horkheimer (2005), 265.

to redirect this knowledge and these organizational capacities towards *universal interests*. It thereby "strives to extend enjoyment to the majority."[58] These pronouncements suggest that the difference between traditional and critical theory involves divergent political commitments or aims, not the inherent structure or nature of scientific activity.

While Horkheimer treats happiness or enjoyment as relatively evident in their nature, Marcuse at least recognizes the need for developing certain rational processes that reveal and articulate our authentic desires or aims. Marcuse thus augments the instrumental function of reason with the hermeneutic processes of psychoanalysis, with a distinctive form of rational self-interpretation that reveals the true and apparently harmonious interests currently repressed and obscured by the norms of contemporary society. Thus reason, in a distinctly hermeneutic register, serves to direct instrumental reason towards aims that such reason cannot itself discover. Marcuse thus fundamentally *augments* the positivist conception of rational inquiry, but he does not directly challenge it: he accepts the formulation of empirical laws as the proper, exhaustive, and intrinsically unobjectionable aim of the social sciences.

By contrast, the critical ontology developed by Lukács directly challenges and rejects the nomological aspirations of the social sciences. Lukács observes that, "modern Western sociology energetically develops itself in the direction of the general theory of the socially conscious manipulation of the masses."[59] He further insists that the inherently manipulative and thus oppressive tendencies of the social sciences do not merely derive from the oppressive ends they contingently serve in the hands of a particular ruling class or other anti-democratic elite. Nor do they simply derive from the biases and special interests that frequently distort the actual development of the social sciences. Instead, Lukács argues that the inherently oppressive tendencies of the social sciences follow directly from the anti-metaphysical presumptions of "neo-positivism," from its "disregard for the rich categories bequeathed to us by the old philosophy, which of course often require revisions." The modern social sciences "dismiss questions regarding the categorial structures of reality as metaphysical pseudo-problems," and they therefore serve only "to enrich the 'language' of manipulation."[60]

Lukács argues that the social sciences must reject the artificial and ideological priority of epistemology and method and reconceive their task in overtly ontological terms:

---

58   Horkheimer (2005), 236.
59   Lukács (1984), 344.
60   Lukács (1984), 357.

> Unless the science [of sociology] remains oriented towards the attainment of the most adequate possible knowledge of reality as it is in itself; unless it strives to deploy its evermore refined method for the discovery of new truths, which must necessarily have an ontological foundation; and unless it strives to deepen and augment this ontological knowledge, its efforts will ultimately be limited to the support of practice in the immediate sense...to the manipulation of the facts that have practical interest.[61]

With the prioritization of epistemology, modern inquiry either pursues the development of a universal method and science, thereby effecting "the radical homogenization of the totality of being," or else it breeds alternative forms or registers of knowing, which, in in their unreconciled plurality, must always remain at a distance from being in itself, and which find only contingent or aggregate unity in the total cognitive practices of humanity.[62] The latter approach finds classic exemplification in Kant's distinction between the registers of theoretical and practical reason and in Habermas' distinction between the "specific viewpoints from which, with transcendental necessity, we apprehend reality," three disparate interests that, "ground three categories of possible knowledge: information that expands our power of technical control; interpretations that make possible the orientation of action within common traditions; and analyses that free consciousness from its dependence on hypostatized powers."[63]

While the strict nomological tendencies of the social sciences may be externally conjoined to the supposed dictates of communicative or pure practical reason, they more naturally suggest the tacit ontological homogenization of positivism. Indeed, the ideal structure of empirical law presupposes an impoverished and ultimately oppressive ontology. As a guiding ideal, the empirical law expresses a universal, exceptionless, and invariant connection between two sets of events, where these sets are each respectively defined by some common property(s) shared by all events in the set, and where every event from set A inevitably leads to an event from set B. In perfected form, they tell us that events of type B always follow events of type A. Of course non-universal or merely probabilistic relations between sets of events have great practical significance. If the administration of some drug leads to the reduction of certain symptoms in seven out of ten cases, this knowledge proves extremely

---

61   Lukács (1984), 344.
62   Lukács (1984), 328.
63   Habermas (2002), 313.

useful. Nonetheless, the universal or exeptionless law remains the regulative ideal. Suppose that events of type A lead to events of type B with eighty percent regularity. The progression of scientific inquiry presupposes either (a) that events of type A can be subdivided into distinct types, A1 and A2, where events of type A1 universally produce events of type B, while events of type A2 have no tendency to do so, or, alternatively, (b) that there is some further relevant variable, some set of events of type C, where the presence or absence of events of this type explains the difference between the eighty times that events of type A lead to events of type B and the twenty times that they do not.

A world exhaustively characterized by empirical laws includes only two basic ontological categories: events and patterns of temporal succession. For at least four reasons, this tacit ontology proves inherently oppressive. First, this ontology renders incoherent all questions regarding the individuation, unity, and temporal persistence of substances, systems, or true entities. What we normally regard as objects or systems become arbitrary collections of events. In the strict language of empirical law, we may observe how events in some conventional collection interact with one another *and* with events beyond this collection. However, neither type of observation can ground the distinction between the unity of the collection and the externality of other causally related events.

Second, this ontology precludes the very conceivability of *self*-determination. In a world of causally related events, every event is either externally caused by some prior event, or else it is simply uncaused. The nomological vision of reality can certainly allow for uncaused or random events, but it cannot show how a thing, substance, or system causes and thus determines some event in a way that goes beyond the standard model of event–event causation. This ontology denies the existence and the agency of individuals, institutions, and classes, which all become conventional collections of events that stand in manifold causal relations with events both within and beyond these collections. Third, this ontology treats beliefs in strictly causal terms. It formulates probabilistic patterns that hold between certain beliefs and the skin color, genitalia, geographical location, and income of the large collections of events we conventionally identify as individuals, but its fundamental categories preclude relations of justification. Obviously, this strictly causal or associative vision undermines all possible justification of belief and the purported rationality of these who hold them.[64]

Fourth, this ontology necessarily precludes all cognitive treatment of the individual qua individual. Laws necessarily focus on sets or classes, on the

---

64   Morris (2016), 36–64.

general properties shared by groups of events. When faced with the apparent distinctiveness of Tolstoy, the French Revolution, or my younger son, the nomological vision of reality sees only collections of simultaneous and successive events, each of which must be considered *separately from* these individuals as unique totalities, though *in relation to* spatially and temporally distant events that have common features and stand in common law-like connections.

The nomological social sciences do not simply objectify individuals and treat them as objects of manipulation: they threaten to render incoherent the very notions of unified selfhood, self-determination, rational responsibility, and unique individuality. Here the defender of the nomological conceptions of the social sciences might of course adopt a Kantian or Habermasian line, attempting to rehabilitate unified selfhood, self-determination, rational responsibility, and individuality at some non-empirical or at least non-scientific level. However, unless they place radical and effective limits upon our collective penchant for rational organization, such strategies devolve into hypocritical platitudes. Strictly linguistic or purely normative reconstructions of selfhood, self-determination, rational responsibility, and individuality remain abstract and largely untethered from the actual practices of the bureaucratic state, the market, the corporate workplace, the schools, the health system, and the domains of public discourse. Alongside and within these domains, we see the luxuriant proliferation of think tanks, academic disciplines, and the paraphernalia of pseudo-expertise. We observe swelling cliques of well-paid and highly trained individuals who, rehearsing progressive pieties all the while, seek to uncover and/or to produce the empirical regularities that facilitate the efficient or otherwise desired direction of single mothers, consumers, workers, students, patients, and voters. If their motives are pure; if their ideals are right; and if their research is effective, then their paychecks and prestige are supposedly merited.

All strictly or predominately nomological social sciences are inherently oppressive. In order to critique and transform this oppression, we need a more general vision of scientific activity that transcends the current clashes between crude scientism and subjectivist anti-realism.[65] We need to transcend both the abstemious postures of modern epistemology and the post-Kantian visions of cognitive activity liberated from all objective constraints. Following Marx, Lukács elaborates his critical ontology as a welcome alternative to these

---

65   For some helpful suggestions, see "Ten Propositions on Science and Antiscience." In Richard Lewontin and Richard Levins, *Biology under the Influence*. (New York: Monthly Review Press, 2007), 87–99.

standard positions, as an approach that prioritizes ontology over epistemology, while shifting attention from the conceptual to the material constitution of the object of knowledge. Lukács deploys his critical ontology in a trenchant critique of the nomological social sciences. This critique rightly emphasizes the intimate connection between empirical laws and the construction of scientific experiments, and it then interprets the process of the experiment from the standpoint of *practice*, the foundational category of Lukács' anthropology and social ontology.

The experiment constructs a closed and highly controlled environment that fixes a few variables or features of a thing in isolation from all forms of external interference. From the beginning, we should note that this controlled isolation is not a process of pure or mere abstraction. In seeking to remove certain influences or factors, it constructs a new, artificial, and complex environment for the variables or objects it studies. If we focus on the purely abstractive function of the experiment, we may be tempted to say that the experimental process shields some events from extraneous distortions and thus reveals the nature of the events in themselves. Of course, this way of viewing the experiment presupposes a discrete or non-holistic ontology. It presupposes that the world consists of discrete features that stand in strictly extrinsic relations to one another. In the world beyond the experiment, there are more moving parts, more factors that stand in interaction, but the conjunction of these factors or parts does not change anything about the factors or parts themselves. Therefore, if we observe them in simplifying isolation and learn their inherent nature, the rules that govern their interaction with other factors or parts, we may eventually be able to predict and thus manipulate their behavior in the motley and more complex world beyond the experiment. On this view, the difference between the experiment and the world is one of complexity, not one of qualitative ontological difference.[66]

Lukács' interpretation of the experiment depends upon his holistic and qualitatively differentiated ontology. Lukács draws a qualitative distinction between three regions of being, each with its own structures or categories. These include: the inorganic, the organic, and the social. The holistic structure of being is most developed at the social level, where "practice, the fundamental grounding category of this new form of being," consists in "the active adaptation to the environment."[67] Organic beings are materially organized complex

---

66 See helpful discussion of these issues, see Richard Lewontin and Richard Levins, *The Dialectical Biologist* (Cambridge: Harvard University Press, 1985), 132–160, and Lewontin and Levins (2007), 101–124.
67 Lukács (1984), 39.

patterns of behavior that allow for the more or less successful navigation of the environment in the pursuit of nutrition, growth, and reproduction. Every individual organic being deploys the generic patterns of its species in slightly different ways, in ways that accord with environmental variations. In non-social organic beings, these patterns adapt over time, but this adaptation depends entirely upon genetic mutation and differential rates of reproduction. In social or human beings, by contrast, the biological species patterns are much looser and more flexible. They are augmented by creative or intentional adaptation that transcends the genetic base of the biological organism, and that must therefore be culturally transmitted.

Moreover, social adaptation differs from merely biological adaptation through what we might describe as its potential cognitive orientation towards totality, an orientation that emerges from and facilitates the human capacity to construct and control complex environments, which themselves function as more or less hermetic totalities. Attempting to sketch the admittedly rough or approximate boundaries between merely biological and relatively primitive sociological ways of being in the world, Lukács observes:

> The collection of plants and the hunting of animals merely demand the careful observation of what is already naturally present. By contrast, agriculture and domestication of animals depend upon the capacity of human practice to create new environments for the required plants and animals, thereby engendering new possibilities and modes of response in them.[68]

This suggests two related points. First, all biological and sociological beings – and to a lesser degree inorganic beings – exist as modes of interaction within an environment. Such beings are not fully given in their discrete or self-enclosed isolation. They only exist through their interaction with broad and defuse swaths of the surrounding world. Second, the social being of humans distinguishes itself from the strictly biological being of other animals through the ability to construct new environments and therefore to call forth new modes of previously non-existent behavior.

If we accept this ontology and anthropology, then the law-like regularities that emerge from experiments do not reflect the true nature of some variables or features of things as they are in themselves. Instead, experiments merely demonstrate the ways that particular things behave in one very specific artificial and self-enclosed environment, itself but one instantiation of a very broad

---

68   Lukács (1984), 168.

human tendency to construct systems or environments that elicit new, stable, and desired responses in particular objects.

> Viewed from the ontological perspective, what is an experiment? It is the artificial, ontological isolation of a particular "if-then" relation from an uncountable array of other such relations, which normally accompany it in the total-complex of being...This pure case of "if-then" necessity exists only in the isolated and teleologically constructed environment of the experiment.[69]

Experiments to do not simply reflect the inherent structure of being. Similarly, the technological control of the world does not consist in the strictly external manipulation of otherwise inert or extrinsically unchanged beings. Stated differently, technological control does not simply rearrange beings. It constructs fundamentally new environments. It thereby qualitatively transforms beings and engenders new possibilities:

> Consider for instance even the very early use of fire for the purposes of human life, such as cooking or heating, and compare this with fire as a mere event of nature, where it only acts in destructive ways...we see here a general characteristic of work...namely, that this process does not simply involve the use of given natural objects or processes for human purposes, but rather that it again and again releases new possibilities, which would never have developed into being in nature as it is immediately given to us.[70]

When placed in constructed contexts and engaged or tended in specific ways, fire behaves in fundamentally new or unnatural ways. Here we may feel the temptation to treat these new possibilities as potential capacities intrinsic to fire itself. More specifically, we may be tempted to treat the intrinsic nature of fire and the intrinsic structure of various possible fire-contexts as ontologically distinct and complete objects that can be exhaustively studied in isolation, and that then, on the basis of this discrete characterization, can be exhaustively characterized in their interaction. Here we should remember that there is no context-less fire; that the possible contexts or environments for fire are endless; and that the supposedly intrinsic properties of fire only ever become manifest within haphazard or carefully constructed environments. These

---

69 Lukács (1984), 152–153.
70 Lukács (1984), 167.

points do not force us to accept a relational and holistic ontology, but they plainly suggest its possibility and strong appeal.

This ontological and anthropological interpretation of the experiment allows us to appreciate the highly oppressive and ironically unstable nature of contemporary society, dominated, as it is, by the activities of instrumental reason. The drive towards efficient organization or control does not simply observe and then manipulate the natural tendencies of individuals. Instrumental reason does not simply discover and then utilize the law-like regularities that intrinsically govern individual human beings. Indeed, if human beings always already behaved in accordance with unchanging natural laws, then it would be hard to fault managers and social scientists for formulating these laws and using them to achieve desired ends. At most, we might fault them for selecting repressive or particularistic ends, but not simply for creating the knowledge of social control. However, once we recognize that biological organisms and even fire always only do what they do in more or less modified interaction with particular and varied contexts, and, once we recognize that law-like regularities reflect the vigilant control of these constitutive contexts, not direct and uncluttered manifestation of the thing or process as it truly is in itself, then we are in a position to see instrumental reason as the active construction of controlling institutional and social environments, not simply as the honest and neutral attempt to register the intrinsic laws that govern human behavior, laws that purportedly precede and guide the construction of institutional and social environments.

The anthropology and ontology of practice further allows us to understand the existential anguish and destructive rage that characterize the instrumentally constructed society. The basic or constitutive human activity involves the active and creative construction of material environments in ways that produce new possibilities. Human freedom is never simply the ability to select between pre-given alternatives. It is not the mere capacity to use objects in different ways within a stable environment. Human freedom, even the very ground or core of human self-hood, consists in the active and creative transformation of material systems in ways that bring forth new possibilities from the objects organized within these systems. Meaningful human freedom does not emerge in the unfettered selection of consumer goods or careers. It does not emerge in the capacity to choose or interpret the symbolic manifestations of my subjective identity. It does not emerge in my ability to select political platforms or representative candidates, who will then control or direct the bureaucratic machinery of the state in accordance with my wishes. In other words, neither the market, nor the construction of personal identity, nor the wildest success of state guided social democracy can fulfill the fundamental human longing for freedom. This freedom demands the decentralized democratization of work. It demands the creative and collective, but non-centralized or only loosely organized – here I frankly depart from Lukács – transformation of the material world.[71]

Only the democratic and decentralized formation of our collective material existence can overcome or preclude the fascistic synthesis of totalizing control and nihilistic destruction. The instrumental regimentation of social existence inevitably breeds the urge to destroy. It breeds the rejection of freedom and human dignity as ideological, hypocritical, or irrelevant ideals. It channels the indestructible human need to form the environment into mammoth political dimensions that radically transcend individual experience and the always fragile and limited boundaries of meaningful consensus. This need thus issues in highly symbolic and ideological political movements, where the reality of change, destruction, and dramatic action take precedence over all specific matters of content. Here the ultimate ends of the political community become eruptive, ephemeral, and largely irrelevant, so long as they are bold. This is the ever-present threat of fascism, a threat that demands the far-reaching transformation of ontology, science, politics, and work. In all four areas of necessary transformation, Lukács still has much to teach us.

---

71 For the best discussion I know of the left's increasing neglect of self-determination of the labor process, see Lasch (1991), 296–368.

CHAPTER 12

Normativity and Totality: Lukács' Contribution to a Critical Social Ontology

Titus Stahl

1   Introduction[1]

In the last twenty years, there has been a resurgence in interest in the ontology of the social, especially on the part of philosophers working in the analytic tradition. In particular, theorists have focused on providing accounts of collective intentionality and collective action.[2]

The debate thus far has remained largely unconnected to prior attempts to develop an ontology of society in traditions ranging from phenomenology to Marxism. It is therefore hardly surprising that Lukács' *Ontology of Social Being* has not attracted the attention of those working in this field. Lukács' book had limited influence even on Marxist scholarship, and it is famous for its occasional inconsistency, not to mention its wordiness, all of which partly explain its contemporary irrelevance. In addition to the more or less accidental circumstances that explain this disregard for Lukács' work on social ontology, there are systematic reasons for why it cannot easily be treated as just another position in the contemporary debate.

One of these reasons consists in the fact that the dominant approaches in the current analytic debate focus on two questions. First, how can we account for social facts from within a broadly naturalist perspective? Second, how can we account for social facts in a way that makes causal explanations possible?[3] Both of these questions frame the debate in such a way that theories that account for social facts in terms of underlying intentional or mental states, which

---

[1] This article is a substantially revised version of a paper that first appeared as Titus Stahl, "Praxis und Totalität: Lukács' Ontologie des gesellschaftlichen Seins im Lichte aktueller sozialontologischer Debatten." *Jahrbuch der Internationalen Georg-Lukács-Gesellschaft*, 14/15 (2015): 123–150.

[2] Cf. David P. Schweikard and Hans Bernhard Schmid, "Collective Intentionality." In *The Stanford Encyclopedia of Philosophy*, ed. Edward N. Zalta, Summer 2013, http://plato.stanford.edu/archives/sum2013/entries/collective-intentionality/; Deborah Tollefsen, "Collective Intentionality." *Internet Encyclopedia of Philosophy*, 2004, http://www.iep.utm.edu/coll-int/.

[3] Cf. John R. Searle, *The Construction of Social Reality*. (New York: Penguin, 1995), 5–7.

are then usually treated as ontologically and explanatorily primary, become attractive.[4]

Lukács' approach to social ontology is clearly animated by different questions and consequently frames the issue in a different way. Even though Lukács is also concerned with presenting a naturalist picture, his framing of the question is focused on how social institutions and social activity fit into a broader picture of exchange between humans and their environment. The theory which Lukács begins to develop in the *Ontology* is in this regard much more ambitious than most social ontological works in the analytic debate: Lukács wants to examine not only the metaphysics of groups and the features of distinctive sorts of collective intentional action but also the way in which almost all activity in a developed society is integrated into a network, or a "totality," that is rooted in the intentional engagement of human beings with their natural environment.

Even if not in the precise way in which Lukács develops it, such a comprehensive theory is of central interest to a critical social ontology, and this for two reasons. First, critical theories famously distinguish themselves from "traditional" theories by adopting a reflexive stance – that is, by including themselves in their object domain. Critical social theories must therefore not only engage in social ontological theorizing in virtue of aiming at social practices in their critiques but also understand their very own activity as one of the social practices they are about, thus adopting a social ontology that includes itself in its object domain. In the history of Western Marxism, such a comprehensive approach was often motivated by the idea that modern capitalist societies form a "totality" – that is, a whole in which no part can be understood in isolation and which thus requires social theory to account for its own place within that totality.

Second, critical theories traditionally distinguish themselves from forms of moral critique by assuming that, rather than approaching their object – society – with norms that have been developed and justified independently of it, they engage in immanent critique. This means that they take up norms and standards which in some sense already exist in social reality. This raises social ontological issues regarding the normative nature of social phenomena for which critical theories must account.

---

4 Authors such a Philip Pettit (cf. Philip Pettit, *The Common Mind. An Essay on Psychology, Society and Politics*. (Oxford/New York: Oxford University Press, 1993), 129ff.) and Michael Bratman (cf. Michael E. Bratman, *Faces of Intention*. (Cambridge University Press, 1999).) make this assumption explicit.

Both issues, normativity and totality, play a major role in Lukács' discussion. The following considerations should be understood as a first attempt to think through the implications of his approach for the possible development of a critical social ontology. Given the many well-known problems associated with his explicit social ontology, the following will not take his pronouncements at face-value or merely attempt to interpret them in the most consistent way possible; rather it will take them as points of departure that allow for insights which can be used in the service of the project of a critical social ontology. The article proceeds as follows: Section 2 examines the theoretical problems faced by critical social ontologies in general. The issues of normativity and totality are then examined. Section 3 discusses the central role that Lukács assigns to work in the emergence of social normativity, and Section 4 does the same for the concept of totality. In both cases, it can be shown that Lukács endorses some intuitions that point beyond contemporary accounts in social ontology but that he does not reject the individualist and objectivist presuppositions of that debate radically enough. The article therefore concludes (Section 5) by discussing the extent to which and the respects in which a convincing critical social ontology must go beyond Lukács.

2   Problems of a Critical Social Ontology

The question at the heart of all theories of social ontology is the question of the *existence of social facts*. Social ontological arguments are grounded in the observation that the most plausible social theories are committed to the existence of institutions, groups, social systems, social rules, collective action, and finally, societies. This raises the question of what it means to claim that such entities exist and in what sense and under what conditions they can exist.

In the contemporary debate, leading theorists defend a number of distinct claims that concern both the question of totality (even if not by that name) and the question of normativity. Regarding the totality issue, most authors in contemporary social ontology assume that it is plausible to assume some form of supervenience of social facts on facts about individuals:[5] At least globally speaking, social phenomena can be taken to supervene not only on the material world but also on the behavior and thoughts of, and the relations between,

---

5   Cf. Brian McLaughlin and Karen Bennett, "Supervenience." In *The Stanford Encyclopedia of Philosophy*, ed. Edward N. Zalta, n.d., http://plato.stanford.edu/archives/fall2008/entries/supervenience/; Frank Hindriks, "The Location Problem in Social Ontology." *Synthese*, vol. 190, no. 3 (February 1, 2013): 414, https://doi.org/10.1007/s11229-011-0036-0.

individual people. If two worlds are the same in all of these respects, they will also be the same with respect to the social entities that exist in them, as social phenomena can only be realized through configurations of material objects and individual human action and thought. As Brian Epstein has noted, this assumption of supervenience motivates the almost universally accepted idea of ontological individualism.[6] While ontological individualism is almost universally accepted, however, it can be spelled out in quite different ways. For example, the "Standard Model" in contemporary social ontology, as defended by John Searle, Raimo Tuomela and many others, takes social facts to depend on the acceptance of constitutive rules that confer a certain status on them. Epstein has recently proposed a more complex theory that combines these views. According to his model, (particular) social facts are ultimately *grounded* in (particular) non-social facts. But this grounding relation (or several relations, in complex cases) depends on there being grounding conditions in place that define the conditions under which non-social facts count as having certain social roles. These grounding conditions are in turn *anchored* in people's collective acceptance of certain frames.[7]

I take it that Epstein's analysis is the most advanced and most plausible interpretation of commitments in contemporary social ontology. However, it is relatively clear that a critical social ontology of the type envisaged by Lukács will not accept this interpretation of the supervenience claim for several reasons, the most important of which has to do with its own reflexive character. Social ontological theorizing, in the philosophical sense, is an extension and part of the way in which we conceptualize social facts in ordinary life. This means that the claims of a social ontological theory are to some extent part of the anchoring of social facts in our societies insofar as social ontological theorizing forms a part of our collectively shared self-understanding. In most cases, however, it will be impossible to neatly divide social phenomena into lower-level phenomena which anchor higher-level phenomena without introducing circularity at some point. This is not only because collective beliefs, such as those we share about the social ontological constitution of our lifeworld, are often rooted in institutions which are anchored by such beliefs and in turn provide anchoring conditions for them. There is also always the possibility that social entities can be ontologically shaped in ways that are independent of our understanding of them. This means that parts of the empirical function of social entities will be determined not by the (anchoring) beliefs we have about

---

6   Brian Epstein, *The Ant Trap: Rebuilding the Foundations of the Social Sciences*, Oxford Studies in Philosophy of Science. (New York, N.Y.: Oxford University Press, 2015), 34.
7   Epstein, 84.

them but by the entire complex of social practices that make up social life. An admittedly not very useful way to describe this issue is to say that social facts must be seen as anchored not only in particular beliefs (of which social ontological theory forms one part) but also in the entirety of the social life of a community. More formally, we can say that it is possible to have a situation in which a particular social fact that anchors a set of social facts S_1 is itself anchored in another set of social facts S_2, where S_1 and S_2 are not distinct sets but share elements with each other. In such a case, both ontological individualism and the standard picture of social reality cease to be useful models of analysis (as does the anchoring model, which combines elements of both), although we can still hold on to a global version of the supervenience claim.

In the Marxist tradition and the tradition of critical theory, this interpretation of the interdependence of social facts has often been referred to by the term "totality,"[8] although there has so far been no attempt to account for the meaning of this term in the vocabulary of social ontology. We should thus expect a critical social ontology to give us insight into this idea.

The normativity issue is a second problem that clearly animates Lukács' social ontology and that sharply separates his analysis from contemporary social ontology. Some contemporary theorists in social ontology – such as Margaret Gilbert – acknowledge that a defining feature of social phenomena such as collective intentions, collective beliefs and institutional rules is their normative character. Gilbert argues, for example, that a genuinely *collective* intention to perform an action A differs from merely *summatively shared* individual intentions to perform A insofar as a collective intention can only exist once the relevant group has "jointly committed itself" to performing A, which generates a "derived" individual commitment on the part of every member of the group to do their part and a corresponding entitlement on the part of other members to demand performance. Such an entitlement is, however, absent in the case of merely accidentally shared individual intentions.[9] Similarly, John Searle argues that social institutions are partly defined by the collective recognition of rules by their members, who thereby impose normatively relevant statuses on actions or objects, which then make certain forms of behavior permissible or impermissible (collectively imposing the status of money on certain objects, for example, means that those objects then fall under rules that regulate how

---

8 See Martin Jay, *Marxism and Totality. The Adventures of a Concept from Lukács to Habermas*. (Berkeley: University of California Press, 1984).

9 Margaret Gilbert, "Walking Together: A Paradigmatic Social Phenomenon." *Midwest Studies in Philosophy*, vol. XV (1990): 3–14.

they can be treated).[10] Both accounts remain deeply problematic, however. In both cases, it never becomes clear how the adoption of individual attitudes (which, as the relevant theorists admit, do not entail normative obligations) can connect up to collective attitudes (which then mysteriously do).[11]

The totality challenge and the normativity challenge are thus two aspects in terms of which current accounts in social ontology are insufficient for the purposes of a critical project. It is these challenges with which Lukács' ontology is also concerned and which justify returning to it, in spite of its difficulties. I will reconstruct Lukács' view on normativity in the next section, before tackling the issue of totality in Section 4.

3 Work, "Teleological Positing," and Normativity

The problem of normativity lies at the center of Lukács' account of a Marxist social ontology, as he argues that "teleological" phenomena are the defining characteristic of the social (which differentiates the latter from both inorganic and organic nature). Lukács explains teleological phenomena in the context of a materialist account by referring to the role played by "teleological positing" – or, put more simply, the anticipation of results of intentional action – in organizing the interchange process between humans and non-human nature through work. In referring to "teleology," Lukács does not thereby want to suggest that society strives towards a goal in its entirety, independently of individual thought and action. Rather, he argues that individuals engage in "teleological positing" in their work, that these individual phenomena can form structures, and that a particular form of structure is a defining characteristic of social entities.[12] It is important to understand that, at its foundation in individual acts of positing, this is a normative phenomenon, which Lukács then takes to explain all normative aspects of social structures (including "objectively existing" social values). All normative social phenomena, in other words, can be traced back to the commitments that individuals undertake in their labor processes.

---

10 John R. Searle, "What Is an Institution?" *Journal of Institutional Economics*, vol. 1, no. 1 (2005): 1–22, https://doi.org/10.1017/S1744137405000020.
11 Titus Stahl, "The Conditions of Collectivity. Joint Commitments and the Shared Norms of Membership." In *Perspectives on Social Ontology*, ed. Hans-Bernhard Schmid, Anita Konzelmann Ziv, and Ulla Schmid. (Dordrecht: Springer, 2013).
12 György Lukács, *Prolegomena zur Ontologie des gesellschaftlichen Seins*, ed. Frank Benseler. (Darmstadt: Luchterhand, 1984). (hereafter cited as OGS), I, 189; II, 52, 464.

To give just a brief overview over some of Lukács' main claims in the *Ontology*, he assigns this central function to labor in his general social ontology on the following grounds: (1) labor, according to him, is the point of transition between nature and society;[13] (2) the positing act in the process of labor has a normative dimension that grounds all normative phenomena in society;[14] (3) the only way to properly understand social institutions and the very idea of history is to view them as being based on such fundamental normativity;[15] and (4) teleological positing and the choice between alternatives are the conditions of existence of human freedom.[16]

In the first instance, the somewhat artificial term "positing" does not refer to much more than the anticipation of a desired result by the worker – in other words, a component of their having an intention.[17] This act of anticipation, Lukács argues, establishes a normative standard for the subsequent work process, or an "ought."[18] Such an "ought," in turn, involves both a dimension of necessity – the regularities described by natural laws, which make choosing one element of a set containing different combinations of means necessary for achieving one's goal – and a dimension of freedom in terms of choosing one's goal.[19] To put it simply: If one wants to achieve X, and if Y is a necessary means to X, then one ought to perform Y. Building on this quite mundane thought, Lukács argues, we can also understand the idea of "unconditioned" normative standards, such as those involved in forms of the moral ought.

Even though this relatively simple thought raises more questions than it answers, it is clear that Lukács attributes a central role to the requirement to choose between goals given available means, together with the emergence of rational planning that is also constitutive of labor – understood here as action in relation to a scope of objects which are governed by natural laws. The concept of "law" that is involved here is located "between" nature and society, Lukács argues, because the relevant ought – i.e., the normative dimension – results from the combination of two non-social components, anticipation of the results of one's action by a desire-driven subject and the relations of natural necessity which govern the rational choice of means, although the resulting normative standard is socially significant insofar as it allows for the intersubjective interpretation of action. One can speculate that other forms of

---

13 OGS II, 9.
14 OGS I, 620.
15 OGS II, 78ff.
16 OGS II, 39ff.
17 OGS II, 18.
18 OGS II, 61.
19 OGS II, 306.

"social-teleological positing" from which Lukács distinguishes his own work,[20] such as institutional and social norms, are not in the same sense "in between" nature and society, because the necessity which has to be incorporated in the choice of means is in these cases no longer natural necessity (i.e., a form of necessity which results from the fact that certain goals, in virtue of the natural features of the relevant context, can only be reached using certain means) but rather socially determined necessity. Similarly, one may say that while in the case of labor the setting of goals is a result of choices between options that are natural kinds (because they can be described as results of non-social action), in the social case the options themselves are socially constituted.

Lukács sometimes also describes the transition between nature and society by claiming that labor leads to a "new form of objectivity."[21] He thereby seems to refer primarily not to the character of the products of work but to the role that objects play in enabling the work process – that is, to tools.[22] Tools can be characterized by their function, which is only intelligible in relation to goals that can be pursued through their use. Hammers are not only suitable for hammering. The fact that it is their function to enable hammering is only intelligible if there are at least possible situations in which hammering is a means to pursuing a goal that someone desires and anticipates before selecting the necessary means. Furthermore, it is a characteristic feature of tools that we can assign essential functions to them which are not fully determined by their natural properties (one could also assign another function to a hammer). Any function that is assigned to them, however, will directly involve their physical properties. This distinguishes them from institutional entities (like advocates or contracts) the functions of which are not such that they are selected from a range that is directly determined by their physical properties. Compared to such entities, the social imposition of a tool's function is more closely bound to its possible roles in causal processes.

Taken together, these elements can help us to grasp a claim that is central to Lukács' (wide-ranging and not always consistent) remarks to the effect that the origin of normativity in society must be located in the attribution of functions to tools, which is only intelligible in a context in which both normative-intentional positing through the (individual) anticipation of the result of an action and the determination of possible routes to achieving that goal by natural laws play a role – in other words, in the context of labor. Lukács seems to assume that it is only labor that can provide a non-mysterious basis (anticipatory

---

20   OGS II, 12.
21   OGS II, 30.
22   OGS II, 35.

imagination of a possible result of one's action and *knowledge* of natural laws) for normative criteria as emerging from broadly natural processes. If we accept this, then we can understand how, through the imposition of functions, tools emerge as the first social entities the internal teleological structure of which also becomes a part of intersubjective reality, as cooperative labor processes require achieving a shared understanding of that structure and thereby form the basis of all other kinds of social normativity.

To put it kindly, this story leaves certain questions open. First, it is unclear why only tools can play this role, and why for, example, communication about goals does not also introduce language as an independent source of normative commitments. Equally unclear, however, is whether Lukács does not merely adopt, after all, a relatively standard Humean idea about normative commitment as the result of a combination of desire and knowledge. Above all, what remains unclear is why labor gives rise to a form of normativity that is, in some non-trivial sense, essentially social. After all, Lukács' conception of labor – at least the way he himself introduces that conception – refers to an activity that can be performed by individuals. If the anticipatory imagination forms the normative standard for labor, it seems entirely possible to explain the resulting normativity even independently of cooperative contexts and as something which can equally apply to a solitary worker. In other words, labor-based normativity does not have social preconditions and does not necessarily lead to socially shared norms. Compared, for example, with the analysis of being-at-hand in Heidegger's *Being and Time,* Lukács' analysis seems to be thoroughly individualistic. Where Heidegger assumes that other people must be included in one's orientation towards the work process, at least as potential consumers of the product,[23] Lukács seems to follow an individualistic path that is quite surprising for one of the most famous Marxist theorists of totality. Society and labor are necessarily linked merely insofar as people create causal connections between each other's activities through the non-intended consequences of their activities, which then gradually form a systemic structure.[24] The *individualist reduction* of labor-based normativity is thus combined by Lukács with a *quasi-system-theoretic analysis* of social integration of individual goals into one overarching structure of production by anonymous laws.[25]

---

23   Martin Heidegger, *Being and Time*, trans. John Macquarrie and Edward Robinson. (Oxford: Blackwell, 1962), 100.
24   Cf. OGS II, 458, 459, 464, 504, but also OGS I, 191–192, 592, 662 and OGS II, 302ff.
25   It is remarkable that a thought that had been prominent in Lukács' reification essay is almost absent in the *Ontology*. This is the idea that the totality can be appropriated by a revolutionary subject and that a merely causally integrated whole can thereby be transformed into one that can itself be understood as the result of intentional positing. It is not

Second, it remains unclear why the structure of work – even if we accept that the interplay of desire and necessity that is characteristic of interaction with nature is the foundation of normativity – should be key to understanding society rather than merely one element within a broader theory of social norms. Even if the normative ought of social rules is always a result, directly or indirectly, of the interaction of human anticipation with natural-law necessity (which is itself not exactly an intuitive thought), it remains possible that social normative structures have a logic of their own which is such that we learn very little about them by examining the structure of the labor process.

There are, however, resources in Lukács' discussion for dealing with these two objections. As to the first problem, concerning the underlying individualism in the description of labor, one might say with some interpretive charity that Lukács not only views work as the realization of individuals' subjective intentions but also views these intentions as in turn subject to social evaluation based on how they contribute (or fail to contribute) to the satisfaction of *needs*.[26] Admittedly, Lukács often seems to endorse a relatively simplistic subjectivist-utilitarian analysis of how work can be evaluated with regard to its effects.[27] That this is not the whole story can be shown, however, if one takes into account his emphasis on the idea that the needs that are relevant to such an evaluation and to judging whether the intention guiding a given labor process has been actualized are needs with a "social character."[28] What does this mean? A first idea is that it could mean that some needs are themselves products of social practices, processes and institutions. Such needs either constitutively depend on social contexts (for example, the need to experience certain forms of recognition or status) or are causally related to social practices (for example, the need to satisfy desires that are the result of a certain kind of socialization).[29] But this cannot be all that Lukács means. Even though such needs are social in some sense, they are not *social* needs in an ontological sense. They are needs of individuals – needs that relate to what individuals require and to what is in some sense essential to their existence or self-realization.

---

entirely clear that this is merely the result of a politically motivated renunciation of the Hegelianism of Lukács' middle period. It could equally well be viewed as the resolution of a tension between the sociological theory of reification and the subject theoretical theory of revolution in that earlier model.

26   OGS II, 39, 42.
27   OGS II, 70.
28   OGS II, 341.
29   OGS II, 242.

There are two passages which are informative for an understanding of the concept of need employed by Lukács and its relation to social normativity. First, he distinguishes between work as a *mere* satisfaction of need and "work as social practice":

> The original intention of the teleological positing is directed, in the first instance, to a mere satisfaction of need. Only within an objectively social context do the work process and the product of work acquire a more general nature which goes beyond the individual person, but is still tied to social practice and thereby to human being.[30]

The distinction between an "original intention" and an "objectively social context" probably refers to the distinction – familiar from Marx[31] – between production that does not involve a division of labor and production that does. While "in the first instance" – that is, in the historically prior form of non-divided labor – individuals work for the satisfaction of their own needs, the norms that govern their labor change in stages where the social environment makes an objective difference to what they do (their actions only being intelligible as part of a larger practice of cooperation), and what they do is different in a social ontological sense.

Earlier in the text, Lukács makes the following argument concerning the "sociality of the determination of purpose" ("Gesellschaftlichkeit der Zielsetzung") within the labor process, which helps to make sense of this idea:

> The homogenization of end and means as set out above, must also be dialectically qualified from another standpoint, and thereby made more concrete. The doubly social character of the positing of the goal – arising as it does from a social need and being called on to satisfy such a need, whereas the naturalness of the substratum of means of realization leads practice directly into a different kind of environment and activity – sets up a fundamental heterogeneity between end and means.[32]

---

30 OGS II, 245, Translation T.S.
31 Karl Marx and Friedrich Engels, "The German Ideology." In *The Marx-Engels Reader*, ed. Robert C. Tucker, 2nd ed. (W.W. Norton & Company, 1978), 158.
32 OGS II, 21. Translation according to György Lukács, *The Ontology of Social Being*. (London: Merlin Press, 1978), vol. 3: 14.

This somewhat opaque passage can be read as follows. Processes of labor are characterized by heterogeneity on an ontological level. On the one hand, they are guided by needs which are socially determined (in a way that still has to be explored). On the other hand, the way in which these needs (as standards for labor) find application is through guiding a choice of appropriate means, whereby the question of which means are appropriate for a given purpose is determined by natural properties and ultimately natural laws, and thus not socially defined. Labor thus requires matching up a standard that is not exhausted by the individual's representation of it with natural facts that are also not exhausted by it, and thus the anticipation which is characteristic of labor has to bring together elements from two ontological spheres which systematically transcend the reach of the individual. If that process succeeds, what the individual's anticipation then establishes is a "homogeneous" (that is, consistent) standard governing their activities. The heterogeneity is homogenized through the labor process, in particular once socially defined and created needs indirectly form the standard for the choice of means.

To fully understand this interpretation, more must be said about the social normative nature of needs. When Lukács talks about social needs that must be satisfied, the social aspect should be taken to refer not only to the *source of the normative significance* of individual needs (for example the way in which the norm of trying to anticipate the widely shared needs of potential customers is established as a rational requirement by the market mechanism) but also to *determining the content* of needs. In other words, what counts as fulfilling a need should also be viewed as something that is socially established.

To use a simple example: The cooperative work of building an apartment complex can be motivated by anticipation of unspecified people's need to have a place to live. We can think of this need as both causally arising from society (for example, if it is assumed that having a place to live is a need that people at least partly acquire through socialization) and as socially determined in terms of its content. For example, there will never be a mere need for a place to live; such a need will always be for an adequate, dignified space. What that means is not determined by the subject of the need alone – as if believing that an apartment is adequate could make it so. Rather, we can assume that people can be mistaken about whether their needs have actually been fulfilled. This entails that those who are trying to fulfill a need – in this example, the builders – can be mistaken about whether they have succeeded in doing so. Not every product that they take to be adequate to satisfy the need involved in the construction of the anticipated result is indeed adequate, and this even holds when there is a consumer who concurs in the judgment that it is. Apparent and actual need satisfaction can be distinguished in the case of socially defined needs.[33] This distinction is socially instituted and can be intersubjectively evaluated.

To be sure, Lukács never explicitly endorses this claim. However, the supposition that the social constitution of needs must extend to their content and the way this content is reflected in the labor-guiding intentions of workers is necessary for making sense of further claims in the ontology. Consider, for example, the following passage, which refers to the character of "positing" (that is, intentionality):

> Epistemologically, a positing that misses its object is still a positing, even if it must be judged to be false. The ontological positing of causality in the complex of a teleological positing, however, must correctly come to grips with its object, or else it is no positing at all, in this sense.[34]

The intentions that guide labor are thus not to be understood as being independent of what they objectively aim at – that is, the product that satisfies anticipated needs and that is produced using specific means. This further entails that, if products and means acquire a specifically historical character through the process of "homogenization," that is, through the imposition of a standard referring to socially determined needs, then (it seems at least reasonable to conclude that) the way in which intentions relate to their satisfactory conditions will be determined by categories that are instituted in a social practice, independently of whether the individual worker adequately represents these conditions to herself.

If this analysis of the social nature of intentions (and underlying needs) is correct, then we can at least make some progress in understanding how the normativity of (in the first instance individual) labor is also a form of social normativity. What remains unclear, however, is the respect in which this normativity can be said to be fundamental to all normative social phenomena – in particular, how it can help us to understand the normativity of social institutions. To put the same question a different way: Why should we assume that labor as a productive practice is special with regard to the social determination of the content of intentional states? There are, after all, many theories of intentional content that assume that all intentional phenomena, mediated through the sociality of concepts, are in fact determined in their content by social practices. For most of these theories, it is discourse, not labor, which is the relevant social practice in which meaning is created.

---

33   OGS II, 70.
34   OGS II, 20. Translation according to Lukács, *The Ontology of Social Being*, vol. 3: 13.

In my opinion, the only way to rescue Lukács' insistence on this primacy is to adopt a relatively risky strategy that again refers to needs and the specific position of labor in the exchange between nature and society. Social practice theories of meaning – such as Brandom's inferentialism – assume that our intentional commitments and explicit linguistic utterances acquire meaningful significance only when we accept the authority of other members of our linguistic community concerning their conditions of satisfaction, which involves relations of recognition between us and them.[35] In Brandom's theory, for example, these others are often imagined in the role of referees or scorekeepers concerning our discursive moves. That picture suggests that they reach their judgment from the perspective of an uninvolved observer or interpreter[36] who imagines counterfactually what moves would be available and correct had they undertaken the commitments of the observed person. From the perspective of such a model, those who engage in "discursive score-keeping" need not be practically involved in the activities of those they interpret.

This "observer" model of the exercise of recognitive authority is intuitively plausible for discursive practices in which descriptive assertions (as in the natural sciences) or the interpretation of norms (as in law or morality) are central to the relevant discourse. It is therefore unsurprising that the examples that Brandom chooses consistently refer to these spheres.[37] The model of a merely observing scorekeeper is less plausible, however, once we focus on the best way to understand the social determination of the intentional states of people engaged in *material labor*. In fact, one can make an argument against the Brandomian conception of social practices which runs parallel to Marx's critique of Feuerbach.[38] According to Marx's critique, an attempt to understand distinctive human capacities on the basis of a conception of social practices will be misleading as long as it describes those practices in terms of interactions that are exclusively guided by epistemic criteria and as long as it understands the relevant actions as epistemic activities. A more appropriate, materialist conception of practice must take into account the fact that much normative human interaction is motivated by the basic fact that humans have needs that can only be satisfied cooperatively and that they therefore cooperatively intervene in their natural surroundings guided by rules that are appropriate for

---

35   Cf. Robert B. Brandom, *Reason in Philosophy. Animating Ideas*. (Cambridge, Mass.: Harvard University Press, 2009), 81ff.
36   Robert B. Brandom, *Making It Explicit*. (Cambridge/London: Harvard University Press, 1994), chap. 3.
37   Brandom, 184; Brandom, *Reason in Philosophy*, 84ff.
38   Karl Marx, "Theses on Feuerbach." In *The Marx-Engels Reader*, ed. Robert C. Tucker, 2nd ed. (W.W. Norton & Company, 1978), 143–145.

social attempts to satisfy such needs. As some of the interpreters of the young Marx have realized,[39] this insight enables us to formulate a different theory of recognition, where the central practice is not the score-keeping in which those who are recognized as authorities engage with regard to the individual, nonsocial behavior of others. Rather, there are also forms of recognition of needs that confer social significance onto those needs and that thereby establish them as standards for essentially other-directed intentional performances. If A not only recognizes B as a competent authority with regard to the disinterested evaluation of whether what A does is compatible with A's stated intentions but also recognizes B's needs as significant, then actions performed by A which are justified and characterized with regard to the goal of fulfilling B's needs are socially determined in a way that is not captured by the score-keeping model. In such a case, it is not B's disinterested evaluation of A's behavior's consistency with A's intentional commitments that is the basic element of the social practice that determines the content of these commitments, but rather the satisfaction of B's needs. It is thus not only the needs referred to by intentions in the labor process that are socially determined; the normative recognition of those needs by those who try to satisfy them is also the basic building block of a social practice of determining the meaning of intentional commitments that can (but need not) be expressed in language. It is this rather speculative suggestion to the effect that we can extend the Brandomian social pragmatist program in the theory of meaning to include a "material" component connected to the structure of labor on which I will draw to make sense of Lukács' claim that *all* social normativity rests on labor.

There is, however, a qualification that must be made here. It is more than obvious that the Lukácsian model presupposes a picture of labor that is focused on the production of consumer goods, as do Marx's early considerations. From both perspectives, it is one of the pathologies of the capitalist market that, while it is driven by normative recognition of the relevance of consumer needs, this recognition appears in the shape of seemingly impersonal laws of supply and demand, blocking workers from understanding their constitutive sociality. That Lukács and Marx do not consider other types of work that are typically not, or only incompletely, subsumed under the market relation in capitalist economies, such as housework, care work, bringing up children and

---

39 Karl Marx, "Auszüge aus James Mills Buch 'Elémens d'économie politique.'" In *Werke / Ergänzungsband, Schriften, Manuskripte, Briefe bis 1844.* (Berlin: Dietz, 1968), 443–463; Daniel Brudney, "Marx' neuer Mensch." In *Anerkennung*, ed. Hans-Christoph Schmidt am Busch and Christopher F. Zurn (Berlin: Akademie Verlag, 2009), 145–180, https://doi.org/10.1524/9783050061566.

informal work in the domestic sector, is a severe deficiency of their account.[40] Including these forms in their analysis would both strengthen their underlying intuitions about how recognition of needs is involved and allow them to analyze pathologies of misrecognition that, even if structurally similar, cannot be ascribed to market dominance.

That being said, there is some plausibility to the idea that a social pragmatist model of linguistic meaning can be extended using the materialist insight. One advantage is that the idea of the social determination of meaning through practices of mutual recognition of needs can much more easily be integrated into a naturalist account. If we assume that human beings can only satisfy their needs through cooperation, and if we also assume that, from a certain point of cultural development onward, the relevant cooperative processes require individuals to engage in complex planning activities, then it becomes completely non-mysterious, first, that the standards of correctness for such planning are socially "administered," and second, that it is useful for humans to be able to make their commitments and entitlements explicit, using language, which also makes it possible for the inferential relations that are constitutive of the meaning of the concepts used to do so to themselves be subject to social standards of correctness. Finally, once we embrace this speculative model of the role of language in the history of the species, Lukács' seemingly reductive claim that we can explain all normativity as being derived from the labor process becomes somewhat less counterintuitive. The conceptual resources that we can use to engage in forms of social cooperation which are not immediately directed towards the satisfaction of needs will then (at the ground level) be those that have already been made available in the social coordination of labor and needs.

In other words, if we assume that the relevant practice of recognition is a recognition of needs as relevant (in the sense that they are accepted as standards for activities which aim at satisfying them), then labor is the basic activity in which such recognition is expressed and which is socially taken to be subject to those standards. This form of recognition then serves as a foundation for other forms of social coordination through an ascription of authority that becomes necessary, at some point, to enable further complexity. It is not necessary to deny that analyses such as Brandom's correctly capture the social practices that underlie discursive practices; rather, the argument is that they make the emergence of relations of recognition mysterious (or attribute it to an unexplained interest in conceptual capacities), which also makes it unclear

---

40   Titus Stahl, "Sharing the Background." In *The Background of Social Reality*, ed. Michael Schmitz, Beatrice Kobow and Hans Bernhard Schmid. (Springer, 2013), 127–146.

whether there are normative standards for determining the rationality of accepting specific forms of social authority. By contrast, if we accept the Lukács-inspired needs-based social pragmatism sketched above, social recognition will be driven, at the most basic level, by an anthropologically rooted interest in living in a society that is structured around the cooperative satisfaction of needs. At a second level, the interest in living in a discursive community in which people recognize each other as equals when it comes to their semantic capacities will then be a cultural development that, even if it ultimately acquires considerable autonomy, can be seen as motivated by and to some extent subject to evaluation with regard to this underlying interest.

This also helps us to answer the second question regarding the link between labor and institutional reality. In the current debate in social ontology, it is often assumed that what lies at the foundation of institutional reality is some kind of collective acceptance of rules. Lukács' theory of "teleological positing" (which, as I have argued, need not be interpreted in an individualistic manner) seems to be an alternative to this view. Again, we have no choice but to engage in speculation given the lack of a clear answer in Lukács' text.

If institutions rest on the collective acceptance of rules, it is plausible to assume that in most cases the answer to the question of what *counts* as a sufficient form of collective acceptance will be determined by institutional rules (which, one might say, "anchor" the fact of collective acceptance). On pain of infinite regress, however, there must be ground-level institutions the rules of which are collectively accepted in a way that is explicable without reference to any further rules. In other words, there must be non-institutional instances of collective acceptance. One example of such a claim is H.L.A. Hart's famous thoughts on the "rule of recognition," a rule which serves to identify valid legal rules but which is not identified as valid by another rule insofar as its force is a pure matter of non-legal social practice.[41] As I have argued elsewhere, the most plausible way to account for such basic forms of shared rule acceptance is to adopt a theory according to which a rule is collectively accepted in a community if the members of that community recognize each other as entitled to criticize each other's behavior with reference to that rule.[42]

I propose that we understand Lukács as advancing the claim that the idea of intersubjective recognition of needs provides the link between such general structures of social reality and processes of labor. Not only does the dependence of human beings on others for the satisfaction of their needs

---

41   Cf. H.L.A. Hart, *The Concept of Law*, 2nd ed. (Oxford: Oxford University Press, 1994).
42   Cf. Titus Stahl, *Immanente Kritik. Elemente Einer Theorie Sozialer Praktiken*. (Frankfurt a. M.: Campus, 2013), 242.

genealogically explain the emergence of historically normative practices that regulate cooperation, but there is also a social ontological point to be made in support of the necessity of including needs in this model. The basic idea is that rules or norms establish a difference between correct and incorrect action. As Wittgenstein famously argued, this distinction cannot be identified with an individual's self-assessment, as there is a difference between applying a rule correctly and merely thinking that one is applying it correctly. This motivates the idea that the distinction between correct and incorrect performance, as a necessary component of any rule-guided practice, can only be rooted in an intersubjective social assessment in which no individual reaction ever settles the matter. This does not entail, however, that there needs to be an infinite regress of rules and rule-applications. Rather, it is plausible to say that there is a standard of correctness embodied in a practice once people accept each other's reactions as having default authority that settles the matter unless there is a challenge to that authority. While the meaning of rules cannot be reduced to whatever community members are disposed to accept as their meaning, their dispositions to accept each other's interpretations as authoritative by default still enables us to think of the whole of assessments in a community as a finite set that determines what is correct or incorrect.[43]

This model entails that, even if the content of institutional rules is not determined by any individual's dispositions, institutional practices are made possible by people's reliable dispositions to apply rules, to assess other people's applications of rules, and so on. Hegelian accounts such as Brandom's typically assume that such dispositions are there and that people are in some way motivated to serve as score-keepers in the social practice game. As sketched above, we may also adopt a more materialist version of this model, in which the basic level of evaluative dispositions is given by needs: When the standard we are asked to apply to other people's performances is whether these performances lead to the satisfaction of our needs, it is easy to see not only why we might be motivated to play that game but also what normative force the game has in its entirety. If we assume that the intersubjective recognition of needs in a cooperative practice is the bottom level of social evaluative practices, we can make more sense of Lukács' claim that all institutional practices are based on labor, as labor is simply the name of a performance that is subject to the standard of whether it satisfies other people's needs (at least this is so once we drop the problematic requirement that all kinds of labor must engage external nature).

Unlike intersubjectivist theories that privilege *discursive* interaction as the main space of recognition – such as those developed by Brandom and, with

---

43   For a longer version of this argument, see Stahl, 325.

some qualifications, Habermas – the materialist theory sketched above does not share the idealist assumption, first expressed by Hegel, that the development of normative orders emerges solely from the internal dialectic between forms and justification and their reflexive self-application.[44] Rather, it will assume that there is also a dialectical relation between individual needs and social institutions, where both elements do not shape each other merely causally but are instead subject to challenges based on the normative meaning of the other element.

What such a theory of labor-based normativity cannot explain, however, is the emergence of types of intentionality by which people create new institutional rules and, concomitantly, new needs emerge. If one assumes that all norms ultimately emerge from needs-directed interaction between people, then there is room to explain how the resulting practices become increasingly complex in their quest to satisfy the relevant needs, and perhaps even how derived needs that relate to the requirements of participation in such practices emerge. The resulting model will still be instrumentalist to a certain extent, however – as Lukács argues, language and institutions are mere means of the "generalization" of more particular forms of action. It will not be able to explain the emergence of new social action types that have goals which are completely divorced from need satisfaction.

Of course, this model has only been briefly sketched here and involves much speculation, although I think that it is ultimately consistent with what Lukács says and provides a foundation for his claims that is missing in his own work. With this said, we must admit that we find no systematic answer to the question of how we can understand labor itself as a social practice and how the structure of this practice fits into the larger framework of a theory of society. His analysis of the individual positing of goals is complemented only by a quasi-system-theoretic model of the emergence of social order through unintentional consequences of action. This does not explain the contribution of labor to the normative structure of society.

4   Social Holism and Totality

In a second step, I wish to discuss Lukács' claims regard the irreducibility of social facts. Lukács develops these claims by connecting his discussion of normativity to a number of other ideas. First, there is the idea that modern

---

44   Cf. Terry P. Pinkard, *Hegel's Phenomenology. The Sociality of Reason*. (New York: Cambridge University Press, 1996), chap. 1.

societies must be understood as totalities – that all specific social phenomena can only be adequately understood if one considers their role and function within society as an overarching structure.[45] Second, there is the idea that individual intentions and beliefs are merely intelligible from within the context of social practices.[46] This leads him to the holistic conclusion that understanding individual beliefs and intentions requires understanding society as a totality.[47]

The development of the concept of totality in Lukács' work involves ontological, epistemological and political aspects. In his earlier work, in particular in the *Theory of the Novel* and in *History and Class Consciousness*, he departs from a specific diagnosis of society. In the former book, he analyzes the modern situation by contrasting it with an earlier historical phase in which individual action could be meaningfully related to a whole, a possibility that disappeared with the emergence of modern individualism.[48] Following his move towards Marxism, he drops this historical narrative and claims that the revolutionary perspective is superior to bourgeois consciousness as it is only from within the revolutionary process that the totality of society, and even the very forms of objectivity of all social phenomena, can be adequately understood, whereas bourgeois thought necessarily regresses into irrationalism.[49] Marxism's capacity to understand totality is linked to its function of expressing the standpoint of the proletariat, which is itself the producer of that totality. Only the link to the possible revolutionary self-constitution of the proletariat accounts for the epistemic possibilities of that form of theory.

All of these aspects return in the *Ontology*, even if in a thoroughly different form. "Genuine" ontologies refer to the totality of everything that exists (as a totality of processes and partial totalities),[50] and this is also the guiding principle for an appropriate epistemology and for the possibility of political action. Political action in particular is understood as a form of acting in which the

---

45 Cf. Georg Lukács, "What Is Orthodox Marxism?" In *History and Class Consciousness. Studies in Marxist Dialectics*, trans. Rodney Livingstone. (1923; repr., MIT Press, 1971), 8; but also OGS II, 252.
46 OGS I, 578–584.
47 Cf. Philip Pettit, "Defining and Defending Social Holism." In *Rules, Reasons and Norms*. (Oxford: Oxford University Press, 2002), 116–135.
48 Georg Lukács, *The Theory of the Novel*, trans. Anna Bostock. (1915; repr., London: Merlin Press, 1971).
49 Georg Lukács, "Reification and the Consciousness of the Proletariat." In *History and Class Consciousness. Studies in Marxist Dialectics*, trans. Rodney Livingstone. (1923; repr., MIT Press, 1971), 110–149.
50 OGS I, 240, 523; OGS II, 155ff.

society's character as a totality, which emerges out of interlocking individual acts of positing, is adequately reflected upon.[51]

Even though this raises all kinds of issues, I wish only to remark that the idea of totality – which, in *History and Class Consciousness*, was still closely linked to the neo-Kantian idea of "forms of objectivity" (*Gegenständlichkeitsformen*) – becomes less plausible once it is integrated into a more traditional theory of ontology. In Lukács' earlier writings, the reference to totality explains not only how certain properties of objects are socially constituted but how the very form under which these objects become accessible to us as objects in the first place is determined by social practices which form a totality and thus rule out other forms of objectivity which might lead to more appropriate forms of engagement with the respective objects. In particular, Lukács there claims that a form of objectivity that "reifies" objects insofar as the constitutive role of social practices for their respective nature becomes inaccessible due to that form also leads to social pathologies.

Compared to this critical employment of the notion of totality, the concept seems to play a less ambitious role later on, that is, in the *Ontology*. When Lukács argues, for example, that we can understand non-organic nature as a totality, this merely seems to mean that we cannot account for material properties except in relation to possible roles in causal explanations.[52] Of course, this notion of totality, which amounts to a quasi-Quinean form of holism, is no longer either controversial or particularly critical; it has lost its connection to the way in which particular kinds of social totality can either allow or block our understanding of the very form of objects.

It might be possible, however, to distinguish remarks where Lukács seemingly accepts this watered-down conception of totality from those passages where totality still has the original meaning of a whole that is constitutive not only of the meaning of experiences but of the very form under which objects can be experienced. In fact, only if we can make such a distinction will it again be possible to examine what role the concept of totality might pay in a critical social ontology.

We can begin this reconstructive work by noting that Lukács primarily uses the concept of totality in the *Ontology* in its social sense to describe the interplay of particular acts of teleological positing which relate to each other in virtue of their reference to objects.[53] Lukács sometimes expresses the issue in an unfortunate way, suggesting that individual acts of positing acquire a social

---

51 OGS II, 432–434.
52 OGS I, 182, 302.
53 Cf. OGS II, 74.

essence when they involve a reference to desired changes in the behavior of other people.[54] The possibility of such "positing" (i.e., intentionality) does not entail any form of social holism, however. At most, it leads to a description of social interaction in terms of the strategic pursuit of goals. That this cannot be Lukács' intended meaning becomes clear when we consider his central examples of the emergence of essentially social forms of positing: the constitution of exchange value and money.[55] In these cases, individuals' intentional acts of positing amount to a totality in a stronger sense, as we can no longer understand the meaning of what is intended without referring to the intentions of others (as would still be possible in the case of strategic interaction). That people form an intention to trade some good they possess in anticipation of the willingness of specified others to match that intention by giving up some specific object desired by them is a plausible reconstruction of the intentionality involved in the most primitive forms of commodity exchange. In any developed form of market exchange, participants' intentions can only be interpreted rationally (at least if we follow Marx this far) if we assume that they share a conception of equal exchange which is independent of their particular desires and which refers to a standard that is only comprehensible as emerging from the social practice in which these intentions play a particular role.[56]

Of course, this particular example might be vulnerable to the standard objections to the Marxist theory of value. What it purports to show is independent of them, however. One can argue that, once individuals' intentions refer to *social* facts such as exchange values, those intentions are social not merely in the sense that their conditions of satisfaction are dependent on the intentions or actions of others (as in the case of strategic interaction) but also in the sense that their *meaning* is determined by larger social practices. In particular, as is obvious in the case of exchange value, people can be capable of reliably applying concepts correctly without being capable of giving a correct or exhaustive analysis of what they mean. In such cases, people's mental states are insufficient to determine the content of their beliefs and intentions, leading to an externalist claim about meaning (the meaning of these terms is not "in their heads").

Furthermore, the social facts that determine the meaning of economic intentions (for example the structures of collective acceptance that fix the meaning of intentions regarding economic value) are typically characterized by

---

54 Cf. OGS II, 47.
55 OGS 78, 123, 206.
56 OGS II, 75.

their dependence on constitutive (or anchoring) relationships to further social facts (for example, the institutional nature of money and value cannot be analyzed without also including the institutional rules determining property, which in turn refer to norms regarding permissible and impermissible forms of exchange), leading to the conclusion that the content of economic intuition depends on a wide set of social practices and is thus social in a more fundamental sense than simple cases of purely strategic intentions.

If it is true that, given progress in the integration of interactions in networks of social practices, people's "positing" intentions – and, once we accept that they are also the source of normativity, the normative standards underlying social interaction – can only be understood if we assume that their content is determined by social institutions or practices, and if it is true that the social institutions involved in this process not only interact causally with other institutions but actually constitute and/or anchor each other, then we can make sense of Lukács' claim that it is indeed the intentional "positings" of individuals which, even if initially isolated from each other, both produce a social totality and, by becoming part of that totality, also become dependent on it for their very content.

This suggests that Lukács' theory can only be made plausible if we accept two assumptions that he himself – lacking the necessary theoretical tools – never makes explicit. The one is a form of social ontological holism that argues that there are no basic social institutions that can be understood without reference to further institutions. The other is an externalist thesis regarding (some) individual intentions that argues that the meaning of such intentions is determined not by the introspective self-understanding of the agent but by the objective social institutions to which those intentions refer, even if the very same intentions are what reproduce and account for the existence of these institutions. Both claims can be understood as forming the basis for a countercurrent to much work in contemporary social ontology.

To raise a last point, one can also relate these suggestions to what Lukács says about language in the *Ontology*. Even though Lukács generally discusses language only very rarely philosophically (apart from his aesthetic considerations), the *Ontology* is extreme in this respect as Lukács mentions the role of language only in passing. Admittedly, there is something like an implicit theory of language to be found, according to which linguistic meaning can be spelled out in terms of reference to objective kinds,[57] and Lukács also emphasizes how

---

57   OGS I, 147.

language can extend social reality by allowing people to refer to new phenomena. In both cases, however, he treats language as an instrument that only allows us to anticipate a relationship with the world that can ultimately only genuinely be realized through work.[58] In other words, for Lukács, language merely has the function of making explicit a world-relation that is always already there in work. The role of language in intersubjective communication (rather than the relation of a individual subject to the world) is only treated superficially. Lukács' theory of language treats communication either as a strategic attempt to influence others' behavior or as a means of transmitting representational content between speakers.[59] He never seriously considers the possibility that language can also enable communication that proceeds via the exchange of reasons and thus transcends strategic interaction insofar as through such exchanges a form of agreement that grounds many forms of social normativity and social institutions can be achieved. Similarly, he also does not consider the many forms of institutional reality the content of which is not explicable without referring to linguistically mediated agreement. One need only think of political action as aiming at generating legitimate power, where legitimacy can hardly be understood other than in terms of potential justifications. Politics and other institutions create spaces of interaction where language has a coordinating function and where, even further, specific forms of intersubjective, linguistically mediated reasoning are indeed constitutive. Even though Lukács stresses that the generalizing capacity of language allows us to think new thoughts,[60] he only considers this in relation to the representation of facts created in other domains of human action,[61] but never as the creation of new forms of interaction.

In relation to the concept of totality which is at issue here, this neglect of the linguistic dimension of the social entails that Lukács can understand the mutual interdependence of institutional contexts (and the action and object types determined by them) merely in the sense that he assumes that institutions are interconnected when agents acting in one institutional context implicitly refer (in some unspecified sense) to the action-guiding intentions of others in other contexts. This prevents him from considering not only the possibility that it is not merely individual intentions that connect different parts of the social whole but also the possibility that such connections already exist

---

58   OGS II, 171.
59   OGS II, 172.
60   OGS II, 165ff.
61   OGS II, 344f.

on the level of meaning. The very notion of a totality of meaning remains unexamined in the *Ontology*.

5   Perspectives for a Critical Social Ontology

This discussion of different fragments of Lukács' social ontology was not so much guided by the intention to make this complex theoretical construction entirely transparent as by the intention to highlight those ideas with which Lukács goes beyond the assumptions of dominant theories in contemporary social ontology and to examine them for their potential contribution to a critical social ontology.

In the introduction, a critical social ontology was defined as a social ontological theory that examines its own historical and social conditions of existence. Such a theory cannot understand itself as being independent of its own object – that is, of social institutions and practices. It must rather analyze all elements of social reality (itself among them) as constitutively interrelated and mutually determined.

Lukács' social ontology contains inspiration for such a theory. If one takes seriously the idea that individual and social forms of teleology are mutually interdependent, there is an argument for also including social ontological theorizing as a norm-guided process in the analysis of this totality. Even if one accepts the ambitious claim that all social normativity is rooted in the labor process, however, it is clear that Lukács' analysis must be extended by an analysis of other forms of social practice that takes their relative autonomy much more seriously.

Even if only in fragments, we can find points of departure for a materialist social ontology in Lukács. I have attempted to sketch how his claims regarding a materialist conception of normativity, a non-reductive conception of the bases of social action and a holistic theory of mutual dependence between social institutions and individual intentions can be developed further and framed in contemporary language. Even if much of that work still has to be done, such a project could be a stepping stone towards a social ontology which would be useful for the purposes of critical theory. In particular, such arguments could prove useful for a theory of society which takes itself to be part of a historical social form of life and thus of a collective project which, at least in theory, can include self-reflection and conscious critical engagement with the basic assumptions that determine its self-understanding. By pursuing this thought, such a critical social ontology could make room for self-reflection and critique in a way that is unavailable to current theorizing.

Even if the way in which Lukács spells out his conception of totality is too objectivist, just as his conception of work remains too individualistic to lead such a project towards the successful challenging of contemporary assumptions, his *Ontology of Social Being* at least illustrates the challenges and unanswered issues faced by a critical social ontology.

CHAPTER 13

Lukács and the Problem of Knowledge: Critical Ontology as Social Theory

Reha Kadakal

Every social theory exists as a paradigm of truth. Its categories express, implicitly or explicitly, how social reality is determined, and how these determinations are to be grasped. Theoretical categories are only meaningful, however, insofar as they can show the difference between how society shows itself to be and how it really is – the difference between its appearance and its truth. Revealing this difference constitutes the normative dimension of any social theory, and as such, theory and its normative implications, or questions of knowledge and questions of truth, are ineluctably interrelated in social theory.

That the positivist paradigm of knowledge prevalent in contemporary social science eliminates this normative dimension of social theory is a truism, although a necessary one. A more recent and perhaps more compelling challenge to the normative orientation of social theory, however, is presented by various tracks of philosophically informed, interdisciplinary movements in social and cultural theory, such as poststructuralism, postmodernism, and post-colonialism. These have not only questioned the legitimacy of a form of social theory with normative ends except as relative to particular cultures, values and subjectivities, but they have also challenged the very relation of knowledge and truth by persistently reiterating the inherent relation of these to power and domination. The relative strengths and weaknesses of their respective critiques aside, these interrelated standpoints in social theory have a common normative implication, namely the demise of the question of true society and the ends of actual freedom within the practice and purview of social theory.

My intent is not to offer a critique of these schools, and much less to dismiss the importance of their insights for developing adequate analyses of historical and ongoing relations of domination. In fact, it is my conviction that the recent prominence of poststructuralist, postmodern and postcolonial critiques of normativity express a fundamental problem of modern social theory, namely the fact that its normative foundations have never successfully been established. The crucial first step in establishing these foundations is a clarification of the relation between knowledge and truth. In the short history of social

THE PROBLEM OF KNOWLEDGE: CRITICAL ONTOLOGY AS SOCIAL THEORY   393

theory, this relation has been predominantly defined either by positivism and its empiricist notion of knowledge that reduces truth to facts, or by various forms of neo-Idealism that, while attempting to establish human subjectivity as the condition of possibility of knowledge, introduced an unbridgeable gap between knowledge and truth.

In Lukács' work on ontology[1] we find the foundations of a social theory with a radically different conception of the relation of knowledge and truth. Although in his seminal work Lukács engages neopositivism and existentialism as his main interlocutors and objects of critique,[2] his method of investigation, the questions such a method sets up, and their resolution nevertheless amount to substantively more than a critique of these two schools of thought. In fact, as I will argue below, Lukács' analysis offers an immanent critique of the relation of knowledge and truth that inform conventional social theory of both positivist and anti-positivist persuasions through an ontological analysis of the relation of categories and reality.

It is the premise of my argument here that such critical ontological analysis and its outcomes can serve as the foundations of social theory capable of overcoming two interrelated problems that have come to constitute the central challenge for a normative grounding of social theory, namely the subject–object antinomy as it has come to define the epistemological pillars of scientific knowledge in social theory, and, second, the separation of theory and practice as it pertains to the question of freedom.

In this chapter, I will delineate these foundations through a close reading of Lukács' ontological analysis. My goal is to trace the underpinnings of critical ontology as a form of social theory, whose analysis of the relation of categories and reality shows their concrete origin in social practice, and which can help to restore the question of true society and actual freedom as an analytic task and normative end of social theory.

In what follows, I will first outline the analytical premises of what Lukács calls the "ontological treatment of reality"[3] against a quickly drawn backdrop of the categories of subject and object as they have come to orient the field of social theory. (1) This ontological account builds on an analysis of human practical activity. More specifically, it is grounded, as I will show, in an analysis of what Lukács identifies as the structural properties of labor as a form of social

---

1 Georg Lukács, *The Ontology of Social Being*. 3 vols. (London: Merlin Press, 1980). This English edition is a partial translation of Georg Lukács, *Zur Ontologie Des Gesellschaftlichen Seins*. (Darmstadt und Neuwied: Hermann Luchterhand, 1984).
2 Georg Lukács, *Zur Ontologie Des Gesellschaftlichen Seins*. (Darmstadt und Neuwied: Hermann Luchterhand, 1984).
3 Georg Lukács, *The Ontology of Social Being*, vol. 3. *Labor*. (London: Merlin Press, 1980), 4.

practice – principally, labor's teleological positing, and the process of "distancing" that the latter involves as its simultaneous outcome. (2) Tracing Lukács' analysis of the structural properties of labor will allow me to demonstrate next their ontological outcomes that culminate in the rise of a new objectivity – what is commonly, albeit erroneously referred to as "reality" in conventional social theory – and an ontologically new form of being, "social being," and its categories, i.e., the subject–object relation. (3 and 4) Identifying these ontological outcomes of labor's structural properties will help to demonstrate, in turn, two interrelated points central to critical ontology as a form of social theory: First, how consciousness appears to itself as different from its onto-genesis, which seeks to discern the socially mediated nature of ontological categories, and second, how social theory in its conventional form becomes oblivious to the relation between categories and social practice. (5) In the final section of the chapter, I will bring together the outcomes of these analyses toward a foundation for critical ontology as a form of social theory that builds on a systematic analysis of categories that ontologically constitute social totality. (6) Lukács' work offers the foundations of such a critical ontology necessary for an analysis of the socio-ontological determination of the present, both for the structure of social reality, as well as for the ontological structure of the modern subject, in their mediation with each other. Such an analysis, I argue, is a necessary first step toward establishing the foundations of normative social theory that can critically engage the ontology of capitalist modernity – the task, although I will not take it up here, toward whose foundations the following analysis would hope to contribute.

1   The Ontological Analysis of Reality

The unique import of Lukács' ontological analysis for the normative foundations of social theory can perhaps be better discerned against a briefly outlined backdrop of the dilemmas that have framed the relation of knowledge and truth in modern social theory.

Although the question of knowledge, its rational foundations, and its relation to truth have been the central questions of modern philosophy since Descartes, as far as social theory proper is concerned, these questions gained a new and specific formulation in the second half of the nineteenth century, when theory of knowledge replaced philosophical metaphysics and the philosophy of history that had ensued from the latter, as the main mode of modernity's self-understanding. Historically, what is known as the Heidelberg neo-Kantianism of Windelband and Rickert represents this shift from metaphysics to theory of knowledge whereby neo-Idealism construed the task of social theory as a demonstration of subjectivity as the condition of possibility of all knowledge and as the key to understanding the meaning of history.

This neo-Kantian turn from metaphysics to theory of knowledge was partly a reaction to nineteenth century positivism. The latter had elevated the empiricist method as the ultimate condition of truth – a method that ultimately transitioned into the scientific rationalism that came to define not only the natural sciences but also the science of society today. Neo-Kantian social theory, in response, had attempted to establish human subjectivity as the ultimate precondition of truth by demonstrating the relation of truth to value. Max Weber's sociology, as is well known, is only an extension of this neo-Kantian paradigm of truth to the science of society. Through this neo-Idealist development in social theory, the question of truth turned into one of inquiring into human subjectivity, transcendentally or culturally conceived, as the condition of possibility of all knowledge, its validity, and its meaning.

Nevertheless, its defense against the positivist elimination of subjectivity notwithstanding,[4] neo-Kantian theory of knowledge retained in its analytical framework the basic epistemological categories that had defined the foundational problems of knowledge and their social-theoretical articulations throughout the history of modern philosophy – categories whose antithetical relation still remains unresolved in social theory – namely the categories of subject and object. That is to say, although positivism and neo-Kantianism occupy opposite sides of the theoretical coin in their pursuits (i.e., general causal laws vs. culturally unique and historically individual causes) and their methodological demands (empiricism vs. valuation), nevertheless, as forms of thought they are in fact equally permeated by the same antinomy of the subject–object distinction. In modern social theory, the efforts to resolve this antinomy of subject and object and its ensuing typologies of knowledge and truth appeared in multiple forms, most notably from Husserl's and Schutz's differing phenomenological accounts of subjectivity, meaning and action, to the brand of pragmatism that guided Mead's sociology, to cite but a few.

In the critical theory tradition, a significant effort to circumvent the subject–object dichotomy within a larger framework of critique came with Habermas' work in his "communicative action" period. What distinguished Habermas' social theory from both the conventional and critical theory traditions alike was its attempt to leave behind what Habermas referred to as "subject-centered reason" in favor of intersubjectivity and linguistic communication as the new

---

4 Andrew Arato, "The Neo-Idealist Defense of Subjectivity." *Telos*, vol. 21 (1974): 108–161.

analytical pillars of social theory.⁵ In so doing, on the one hand, Habermas argued for communicative action, its inherent rationality and the sphere of the lifeworld as central components in the constitution of society. On the other hand, his theory also upheld the existence of the system-like objectivity of economic processes with their distinctive purposive-rational domain of action in the evolution of modern society. The conception of this duality of lifeworld and system allowed Habermas a point of critique, namely the "internal colonization" of the communicative structures of the lifeworld by the steering media – money and power – of the system.

Essentially a neo-Idealist model at its analytical core, and Weberian in its theoretical premises, a social theory that is premised on the idea of the differentiation of the two distinct domains of social life (i.e., lifeworld and system) nevertheless had two fundamental shortcomings: it could not successfully establish the existence of two domains of social life as distinct from each other in terms of their underlying governing forms of rationality, nor could it establish that they are not determined by one another. While the premises of Habermas' social theory catalyzed stimulating debates that transitioned into the question of law as a framework to reconcile otherwise contentious political standpoints on rights and democracy, the normative grounding of social theory was its casualty.⁶

Nevertheless, the idea of the inherent rationality of language and communicative action as a model for social theory is in fact a continuation of Habermas' earlier attempt at a critique of labor in Marx's social theory. This earlier critique is most instructive, not because it offers an adequate critique, but quite to the contrary, because it represents a fundamental misconception of labor as social practice in Marx's analysis.

In this critique, Habermas argues that Marx's social theory as a materialist study of "societal categories" conceives social labor as a "synthesis of man and nature"⁷ revealed through self-reflection of consciousness on the structures of social labor. He then claims that, at the "*categorial level*," social labor in Marx's analysis is conceived as "instrumental action," or "labor in the sense of material activity," whereas relations in social practice take place in a medium of the "linguistic communicative structure on the basis of which subjects interpret both nature and themselves."⁸ For Habermas, however, if the synthesis takes place through labor, its effect would be in the "system of social labor" rather

---

5   Jürgen Habermas, *The Theory of Communicative Action.* 2 vols. (Boston: Beacon Press, 1984).
6   See Jürgen Habermas, *Between Facts and Norms.* (Cambridge: MIT Press, 1996).
7   Jürgen Habermas, *Knowledge and Human Interest.* (Boston: Beacon Press, 1972), 31–32.
8   Ibid., 52–53.

than in the system of symbols.⁹ Accordingly, against what he sees as the reduction of "the nature of reflection to labor" in Marx's social theory, Habermas presents the "structure of symbolic interaction" and culture as the dimensions of social life within which the subject's "phenomenological experience moves."¹⁰ The fundamental flaws of such a Kantian reading of Marx's categories aside, Habermas in fact conflates how labor is represented in consciousness, that is, how consciousness represents its laboring activity in the experience of the subject, with labor as an objective form of practice whose objective outcomes are integral to the processes of consciousness' own becoming. This is a necessary Hegelian distinction that I will demonstrate later with reference to Lukács' ontological analysis.

This last point brings us, finally, to the project of critical ontology and the necessity of understanding labor's centrality in guiding us beyond the antinomies of the subject–object relation, and the consequences of this analysis for social theory, its categories, and its normative foundations.

A close reading of Lukács' account shows us that what is common to conventional forms of social theory in its positivist and neo-Idealist versions alike is a fundamental flaw residing in the antinomies that frame their analyses: they represent epistemological treatments of what are in fact ontological categories, and as such, not only do their analyses conceive of truth as immediacy, but also by substituting epistemology for ontology, they fail to provide an account of the determination of their own categories. The core of critical ontology as social theory, in contrast, consists in analyzing the onto-genesis of the fundamental categories of social being, (such as consciousness and reality, knowledge and action, and nature and society), as well as the critical analysis of the specific antinomies with which these relationships are grasped (i.e., subject and object, theory and practice, and determination and freedom).¹¹ This mode of analysis seeks to demonstrate how categories develop as an outcome of concrete human practical activity, and how mediations of the categories constitute, as I will try to show, the elements of a "complex level of being" to which Lukács refers as "social being."¹² As such, Lukács' analysis pursues an ontology of categories as historical becoming and development of thought determinations within and as a part of the ontological self-constitution of human beings. This reorientation of theory from the formal-logical account

---

9   Ibid., 31.
10 Ibid., 42.
11 Lukács already shows this distinction as a form of reflection of reality in theoretical consciousness in "Reification and the Consciousness of the Proletariat." In *History and Class Consciousness*. (Cambridge: MIT Press, 1971).
12 Georg Lukács, *The Ontology of Social Being*, vol. 3, *Labor*. (London: Merlin Press, 1980), 21.

offered by an epistemology of categories toward an inquiry into their onto-genesis is at the center of critical ontology as a form of social theory.

What underlies this general theoretical framework, and hence the core of what Lukács refers to as an "ontological treatment of reality," is what he identifies as one of Marx's central insights into the relations of categories to history: "A non-objective being is a non-being. And within the object history is the history of the changes which take place in the categories."[13] In fact, a well-known statement from Marx's early writings, whose ontological significance is often overlooked, needs to be understood as pointing to such a relation of categories and history, and the ontological significance of practice, more specifically, the social practice of labor in that relation: "an objective being acts objectively, and he would not act objectively if the objective did not reside in the very nature of his being."[14] These assertions regarding the relation of categories, history, and practice in fact capture in the language of materialist philosophy (as distinct from "vulgar materialism"[15]) the relation of consciousness and reality as a matter of ontological self-constitution of human beings with its concrete foundations in the social practice of labor. This significance of labor in the ontology of human beings consists in what Lukács refers to as the "structural properties of labor," and more specifically, in labors' "teleological positing" and the process of distancing that is simultaneously involved in the realization of this teleology. In what follows next, I will outline the structural properties of labor as Lukács defines them, from the standpoint of their outcomes for the ontology of human beings as a first step toward building critical ontology as a form of social theory.

It is crucial to note from the outset, however, that the following analysis builds at its core on the notion of what Lukács refers to as "simple labor," understood analytically as labor in its prime case, that is, laboring activity directed toward the creation of use-values. This analysis should not be understood as a reduction of complex forms of social practice of labor to "primitive" laboring activity. Rather, In Lukács' analysis, the structural properties of simple labor constitute the "ontological precondition" of its more advanced forms. That is to say, the transformation of the subject of labor, labor's further development, the mediation of its relations, and, in return, their further transformation of the subject of labor, must already assume, as their "ontological precondition,"

---

13   Georg Lukács, *Record of a Life*. (London: Verso, 1983), 142.
14   Karl Marx, *The Economic and Philosophic Manuscripts of 1844*. (New York: International Publishers, 1964), 180.
15   Georg Lukács, *The Ontology of Social Being*, vol. 3, *Labor*. (London: Merlin Press, 1980), 68.

simple labor as the prime case.[16] Second, however, the analysis of labor as an analytically prime case does not denote a notion of labor in its "natural form," whatever the connotations of the term "natural" might be. Rather, in Lukács' analysis, labor denotes a social practice; that is to say, in its prime case and its historically complex forms alike, labor is always already the "social practice" of labor.[17] This ontological analysis, as I will try to show, reveals labor as a social, ontogenetic process with implications beyond the simple satisfaction of needs through labor's utilization of nature, and as such, it asserts the fundamental place of labor in the constitution of human being, or better, in its self-constituting ontology.[18]

2   "The Ontological Facticity of Labor"

In Lukács' ontological analysis, labor is not simply the control and change of nature for biologically determined needs. In his reinterpretation of Marx's analysis of labor, Lukács shows how laboring activity involves a radically new phenomenon vis-à-vis nature. This radically new phenomenon consists in labor's teleological positing – in the positing of goals, and the possibility of alternative decisions involved in the labor process, whose outcomes constitute labor as the central category in the ontology of human beings.[19] The realization of labor's teleological positing, accordingly, constitutes an "ontologically new social being."[20]

As Lukács states from the outset, "teleology is by its very nature a posited category."[21] It expresses an objective, concrete process of "goal positing consciousness" that initiates a concrete "real process."[22] As Lukács reminds us, however, the notion of "goal positing consciousness" is not an unfamiliar idea in the history of human thought. In fact it is observable in both the religious conception of the world with the notion of a "conscious creator,"[23] as well as in various philosophical conceptions of history. Aristotle's conception of the processes of nature in its totality, and Hegel's notion of the objective logic

---

16   Ibid., 40–41.
17   Ibid., 24.
18   Ibid., 3.
19   Georg Lukács, *The Ontology of Social Being,* vol. 3, *Labor.* (London: Merlin Press, 1980), 20–21.
20   Ibid., 122–123.
21   Ibid., 5.
22   Ibid., 5.
23   Ibid., 5.

determining the unfolding, movement, and direction of human history embody two familiar conceptions of teleology in the form of philosophical comprehension of the world and of human beings' place in it. The central feature of the notion of teleology common to philosophy and religious thought alike consists in the fact that it conceives of the act of teleological positing, as well as positing consciousness itself, as a "general cosmological category."[24] Although the development of scientific thought and its underlying form of rationality overshadowed these religious and philosophical conceptions of general cosmology, nevertheless, as the history, development and the current, often contested status of scientific truths have shown us, scientific explanations could not address the specific need served by such general cosmology and its underlying metaphysics, namely, as Lukács puts it, "the need to make sense of existence, from the course of the world down to the experiences of individual life."[25] In fact, the positivist philosophy of history, from Condorcet to that of Comte and beyond, expresses this need articulated in rationalist and secular forms.

At an analytical level, what is common to religious, philosophical and positivist versions of teleological explanation is the fact that the objective processes they purport to express are articulated at the expense of human agency and the latter's role in the causal processes of history. In fact, the antagonism between the objective processes of history and human agency finds its expression in the antinomy of freedom and determination – categories I will revisit in the final section below to reiterate how an ontological analysis of labor's teleology cuts through these antinomies. The teleology involved in human labor, however, is fundamentally different from the conventional notion of teleology as it has been conceived throughout the history of Western philosophy. In contrast to these conventional notions of teleology, in Lukács' ontological account of reality, the only form of "teleologically produced existence,"[26] – that is to say, existence where teleology is in fact an "effective category" in the ontology of social being – is confined to human practice, to the concrete practice of labor.[27]

Labor's teleology as an ontologically effective category consists in the fact that labor as a concrete, practical activity entails the recognition of the natural properties of the object of labor as "adequate objective knowledge of the material and its processes," and identifying "the suitability of certain properties of

---

24 Ibid., 4.
25 Ibid., 5.
26 Ibid., 20.
27 Ibid., 8–9.

an object" from the standpoint of positing goals.[28] Put differently, labor's realization transforms "existent possibility" into reality – a transformation without which labor would not be possible.[29]

One should note, nevertheless, that in pointing out this transformation of possibility to reality in labor, Lukács does not subscribe to a notion of "necessity" in the sense of simply raising an inherent necessity into a conscious one through labor.[30] Rather, labor's realization transforms a "latent possibility" – a possibility that "without the labor process will always remain latent."[31] That is to say, labor's realization, if it is to be successful, involves the recognition of the properties of reality adequate to the goal posited – what Lukács refers to as the "correct reflection of reality" in consciousness. The very act of positing in human labor involves, accordingly, making decisions among alternative possible casual relations, a process that transforms "natural causalities" which are independent and "heterogeneous" in nature, into "posited" ones.

This notion of "alternatives" in making decisions among causal relations requires a further reiteration, as it is central to the specific goals involved in labor and their outcomes as analyzed here.[32]

From the standpoint of labor's positing, the "alternative causal relations" involve a "moment of decision."[33] As Lukács puts it, "For every positing in labor has its goal concretely and definitely fixed in thought; without this no labor would be possible."[34] That is to say, the process of transformation of heterogeneous causalities to posited ones is only possible through a moment of consciousness – an arising consciousness that the process must include as its moment, and through its mastery over what is immediate. Human consciousness, in other words, emerges as the central moment of this process of labor's positing, where labor mediates between needs and their satisfaction, a process of mediation that in order to be successful must involve making decisions, in selecting means as a moment of consciousness with a view to causal relations and the outcomes they entail from the standpoint of labor's goals. Equally

---

28 Ibid., 116–123.
29 Ibid., 123–124.
30 As Lukács notes, it was Hegel's system building, his logicistic understanding of his own analysis that led him to elevate the category of "necessity" to a "logically exaggerated significance" at the expense of the "categorically privileged specificity of reality" itself as a result of which he "investigated" freedom as a part of a system, but not in relation to reality. See ibid., 123.
31 Ibid., 123.
32 Ibid., 115–116.
33 Ibid., 39.
34 Ibid., 116.

important, this interpolation between needs and their satisfaction is also the moment of the domination of consciousness over instincts and emotions, and as such, it expresses the predominance of consciousness in the "concrete realization of teleological positing."[35] Labor's process, then, consists in transforming possibility to reality and in so doing, realizing labor's teleology "as an adequate, considered and willed result."[36] This process constitutes the "objective method of labor's existence," what Lukács calls the "ontological facticity of labor": labor's realization of a posited goal, independent of the forms of consciousness or the "inner motive of the subject," as a process by means of which the reflection of reality in consciousness adequate to the goal posited transforms otherwise "natural causalities" into posited ones from the standpoint of labor's teleology.[37] As an "objective ontological category" then, labor's teleology constitutes a "real moment of material activity,"[38] and as such, it is the only form of teleology that can have actual relevance in the ontology of human beings, with its real ontological outcomes for human beings' existence.[39] The ontological significance of this teleology, its material outcome, is not simply the change it effects in nature. Rather, as I will show next, with labor's teleology and its realization, there is a concrete change in the *subject* of labor.

3   Labor and the Rise of a New Objectivity

In labor's teleology, both the positing of goals, as well as consciousness as an arising moment of labor, form parts of the same teleology. This positing "as a willed result"[40] offers a key to the onto-genesis of consciousness in its relation

---

35   Ibid., 42. To reiterate the point I emphasized earlier, the forms of consciousness in this analysis of labor as a prime case, "simple labor," are not to be understood in terms of the characteristics of modern forms of consciousness. Although the analysis is specific to simple labor and its subject, nevertheless, consciousness and its processes of reflection of reality as a moment of this process still mediate between needs and their satisfaction.
36   Ibid., 20.
37   Ibid., 42.
38   Ibid., 8.
39   It is also important to note, although I will not expand on it in this chapter, that it is because of this ontological character of labor's teleology, independent of the forms of consciousness, that in its advanced and more complex forms, i.e., in capitalist modernity, laboring activity becomes a form of domination constituted by the structural framework of labor-time and value as a social form, i.e., the commodity form, and as a model on which society is organized. See Moishe Postone, *Time, Labor, and Social Domination: A Reinterpretation of Marx's Critical Theory*. (New York: Cambridge University Press, 1993).
40   Georg Lukács, *The Ontology of Social Being*, vol. 3, *Labor*. (London: Merlin Press, 1980), 20.

to reality. For, consciousness in this process "ceases to be an epiphenomenon,"[41] i.e., an epiphenomenon of organic being and its biological existence and reproduction. Rather, as part of labor's teleology, the very activity of consciousness, which structures its own relation to the environment, becomes its own ontological transformation, one that is ontologically objective in its outcome: the "overcoming of the epiphenomenal consciousness determined merely by biology."[42] With teleological positing and its realization, then, human practical activity constitutes what Lukács calls "the humanization in labor."[43]

This overcoming of epiphenomenal consciousness through labor's teleology, however, is not only the overcoming of instinct by consciousness, but also the overcoming of conditions of existence defined by heterogeneous and indifferent natural causalities, by those that are self-created through human practical activity and its material outcomes. It is only on the basis of this new sphere of social practice within which further teleological positings take their concrete form that the practice of social being, its conscious organization and the realization of its goals become possible. The new form of being that emerges through labor's teleology, in other words, moves away from biological determination toward a sphere of self-determinations through the practice of labor. Put differently, labor's teleology is realized materially, in the constitution of a "new form of objectivity,"[44] social objectivity whose processes and boundaries are defined not by natural determinations but by determinations of a new kind: the social practice of labor. Neither in its goals and orientation, nor in its concrete decisions as a means to realize them, would the practice of labor refer to "reality in general"; rather it refers to social objectivity. In its teleological positing in its totality (its goal, its orientation and its means), labor takes place not as an act of the individual human in isolation but as a practice of the social being within which the human individual exists.

The overcoming of reality by social objectivity in the ontology of social being has three main implications for social theory and its categories.

First, "reality as such" can never serve as a category of social theory or as a reference point of its analyses. Rather, by the very ontology of social being, it is social objectivity and the conditions of existence produced by social practice that social theory must have, both as a category and as a reference point in its analyses. Second, the consciousness involved in making decisions from the

---

41 Ibid., 21.
42 Ibid., 21.
43 Ibid., 35. I will revisit this "humanization" as a "leap" in the discussion of language, that is, the overcoming of consciousness determined by biological being and its needs.
44 Ibid., 32.

standpoint of labor's teleology is never a matter of "abstract and pure freedom" or "simple reason"[45] of the subject as Idealist philosophy would have it. Rather, consciousness and its categories, and the direction they provide to labor's teleology are part of the social practice of labor and the new form of objectivity which it creates. The forms of consciousness concretely realized through practice, then, are ontologically social. Third, in social objectivity and social forms of consciousness, the ontological outcomes of labor's teleology – the overcoming of consciousness as epiphenomenal to biology – acquires a "specifically fixed form," a social form.[46] As the humanization in labor attains a social form, however, what made this social form possible in the first place – the realization of labor's teleology – disappears from the reflection of this reality in the consciousness of social being: human being appears to itself as if "it was already social being by its own inherent nature,"[47] rather than becoming so through its labor, through its own practical activity.

Such is the self-constituting ontology of human beings as social beings. The outcomes of labor's teleological positing transforms reality into social objectivity, and in so doing, labor's teleology also changes the *subject* of laboring activity. With the realization of labor, human beings are reconstituted as "a new and self-founded being, into social-being."[48] This is the ontological process that constitutes the rise of a new objectivity, objectively as well as for the subject.

If labor's teleology is the ontological foundation of new objectivity, how does consciousness that arises as a moment of labor's teleology experience the process itself? In the next section, I will address this question, followed by a discussion of its implications for social theory adequate to comprehending social objectivity and its categories in their truth.

4   Ontological Foundation of the Categories of Social Being

Earlier I argued, following Lukács, that labor's teleological positing transforms heterogeneous and independent causalities to homogenized causal relations from the standpoint of labor's goals, a process that involves making decisions among alternative causal relations. This teleology as exclusive to labor involves two reciprocal processes central to its successful realization, and ontologically central to consciousness and its experience of the outcomes of this teleology.

---

45   Ibid., 37.
46   Ibid., 35.
47   Ibid., 35.
48   Ibid., 46.

First, labor's positing "distances" the subject from the object "in the reflection of reality."[49] Second, it is only through such a distancing of the subject of labor from the object in the reflection of reality that the very subject–object relation becomes possible. That is to say, the positing of labor involves the "simultaneous positing of subject and object,"[50] which is also their distinction from each other. These two moments of labor's teleology – distancing and the rise of the subject–object relation – as reciprocal processes can only be separated analytically (rather than as a matter of ontological priority) as the "ontological conditions of the rise of labor"[51] and its successful realization.

In the experience of the subject of labor, these ontological conditions of labor appear in the form of subject's "complete independence"[52] from its own concrete practical activity. Indeed, the very process of the rise of the subject–object relation appears to consciousness as its own independence from its concrete ontological conditions. Consciousness, then, experiences what is in fact its ontologically only relative independence from its practical activity as complete independence in an objectively effective way. This form of appearance of consciousness as completely independent from its concrete conditions also becomes the precondition of further antinomies of thought, such as theory and practice, and freedom and determination – antinomies that inform, in their general form, the major epistemological, ethical and normative questions of European philosophy and social theory.

Nevertheless, the distancing of subject and object in the reflection of reality, and the rise of the subject–object relation as the ontological conditions of the rise of labor, are not merely epiphenomenal to reality. Rather, they become ontologically central to social objectivity itself. For, the emergence of the subject–object relation is not only a matter of individual labor and consciousness; rather, the process becomes a socially generalized ontology.[53] In Lukács' account, language itself expresses this social generality of distancing, as distancing posited in language is not only the distancing of subject from object, but also simultaneously the abstraction of a concept from its concrete object. As Lukács puts it, "what is depicted by the verbal sign is separated from the object it describes, and hence also from the subject uttering it…"[54] Language, in other words, not only expresses the distancing involved in labor's teleology, but also reproduces it symbolically, as "mental distancing," and thus makes it

---

49   Ibid., 48, 101.
50   Ibid., 101.
51   Ibid., 59.
52   Ibid., 111.
53   Ibid. 102.
54   Ibid., 100.

"communicable socially."[55] Perhaps the most clear representation of this social generality of distancing is the notion of time as expressed in language. For, with time we find a socially generalized notion by means of which the common coordination of successive teleological positings and their further mediations become possible. Through time as a succession of positings, in other words, distancing becomes the "common possession"[56] and common structural property of society. For Lukács, the social generality of distancing and its reproduction in language as socially generalized ontology expresses a fundamental internal transformation within the human being in both their social and self-relations. In Lukács' terms, this represents "a leap from natural to social being."[57]

We should immediately note here that this ontological account of the categories of social being is not a reduction of language and thought to epiphenomena. Rather, the ontological analysis of categories points to a continuous reciprocity of labor, language and thought in the ontology of social being. As Lukács puts it: "word and concept, speech and conceptual thought belong together as elements of a complex, the complex of social being, and they can only be grasped in their true nature in the context of an ontological analysis of social being, by knowledge of the functions that they fulfill within this complex."[58] Labor constitutes the predominant moment of this process, but only within the totality of social being. Put differently, in critical ontology, labor does not denote a transcendental category. Rather, labor's predominance in the ontology of social being expresses the concrete, practical activity of labor and its outcomes as the ontological facticity of the "complex of social being" itself. In an adequate ontological analysis, the totality of social being has primacy over the elements that constitute it. It is thanks to this emphasis on totality that in the critical ontology of social being neither language nor conceptual thought can be understood in separation from each other. Rather, they constitute the elements of social being, where the latter, in its total social objectivity, has primacy over its elements. As Lukács points out, however, within the totality of social objectivity, the process of distancing subject and object lead to further differentiations through the social mediations of labor's positings, and through language and thought as "psychophysical abilities and possibilities"[59] reconstructed into word and concept. This social mediation of

---

55   Ibid., 102.
56   Ibid., 102.
57   Ibid., 102.
58   Ibid., 49.
59   Ibid., 49.

labor's positings requires further explanation, as it is central to the account of the development of categories through social practice.

In pursuing the foundations of critical ontology as a form of social theory following Lukács, I have so far focused on the analysis of labor in its prime case, that is, of simple labor as "the producer of use values."[60] Framing the analysis around simple labor – rather than around complex structures of social production presented by historically advanced social forms – allows for an analytical separation and outline of the structural properties of labor's teleology and their outcome in the self-constituting ontology of human beings as social beings. Although this account builds on labor as the production of use values, nevertheless, it still serves as a model for an analysis of more complex forms of social production, i.e., exchange value, and their accompanying social forms of consciousness. This is not because all forms of social production are to be reduced to the production of use values, but because the latter already contains labor's teleology as the ontological kernel of social production. Put differently, the analytical focus on simple labor as the production of use values does not imply a linearly conceived history of labor that progresses from the production of use value to that of exchange value. Rather, Lukács' "mode of presentation,"[61] points to the production of use values as a moment, ontologically central in labor's teleology nevertheless, of the socially mediated process of social production.

The key to this socially mediated process resides in the antithetical nature of labor and the mediation of teleological positings themselves. While labor as social practice, in its immediacy, is aimed at the production of use values, this immediacy already has a mediated content, namely the social practice of labor preceding it. Considered from the standpoint of the satisfaction of needs, the concrete realization of labor's teleology simultaneously creates new relations of immediacy and mediation, as "every product of labor, when finished, poses new and no longer natural immediacy for the man using it..."[62] With these mediated positings, labor in social practice, if its teleology is to be realized, requires the subject – as the subject of social being – to "reconstruct" its already developing abilities into speech and thought where, as Lukács puts it, "the posited goal is directly the positing of a goal for other people..."[63] Both language and thought, accordingly, in their ontology, in their "coming to be,"

---

60 Ibid., 39.
61 Ibid., 46.
62 Ibid., 101.
63 Ibid., 47–49.

have positings for other subjects, what Lukács calls "secondary teleological positings," when positing has as its orientation not simply nature or natural reality but social being itself.

This mediated nature of simple labor, and the "secondary character of its teleological positing" that comes with the socialization of labor, have as their object and their orientation "the consciousness of group life," or, consciousness in its social form. In this analytical separation of positings, accordingly, while labor as the production of use values acts upon nature, in more developed forms of social practice, labor aims at coordinating or transforming the labor of other human beings. In both forms, however, labor involves the social life and consciousness of others. Indeed, the teleological positing of labor in its "essential content" and structure involves not the individual being in isolation, but social life in general. Put differently, in their mediated forms, teleological positings are essentially social; they aim to bring about a form of consciousness as their means. However, the mediated forms of the teleological positing of labor provide the immediate conditions for the further teleological positing of labor in social practice. Thus, more complex forms of social practice develop from what is in effect the dialectical outcomes of the structural properties of labor and its socially mediated teleological positings.

To reiterate, then, as Lukács' ontological analysis shows, labor is not simply a matter of the control and change of nature for the satisfaction of needs. The realization of labor's teleology simultaneously leads to the distancing of subject from object. This subject–object relation, as the outcome of labor's teleology, becomes the general form within which conscious activity is structured as it is reproduced in language and thought. Labor's teleology and its concrete realization, accordingly, constitute the ontological foundations of the categories as well as the conditions of the further development of social practice. However – and this is where the task of critical ontology as social theory becomes most pivotal – both social being and its categories have the structural properties of labor in their onto-genesis, and yet this is not necessarily how consciousness experiences its own onto-genetic processes. Quite to the contrary, categories appear to consciousness as objectively existing and independent of human practice – a process whereby consciousness in effect hides its origin by misapprehending its emergence from labor's teleology and its realization.

Recognizing this fact – the fact that consciousness hides its origin – is central to understanding the relation of knowledge to truth. It also leads to the next necessary question: what kind of theory is adequate to comprehend this process and its outcomes, which culminate not only in social objectivity, but also in the categories through which consciousness conceives of such reality.

In the next section of this chapter, I will seek to lay the groundwork toward answering this question.

5 Social Theory and the Contemplative Form of Thought

Starting from the analysis of labor's teleology, so far I have pursued its ontological outcomes as they result in what Lukács refers to as the "genuine humanization in labor," a process that involves the overcoming of reality by social objectivity and the transition to conditions of existence that are self-determined through practice. In this analysis, consciousness, as I have pointed out, emerges as an arising moment of this process in transforming heterogeneous and independent causalities into homogeneous causes, making decisions among causal alternatives, and among their means and ends from the standpoint of labor's teleology. Such positings become possible, as I pointed out earlier, only if there is a reflection of reality in consciousness in a materially correct form from the standpoint of labor's goals.

Lukács' analysis of this process points to two implications central to the ontology of consciousness and its relation to practice, and to critical ontology as an adequate comprehension of this relation. First, consciousness is in fact "called into being in labor," and it involves a process of "checking and perfection of the acts of reflection" as central to labor's teleology.[64] Second, however, labor's further development becomes dependent on the further development of consciousness itself and on the relative independence of consciousness from the immediacy of labor. Consciousness, then, which arises in practice as a moment of labor's teleology now becomes not only independent of labor, but in fact intervenes in the teleology itself and in the very practice from which it emerged. This intervention essentially consists in the control and domination of human beings – their self-control – from the standpoint of labor's realization. Through such domination, consciousness becomes a central and integral moment of the social practice of labor and its further mediations. As Lukács has it, "human consciousness, called into being in labor, for labor, and by labor, intervenes in the activity of man's own reproduction."[65] In Lukács' ontological analysis, accordingly, the consciousness of social being emerges out of the reproduction of social being's own processes, practically, "out of the reproduction of his own existence,"[66] and as such, even if consciousness becomes

---

64 Ibid., 51–52.
65 Ibid., 52.
66 Ibid., 51.

gradually but increasingly independent of labor, it is still a product of social being's own material reproduction in its onto-genesis. By the same process, however, labor's development becomes dependent on the development of consciousness and its independence from the immediacy of labor, as a result of which consciousness now intervenes in the further teleological positing of labor in the form of independent and original teleological positings and through the form in which reality comes to be reflected in consciousness. This relationship between practice and consciousness has direct implications for the ontology of consciousness itself, for categories as thought-determinations, and for the question of the relation of knowledge to truth. Through an ontological analysis of labor's teleology, then, we come to see what is in fact the mediation of consciousness and practice with ontologically material outcomes.

The apparent independence of categories is only made possible through the forms in which social objectivity is reflected in consciousness, that is to say, only when the conceptual thought involved in these forms is sufficiently general to grasp generalized causal relations. This generalization becomes materially possible as the experience of one moment of concrete labor, which involves the materially correct reflection of causality in consciousness, would inform another labor in the realization of its goal. Through this socially mediated process of labor's positing, the correct reflection of reality becomes relatively independent of one particular instance of labor and instead becomes increasingly general. The reflection of causality, in other words, in its autonomous, "universal character"[67] is in fact a socially mediated process that transforms causality into a general, autonomous category. Categories, then, even in their general autonomy, are socially mediated through the mediated nature of labor's positings. Put differently, the increasing generalization and autonomy of categories expresses not the inherent, independent nature of "reality" as such (for reality as such is already overcome by social objectivity); rather it expresses the social experience of labor, that is, labor's teleology and the consciousness that such teleology involves. If categories have universal validity, then, such validity expresses not the nature of reality, nor the transcendental nature of reason, but the fact that categorical relations relative to the goal of labor and its teleology are socially generalized.

The development of scientific reason and theory, if with which we understand the conception of generalized causal relations, expresses this development of the seemingly autonomous forms of thought within which social objectivity is reflected in consciousness. Furthermore, this relative autonomy of

---

67 Ibid., 50.

theory, its reflection of reality in the form of competing causal relations, become labor's own precondition in social production, and as such, it becomes "an indispensable precondition for the rise and further development of labor."[68] Needless to say, this is only a seeming independence, for neither science nor theory, in their truth, can be absolutely independent from the original ontological connection to the positing of labor, needs, and their social mediation through the antithetical character of labor. On one hand, science and theory must serve as "self-acting and autonomous forms of the original teleological and causal positings."[69] On the other hand, neither science nor theory can ever be detached, in their truth, from their relation to socially mediated needs, "no matter how complicated and ramified the mediations that link them to this."[70]

In the history of human thought, as Lukács points out, this "paradoxical relationship"[71] finds its expression in the question of "theory and practice" that hitherto had been understood in their separation. From the standpoint of critical ontology as a form of social theory, the separation of theory and practice expresses the fact that the increasing autonomy of categories from the immediacy of labor in the experience of consciousness resulted in a form of thought within which theoretical reason appears to itself as autonomous and independent of human practice in its onto-genesis. The ultimate examples of this form of thought include the moral philosophy of Kant, neo-Kantian notions of concept formation, and their translation into social theory that builds on "understanding" and forms of rationality differentiated according to their interest-bound orientations.

More importantly, however, in this unreflective separation, while theoretical reason conceives of itself as autonomous and independent of practice, it can do so only by imparting, at the same time, an equally independent status to social objectivity in the form of "reality," whose causal relations it purports to explain through its categories. Social theory that builds on the separation of theory and practice in effect replaces social objectivity with reality as such, constituted independently of human practice, and detached from human practical activity in its ontological roots.

Positivist and neo-Idealist social theories, whose equally problematic conceptions of the relation of knowledge to truth I criticized earlier, occupy the two sides of this contemplative form of thought. The positivist paradigm of knowledge, where reality is conceived as external to and independent from

---

68   Ibid., 52.
69   Ibid., 52.
70   Ibid., 52.
71   Ibid., 52.

human practice, reduces truth to an empiricist notion of facts, and knowledge to their passive register. Such a conception of reality conceals the very truth that facts are but products of social objectivity.

Conversely, neo-Idealist social theory, where subjectivity becomes the epistemological center of knowledge, transforms truth to value-relations – a theoretical model that recasts values as transcendent determinations at the foundation of ethical orientations, and subjectivity as the center of this process.[72] From Weber's analysis of the Protestant work ethic to Habermas' differentiation of spheres of reason, this neo-Idealist framework expands on Kant's notion of practical reason and the idea of the "categorical imperative," represents an example of what Lukács identifies as the "idealist conception of socio-historical processes."[73] Here the causal change in the development of history is explained through ethical, ideal or communicative-rational interests of the "human understanding" or the inherent rationality of inter-subjective communication. Driven by a search for a unitary and rational system, social theory that builds on the notion of reason as "understanding," one that imparts validity to truth in both epistemological and moral realms, identifies the categories of subjectivity, understanding, and valuation with the conditions of possibility of freedom.

This neo-Idealist framework and its emphasis on subjectivity in the form of "understanding" – linguistic, communicative or otherwise – comes to obscure the fact that the apparent objectivity of values is but history that has already imparted significance to subjectivity as its means of social development. It ignores that it is the workings of history as social objectivity that assign importance to subjective and ethical understanding, and not the other way around.[74] Social theory that builds on this neo-Idealist framework loses the ontological distinction between social objectivity and its form of appearance, and thus conflates the appearance of subjective autonomy and freedom with their truth. Put differently, theory becomes oblivious to the fact that "the subject came to be an ideology."[75]

Within both neo-Idealist and positivist forms of thought, in effect, knowledge becomes detached from truth, and freedom becomes unmoored from its onto-genesis in human practice. That is, knowledge becomes separated from its practical possibility, and the outcome is the contemplative form of thought

---

72 See Max Weber, *The Methodology of the Social Sciences*. (New York: Free Press, 1949); and Max Weber, *Roscher and Knies: The Logical Problems of Historical Economics*. (New York: Free Press, 1975).
73 Georg Lukács, *The Ontology of Social Being*, vol. 3, *Labor*. (London: Merlin Press, 1980), 133.
74 Ibid., 133–134.
75 Theodor Adorno, *Negative Dialectics*. (New York: Continuum, 1973), 66.

that not only "hindered a concrete understanding of practice (labor)"[76] but also obfuscated the relationship of the subject to social objectivity. This contemplative form of thought, in its positivist and neo-Idealist versions, has oriented conventional social theory since the second half of the nineteenth century in its epistemological and moral grounding, in each case on one naturalized half of a specific subject–object antinomy. In this contemplative form, social theory is inadequate not only to the task of accounting for the conditions of it own emergence but also for the possibility of its normative grounding. The solution to this contemplative form of thought and its detachment of knowledge and truth resides in an ontological account of practice itself and its outcomes, "in its real and material form of appearance."[77] To that end, in the next and final part of this chapter I will gather some of the outcomes of the preceding account of Lukács' ontological analysis toward an outline of critical ontology as a form of social theory.

6   Critical Ontology as Social Theory

In critical ontology, the ontological priority of labor is not ascribed from without, i.e., by a theoretical value-relation as neo-Idealist social theory would have it for its theoretical categories, nor is labor's practice conceived of simply as the expression of reason that exists transcendentally and applies itself practically in human action – an abstract logic of reason that can only conceive of truth through an abstractly general epistemology. Rather, as the preceding account shows, the ontological outcomes of labor's teleology appear in "real and material form."[78] Labor as an ontologically effective category emerges out of the structural properties of the social practice of labor itself, and more specifically, out of the structural processes involved in the realization of labor's teleology. That is to say, practically as well as in thought, labor's processes "contain real [onto-genetic] tendencies that necessarily lead far beyond this original condition."[79] I limited the task of this chapter to investigate these outcomes as a necessary first step for social theory and the grounding of its normative ends.

These outcomes are neither a part of the teleology of nature, nor that of history. Rather, the social practice of labor and the realization of its teleology transforms the material conditions of human beings' existence into social

---

76   Georg Lukács, *The Ontology of Social Being*, vol. 3, *Labor*. (London: Merlin Press, 1980), 53.
77   Ibid., 54.
78   Ibid., 54.
79   Ibid., 136.

objectivity, toward conditions that are self-determining in practice, a process that at the same time involves consciousness as its arising moment. This account of labor's teleology and consciousness as a moment of its positing would seem circular to conventional social theory and its contemplative form of thought, but this is only because the latter submits to a logicistic account of reason that substitutes epistemology for ontological categories. Critical ontology, in contrast, builds on material ontology with real, material outcomes.

The first material outcome of this ontology is in fact an act of arising freedom that the positing of a goal involves as a moment of concrete practical activity, as a moment of concrete reality. Such a moment consists in the act of decision, whose "'place' and 'organ' is consciousness,"[80] in labor's teleological positing between concrete alternatives and the causal links they involve in realizing posited goals. Consciousness as an arising moment of this teleology has concrete material outcomes, namely the overcoming of reality by social objectivity and the change it effects in the subject itself, as well as in the consciousness of others through the antithetical nature of labor's teleology and its socially mediated teleological positings. When the teleological process of labor is directed toward a change in the consciousness of others, the posited goal is not only that of simple labor but an outcome of social objectivity, mediations of its social relations and the alternative positings they involve. In critical ontology, accordingly, the socially mediated teleological positings of labor become the "predominant moment"[81] of practice and its outcomes.

With its grounding in concrete practical activity and its ontological outcomes, critical ontological analysis can guide us to overcome theoretical categories that remain in the immediacy of social being by those whose objective basis is in human beings' ontology and its concrete processes in practice. It is only with such an objective basis and with the ontological foundations of truth in practice and its mediations that social theory can build toward its normative ends. This is the fundamental difference, I argue, between critical ontology as a form of social theory – what Lukács refers to as "genuine knowledge of being," – and the forms of knowledge that are ineffectual before the "practical manipulation of concretely recognized causal connections."[82] This is not simply an abstract or theoretical difference, however. Rather, it entails an antithesis that is deeply embedded in labor's practice, between "every labor process"

---

80   Ibid., 39.
81   Ibid., 131.
82   Ibid., 63.

and consciousness in its present social form – the commodity form in a society that "should learn to satisfy all its needs in terms of commodity exchange."[83]

The foremost implication of this antithesis of practice and social forms of consciousness concerns the question of freedom, the question that is at the core of the category of subject. In critical ontology, the antithesis of practice and consciousness does not imply an antithesis of freedom and determination – an abstract antithesis where freedom could only be attained abstractly. Rather, freedom as a category can only be conceived through determined mediations, for, "A non-objective being is non-being."[84] Freedom, in other words, cannot be conceived as an antithesis of determination but rather must be conceived in reciprocity with it; as such, freedom is in fact "determined directly by the need itself."[85] This is because, as I have tried to show in the preceding account, laboring activity not only gives rise to social objectivity – the totality of the concrete and mediated outcomes of the social practice of labor – but also to social being, its transformation in the form of "control over oneself."[86] That is to say, the concrete outcome of the social practice of labor's teleology, and the concrete changes it effects in the constitution of human being, transforms the latter into social being by means of self-mastery, and through the overcoming of the biological determination of needs by socially and practically self-determined ones. "With labor [there is a] qualitatively new category in the ontology of the social being."[87] In this conscious self-determination, whatever its form might be, human being also reproduces itself not as a particular organic being, a being determined by its nature, but as a member of the social being.[88] This is a process that involves not only other subjects, but the subject of labor itself, that is, human beings' own subjectivity when subjectivity itself becomes the object of its own teleological positing.[89] Subjectivity as such, in its transcendental, communicative or pragmatic formulations, can never be the key to truth, as the subject as "being" is not an autonomous ontological category but a category of social objectivity, and in an ontologically determined form.

---

83   Georg Lukács, "Reification and the Consciousness of the Proletariat." In *History and Class Consciousness*. (Cambridge: MIT Press, 1971), 91.
84   Georg Lukács, *Record of a Life*. (London: Verso, 1983), 142.
85   Georg Lukács, *The Ontology of Social Being*, vol. 3, *Labor*. (London: Merlin Press, 1980), 117.
86   Ibid., 135.
87   Ibid., 20.
88   The idea that Feuerbach tried to capture in the notion of "species being." See Ludwig Feuerbach, *The Essence of Christianity*. (Buffalo: Prometheus Books, 1989), 281.
89   Georg Lukács, *The Ontology of Social Being*, vol. 3, *Labor*. (London: Merlin Press, 1980), 128.

Second, as I have tried to show, in Lukács' analysis, consciousness arises as a moment of this ontologically structuring process, as an ontological outcome of labor's teleology objectively as well as within the subject. This process is also the ontological foundation of the ideas social beings then form of themselves, their self-consciousness. As labor's teleology and the means of its realization become socially mediated, the social practice of labor orients itself to the conscious organization of group life. At the same time, however, these means and the decisions they involve can be successful only if they are bound by social objectivity – its seemingly independent, objective causal relations. That is to say, the more the means of labor's realization become "socially relevant,"[90] the more decisions and positings now appear to be independent of human beings' own practice. Social objectivity, then, confronts human beings as objective reality, whose processes appear to be law-like and independent of practice.[91] Consciousness of this social objectivity becomes the "ontological fact of social being,"[92] and as such, the relation of consciousness and social objectivity is central to the ontological analysis of categories, and to any social theory adequate to its task. In critical ontology, categories are not epiphenomenal. They have their essential ontogenesis in practice. And yet, "essence must appear."[93] In critical ontology, accordingly, categories are "never completely free from determination."[94] Categories, in other words, must be comprehended ontologically, as "forms of being,"[95] and history itself must be comprehended as the history of their coming into being, development and transformation. An adequate comprehension of categories in their ontological truth resides not in their form of appearance (i.e., subject–object, freedom and determination) but in their "ontological specificity" and their "socio-historical genesis"[96] in the social practice of labor.

Third, this ontological specificity of categories is the key to the relation of knowledge and truth in social theory. From the perspective of critical ontology, truth can only be comprehended as a moment of concrete processes of social objectivity, where subject and object, and freedom and determination, are not antithetical but rather determined mediations of this social objectivity. Categories can only be comprehended through an analysis of these determined mediations of social objectivity, social development and its material relations.

---

90 Ibid., 129.
91 Ibid., 130.
92 Ibid., 103.
93 G.W.F. Hegel, *Hegel's Science of Logic*. (New York: Humanity Books, 1998), 479.
94 Georg Lukács, *The Ontology of Social Being*, vol. 3, *Labor*. (London: Merlin Press, 1980), 115.
95 Georg Lukács, *Record of a Life*. (London: Verso, 1983), 142.
96 Georg Lukács, *The Ontology of Social Being*, vol. 3, *Labor*. (London: Merlin Press, 1980), 88.

When positing takes as its object the transformation of subjectivity itself, categories can no longer simply be comprehended through the processes unfolding through simple labor. Rather, they must be understood through the forms of positing that emerge through the transformation of subjectivity. As such, they express the historical development of social objectivity.

Such history as the history of categories has a direct bearing on social theory. Social theory is a modern endeavor. It came into being along with modern society, and it understood itself to be founded upon a rational pursuit of knowledge that came to be identified with scientific disciplines. It is perhaps the irony of the modern form of consciousness that what made an unfettered mastery of material production possible – scientific knowledge and its generalized, universal categories – also became the greatest impediment, as Lukács asserts, to "genuine knowledge of being."[97] For in its seeming independence, scientific knowledge oriented toward the mastery of production not only hides its onto-genesis in the social practice of labor, but it itself becomes the vey means of the manipulation of social being.[98] The seemingly independent categories of scientific knowledge, accordingly, express more generalized and abstract expressions of real, material relations, whose ontogenesis is the development of labor's teleology as socially mediated practice.[99] This represents as state of social objectivity where, as Lukács puts it, a "genuine ontological investigation of being…has to be directed, but rather against its own confinement on the basis of its own practical universality."[100] Such ontological investigation, directed against social being's own confinement, its self-domination in practice and in thought, is the task of critical ontology as a form of social theory. For it is also such ontological analysis – as the analysis of the material self-constitution of human beings – that also makes freedom a practical possibility, and reveals social practice as the ontological kernel of such freedom.

I began this chapter by arguing that the categories of social theory express how reality is determined, and how these determinations are to be grasped. I also argued that the relation of categories to reality is the foundation of every social theory, its claim to truth, and its normative ends. By building on Lukács' ontological analysis, I have tried to demonstrate the onto-genesis of categories in the social practice of labor and its teleology. That teleology and its realization involves an "act of rising freedom" as its moment in human ontology, in the moment of decisions among alternatives in the transformation of

---

97 Ibid., 63.
98 Ibid., 127.
99 Ibid., 118.
100 Ibid., 127.

heterogeneous and indifferent causalities into posited ones from the standpoint of the goals of labor. As I have tried to show, the outcomes of this process are most crucial for social theory, as they involve categories in the form of thought-determinations, how these determinations appear in the experience of consciousness, and how these appearances transform into conceptions of theory and practice. In laying out a framework of critical ontology as a form of social theory adequate to comprehending this "ontological kernel of freedom,"[101] I have limited my discussion to the structural properties of labor as social practice, their outcomes, and their further mediations. The preceding account, however, could only serve as a possible beginning point for a critical ontology of the present, whose task is to systematically investigate social objectivity and its reproduction, social forms of consciousness, and the outcome of their mediation in the form of categories. Critical ontological analysis of this mediation of consciousness and social objectivity, one that comprehends categories in their onto-genesis, in their coming to be, can offer a standpoint for their true critique, and can reestablish a relation between knowledge and truth in social theory.

---

101   Ibid., 39.

CHAPTER 14

Marx, Lukács and the Groundwork of Critical Social Ontology

Michael J. Thompson

1   Introduction

One of the core problems faced by Marxist theory has been the cultivation and maintenance of a critical insight into the forms of domination and control that pervade capitalist society that would allow for the formation of a radical, critical form of political agency. Whatever the mantras and tired slogans about the interests of a working class may have been, and for some, may continue to be, there is little question that the twentieth and early-twenty-first centuries have demonstrated a secular decline in that kind of political agency requisite for social transformation. Georg Lukács saw this to be the case about a century ago when he articulated the problem of reification as a kind of pathology of consciousness that resulted from the increasing penetration of the commodity form and the rationalization of productive and consumptive practices. The deformation of critical consciousness hid from view what he saw as the core insight of Marxian theory: that human praxis lay at the core of any rational and valid conception of what it meant to be a human being. Critical consciousness could only emerge in the context of the realization on behalf of working people that the society around them was in fact a collective creation and, as such, exploded the legitimacy of the private control over it and the rest of society as a whole.

Although this may strike some as an out-dated and out-moded means of articulating the problem, what I would like to suggest here is that only a return to this kind of thinking will be able to make Marxian theory into a theory capable of judgment and of action. More specifically, my thesis here will be that a form of politically relevant critical judgment can be most fruitfully explored by the construction of a critical social ontology. Lukács, later in life, returned to this project since he saw that there was no way to get away from the central problem of ethics. He saw, as did members of the Frankfurt School and other trenchant critics of modern administrative-capitalist society, that the domination of neopositivism and analytic frames of thought were dissolving the capacity to think critically – that is, to think in terms of the totality of social reality.

But we should be clear about what a turn to ontology means in the context of modern society. What Lukács clearly saw as attractive in this project was the need to create a categorial scheme that enables us to grasp the nature of social reality in such a way that we can diagnose and overcome the pathologies of capitalist society. Problems such as alienation, reification, exploitation, oligarchic inequality, among others, are endemic to capitalism. But what is increasingly lacking is a critical theory of capitalism that can provide a unified theory of critique and judgment. By this I mean a theoretical approach to social reality that will be able to grant us rational insight into the nature of social pathologies as well as the dialectical means to have judgment about what is required and desired for social transformation. What current theory and philosophy have evinced is an increasing lack of insight in this regard. Lukács saw that it was essential to keep an essentially humanist core in tact in any expression of Marxian philosophy. This meant that the purpose of Marxist theory was not only a diagnosis of the negative forces and effects of capitalist society, but also an emphasis on the need for social transformation that would enhance human progress at the social and individual level.

But the trends of current theory have turned against this tradition of thought. From nihilistic critiques of progress to vapid theories about "justification" as a means for critique, the project of critical theory has become increasingly domesticated and detached from efforts for social transformation. What has been lost from view is a comprehensive theoretical grasp of the reality of human life. In this sense, we can see a return to Kantian themes that were once the focus of Hegelian-Marxist critiques. Now, theories of communication, discourse, justification and recognition – all products of the post-metaphysical turn in moral and political philosophy – have gained sway. They embrace what I think we can call a form of "noumenalism," or a philosophy of human reality that grounds the essence of human sociality as restricted to the mental and cognitive domain of consciousness. What unites these various programs is a neo-Idealist paradigm where sociality is reduced to intersubjectivity and pragmatic forms of moral-cognitive "development."[1]

But this post-metaphysical and neo-Idealist paradigm cannot bear the weight of the kind of critique needed to confront the realities of modern forms of social power and domination that are rooted in the logics of rationalized forms of global capitalism and the culture and politics it generates. There is no

---

1 Elsewhere I have critiqued this neo-Idealist paradigm. See my *The Domestication of Critical Theory*. (London: Rowman and Littlefield, 2016).

ballast to forms of practical reason that rely only on our intersubjective noumenal faculties. Given the high level of efficiency of modern institutions to socialize agents and reify their consciousness with respect to the general goals and processes of global capitalism, the need for a more robust form of critique is required. As Nicolai Hartmann once insightfully remarked, "philosophers, time and again, come to think they can go their way without an ontological foundation."[2]

2 Marx's Materialism as Critical Ontology

What I would like to do first is frame Marx's ideas about human sociality and show that they conform to a critical social-ontological project. For Marx, any critical science of society would have to begin with the proper establishment of its object of study. Ideology or other forms of false consciousness take root in the fertile soil of corrupt conceptions about human beings and their actual existence. Marx saw in Hobbes and Locke theoretical justifications for the kind of market society that would mature into capitalism. Indeed, thinkers at the root of the liberal tradition did invest in overturning the older ontology of individual and community that had its roots in Aristotle and Scholasticism and to ground a new theory of rights, social action and a justification for property and personal acquisition based on new metaphysical commitments. But Marx also saw that Hegelian Idealism pushed a conception of human life that was also one-sided and lacking in fuller richness. Thus, Marx's social ontology contains several features all of which need to be taken together to fill out his systemic understanding of human sociality and the ontological features of human social life.

Briefly stated, we can see the framework of Marx's critical social ontology as consisting in his idea that: (i) human activity as *praxis*, or a special kind of activity that has teleological force; (ii) human individuals are *social-relational* and form an interdependent nexus of structures that organize praxis and orient it toward certain collective ends and purposes; (iii) these social relational-structures of practical activities constitute society as an objective entity with *processual* properties; and (iv) all social process have *ends and purposes* toward which previous features are oriented. From this we can see that the implication is that Marx's social ontology is a theory of nested or layered dimensions of social reality that are not natural or objective in any physical sense, but rather are ontological in the sense that they are rooted in human practices and

---

2 Nicolai Hartmann, *The New Ways of Ontology*. (Chicago: Henry Regenry Co., 1953), 4.

constitute a reality that is not natural but distinctly social in nature.³ This latter point is of particular importance since for Marx practices constitute the basic nucleus of an ontology of sociality. Marx takes after Aristotle's thesis that thought requires activity in the world for it to be an effective reality. As Aristotle argues the matter: "Thought (διάνοια) by itself however moves nothing, only thought directed toward an end and concerning action (πρακτική) does."⁴ Praxis is not simply activity, but activity that is directed toward an end and which is therefore the basis of "productive activity," or of making and doing things in the world (τῆς ποιητικῆς).

For Marx, this basic idea is taken over from Aristotle in order to obtain a more comprehensive grasp of human activity. For Marx also sees that human praxis (πρακτική) and human labor (ποιητική) are both to be understood as a more complex way of understanding the way that thought and the world are united. Unlike Hegel who saw thought working itself out via cognition and, therefore, as an essentially passive, contemplative position, Marx pushes this idea further in order to show that the world must be activley shaped by reason and therefore by activity in the world. Marx's revolt against Hegel, in this sense, pivots on a more radical understanding of how reason interacts with the world. For Marx, it is clear that praxis is the very means by which humans are able to rationalize the world they live within. It is not a matter of an instrumental treatment of nature, but as a means of understanding the ways that capitalist society misshapes and distorts the ontological reality of human life that is at issue. For Marx, the great insight is that we need to have insight into the essential metaphysical structure inherent within human sociality if we are to be able to achieve this kind of radical transformative power.

Marx makes many of these ideas explicit in the *Theses on Feuerbach*. In the first thesis, he posits a new kind of relation between subject and object: "The chief defect of all previous materialism ... is that the object, actuality, sensuousness is conceived only in the form of the *object of perception (Anschauung)*, but not as *sensuous human activity, Praxis*, not subjectively."⁵ Marx complains that "Feuerbach wants sensuous objects actually different from thought objects: but he does not comprehend human activity itself as objective."⁶ Further, Marx claims that: "In practice (*Praxis*) man must prove the truth, that is,

---

3 Cf. Vardaman R. Smith, "Marx's Social Ontology, His Critical Method and Contemporary Social Economics." *Review of Social Economy*, vol. 42, no. 2 (1984): 143–169.
4 Aristotle, *Nicomachean Ethics*, VI, ii. 5.
5 Karl Marx, "Theses on Feuerbach." In Lloyd Easton and Kurt Guddat (eds.), *Writings of the Young Marx on Philosophy and Society*. (New York: Doubleday, 1967), 400.
6 Marx, *Theses on Feuerbach*, 400.

actuality and power, this-sidedness of his thinking."[7] Putting these ideas together gives us a first step in Marx's ontological conception of man. Thinking and being are united in the concept of *praxis* just as in the Aristotelian thesis that cognition cannot be complete without activity. For Marx, too, this is a critique of Idealism in that only the dialectic of subject and object can be made complete through praxis, i.e., through the externalization of thought into the world. This makes the objective world actual (*Wirklich*), or "active" in that things realize their active completion via this dialectic.[8]

This thesis is distinctly ontological as opposed to material and Idealist. It is obvious that a book is not merely paper, that paper is not merely a tree. It is only via the idea of bookness synthesized with the practical working of natural substrates into a specific form that the *telos*, or aim of practice, an actual book, is possible and achieves any kind of reality.[9] In contrast to mechanical forms of materialism, Marx is arguing that human praxis conceived as the externalization of human thought into the world can be understood as proper human activity. Hence, Marx argues that: "The coincidence of the change of circumstances and of human activity or self-change can be comprehended and rationally understood only as *revolutionary practice*."[10] This means that the very capacity to understand and grasp what we are as human requires that we understand our world as created by us. But there is more. In a next step, Marx wants us to see that practice is not simply a feature of us qua individuals. Rather, praxis is social just as society itself is practical: "All social life is essentially practical. All mysteries which lead theory to mysticism find their rational solution in human practice and the comprehension of this practice."[11]

Marx now begins to build out a model of social ontology that comprehends the essence not as an individual object, but rather as essentially social: "the essence of man is no abstraction inhering in each single individual. In its actuality it is the ensemble of social relationships."[12] Now we see that practical

---

7 Marx, *Theses on Feuerbach*, 401.
8 For a more textured discussion of the Aristotelian concept of "activity," upon which Marx draws, see Aryeh Kosman, *The Activity of Being: An Essay on Aristotle's Ontology*. (Cambridge, Mass.: Harvard University Press, 2013), specifically 87ff.
9 Norman D. Livergood argues on this point that: "Reality, according to Marx, must be viewed as the result of the redirective activity of human beings in relation to changing conditions in external reality. Both the object and the subject are continually active; human history may be seen as a process in which changes in material reality create new needs which in turn bring about human transformations of material reality." *Activity in Marx's Philosophy*. (The Hague: Martinus Nijhoff, 1967), 20.
10 Marx, "Theses on Feuerbach," 401.
11 Marx, "Theses on Feuerbach," 402.
12 Marx, "Theses on Feuerbach," 402.

activity is not merely a property of the self, of a given individual but is rather itself activated by our interactions with others. In our relations with others our practices are themselves shaped and oriented toward ends and purposes. Things are what they are because of the ways we act upon them; each of us do not act alone, but in concert with others. Hence brute natural facts are transformed into human, social facts. Trees and grass exist as brute facts of nature; parks and lawns do not. And parks and lawns only have meaning because we have externalized the ideas of parks and lawns into a transformed physical organization of matter that corresponds with the idea of a park or lawn – it achieves an ontological reality as a result of the synthesis of the two. No one does this alone, but rather it is always *essentially social*. Hence Marx writes in the *Economic and Philosophical Manuscripts*:

> Even when I carry out *scientific* work, etc. an activity which I can seldom conduct in direct association with other men, I perform a *social*, because *human*, act. It is not only the material of my activity – such as the language itself which the thinker uses – which is given to me as a social product. *My own existence* is a social activity. For this reason, what I myself produce I produce for society, and with the consciousness of acting as a social being.[13]

Marx's radical thesis here now comes more clearly into view. If we see human beings as essentially social, this means that our sociality is constituted by the interdependent practices that engage us and within which we participate. Marx reaches back to Aristotle and his thesis about the essence of human life being social and constituted by a series of relations to others forming a coherent whole. As Marx notes in the *Grundrisse*: "The human being is in the most literal sense a ζῷον πολιτικόν, not merely a gregarious animal, but an animal which can individuate itself only in the midst of society."[14] Practices are therefore not reducible to an individual alone working on nature with some teleological purpose since the nature of these practices and the capacity to engage in them find their origins in our relations. Language, speech, the use of tools, etc. – all are social properties that emerge within us as individuals. But the key idea here that is crucial is nevertheless an ontological one: our practices and

---

13　Karl Marx, *The Economic and Philosophical Manuscripts*. (New York: Frederick Ungar Publishing, 1964), 130.
14　Karl Marx, *Grundrisse*. (New York: Penguin, 1973), 84.

relations are not material in some natural sense, they are social in an *ontological sense*.[15]

But practices and relations are not sufficient categories on their own to comprehend Marx's ontological thesis. One reason is that practices and relations are not static, but rather are inherently in motion. Once we begin to transform nature and embed it with human, social forms of meaning, then new dynamics of change begin to take effect. So, in the *Grundrisse*, Marx makes a brief comment that displays a distinctively ontological commitment: "A railway on which no trains run, hence which is not used up, not consumed, is a railway only δυνάμει, and not in reality.... [A] garment becomes a real garment only in the act of being worn; a house where no one lives is in fact not a real house."[16] Even capital is itself a process; one whereby the entirety of society is put into motion. Hence, the social reality that we create itself creates certain needs, logics and forms of motion on their own. The structures of practices that we form are therefore also *processual* in nature by which is meant that these structures of practices are transformative in nature. Materia can be put into different forms to create new content; the change of our relations over time constitutes a change in the content of our society as a whole. Here we have a premise that allows us insight into a historical dimension of social reality.

Freedom is therefore to be understood in a new way. Human life that is able to comprehend and to shape actively these ontological properties constitutes a new kind of freedom that is not merely abstract in an Idealist sense, but will be made concrete via the actual social facts that are constitutive of our social reality. What is crucial here is the insight that free individuality is a function of free sociality. In turn, free sociality is one where the relations, processes, ends and purposes of our social world are oriented toward the development of such a free individuality.[17] It is not simply a mastery over nature that is of concern, but a comprehension of the social-ontological structures requisite for the

---

15 It is important to stress the extent to which Marx's critical, dialectical theory of ontology is distinct from the pre-critical, non-dialectical form of ontology. As Jindrich Zeleny has argued: "in Marx's scientific work the materialist – *sit venia verbo* – relativist-substantialist logic is employed. But it is so constructed that it has nothing in common with a realtivism which disputes the possibility of perceiving objective reality correctly. It is rather a presupposition of true objective knowledge, following on the collapse of anti-dialectical conceptions of the ontological structure of reality." *The Logic of Marx*. (Oxford: Basil Blackwell, 1980), 23 as well as 187ff.

16 Marx, *Grundrisse*, 91.

17 Carol Gould insightfully remarks that: "for Marx freedom arises through interaction with these empirical conditions, that is, by a transformative process in which a subject who is originally heteronomous becomes autonomous by achieving mastery over nature, and

articulation of a free sociality. Of course, such comprehension is only concretely free if it instantiates itself *practically* in the world: only once our actual lived lives unfold within relations of practices that are oriented toward common ends and purposes that cultivate a common, social form of wealth that has its purpose and end, its *telos*, the full development of each individual. Since Marx's social ontology dialectically sublates the concepts of individual and community insofar as it sees our individuality as functionally related to the particular shape of interdependencies within which it is embedded, then the concept of freedom must become a social category, not merely an individual one.

Marx's critical social ontology therefore has within it a conflation between descriptive and normative claims: by comprehending the essential structure of human life as interdependent and practical, we see that those ends and purposes that such descriptive categories are put toward also can be seen as having evaluative categories embedded within in it. The key idea seems to me that any proper, rational cognition of an object also provides us with the evaluative categories for that object. The reason for this lies in the structure of teleological reasoning that Marx elaborates. This is not a pre-modern, transcendental form of teleological reasoning. Rather, it is one that is confined to the activity of labor – but labor itself is an expression of praxis, of the capacity of an idea in the mind of the individual to orient actual human actions and activities and the production of some kind of end. In this sense, it need not be confined to physical labor but can be seen as a basic capacity within the human species that enables the projection and the realization of some conscious end, some idea, some telos. It is Marx's philosophical innovation to buttress his philosophical anthropology with a new conception of teleology: one that is based solely on human intentionality and the capacities inherent in human action (praxis) to realize those intentions in the world. But this also means a modification of the kind of reasoning that modern forms of reason sought to undermine. Primarily among these was that of teleological reasoning. Marx's reworking of this idea entails the thesis that *telos* is not a structure of nature or of history; it has no transcendental metaphysical warrant at all. At the same time, various forms of rationalism and Idealism that seek to eviscerate teleology also miss the mark because they cannot account for the structure of practice itself; they are unable to comprehend the true, i.e., concrete structure of human activity and, as such, of human life and sociality more generally.

---

freedom from social domination." *Marx's Social Ontology: Individuality and Community in Marx's Theory of Social Reality*. (Cambridge, Mass.: MIT Press, 1978), 107.

What Marx is after here is an account of human praxis that is able to inform a new framework for social critique. Once we posit the thesis of human praxis as a concrete activity of projecting ends and social relations as more complex evolutions of praxis, we can then inquire in a critical sense about the purposes and ends for which those practices are instantiated. Far from being a mere descriptive exercise, then, Marx's thesis about human praxis (i.e., labor) entails the inquiry into what kinds of ends, what *teloi*, do any community orient its various levels of praxis. For Marx, the question of human emancipation now becomes tied to the structure of human practices and the kinds of social reality that both create them and that are created by them. The essential point seems to be that the structure of praxis contains within it the nucleus for a kind of social critique that can call into question the objective social structures, relations and processes that any community manifests. The reason for this can be found in the kind of reasoning distinctive of a critical ontology that takes ends or purposes as decisive for critical judgment. Marx sees the theory of value – value taken to mean the various social objects that result from nature transformed by the practice of labor – as the conceptual space of judging the ends or purposes of labor (individual or collective). His distinction between "use value" and "exchange value," taken over from Aristotle, is an example of how Marx's social ontological categories are both descriptive and evaluative.[18] The importance of the theory of value is therefore ontological rather than material since it can only be comprehended as a social form and not a form of nature or matter.

This point deserves further development. To say that value is a social form is to say that it is a particular outcome of our practices. The question of value is therefore an ontological question because any object can only have value once it is endowed with labor. Since labor is a distinctively human form of activity, value is therefore the result of some intentional, some teleological activity. But then again, the more complex the levels of praxis (say of labor) are that produce the object, the more density of value it possesses. At last, we can evaluate the value of the object based on the role it plays within society as a whole. To say that many human beings organize themselves into productive forms of activity to produce shoes to sell the shoes in order to produce surplus profit, means that we can judge the way that such a community organizes its layers of praxis – of sewing, shipping, distributing, such shoes – according to the ends

---

18 Elsewhere I have tackled the issue of the sublation of descriptive and evaluative forms of knowledge in Marx's thought in my paper "Philosophical Foundations for a Marxian Ethics." In M. Thompson (ed.), *Constructing Marxist Ethics: Critique, Normativity, Praxis*. (Leiden: Brill, 2015): 235–265.

that are produced. Capitalism itself constitutes a system of power that is thoroughly ontological in the sense that its very way of organizing the practical activities of society is a regime of power.[19] The power consists in the capacity of capitalists to orient the community toward their ends and purposes rather than democratic, or common ends and purposes. The relevant question for critical consiousness therefore becomes: Do such ends serve common, social goals or particular, private goals? Capitalism's logic of producing for surplus value now becomes a social ontological question: is society organized according its common ends, judged according to some conception of human progress in an emancipatory sense, or is it organized according to the domination logics of inequality and surplus extraction?

Freedom as a form of self-determination now takes on a very different form: it is now only possible within a kind of social totality that places the comprehensive development and good of that totality as the premise of the development and fulfillment of the individual members of that association. In opposition to liberal or individualist conceptions of self-determination, the self is now embedded in a context of sociality and must live in a world where the relations, processes and ends of that reality reinforce and enrich one's personhood. Indeed, as Nicolai Hartmann rightly observed: "What is hidden ontologically in the so-called freedom of the will is nothing less than a new, unique, and obviously higher form of determination."[20] It is this insight that helps us transition from Marx's critical social ontology to its expansion in the work of Lukács. For Lukács, the concept of labor is the central master concept for a more comprehensive social ontology, or comprehension of human social being and social reality itself. But even more, he sees this ontology as the basis for a form of judgment, an ethics that will be able to grant Marxism a distinctive power of critique and evaluative capacity.

3   Lukács and the Expansion of Critical Social Ontology

The reception of Marx's thought throughout the twentieth century lost track of the distinctively ontological character of his thought and the kind of foundational role it played in the coherence of his through more generally. Lukács not only knew this to be true; he insightfully realized that only through a systematic

---

19 On the idea of capitalism as manifesting an ontology of power, see the important discussion by Giulio Palermo, "The Ontology of Economic Power in Capitalism: Mainstream Economics and Marx." *Cambridge Journal of Economics*, vol. 31 (2007): 539–561.

20 Hartmann, *The New Ways of Ontology*, 72.

exploration of this social ontology would we be able to construct a form of judgment rooted in Marxian thought. At the heart of his project is the desire to get at a categorial scheme that will enable us to comprehend human reality but also to be able to activate a higher sense of critical judgment and reflection. Indeed, although Lukács sees the basic categories that Marx laid out as basic, he also saw that more was needed if we were going to be able to construct an ethical system. First, it is important to see in his earlier works the implicit way that a social ontology is in fact operative in his ideas. If we go back to the thesis of *History and Class Consciousness*, we see that Lukács adds a crucial category to Marx's own scheme. Lukács sees the basis of his ontology as constituted by the structure of labor. This he sees as a kind of generative nucleus for all forms of social reality. Labor is a unique human capacity that generates higher and more complex forms of social reality that can be seen as distinct from nature and as a reworking of the natural-material world into objects that are uniquely human.

Lukács sees Marx's distinctive contribution to a social ontology as his conception of human labor. Taking Marx's Aristotelian conception of labor/praxis as a core concept, he proposes that we see in labor as the constitutive causal activity for all forms of social reality. Once we see labor as both efficient cause and final cause, we can begin to glimpse the ontological ground that Lukács proposes as the fundamental principle. The essential component of labor is the core concept of "teleological positing" or "projection" (*Setzung*). Lukács defines this as:

> a mental plan achieving material realization, in the projection of a desired goal bringing about a change in material reality, introducing a material change in reality that represents something qualitatively and radically new in relation to nature. Aristotle's example of the building of a house shows this very concretely. The house is just as material an existence as the stone, wood, etc., of which it is constructed. Yet the teleological projection gives rise to an objectivity that is completely different from that of its elements…. What is necessary for the house is the power of human thought and will, to arrange these properties materially and actually in an essentially quite new connection.[21]

---

21 Georg Lukács, *Zur Ontologie des gesellschaftlichen Seins*, vol. 2. (Darmstadt: Hermann Luchterland, 1986), 51.

From this Lukács derives what he calls the "fundamental ontological ground": "causality set in motion through teleological decisions (*teleologische Alternativenetscheidungen*) where choice enters into play."²²

The key idea here is that our social being is determined not by our biological capacities but by the social mediations that are used to shape our activities. Labor is not to be narrowly construed as "work" or some kind of ideological category but rather as the central category of any ontology. The reason for this is that: "Through labor a teleological positing is realized within material being as the realization of a new objectivity. The first consequence of this is that labor becomes the model for any social practice (*Praxis*), for in this – no matter how widely ramified its mediations – teleological projections become realized and in the end, realized materially."²³ Since Marx had posited that the only valid form of teleology was the teleology of labor, it follows that all human praxis be conceived as "a mental plan achieving material realization, in the positing of a desired goal bringing about a change in material reality, introducing a material change in reality which represents something qualitatively and radically new in relation to nature."²⁴

As a basis for building a more complex understanding of social reality, Lukács takes pains to emphasize that the desires goal, the mental plan that exists prior to the realization of this new objectivity is followed by the means by which this new objectivity is brought into being. We begin to unfold new forms of social reality – language, conceptual thought, cooperation, etc. – from this core capacity of human being. Society is therefore a series of overlapping forms of praxis that have their origin in human practical relations with nature – "the transformation of natural objects into use value."²⁵ Group cooperation then follows as a result of this basic capacity, and the basis of human society based not on biological drives, but a capacity that has choice at its center now becomes the space within which the human community realizes itself. Lukács is clear that this latter point – the capacity to choose or to decide the means by which we realize our posited *teloi* – is distinctive in that different means can be developed to solve problems and create new forms of social reality. The complexity of social forms therefore becomes seen as a complexity of decisions of how to realize certain ends.

---

22 Georg Lukács, "The Ontological Foundations of Human Thinking and Action." In Ernst Joos, *Lukács' Last Autocriticism: The Ontology*. (Atlantic Highlands, N.J.: Humanities Press, 1983), 144.
23 Lukács, *Zur Ontologie des gesellschaftlichen Seins*, vol. 2, 12.
24 Lukács, *Zur Ontologie des gesellschaftlichen Seins*, vol. 2, 18.
25 Lukács, *Zur Ontologie des gesellschaftlichen Seins*, vol. 2, 46.

Lukács gives an example of this, in somewhat rudimentary fashion, when he describes the emergence in hunter societies of their cooperative activities:

> The size, strength and danger of the animals hunted made group cooperation (*Kooperation einer Menschengruppe*) necessary. But if this cooperation was to function successfully, there had to be a division of functions among the individual participants (beaters and hunters). The teleological projections that follow from this have a secondary character from the standpoint of the immediate labor itself. They must be preceded by a teleological positing that defines the character, role, function, etc., of the individual concrete and real positings that are oriented to a natural object. The object of this secondary goal positing, therefore, is no longer something purely natural, but rather the consciousness of a human group; the posited goal is no longer designed directly to change a natural object, but rather to bring about a teleological positing that really is oriented to the natural objects.[26]

This indicates how the various layers of social reality can be seen as the nested layering of forms of *Praxis* in that each form of social reality contains webs of teleological projections. Lukács is therefore saying that for us to act together, we possess a shared form of teleological positing or, as some contemporary social ontologists would argue, a sense of "shared agency" rooted in our shared capacity for intentionality.[27] But as societies become more complex, the root capacity to realize teleological positing at the individual level becomes lost. "The internal discrepancy between teleological projections and their causal consequences increases with the growth of societies and the intensification of socio-human (*gesellschaftlich-menschlichen*) participation."[28] The critical potency of this social ontology now begins to be glimpsed. Once we place the ends or purposes of our activities at center stage, we begin to open up the way that social values can be assessed as either promoting social ends or private ends. We now have an objective criterion for the evaluation of the kinds of activities, relations, institutions and norms that constitute our social reality.

Instead of exploring the nuances of Lukács' social ontology, I would like to develop his core ideas into a more systematic and organized theory of social

---

26   Lukács, *Zur Ontologie des gesellschaftlichen Seins*, vol. 2, 47.
27   The parallel ideas between Lukács' argument here and the theory of shared agency and planning in group activities is striking. Cf. Michael E. Bratman, *Shared Agency: A Planning Theory of Acting Together*. (New York: Oxford University Press, 2014), with Lukács' thesis here.
28   Lukács, "The Ontological Foundations of Human Thinking and Action," 143.

reality. After this, I will attempt to provide a framework for what Lukács was never able to develop: that of an ethical theory rooted in this critical social ontology. What I hope to make clear is that Lukács' groundwork for a critical social ontology requires that we see the centrality of the kinds of ends toward which forms of social organization and the various ways that our praxis is shaped and fitted into these forms as the core *explanandum* for a critical social ontology. I then want to show how the centrality of teleology and human praxis can be used to develop a conception of practical reasoning that can aid in the project of constructing a Marxian theory of ethics.

4   Foundational Categories for a Critical Social Ontology

As I see it, there is much more work to be done if a critical social ontology along Marxian lines is to be established. To be sure, Lukács was able to provide a kind of justification for an ontology, but his work leaves us bereft of a more systematic and more comprehensive theory. What I want to concentrate upon for the remainder of this essay is the elaboration of a critical social ontology that expands on Marx's own insights and takes on those of Lukács as well as some of the ideas that have been introduced in more contemporary work in social ontology. As I see it, the task here is not a categorical scheme that will be in some sense exhaustive in a logico-deductive sense, but rather to produce a set of categories that will enable us to tease out the intrinsic logic of social forms. By this I mean a set of categories that will be able give theoretical mediation to the inherited and socialized forms of practices, relations and ends toward which any given society predisposes us. Lukács' thesis of reification seems to me to remain salient in the sense that the essential power of modern society lay in its capacity to co-opt the forms of legitimation and consciousness to the extent that its purposes and goals can be fulfilled. To the extent that this is true, the actual dynamics of the social world in its totality remain obscure. Even barring weak forms of ideological bias, there is simply a basic incapacity to view the modern world as a systematic totality and, even more, to be able to comprehend the pathologies that one experiences phenomenologically as rooted in broader systemic causes. A social ontology becomes critical to the extent that it can mediate these experience rationally and lead reflective agents to the roots of societal pathologies in the organizing principles and interests that govern their social reality.

We can take the ideas of Marx and Lukács and make them part of a larger, more comprehensive critical social ontology that can serve as the ground for a critical theory of judgment only once we examine with more clarity the ideas that have been elaborated in recent years by theorists working in social ontology. As I see it, a critical social ontology can only be formulated by synthesizing these two theoretical fields in order for us to be able to service the thesis outlined by Lukács that reification can only be overcome by keeping the totality in view. In this sense, what I would like to do now is sketch a theory of a critical social ontology that can allow not merely a descriptive capacity to understand social reality, but, more importantly, grant us access to a critical theory of judgment. My thesis here will be that a social ontology is only critical when it can inform normative judgments. These normative judgments have in view not only a rational grasp of our social reality, but also the potentialities inherent in the defective social forms that we inhabit and which we re-create. This will therefore provide us with the requisite social theory to be able to construct a critical theory of judgment.

4.1 Properties of Social Ontology

We should first distinguish between the *properties* and the *modes* of a critical social ontology. The *properties* of a social ontology describe the features of what counts as social ontological whereas the *modes* of the social ontology are the constitutive categories of society and, when taken together, can help up grasp the social totality and its dynamics. The basic properties of what allow us to account for a social ontology must be the following. First, it must be *objective* in the sense that it is a shared reality among members of the community itself. This should be sharply contrasted to what is *material* in the traditional sense. A legal code, money, rules and the kind of rule-following that allows for the game of baseball or checkers – all are objective social facts that constitute objects that possess social facticity rather than material (or natural) facticity. Hence, John Searle's conception of "constitutive rules" means the normative rule-following that creates certain objective social facts. The game of baseball is not a material fact, but a social fact constituted by certain rules and rule-following behavior accepted by all who participate in it. But we can also say, after Marx and Lukács, that there are objective social facts that are material: hence, the human interaction with nature and the resulting transformation of nature into human products is itself an expression of the objective sociality.

We therefore have to distinguish between those aspects of social ontology that are *active* and those that are *congealed* in the material world. Both are significant. We can say that an *active* aspect of social ontology would possess objectivity but not materiality. Whenever I follow a rule or norm in tandem with others I create an objective social fact as in the case when students and teacher behave in different ways according to different statuses and norms toward one another. This creates the category of teacher and student as an objective but not a material social fact. But practices that manipulate the natural world into socially meaningful objects possess an objective social reality as well as a social-material reality. A violin or a baseball bat are essentially, in a brute material sense, pieces of wood, plastic and other materials. But it has an objective social meaning in the sense that that particular object of a violin as purposes and meanings that are assigned to it by us cognitively. At the same time, it is a the product of an ensemble of social relations and practices that have manipulated the natural world – trees into wood, plastic into tuning keys, and whatever – that have brought those elements from the sphere of nature into the sphere of the social. The material world of cities, electric power stations, paintings, paint, parks, etc., are all the result of socio-human praxis in a congealed, material form. Hence, the first property of social ontology embraces what is objective and material, although not necessarily both at the same time.[29]

A second property of social ontology is that it possesses *causal powers* over social agents. A social fact must have causal powers in some basic sense for it to be social ontological. Searle says, for instance, that social facts possess "deontic power" which means that the norms we accept as constitutive of social facts make demands on us and our commitments, behavior and conscience. Searle calls this "deontic power," and it entails the capacity of any social fact to be able to cause us to perform, think or feel in some way. Social reality would not be real in any efficacious sense if it were not able to have some causal power. This can come in a myriad forms. On the one hand, they can be embedded in norms of behavior in the sense that the roles, functions and statuses of individuals within a given social context will entail certain expectations, behaviors and additional norms as well. Social power is therefore intricately entwined with these causal powers, for the capacity to shape and develop efficacious forms of deontic power carry with it the capacity to control and shape others. In this sense, capital, for instance, is not a material reality, but a social-ontological one: it is a structural and processual set of congealed norms that force certain kinds of behaviors and expectations. It only has power to the extent that it is embedded in the basic background world-view and institutional logics of the society as a whole. But herein lies its essentially *ontological constitution*: it is constituted by the kinds of rule-following (coercive or tacit) that the institutions shaped and affected by capital absorbed and enacted by agents.

---

29 In this sense, unicorns, for instance, are not possible via an ontological scheme because it makes claims about material reality whereas *merely objective* social facts are forms of reality that possess objectivity because we accept their reality (say interest rates on a loan) but make no claims about the organization of matter.

As a result of the complex activities of objective forms of social reality that have the capacity to shape and orient our behavior, we can see as these kinds of activities congeal into more complex social forms, they further develop their ontological sophistication and reality. We can therefore see that there is a third property of social ontology: that social reality is *systemic* meaning that they are not static things of reality, but operate within a context of other social facts (relations, structures, processes and so on). Given the interrelatedness of social facts, their constitution as a system brings us to higher levels of complexity and toward the totality itself. As David Weissman has argued, "Systems take causality one step further: mutual activation and inhibition – causal reciprocities – stabilize interactions that have created a system."[30] Systems are not aggregates of the smaller elements that constitute them, they are composed of elements that are related via mutual forms of determination. In this sense, higher, more complex forms of reality can be articulated by enlarging the web of mutually related elements.

4.2 *Modes of Social Ontology*

These three basic properties of social ontology therefore describe what counts as social-ontological as opposed to natural. They are descriptive of the qualities that inhere to any social-ontological phenomenon. We can now turn to the basic categories that are constitutive of social reality itself, i.e., those categories that essentially account for social-ontological phenomena. As I see it, these will have to expand beyond the basic ideas described by Marx and Lukács. First we must keep in mind that we can understand these categories by breaking them down analytically but in reality they operate dialectically, as will be shown. The first fundamental analytic division must be made between what we can call subjective and objective modes of social ontology. I take these respective terms to indicate not a separately delineated sphere of reality, but that what are subjective and objective interpenetrate dialectically, i.e., are mutually causal of the other. A subjective facet of social ontology is therefore nevertheless rooted in social forms and reality. But it can manifest itself without external agents. Hence, Robinson Crusoe could utter a language and perform other practices that he absorbed through socialization without having others around him. However, objective facets of social ontology cannot exist without others: relations, structures, processes and ends all have an ontological objectivity that transcend any given individual and which require multiple agents for their emergence.

---

30   David Weissman, *A Social Ontology*. (New Haven, Conn.: Yale University Press, 2000), 64.

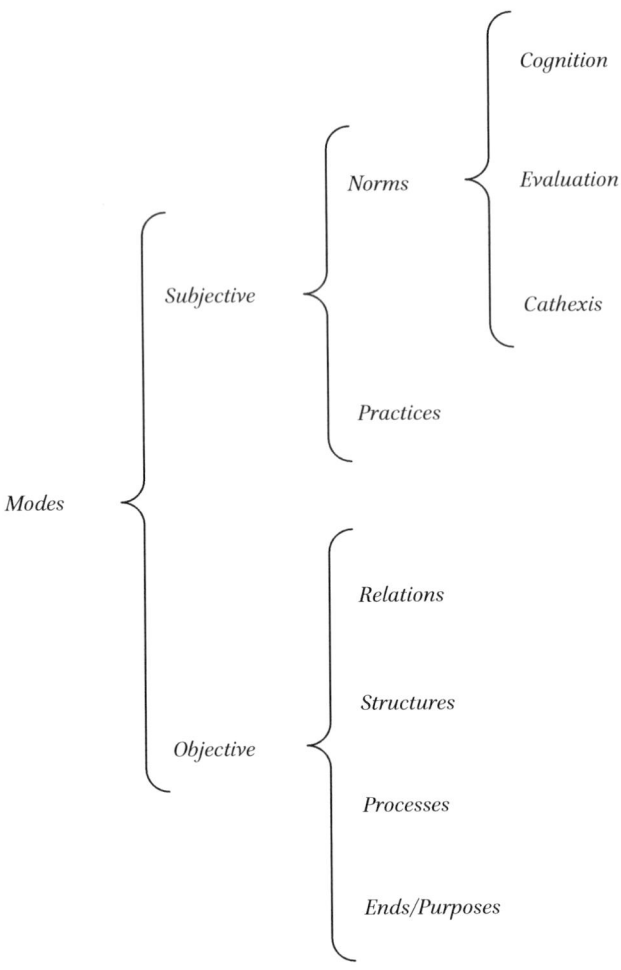

FIGURE 14.1 Analytical breakdown of modes of social ontology

What is crucial here is to see that any practice is, even if performed by an individual, is a socially mediated activity. The capacity for language, for instance, is innate, but language, communication, and so on, are socially mediated developments. These become social-ontological realities, social facts that possess objectivity, causal powers and the status of a system. But since practices are socially mediated forms of activity, more developed forms of praxis are essentially social and, as such, require cooperation with others. In this sense, social facts are constituted by relations between individuals performing collective praxis. A conversation has ontological status as a social fact constituted by a cooperative interplay of the practice of speaking. Now, going further, these relations can become structured in that they are patterned by rules, norms, status functions and so on. Producing a commodity in a factory is therefore entails a structural relationship in that each productive members depends in an interdependent fashion on the activities of others.

Relations are only discernable analytically, they do not exist in reality in that form. Any relation can be understood to exist ontologically, but it is also a process in that each relation is also an activity. A marriage is not simply a relation, it is also a process in that it is constituted by relations of activity.[31] A family is a larger structure of relations than a mere marriage, but it, too, is a structure of relations of activity and its ontological status can be seen in the activities that take place within that structure. It is, for all intents and purposes, a *process*. In this sense, emphasis on a relational sociology is necessary but insufficient to account for the reality of social facts. Take as an example of this thesis Margaret Archer and Pierpaolo Donati's contention:

> The term *"Relational Subject"* refers to individual and collective social subjects in that they are *"relationally constituted,"* that is, *in as much as they generate emergent properties and powers through their social relations*. These relational goods and evils have internal effects upon the subjects themselves and external effects upon their social environments.[32]

Although it is clear that relations are constitutive of social facts, they alone cannot account for a social ontology in any comprehensive sense. Archer and Donati are right to see relations as constitutive of social facts and, in Donati's case in particular, quite right to see the goods produced and shared by society as "relational goods."[33] But the limitation here is the in the constricted social metaphysics that such a perspective confines us. Relations are themselves constitutive of higher social-ontological forms and in parsing these various modes, we can grasp a more total conception of social reality. More to the point, once we see that relations constitute structures, that structures constitute processes, and that processes constitute ends and purposes, we are on our way to a

---

[31] See the important discussion by Richard T. De George, "Social Reality and Social Relations." *Review of Metaphysics*, vol. 37, no. 1 (1983): 3–20.

[32] Pierpaolo Donati and Margaret S. Archer, *The Relational Subject*. (Cambridge: Cambridge University Press, 2015), 31. Also cf. Dave Elder-Vass, "Social Structure and Social Relations." *Journal for the Theory of Social Behaviour*, vol. 37, no. 4 (2007): 463–477.

[33] See Pierpaolo Donati's excellent paper "The Common Good as a Relational Good." *Nova et Vetera*, vol. 7, no. 3 (2009): 603–624, as well as his "Social Capital and Associative Democracy: A Relational Perspective." *Journal for the Theory of Social Behaviour*, vol. 44, no. 1 (2013): 24–45, as well as his discussion in *The Relational Subject*, 198ff.

more comprehensive and critical grasp of social reality, or social reality as a totality.[34]

Social Structure now can be understood not as static forms of relations, but as a *process*: that is, as collective, interactive activities that are oriented toward an end or purpose. Processes are a higher ontological form than relational structures insofar as they are *defined by reciprocal causes among the component parts of the structure*. In this sense, structures evolve into processes once the component parts of the structure act on one another to form a coherent system with its own ontological properties – ontological properties that are irreducible to the component parts or elements of the structure that constitute them.[35] Social facts can be seen as constituted by processes once we see that they are the result of a complex of practices.[36] But processes are themselves dialectically related to *ends* or *purposes*. Indeed, just as relations are dialectically related to structures, and structures to processes, so are processes defined in some basic sense as essentially related to the ends or purposes that they are organized to produce.

Families are an example of this. Although they do not, necessarily, produce some concrete commodity or good, they can still be seen as relational structures where each component member acts in particular ways toward others in some reciprocal fashion thereby constituting a system or process that produces some end or set of ends – mutual emotional support, raising of children, and so on. Clearly we can see that the more we expand the horizon of what counts as social facts we see that we are increasingly ensconced in overlapping systems of relational structures that generally have some kind of purpose or end which gives them their coherence and defines in some basic sense their activities. The end or purpose can also be seen to shape and organize the other modes that lead up to it: the nature of relational structures and processes. Hence, the imperative to increase productive efficiency in an economic activity may entail transforming the relational structures of the factory which, in

---

34 I have outlined the Hegelian foundations for this approach in my paper "The Metaphysical Infrastructure of Hegel's Practical Philosophy." In M. Thompson (ed.), *Hegel's Metaphysics and the Philosophy of Politics*. (New York: Routledge, 2018): 101–141.

35 David Weissman notes on this aspect of social ontology that: "High-order systems are formed when reciprocal causal relations are established between lower-order systems (starting with elementary particles). Causal reciprocity is the relation of agents whose characters or behaviors are mutually determining, hence mutually controlling, over a cycle of back-and-forth interactions." *A Social Ontology*, 46.

36 As Lukács notes: "Thus the knowledge that social facts are not objects but relations between men is intensified to the point where facts are wholly dissolved into processes." *History and Class Consciousness*, 180.

turn, changes the processes that constitute it. Indeed, the more general point I want to point to here in discussing the objective aspects of social-ontological modes is that when the *totality* of these modes is taken into account, we are able to approach a comprehensive grasp of the social totality.

The objective modes of social ontology are dialectically related to the subjective modes. As I point out in Figure 14.1, the subjective modes are made up of individual practices as well as norms make up the basic structure of the subjective dimension of social reality. The reason is that for the objective modes to achieve ontological activity, they must be enacted by agents. At the same time, already existing ontological social forms are acting upon agents, integrating them into the norms and practices requisite for the reproduction of those institutions and structures. At the level of the subject, therefore, we need to see that the cognitive, evaluative and cathectic levels of the subject need to be shaped and brought into compliance, to some basic degree, with the norms and rules that institutions deploy. When an institution is unable to achieve this level of social conformity, it begins to disintegrate. Once agents no longer think in terms of the dominant institutions, judge the world according to the norms that it emanates and feels no personal investment in them, they will begin to fall apart. Hence, the ontological forms a kind of system involving the objective and subjective into a higher totality. When whole societies are affected by the disintegration of this social system, it will collapse, as in the fall of Soviet communism in the late-twentieth century.

4.3 *Relation between Modes*

When considering the subjective modes of social ontology we enter into a more complex and more interesting discussion. Each social agent requires a set of norms that will guide his or her practices and in many instances mediate our practical capacities to serve social ends and purposes. What needs to be explained now is the relation between structure and agency or the ways that the subjective features of the individual relate to the objective social-ontological modes described above.

Let us begin with the concept of intentionality. In some basic sense, three different theories of social ontology – Lukács', critical realism and John Searle – all see intentionality in some form as the root of our social reality. There must be some conscious form of meaning that is realized in the external world for there to be some social reality. For Lukács, as we saw, this is the basic thesis of teleological positing where the *Vorbild* is the origin of the labor practice of external realization. But this too can be understood as a form of intentionality. The core question I would like to address now is the relation between the subjective and objective modes of social ontology schematized above. My basic thesis here will be that the subjective dimensions of social reality require an awareness of the objective modes for there to exist any form of critical consciousness of one's social reality. The problem in modern societies remains the colonization of the subjective modes by the objective modes. In other words, reification of consciousness emerges as a pathology once we can see that the objective mechanisms of social reality – e.g., the relations, structures, processes and purposes of that society – do not possess conscious awareness within the subjects that re-create those realities and which also shape them.

Intentionality is therefore one place to begin this discussion since it is a convergent concept for social ontology. John Searle's theory of social reality places emphasis on the intentional capacity of individuals as the root of all social reality. For Searle, the essence of any social reality begins with our attributing a status to the external world, some sense of meaning that it does not possess by nature. As Searle argues, "humans have the capacity to impose functions on objects and people where the objects and people cannot perform the functions solely in virtue of their physical structure."[37] The attribution of a status function achieves a social-ontological status once we collectively accept that object or person as possessing that status or function. This then becomes a matter of collective intentionality, or the fact that objects such as money, professors, or whatever "have a collectively recognized status that enables them to perform those functions in a way they could not do without the collective recognition of the status."[38] These become rules of consciousness, not only of behavior. For Searle, these "constitutive rules" produce the reality of the social world since they organize the intentional structures of consciousness and endow social reality with "deontic powers" that individuals accept from the collective acceptance of various status and function attribution.

Deontic powers result from the ways that collective intentionality ascribes statuses and powers to certain people in that the status function presses some obligation on us. As Searle describes this, deontic powers "involve getting people to do things without using force."[39] So, a student will act in certain ways toward a teacher that endows that teacher with a certain range of powers over that student. But this power is an emergent property of the status function attributed to the teacher by students and teachers alike. It structures certain obligations and norms without the use of force or coercion. Searle is therefore able to extrapolate a complex theory of social ontology

---

37   John Searle, *Making the Social World: The Structure of Human Civilization*. (New York: Oxford University Press, 2010), 7.
38   Searle, *Making the Social World*, 7.
39   Searle, *Making the Social World*, 147.

from a single mechanism: from our ability to use language and from speech-acts. All institutional facts and the ontology of the social world are created from the use of "one formal linguistic mechanism, and we apply it over and over with different contents."[40]

The problem here is that Searle's theory is too reliant on the cognitive faculties of the mind, and a conception of intentionality as circumscribed by the capacity to use language. There is no sense that the actual, objective social structures that are the product of these collective-intentional rules have any causal powers back onto the formation of subjectivity and agency itself. As Margaret Archer has correctly maintained, we need to see that there is an "analytical dualism" between agency and structure such that social structures possess a causal power over the agents that structure them as well as agents possessing the capacity to alter those same structures. As she puts the matter:

> Society is that which nobody wants, in the form in which they encounter is, for it is an unintended consequence. Its constitution could be expressed as a riddle: what it is that depends on human intentionality but never conforms to their intentions? What is it that relies upon people's concepts, but which they never fully know? ... At any given time, structure itself is the result of the result of prior social relations conditioned by an antecedent structural context. As such it is molded and re-molded but conforms to no mold.[41]

This critical realist approach therefore seeks to solve the problem of the relation between agency and structure, between the objective social structures that exist ontologically and the forms of subjective agency that shape it and are shaped by it. This is an important development in the search for a more general critical social ontology insofar as it sees as its crucial concern the explanation of the relation between the objective and subjective modes I outlined above.

---

40 Searle, *Making the Social World*, 7.
41 Margaret S. Archer, *Realist Social Theory: The Morphogenetic Approach*. (Cambridge: Cambridge University Press, 1995), 165. Roy Bhaskar makes an anti-Searlian position clear when he argues that: "people do not create society. For it always pre-exists them and is a necessary condition for their activity. Rather, society must be regarded as an ensemble of structures, practices and conventions which individuals reproduce or transform, but which would not exist unless they did so." Roy Bhaskar, *The Possibility of Naturalism: A Philosophical Critique of the Contemporary Human Sciences*. (Atlantic Highlands, N.J.: Humanities Press, 1979), 45.

The solution to this dilemma for critical realists is what Roy Bhaskar called the "position-practice system" by which is meant the ways that the social structure encounters the subject. As he argues:

> [W]e need a system of mediating concepts, encompassing both aspects of the duality of praxis, designating the "slots," as it were, in the social structure into which active subjects must slip in order to reproduce it; that it, a system of concepts designating the "point of contact" between human agency and social structures. Such a point, linking action to structure, must *both* endure and be immediately occupied by individuals. It is clear that the mediating system we need is that of the *positions* (places, functions, rules, tasks, duties, rights, etc.) occupied (filled, assumed, enacted, etc.) by individuals, and of the *practices* (activities, etc.) in which, in virtue of their occupancy of these positions (and vice-versa), they engage.[42]

Now we are presented with a theory of social ontology that takes structures dialectically with subjectivity. Indeed, Bhaskar rightly points to the idea that our agency is shaped by the socialization and integration into the various antecedent structures, and, to be sure, he and Archer also highlight the thesis that these structures not only shape agency but are in turn shaped by our agency (hence the concepts of "morphogenesis" and "morphostasis").[43] But what is missing here is a theory of power. Indeed, although Searle's account may be taken to be too linked to a theory of mind, he nevertheless has a promising account of how power works in terms of the ways it shapes the intentional structures of consciousness. In other words, the key for Searle's concept of power is that we attribute statuses to things/people that grant them power over us via our own capacity to attribute obligations and duties to perform certain acts or enact certain practices.

But notice, again, that Searle's account is essentially socially weightless: there is no sense that the structures within which we are socially integrated are the conceptual and normative fields that endow our subjective norms and values with a conceptual-normative basis for how we shape and orient our practices as well as the epistemic frames that reflect that external world back onto us. But power even in this sense is not really satisfying. Indeed, no one would quarrel with the notion that social structures emanate power relationships and that they are indeed constituted by such relations. Going to school or

---

42 Bhaskar, *The Possibility of Naturalism*, 51; also cf. Archer, *Realist Social Theory*, 170ff.
43 See Archer, *Realist Social Theory*, 165ff.

work, living in a family, let alone becoming a member of some larger organization confronts each individual with antecedent social structures that socialize our subjectivity and personality to the degree needed for those ontological entities to carry out their purposes. But the larger scale issue of the control of those organizations and institutions is what is needed for a critical understanding of social reality – i.e., a conception of the social world that can unmask the roots of power relations and give insight for emancipatory struggles.

For now we can see that Lukács' thesis about the nature of reification can be understood in a more compelling way. For now, reification becomes that pathological state of consciousness that is shaped by the collective-intentional constitutive rules that orient our cognitive and evaluative structures of consciousness.[44] The norms and the values that we absorb as the result of being socialized into the objective social structures entails a shaping of our cognitive, evaluative and cathectic subjective structures. Since this socialization process shapes and instills norms, these norms become rooted in consciousness – some at a more basic level than others. But the key issue here is we can now begin to see the deeper entanglement of the subjective and objective modes; and once we introduce the concept of power into this matrix, we can see that social power becomes a kind of *constitutive power* or a kind of power that can shape and orient our agency by having us adopt norms and values that will come to underwrite our consciousness (i.e., our cognition, our capacity to judge the normative validity of the world and how we emotionally invest ourselves in these values, norms and institutions). But once we bring this discussion of Searle and critical realism back into dialogue with Lukács' thesis, we see that the concept of teleology and of social reproduction can help us elaborate a more comprehensive critical social ontology.

4.4 *Critical versus Descriptive Social Ontology*

Now we have some of the necessary conceptual pieces needed to construct a critical social ontology, one that will be able to serve as the ground for a critical theory of ethics and a critical theory of judgment. My thesis here will be that a critical social ontology is possible only once we are able to put the concepts of teleology and totality as the final conceptual elements of our comprehension of social reality. The reason for this is that, as Lukács pointed out in his attempt

---

44 I have explored this thesis elsewhere with more technical rigor in my paper, "Collective Intentionality, Social Domination and Reification." *Journal of Social Ontology*, vol. 3, no. 2 (2017): 207–229. Also see my forthcoming paper "Reification, Values and Norms: Toward a Critical Theory of Consciousness." In Gregory R. Smulewicz-Zucker (ed.), *Confronting Reification: The Revitalization of a Concept in Late Capitalism*. (Leiden: Brill, forthcoming).

to understand reification, the only adequate means to explode reification was to embed the experience we have of particular social facts into the social totality as a whole. As he puts it in *History and Class Consciousness*: "Every contemplative, purely cognitive stance leads ultimately to a divided relationship to its object…. For every purely cognitive stance bears the stigma of immediacy. That is to say, it never ceases to be confronted by a whole series of ready-made objects that cannot be dissolved into processes."[45]

Lukács' thesis here is that any valid, true knowledge of an object (a social fact) is one that will understand it as the product of praxis, and as praxis as processual, as encompassing the structures of relations and ends toward which those structures have been activated to achieve. This capacity to see each social fact around us as linked to these larger objective ontological modes of practices, relations, structures, processes and ends entails a capacity to explode reification, or the state of cognition that remains fixed in the ready-made instituted norms and concepts generated by the prevailing social reality. In contrast to the "purely contemplative stance" Lukács asks us to consider a stance informed by praxis. I suggest that we see this as an implicit argument to adopt a critical social ontology. Once we take the stance of praxis we are moving in a categorial scheme very different from pure cognition. The reason is, as we saw above, the concept of praxis is a structure that combines activity and thought in the form of a *telos* or teleological positing. Now, for Lukács this means that reification is the negation of this form of comprehension; it means seeing the world as disarticulated particulars, or even as chunks of reality rather than as a totality. Any social fact is the product of practice: it is therefore underwritten by human activity, human relational structures and processes. Once we see this, we can then assess the validity of these practices and the ends toward which they are organized.

Now, herein lies a crucial split between what I am calling *descriptive* and *critical* social ontologies. In the case of the former, we are asked to understand features of sociality that lack any sense of power that shapes the totality of social forms. They are descriptive because they offer us no sense of the social whole and how we can evaluate it critically. A critical social ontology, in contrast, seeks to understand how power relations within the society also shape and organize the social totality itself. It seeks to comprehend the ways that social relations, structures, processes and purposes are shaped or possibly contested. The core idea here is the concept of an end or purpose – the *telos* of our social activities. This was what Lukács highlights in his ontological scheme and we can see why once we inquire into the ways that the *telos* is the active cause

---

45 Lukács, *History and Class Consciousness*, 205.

of the ways social reality is shaped. In descriptive social ontologies, emphasis is not placed on the ends in any systematic sense, but on the means. Take the following from Michael E. Bratman as an illustration of my thesis:

> Think of the coordinated activities of the thousands of employees around the world involved in making iPhones. Here the source of the organization is not likely to be an intention shared by the participants. Instead, the complex social coordination is externally orchestrated by a managerial group.[46]

For Lukács, the problem with the account given here is that there is no sense that the ultimate aim of the total organization of this kind is capacity of some agents to direct and organize the intentional agency of others; to be able to create the structures of organization and production, and the social-relational structures and processes that go along with them, that are ultimately oriented toward the extraction of surplus from the participants involved. In this sense, the descriptive ontology simply re-creates the social reality in a one-dimensional sense. We merely describe the prevailing order, we have no conceptual means to contest it.

As I see it, Lukács was seeking to pursue this latter form of social ontology – i.e., to provide us with a set of categories that would enable us to open up a critical stance to the world that was also grounded in the rational comprehension of the social totality. He saw that the concept of labor was not to be construed in some narrow, ideological sense – say, as proletarian "work" or whatever – but rather as the nucleus for the generation of larger social forms and complexes. More crucially, the concept of labor constructed as a form of praxis entails dialectically a sublation of description and evaluation or, to put it in different terms, to merge fact and value into a higher form of critique. This can occur once we see that the teleological positing of labor (human praxis) is a structure that contains activity and purpose; it is an activity that can be broadened to encompass social relations and structures as well as processes. But the very act of positing a *telos*, or constituting social relations for the purpose of such an activity – whether they be conversations, orchestras or factories – entails the capacity to *judge*, to *evaluate* that *telos* as well as the activities, relations, structures and processes that brought it into being. Here is the point where a critical theory of ethics can be seen grounded in a critical social ontology.

---

46   Bratman, *Shared Agency*, 10.

5 Ontology and Ethics: A Theory of Critical Judgment

The categories of a critical social ontology explored above delineate a means to comprehend human reality *as a totality*. The significance of this is not to articulate a rigid categorial scheme, however, but rather to serve as a means to further construct a robust epistemic and normative basis for a critical theory of society. As I stated earlier, the central flaw that plagues contemporary trends in critical theory can be understood as resulting from a retreat to an intersubjective epistemology based either on language, forms of justification or recognition. What these projects have been defined against is the Marxian premise of materialism: of the idea that we need to have a critical comprehension of the objective features of human sociality and society itself as an object of investigation. Without this, there can be no basis for a theory that can have genuine emancipatory aims. Just as Marx had critiqued Kant, Fichte and Hegel before him for their lack of a philosophy that would concretize human freedom in objective (i.e., socially-transformative terms), so we must make a similar move against the post-metaphysical paradigm. A critical social ontology can enable this not because it abandons normative or epistemological concerns, but because it gives those concerns ontological and, hence, *objective* ballast:[47] we can therefore return to the political project of engaging in the need for objective social transformation – i.e., the transformation of concrete social relations, structures, processes and ends that underwrite the norms and forms of consciousness that re-create the prevailing social order.

5.1 *The Concept of Totality and Judgment*

This means we can now turn to the most essential question of this investigation, that of a unification of the descriptive and normative dimensions of a critical theory of society. As I see it, this is what Lukács rightly saw as the essential purpose of a critical social ontology, its capacity to structure a critical theory of judgment. This theory of judgment is one that is rooted in the reflective capacities of the subject, but allows for a more critical and more rationally grounded form of reflection because of its ability to be allow cognition to extend beyond the mere empirical and phenomenological domain and into the

---

47   Nicolai Hartmann remarks on this role of a critical ontology: "It is precisely the problem of knowledge, and in it, furthermore, precisely the problem of a priori knowledge, which most urgently needs an ontological foundation. Without it everything here is hovering in mid-air. Without it one cannot distinguish representation from knowledge, thought from insight, fancy from truth, or speculation from science." Nicolai Hartmann, "How Is Critical Ontology Possible? Toward the Foundation of the General Theory of the Categories." *Axiomanthes*, vol. 22 (2012 [1923]): 315–354, 317.

deeper, ontological realm thereby granting us access to the totality of the structures and processes of social reality. My thesis here is that we can derive a theory of critical judgment from a critical social ontology by going back to the basic thesis Lukács laid out in 1923 in *History and Class Consciousness*. There Lukács argues that the only way we can shatter the effects of reification and its muting effect on critical consciousness is by a return to an implicitly ontological thesis that sees the totality as the central category of any form of social cognition or reflection. The apex of this argument is worth quoting in full:

> Reification is, then, the necessary, immediate reality of every person living in capitalist society. It can be overcome only by *constant and constantly renewed efforts to disrupt the reified structure of existence by concretely relating to the concretely manifested contradictions of the total development, by becoming conscious of the immanent meanings of these contradictions for the total development*. But it must be emphasized that (1) the structure can be disrupted only if the immanent contradictions of the process are made conscious…. (2) What is crucial is that there should be an aspiration toward totality, that action should serve the purpose, described above, in the totality of the process… Hence (3) when judging whether an action is right or wrong it is essential to relate it to its function in the total process.[48]

Unpacking this, we see that the basic idea here can be filled out only through an ontological scheme that grants us knowledge of the totality of the social system – totality understood as the relations, structures, processes and purposes – that are constitutive of our social forms will we be able to penetrate beyond the phenomenological membrane of reified reality. The core essence of critical judgment now becomes hinged to the cognitive capacity to view this totality.

Even though this is the case, the relation between the categorial scheme of critical social ontology and the normative assessment of one's social reality is not a deductive procedure. Rather, it is only through a synthetic operation of consciousness where we are able to assess our phenomenological state via the rationalizing categories of the ontology that a critical consciousness of the social manifold can be established. Our critical assessment of the world can only become concrete, in this sense, when we theorize about the ways that the structures of relations that constitute our world also constitute the social processes that we inhabit and which shape our lives. This in turn has to be assessed

---

48   Lukács, *History and Class Consciousness*, 197–198.

via the social purposes and ends toward which those relations, structures and processes are oriented in order for us to go deeper into the structure of the totality. What we come to grasp is the ontological shape of our social reality. The concept of an ontological shape of reality is important here for it forms a comprehensive picture of the ontological form of the world we inhabit and allows us to assess it critically.

In this sense, the role of ontology in the practice of critique and judgment is to serve as the categorial structure of a new space of reasons within which synthetic-critical judgments can be constructed. Synthetic-critical judgments are those that are able dialectically to grasp the ontological categories that constitute any given object of social reality. By this I mean a kind of ethical or practical reasoning that evaluates the phenomena of social reality based on the ways that social reality and the relations, structures processes and ends that constitute its ontological reality serve the development of the social totality itself – a social totality that can be understood as having a specific "shape" or form in terms of the structures of its social relations, its processes and designated ends and purposes. A synthetic-critical judgment is one that takes this ontological structure as the basis for evaluation as opposed to the application of norms or values that are seen as separate from that reality (neo-Kantianism) or which can be agreed upon as "working" within any given social context (pragmatism). This is why Lukács argues that "categories do nor predicate something about a being or that which is becoming; nor are they the (ideal) principles that shape matter. They are rather the moving and moved forms of matter itself."[49] Ontological categories are therefore to be understood as the constitutive features that produce any object, that shape matter and move it into the forms that we comprehend via the processes of human praxis. But we have seen, this need not be restricted to matter alone, but can also be applied to the norms and values that are used to shape and structure social relations as well. But Lukács' point here seems to be that the forms of social relations and other objective ontological modes are in service of the practical shaping of brute nature into social reality.

Now, any *telos* can be judged not by some abstract, arbitrary set of standards of evaluation, but by the purpose that such a *telos* is supposed to serve. Normative concepts are not, in this sense, sealed off in some neo-Kantian sphere of values but is internal to the very structures of praxis that constitute our social being. In this sense, it seems to me that Lukács' contention that there can be "no ethics without ontology" (*keine Ethik ohne Ontologie*), is an expression of the thesis that the evaluative categories that can bring our social reality to

---

49   Lukács, "The Ontological Foundations of Human Thinking and Action," 136.

critical consciousness. The concept of social value now becomes a crucial category. To judge the products of our social world critically means, on this view, to be able to judge them according to their capacity to fulfill some kind of valid social purpose or end. Lukács states that:

> Generally speaking, in our way of knowing, we make a clear distinction between the existence of objects in themselves and their being-for-us (*Fürunssein*), which is merely thought in the process of knowing. But in labor, the being-for-us of the product of labor realizes in itself its objective ontological character and becomes exactly that being through which, when properly thematized, the product can fulfill its social functions. It is in this way that the product becomes valuable (in case of failure, valueless).[50]

What Lukács seems to be suggesting here is that the *telos* of the production of any object is part of the criterion that can be used to evaluate it. But when we think in non-ontological terms, we separate out the object from its use for us. The essence of social objects are the objective ontological modes elaborated above: that is, we come to see that our evaluation of social fact must be tied to the way we cognize it. In other words, the thesis here is that true knowledge of social facts provides us with the requisite criteria for their evaluation.

An example here may be necessary, for this way of thinking is in strong contrast to the reified forms of thought that Lukács saw as predominating capitalist society. To link critical reflection and judgment to a critical social ontology means that we grasp what is essentially human or essentially social about any given social fact. It makes no sense to do this for, say, mountains or stars or orangutans. But it does when it comes to organizations, commodities, ideas, or whatever else we can conceive as a social fact. For all of them are linked to some larger system with its own ends and purposes and logics. They are embedded in and emanate from, a particular web of relations, structures, and processes that are themselves constituted for the production or maintenance of some end or purpose. Capitalism is therefore a unique form of social organization because it is a logic that colonizes and transforms existing social institutions. The ontological structure of society begins to transform: economic life shifts toward large-scale manufacturing, personal life becomes organized according to a new set of norms and values, the practices that constitute our activities are also transformed according to its logic. Capital is, as Harry Dahms has argued, a kind of social "artificial intelligence" that re-shapes the social

---

50   Lukács, "The Ontological Foundations of Human Thinking and Action," 140.

reality. To say this means that the structure of social relations, their processes and ends are all re-made according to private interest – the interest to accumulate and expand surplus value.

Power is therefore a crucial variable in grasping a critical social ontology since it is the efficient cause giving new shape to the ontological forms of our sociality. Consider one of the basic critiques issued by Marx of capitalist society: the capacity of private individuals to organize the social-relational structures and activities of society as a whole according to their interests, i.e., the maximization of surplus value as opposed to valid social ends and purposes. As he puts it in volume one of *Capital*:

> [T]he co-operation of wage laborers is entirely brought about by the capital that employs them. Their unification into one single productive body, and the establishment of a connection between their individual functions, lies outside their competence. These things are not their own act, but the act of the capital that brings them together and maintains them in that situation. Hence, the interconnection between their various labors confronts them, in the realm of ideas, as a plan drawn up by the capitalist, and, in practice, as his authority, as the powerful will of a being outside them, who subjects their activity to his purpose.[51]

This passage is imbued by the kind of critical social-ontological reasoning that I have been exploring here. The last line of the passage quoted tells us much when he argues that the capitalist "subjects their activity to his purpose." Here we can see that the objective ontological modes of relations, processes, and ends come into play since it is the power of capital to enable its owner to shape those modes according to his designs and ends. Once reification is shattered in the consciousness of the agents that reproduce the system, the immediacy of it dissolves and we begin to move in a critical space of reasons: one where we begin to inquire to the validity of the ends and purposes of the social forms that shape our lives. This is why Lukács' emphasis on practice, on labor as teleological positing is so crucial: it entails seeing that the structure of social reality as ontological means seeing that the ends toward which our individual and social-relational activities are put in service are determinative of our broader social reality. If we do not think in these *praxiological* terms, we will not be able to think in *ontological* terms, and this implies that our consciousness and cognition will be collapsed into the prevailing structure of the objective world.

---

51   Karl Marx, *Capital*, vol. 1. (New York: Vintage, 1977), 450.

Critical reflection will remain inert and impotent.[52] Hence the importance given to teleological reasoning, which deserves some discussion.

5.2 The Structure of Teleological Reasons

At the core of Lukács' model of social ontology as well as that of Marx, as I have shown above, was a distinctive interpretation of the concept of teleology. For Marx, the concept of teleology that was at the heart of pre-critical philosophy as well as what marked Hegel's socio-historical conception of teleology was to be deflated and circumscribed to contain the practical activities of labor as well as the coordinated praxis of more complex group activities. The *telos* was now to be understood not as a feature of nature nor of anything extra-human. Rather, it was a posited idea (*Vorbild*) that was to serve as the organizing principle of human activity as such. In this sense, the account of Marx and Lukács highlight what Hegel saw as definitive of human practice itself: the need for a dialectic between subjective and objective worlds.[53] But Marx's important turn was to see actual concrete forms of practice – labor being only one of multiple expressions of this structure of practice – where the cognitive structures of thought and the shaping of nature provide us with a basic conception of how to understand human life. Lukács' emphasis on this allows us to see how the various modes of social reality are woven together into a functionalist totality. The key idea here again comes back to the problem of teleological reasoning: how can we accept the validity of a kind of logic that was decisively rejected by modern rationalism?

Lukács seems to have solved this problem by placing the question in a very different frame. In his discussion of Hegel's ontology, he shows how teleology has to be taken out of the structures of nature and history and placed into the

---

52   Lukács seems to indicate precisely this thesis when he writes: "From the fact of this rigid confrontation it follows (1) that thought and (empirical) existence cannot reflect each other, but also (2) that the criterion of correct thought can only be found in the realm of reflection. As long as man adopts a stance of intuition and contemplation he can only relate to his own thought and to the objects of the empirical world in an immediate way. He accepts both as ready-made – produced by historical reality. As he wishes only to know the world and not to change it he is forced to accept both the empirical, material rigidity of existence and the logical rigidity of concepts as unchangeable." *History and Class Consciousness*, 202.

53   As Willem de Vries correctly notes: "Practical reasoning and the proper formulation of intentions require an understanding of the world's independence of us, of its universal patterns. Our subjective intentions make sense against an independent, objective world. But this means that a language of pure practice is impossible; it must be conjoined with a theoretical language." Willem de Vries, *Hegel's Theory of Mental Activity: An Introduction to Theoretical Spirit*. (Ithaca, N.Y.: Cornell University Press, 1988), 6.

framework of human practice. But this also needs to be expanded outward into the various complexes of society via our relations with others and the collective ends and purposes that organize the society as a whole. The basic thesis here is one where ends and purposes are the crucial feature of a social ontology: i.e., things are genuinely social if and only if they have been shaped by conscious expressions of practice that shape and constitute social reality. Now, this only makes sense if teleology is the governing principle of any practice. This is because Lukács sees the concept of teleological positing as that which distinguishes our human form of activity form merely biological forms of activity. How we connect this with the concern with evaluative or critical forms of judgment that Lukács himself was after?

Before answering this question, we need to be aware of what the structure of teleological arguments actually are. If we take any argument to be teleological it means seeing any social fact as the result of an intentional act – individual or collective – and that this social fact was both (a) constituted by a series of set of social practices and (b) these same social practices were constituted to produce that social fact as an end. As such, the *telos* of the practice determines the *structure* of the practice. When read back through the social ontological scheme advanced above, we can then see that the whole complex of social-ontological modes is oriented toward that end or set of ends as well as the maintenance of the production of those ends. The division labor, structures of relations, and so on are all now to be understood in relation to the end or purpose toward which they are oriented. Hence, the ends produced need to understood in terms of the kinds of value that they achieve. To say that a social end is, in some sense, valid or good, is not to apply a predicate (valid or good) to that end but rather to see ends as good when they achieve the development of human ends. To privilege use value over exchange value is therefore an argument about the socially valid purposes toward which our activities and institutions are oriented.[54] The good is therefore an objective feature of the kind of life that one lives where the ends and purposes of our individual and collective activities, institutions and norms cultivate our developmental capacities and enhance the common, public goods that in turn enrich us as individuals as well as the common complex interdependent structural relations that enhance and progress our individuality. In capitalist society, the ends that are maximized are private, the extraction of surplus value. Hence, *the ends come to define the antecedent relations, structures and processes that produce and maintain them.*

---

54 Cf. the discussion by Daniel Brudney, "Justifying a Conception of the Good Life: The Problem of the 1844 Marx." *Political Theory*, vol. 29, no. 3 (2001): 364–394.

This opens up for us a way in to a more critical and more comprehensive way of thinking about claims to validity in ethical reasoning. The reason for this is that once we see that valid reasons have to have some account of the way the world works, what purposes the social facts in question are intended to realize, we see that teleological reasoning within a critical social-ontological context means a very different sense of reason and normative validity than neo-Idealists such as Habermas would have us believe. For now, the validity of a normative claim must be seen as based not on others' capacity to agree with it, but rather according to the extent to which it is able to inquire into the purposes and ends that the social fact in question serves. The problem with the neo-Idealist approach of discourse ethics is simply that it cannot secure a form of reasoning that would be immune to the distorting pressures of reification as I discussed the concept above. In other words, neo-Idealist theories of exchanging reasons, of justification, or whatever, is based on a pragmatist paradigm that eschews the social-metaphysics requisite for valid social knowledge. Since our norms underwrite consciousness and our cognitive and evaluative capacities for reasoning, and these norms are largely absorbed from our socialization into the social structures they were meant to sustain, we must have a means by which to counter and shatter the accepted normative frameworks that are constitutive of our reality and subjectivity.

5.3   *Toward a Materialist Theory of Ethics*

Hegel's thesis of "ethical life" elaborated in his *Philosophy of Right* was an important attempt to bring back the conception of an objective ethics into the modern world. The connection between our capacity to judge the world (our ethical concepts) and the ontological structures of the social reality we inhabit are both enmeshed with one another, as we have seen. But the critical capacity to evaluate this social reality is itself tied up with the kind of teleological form of thinking explored above. As Willem de Vries correctly argued, in the context of Hegel's thought: "In all teleology there is at least implicit reference to the good. In intentional teleology this reference is itself intentional; intentional action aims at a subjectively valued end. In natural, objective teleology activity aims at the objective good of the organism."[55] But we can go another step toward a different category of teleology: *socio-ontological teleology* that can be described as the kinds of ends and purposes toward which our social practices (both individual and collective) are oriented. Marx and Lukács open up this category in their category of labor/praxis that, as we have seen, is itself

---

55   De Vries, *Hegel's Theory of Mental Activity*, 8. Cf. Lukács' critical discussion of Hegel's teleological theory in *Zur Ontologie des gesellschaftlichen Seins*, vol. 1, 515ff.

constitutive of the totality of our social reality. Indeed, the ontological structures of this social reality are rooted in this "fundamental ontological ground" as Lukács refers to it – i.e., to the actual structure of labor as the activity of teleological positing.

A materialist theory of ethics is therefore one that can conceive of our normative-evaluative premises as rooted in the ends and purposes of our collective activities. One of the central pathologies of modern, technologically advanced societies is the loss of the knowledge of ends and the centrality of the means as the organizing criteria of our evaluative concepts. A materialist ethics is therefore concerned with the concrete ends and purposes that our material social relations are organized to attain. Once we make a turn toward *praxis* (or labor as Lukács expresses it) as the nucleus of an evaluative scheme we are moving in a structure of thought that takes us away from a detached noumenalism characteristic of pragmatism, discourse ethics, recognition, or whatever, and we are placed firmly back into a realm of thinking about the concrete ways that social reality is organized and the ways that these forms of organization can shape consciousness as well. Indeed, once social agents begin to absorb the norms and rule-following necessary for technological and administrative institutions to function, their capacity to generate rational critical consciousness withers. The category of a common good, in this sense, can be conceived not as a predicate of some object or social fact, but rather as constitutive of its capacity to fulfill ends that are appropriate to a common structure of relations that enhances the developmental capacities of its members.

Once we view the essence of human life as consisting of the various shapes and forms that our interdependent relationality can take at any given time in history according to a given set of ends and purposes, we can see that a critical social ontology is a means by which we can achieve some kind of critical cognition of the social totality. Any struggle for emancipation must elaborate new ontological social forms that can achieve the fullest development of the capacities and ends and purposes of that community. Any struggle for emancipation, to qualify as radical and rational must consequently examine the ways that social organization is structured and struggle for more humane forms of social relations. This project cannot be undertaken unless we comprehend the ways that social power maintains not only the prevailing orders of institutional logics and the normative webs that underwrite them, but also the ends and purposes of the social order as well. A shadow of Plato's thesis in the *Republic* therefore informs the Marxian thesis about what a good, free, or just society would look like: a structure of associational life where both personal good and common good are maximized through the organization of social structures and processes according to common needs of the community.[56] For only once there exists the free development of each can we speak in any terms about the free development of all.

---

56 I explore this thesis in more detail in my essay "Erich Fromm and the Ontology of Social Relations." In Joan Braun and Kieran Durkin (eds.), *Erich Fromm's Critical Theory: Hope, Humanism and the Future*. (New York: Bloomsbury, 2019).

Index

Adorno, T.W.   61, 156, 167, 223–224, 232–234, 237, 248, 257, 263–265, 322–324, 352, 354, 412
alienation   2, 5, 7, 34, 50, 116–133, 135, 137–151, 160–162, 189, 195, 211, 222, 238–241, 310, 316, 420
Archer, Margaret   3, 308, 437, 441–442
Arendt, Hannah   322–323, 337–341
Aristotle   2, 14–15, 25, 51, 154, 287, 289, 333, 399, 421–424, 427, 429

Bhaskar, Roy   3, 190, 265, 279, 281–282, 441–442
Borges, J.L.   267–277, 279, 281, 283, 285–287
Brandom, Robert   45, 47–48, 55–56, 75, 379, 381, 383
Brentano, Franz   42–44
Butler, Judith   226, 228, 231, 297

Capital (Marx)   1, 8, 22, 34, 57–60, 63–64, 72, 74, 89, 91, 96, 99–101, 103–104, 106–110, 112–114, 118, 133, 137, 139, 143–145, 147, 212, 228, 231, 278, 288, 304, 316, 425, 434, 437, 449–450
capitalism   1, 8, 19, 39, 63–65, 74, 81–82, 96, 98–99, 101–102, 105, 107–110, 113–115, 144–146, 157, 159, 161, 164, 189, 228, 230, 232, 234–236, 241, 246, 265, 311, 336, 420–421, 428, 443, 449
collective intentionality   4, 10, 208, 246–247, 366, 440, 443
commodity fetishism   99
critical ontology   55–56, 161, 168–169, 190, 246–247, 249, 308, 321, 323–325, 327, 329–335, 337, 339, 341, 343, 345, 347, 349, 351, 353, 355, 357, 359–361, 363, 365, 392–395, 397–399, 401, 403, 405–409, 411, 413–418, 421, 427, 446
critical social ontology   6–7, 9–10, 154–155, 223, 225–227, 229, 231, 233, 235, 237, 239, 241, 243, 245, 247, 249, 251, 253, 255, 257, 259, 261, 263, 265, 319, 366–371, 373, 375, 377, 379, 381, 383, 385–387, 389–391, 419, 421, 423, 425–429, 431–433, 435, 437, 439, 441, 443–447, 449–451, 453–455

Economic and Philosophical Manuscripts (Marx)   17, 424
epistemology   3, 6, 29–30, 35–37, 39–40, 54, 187, 215, 227, 229, 236, 249–250, 255, 262, 289, 291–292, 297–299, 301, 305–307, 310, 325–335, 341–342, 345, 349, 351, 355, 357–358, 360–361, 385, 397–398, 413–414, 446
Epstein, Brian   7, 246–247, 369
ethics   1–2, 10, 13–15, 17, 20, 40, 82, 114, 121, 150, 159, 184, 192, 216, 250, 262–263, 294, 302, 305–306, 308, 314, 325, 419, 422, 427–428, 432, 443, 445–446, 448, 453–454

freedom   9, 17, 19, 21, 41, 77, 86, 135, 137, 143–145, 147, 167, 179, 219–222, 224, 249, 251, 263, 309–310, 323–324, 341, 343–344, 348, 353, 364–365, 372, 392–393, 397, 400–401, 404–405, 412, 414–418, 425–426, 428, 446
Frege, Gottlob   44–46, 73, 194

Goldmann, Lucienn   2, 234–239, 243, 264
Grundrisse (Marx)   57, 64, 93–94, 96–97, 102–104, 106, 111–113, 286, 424–425

Habermas, Jürgen   10, 16, 61, 74, 179, 194, 216, 221, 232–234, 291, 305, 308, 356, 358, 370, 384, 395–397, 412, 453
Hartmann, Nikolai   22, 28–39, 51, 82–83, 163, 183, 187, 191, 194–195, 197, 204–205, 215, 287, 289, 291, 307, 312–313, 316, 421, 428, 446
Hegel, G.W.F.   2, 6–9, 14–15, 18–20, 22–25, 30, 32, 39, 46–57, 59, 62, 65, 83, 124, 126, 130, 134, 152–175, 177–179, 194–195, 203–205, 215, 228, 238, 241, 247, 289–290, 299–301, 307, 311, 314, 327–328, 348, 350–351, 384, 399, 401, 416, 422, 438, 446, 451, 453
Heidegger, Martin   2, 120, 164, 183, 191, 235, 239, 241, 254, 298–299, 301, 305, 311, 374
Heller, Agnes   16, 18, 178, 239, 291
Honneth, Axel   61, 118–120, 228, 233–234, 246

Horkheimer, Max   61, 232–234, 321–324, 331–332, 352–357
Husserl, Edmund   44, 210, 291–292, 299–300, 305, 328, 332, 395

Idealism   37, 45, 55, 57, 87, 154, 157, 162, 168–169, 184, 187–189, 191, 202–205, 223, 240, 300, 306, 311, 393, 395, 421, 423, 426
intentionality   4, 10, 41–44, 48, 51, 55–56, 59, 65–67, 71, 73, 77, 192, 199–200, 202, 206, 208, 211, 219, 246–247, 252, 366, 378, 384, 387, 426, 431, 439–441, 443

Kant, Immanuel   6, 26, 37, 39–40, 45, 51, 54, 74, 159, 170, 191, 240, 249, 289, 331, 355–356, 358, 411–412, 446
Kuhn, Thomas   267, 269, 271, 273, 275, 277–279, 281–287

labor   1, 4–6, 8–9, 13, 15, 17–27, 41–42, 51, 53, 56–59, 62–77, 81–83, 85–115, 117, 121, 124, 128, 132–144, 147–148, 152, 154–159, 161–163, 169, 173–179, 225, 235, 239–245, 264, 286–288, 305, 309–310, 315, 332, 340, 356, 365, 371–384, 390, 393–394, 396–418, 422, 426–431, 439, 445, 449–454
Lakatos, Imre   267, 269, 271, 273, 275, 277–279, 281–287
language   6, 10, 16, 21–22, 44, 66, 68, 72, 76, 83, 122, 159, 176, 185, 192–194, 201, 208–210, 212, 214–216, 218–219, 221, 250, 268–269, 271–273, 275, 278, 295, 301, 309, 313, 315, 324, 326–327, 330, 342–343, 355, 357, 359, 374, 380–381, 384, 388–390, 396, 398, 403, 405–408, 424, 430, 435–436, 441, 446, 451
Latour, Bruno   223, 226, 254–255, 261–263, 265, 289–317
Lenin, V.I.   32, 57, 127, 157, 170, 196, 199, 203–205, 228
liberalism   31, 322, 324–325, 335–336, 339–347, 349, 351–352
Lukács, Georg   1–2, 4–6, 8–11, 13–45, 47–77, 79, 81–100, 102–105, 107–114, 116–179, 181, 183–187, 189–191, 193–201, 203–207, 209, 211–219, 221–232, 234–236, 238–245, 247–252, 255–265, 267, 270, 285–289,
291–293, 295–297, 299, 301, 303–313, 315–317, 321, 323–329, 331, 333–335, 337, 339, 341, 343, 345–347, 349–351, 353, 355, 357–363, 365–394, 397–409, 411–417, 419–421, 423, 425, 427–433, 435, 437–439, 441, 443–455

Marcuse, Herbert   155–156, 234, 322, 324, 354, 356–357
Marx, Karl   1–2, 6–8, 15, 17–19, 22, 24–25, 29–32, 34–44, 48–49, 51–52, 54, 56–60, 62–65, 67–68, 71–72, 74, 81–85, 87, 89, 91–115, 118–119, 123–124, 126–128, 130, 132–134, 137–141, 143–148, 150–151, 157, 162–164, 189, 193, 195, 202–204, 206, 212, 214, 221, 228, 235–236, 238–243, 246–247, 250–251, 258, 260, 265, 286–288, 292, 294–298, 300, 309–312, 314, 316, 329–330, 340, 345, 350, 360, 376, 379–380, 387, 396–399, 402, 419, 421–433, 435, 437, 439, 441, 443, 445–447, 449–453, 455
materialism   1, 7, 10, 57, 60, 88, 97, 134, 152–158, 164, 167–169, 174, 178, 187, 189, 196, 202–206, 230, 253–254, 306, 398, 421–423, 446
McDowell, John   45, 47, 56
Mészáros, István   81, 102–104, 107–108, 113
metaphysics   2–3, 6, 14, 16–17, 51, 55, 73, 167, 223, 255, 258, 265, 279, 289, 293, 325, 331, 345, 352, 367, 394–395, 400, 437–438, 453

Neo-Kantianism   29, 40, 73, 395, 448
norms   4, 9, 48, 71, 75, 233, 255, 300, 347, 349, 357, 367, 371, 373–376, 379, 383–385, 388, 396, 431, 433–434, 436–437, 439–440, 442–444, 446, 448–449, 452–454

objectification   7, 26, 34, 50, 85–88, 124, 126, 138, 140–141, 145, 238, 244, 248

Phenomenology of Spirit (Hegel)   6, 24, 50, 154, 156–157, 160–163, 175, 178, 289, 327, 384
positivism   30–34, 38–40, 73, 191, 223, 249, 253, 267, 278–283, 285–286, 325,

INDEX

331–332, 334–335, 341–342, 346,
351–352, 354–355, 357–358, 393, 395
praxis   1, 5–7, 10, 18–19, 24–25, 27, 85, 87, 112,
141, 150, 153, 159, 210, 246, 257, 261, 267,
284, 286, 288, 308, 313, 334, 366, 419,
421–423, 426–427, 429–432, 434, 436,
442, 444–445, 448, 451, 453–454

reification   2, 18, 61, 116–120, 123–124, 126–127,
135, 153, 155, 159, 161, 223–229, 231–235,
237–245, 247–249, 251, 253, 255, 257,
259, 261, 263–266, 310, 329–330,
374–375, 385, 397, 415, 419–420,
432–433, 440, 443–444, 447, 450, 453

Searle, John   4, 183–203, 205–222, 366,
369–371, 433–434, 439–443
Simmel, Georg   118
social being   1, 4–5, 10–11, 13–18, 20–21,
26–27, 41, 43–45, 47, 49, 51–53, 55–57,
59–63, 65–73, 75, 77, 81–96, 98, 100, 105,
114, 116, 120–121, 125–126, 128, 132–138,
148, 150–151, 153, 155, 163–165, 167–170,
172, 174–179, 185–187, 189, 193–196, 198,
200–202, 206, 209–216, 218, 221–222,
225, 229, 238–241, 245, 249, 251,
256–257, 259–265, 268, 270, 287, 289,
304, 309, 328–329, 345, 356, 362, 366,
376, 378, 391, 393–394, 397–400,
402–404, 406–410, 412–417, 424, 428,
430, 448
social ontology   1, 3–4, 6–10, 36, 79, 153–155,
174, 178–179, 181, 183–185, 187, 189,
191–195, 197–199, 201, 203, 205, 207–211,
213, 215, 217–219, 221, 223, 225–227, 229,
231, 233, 235, 237, 239, 241, 243, 245–249,
251, 253, 255–257, 259, 261–265, 290,
319, 332, 361, 366–373, 375, 377, 379,
381–383, 385–391, 419, 421–423,
425–429, 431–447, 449–455
socialism   16–17, 29, 38, 103, 105, 108–109, 123,
126, 128, 151, 162, 227, 289
sociality   3, 8, 10, 25, 36, 75, 77, 94–95, 308,
339–341, 376, 378, 380, 384, 420–422,
424–426, 428, 433, 444, 446, 450

teleological positing   4–5, 25, 68–71, 74,
86–87, 89, 92, 98, 100, 133, 140, 152, 156,
169, 174, 177, 215, 371–373, 376, 378, 382,
386, 394, 398–400, 402–404, 408, 410,
414–415, 429–431, 439, 444–445, 450,
452, 454
teleology   8, 22–24, 36–37, 53, 56–57, 62, 68,
70, 85–86, 89, 91, 133, 150, 159, 162–163,
170, 172, 179, 195, 202–203, 219, 225, 258,
371, 390, 398–400, 402–405, 407–410,
413–417, 426, 430, 432, 443, 451–453

value   8–9, 14, 21, 25, 35, 60, 62–63, 67, 72,
81–83, 85–101, 103–115, 122, 128, 135, 138,
140, 144, 164, 175, 178, 212, 233, 237,
243–244, 250, 303, 305, 311, 343, 368,
387–388, 395, 402, 407, 412–413,
427–428, 430, 445, 449–450, 452

Weber, Max   118, 156, 240, 305, 395, 412

Printed in the United States
By Bookmasters